ARAMAIC PAPYRI

OF THE

FIFTH CENTURY B.C.

ARAMAIC PAPYRI

OF THE

FIFTH CENTURY B.C.

EDITED, WITH TRANSLATION AND NOTES,

BY

A. COWLEY

OXFORD
AT THE CLARENDON PRESS
1923

Oxford University Press
London Edinburgh Glasgow Copenhagen
New York Toronto Melbourne Cape Town
Bombay Calcutta Madras Shanghai
Humphrey Milford Publisher to the UNIVERSITY

Printed in England

PREFACE

No apology need be made for re-editing these texts, for every fresh examination sheds fresh light on them, and in spite of the very extensive literature to which they have given rise, much still remains to be done. Moreover, it is obviously convenient to have them all collected in one volume and arranged as far as may be chronologically. Professor Sachau himself suggested to me in 1912 that we should collaborate on a new edition, and in 1913, with this object in view, I began to make a careful study of the facsimiles and of the articles and reviews which had appeared up to that time. During the war I continued the work, with many interruptions, as far as the anxieties of the time allowed. It no doubt shows many inconsistencies for that reason. I had originally intended going to Cairo and Berlin when the work was more advanced, to verify some of the readings on the originals, and to discuss difficulties with Professor Sachau. As this was impracticable, the present edition has been finished without that advantage. Fortunately, however, the previous editions contain such excellent facsimiles of all the texts (except nos. 79, 80, 83) that it was possible to work on them with confidence, and it was unnecessary to re-issue facsimiles with this volume.

As a first result of the revision of the texts, I published in 1919 translations of thirty-six of the most important of them, together with the 'Words of Aḥiḳar' and the fragments of a version of the Behistun inscription (*Jewish Documents of the time of Ezra*, London, SPCK., 1919). The present volume contains the Aramaic texts from which these translations were made, together with others, and a commentary in support of the readings and interpretations adopted. Consideration of expense has obliged me to restrict the commentary so that many interesting questions have been left undiscussed. Further treatment of many of these will, however, be found in the special articles to which reference is made.

I acknowledge gratefully the help obtained from Sachau's original edition, and from Ungnad's small edition, though often differing from both of them. I also wish to thank Mr. F. Ll. Griffith for help in matters relating to Egypt, Professor Langdon and Mr. G. R. Driver for help in Assyriological questions, and the staff of the Clarendon Press for the care they have bestowed on the production of the book.

A. COWLEY

MAGDALEN COLLEGE, OXFORD,
January, 1923

CONTENTS

	PAGE
LIST OF BOOKS AND ARTICLES . .	viii
TABLE OF THE PAPYRI	xi
INTRODUCTION	xiii
ARAMAIC PAPYRI TEXTS .	1
INDEX OF WORDS AND NAMES	273

LIST OF BOOKS AND ARTICLES

The following are some of the books and articles which have been consulted, besides those mentioned in the notes:

Anneler, Zur Geschichte d. Juden in Elephantine. (Diss.) Bern, 1912 (with bibliography).
Arnold, Journal of Biblical Literature 1912, p. 1 (on pap. 21).
Barth, Jahrbuch d. Jüdisch-Literarischen Gesellschaft 1907, p. 323 (on Sachau's Drei aramäische Papyrus).
—— Revue Sémitique 1907, p. 522 (on no. 15); 1909, p. 149 (on אגר or אגד).
—— Zeitschrift f. Assyriologie 1908, p. 188 (on pap. 30).
—— Orientalistische Literaturzeitung 1912, p. 10.
Blau, Magyar-zsidó Szemle 1912 p. 41; 1921, p. 44.
—— in Festschrift H. Cohen. Berlin, 1912, p. 207.
Bornstein in Festschrift Harkavy. St. Petersburg 1908, p. 63 Heb. (on dates).
Boylan, Irish Theological Quarterly 1912, p. 40.
Bruston, Revue de Théologie et de Philosophie 1908, p. 97.
Büchler, Orientalistische Literaturzeitung 1912, p. 126 (on pap. 26).
Burney, Expositor 1912, p. 97.
—— Church Quarterly Review 74 (1912), p. 392.
Chabot, Journal Asiatique 14 (1909), p. 515 (on dates).
Clermont-Ganneau, Recueil d'Archéologie Orientale vi (1905), pp. 147, 221.
—— Revue Critique d'histoire 1906 (2), p. 341.
Cook (S. A.), American Journal of Theology 1915, p. 346.
—— Expositor 1912, p. 193.
Cooke (G. A.), Journal of Theological Studies 1907, p. 615.
Daiches, Zeitschrift für Assyriologie 1909, p. 197.
—— Proceedings of the Society of Biblical Archaeology 1912, p. 17.
Desnoyers, Bulletin de Littérature Ecclésiastique 1907, pp. 138, 176; 1908, p. 235.
Döller, Theologische Quartalschrift 1907, p. 497.
Eerdmans, Theologisch Tijdschrift 1908, p. 72.
Elhorst, Journal of Biblical Literature 1912, p. 147.
Epstein (J. N.), Jahrbuch d. Jüdisch-Literarischen Gesellschaft 1909, p. 359.
—— Zeitschrift d. Alttestamentlichen Wissenschaft 1912, pp. 128, 139; 1913, p. 138.
Fischer (L.), Jahrbuch d. Jüdisch-Literarischen Gesellschaft 1911, p. 371 Heb. (on legal forms); 1912, p. 45.

Fotheringham, see Introduction, p. v, note 5.
—— Journal of Theological Studies 14 (1913), p. 570 (on dates).
Fränkel, Zeitschrift f. Assyriologie 1908, p. 240.
Freund, Vienna Oriental Journal, *or* Wiener Zeitschrift f. d. Kunde d. Morgenlands 1907, p. 169 (on pap. 15).
von Gall, Vorträge d. theologischen Konferenz zu Giessen 1912, no. 34.
van Gelderen, Orientalistische Literaturzeitung 1912, p. 337.
Ginzel, Handbuch d. Chronologie ii, p. 45; iii, p. 375.
Gray (G. B.) in Studien Wellhausen, Giessen 1914, p. 163 (on names).
Grimme, Orientalistische Literaturzeitung 1911, p. 529, (on Aḥiḳar); 1912, p. 11.
Guillaume, Expository Times 32 (1921), p. 377.
Gunkel, Expositor 1911, p. 20.
Gutesmann, Revue des Études Juives 53 (1907), p. 194 (on dates).
Halévy, Journal Asiatique 18 (1911), p. 658; 19 (1912), pp. 410, 622.
—— Revue Sémitique 1911, p. 473; 1912, pp. 31, 153, 252.
Holtzmann, Theologische Literaturzeitung 1912, p. 166 (on Sprengling, AJSL 1911).
Hontheim, Biblische Zeitschrift 1907, p. 225 (on dates).
Jampel, Monatschrift f. d. Geschichte d. Judentums 1907, p. 617.
Jirku, Orientalistische Literaturzeitung 1912, p. 247.
Knobel (E. B.), see Introduction, p. v, note 4.
Knudtzon, Orientalistische Literaturzeitung 1912, p. 486 (on יהו).
Köberle, Neue Kirchliche Zeitschrift 1908, p. 173.
Lagrange, Revue Biblique 1907, p. 258; 1912, p. 575.
Leander, Orientalistische Literaturzeitung 1912, p. 151 (on יהו).
Lévi (Isr.), Revue des Études Juives 54 (1907), pp. 35, 153; 56 (1908), p. 161; 63 (1912), p. 161.
Lidzbarski, Ephemeris ii (1906), p. 210; iii (1909), p. 70; (1912), p. 238.
—— Deutsche Literaturzeitung 1906, p. 3205; 1907, p. 3160; 1911, p. 2966.
Mahler, Zeitschrift f. Assyriologie 1912, p. 61 (on dates).
Margolis, Jewish Quarterly Review, new series ii (1911–12), p. 419.
Meyer (Ed.), Sitzungsberichte d. k. Preussischen Akademie 1911, p. 1026.
—— Der Papyrusfund von Elephantine. Leipzig, 1912.
Mittwoch in Festschrift A. Cohen. Berlin, 1912, p. 227.
Montgomery, Orientalistische Literaturzeitung 1912, p. 535 (on Aḥiḳar).
Nau, Journal Asiatique 18 (1911), p. 660.
—— Revue Biblique 1912, p. 68.
Nöldeke, Zeitschrift f. Assyriologie 1907, p. 130; 1908, p. 195 (on pap. 30).
—— Literarisches Zentralblatt 1911, p. 1503.
Peiser, Orientalistische Literaturzeitung 1907, p. 622; 1908, pp. 24, 73 (on Staerk).
Perles, Orientalistische Literaturzeitung 1908, p. 26; 1911, p. 497; 1912, p. 54.
Peters, Die jüdische Gemeinde von Elephantine . . . Freiburg i. Br. 1910.

Pognon, Journal Asiatique 18 (1911), p. 337 (on dates).
Poznański (S.), Życie Żydowskie 1907 (nos. 13, 14), p. 219.
—— Orientalistische Literaturzeitung 1921, p. 303.
Prašek, Orientalistische Literaturzeitung 1912, p. 168 (on Sprengling AJSL 1911).
Pritsch, Zeitschrift f. Assyriologie 1911, p. 345 (on pap. 20).
Sachau, Drei Aramäische Papyrusurkunden. Berlin, 1908.
—— in Florilegium de Vogüé. Paris, 1909, p. 529 (on pap. 35).
Sayce, Expositor 1911, pp. 97, 417.
Schultess, Göttingische Gelehrte Anzeigen 1907, p. 181.
Schürer, Theologische Literaturzeitung 1907, pp. 1, 65.
Schwally, Orientalistische Literaturzeitung 1912, p. 160.
Seidel, Zeitschrift d. alttestamentlichen Wissenschaft 1912, p. 292.
Sidersky, Journal Asiatique 16 (1910), p. 587 (on dates).
Smyly, see Introduction, p. xiii, note 6.
Spiegelberg, Orientalistische Literaturzeitung 1913, p. 15; 1912, p. 1 (on names).
Sprengling, American Journal of Semitic Languages 27 (1911), p. 233.
—— American Journal of Theology 1917, p. 411; 1918, p. 349.
Staerk, Die jüdisch-aramäischen Papyri . . . in Kleine Texte, nos. 22, 23. Bonn, 1907, and no. 32, 1908.
—— Orientalistische Literaturzeitung 1908 (Beiheft).
Torczyner, Zeitschrift d. Deutschen Morgenländischen Gesellschaft 1916, p. 288 (bibliography).
—— Orientalistische Literaturzeitung 1912, p. 397.
Ungnad, Aramäische Papyrus . . . kleine Ausgabe. Leipzig, 1911.
de Vogüé, Comptes Rendus de l'Académie des Inscriptions 1906, p. 499.
Wensinck, Orientalistische Literaturzeitung 1912, p. 49 (on Aḥiḳar).

TABLE OF THE PAPYRI

AS ARRANGED IN PREVIOUS EDITIONS, SHOWING THEIR NUMBERS IN THIS EDITION.

Sayce and Cowley	This edition
A	no. 5
B	6
C	9
D	8
E	13
F	14
G	15
H	20
J	25
K	28
L (Ungnad, no. 88)	11

Sachau		Ungnad	This edition
Plate	Papyrus		
1, 2	1	no. 1	no. 30
3	2	2	31
4	3	3	32
4	5	4	33
5	4	5	17
6	6	6	21
7	7	7	16
8, 9	8	8	26
10	9	9	36
11	10	10	37
12	11	11	38
13	12	12	39
13	14	13	40
14	13	14	41
15	15	16	34
15	29	15	29
16	16	17	42
17	17	18	12
17–20	18	19	22
21, 22	19	20, 21	24
23	20	22	23
23	21	23	19
23	23	24	51
24	22	25	52
24	24	26	53
25, 26	25	27	2
26	27	28	7

Sachau Plate	Sachau Papyrus	Ungnad	This edition
27	26	no. 29	no. 3
28, 29	28	30	10
30	30	31	1
31	31	32	46
32	32	33	44
32	36	34	45
33	33	35	43
33	34	36	18
34	35	37	35
35	37	38	47
35	38	39	48
36	39	40	54
36	40	41	55
36	41	42	4
37	42	43	58
37	43	44	56
38	44	45	49
38	45	46	57
38	46	47	50
39	47	48	60
39	47	49	59
40-50	49-59	50-63	Ahiḳar (pp. 212-20)
51	60	64	69
52, 54-57	61, 62 &c	65-68 D	Behistun (pp 251-4, 265-9)
53	61 rev	69	63
55 col 2		67, 11	61
56 rev.		68 E	62
57		70 B	64
58		71	65
59		72	66
60		73	67
61		74	68
75 (Euting's papyrus)		2a	27
CIS. ii 1, no	144		70
	145		71
	146		72
	147		73
	148		74
	149	(Ungnad, no. 64)	69
	150		75
	151		76
	152		77
	153		78
Ungnad, no	89		79
	90		80
PSBA 1907, p. 260			81
1915, p 217			82
Harrow Papyrus			83
Giron's Papyrus			Appendix, p. 316.

INTRODUCTION

THE present volume comprises all the legible pre-Christian Aramaic papyri known to me.[1] The best preserved and the most important are nos. 5, 6, 8, 9, 11, 13–15, 20, 25. 28, published by Sayce and Cowley in *Aramaic Papyri Discovered at Assuan* (London, 1906); no. 27 published by Euting in *Mémoires présentés . . . à l'Académie des Inscriptions* (Paris, 1903); and many of those published by Sachau in *Aramäische Papyrus* . . . (Leipzig, 1911). The rest are fragments from Sachau, some much mutilated texts from the *Corpus Inscriptionum Semiticarum* ii, 1, two others published by me in *PSBA* 1907, p. 263 (with notes by Sayce), and 1915, p. 217, and one fragment of accounts, not previously published, which was brought to my notice by Mr. F. Ll. Griffith, in the Harrow School museum.[2] The genuineness of the papyri published by Sayce-Cowley and Sachau has been questioned[3] on the ground that the double dates in some of them do not seem to be consistent. I do not propose to deal with the dates, because they have been discussed by such competent authorities as Mr. Knobel,[4] Dr. Fotheringham,[5] and Dr. Smyly,[6] and the possible errors are not a sufficient ground for condemning the texts. A more serious attack has been made by Prof. Margoliouth,[7] whose opinion deserves every consideration. His arguments however have not gained acceptance, and a careful study

[1] For a bibliography of the texts known up to 1906 see Seymour de Ricci in Sayce and Cowley, p. 25. Some post-Christian pieces were published in the *Jewish Quarterly Review*, xvi (1903), p. 1.

[2] The late Mr. B. P. Lascelles kindly procured photographs of this for me.

[3] By L. Belléli in *An Independent Examination* . . . 1909, and by G. Jahn in *Die Elephantiner Papyri*, 1913; reviewed by Rothstein in *ZDMG* 1913, p. 718, to whom Jahn replied in *ZDMG* 1914, p. 142.

[4] *Monthly Notices of the R. Astron. Soc.*, March 1908, p. 334, and Nov. 1908, p. 8.

[5] Ibid., Nov. 1908, p. 12; March 1909, p. 446; June 1911, p. 661, against Ginzel's *Handbuch der . . . Chronologie* ii (1911), p. 45.

[6] *Proc. R. Irish Academy* 1909, C, p. 235.

[7] *Expositor* 1912, p. 69.

of the texts will furnish the unprejudiced reader with answers to them.

The collection consists of letters, legal documents, lists of names, accounts, and three literary pieces. Some of these are complete, others are more or less fragmentary. A large proportion of them are dated, unmistakably, and these have been arranged here chronologically, so as to form an historical sequence. In many cases the date is given both in the Egyptian and the Jewish reckoning, and there may be errors in these equations (see above, p. xiii). Some texts which are not dated can be fitted into the sequence from their contents: others, which give no certain clue as to date, are put at the end. The dated texts cover practically the whole of the fifth century B.C., and on palaeographical grounds the undated texts (with a few exceptions) may be assigned to the same century. They thus confirm the brilliant discovery of Mr. Clermont-Ganneau[1] that the similar texts in the *CIS* (which were all he had to go upon) belong to the period of the Persian rule in Egypt. The exceptions are nos. 81–83, in a much later style of writing. Since, however, it is unlikely that Aramaic continued in popular use in Egypt long after the time of Alexander the Great, we may with some confidence date these before or about 300 B.C.

The interest of documents such as these is that they are contemporary with the events to which they relate. They present therefore a trustworthy picture of their surroundings, not distorted by lapse of time, nor obscured by textual corruption. These particular documents have the additional interest that they were written by Jews. They are therefore the earliest Jewish texts we possess, with the exception of the Siloam inscription and the ostraka from Samaria, and (with those exceptions) the only Jewish literature of so early a date, outside the Old Testament. The literary pieces, it is true, are evidently of non-Jewish origin, but they show nevertheless the kind of literature which was current in the community. And their interest consists not only in what they say but in what they omit: in

[1] 'Origine perse des monuments araméens d'Égypte', in the *Rev. Archéol.* New Series 36 (1878), p. 93, and 37 (1879), p. 21.

the light they give and in the darkness in which they leave us (see below).

The language in which they are written is Aramaic, the same (with some reservations) as that of parts of the book of Ezra. Though there are Hebraisms in it and the names are Hebrew, there is no document in Hebrew, nor any direct evidence that Hebrew was used by the community for any purpose. (But see p. 119). As long as the Oriental empires continued to dominate the civilized world, Aramaic was the language of commerce and diplomacy, succeeded in Ptolemaic times by Greek. We have proof of its use in Assyria in the 'dockets' written in ink on the edge of cuneiform tablets as early as the seventh century B.C.[1] It was no doubt used even earlier, since Babylonian sculptures show scribes writing on scrolls, which would not be used for cuneiform, and it was not used only by Jews, nor (in this community) because it was in any sense a Jewish language. Assurbanipal had Aramaean scribes in his employ, Darius apparently sent abroad an Aramaic version of his great inscription at Behistun, and (in no. 26) a Persian satrap sends his orders to an Egyptian boat-builder in Aramaic.[2] It was evidently also an official language in the law-courts. It was only in Egypt, however, that papyrus could survive. Early documents on any such material inevitably perished in the climate of Mesopotamia or Palestine. In Egypt Aramaic probably gave way to Greek by about 300 B.C. In the East it continued, gradually becoming more corrupt, among the Jewish schools down to mediaeval times, and in some Christian communities to the present day.

The authors of most of these texts were Jews if names mean anything—not Samaritans, as argued by Hoonacker[3]—nor Israelites. They call themselves יהוריא 'the Jews', and their community חילא יהוריא 'the Jewish force'. Sometimes the term ארמי is used, but no other designation is found, and the name

[1] See Clay, 'Aramaic Indorsements', in *O. T. Studies in Memory of W. R. Harper* 1908, p. 285, and Delaporte, *Épigraphes araméens*, 1912, &c.

[2] In Ezra 6[2] the official record of the decree of Cyrus was on a מגלה (a scroll) which probably implies Aramaic writing.

[3] In his Schweich Lectures for 1914 (*Une Communauté Judéo-Araméenne . . .*, London, 1915).

Israel does not occur. These Jews seem to have been domiciled specially in Elephantine. Other western Asiatics were settled in Syene under the general name Aramaean. But 'Aramaean' might also include Jews,[1] so that we sometimes find a man described in one place (correctly) as a Jew of Elephantine, and in another (more loosely) as an Aramaean of Syene when he had in some way become connected with that station. Three times (25^{2}, &c.) we find an 'Aramaean of Elephantine', where the man is evidently a Jew, but the description may be due to mere carelessness. See on 5^{2}.

How did they get there? The Jewish force, or garrison, can only have been a military settlement, and there was no doubt likewise an Aramaean garrison at Syene. They were therefore mercenaries in the employment of the Persian king. This is corroborated by several indications. They were divided into דגלן 'companies' or 'regiments', each bearing a name, Babylonian or Persian, probably that of the commander.[2] Another division was מאתא 'centuria' ($22^{19.20}$), but whether larger or, more probably, smaller than the *degel* is not clear. They were under the supreme command of the רבחילא 'commander of the garrison', and they received rations (פתפא, see e.g. 24^{39}) and pay (פרס 11^{6}, &c.) from the government.

The writer of the Letter of Aristeas mentions (§ 13) that Psammetichus used Jewish mercenaries in his campaign against Ethiopia. If this means Psammetichus ii (cf. Herodotus ii, 30) their employment would have begun between 595 and 590 B.C. —therefore just before the fall of Jerusalem and the beginning of the Exile. They were afterwards apparently put in charge of the fortresses of Elephantine and Syene as a defence of the southern frontier of Egypt against Ethiopia, for when Cambyses came into Egypt, in 525, they were already settled in Elephantine (30^{13}). With the passing of the government of Egypt, these mercenaries must also have passed under Persian control.

When these papyri begin, early in the fifth century, the colony, while retaining its military organization, had become a settled community. Its members could buy and sell land and houses,

[1] Cf. Deut. 26^{5} ארמי אבד אבי.

[2] But see note on ו[רין]ת, 28^{2}, and on דגל, 5^{2}.

they engaged in trade, they could go to law before the civil courts and they held civil posts under government. Moreover they had their wives and families, and the women could hold property and take legal action in their own right, and were even reckoned as belonging to the *degel*, whether through their relation to the men, or independently, does not appear. We have thus the outline of a picture of a Jewish community, its life and manners, in the fifth (and sixth) century B.C., which is the more valuable because it is not an intentional description, and therefore need not be discounted as *tendencieux*.

They lived on equal terms with the Egyptians, transacted business with people of various races, intermarried,[1] and sometimes bore alien names (cf. OT names in -baal). But they aroused anti-Jewish feeling, and suffered violence which they ascribed, as always, and probably with as little reason then as now, to hatred of their religion. No doubt their animal sacrifices offended Egyptian susceptibilities, but much is also to be ascribed to natural suspicion of a community with customs differing from those of its neighbours, holding aloof from the common pursuits of its fellow-citizens, and showing contempt or hostility to everything outside itself. The great pogrom described in nos. 27, 30–34 may have brought the colony to an end.

The internal affairs of the community were directed by a head-man with 'his colleagues the priests', very much as at the present day by the chief rabbi and his beth-din. In the latter part of the fifth century the chief man was Yedoniah b. Gemariah. It was to him that the edict of Darius (no. 21) was addressed in 419; it was he who received the contributions to the temple funds ($22^{120.121}$) in the same year; it was he who drew up the petition to the governor of Judaea (no. 30) in 408, and a similar petition (no. 33) about the same time, and he was one of the notable prisoners mentioned in no. 34 about 407 B.C. Whether he was a priest is not certain, but it is probable on general grounds, and also from his connexion with religious affairs (21, 22). At any rate he was politically recognized by the Persian government.

[1] But cf. introduction to no. 14.

But to most students of this dark period the papyri will be chiefly valuable for the indications they give as to the state of Jewish religion in the colony. It would no doubt be still more interesting to have similar documents relating to Jerusalem in the fifth century, or indeed any early century, but the state of things in the colony may to some extent be taken to represent what had been in Judaea before the days of Ezra. The colonists were not better than their fathers—nor perhaps much worse. To begin with, they regarded themselves as specially devoted to the worship of the national God, whom they call יהו. This name, as I have argued elsewhere,[1] is not an abbreviation of יהוה, but an earlier form, and only another way of writing the earliest form יה. As the ה seems to be a mere vowel-sign, or perhaps *hamza*, I have adopted here the transliteration *Ya'u*, as an approximate pronunciation, rather than the customary *Yahu* or *Yeho*, which are no forms. He is generally called, between Jews, simply 'Ya'u the God' (13^{14}, 22^{1}, 25^{6}); in dealings with Persians, 'the God of heaven' or 'Ya'u the God of heaven' ($30^{2.15.27}$ [but cf. $30^{6.24.26}$], 32^{3} [but cf. 33^{8}]), and often in letters. Yet we also find other gods mentioned besides Ya'u. The most explicit case of this is in $22^{123-125}$ where the temple-fund is to be divided between Ya'u and 'Anathbethel in nearly equal shares, and Ishumbethel who receives much less. In the law-courts they swear usually by Ya'u, but in 44^{3} an oath is recorded 'by the temple and by 'Anathya'u', and in 7^{7} a man is challenged to swear 'by Ḥerembethel the god'. There are also personal names like Ḥeremnathan and Bethelnathan (18^{4}), formed like the orthodox Jonathan and Elnathan. Whether other gods were recognized besides these, whether these were all distinct or e.g. 'Anathbethel was the same as 'Anathya'u, what was the meaning of the various compounds, and what relation the different divinities bore to one another, the evidence does not show. It would seem that besides Ya'u they recognized 'Anath, Bethel, Ishum and Ḥerem. There may have been others, but it is at least a coincidence that we have the names of five gods and that there were five gates to the temple (30^{9}).

[1] *JRAS* 1920, p. 175.

Of these names 'Anath is known as that of a goddess in Syria and elsewhere, so that it has been suggested that 'Anathya'u was intended as a consort of Ya'u—the Queen of heaven (Jer. 44¹⁷), as He was the God of heaven. Bethel has long been recognized as an early Canaanite god (cf. Gen. 31¹³). These two therefore may well have been brought by the colonists with them from Judaea. It was not a case of falling away from a monotheistic ideal, but a continuation of the pre-exilic popular beliefs. Ishum (if that is the pronunciation of אשם) may be the Babylonian demon of that name, but it is also worth while to remember the persistent tradition that the Samaritans worshipped a divinity called Ashima, to whom it has been thought reference is made in Amos 8¹⁴ by a play on the word אשמה. If this was true in the time of Amos, the tradition continued long after it had ceased to be so, perhaps encouraged by the later Samaritan pronunciation of שמה 'the name' (which they still read instead of יהוה) as *ashma*[1] Lidzbarski also cites[2] from a late Syrian-Greek inscription a god Συμβέτυλος, whose name looks very like Ishumbethel. Thus it seems probable that a god אשם was worshipped in Syria and was brought by the colonists to Egypt with the others.

As to Ḥerem I have no suggestion to make.

Since these five gods are mentioned by name, there can be no question that the word אלהיא used in these texts, and sometimes as subject to a verb in the *plural*, is to be taken as 'gods' and not as God (אלהא) on the analogy of Hebrew. It is most often found in the beginnings of letters: note especially 39¹, and oddly enough 21² in the edict about the Passover, from one Jew to another. Further, in one place (14⁵) a Jewess swears by Sati the Egyptian goddess, in a transaction with an Egyptian

It is thus evident that the description in Jeremiah (44¹⁵ &c) of the religious practices of the Jews in Egypt in his time is in the main corroborated by what we find in these texts a century later, and the explanation is supplied by Jeremiah himself (44¹⁷). It was no new heresy that they invented for themselves—people do not invent much—but they did 'as we have done, we and our fathers . . . in the cities of Judah.' They took with them in all

[1] See Cowley, *Samaritan Liturgy* (1909), p xli

[2] *Ephemeris* iii (1912), p 247

sincerity the old religion of pre-exilic Judah, and continued to practise it after the exile (and Ezra) had made it impossible in the mother-country. Thus, as a picture not only of their own time but also of pre-exilic Judaism—the religion against which all the prophets protested—these papyri are specially instructive.

Yet the national God was Ya'u. Whatever may have been their doctrine as to his relation to the other gods, there is no sort of doubt that he was pre-eminent. It was to him that the temple belonged, although it seems that other gods were also worshipped there. The temple of Elephantine was not a mere synagogue, but a considerable building, with an altar and all the appurtenances of sacrifice (30[9–12]). It is called אגורא (meeting-place?) and מסגדא (place of worship), and is first mentioned (13[11]) in 447. But it had been in existence at least as early as 525 (30[13 14]). This is a very surprising fact, quite contrary to the law of Deuteronomy (12[5 6] &c.). The case of the Onias-temple, built at Leontopolis about 154 B.C., was on an altogether different footing. That was definitely schismatic, and in whatever way the supporters of it might defend their action, they knew at least that it required defence. The colonists of Elephantine had no such misgivings. After their temple was destroyed in a riot of the Egyptians (in 411), they sent a petition to the High Priest at Jerusalem, asking for help to rebuild it. When this was disregarded (30[18 19]), they appealed to the Persian governor at Jerusalem. There is no hint of any suspicion that the temple could be considered heretical, and they would surely not have appealed to the High Priest at Jerusalem if they had felt any doubt about it. On the contrary they give the impression of being proud of having a temple of their own, and as pious devotees of Ya'u (no other god is mentioned in the petition) seriously distressed at the loss of religious opportunities caused by its destruction.

The explanation seems to be that in this respect, as in the worship of strange gods, their practice was a continuation of that of pre-exilic Judaism. It is now generally held that the book of Deuteronomy was first promulgated under Josiah (about 621 B.C.). Previously, as we learn from e.g. the books of Samuel, sacrifice was habitually offered at various places, and indeed until the reign of Solomon no temple existed at Jerusalem [1] to mark it out as the place which the Lord had chosen. It cannot be supposed that the book of Deuteronomy was at once accepted everywhere, even in Judaea, or that it at once put a stop to popular practices which it condemned. Still less should we expect these colonists if they left the country soon afterwards, or perhaps were already abroad, to feel bound by the new and stricter enactments. The exile followed in 588, breaking all continuity, and Judaea was left without religious direction. We need not wonder then that in the complete collapse of religious institutions, the colonists, deprived of any central authority and despairing of its restoration, decided to work out their own salvation and naturally on the lines with which they were familiar. What was their attitude towards the changes in Judaea, or whether they knew of them, we cannot tell. They may even have taken the view of Rabshakeh (2 Ki. 18^{22}, cf. Elijah in 1 Ki. 19^{10}), regarding the abolition of local sanctuaries as an act of disrespect to Ya'u. But it is quite intelligible that the High Priest took no notice of their appeal. We can also understand why they afterwards wrote to the Persian governor, who had no interest in Deuteronomy, and to the Samaritans, who interpreted it in their own way, and that they received a reply.

On the persons concerned with the petition, and the difficulty of reconciling various accounts of the history, see the introduction to no. 30.

Before leaving the subject of the temple a word must be said about the difficult passage in Isaiah 19^{19+}, 'In that day shall there be an altar to the Lord in the midst of the land of Egypt, and a pillar (מצבה) at the border thereof to the Lord', &c. This has generally been taken as a prophecy, before or after the event, of the Onias temple, that having been hitherto the only foreign temple known. It is dangerous to argue as if we knew all the facts, for the passage might equally well refer to the temple at Elephantine—on the border of Egypt. Then the date of the prophecy may be put considerably earlier than has been supposed. It is in fact not unreasonable to suggest that it was

[1] It must be remembered that the name does not even occur in the Pentateuch.

written before the promulgation of Deuteronomy. If there was, say just before 621, any considerable migration of Jews to Egypt, the prophecy may have been intended as an encouragement to the emigrants. 'Though you are leaving your native land, you shall make a new home in Egypt and follow there the faith of your fathers (Is. 19^{21}). It is a great opportunity for you'. Note also another strange coincidence five gods, five gates of the temple, and five cities speaking the language of Canaan

Thus there are several indications that the colonists in the fifth century B.C. remained at the same stage of religious development (if that is what we ought to call it) as their fathers in Judaea in the seventh century. It is consequently of particular interest to collect from these papyri all possible evidence as to their beliefs and practice, always remembering that in the course of two centuries some things may have changed for better or worse. Unfortunately the inquiry depends largely on an *argumentum e silentio*, which must not be unduly pressed, since we cannot be sure that what is not mentioned did not exist. Two thousand years hence if a part of English literature exists, it might well be a considerable part and yet contain no reference to King Alfred, or the Norman conquest, or the Reformation, or the doctrines of the Church, or to a number of questions which agitate us at the present day.

We have positive evidence that sacrifices, including animal sacrifices (מנחה ולבונה ועלוה) were offered ($30^{21\ 25\ 28}$). This indeed was the express purpose of the temple with its altar (מדבחא), for when the temple was destroyed their chief complaint is that they can no longer offer sacrifice. One would suppose that such offerings would be the duty of the priests, the sons of Aaron, or at any rate of Levites. But although priests[1] are frequently mentioned, they are nowhere called sons of Aaron, nor does the name Aaron ever occur, nor that of Levi or the levitical order. It seems difficult to explain away this omission and at the same time to maintain that the 'house of Aaron' and the levites were recognized in the seventh century in Judaea as they were later. The question is too large to be discussed here. I will only call

[1] כהניא. For the priests of the Egyptians they use כמריא, as in the OT and elsewhere.

attention to the fact that apart from the Hexateuch (*de quo videant critici!*) the name Aaron occurs only in Psalms, Ezra, Nehemiah, Chronicles, and once in Judges, twice (really once) in Samuel, and once in Micah. The passage in Micah (6^4) is probably an addition, in 1 Sam. $12^{6,8}$ the name is certainly added as the natural accompaniment of Moses,[1] and in Judges (20^{28}) it is a gloss to complete the genealogy. That is to say, it does not occur for certain in any undoubtedly early writer, not even in Ezekiel! There is an explanation of this, which I leave the reader to discover. It certainly looks as if the house of Aaron were a late post-exilic invention, and if so, the colonists would naturally know nothing of it.

What precisely constituted a *kahen* at Elephantine does not appear. One of their prerogatives, we might suppose, would be to possess the Law of Moses and to administer it. Yet there is no hint of its existence. We should expect that in 30^{25} they would say 'offer sacrifice according to our law', and that in other places they would make some allusion to it. But there is none. So far as we learn from these texts Moses might never have existed, there might have been no bondage in Egypt, no exodus, no monarchy, no prophets. There is no mention of other tribes and no claim to any heritage in the land of Judah. Among the numerous names of colonists, Abraham, Jacob, Joseph, Moses, Samuel, David, so common in later times, never occur (nor in Nehemiah), nor any other name derived from their past history as recorded in the Pentateuch and early literature. It is almost incredible, but it is true.

Again, that essentially Jewish (though also Babylonian) institution, the Sabbath, is nowhere noticed. Even if there were no occasion for mentioning it explicitly, we should expect that it would sometimes interfere with the transaction of business when that involved the drawing up of a document. At the present day no practising orthodox Jew would write on the Sabbath. Dr. Fotheringham, in a note on the subject in *JTS* 14 (1913), p. 574, concludes from a calculation of the dates that 'they do not

[1] The LXX in v. 8 has κατῴκισεν, 'He (i.e. God) made to dwell', rightly, for Moses and Aaron did not go into the land. For 'brought forth' Cod. A has the singular (ἐξήγαγεν) as if of Moses alone.

prove the existence of such a scruple, nor indeed the absence of it, for no document between Jews seems to be *certainly* dated on the Sabbath. There is in fact a complete silence on the subject.

Another of these negative instances concerns the festivals. None of them is mentioned except, in one papyrus, the feast of Unleavened Bread and possibly the Passover. Even in the case of these it is difficult to explain the fact. No. 21 is an edict of Darius ordering[1] an observance of the feast of Unleavened Bread, and, if the proposed restoration is right, the Passover. This can only mean either that the festivals in question were unknown in the colony, or that they had fallen into desuetude. It might even be taken as an argument that Josiah's great celebration of the Passover ('Surely there was not kept such a passover from the days of the Judges' 2 Ki. 23^{22}) was the first institution of it, and that the colonists, having left their country before 621, knew no more of it than they knew of Deuteronomy. That, however, is not proved and is hardly probable. It is more likely that the Passover in early times was irregularly observed, that Josiah really revived it after a period of neglect, and that its yearly celebration was only established, like so much else, under Ezra. This would equally well account for the edict (no. 21). Though the colonists would have vaguely known of the institution, they would have been accustomed to neglect it, as their fathers did before Josiah's time. The issue of the edict thus again suggests that they may have already left Judaea before 621. The important thing however, about which there is no doubt, is that the order came from the Persian king. It was a curt command (if my restoration is approximately correct): 'In the month of Tybi (?) let there be a Passover for the Jewish garrison'. That is the whole of it—from the king to Arsames the governor of the province. The details are added by the messenger, who was clearly a Jew—'your brother Hananiah'. Various reasons may have induced the Great King to intervene in the religious affairs of an obscure settlement, but whatever they were, the case is exactly parallel to that of the letter of

[1] Blau, in Magyar-zsidó Szemle 1921, p. 44, argues that it was only permissive, granting exemption from military duties during the festival.

Artaxerxes in Ezra 7^{12+}, and shows that we need not doubt the authenticity of the latter document. The similarity of the style of the letter in Ezra to that of texts in this collection is striking. No doubt in both cases the king was only responsible for the general order or permission. The details are due to his Jewish protégés. See further in the introduction to no. 21. Apparently they did keep the Passover on this occasion, as directed, for it is mentioned at least on two ostraca[1] (not included in this volume), of about the same date as no. 21, though of course these may refer to another celebration of it. It is worth noting also that the great list (no. 22) of subscriptions to the temple funds was drawn up in the same year (419) as the Passover edict, and it is difficult to believe that they are not connected. This again would seem to indicate that the Passover was an exceptional event. On the other hand, in no. 21 there cannot have been any directions for the ceremony, for there is no room on the papyrus, whereas the rules for the feast of Unleavened Bread occupy half the document. Did they know all about the one (choosing the lamb, bitter herbs, eating in haste, &c.) and not about the other? It will be seen that the conclusions to be drawn from no. 21 are not all certain. What is certain is that the celebration of the (Passover and) feast of Unleavened Bread was ordered by the Persian king, and that these are the only festivals[2] mentioned (and that exceptionally) in these papyri.

If the arguments here adduced are at all well-founded, it follows that the religious condition of Judaism before the exile, so far as we can draw deductions about it from these papyri, was very different from what has been usually assumed. To sum it up, we may picture the historical development somewhat as follows. From early times documents[3] which eventually formed part of the Tora, no doubt existed. They were partly historical, partly legal and theological, and were composed at various dates. But they were the possession of a priestly or learned class.

[1] Ungnad no. 77 A 5 and *PSBA* 1915, p. 222, perhaps both by the same hand.

[2] In Ungnad no. 77 A 3 even if מכביא = סכות, I cannot think that it refers to the feast of Tabernacles. In Neh. 8^{17} we are practically told that the feast had never been kept before.

[3] I think there is no doubt that they were written in cuneiform and probably in the Babylonian language, though this is not necessary to the argument.

necessarily limited in number. In the earliest times, down to, say, the reign of Solomon, owing to the disunion of the inhabitants, the unsettled state of the country and the difficulty of communication, the possessors of these documents can have had little influence on the mass of the people, who lived in isolated groups, without knowledge of any Law, following the religious customs and beliefs with which they happened to be in contact. Later on we find the prophetic class becoming important and using its influence to promote the exclusive worship of Ya'u among the people, though still with little reference to a written Law or to the early history. Then came the exile, and we cannot know what ferment of mind and spirit took place in Babylon or in Judaea. No sooner is the exile ended and order to some extent restored in Jerusalem, than we find in Nehemiah frequent insistence on the Law of Moses, in striking contrast to the earlier literature, which ignores it. It had suddenly sprung into full existence, and a definite effort was made to spread among the people the knowledge of it, which had previously belonged to the few, by reading[1] it in public (Neh. $8^{8.13}$ &c.). Apparently such readings were made a regular institution, for we find them mentioned again in Neh. 9^3, 13^1. What was it they read? I believe it was the Tora very much as we have it to-day. The constant insistence, especially in the latter part of Nehemiah, on details required by the Pentateuch, seems certainly to point to this. Moreover, the existence of the Samaritan recension of the Pentateuch, practically identical with the Masoretic, can hardly be explained in any other way. If the Samaritan schism occurred, as tradition states, somewhere about 430 B.C. (Josephus makes it a century later), the hostile community was not likely to adopt a body of Jewish law compiled after that date. We can only suppose that, at the time, the Pentateuch was already in existence, and had gained such general acceptance that the deserting priest Menasseh felt it advisable to carry the Law with him. Who then was responsible for this fruitful innovation? I think the answer is given by the

[1] The much-quoted passage, Neh. 8^8, is generally taken to mean that they translated it extempore into Aramaic—the beginning of Targum. There is no reason why it should not mean that they read a Hebrew translation from cuneiform Babylonian.

persistent rabbinical tradition [1] that the Law was lost and Ezra restored it. Only it would be more correct to say that the Law did not exist in its present form until Ezra drew it up, compiling it from existing separate sources, and completing it. He is described specially (Ezra 7⁶) as 'a ready scribe in the law of Moses', who 'had prepared his heart to seek the law of the Lord . . . and to teach' it (7¹⁰). Having been educated in Babylonia he must have been familiar with the difficult cuneiform writing, as well as with the Babylonian language, with Aramaic and, no doubt, with Hebrew. He was therefore able, with the help of 'his colleagues the priests' to put in order the [cuneiform] tablets containing the various sources of the Pentateuch, to translate them into Hebrew, to weld them together into a more or less consistent whole, and to write down the result in the simple Aramaic alphabet which he had learned in Assyria (אשורית). This would account alike for the general uniformity of language and for the idiosyncrasies of various parts, which were due partly to the diverse characteristics of the original documents, and partly to differences in the style of the various collaborators. In enforcing the Law, Ezra was helped by the powerful support of the Persian king (7²⁶), without which it could never have obtained general and immediate acceptance.[2]

It may be objected that the above account is merely imaginary. It is true that many of the details of it are nowhere explicitly recorded. Nor should we expect that even the central fact of Ezra's redaction of the Law would be described. It was necessary to his success that the newly promulgated code should be represented as that which was originally revealed to Israel by the hand of Moses—which, in its essence, it may have been. The strength of Ezra's moral appeal (apart from the political support of the Persian king) lay in his insistence that the Law had hitherto been neglected, that this neglect was the cause of the national misfortunes, and that the only hope for the future was to be found in a return to the supposed faith of an ideal past. To have admitted that the Law was a new thing, invented even with the best objects, would have defeated his whole purpose

[1] e.g. in B. T. Sanhedrin, f. 21ᵇ and Sukka, f. 20ᵃ.

[2] So too Ed. Meyer, *Die Entstehung des Judentums*, 1896.

And perhaps it was not new. Various documents, of different dates, must or may have been in existence, from which the complete work was produced very much in the manner on which modern criticism insists—only that previously the documents had not been generally accessible, and that the final redaction took place at one definite time, and not as a gradual and rather undefined process. This view, though many difficulties still remain, and though its details may require modification, does on the whole provide an intelligible explanation of the facts.

I have digressed at some length upon it, because the problems which it seeks to explain are the most important arising from a study of these papyri. Regarded without prejudice, these texts lead to the conclusion that the Pentateuch, both in its historical and legal aspects, was unknown in the fifth century to the Jews of Elephantine, and it is probable that the populace in Judaea in the seventh century was no better informed. But in the book of Nehemiah we find the Pentateuch being made known and accepted—and we are bound to seek an explanation. The importance of the new revelation is that in it we see the birth of modern Judaism, which could never have developed by natural process from pre-exilic Judaism. The subsequent development of it down to the present day is easily traced, in the gradual elaboration of halakha and the exaltation of it by the suppression of all else—its systematization in the Mishna—its discussion in the Talmud—its codification again by Maimonides—its extension by Jacob b. Asher and Joseph Ḳaro—with its final reduction *ad impossibile* in the *pilpul* of the eighteenth century—the moderation of it by Moses Mendelssohn—and the revolt against it by the modern 'reformed' Jews. All this is the natural growth of the system born under Ezra: it could not have grown out of a religious system such as that of the colonists of Elephantine.

Now to return to our texts. The internal affairs of the colony, as mentioned above, were directed by the head man of the community, who was Yedoniah in 419. No reports of his court are preserved and no mention is made of his administering the Mosaic law. Even when both parties were Jews they appeared before the Persian-Egyptian court (1^{3}, 25^{2}) though the composition of the court is usually not stated. Perhaps the head of the *degel* exercised magisterial functions, and this would account for the mention of the *degel* of the parties at issue; see on no. 25^{2}. As a military body they were under the רבחילא 'the commander of the garrison', who was in turn subordinate to the פרתרך, a Persian title. That the latter was superior to the former appears from $20^{4.5}$, where Waidrang is רבחילא, compared with 30^{5}, where he has become (twelve years later) *fratarak*, and his son (30^{7}) is רבחילא. The *fratarak* was no doubt governor of the province (of Tšṭrs). The governor-general of the country is usually called simply מראן 'our lord', without any more specific title. In the latter part of the period he was named ארשם, O P Aršâma, Bab. Aršam (Ungnad), Arsames. He was directly responsible to the king.

Several minor officials are mentioned, as דיניא ($16^{4.5}$), ספרי מדינתא ($17^{1.6}$), אזדכריא ($17^{5.7}$), המדכריא ($26^{4.23}$), פרמנכריא ($26^{4.8}$), תיפתיא גושכיא (27^{9}), on whom see the notes on the passages.

The courts over which the רבחילא and the פרתרך presided, with their assessors (דיניא), administered no doubt the law of the Persian empire, but this law, like so much else, was evidently taken over by the conquerors from the Babylonians, or was based on their system. Thus we find the enumeration of relatives of the parties, the fine for breach of contract (ינתן כסף, *kaspi iddin*), the definition of the boundaries of property: special phrases like דין ודבב (*dînu dabâbu*), טב לבב, באבני מלכא, with their variants: particular words, like גרי (Bab. *garu*) 'to bring an action' and many more. See e.g. Meissner, *Beitr. zum altbab. Privatrecht* (1893). The method of preparing a document may be compared with that described by Jeremiah (32^{9+}) drawn up in 586. The money was weighed on the scales (pap. 15^{24}), the deed was written, signed by (or for) the witnesses, and sealed. One deed (no. 5) was actually found rolled up, tied with string and with the clay seal still intact. But Jeremiah's document was evidently on a clay tablet, placed in an envelope, and an 'open' duplicate was also made. The same practice may have been followed at Elephantine, and this would account for the duplicate of no. 2. The deed was then delivered to the interested party (ספר זי כתב פלוני לאלמוני) in the presence of the witnesses, and was stored in a clay pot (Jer. 32[14]) or in a box (as some of the papyri were found) 'that it might last many days'.

In general the connexion with Babylonian law is well worthy of a thorough study, as is also the question of the double dating of documents and the chronology generally. This has not been attempted here, partly because of the necessity of restricting the limits of this volume, and partly because it would require special knowledge which I do not claim to possess.

Finally a word must be added as to the money. The most important text in this connexion is no. 15, a marriage contract in which the value of various items of the gift to the bride is stated and the total given at the end. The items are valued as follows:

In line	5,		5 shekels	
,,	6,	1 karash,	2 ,,	
,,	8,	2 ,,	8 ,,	
,,	10,		8 ,,	
,,	11,		7 ,,	
,,	12,		1 ,,	2 R
,,	12,		1 ,,	2 R
,,	13.		2 ,,	
,,	13.			2 R
Total.		3 kerashin	34 shekels	6 R

In line 14 the total is given as 6 kerashin, 5 shekels, 20 ḥallurin. Now the standard (see below) of the silver is given sometimes as לעשרתא II ר and sometimes as I לכרש II ר (cf. e.g. $15^{7.14}$ with 20^{15}). Hence it seems probable that 1 karash=עשרתא 'the ten-piece' or presumably the piece of 10 shekels. If so, then 30 shekels= 3 kerashin. Applying this to our first total we have 3 kerashin 34 shekels 6 R=6 kerashin 4 shekels 6 R, which should be equal to 6 kerashin 5 shekels 20 ḥallurin. The next question is, what is the value of R? It might of course also be a D, and it has been taken to stand for דרכמון drachma, but this would hardly be found in the earlier texts. Taken as R, it might stand for רעי, which seems to be a money term in 73^{6}, &c., of unknown value. The simplest explanation, however, is to take it for רבע(א) 'a quarter' sc. of a shekel. (A corroboration of this may be found in 15[24]. If the wife divorces her husband, she is to pay back 7 shekels 2 R, i.e. $7\frac{1}{2}$ shekels, which are equal to the price he originally paid for her (15[5]) plus 50 per cent.) Then in the above equation (4 sh. 6 R = 5 sh. 20 hal.) since 4 R = 1 shekel, it follows that 2 R = 20 hallurin, and we have the following table

1 karash = 10 shekels.
1 shekel = 4 quarters ר
1 quarter = 10 hallurin.

As to the names, *karash* is Persian, no doubt the same as *karša* on a trilingual weight in the British Museum. In the Babylonian inscription the 2 karšā are given as $\frac{1}{3}$ of a mina, see Weissbach, *Keilinschriften der Achameniden* (1911), p. 105, so that 6 kerašin = 60 shekels = 1 mina. (The reading כבש in Sayce and Cowley is wrong, and the conclusions drawn from it need not be considered.)

No satisfactory derivation of the name karša has been proposed.

Shekel and *rebhaʿ* (*ribhʿa*) are both common Semitic.

Ḥallûru is a small Babylonian money term (see the Lexicon), not previously found in Western Semitic. Cf. *PSBA* 25 (1903). p. 206.

The larger amounts are generally reckoned by royal weight (באבני מלכא, cf. 2 Sam. 14[26]), as also in Assyria (Köberle, *NKZ* 1908, p. 178), and are further defined as ר וו לעשרתא or ר וו לכרש ו. If the above calculations are correct, this would imply an alloy of 2 quarters, or $\frac{1}{2}$ a shekel, in 10, that is 5 per cent. Money is also sometimes described as כסף צריף (5[7], 28[11.12]), where it is likewise paid באבני מלכא. This must mean pure silver as distinguished from silver with 5 per cent alloy, and 'royal weight' must refer to weight only and not to standard. Specimens of certified weights with Aramaic inscriptions[1] are known, e.g. *CIS* ii, 1, no 108 (from Abydos) and no 1 (from Nineveh) The higher sums (or weights) מנן 'minae' and כנכרן 'talents' are rarely found The business transactions are as a rule not on that scale. Also gold was apparently not used as currency

In the later documents (35[4.7], 37[12]) we find another term used,

[1] Where the ב cannot mean 'double', but is to be taken as in באבני מלכא, so that בזי ארקא is 'according to (the weight) of the country' and [בז]י מלך 'according to the weight of the k[ing]'

סתתרי, which is no doubt the Greek στατήρ, and is given as the equivalent of two shekels (35^4).

On the literary pieces reference may be made to the special introductions to the Aḥiḳar fragments and the version of the Behistun inscription.

For the grammar, see the introduction to the edition of Sayce and Cowley, supplemented by the *Anhang über den aramäischen Dialekt* in Sachau (p. 261). I hope to publish a detailed treatment of the grammar in comparison with biblical Aramaic at a future date.

My main object in this volume has been to contribute something to the establishment of the text and translation, as the only sure basis for future investigation, rather than to attempt a discussion of all the questions involved.

To avoid complication, letters which are broken in the text but are nevertheless certain are not marked. Doubtful letters are overlined. Letters restored are enclosed between square brackets. The readings have been tested over and over again with the facsimiles. In the translation, restorations are indicated as far as possible by italics. Such restorations were necessary in order to show the connexion of the sentences. They have been made with great care and after much thought, and are in many cases certain. Others of course represent only my personal view and are open to question. I have tried in the notes to distinguish between what is certain and what is conjectural.

Where the restored letters or words are not my own, I have tried in the notes to ascribe them to their originators, but I fear that I have not always succeeded in doing so. The literature dealing with these papyri is large and scattered, so that some proposals may have escaped me, or been adopted unconsciously, while some readings have been suggested by more than one scholar.

Words inserted for clearness, owing to the difference of idiom between the two languages, are put in parentheses.

Proper names found in the O.T. have been spelt as in the R.V., though this causes some inconsistencies.

Where the vocalization of a name is unknown, its consonants only are printed, in capitals.

Unknown words, introduced to show the form of the sentence, are transliterated (consonants only) in small capitals.

ARAMAIC PAPYRI

No. 1.

Agreement dated 495 B.C.

The numeral after שנת in line 1 is a very carelessly written 𐡟 (=20). It cannot be 𐡞 (=10) The year is therefore the 27th of Darius, and since Darius II reigned only twenty years, the king must be Darius I and the date 495 B.C. The papyrus is thus the earliest in the collection. This conclusion is supported by the style of the writing, with which cf. that of no. 2 (484 B.C). Sachau also compares no. 3, which is less like. Note also the spelling דריוש, as in O. T., which seems to be earlier than דריהוש and דריוהוש as in the later papyri, under Darius II This is the only place in these papyri where it has this form A characteristic of the early writing seems to be the pronounced difference between thick and thin strokes. The formulae also differ from those of later documents

This is a contract or agreement arising out of a previous decision of the court, of which no 67, 3 is perhaps a fragment. Certain property had been divided between two parties (cf. no. 28) who now agree to an exchange of half of their respective shares. The names of the parties are all feminine, Selua and Yethoma of the one part and Ya'a'or of the other part, showing that in 495 B.C. in this colony women could hold property in their own right, and could go to law about it.

Sachau, plate 30. Ungnad, no. 31.

1 בי[ו]ם II ל[י]רח אפף שנת 𐡟 III III I לדריוש מלכא אמרת סלואה ברת
2 קניה ויתומה אחתה ליההאור ברת שלומם אנחן יהבן לכי פלג
3 מנ[ת]א זי יהבו לן דיני מלכא ורוך רבחילא חלף פלג מנתא זי
4 מטתכי עם נאהבת לׄמׄחר יום אחרן לא נכל נגרכי במנתא זכי
5 [ו]נׄמׄ[ר] לא אנחן יהבנה לכי לא יכל אח ואחה בר וברה קרב
6 ורׄחׄיׄקׄ יׄגׄרׄנׄכׄי וׄזׄי יגרנכי במנתא זכי זי יהבן לכי ינתן לכי
7 כסף כרשן III II ומנתא זילכי תוב
8 שהדיא
9 [ה]ושע בר הׄוׄדׄויה
10 שלומם בר עׄזׄר[י]ה
11 צפניה בר מכי

[1] On the 2nd day of the month Epiphi of the 27th year of King Darius, said Selua daughter of [2] Kenaya and Yethoma her sister to Ya'a'or daughter of Shelomim, We have given to you half [3] the share which was granted to us by the king's judges and Ravaka the commander, in exchange for half the share which [4] accrued to you with Ne'ehebeth. Hereafter, on a future day, we shall not be able to sue you in the matter of this your share, [5] and say, We did not give it to you; nor shall a brother or sister (of ours), son or daughter, relative [6] or alien be able to sue you; and whoever shall sue you in the matter of this your share which we have given you, shall pay to you [7] the sum of 5 karash and the share is yours: and [8] the witnesses (are) [9] Hosea b. Hodaviah, [10] Shelomim b. Azariah, [11] Zephaniah b. Machi.

Line 1. Usually the equivalent day of the Jewish month is also given. Its omission here and in no. 2 may be merely accidental. In no. 5 (471 B.C.) it is added, but in no. 7 (461 B.C.) it is omitted. סלואח (elsewhere סלוא, סלוה) as a fem. name, is only known from these papyri. Masc. סלוא, סלו in O.T.

Line 2. קניה, only here. It may be קְנָיָה (so Sachau), cf. אלקנה, or for קוניה as in 4^{2}. יתומה only here and in 67, 3 (with סלואח). The masc. יתום and יתמא also occur. יההאור only here. No doubt to be divided יהה = יהו and אור 'light' (so G. B. Gray). On יהה = יהו see 13^{14} note. Before אנחן it would be usual to have לאמר.

Line 3. מנ[ת]א something allotted. In Hebrew cf. Pss. 11^{6}, 16^{5}. In Talmud it is a common legal term for 'share' (= חלק in 28^{3}) assigned by the court. There is nothing to show the nature of the property. דיני מלכא. The previous action was taken before the royal (i.e. Persian) court, not the *beth din* of the colony. ורוך. In this alphabet there is no certain distinction between ר and ד, except that ד *seems* generally to have a shorter down-stroke. The first ו is unusual in form, but probable. The word can only be a preposition 'by order of' &c. or a proper name with 'and'. The latter is more probable, but the name is unknown. Justi gives Rawai. Cf. perhaps Zend *rava*, 'pleasant' with the OP termination *-ka*. This is another argument for the early date, since in 408–7 (the alternative date) the רבחילא was נפין (30^{7}). רבחילא one word, as usually. He sat with the (civil?) court. Cf. also 16^{7}.

Line 4. נאהבת, elsewhere נהבת. It seems to be a Hebrew Niphal form, 'beloved'. The meaning of עם is not clear. It may mean that N was co-partner with Ya'a'or, when it would be equivalent to 'and' (so Sachau), or N was a slave and part of the property divided (cf. no. 28). The former is the more probable, but her father ought to be named. לְמָחר. There is a trace of ל and a down-stroke after it. Sachau disregards both, and reads וחד 'and one other day'. So Torczyner, 'one day hereafter'. We should expect או before יום as elsewhere.

It must mean 'hereafter, on some later day', a variant of the usual 'to-morrow or another day'. For ל cf. Ahikar, l. 39. נכל usually taken as נְכֻל with first radical assimilated, from יכל. More probably from a stem כול (כל), of which כהל is only another spelling. נגרכי ought to be (Sachau says a mistake for) נגרנכי Note the construction, which is usual. The root גרה, cf Hebrew (Piel) and Aramaic, means to 'stir up', hence to institute legal proceedings against, with an accusative of the person. It is a Babylonian legal term. זני 'this of thine', speaking to a woman, as זך to a man

Line 5. [ו]נ̇מ[ר], so Epstein. Sachau's ומה (for וזי) gives no satisfactory sense. נמר for נאמר is not wholly convincing, since the form does not occur elsewhere (but cf. לממר in 32^{2}) A נ alone does not quite fit the space, for the lines begin very evenly, but there is a trace of the tail of a נ. Therefore not נאמר We should expect לאמר, but that cannot be read יהבנה. The ה is a suffix, 'we have given it'. קרב defectively for קריב 'related or not related' (רחיק), the regular formula, and similarly in Babylonian law.

Line 7 כרשן The karash was worth 10 shekels (see p. xxii) This is not an unusually high penalty, as Sachau suggests. As a rule the money is defined as being באבני מלכא. תוב. The reading is clear, but it looks as though added as an afterthought. Elsewhere we have ולא דין ולא דבב. In later Aramaic תוב or תו means 'again', 'further'. I doubt if it can mean here 'nevertheless'. More likely it introduces שהדיא, 'moreover the witnesses are'.

Lines 9–11 The witnesses' names here, as in no. 11, were written by the scribe. הושע בר הודויה occurs almost certainly in no. 2. הוד̇ו̇יה is fairly certain, not ירחיה (as Sachau), an unknown name. The pronunciation Hodaviah is attested by the Masoretes.

Line 10 שלומם possibly the same as in l. 2, witnessing on behalf of his daughter עֲזַר[יה] uncertain, but probable. Hardly the same as in 20^{6} (420 B.C.), but perhaps his grandfather There is some evidence of the practice of calling a child after his grandfather.

Line 11. מכי only here (and in Num. 13^{15})

No. 2.

Contract for supplying Corn to the Garrison 484 B.C

There is a slight uncertainty as to the number of the year, owing to a break in the papyrus It must be either 2 (as Sachau) or 3 There is hardly room for ||→, since in this papyrus the → is made rather large, cf. l 4 and l. 6. Year 22 is impossible, because Xerxes reigned only 20 or 21 years. On the whole 2 is the more probable, and the date is therefore 484 B.C. The style of the writing in general resembles that of no. 1.

This is a contract, of which the precise terms are obscure owing to the loss of the ends of all the lines (about 18 letters missing in each line). The main points are that Hosea and Aḥiab received from Espemet a consignment of barley and lentils which they undertake to deliver (at Syene) to the government officials for the use of a section of the garrison.

The similar document, no. 3, may be a duplicate, but it differs in form and thus throws little light on the details of the transaction. Epstein has endeavoured to combine the two, and on the assumption of their identity has restored the ends of most of the lines, but he is not convincing. It seems best not to attempt the restoration of most of the lines.

Sachau, plates 25, 26. Ungnad, no. 27.

1 ב 𐡜 III III II לירח פאפי שנת 𐡙 חשיריש [מל]כ[א ביב בירתא אמר הושע
2 בר הודויה ואחיאב בר גמריה לאס[פמט בר פפטעונית מלחא ......
3 זי] חנני נגרא לאמר יהבת על ידן שע[רן
4 III III II וטלפחן ארדב 𐡛 לש[ער]ן ארדבן [𐡜 III I
5 כל שערן וטלפחן מערב ארדבן 𐡜𐡛 III I[I
6 ש̄ק̄ [גבר]ן זי מאתה זי ביתאלתקם 𐡛 כ[ל III II ארדבן לכבול
7 גברן II לגבר לגבר I שערן ארדבן II נ 𐡛 ג[ברן 𐡛
8 זי] מאת נבושלו גברן II לשערן ארדבן [III II
9 וטיב לבבן בגו אנחנה נבל עבורא [זנה זי אנת יהבת על ידן
10 לחי]לא זנה זי מאתה זי ביתאלתקם וזי מ[אתה זי נבושלו זי
11 כתיבן בספרא זנה אנחנה ננתן די[ן קדם רב מאתא ורבני
12 בית מלכא וקדם ספרי אוצרא ינ[תנו עבורא זי אנת יהבת
13 עליכן למובל לגבריא אלה זי כתיבן [מנעלא והן לא ננתן כל עבורא זי
14 לך במנין בבית מלכא וקדם ספרי א[וצרא
15 אנחנה נחוב לך כסף כרשן 𐡛 כסף צ[ריף
16 אלהא ואנת שלט בפרכן זי בית מלכא [ובי זי לבנן וכל זי
17 לן אנת שלט למאחד עד תחטלא בעבורא [זי כתיב מנעלא ולא דין
18 כתב הושע על פם אחיאב
19 שהדיא כיא בר אסכישו נשכעדרי בר נ[בג
20 דוכל בר אביהו שורי בר כדו אתעדרי בר[
21 אסורת בר יהנתן שבתי בר נבדא

Endorsement. 22 ספרא זי] כתב הושע וא[חיאב] לאספ[מט

[1] On the 28th of the month Paophi in the 2nd year of King Xerxes *in the city of Yeb, said Hosea* [2] b. Hodaviah and Aḥiab b. Gemariah to

Espemet b. Peft'onith the sailor ... [3] *of* Hanani, the carpenter, saying, You have delivered to us barley ...... [4] 8 (?) and beans, 11 ardabs to *44* (?) ardabs of barley .... . [5] total barley and beans together 55 ardabs ...... [6] ... 11 men of the company of Betheltakem *every 5 ardabs for the ration of* [7] 2 men, to each man 2 ardabs of barley and 2 G . . *also 11 men* [8] *of* the company of Nabushalliv, 2 men to *5* ardabs of barley, *we have accepted it* [9] and our heart is content therewith We will convey *this* corn *which you have delivered to us* [10] *to* these *tr*oops of the company of Betheltakem and of the *company of Nabushalliv as* [11] written in this document We will render an acc*ount before the company commander and the authorities of* [12] Government House and before the clerks of the treasury (and) they shall *give out the corn which you have delivered* [13] to us to be conveyed to those men who are described *above, and if we do not deliver all the corn that is* [14] yours in full at Government House and before the clerks of the tr*easury, as aforesaid,* [15] we shall be liable to you in the sum of 100 karash, p*ure* (?) silver *as we swear by Ya'u* [16] the God, and you have a right to our payment from Government House *and the counting-house, and all that is* [17] ours you have a right to seize until you are indemnified in full for the corn *as aforesaid, and no suit shall lie.* [18] Written by Hosea at the dictation of Aḥiab. [19] Witnesses· Ki' b. Iskishu: Nushku-idri b N . . . [20] Dukal b. Abijah, Shuri b. Kadu; Ata-idri b . . . [21] Asvadata b. Jonathan, Shabbethai b Nabda [22] (Endorsement.) *Deed which* Hosea and A*hiab* wrote for Esp*emet*

Line 1. Date, see on 1^1. חשירש, in no. 5 (thirteen years later) חשיארש, O P Khshayârshâ. The place, יב or סון, was probably mentioned in the lost part of the line. הושע must be the name of the first party. Cf l. 18 and l. 22, and 3^2. He is perhaps the same as in 1^9

Line 2 לאס[פמט], in 3^3 . . לאספ In 4^7 (a similar document) אספמט is mentioned, and in 6^{10} אספמת is son of פכטעונית (see 5^{13}).

Line 3 As Epstein points out, there is not room for בר (as Sachau) at the beginning. He suggests זי, which requires some word like 'servant' at the end of l. 2 Also יהבת (sing) shows that only one person is addressed. נגרא, cf. 26^9 נגריא, 'ship's carpenters'. Espemet in 6^{10} is a sailor. However the ר has a short tail and should be a ד. ש[ערן] cf 3^4.

Line 4. It does not seem possible to read anything but ||| at the beginning. Can the numeral be divided between the two lines? I do not remember any other case. The connexion is obscure.

Line 5. מערב, though singular, must mean 'taken together'. The barley and beans being regarded as a quantity, not as plural. כדין |||]|[
The first figure is badly made or defaced, but ב is the only possibility. | (as Sachau) is out of the question The numeral might be 54 to 59, but see on l. 7.

Line 6. שׁ־ is very uncertain. If right, is it the price per ardab (10 shekels)? ק is very uncertain. The first letter may be א. [גבר]; only the tail of a letter remains. מאתה 'centuria' (with suffix).

Probably a subdivision of the רגל. ביתאלתקם, as in l. 10, the name of the centurion. The numeral refers to the preceding גברן. The trace of the next letter suggests a כ, which again suggests the words restored.

Line 7. לגבר לגבר, cf. 22^1. ג is a subdivision of the ardab, probably a quarter. The trace at the end may belong to a ג. We want גברן somewhere here, but it is difficult to see how to complete the line. If the number of men is the same as in the other company, with the same allowance, they would account for the 55 ardabs in l. 5. Then, since there are, in all, 11 ardabs of beans in l. 4 for 22 men, the half ardab (II ג) would be the allowance of beans per man.

Line 8. [זי] hardly room for anything else. נבוישלו, cf. CIS. ii. 25 נבושלם, ו = ם in Babylonian. The construction here (2 men to [5] ardabs) differs from that in l. 7 ($2\frac{1}{2}$ ardabs to 1 man). At the end something must be supplied like 'we have received the goods'.

Line 9. בנו as frequently, without a suffix, in these papyri. Bab. *ina libbi*. At the end Epstein restores [זנה סון] עבורא from 3^9, but whatever the construction may be there, סון can hardly mean '*to* Syene' here.

Line 10. At the end there is a trace of מ. As only two companies have been mentioned the restoration is fairly certain.

Line 11, end. Epstein proposes [נן]די. There is no other word beginning with די. He completes the line from 3^{11}. My translation of נתן דין by 'render an account' (or 'give instructions'?) is only a guess.

Line 12. בית מלכא must be 'Government House', since the king did not live at Elephantine or Syene. ינתנו, asyndeton, as in l. 11, or final, 'that they should give'. The restoration (from 3^{12}) is Epstein's. It must be nearly right, though rather confused.

Line 13. למובל 'give it (to some one) to convey', i.e. send it. At the end something of the kind is required to introduce the penalty in l. 15.

Line 14. במנין 'according to number', i.e. exactly, in full. It cannot be 'in minae' (as Sachau alternatively) which would be במנן and meaningless. At the end Epstein proposes זי לא חלקה (cf. 3^{15}), but his meaning is not clear.

Line 15. נחוב is unusual, but quite certain. 𐡝 the sign for 100 has an unusual (perhaps early) form. The penalty is very heavy. If 10 shekels per ardab (l. 6) was really the cost of the goods, this is nearly double the total value. The end should define the standard of the money. Epstein restores כסף זי [שב לר׳ באבני פתח] אלהא, cf. 11^2 and the demotic deed of 493/2 B.C. cited by Staerk (*Die Jüd. Aram. Papyri* . . . p. 26). But זי is not used in this formula, nor is אלהא added to Ptaḥ in no. 11. For כסף צריף cf. 5^7, 28^{11}, but there is not sufficient ground for restoration.

Line 16 אלהא the connexion is obscure. Sachau thinks it may belong to an oath: 'we swear by the god X'. בפרסן 'our share' or 'payment'. Possibly a percentage on the deal—or as in no. 11, their military pay The construction with זי is awkward. The restoration is Epstein's, from 3^{18}, where see note.

Line 17. תתמלא, i. e you receive in full the value of the coin The end is restored from 3^{20}

Line 18 על פם 'at the dictation or direction of' is a common expression, cf 11^{16}, but it is unusual to find a man writing for his partner. הושע no doubt the partner whose name is lost in line 1. He acts as scribe If he were a new person he would be further described here. So also in l. 22.

Line 19. The witnesses' names are not written by the scribe, and are very difficult to read. כיא or ביא, cf. פיא in 14^{1}. Egyptian? as his father's name

Line 20. דוכל is more probable than רוכל. Otherwise the reading is certain. Neither name is known. שורי Sachau cites CIS. ii. 1, 154^{2}. כדו (or כרו) probable. Unknown.

Line 21. אסֿודת (or ־רת). Sachau אמודת. Cf. Persian Aspadata? יהנתן a mistake? for יהונתן. נבדא or כברא

Line 22 is incomplete at both ends. It is the endorsement written on the outside after the document had been rolled up, tied, and sealed. This is the usual formula, sometimes with a word added to indicate the nature of the transaction (ספר מרחק &c.). Being outside, the endorsements are generally much defaced.

No. 3.

A Duplicate (?) of No 2

Beginnings of lines of a document very similar to no. 2, but perhaps relating to a different transaction Much of what is missing could evidently be restored from no. 2, though the details remain obscure in both. As so much is lost, it seemed best not to attempt restoration

Sachau, plate 27. Ungnad, no. 29.

1 ב ד III III II ל[ירח
2 ב[ר הו]דויה ואח[יאב
3 מה[חסנן ביב] לאספ[מט
4 על ידן שערן [

5 טלפחן ארדבן ד [

6 כל [שער]ן וטלפח[ן

7 לנברן [ו]וו ||| || .[

8 טלפחן ארדב ו [

9 עבו[רא] זנה סון [

10 בספר[א ז]נה וי. [

11 מאתא ורבני [

12 עבורא זי נתנת [

13 במנין [בב]ית מל[כא

14 זי יהבת על יד[ן

15 זי לא הילן [

16 אוצ[רא

17 אלהא בסף . . . [

18 ובי זי לבנן ו[

19 לי [ואנת של]ט למ[אחד

20 זי בתב מנעלא ו[

21 בתב ה[ושע] בכפי א[

22 שהדיא שורי בר [בדו

23 נשבעד[ר]י בר נבנ[. . .

24 בגד[ת בר] אסמשד[

[1] On the 28th of . . . . . . [2] b. Hodaviah and Aḥ*iab* . . . . . . [3] pro*perty-holders in Yeb* to Esp*emeṭ* . . . . . . [4] to us barley . . . . . . [5] lentils, 20 ardabs . . . . . . [6] total *barley* and lentils . . . . . . [7] to 5 (?) men . . . . . . [8] lentils, 1 (?) ardab . . . . . . [9] this co*rn* Syene . . . . . . [10] in this deed and shall . . . . . . [11] the company, and the officers . . . . . . [12] the corn which you gave . . . . . . [13] in full *at Gov*ernment Hou*se* . . . . . . [14] which you delivered to us . . . . . . [15] which does not belong to us . . . . . . [16] treas*ury* . . . . . . [17] the god, silver . . . . . . [18] and the counting-house and . . . . . . [19] mine *and you have a ri*ght to *seize* . . . . . . [20] as aforesaid, and . . . . . . [21] Written by Hosea at the hands (?) of A*ḥiab*. [22] Witnesses: Shuri b. *Kadu* . . . . . . [23] Nushku-idri b. Nabn*itu* . . . . . . [24] Bagada*ta b.* ISMSHD . . .

Line 1. The day of the month is the same as in no. 2. Perhaps the two documents were drawn up on the same day.

Line 2. The form differs from that of no. 2. This line probably contained a description of the parties, e.g. 'both Jews of the regiment of X', which is continued in l. 3.

Line 5. Ardabs 20+, a quantity not mentioned in the extant part of no 2

Line 7. The numeral can hardly be II II (as Sachau), since that would be I III It must be 5 or 6 or 8 (cf. 2^4) or 9. If it is 5 the ration is the same as in no. 2.

Line 8. The I is very uncertain. Perhaps \ר as in 2^4?

Line 9. סון seems certain, but construction?

Line 15. לא is doubtful. After it Sachau reads חלק, but only ל is certain.

Line 17 After כסף the definition of standard is quite uncertain (צריף?). The fact that this follows אלהא no doubt supports Epstein's restoration באבני פתח in 2^{15}.

Line 18, as in 10^9. The reading in both places is clear. בי as absolute form of בית is found several times We should not expect בי ז׳, cf. בית מלכא in l. 13 Sachau takes לבנן as 'tiles', but there is not much point in that as a description. From its association with the treasury it must be some sort of bank or counting-house In Ezra 6^1 there is a בית ספריא, a record office to which the treasury was attached, and this must be something of the same sort. There is no word in O T. specially denoting a cuneiform clay tablet (לוח has various meanings) In Ezek. 4^1 לבנה may be such a tablet, on which a plan of the city was drawn. Probably here לבן means a tablet, and the 'house of tablets' was the place where records of payments were stored—even though they may have come to be written on papyrus. This would suit 10^9 also.

Line 19. לי by an oversight for לן.

Line 21. בכפי instead of על פם as in 2^{18}. Sachau 'by the hands of', i e. Aḥiab wrote it. It is not in the same hand as no. 2, written by Hosea. Seidel thinks it is for כפי = כפם, the כ having become otiose, and ב being added But פי is never found (as a Hebraism) for פם in these texts

Lines 22, 23 These two witnesses also appear in no. 2. נבנ̇. . . Ungnad suggests Bab. Nabnîtu.

Line 24. [ת]בגד (probably) = Persian Bagadata. His father's name (Egyptian?) is unknown.

No. 4.

A small Fragment, apparently connected with Nos. 2 and 3.

Written on both sides. Fragment probably of a letter. It is not dated, but seems to relate to the transactions recorded in nos 2 and 3 Beginnings and ends of lines lost.

Sachau, plate 36. Ungnad, no. 42.

Obverse.

1 [עבדו לי נ̊]

2]שין ואף ל̊]

3 [הקשט אף]

4 [זי צ̊בית בנו

Reverse.

5 ה]שכחן שערן]

6 [תנה כענת]

7 [אספמט הל̊]

8]לין מן זי נ̊ו .]

[1] . . . . . . they made for me . . . . . . [2] . . . . . . s, and also for . . . . . . [3] . . . . . . he prepared, also . . . . . . [4] . . . . . . what you wish with it . . . . . . [5] . . . . . . we have found barley . . . . . . [6] . . . . . . here. Now . . . . . . [7] . . . . . . Espemeṭ . . . . . . [8] . . . . since we . . . . . .

Line 2. Sachau suggests [כר]שין, but this would surely require a numeral after it.

Line 3. הקשט Haphel, 'make ready' (Sachau). Only here.

Line 4. זי is almost certain. Not א, as Sachau. בנו, cf. on 2^9.

Line 5. [ה]שכחן 'we have found', not אנחן as Sachau. שערן as in nos. 2 and 3.

Line 7. אספמט, cf. 2^2, 3^3.

Line 8. -לין. Ungnad -טין which Seidel restores to [חנ]טין, but the ל is almost certain.

No. 5.

Grant of Building Rights. 471 B.C.

The date is quite certain, 471 B.C. When found it was still rolled up, tied and sealed.

This is an agreement between Ḳoniya and Mahseiah, allowing the former to build some kind of structure (אגר or אנר, see note) between his house and Mahseiah's, which are adjacent.

It is the first of a series of documents in which Mahseiah and his family are concerned. It is perfectly preserved.

Sayce and Cowley, pap. A.

1 ב ־/// /// || לאלול הו יום ד /// /// || לפחנס שנת ־ /// /| חשיארש מלכא אמר

2 קוניה בר צדק ארמי זי סון לדגל וריזת למחסיה בר ינדיה ארמי זי סון

3 לדגל וריזת לאמר אנה אתית עליך ויהבת לי תרע ביתא זילך למבנה
4 אנר I תביה אגרא זך זילך הי זי דבקה לביתא זילי לזויתה זי לעליה
5 אגרא זך תדבק לשטר ביתי מן ארעא ועד עלא מן זוית ביתי זי לעליה ועד
בית זכריה
6 מחר או יום אחרן לא אכהל אכלאנך למבנה עלוי אגרא זך זילך
7 הן כליתך אנתן לך כסף כרשן /// II באבני מלכא כסף צריף ואגרא זך
8 אפם והן מית קוניה מחר או יום אחרן לא יכהל בר וברה אח ואחה
9 קריב ורחיק בעל דגל וקריה יכלא למחסה או לבר לה למבנה עלוי
10 אגרא זך זילה זי יכלא מנהם ינתן לה כספא זי כתיב מן עלא ואגרא
11 זילך אפם ואנת שליט למבנה עלויה עד עלא ואנה קוניה לא אכהל
12 אמר למחסה לאמר   תרעא זך לא זילך הו ולא תנפק בשוקא זי
13 בינין ובין בית פפטעונית מלחא הן כליתך אנתן לך כספא זי כתיב מן עלא
14 ואנת שליט למפתח תרעא זך ולמנפק בשוקא זי בינין
15 כתב פלטיה בר אחיו ספרא זנה כפם קוניה   שהדיא בגו
16 שהד מחסה בר ישעיה . שהד שתברזן בר אתרלי
17 שהד שמעיה בר הושע שהד פרתפרן בר ארתפרן
18 שהד בגדת בר נבוכדרי . נבולי בר דרנא
19 שהד בנתרש בר רחמרע שהד שלם בר הושעיה

Endorsement. 20 ספר   אגרא זי בנה זי כתב קוניה למחסה

[1] On the 18th of Elul, that is the 28th day of Paḥons, year 15 of King Xerxes, said [2] Ḳoniya b. Zadok, an Aramaean of Syene, of the detachment of Warizath, to Mahseiah b. Yedoniah, an Aramaean of Syene, [3] of the detachment of Warizath, saying: I came to you and you have given to me the gateway of your house to build [4] 1 portico (?) there. This portico is yours. It adjoins my house at its upper corner. [5] This portico shall adjoin the side of my house from the ground upwards, from the corner of my house at the upper end to the house of Zechariah. [6] To-morrow or on any later day I have no power to restrain you from building above (*or* upon) this portico of yours. [7] If I restrain you, I will pay you the sum of 5 karash, royal weight, pure silver, and the portico is yours [8] assuredly. If Ḳoniya dies to-morrow or on a later day no son or daughter, brother or sister, [9] relative or stranger, soldier or citizen, shall have power to restrain Maḥseh or his son from building above [10] this portico of his. Whoever restrains one of them shall pay him the sum aforesaid, and the portico [11] is yours assuredly, and you have the right to build above it upwards, and I Ḳoniya have no power [12] to speak to Maḥseh saying: This gateway is not yours, and you shall not go out (by it) into the street which [13] is between us and the house of Peft'onith, the boatman. If I restrain you, I will pay you the sum aforesaid. [14] And you have the right to open this gate and go out into the street which

is between us. [15] Pelatiah b. Ahio wrote this document at the dictation of Koniya. Witnesses thereto: [16] Witness Mahseh b. Isaiah. Witness Satibarzanes b. Atharli. [17] Witness Shemaiah b. Hosea. Witness Phrataphernes b. Artaphernes. [18] Witness Bagadata b. Nabukudurri. Nabuli b. Darga. [19] Witness Bentirash b. Raḥamrea' (?) Witness Shallum b. Hoshaiah. [20] (Endorsement.) Deed (relating to) the portico which he built, which Koniya wrote for Maḥseh.

Line 1. Elul = Paḥons. The equation of the Jewish and Egyptian dates is usual. See Introduction, p. vi. חשיאריש, in 2^1 חשירש.

Line 2. The parties are both described as Aramaeans of Syene. In 6^3 &c. Mahseiah is called a 'Jew in Elephantine', and in 6^3 Koniya is also called a Jew. The terms seem to be used almost indiscriminately, but it is noticeable that, although we have six instances of יהודי זי ביב, we never find יהודי זי סון, and though there are ten cases of ארמי זי סון, there are only three of ארמי זי ביב. This can hardly be accidental, and points to Elephantine as the specially Jewish settlement. לרגל, a frequent term. S-C לרגל in the sense of 'depending on', in which case the בעל רגל (l. 9) was a *cliens* depending on a *patronus*. Cf. Exod. 11^8. Though this view might be defended, it is perhaps better to read, as is now generally agreed, לדגל, cf. G. B. Gray in *J. Q. R.*, II, p. 92+. It is then a military term (1) 'standard', (2) 'detachment',[1] commanded by the man whose name (always Persian or Babylonian) follows it. Cf. the σημέα (σημαία, σημεῖον) in Ptolemaic Greek papyri. The explanation is not without difficulty, for the *degel* of Warizath here (in 471) appears also in 15^3 (441), and perhaps in 28^2 (410), in each case relating to Aramaeans of Syene. We can hardly suppose that any one man could command it for sixty-one years. Several men are described in different documents as belonging to two *degalin*, which may mean that they were transferred from one detachment to another. The persons belonging to a *degel* nearly all have Jewish (or other foreign) names, but see 7^3 (reading not certain). Native Egyptians are never so described. This may be accidental, but it may also be that Egyptians were not employed as soldiers in the garrison. The *degalin* (composed of Jews) formed the garrison (חילא), or an important part of it, in Elephantine-Syene. They were settled there with their families, and were capable of holding property (κάτοικοι). Their military duties seem to have been secondary and slight, though they received rations and pay, as a retaining fee. The native population seems to have been purely civil. See further in the Introduction, p. viii, and for σημέα, see Lesquier, *Les Institutions militaires de l'Égypte* (1911), p. 103, &c. ורייזת, a Persian name. The parties

[1] This vague term is used because there is no indication of its number.

belonged to the same detachment. ינדיה a mistake for ידניה, one of the many mis-spellings in these texts. Stenning compares בלגרי for ברגלי in Sinjirli, P 16.

Line 3. לאמר. A Hebraism, commonly used to introduce the business.

Line 4. אגר or אנר is feminine. The word has been much discussed, but no convincing explanation has yet been found. As אגר it has been compared with Bab. *agurru* 'brickwork', or איגר 'roof'. As אנר, Barth (*Rev. Sém.*, 1909, p. 149) compares اجاد, and אֲגֻדָּתוֹ (Amos 9[6]), a lower building contrasted with מעלותיו. Lidzbarski thinks it was possibly a *succa* (in Elul), but it seems to be something more permanent. From the description it must be some sort of archway or covered passage on or over which the lessor has the right to build. The following plan of the buildings has been made by Hoonacker (*Schweich Lectures*, p. 14):

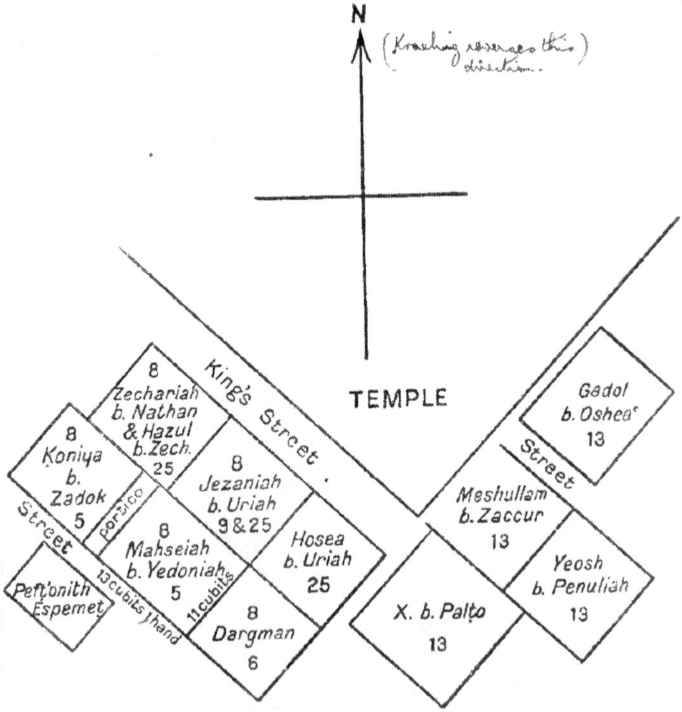

The passage between the houses is called תרע in l. 3, meaning the gate and the way to it. The lessor Mahseiah grants the right to build there, but the building, as a fixture, is to be his property as ground landlord (or tenant-in-chief?). לעליה. The 'upper part' is the end remote from the house of Zechariah, i. e. at the South.

Line 5 was inserted after l. 6 was written, because l. 4 was not sufficiently definite. Hence it is partly a repetition. מן ארעא וכ׳. The posts or pillars supporting the אגר were to be fixed against the side of the house (רבק 'attached' to it). זכריה was son of Nathan (8^7). The house afterwards passed to his son הצול (25^5).

Line 6. The usual formula. אכהל. Only the imperfect occurs in these texts, and in the forms יכהל and יכל (cf. 1^4), which are probably only varieties of spelling. In BA the participle alone has the fuller form (כָּהֵל): the other parts have been influenced by the Hebrew יכל. See further *JRAS*, 1920, p. 182. In these texts it is always followed by an imperfect. עלוי either 'upon' or 'above'.

Line 7. On the money see Introduction, p. xxii. A penalty is part of the common form. זך a mistake for זילך, cf. ll. 10, 11.

Line 8. אפם a strengthened form of אף, as זכם (9^2) of זך. בר וברה וכ׳ is again common form.

Line 9. וקריה for ובעל קריה, a full citizen as distinguished from בעל דגל, κληροῦχος (here translated 'soldier' for convenience). למחסה. The use of ל to mark the object is not common in these texts. It is probably inserted here for greater clearness, and then repeated in לבר. Note the change to the third person. The name is shortened (familiarly) from Mahseiah.

Line 10. זי . . . מנהם 'whoever of them' restrains? or 'whoever (restrains one) of them'?

Line 11. עד עלא repeated for greater precision. Mahseiah was free to build on top of the portico, but not under it.

Line 12. אמר, 1st pers. sing. imperf. The right to build above it being settled, the next clause deals with the right to use the gate and passage under it.

Line 13. פפטעונית, an Egyptian name. The Jews were not restricted to a particular quarter or ghetto. מלחא. He was a Nile boatman. His son ($6^{10,11}$) followed the same calling.

Line 14. זי בינין is used inaccurately. The *street* was not between the houses of Ḳoniya and Mahseiah, but only a passage (with the אגר), unless that is now called a שוק. The phrase no doubt means (as in l. 13) the street 'between our houses and that of Peft'onith'.

Line 15. The deed is drawn up at the direction of the lessee. בר אחיו. The family may have been professional scribes, since no. 11 was written by Gemariah b. Ahio. In 10^{22} Ahio b. Pelaṭiah, a witness, is probably a son of the present scribe. כפם or על פם the regular phrases, 'at the dictation of'. בנו cf. on 2^{9}.

Lines 16–19. The names are signed by the witnesses themselves, and are therefore difficult to read. Note the mixture of Jewish, Persian, Babylonian, and perhaps other names.

Line 16. שתברזן a Persian name, of which שתר־בוזני (Ezra 5^{6}, &c.) is no doubt a corruption. אתרלי (though מתרלי is possible), as in 13^{18}. Halévy, however, points out that if it is Assyrian it should be אשתרלי, if Aramaic or Arabic, עתרלי. Peiser suggests Atarlîu. Cf. נבולי, l. 18.

Line 17. פרתפרן is no doubt intended, but it is written פרתנזן.

Line 18. בגדת Persian. His father's name is Babylonian. נבולי 'Nabu is my god' or 'is mighty'. The mark before it may be a false start, or a mark of division. Stenning suggests that it is a bad ש, for שהד which stands before the other names. דרגא. Lidzbarski thinks a short form of Dargman (6^{2}), cf. 13^{19}. It may be דדגא Δαδάκης, Persian.

Line 19. בנתרש a strange name. There seems to be no other way of reading it. רחמרע uncertain. The papyrus is broken. Cf. CIS. ii. i. 154^{7}.

No. 6.

Conveyance. 465 B.C.

The date is the 21st year of Xerxes, which is stated to be the 1st year of Artaxerxes (i), i.e. 465 B.C.

It is an agreement between Dargman and Mahseiah (cf. 5^{2}) concerning the right to certain property. Dargman claimed a piece of land which Mahseiah also claimed. The matter being brought before the court, Mahseiah was required to take an oath in support of his claim, presumably because there was no evidence. Dargman now submits to the ruling of the court against him, and this deed is drawn up at his direction. Reference is made to it in 8^{23}, when the property passed to Mibṭaḥiah. Such an oath was a common form of legal procedure, see nos. 7, 44, 45. It was used in Babylonian law, see the Code of Ḥammurabi (ed. Winckler) §§ 20, 249, &c. Clermont-Ganneau compares also *'ankh* (*sankh*) in Egyptian law.

The writing is not very skilful. Note too the great variation in the number of letters in a line. The papyrus is almost perfect. (Some letters incorrectly transliterated)

Sayce and Cowley, pap. B.

ב ר/// ||| || לכסלו הו י[ום |||] ||| ∖ לתחות שנת ד ∖ ראש מלוכתא כזי
ארתחשסש מלכא יתב בכרסאה אמר דרגמן בר חרשין חרזמי זי אתרה
ביב בירתא עביד לדגל ארתבנו למחסיה בר ידניה יהודי זי בבירת יב
לדגל וריזת לאמר י[מא]ת לי ביהו אלהא ביב בירתא אנת ואנתתך
וברך כל ||| על ארקא זילי זי אנה קבלת עליך עלדברה קדם
דמידת וכנותה דיניא וטענוך לי מומאה למומא ביהו עלדבר ארקא
זך כזי לא הות ארק לדרגמן זילי הא אנה אף הא תחומי ארקא זך
אנה
זי ימאת לי עלדברה ביתי דרגמן למוע שמש מנ[ה] ובית קוניה בר צדק
יהודי לדגל אתרופרן למערב שמש לה ובית [יז]ניה בר אוריה
יהודי לדגל וריזת לתחתיה לה ובית אספמת בר פפטעונית
מלח זי מיא קשיא לעליה לה ימאת לי ביהו והוכבת
לבבי על ארקא זך לא אכהל אגרנך דין ודבב אנה וברלי וברה
את ואחה לי קריב ורחיק
לי על ארקא זך אנת וברלך וברה לך אח ואחה לך קריב ורחיק
על
זי יגרנך בשמי ארקא זך ינתן לך כסף כרשן ד הו עשרן באבני
מלכא כסף ר || לעשרתא וארקא אפם זילך ואנת רחיק מן
כל דין זי יקבלון עליך עלדבר ארעא זך כתב איתן בר אבה ספרא
זנה בסון בירתא כפם דרגמן שהד הושע בר פטחנום שהד
גדול בר יגדל שהד גמריה בר אחיו משלם בר הושע
סינבשר בר נבוסמסכן שהד הדגורי בבליא
שהד גדליה בר ענניה
שהד אריישא בר ארוסתמר

Endorsement. ספר מרחק זי כתב [דרגמן] בר חרשין ל מחסיה

[1] On the 18th of Chisleu, that is the 7th day of Thoth, in year 21, the beginning of the reign when [2] King Artaxerxes sat on his throne, said Dargman b. Ḥarshin the Khorasmian, whose station [3] is fixed in Yeb the fortress, of the detachment of Artabanu, to Mahseiah b. Yedoniah a Jew who (lives) in the fortress of Yeb, [4] of the detachment of Warizath, saying: You have *sworn* to me by the God Ya'u in Yeb the fortress, you and your wife [5] and your son, three in all, about my land in regard to which I lodged a complaint against you before [6] Damidata and his colleagues the judges, and they imposed upon you an oath to me, to swear by Ya'u in regard to this land, [7] that it was no longer the land of Dargman, mine, that is (belonging to) me. Now these are the boundaries of this land [8] in regard to which you swore to me: My house, of me Dargman, is to

the east of *it*, and the house of Ḳoniya b. Zadok, [9] Jew, of the detachment of Athroparan, to the west of it, and the house of *Jezaniah* b. Uriah, [10] Jew, of the detachment of Warizath, at the lower end of it, and the house of Espemet b. Peftʻoniih, [11] boatman of the cataract, at the upper end of it. You have sworn to me by Ya'u, and have satisfied [12] my mind about this land. I shall have no power to institute suit or process against you, I and my son and my daughter, [12a] brother and sister of mine, relative and stranger, [13] concerning this land, (against) you and your son and your daughter, brother and sister of yours, relative and stranger. [14] Whoever sues you in my name concerning this land, shall pay you the sum of 20 (twenty) karash royal weight, [15] at the rate of 2 R to the ten, and the land is assuredly yours, and you are quit of [16] all claim that they may bring against you in regard to this land. Ethan b. Aba wrote this deed [17] in Syene the fortress, at the dictation of Dargman. Witness, Hosea b. Peṭekhnum. Witness, [18] Gadol b. Yigdal. Witness, Gemariah b. Ahio. Meshullam b. Hosea. [19] Sinkashid b. Nabusumiskun. Witness, Hadadnuri the Babylonian. [20] Witness, Gedaliah b. Ananiah. [21] Witness, Aryisha b. Arusathmar. [22] (Endorsement.) Deed of renunciation written by *Dargman* b. Ḥarshin for Mahseiah.

Line 1. The number in the Egyptian mouth is broken, and the space requires something before \III, most probably III, but it might be ⌐ (making 14). Gutesmann and Hontheim calculate that it should be 17, but there is hardly room for III ⌐.

Line 2. דרגמן בר חרשין apparently Persian names. חרזמי if it means 'of Khwarizm' is a strangely modern form, for خو in the Persian of to-day is pronounced *kh*. אתרה. Nöldeke is probably right in taking this as 'place', i. e. 'his station'. So I. Lévi and Clermont-Ganneau. Halévy, 'whose land is cultivated in Yeb'. Cf. 13^{19}, where see note.

Line 3. עביד must then be 'made', 'fixed', as Nöldeke. But the expression is strange. מחסיה in 5^{2} was an Aramaean of Syene, but in both places he belongs to the *degel* of Warizath. The property was evidently in Elephantine.

Line 4. י[מא]ת. Traces of מא make this certain. Mahseiah, as a Jew, swears by Ya'u before a Persian court, and his oath is accepted by the court and by his opponent, who was not a Jew. On the name, see Introduction, p. x. בירתא is probably right. It looks like בארקי, but the tail is too long for ק, and the preposition would then be על. Moreover, l. 5 makes it superfluous.

Line 5. ברך probably Gemariah, 9^{18}.

Line 6. Damidata, a Persian, was president of the court. כנותה

are his assessors, cf. Ezra 5^{6}, &c. דיניא as Ezra 4^{9}. מענוך 'they laid upon you', i. e. required you to take.

Line 8. 'ביתי אנה ד. The scribe originally wrote 'בית ד, and altered it for greater clearness, since Dargman retained the adjoining house. He forgot at first that he was writing in Dargman's name. The boundaries of the property, to be consistent with no. 5, must include Mahseiah's house, which may have been the cause of the action. As the properties are in the same group as in no. 5, it is probable that Darga there (5^{18}) is a short form of Dargman. קוניה in 5^{2} is an Aramaean of Syene, of the detachment of Warizath.

Line 10. לתחתיה, the lower side is the north, as לעליה (l. 11) is the south. פפטעונית, not 'פוט as S–C, is no doubt the same as in 5^{13}. His son Espemet carried on the same business, cf. 2^{2}, 3^{3}, 4^{7}.

Line 11. מיא קשיא 'the difficult waters', no doubt the cataract of Assuan. On the navigation of it, see Hdt. 2^{29}.

Line 12. אגרנך, cf. on 1^{4}. Here with double accusative. ברלי as one word, so ברלך l. 13, עלדברה l. 8, and often.

Line 12^{a} inserted as an afterthought.

Line 13. אנת &c. resuming the pronoun in אגרנך. The construction is clumsy but clear.

Line 14. בשמי i. e. acting for me. ינתן not אנתן as S–C. ב is badly made. It is like that in 1^{1}, and confirms the reading there.

Line 15. ר II לעשרתא. See Introduction, p. ~~xxiii~~ p. xxxi. רחיק 'removed from', i. e. quit of, or guaranteed against.

Line 16. יקבלון, cf. l. 5, a technical term, 'lodge a complaint', 'bring an action'. Here with a cognate accusative. ארעא as in no. 5, though ארקא is used in l. 15 &c. איתן probably, cf. 1 Kings 4^{31}. Not איתו, which is not a known name.

Line 17. בסון. The court was held in Syene, though the parties both belonged to Elephantine, and the property was also there. The names are written by the witnesses themselves. הושע בר פטחנום a Jew whose father has an Egyptian name. Was he a proselyte? Or did a Jewess marry an Egyptian and give her son a Jewish name? In later times Jews had no objection to using foreign (even theophoric) names, as Isidore, sometimes as alternatives to their Hebrew names, so that Petekhnum may have been a Jew. Cf. 15^{2}, and note on 25^{3}.

Line 18. נמריה בר אחיו, the scribe of no. 11.

Line 21. The names are unknown.

Line 22. מרחק 'withdrawal' or 'renunciation' of claim.

No. 7.

A Case of Burglary. 461 B.C.

The date is the fourth year of Artaxerxes. Sachau takes this to be Artaxerxes I, on the ground that in the time of Artaxerxes II (404–358) Egypt was in revolt and therefore documents would not be dated by Persian regnal years. Cf. no. 35, dated in the fifth year of Amyrtaeus, about 400. The argument is not conclusive, because the history of the revolt is obscure and we do not know how far the Persians may have retained a hold on the country, e. g. in the south at Elephantine, or whether some sections of the people (e. g. the Jews) may have remained faithful to Persia. On the whole, however, the earlier date (461 B. C.) is more probable than the later (401). The name of the defendant, Phrataphernes b. Artaphernes (l. 3), about which there can be little doubt, occurs also in 5^{17} as a witness in 471 B. C. (The Malchiah, whose son is a witness in nos. 8 and 9, in 460, may or may not be the same as the plaintiff here). The style of the writing, though at first sight it appears to be late, is not decisive. On the other hand the *degel* of Nabukudurri occurs elsewhere only in 29^2 (about 409 B. C.) and 35^2 (about 400 B. C.). It seems, however, that the name of a *degel* could go on for a long time, whatever the explanation, since that of Warizath is mentioned in nos. 5, 6, 14, 15, 28, i. e. from 471 to 410 B. C. It is therefore more probable that the *degel* of Nabukudurri should have lasted for sixty years than that there should have been two men of the name of Phrataphernes b. Artaphernes (if that is right) with an interval of seventy years between them. Still it must be admitted that the date is not certain.

The precise form of procedure here is not clear, owing to the broken state of the papyrus. It is usually taken as a case of an oath of exculpation, where, if evidence was not obtainable, the defendant was required to swear that he had not committed the offence alleged against him. Cf. no. 6. If, however, the restorations proposed here are correct, the case is rather thus: Phrataphernes had boasted that he had trespassed on Malchiah's property, &c. Malchiah now requires him to retract his statements on oath, and will then have the right to take further proceedings, the nature of which is unknown owing to the loss of part of the papyrus.

In general compare nos. 6, 16, 44, 45.

Sachau, plate 26. Ungnad, no. 28.

1 ב ־ /// /// // לפאפי שנת \/// ארתחשסש מלכ[א] ביב

2 בירתא אמר מלכיה בר ישביה ארמי מהחסן ביב

ב[ירחא לד]גל נבוכד[רי לפר]תפרן [בר ארתפ]רן לדג[ל
נבו[כדרי לא]מר [א]נת קר[ית עלי] בנפא [הן על]ת [בביתי
כחסן וכתשת לאנתתי ונכסן כחסן הנפקת מן ביתי
ולקחת לנפש[ך] עבדת שאיל[א] ומקריא על אלהן
מטא עלי בדינא אנה מלכיה אקרא לך על חרמביתאל
אלהא בין [נק]מן ///\ לא[מר] כחסן בביתך [לא] עלת
ולאנתתא [זילך] לא כתשת ונכסן מן ביתך כ[חס]ן לא לקחת
והן [אנה] קרית לך בין [נ]קמיא אלה [אכה]ל אף אק[רא

[1] On the 18th of Paophi, in the 4th year of Artaxerxes the king, in Yeb [2] the fortress, said Malchiah b. Joshibiah, Aramaean, holding property in Yeb [3] the for*tress*, *of the detach*ment of Nabukudurri, *to Phrata*phernes *b. Artaph*ernes of the detachme*nt* [4] of Nabu*kudurri*, *say*ing: You decl*ared concerning me* in Nepha *that you entere*d *my house* [5] by force, and struck my wife, and removed goods from my house by force, [6] and took them for *your*self. I have made a petition and the appeal to our god [7] has been laid upon me by the court, on me Malchiah, that I should challenge you by Herembethel [8] the god, before 4 *jud*ges (?), thus: 'I did *not* enter your house by force, [9] and did not strike *your* wife, and did not take goods from your house by *for*ce.' [10] And if *I* challenge you before these *ju*dges (?) *I am enti*tled also to chal*lenge* . . .

Line 2. מהחסן, the regular word for 'holding property'.

Line 3. The beginning is certain. In the defendant's name the letters תפרן are certain. Of his father's name only רן remains. It is not מ, as Sachau and Ungnad read, and what they take as י after it is an accidental mark, of which there are several in this papyrus. Also their proposed [אר]מי would not fill the space, nor would there be room for anything between it and the name. A name ending in תפרן must belong to a Persian, who would not be described as an Aramaean. Hence רן . . . . תפרן בר . . ל seems certain, and the restoration highly probable.

Line 4. נבו[כדרי]. Sachau and Ungnad read מר . . . In this hand נב are very like מ, but נבו is more probable, though it need not necessarily be completed as in l. 3. If it is Nabukudurri, both parties belonged to the same *degel*. This is expressed in 20[4] by לזכם דגלא, cf. 9[2]. [לא]מר. The tails of מר are clear. קר[ית לי] or עלי. The restoration is quite conjectural. The preceding [א]נת can hardly be anything else. Then these words must introduce the accusation, and the introduction is put into the mouth of the accused. Since he is afterwards required to deny the charge, it should be introduced here by something like 'you stated' or 'you did'. But of course it might be another clause in the charge, which is not recited in ll. 8, 9. It might, however, be [קד[ם,

or 'you attacked me' (or something similar) in N. and entered. בנפא is fairly certain Traces of פ are visible. In 20[4] there is ברין נפא Here it seems to be a place-name. הן is quite conjectural The traces of letters make nothing The fragment of papyrus here and in l. 3 seems to be out of place as the traces are not in the line. [על]ת [בביתי] is required by l. 8. So Sachau Ungnad reads . . . ב . (i. e [ב[ב]יתי]), but the mark is merely accidental

Line 5 כחסן cf. כעשק in 16[5, 8, 9], where Seidel takes the כ as otiose. It seems here to be like a *kaph veritatis* (perhaps כחוסן) 'as (with) violence', i. e. violently

Line 6. עבׄדׄת. So Sachau and Ungnad. The בר are badly written, but nothing else seems probable. שאיל[א] ומקריא evidently technical terms. They belong to different clauses. אלהן 'our god' (as Sachau). Not אלהיא 'the gods'. It can hardly be a Hebraism, like אלהים used as a proper name.

Line 7. אנה, asyndeton, 'so I M challenge'. חרמביתאל. On this and other gods, see Introduction, p x.

Line 8. [נק]מן 'avengers', i. e. judges, is Sachau's suggestion, and so in l. 10. It is not very satisfactory. Ungnad points out that one would expect קדם before it, but בין is not impossible.

Line 10. After והן Ungnad suggests לא, but the apodosis with אף makes this impossible 'if I do not challenge, then I shall also challenge'. Sachau suggests לא or אנה. I thought of והן לו as in Aḥikar, l. 81, &c., but there seem to be faint traces of אנה. It is much to be regretted that the rest is lost, so that we do not know the subsequent procedure.

No. 8.

Conveyance. 460 B.C.

The papyrus is almost perfectly preserved, except for a crease in the last third of the breadth which causes a doubt as to a few letters.

The date is the 6th (Gutesmann and Hontheim 5th) year of Artaxerxes I = 460 B.C. Artaxerxes I (not II) is certain because it relates to the same persons who appear in no. 6, of the first year of Artaxerxes I = 465.

The sentences are sometimes divided by extra space.

Mibtaḥiah, daughter of Mahseiah, was about to be married, or had just been married (l 7), to Jezaniah b. Uriah. Her father gives her as dowry a property in Elephantine, with full powers to dispose of it. The property is carefully described, and Mibṭaḥiah's rights are elaborately safeguarded. It is the same estate to which Dargman had laid claim in no. 6. That document is now handed over to Mibṭaḥiah as part of the title-deeds.

Sayce and Cowley, D.

ב 3 | לכסלו הו יום | למסורע שנת /// \ /// \ ארתחששש מלכא אמר מחסיה
בר ידניה יהוד[י] מהחסן ביב בירתא לדגל הומדת לנשן מבטחיה
ברתה לאמר אנה יהבת לכי בחיי ובמותי בית \ ארק זילי הוה
משחתה ארכה מן תחתיה לעליה אמן 10 /// \ ופשך | פתי מן מועא
למערב אמן 10 | בעשתא תחומוהי עליה לה בית דרגמן בר חרשין
דבק[תחתיה לה בית קוניה בר צדק מועא שמש לה בית יזן בר
אוריה בעלבי ובית זכריה בר נתן מערב לה בית אספמת בר פפטעונית
מלת זי מיא קשיא ביתא זנך ארק אנה יהבתה לכי בחיי ובמותי
אנתי שליטה בה מן יומא זנה ועד עלם ובניכי אחריכי למן זי
רחמתי תנתנן . לא איתי לי בר וברה אחרנן אח ואחה ואנתה
ואיש אחרן שליט בארקא זך להן אנתי ובניכי עד עלם זי
ירשנכי דין ודב[ב] אנתי ובר וברה לכי ואיש זילכי בשם ארקא
זך זי יהבת לכי ויקבל עליכי סגן ודין ינתן לכי ולבניכי
כסף כרשן 10 הו עשרה באבני מלכא ככף ר || לעשרתא ולא דין ולא דבב
וביתא ביתכי אפם ולבניכי אחריכי / ולא יפהלון יהנפקון עליכי
ספר חדת ועתיק בשמי על ארקא זך למנתן לאיש אחרן זך]ספרא
זי יהנפקון עליכי כדב יהוה]לא אנה כתבתה ולא יתלקח בדין
וספרא זנה בידכי , ואף אנה מחסיה מחר או יום אחרן לא אהנצל
מנכי למנתן לאחרנן ארקא זך זיליכי) בני והבי למן זי רחמתי
הן מחר או יום אחרן ארשנכי דין ודבב ואמר לא יהבת לכי
אנה אנתן לכי כסף כרשן 10 באבני מלכא כסף ר // לעשרתא . ולא דין
ולא דבב . וביתא ביתכי אפם , ואהך בדין ולא אצדק וספרא זנה בידכי
אף איתי ספר מרחק | זי דרגמן בר חרשין חרזמיא . כתבלי . על
ארקא זך כזי רשה עליה קדם דיניא . ומומא טעינתלה . וימאתלה ,
כזי זיליהי וספר מרחק כתב ויהבלי ספרא זך אנה יהבתה לכי
אנתי החסנהי הן מחר או יום אחרן דרגמן או בר זילה ירשה
על ביתא זך ספרא זך הנפקי ולקבלה דין עורי עמה כתב עתרשורי
בר נבוזראבן ספרא , זנה בסון בירתא כפם מחסיה . שהדיא בגו
שהד גמריה בר מחסיה שהד זכריה בר נתן

30 שהד הושע בר פלליה שהד זכריה בר משלם   שהד מעויה בר
31 מלכיה שהד שמעיה בר ידניה שהד ידניה בר מחסיה
32 שהד נתן בר ענניה   זכור בר צפניה
33 שהד הושע בר רעויה שהד מחסה בר ישעיה
34 שהד הושע בר יגדל
35 ספר   בי[ן זי יהב] מחסה בר ידנ[יה   Endorsement.
36 למבטח ברת מחסה

[1] On the 21st of Chisleu, that is the 1st day of Mesore, the 6th year of Artaxerxes, the king, said Mahseiah [2] b. Yedoniah, a Jew holding property in Yeb the fortress, of the detachment of Haumadata, to Mibtahiah, spinster (?), [3] his daughter, as follows: I give to you for my lifetime and after my death a house and land of mine. [4] Its measurement is: its length from the lower to the upper end 13 cubits and 1 handbreadth; width from east [5] to west 11 cubits by the measuring-rod; its boundaries, at the upper end of it the house of Dargman b Ḥarshin [6] adjoins it, at the lower end of it the house of Konya b. Zadok; east of it the house of Jezan b. [7] Uriah, your husband, and the house of Zechariah b. Nathan, west of it the house of Espemet b Peft'onith [8] boatman of the cataract This house and land I give to you for my lifetime and after my death; [9] you have full rights over it from this day for ever, and your children after you. To whom [10] you wish you may give it. There is no other son or daughter of mine, brother or sister, or other [11] woman or man who has rights over this land, except you and your children for ever. Whoever [12] shall institute against you suit or process, against you or son or daughter of yours or any one belonging to you on account of this land [13] which I give to you, and shall appeal against you to governor or judge, shall pay to you or to your children [14] the sum of 10 (that is, ten) kerashin, royal weight, at the rate of 2 R to the ten, and no suit or process (shall lie), [15] and the house is your house assuredly and your children's after you; and they shall have no power to produce against you [16] any deed new or old in my name concerning this land to give it to any one else Any deed [17] which they produce against you will be forged. I shall not have written it and it shall not be accepted by the court [18] while this deed is in your hand. And further, I, Mahseiah will not to-morrow or on any other day take it away [19] from you to give it to others. This land is yours. Build (on it) or give it to whom you will. [20] If to-morrow or on any other day I institute against you suit or process, and say I did not give it to you, [21] I will pay you the sum of 10 kerashin, royal weight, at the rate of 2 R to the ten, and no suit [22] or process (shall lie), but the house is your house assuredly, and (if) I go into court I shall not win my case while this deed is in your hand [23] There is also a deed of renunciation which Dargman b. Harshin the Khorazmian wrote for me concerning [24] this land, when he laid claim to it before the judges and I took an oath to him and swore to him [25] that it was mine, and he wrote and gave me a deed of renunciation. This

deed I give to you. [26] You are to take charge of it. If to-morrow or another day Dargman or his son should lay claim [27] to this house, produce this deed and in accordance with it contest the case with him. 'Atharshuri [28] b. Nabu-zira-ibni wrote this deed in Syene the fortress at the dictation of Mahseiah. Witnesses hereto: [29] Witness, Gemariah b. Mahseiah. Witness, Zechariah b. Nathan. [30] Witness, Hosea b. Pelaliah. Witness, Zechariah b. Meshullam. Witness, Ma'uziah b. [31] Malchiah. Witness, Shemaiah b. Yedoniah. Witness, Yedoniah b. Mahseiah. [32] Witness, Nathan b. Ananiah. Zaccur b. Zephaniah. [33] Witness, Hosea b. Re'uiah. Witness, Maḥseh b. Isaiah. [34] Witness, Hosea b. Yigdal. (Endorsement.) [35] Deed of a house *which* Maḥseh b. Yedon*iah gave* [36] to Mibṭaḥ daughter of Maḥseh.

Line 2. Mahseiah here belongs to the *degel* of Haumadata. In nos. 5 and 6 he is of the *degel* of Warizath. נשן applied to Mibṭaḥiah on her first marriage must be equivalent to Heb. בתולה. Elsewhere only in 10^2. S–C suggested a connexion with Arab. ناشى 'a young grown-up person'.

Line 3. בית̄ ⁄ ארק. In 9^3 ארק בי ⁄. S–C read בי here also, but there is an additional stroke, which seems to be part of a ת lost in the crease. The word is apparently used almost as a measure 'one house of land', i. e. the amount of land sufficient for one house, including the house upon it, and hence much the same as 'a house and land'. It was a freehold house, as no ground-rent is mentioned. בחיי ובמותי. Epstein compares B. T. Baba B. 153^a.

Line 4. אֻרְכַּהּ 'its length', though פתי has no pronoun. Cf. תחומוהי, l. 5. מן תחתיה לעליה, cf. 6^{10}. The ground was higher on the south.

Line 5. בעֲשתא is not very distinct, but certain from 9^5. It must be some sort of measuring rod, though the Hebrew עשת means rather a lump or plate of metal. Perhaps it was originally a plumb-line, and then any sort of measuring line. Or it may be from the root עשת ('think', 'calculate') if that ever meant to 'measure' (so Nöldeke). Jampel proposes 'singly', 'each' (cf. עשתי עשר), which does not seem to give much sense. Clermont-Ganneau thinks it may mean 'eleven', repeating the numeral, as in 9^5, but the ב would be difficult.

Line 6. ין a short form of יזניה, as Maḥseh for Mahseiah in 5^9 &c.

Line 7. אספמת cf. 6^{10}.

Line 8. מיא קשיא cf. 6^{11}. ביתא זנך ארק. S–C 'this house (*istam domum*) as an estate', but cf. l. 3. It probably is used loosely to mean house *and* land. זנך is not זך with נ inserted (as Staerk), but זנה with ך added, 'this of yours', though, speaking to a woman, it should be זכי.

Line 10. חנתנן has been taken (by Staerk and others) as a mistake for חנתננה. But see note on אשבקן Aḥiḳar 82.

Line 11 ארקא = ארקא ∖ בי in l 3 The land was the important part. The house went with it Note that land could be conveyed.

Line 13 סגן a Babylonian term (*šaknu*), properly 'deputy' or 'representative' of the king. If דין means 'judge', the two words indicate two different authorities, the high court (of the רבחילא, cf 20^4), and the local court. But it may mean 'magistrate and (his) court'. יקבל, lit. 'complain against you [to] governor or judge' It is used like אגרנך, 6^{12}. In 6^{16} it is connected with דין 'law-suit'.

Line 17 בדין, in a court, i. e. in any court

Line 18. וספרא as in l. 22, 'while you hold this'.

Line 19. The space before ארקא shows that it begins a new sentence. בני 'build (upon it)', i e. lay it out.

Line 23 ספר מרחק, i.e. no. 6, which is so called in the endorsement. כתבלי as one word, and so in ll. 24, 25

Line 27 עׄדרי probably so. The ו is in the crease. From עדר in the same sense as רשה or גרה.

Line 28. Noldeke נבוזראדן, but cf. on 9^{16}.

Lines 29–34. The names are signed by the witnesses themselves.

Lines 35, 36. The endorsement is much broken. There is a trace of ב before מחסה. Note the forms Maḥseh and Mibtaḥ, which are certain. Was the divine name avoided on the exposed part of the document? Of the witnesses Gemariah (l. 29) and Yedoniah (l. 31) were the sons of Mahseiah, the donor, and Shemaiah (l. 31) his grandson. Shemaiah's writing is that of a young man. Yedoniah has the same name as his grandfather.

No. 9.

Deed relating to the Reversion of the Property in No. 8. 460 B.C.

The papyrus is unusual in being written on both sides.

The year is the same as in no. 8, namely 460 B C, and probably the rest of the date, which is broken, also corresponds

This is the complement of no. 8, dealing with the position of Jezaniah with regard to the property settled on his wife by no. 8. By that deed Mibtaḥiah was to have full rights to dispose of the property as she wished. This is modified here by the provision that such rights only held good so long as she remained the wife of Jezaniah. If Jezaniah improved the property and Mibṭahiah subsequently divorced him, the property was to go to the children. If he divorced her, she was to take one half (of the house) absolutely, and he was to have rights over the other half with remainder to the children. In no case had Jezaniah power to dispose of the property. As no provision is made for Jezaniah in the event of Mibtaḥiah's dying while in possession of the property, it would apparently go to the children. On the legal points as compared with later Jewish practice, cf. Epstein, *Jahrb. d. jüdisch-lit. Gesellschaft*, 1909, p. 359. The document does not seem to intend a distinction between the house and the land, since the property is described first as one and then as the other. This is intelligible if the explanation of בית \ ארק in 8[3] is correct. The land was the important thing. Or does l. 11 imply that the *house* could be divided but not the *land*? The precise nature of land-tenure, whether freehold or some sort of copyhold, is not stated. At any rate there is no mention of a ground-rent or of a ground-landlord (the State?).

Sayce and Cowley, C.

1 ב[ר I] ל[כס]ל[ו הו יום I] ל[מסור]ע שנת III III ארתחשסש מלכא אמר
מחסיה
2 בר ידניה י[הודי זי ב]אב לדגל הומדת ליזניה בר אוריה בזכם דגלא
3 לאמר איתי ארק בי \ זילי מערב לביתא זילך זי אנה יהבת למבטחיה
4 ברתי אנתתך וספר כתבתלה אחרוהי משחת ביתא זך אמן ר III ופשך
5 ב ר \ בעשתא כען אנה מחסיה אמרתלך ארקא זך בני ועתר בהמיתה
6 ותב בנו עם אנתתך להן ביתא זנך לא שליט אנת לזבנה ולמנתן
7 רחמת לאחרנן להן בניך מן מבטחיה ברתי המו שליטן בה
8 אחריכם הן מחר או יום אחרן ארקא זך תבנה אחר ברתי תשנאנך
9 ותנפק מנך לא שליטה הי למלקחה ולמנתנה לאחרנן להן בניך מן
10 מבטחיה המו שליטן בה חלף עבידתא זי אנת עבדת הן תהנצל
11 מנך פלג ביתא [יהוה] לה למלקח ופלגא אחר[נא] אנת שליט בה חלף
12 בנויא זי אנת בנית בביתא זך ותוב פלגא הו בניך מן מבטחיה
13 המו שליטן בה אחריך הן מחר או יום אחרן ארשנך דין ודבב
14 ואמר לא יהבתלך ארקא זך למבנה ולא כתבתלך ספרא זנה אנה
15 אנתן לך כסף כרשן ר באבני מלכא כסף ר // לעשרתא ולא דין ולא דבב
16 כתב עתרשורי בר נבוזראבן ספרא זנה בסון בירתא כפם מחסיה שהדיא
17 בגו שהד הושע בר פלליה שהד זכריה בר נתן
18 שהד גמריה [ב]ר מחסיה שהד זכריה ברמשלם
19 שהד מעזיה בר מלכיה שהד שמעיה בר ידניה
20 שהד ידניה בר מחסיה שהד נתן בר ענניה שהד זכור בר צפניה
21 שהד הושע [בר] רעויה שהד מחסה בר ישעיה
22 שהד הו[שע בר יגד]ל

Note the absence [illegible] endorsement in this document

[1] On the *21st of Chisleu, that is the 1st* of *Mesore*, the 6th year of Artaxerxes the king, said Mahseiah [2] b. Yedoniah *Jew, of* Yeb, of the detachment of Haumadata, to Jezaniah b. Uriah, of the same detachment [3] as follows: There is the land of 1 house belonging to me, west of your house, which I have given to Mibtaḥiah [4] my daughter, your wife, and I have written for her a deed concerning it. The measurement of this house is 13 cubits and a hand-breadth [5] by 11, by the measuring rod. Now I, Mahseiah, say to you, lay out this land and rear cattle on it (?), [6] and dwell on it with your wife, but you have no power to sell this house, or to give it [7] as a present to others; but your children by Mibṭaḥiah my daughter have power over it [8] after you. If to-morrow or another day you lay out this land and then my daughter divorces you [9] and goes away from you, she has no power to take it or give it to others, but your children by [10] Mibtaḥiah have power over it in return for the work which you have done. If you put her away [11] from you, half the house *shall be* hers to take, and as to the oth*er* half you have power over it in return for [12] the improvements which you have made in this house. And again as to that half, your children by Mibṭaḥiah [13] have power over it after you. If to-morrow or another day I should institute suit or process against you [14] and say I did not give you this land to develop, and did not draw up this deed for you, I [15] will pay you the sum of 10 kerashin by royal weight, at the rate of 2 R to the ten, and no suit or process (shall lie). [16] 'Atharshuri b. Nabu-zira-ibni wrote this deed in Syene the fortress at the dictation of Mahseiah. Witnesses [17] hereto: Witness, Hosea b. Pelaliah. Witness, Zechariah b. Nathan. [18] Witness, Gemariah *b.* Mahseiah. Witness, Zechariah b. Meshullam. [19] Witness, Ma'uziah b. Malchiah. Witness, Shemaiah b. Yedoniah. [20] Witness, Yedoniah b. Mahseiah. Witness, Nathan b. Ananiah. Witness, Zaccur b. Zephaniah. [21] Witness, Hosea *b.* Re'uiah. Witness, Maḥseh b. Isaiah. [22] Witness, Ho*sea b. Yigda*l.

Line 1. [ו]ל[כם]ל, the tops of the ל's make this certain. The other restorations are from no. 8.

Line 2. בא[ב] for ביב only here. The א is probable. וכם 'that very' = 'the same'. The same intensive suffix as in אפם 5^8.

Line 3. ארק בי ׀, cf. 8^3. The בי is certain here.

Line 4. כתבתלה one word, as often in these two deeds. אחרוהי 'after it', i.e. in consequence, or respecting it.

Line 5. ב ר ׀. The second dimension is introduced by ב of which the precise meaning is not clear. כען as frequently in letters, introduces the business after preliminaries. ועתר. Probably ד. S-C read ועתר and translate (from the context) 'stock (it) with', cf. Prov. 24^{27}. So Halévy 'multiply'. Nöldeke reads עַתֵּר but does not explain the connexion. He thinks the site was too small to support cattle, but the dimensions of the *house* only are given. There may have been plenty of land attached to it. We may perhaps compare the root of Hebrew עתודים (Ass *attûdu*, Arab. عتود) 'he-goats', a good Semitic word, which can be only artificially explained from עתד 'to be ready'. In Ps 50[9] it is parallel to פר and in 50[13] to אבירים, in both cases implying animals that are *strong*, i e well-fed or fattened. So also in explaining عتود and عتد ('a well-bred horse') the Arab lexicographers (see Lane) lay stress on the quality of strength. Hence we may assume an extension of the meaning of √ עתד, or a separate root meaning 'to feed', 'make strong', 'rear (cattle)'. Cf. perhaps the various senses of √ זון. [Also perhaps Sumerian *tud* 'beget' or 'bring forth', *utud* 'offspring', *udu* 'sheep'] In general cf. Prov. 27[23-27]. בהמיתה is very difficult. In the first place בהמה is not used in Aramaic. If it is a Hebraism, which is possible, the form is strange. The י is clear It may be a false start in making a ת, or the scribe may have been going to write an א to mark the long vowel of the plural (בהמָתה). Then the final ה cannot mark the emph st., which always ends in א. It can only be '*its* cattle' referring to ארקא if that be possible, for 'rear cattle *on it*' Noldeke alternatively suggests בה מיתא but does not explain. Or is it a Persian compound of *ham-*, with the preposition ב? Then we should have to find another meaning for עתד (עתּד), such as 'be happy in unity', but that is hardly probable

Line 6. לזבנה. Staerk's note here is very bad. לְזִבְנָהּ is an impossible form. Only the Peal happens to occur in BA, of course in the sense of 'buy'. This is Pael, which quite naturally means to 'sell'. It is to be pointed לְזַבָּנָה. The ה is part of the form, not the pronominal suffix For the omission of the suffix cf e.g. 8[19] למנתן.

Line 7. רחמת 'as a gift', cf. 24[11.14] ברחמן 'in friendship'.

Line 8. תשנאנך 'shall express her dislike for you' and separate from you. If it was her act, she was to have none of the property, but it was to go to the children. No provision is made for the case of there being no issue, nor for a trust if they were infants. שנא, as in 15[23], is a legal term for 'divorce'. Staerk quotes an Egyptian document of the fourth century B.C. in which 'hate' is similarly used. In Hebrew cf. Deut. 21[15], &c. In Ecclus. 42[9] μή ποτε μισηθῇ where the Heb (margin) has תשׂנא. On the legal form, cf. Epstein, *Jahrbuch d. judisch-lit. Gesellschaft*, 1908, p. 368

Line 10. תהנצל. Haphel as in 8[18]. It should mean here, as there, 'take away', and Epstein and Noldeke translate 'if she takes away from you' half the house, she has a right to do so. This seems very unlikely, for the circumstances are not described under which she might take half the house. The verbal form may be either 2nd or 3rd (fem.) person. In BA, as in Hebrew, its natural meaning is to 'set free'. Provision has already been made for the case of her divorcing him, and we want a clause providing for the case of his divorcing her. In no. 15 there is provision for three cases; if she divorces him, she loses everything; if he divorces her, she gets compensation; if he violently ejects her, she gets a larger compensation. The two cases here must be the same as the first two in no. 15. Then we must take תהנצל as another term for divorce, and translate 'if you set (her) free (i. e. put her away) from you'. (For the idea of 'freedom' cf. the phrase in 15^{25-28} 'she shall go away whither she will'.) The suffix is omitted as in 8^{18}, though one would expect it in both places.

Line 12. ותוב as in Syriac and late Hebrew, cf. 1^{7}. פלגא הו = Heb. הפלג ההוא. Only here and in 22^{120}. Epstein thinks the insistence on children *by Mibṭaḥiah* shows that Jezaniah had another wife and perhaps children.

Line 16 sqq. The scribe and witnesses are the same as in no. 8. נבוזראבן. The ־אבן is certain here and hence to be so read in 8^{28}.

No. 10.

Contract for a Loan. 456 B.C.

A long document almost perfectly preserved. It was found (like no. 5) still folded, tied and sealed. The writing is coarse, and several characters (ק, ם, ת, &c.) are badly formed, so that there would be a difficulty in reading some passages if the text were at all obscure or unusual.

The date is the 9th year of Artaxerxes I = 456 B. C. The document is a contract for a loan to Ya'uḥan, daughter of MŠLK, from Meshullam b. Zaccur (cf. 13^{3} in 447 B. C.) and the conditions are set out with the utmost care. They resemble those of no. 11. If the interest was not paid (by the end of the year?) it was to be added to the capital and to pay interest in the same way. If interest was outstanding at the end of the second year, Meshullam could distrain on Ya'uḥan's property. The sum is only 4 shekels and the interest is 8 ḥallurin per month—as in no. 11. If the relative values are rightly determined (see Introduction, p. xxiii), this would be 60 per cent. per annum, a high but not unusual rate at that date.

Sachau, plates 28, 29. Ungnad, no. 30.

ב /// ||\ | לכסלו הו יום ||\ | לירח תחות שנת ||\ ||| ||\ ארתחשסש

מלכא אמרת יהוחן ברת מישלך נשן זי יב בירתא למשלם בר

3 זכור יהודי זי יב בירתא לאמר יהבת לי זפת כסף שקלן
4 /// | הו ארבעה באבני מלכא במרביתה ירבה עלי
5 כסף חלרן II לתקל I לירח I הוה כסף חלרן III III II
6 לירח חד הן מטת מרביתא לרשא ירבה מרביתא כרשא,
7 חד כחד, והן מטא תנין שנה ולא שלמתך בכספך .
8 ומרביתה זי כתיב בספרא זנה אנת משלם. ובניך שליטן
9 למלקח לך כל ערבן זי תשכח לי בי זילבנן, כסף ודהב
10 נחש ופרזל עבד ואמה שערן כנתן וכל זן זי תשכחלי
11 עד תתמלא בכספך ומרביתה ולא אכל אמר לך שלמתך
12 בכספך ומרביתה וספרא זנה בידך ולא אכל אקבל
13 עליך קדם סגן ודין לם לקחת מני ערבן וספרא
14 זנה בידך והן מיתת ולא שלמתך בכספא זנה ומרבית
15 בני המו ישלמון לך כספא זנה ומרביתה, והן
16 לא שלמו לך כספא זנה ומרביתה, אנת משלם שליט
17 למלקח לך כל זון וערבן זי תשכחלהם עדתתמלא
18 בכספך ומרביתה ולא יכלון יקבלון עליך קדם סגן
19 ודין וספרא זנה בידך אף יהכון בדין ולא יצדקון
20 וכפרא זנה בידך כתב נתן בר ענני ספרא, זנה
21 כפם יהוחן ושהדיא בנו שהד אושע בר גלגול
22 הודויה בר גדליה אחיו בר פלטיה אגור בר אחיו

Endorsement.

23 ספר כסף דנה זי כתבת יהוחן ברת משלך
24 למשלם בר זכ[ור]

[1] On the 7th of Chisleu, that is the 4th day of the month Thoth, the 9th year of Artaxerxes [2] the king, said Ya'uhan daughter of Meshullak, spinster (?), of Yeb the fortress, to Meshullam b. [3] Zaccur, Jew, of Yeb the fortress, as follows. You have given to me as a loan the sum of 4 shekels, [4] that is four, by royal weight, at interest, which shall be due from me [5] at the rate of 2 hallurin per shekel per month, being at the rate of 8 hallurin [6] for each month. If the interest is added to the capital, it shall pay interest like the capital, [7] both alike, and if there come a second year and I have not paid you your money [8] and interest on it as written in this deed, you, Meshullam, and your children, have the right [9] to take for yourself any security which you may find of mine in the counting-house, silver or gold, [10] bronze or iron, male or female slave, barley, spelt or any food that you may find of mine, [11] till you have full payment of your money and interest thereon, and I shall have no power to say to you that I have paid you [12] your money and the interest on it while this deed is in your hand, nor shall I have power to lodge a complaint [13] against

you before governor or judge on the ground that you have taken from me any security while this deed [14] is in your hand. If I die without paying you this money and interest thereon, [15] my children are to pay you this money and interest thereon. If [16] they do not pay you this money and interest thereon, you Meshullam have a right [17] to take for yourself any food or security that you may find of theirs until you have full payment [18] of your money and interest thereon, and they shall have no power to lodge a complaint against you before governor [19] or judge while this deed is in your hand. Even if they go to law they shall not win their case [20] while this deed is in your hand. Nathan b. 'Anani wrote this deed [21] at the dictation of Ya'uḥan. Witnesses hereto: Witness, Oshea' b. Gilgul. [22] Hodaviah b. Gedaliah. Ahio b. Pelaṭiah. Agur b. Ahio. (Endorsement.) [23] Deed of money lent (?), which Ya'uḥan daughter of Meshullak wrote [24] for Meshullam b. Zaccur.

Line 2. יהוחן fem. occurs several times. Cf. יהוחנן masc. מישלך occurs several times, but its meaning and vocalization are unknown. Sachau compares Phoenician or Punic בעלשלך, and Ungnad שמשלך in 26^{8}. If it is formed from a √ שלך (Meshullakh) that can hardly have the meaning of the Hebrew שלך. נשן as in 8^{2}. She could do business in her own right.

Line 3. זפת from √ יזף, only in these papyri. Cf. Aḥiḳar 130, &c.

Line 4. במרביתה 'as *its* interest'.

Line 5. לתקל the proper Aramaic form, cf. Dan. 5^{25}. In l. 3 and elsewhere שקל is always used = Bab. *Šiklu*. הוה. The reading is clear, but the asyndeton is strange. We should expect הו. Perhaps a mistake.

Line 6. הן מטא, pregnant, if it (is not paid and therefore) is added. In 11^{5} more explicitly יהוה ראש. No doubt this was the usual practice and is here taken for granted. רשא i.e. רֵישָׁא. ירבה attracted to the gender of רשא, cf. on 11^{5}.

Line 7. חד כחד 'one like one', i.e. both alike. תנין שנה. The construction is strange for 'a second year'. Sachau and Ungnad say ת' means 'repetition'. For the first year unpaid interest (96 ḥallurin) added to the principal would amount to a total of 6 sh. 16 ḥal.

Line 9. ערבן, Heb. ערבון, 'pledge', anything which represents money. תַשכח, cf. ll. 10, 17. No doubt to be so pointed, since it is always used in Haphel. The ה is frequently not written. Cf. 37^{10}, 13^{12} (ינפק) and Aḥiḳar 96 (תחוה), &c. לי, i.e. 'belonging to me'. בי וילבנן as in 3^{18}. Note no preposition.

Line 10. זון apparently for מזון, but not known elsewhere as a noun.

Line 11. תתמלא as in 2^{17}. כספך is 'capital'. לם is added above the line as an afterthought.

Line 14. ומרביתה. The ה is added above the line for want of space.

Line 17. תשכח no doubt to be so read, as in ll. 9, 10. There is a mark before the ת which might be י if the form יתשכח were possible. It is like that in בהמיתה 9[5], so that both may be unintentional.

Lines 19, 20. Cf. 8[22].

Line 20. The same scribe as in 13[17], &c.

Line 23. דנה (not רבה). Ungnad says = זנה, but this is impossible. In CIS ii, 1, 17 + דנת is explained as = Bab. *dannitu* = *duppu* 'document'. Perhaps דנה is the abs. st. of this, in the special sense of 'contract' (loan or sale), and was borrowed by Greek as δάνος (for which there is no satisfactory etymology); cf. ἀῤῥαβών from ערבון.

Frequently in endorsement ספר is followed by a word indicating the nature of the document. But cf the endorsement of #2.

No. 11.

Contract for a Loan. About 455 B.C.

This was the first of the papyri brought from Elephantine and was published in 1903 (see the account of it in *PSBA* 1903, p. 205) just after no. 27 (ed. by Euting).

The writing is good, but the papyrus is badly broken, especially at the beginning (the outside of the roll) so that some details are uncertain. Several points, however, are cleared up by comparison with similar documents in this collection. In general cf. no. 10. The date is lost at the beginning, but there can be little doubt that it was written about 460–450 B.C. At that time Egypt was in revolt against the Persians, and this may be the reason why the money is described as 'of the weight of Ptaḥ' (l. 2) instead of 'royal weight' as usually. The phrase would equally well suit the time of the revolt about 400 B.C., but the earlier date is required by the names. The scribe Gemariah b. Ahio is a witness in 6[18] (465 B.C.) but is not mentioned in later dated documents, and one of the witnesses here, Mahseiah b. Yedoniah, is a party to no. 5 (471 B.C.) and no. 15, but must have died soon after that (441 B.C.). In 25[18] the witness Mahseiah b. Yedoniah is probably the grandson (416 B.C.). The deed must have been dated somehow. In the present first line there is just room for אמר פלוני בר אלמוני לפלוני and no more. Hence it seems that there must originally have been a line before it containing the date. [The small fragments at the top are merely loose scraps which were put together there because they could not be fitted in anywhere. They do not belong there and are not consecutive, so that it is useless to try to make anything out of them.] In l. 8 the debt is to be paid by the 9th year (probably). As M. Clermont-Ganneau points out, this can hardly be the year of a king, because he might die in the meantime. It might be the 9th year 'of the freedom of Egypt', or the 9th year after the deed was written. In the last case it implies a date at the beginning.

M. Clermont-Ganneau, who makes the shekel = 192 ḥallurin, remarks that the interest would be $12\frac{1}{2}$ per cent. per annum, and would therefore in eight years amount to as much as the original capital. This would give a meaning to the number 9, and to יעקף (l. 8), and it is possible that the values here differ from those in the other documents. Comparing no. 10, however, it is unlikely that the creditor would allow outstanding interest to accumulate for eight years without distraining. See note on יעקף (l. 8). If the values are the same as elsewhere and are rightly ascertained in the Introduction (p. xxiii) the interest would be 60 per cent. per annum, and the above argument does not hold.

Sayce and Cowley, L. Ungnad, no. 88.

. . . .

. . . . ר בר יתמא [לאמר] נתנת לי כסף
[שקלן III]I [בא]בני פתח כסף ש 𐡘 ל 𐡛 וירבה עלי כסף חלרן II
לכסף ש 𐡘 לירחא עד יום זי אשלמנהי ל[ך] ותהוה מרבית
כספך חלרן III [III II] לירח 𐡘 וירחא זי לא אנתן לך בה
מרבית יהוה ראש וירבה ואשלמ[נה]י לך ירח בירח
מן פרסי זי ינ[ת]נן לי מן אוצרא ותכתב לי נבז על כל
כסף ומרבי זי אהוה משלם לך והן לא שלמת לך כל
כספך ומרביתה עד ירח תחות שנת [III] III II𐡘 יעקף כספך
ומרביתה זי יִשְׁתְּאַר עלי ויהוה רבה עלי ירח לירח
עד יום זי אשלמנהי לך
שהדיא
עקבן בר שמשנורי
קצרי בר יהההדרי
מחסיה בר ידניה
מלכיה בר זכריה
כתב ספרא גמריה בר אחיו על פם שהדיא זי על ספרא זנה

[1] *Said X b. Y to Z* b. Yathma *as follows:* You have given me the sum of [2] *4 shekels by the wei*ght of Ptaḥ, at the rate of 1 shekel to 10, and interest shall be due from me at the rate of 2 ḥallurin [3] for the sum of 1 shekel per month, till the day when I repay it to *you*, so that the interest on [4] your money shall be *8* ḥallurin each month. Any month in which I do not give you [5] interest, it shall be (added to the) capital and shall bear interest. I will pay it to you month by month [6] out of my

salary which they give me from the treasury, and you shall write me a receipt for all [7] money and interest which I pay to you. If I do not pay you all [8] your money and the interest thereon by the month of Thoth in the 9th year, your money shall be doubled (?) [9] and the interest on it which is outstanding against me, and interest shall be due from me month by month [10] until the day when I repay it to you. Witnesses: [11] 'Uḳban b. Shemesh-nuri. [12] Ḳoẓri b. Ya'hadari. [13] Mahseiah b. Yedoniah. [14] Malchiah b. Zechariah. [15] Gemariah b. Ahio wrote the deed before the witnesses who(se names) are upon this deed.

Line 1. [לאמר] can be restored with certainty from other deeds. There is perhaps a slight trace of ל.

Line 2. [שקלן] must be restored, since the interest is in ḥallurin, but the number of them is less certain. Four is most likely. When the text was first published this seemed too small a sum for so formal a document, but no. 10 now removes that objection. [בא]בני פתח is right. Elsewhere always באבני מלכא. The 'weight of Ptaḥ' would be that used in his temple at Memphis and no doubt represents the Egyptian scale (of the revolt) as distinguished from the Royal (Persian) weight. (So in demotic documents frequently 'of the double house of Ptaḥ.)' The standard is here described as 1 shekel to 10, whereas the ordinary standard is 2 R to 10. If this means the proportion of alloy, the standard of the revolt had twice as much alloy as before. ש \ is not found in legal documents usually for 1 shekel.

Line 3. ותהוה i.e. 'so that it shall be'.

Line 4. The numeral must be under 10 and must be divisible by 2. Therefore either 4 or 6 or 8. The space best suits 8. Therefore the shekels in l. 2 must be 4.

Line 5. יהוה ראש. The grammar is inaccurate. It ought to be מרביתא(־ה) and תהוה as in l. 3. The verb is no doubt attracted to the gender of ראש (cf. ירבה in 10^6). ראש is the Hebrew form.

Line 6. פרסי 'share' 'portion', i.e. wages. The debtor was still in the employment of the provisional government, as he had been under the Persian régime, and the same terms are used. Cf. 2^{16}, but there is no mention here of בית מלכא or בי זי לבנן. נבז must mean a 'note', i.e. a receipt. As an Aramaic word it occurs in the Samaritan Targum Lev. 16^{8-10} for Heb. גורל, and is no doubt there a loan-word from Arab. نبذ. The meaning is hardly the same here, and I am still inclined to take it (against Halévy) as a Persian form from نوشتن (see *PSBA* 1903, p. 207), a 'written' receipt. Johns (*PSBA* 1905, p. 187) cites an Assyrian word *nibzu* in this sense, but with no Semitic etymology.

Line 7. מרבי should be מרביתה as in ll. 8, 9 and in no. 10.

אהוה משלם not common in this Aramaic (as later) for אשלם. Cf. l. 9 יהוה רבה for ירבה.

Line 8. The numeral is certain since units are always grouped in threes as far as they go. But the point of naming the 9th year is not clear. The 9th year from the date of writing is a long time for so small a loan. If the deed was dated in the *n*th year of the freedom of Egypt (cf. the Jewish coins of the revolt) the loan would only be for 9–*n* years. The nature of the penalty is not clear enough to help. It can hardly be the 9th year of a king, though the 9th year of Artaxerxes I (456 B.C.) would be a suitable date. יעקף is very difficult. In ll. 4, 5 the outstanding interest is to be added to capital. Ll. 8, 9 are therefore unnecessary unless יעקף adds a further penalty. In no. 10 the outstanding interest in the first year is to be added to capital, but in the second year the creditor might distrain. Here distraint is not mentioned, but one would expect something corresponding. Perhaps עקף = ضعف in the sense of 'be doubled'.

Lines 11–16 are not arranged in the usual manner. L. 16 should complete l. 10, and the witnesses' names be written continuously. Cf. no. 1 and frequently.

Line 13. יההדרי. Probably for יהו הדרי 'Ya'u is my glory'.

Line 16. ספרא is 'document' not 'scribe' in both places. עלפם שהדיא is unusual. It is generally עלפם or כפם of one of the parties 'according to (instructions from)'. The interested party said what he wanted written, and the scribe put it into formal language. The witnesses would hardly give such instructions, so that here perhaps עלפם means rather 'in presence of'. Why the name of the debtor is not given (as in no. 10), is not evident.

No. 12.

List of Names, undated.

There are several lists of names in the collection, but the purpose of them is not always apparent. Some are connected with accounts. In mediaeval Jewish communities lists of this kind were often drawn up to commemorate members of the congregation who had suffered for their religion.

It is undated. If it is a memorial list it may be related to no. 34 (about 407 B.C.), which is probably connected with no. 30. Sachau, however, points out that the sons of Menahem b. Posai (l. 7) are mentioned in $22^{78,79}$. As the name Posai occurs only in these two documents, the persons are probably the same and this papyrus belongs to the generation earlier than no. 22 (420 B.C.) i.e. about 440–450 B.C.

The writing is not very careful, and the reading of it is the more difficult because the context affords no help.

Sachau, plate 17. Ungnad, no. 18.

1 חגי בר נתון
2 חרמן בר אושע
3 אושע בר יתום
4 אושע בר הודו
5 שמוע בר חגי
6 נתן בר נריה
7 מנחם בר פוסי
8 יאוש בר אזניה
9 ביתאלעקב בר עכר
10 כל ג[בר]ן /// /// ///
11 נבועקב בר

[1] Haggai b. Nathan. [2] Ḥarman b. Oshea'. [3] Oshea' b. Yathom. [4] Oshea' b. Hodav. [4] Shamua' b. Haggai. [6] Nathan b. Neraiah. [7] Menahem b. Posai. [8] Yeosh b. Azaniah. [9] Bethel'aḳab b. Achar. [10] Total 9 men. [11] Nabu'aḳab (?) b.

Line 1. Cf. 34^5, Hosea b. Nathum and Haggai his brother.

Line 2. חרמן (or חדמן). The second letter is more like a ד. Sachau compares חרמון. It may be related to חרמנתן, &c. It occurs also in 22^4 (the son of this man?). אושע. The ו is very unusual and the ש broken. אבישע is not possible.

Line 3. Cf. 34^6.

Line 4. הודו, as in 34^3, &c. A short form of Hodaviah.

Line 8. אזניה, in Neh. 10^{10} the father of ישוע, which looks like an improvement of יאוש here. It is parallel to י(א)זניה. יאוש Sachau thinks = יאשיה.

Line 9. עכר. Sachau and Ungnad עזר, but ז is impossible. It might be a נ. In 1 Chron. 2^7 Achar is a variant of Achan in Jos. 7^1.

Line 10. The total shows that the list is complete.

Line 11 is not Egyptian (Ungnad), but Aramaic written upside down.

No. 13.

Conveyance of a House. 447 B.C.

The end is somewhat broken.

Its date is the 19th year of Artaxerxes (I) = 447 B.C.

It is a deed of gift of a house from Mahseiah to his daughter Mibṭaḥiah, in return for value received from her. As the parties are known from previous documents, there can be no doubt that the year is that of Artaxerxes I, not II.

It is another proof that a woman could hold property and transact business independently of her father or (since Mibṭaḥiah was married in no. 8) her husband.

A peculiarity of this text is the number of mistakes in spelling, though the scribe, Nathan b. Ananiah, must have been a professional notary, since he also wrote nos. 10 and 15. The following are probably such slips: l. 2 מפטחיה (also elsewhere), l. 4 בבירת?, l. 7, &c. דילבי, l. 10 ובב, קרב, l. 11 אם, l. 12 ועתק, ינפק?, ספ, l. 14 יהה, ושקא?

Sayce and Cowley, E.

1 ב III לכסלו הו יום 𐡛 לירח מסורע שנת 𐡛 III III III ארתחשסש מלכא אמר מחסיה בר

2 ידניה ארמי זי סון לדגל וריזת למפטחיה ברתה לאמר אנה יהבת לכי לביתא

3 זי יהב לי משלם בר זכור בר אטר ארמי זי סון בדמוה[י] וספר כתב לי עלא

4 ויהבתה למפטחיה ברתי חלף נכסיא זי יהבת לי כזי הנדז הוית בבירת אפלת

5 המו ולא השכחת כסף ונכסן לשלמה לכי אחר אנה יהבת לכי לביתא זנה

6 חלף נכסיכי אלבי דמי כסף כרשן /// // ויהבת לכי ספרא עתיקא זי [כתב]

7 לי משלם זך אחרוהי זנה ביתא יהבתה לכי ורחקת מנה דילבי הו ולבניכ[י]

8 מן אחריכי ול[מן זי רחמ]תי תנתננה לא אכל אנה ובני וזרע זילי ונבר

9 אחרן ירשנכי דין ודבב בשם ביתא זך זי אנה יהבת לכ[י] וספרא כתבת לכי

10 עלא זי ירשנכי דין ובב אנה ואח ואחה קרב ורחי[ק בע]ל דגל ובעל קריה

11 ינתן לכי כסף כרשן 𐡛 ובית אם דילכי אפלא יכל גבר אחרן יהנפק עליכי ספר

12 חדת ועתק להן זנה ספרא זי אנה כתבת ויהבת לכ[י ז]י ינפק עליכי ספ לא אנה כ[תבתה]

13 אף הא אלה תחומי ביתא זך עליהלה בית יאו[ש בר פ]נוליה תחתיאלה

14 אגורא זי יהה אלה מועאלה בית גדול בר אושע ושקא בניהם

15 מערב שמש לה [אר]ק אסרוך בר פלטו כמר זי חנ[ום ומ]תי א[ל]היא זך ביתא

16 יהבתה לך ורחקת מנה דילכי הו עד עלם ולמן [זי] תִצבִין הבהי כתב

17 נתן בר ענניה ספרא זנה· כפם מחסיה ושהדיא בגו כתב מחסיה בנ̄ׄי

18 נפשה מתרסרה בר מתרסרה ו[׳שתברזן] בר אתרלי כספי

19 שהד ברברי בר דרגי כספי זי אתרא [שׁהד , . . .] בר שמעיה

20 זכור בר שלם

Endorsement. 21 ספר במחסיה בר ידניה [ומפטחי]ה ברתה

[1] On the 3rd of Chisleu, that is the 10th day of the month Mesore, year 19 of Artaxerxes the king, said Mahseiah b. [2] Yedoniah, Aramaean of Syene, of the detachment of Warizath, to Miphtaḥiah his daughter, as follows: I give you the house [3] which Meshullam b. Zaccur b. Atar, Aramaean of Syene, gave me for its price, and wrote a document for me about it, [4] and I give it to Miphtaḥiah my daughter in return for the goods which she gave me when I was inspector (?) in the fortress. I acknowledged (?) [5] them but did not find money and goods to pay you. Consequently I give you this house [6] in return for those your goods of the value of 5 kerashin, and I give you the original document which [7] the said Meshullam *wrote* for me about it. This house I give to you and I resign all claim to it. It belongs to you and to your children [8] after you and to *whomsoever you please* you may give it. I have no power, I or my children or my descendants or any [9] other man, to bring against you suit or process in the matter of this house which I give you, and have written the document for you [10] about it. Whoever raises against you suit or process, (whether it be) I or a brother or sister, relative or strang*er*, *sol*dier or citizen, [11] shall pay you the sum of 10 kerashin, and the house is assuredly yours. Moreover no other man shall produce against you a document [12] new or old, other than this document which I have written and given to *you*: *who*ever produces against you such document, I have not wr*itten it*. [13] Moreover note, these are the boundaries of this house. At the upper end of it is the house of Yeo*sh b. Pe*nuliah, at the lower end of it is [14] the temple of the God Ya'u, at the east of it is the house of Gadol b. Oshea' and the street between them, [15] on the west of it is the *land* of. . . . b. Palṭo, priest of the gods Khn*um and Sa*ti (?). This house [16] I give you and resign all claim to it. It is yours for ever. To whom*soever* you wish, give it. [17] Nathan b. Ananiah wrote this document at the direction of Mahseiah and the witnesses hereto. Mahseiah signed for [18] himself (?). Mithrasari (?) b. Mithrasari (?), and *Satibarzanes* b. Atharli, silversmith. [19] Witness, Barbari b. Dargi, silversmith of the place (?). *Witness*, ... b. Shemaiah. [20] Zaccur b. Shallum. (Endorsement.) [21] Document concerning Mahseiah b. Yedoniah *and Miphṭaḥi*ah his daughter.

Line 1. ///ב is probable. According to Gutesmann it should be Chisleu 2 = Mesore 10, or Chisleu 3 = Mesore 11. Hontheim reads 2.

Line 2. In nos. 8, 9 Mahseiah is a Jew of Yeb, of the *degel* of Haumadata. לביתא. The ל marks the accusative, as occasionally in these texts. The house was at Elephantine, since it adjoins the temple (l. 14), though the owner and former owner are both 'of Syene'.

Line 3. Meshullam is a party to no. 10. עלא adverbially 'concerning (it)', cf. בנו. אטר as Ezra 2^{16}.

Line 4. הנדז has been much discussed, but nothing has yet been suggested which seems better than the original explanation in S-C. A word הנדז or הנדס is fairly common in late Hebrew, and in Arabic (هندس) in the sense of 'measuring'. It is clearly *not* Semitic, and it seems an impossible coincidence that there should be two loan-words identical in form, but differing in meaning and origin, even if they are found 1000 years apart. Other words in these documents occur elsewhere not earlier than the Talmud. The common ground is to be found in the Persian انداختن. A Persian loan-word is as natural here as in modern Arabic, where هندس is explained as being from the Persian اندازه (from انداختن). The precise meaning here, however, is still not clear. The modern Arabic هندسة (and so modern Hebrew) means 'geometry' or 'measurement' as applied to various arts, such as drawing, engineering, architecture, astronomy. In the Talmud the verb is used of the marks on measures of liquid &c. Hence it ought to mean here something like 'inspector of weights and measures' or 'controller of the water supply' for drinking or irrigation. In 27^7 הנדזין is apparently a verb. Andreas takes it to mean 'heap', i. e. 'many' in 27^7, but that is unsuitable here. Clermont-Ganneau doubtfully suggests 'crowd'. Nöldeke rejects this and proposes 'einberufen' (so Smend) or 'answered'. Lagrange, 'chargé des rations'. בבירת either a mistake for בבירתא, or a name (יב?) has been omitted. אפ̄לח Lagrange, 'in the fortress of Apalt'. Nöldeke also takes it as a name, and makes המו (l. 5) refer back to זי יהבת. This is impossible. It must be a verb governing המו. Bab. *apâlu* means 'answer', 'announce'. Can it mean 'I acknowledged them'? It might possibly be אכלת ('I consumed'), but the tail is hardly straight enough for כ.

Line 5. המו the separate pronoun as accusative, cf. 15^{35} &c. אחר, commonly in Aḥiḳar and Behistun, 'and then'.

Line 6. ה̄ל̄ף̄ restored from l. 4, but very uncertain. There seems to be something (א or י) after the פ, but it is difficult to guess what other word would suit the passage. נכסיכ̄י (S-C נכסיך) is correct and fairly certain. אלכ̄י is correct and probable, as in 14^8. There is a slight trace of י. [כתב] a trace of ת.

Line 7. אחרוהי 'about it', as in 9^4. דילבי as in ll. 11, 16, for the usual זי־. There is no evident reason for די־. Both forms must have been in use, and די־ is not necessarily later or popular, since זי־ is used in the Ptolemaic papyrus no. 81, which is not formal.

Line 10. ובב a mistake for ורבב, as קרב for קריב.

Line 11. אם a mistake for אפם, as in 6^{15}.

Line 12. ינפק is practically certain. This spelling (as against יהנפק in l. 11) is due to carelessness rather than error. The usual ה is merely a vowel-letter indicating the pronunciation יַנפק as distinguished from יִנפק. There was no reason why it should not be omitted from a word which was *always* used in the (H)aphel (as תַשכח $10^{9,10}$), or was evidently causal since it has an object, as here. ספ for ספר, another mistake.

Line 13. יאו[ש] is probable, as there is a slight trace of ש, and the name occurs several times. S–C יאור which does not occur, though יההאור is found in 1^2. The house was near that conveyed to Mibṭaḥiah in no. 8. See the plan in no. 5.

Line 14. אגורא is the temple, cf. no. 30, and notes there. It was not merely a chapel or shrine, as conjectured by S–C before the discovery of Sachau's papyri. Other speculations as to its character may now be disregarded. יהה for יהו only here (and in יההאור, 1^2?). The form, which is certain, has been much discussed, but it is probably a mere slip, considering the many errors in this document. מועאלה, in 8^6 more fully מועא שמש לה. ושקא for ושוקא by a mistake? בניהם a mistake for ביניהם? There may be something after it, but nothing is wanted.

Line 15. ק[אר]. The ק is probable. It seems not to be בית. ...זך The reading מרדוך (S–C) is hardly probable. The papyrus is slightly out of position. ברוך is unlikely. We should expect an Egyptian name (אסרוך?) though the father's name is Jewish. פלטו, cf. late Hebrew פלטוי and O.T. פלט, פלטי, &c. חנ[ום וס]תי are not quite certain as the space is barely sufficient even if the papyrus is re-adjusted. But the reading is probable, because Khnum and Sati were associated as the divinities of the cataract, there must be two names since אלהיא is fairly certain (not אלהא), and כמר is correctly used in these texts (cf. 30^5, כמריא זי חנוב), as later, of the priest of a foreign god. זי is probable (not as S–C). It might be וילחנום or חנֻם or חנוב (as in 30^5).

Line 16. לך another mistake for לבי. הבהי defectively, or a mistake, for הביהי.

Line 17. The sentence ends with בנו, unless כתב מח׳ וכ׳ is an intrusion. As it stands, we must translate 'at the direction of M. and the witnesses hereto'. But the formula is unusual. בבי נפשה. It must be a כ,

not ר (as S–C), cf. the כ in כתב just before. It cannot then be for בר י[דניה]. The meaning is quite obscure. It looks as if Mahseiah had become impatient, seized a pen and written something hastily. If so, he probably meant (as S–C) 'M. wrote for himself', but it is not clear how the words can mean that.

Line 18. מתרסרה. The רס are run together, and might be חס as in מחסיה. Hence S–C מתחסרה. It may be the Persian name Mithrasari. ו[יתברזן] is restored from 5^{16}. There is perhaps a trace of ת. אתרלי is certain here. The name is no doubt the same as in 5^{16}, where see note. כספי. Lagrange suggests 'Caspian', but if such a gentilic name were found it would be כספיא, as בבליא in 6^{19}.

Line 19. ברברי. Unknown as a name. דרגי, cf. דרגא 5^{18} (for דרגמן), or it may be דדגי, cf. Δάδαγος, Δαδάκης. אתרא. 'Silversmith of the place' is a strange expression, cf. אתרה 6^2, of Dargman. Lagrange, 'Caspien de Athra' (as in 6^2), cf. Atropatene. He also compares Ezra 8^{17}, which, however, does not help. The very slight traces remaining do not fit any of the known names of sons of Shemaiah.

Line 21. במחסיה. The formula is unusual.

No. 14.

Settlement of Claim. 441 B.C.

The date is 441 B.C., probably the year before, and in view of, Mibṭaḥiah's third (?) marriage (in no. 15).

Halévy thinks that Mibṭaḥiah had married Pi', an Egyptian, and adopted his religion. She swears by Sati in l. 5. Among the witnesses here there is no one with a Jewish name, because the community refused to recognize her. On her divorce she would return to the Jewish faith. This document is the act of separation following on the divorce pronounced by the court, cf. l. 3. If ספר אנתו is right in l. 4, she must have been married to him, and Halévy's explanation must be in the main correct. They now have to divide their possessions and she is required to take an oath, the object of which is not clear. It would seem to relate to the amount of stock in her hands or to their joint credit, she having carried on the business of ארדיכל with Pi'. He declares himself satisfied with her statement, and the division of property is completed. The terms had evidently been settled in the previous suit (l. 3).

The papyrus is in an excellent state of preservation.

Sayce and Cowley, F.

1 ב ר ///\ לאב הו יום ר /// /// /// /// לפחנס שנת ד /// // ארתחשסש
מלכא אמר פיא
2 בר פחי ארדיכל לסון בירתא למבטחיה ברת מחסיה בר ידניא
3 ארמיא זי סון לדגל וריזת על דינא זי עבדן בסון נפלגת על כסף
אפתו
4 ועבור ולבוש ונחש ופרזל כל נכסן וקנין וספר אדין מומאה
5 מטאה עליכי וימאתי לי עליהם בסתי אלהתה וטיב לבבי
6 במומאה דכא זי עבדתי לי על נכסיא אלכי ורחקת מנכי מן
7 יומא זנה ועד עלם לא אכהל אגרנכי דין ודבב אנתי ובר
8 וברה לכי בשם נכסיא אלכי זי ימאתי לי עליהם הן גריתכי
9 דין ודבב וגרכי ברלי וברהלי בשם מומאה דכי אנה פיא ובני
10 אנתן למבטחיה כסף כרשן /// // באבני מלכא ולא דין ולא דבב
11 ואנה רחיק מן כלדין ודבב כתב פטאסי בר נבונתן ספרא זנה
12 בסון בירתא כפם פיא בר פחי שהדיא בגו נבורעי בר נבונתן
13 לוחי בר מנכי עדנהר בר דומא נבורעי בר וישתן

Endorsement. 14 ספר מרחק זי כתב פיא למבט[חיה]

[1] On the 14th of Ab, that is the 19th day of Paḥons, year 25 of Artaxerxes the king, said Pi' [2] b. Paḥi, builder, of Syene the fortress, to Mibṭaḥiah daughter of Mahseiah b. Yedoniah [3] Aramaean of Syene, of the detachment of Warizath (as follows): In accordance with the action which we took at Syene, let us make a division concerning the money [4] and corn and garments and bronze and iron, all goods and possessions, and the marriage-document. Then an oath [5] was imposed on you and you swore to me concerning them by the goddess Sati and my heart was content [6] with that oath which you took to me concerning those your goods and I renounce all claim on you from [7] this day for ever. I have no power to institute against you suit or process, you or son [8] or daughter of yours in the matter of those your goods concerning which you have sworn to me. If I institute against you [9] suit or process, or my son or daughter sue you in the matter of that your oath, I, Pi', or my son [10] will pay to Mi*b*ṭaḥiah the sum of 5 kerashin, royal weight, without suit or process, [11] and I renounce all suit and process. Peṭisi b. Nabunathan wrote this document [12] in Syene the fortress, at the direction of Pi' b. Paḥi. Witnesses hereto: Nabure'i b. Nabunathan. [13] Luḥi b. Mannuki. 'Odnahar b. Duma. Nabure'i b. Vashtan. (Endorsement.) [14] Deed of quittance which Pi' wrote for Mibṭ*aḥiah*.

Line 1. פיא בר פחי. Probably Egyptian, but the meaning of the names is obscure. Note that he does not belong to a *degel*.

Line 2. ארדיכל. Bab. *arad-ekalli*, 'servant of the palace'. In later Aramaic it means 'architect' or 'builder'. In 15[2] Asḥor is ארדיכל זי מלכא. Halévy compares Persian *ardikar*, 'wall-maker'. ידניא for ידניה.

Line 3. על 'in accordance with'? We should expect לאמר before it. עבדן not עבדן as S–C, but the phrase is strange. The last letter is really a ף, or ן with the top broken. על after נפרת is also strange, but the meaning of נפרת is certain. Nöldeke says 'let us separate', and supplies לאמר before it. Halévy compares نفر 'I withdrew' (unsuitable).

Line 4. ספר אנתו (not אנתן as S–C), a 'deed of marriage', cf. 15[3]. He gave up the deed on his divorce, showing that he had no longer any rights over her. She re-married in the next year.

Line 5. מטאה 'came upon you', i.e. was imposed upon you. בסתי. There is no question of the reading or meaning. She was required to swear by the Egyptian goddess because her opponent was an Egyptian. (I. Lévi compares B. T. Sanhedrin 63^b, אמר אביה דשמואל אסור לאדם שיעלה שותפות עם ע"כ שמא יתחייב לו שבועה ונשבע בע"כ שלו. Samuel belonged to the third century A. D.). The case is different from that in which other divinities are mentioned in connexion with Ya'u and the temple. This concerns a definitely foreign deity (cf. the 'queen of heaven' in Jer. 44), not one who had been accepted or imagined as Jewish.

Line 6. דכא. Note ד again sporadically for ז. It is perhaps a mistake for דכי as in l. 9, elsewhere זכי, which would be correct in speaking to a woman. אלכי would be correct, as in l. 8. There is room for י, and possibly some trace of it.

Line 9. וגרבי perfect, as גריתבי (l. 8), depending on הן. There is a mark above the י, which seems to be unintentional. ובראלי, cf. ידניא, l. 2. Here the א is for ה of the feminine. ובני added parenthetically without affecting the construction.

Line 10. למטחיה a mere mistake.

Line 11. פטאסי וכ׳, a man bearing a pure Egyptian name whose father has a Babylonian name.

Lines 12, 13. The witnesses' names are in their own writing.

Line 13. מנכי, shortened from Bab. *Mannuakiilani* = מיכאל. עורנהר וכ׳ can hardly be read otherwise, but the names are unknown. נבורעי is Babylonian, while his father's name is Persian.

Line 14. מרחק 'withdrawal' or renunciation of claim. It was not the actual divorce, but the sequel to it.

No. 15.

Marriage Contract. About 441 B.C.

The number of the year is lost, line 1 being much broken. There are, however, reasons for putting the document at about the same date as no. 14, or soon after. The scribe Nathan was a witness to nos. 8 and 9 in 459 B.C. and wrote no. 10 in 456 and no. 13 in 447. In 459 Mibṭaḥiah was the wife of Yezaniah, her first marriage. In no. 13 (447) he is not mentioned, and was therefore probably dead or divorced. In no. 20 (420) Asḥor, the present bridegroom, was apparently also dead, leaving two sons old enough to act as principals in an action at law. Supposing them to be then about 18 years of age, the present marriage cannot have taken place much after 440. If the interpretation of no. 14 is right and Mibṭaḥiah was then (in 441) just divorced from her second husband, we are forced to date this document in or after 441. At any rate Asḥor is not mentioned in no. 14. [Gutesmann calculates the date as 447–449.]

One of the witnesses here is Penuliah b. Yezaniah, and in no. 20 (420) a witness is Yezaniah b. Penuliah, probably his son, as a child was often named after his grandfather.

This is a כתובה or marriage settlement (cf. demotic marriage contracts in *Journal Asiatique* 1906, p. 351), giving lists of the mutual gifts with their values, very important for determining the relative values of the money terms. See Introduction, p. xxii. It then states the terms of succession in case the marriage is dissolved. Cf. no. 9. Unfortunately the text is very difficult, partly owing to its broken condition, and partly to the many unknown words.

cp Document 36.

Sayce and Cowley, G.

1 ב ד̄ [//// // ל]תשרי [הו יום] III III לירח אפף [שנת . . . ארתחשס]ש מלכ[א]

2 אמר אסחור בר [צחא] ארדכל זי מלכא למח[סיה א]רמי זי סון לדגל

3 וריזת לאמר אנה [א]תית ביתך למנתן לי [ל]ברתך מפטיה לאנתו

4 הי אנתתי ואנה בעלה מן יומא זנה ועד עלם יהבת לך מהר

5 ברתך מפטחיה [כסף] שקלן III II באבני מלכ[א] על עליך וטב לבבך

6 בגו הנעלת לב[רתך] מפטחיה בידה כס[ף] תכונה כרש I באבני שקלן II

7 מלכא. כסף ר II ל ר הנעלת לה בידה לבש I זי עמר חדת חטב

II III III

8 צבע ידין הוה ארך אמן III III II ב III II [ש]וה כסף כרשן II שקלן

באבני מלכא שביט | חדת הוה ארך אמן ||| ||| ||| ב ||| || שוה
כסף שקלן ||| ||| || באבני מלכא לבש אחרן זי עמר נשחט הוה
ארך אמן ||| ||| ב |||ʌ שוה כסף שקלן ||| ||| | מחזי | זי נחש שוה
כסף שקל | ר || תמ[חי] | זי נחש שויה כסף שקל | ר || כסן זי נחש ||
שוין כסף שקלן |[|] זלוע | זי נחש שוה כסף ר || כל כספא
ודמי נכסיא כסף כרשן ||| ||| שקל||| || חלרן ד כסף ר || ל ר באבני
מלכא על עלי [וט]יב לבבי בנו שוי | זי גמא בה נעבצן
תקם ח ||| ||| || שנן משאן |
זי אבן |||ʌ פק | זי סלק כפן || פרכס | זי חצן חדת
מחר או יום א[חר]ן ימות אסחור ובר דכר ונקבה לא
איתי לה מן מ[פטח]יה אנתתה מפטחיה הי שליטה בביתה
זי אסחור ונכס[והי] וקנינה וכל זי איתי לה על אנפי ארעא
כלה מחר או יום תמות מפטחיה ובר דכר ונקבה לא
איתי לה מן אסחור בעלה אסחור הו ירתנה בנכסיה
וקנינה מחר [או י]ום אחרן תקום [מפ]טחיה בעדה
ותאמר שנאת לאסחור בעלי כסף שנאה בראשה תתב על
מוזנא ותתקל ל[אס]חור כסף שקלן ||| |||ʌ ר || וכל זי הנעלת
בידה תהנפק מן חם עד חוט ותהך [ל]האן זי צבית ולא
ידין ולא דבב מחר או יום אחרן יקום אסחור בעדה
ויאמר שנאת [לאנ]תתי מפטחיה מהרה [י]אבד וכל זי הנעלת
בידה תהנפק מן חם עד חוט ביום חד בכף חדה ותהך
לה אן זי צבית מן לא דין ולא דבב ו[הן] יקום על מפטחיה
לתרכותה מן ביתה זי אסחור ונכסוהי וקנינה ינתן לה
כסף כרשן ד ויע[די] לה דין ספרא זנה ולא אכל אמר
איתי לי אנתה אחרה להן מפטיה ובנן אחרנן להן בנן זי
תלד לי מפטחיה הן אמר איתי לי ב[נן] ואנתה אחרן להן
מפטחיה ובניה אנתן למפטחיה כס[ף] כרשן ד באבני
מלכא ולא אכל [אהנ]תר נכסי וקניני מן מפ[טח]יה והן העדת המו
מנה (קבל ס[פר אחר]ן) אנתן למפטחיה [כסף] כרשן ד באבני מל[כא]
כתב נתן בר ענניה [ספרא זנה כפם אסחור] ושהדיא בגו
פנוליה בר יזניה [. . .]יה בר אוריה מנחם בר [ז]כור
שהד רעיבל ב[ר . . . .

[1] On the 25th (?) of Tishri *that is* the 6th *day* of the month Epiphi, *ear . . . of Artaxerx*es the king, [2] said Ashor b. *Zeho*, builder to the king, o Mah*seiah A*ramaean of Syene, of the detachment of [3] Warizath, as

follows: I came to your house that you might give me your daughter Miphṭaḥiah in marriage. [4] She is my wife and I her husband from this day for ever. I have given you as the price [5] of your daughter Miphṭaḥiah *the sum* of 5 shekels, royal weight. It has been received by you and your heart is content [6] therewith. I have delivered to your *daughter* Miphṭaḥiah into her hand for the cos*t of* furniture 1 karash 2 shekels royal [7] weight, of the standard of 2 R to 10. I have delivered to her into her hand 1 woollen robe, new, striped, [8] dyed on both sides, (whose) length was 8 cubits by 5, *w*orth the sum of 2 kerashin 8 shekels, [9] royal weight; 1 closely-woven (shawl) new, (whose) length was 8 cubits by 5, worth [10] the sum of 8 shekels royal weight; another woollen robe, finely woven, (whose) length was [11] 6 cubits by 4, worth the sum of 7 shekels; 1 mirror of bronze, worth [12] the sum of 1 shekel 2 R; 1 tray of bronze, worth the sum of 1 shekel 2 R; 2 cups of bronze, [13] worth the sum of 2 shekels; 1 bowl of bronze, worth the sum of 2 R; total money [14] and value of goods being the sum of 6 kerashin 5 shekels 20 ḥallurin, of the standard of 2 R to 10, royal weight. [15] I have received, and my heart is *con*tent therewith, 1 couch of reeds with 4 supports (?) [16] of stone; 1 PK of SLK; 2 ladles, holding (?) 8 Ḥ; 1 MŠ'N knife (?); 1 cosmetic box of ivory, new. [17] To-morrow or a*noth*er day (if) Asḥor should die and there is no child male or female [18] belonging to him by Mi*phṭaḥ*iah his wife, Miphṭaḥiah has a right to the house [19] of Asḥor, *his* goods and his chattels and all that he has on the face of the earth, [20] all of it. To-morrow or (another) day (if) Miphṭaḥiah should die and there is no child male or female [21] belonging to her by Asḥor her husband, Asḥor shall inherit her goods [22] and her chattels. To-morrow *or* another day (if) *Miph*ṭaḥiah should stand up in the congregation [23] and say, I divorce Asḥor my husband, the price of divorce (shall be) on her head; she shall return to [24] the scales and weigh out to *A*sḥor the sum of 7 shekels 2 R and all that I have put [25] into her hand she shall give up, both shred (?) and thread, and she shall go away whither she will, without [26] suit or process. To-morrow or another day (if) Asḥor should stand up in the congregation [27] and say, I divorce my *wi*fe Miphṭaḥiah, her price shall be forfeited, but all that I have put [28] into her hand, she shall give up, both shred (?) and thread, on one day at one time, and she shall go [29] away whither she will, without suit or process. But if he should rise up against Miphṭaḥiah [30] to drive her out from his, Asḥor's, house and his goods and chattels, he shall give her [31] the sum of 20 kerashin, and the provisions of this deed shall be an*nulled*, as far as she is concerned. And I shall have no right to say [32] I have another wife besides Miphṭaḥiah and other children than the children whom [33] Miphṭaḥiah shall bear to me. If I say I have children and wife other than [34] Miphṭaḥiah and her children, I will pay to Miphṭaḥiah the su*m* of 20 kerashin, royal weight, [35] and I shall have no right to *take* away my goods and chattels from Miph*ṭaḥ*iah; and if I remove them [36] from her [erasure] I will pay to Miphṭaḥiah the *sum of* 20 kerashin, roy*al* weight. [37] Nathan b. Ananiah wrote *this deed at the direction of Asḥor* and the witnesses hereto: [38] Penuliah b. Jezaniah. . . . iah b. Uriah (?). Menahem b. *Za*ccur. [39] Witness, Re'ibel (?) b. . . .

Line 1 can now be restored with some certainty, except the number of the year. [/// ///]בּ. The lower part of ב is visible and is fairly certain. It might be ר, less probably. There is then room for about five units. חשרי. There is enough remaining of the lower parts of letters to make this certain now that the rest is explained. S-C marked it as doubtful because the facsimile shows traces of letters after it which were read זי מלא, and it was thought that this was part of some new formula. The remnants, however, are certainly to be read [ארתחשס]ש מלכ[א], and the loose fragment on which they are written should be transferred to the end of the line. שנת. There are again traces which fit this, and room for about /// /// ב after it.

Line 2. אסחור seems to have afterwards taken the name of Nathan, but whether as a proselyte or not, does not appear. Cf. 25^3, 28^2 with 20^3. This name and his father's are pure Egyptian. ארדכל זי מ׳, see on 14^2. He was a government contractor like Pi' b. Paḥi.

Line 3. The constructions are curious, though the sense is clear. אתית with an accusative. למנתן לי 'to (ask you to) give me'. לברתך accusative as in 13^2, with another ל marking the dative. מפטיה a mere mistake, cf. 14^{10}. לאנתו 'for wife-hood', i.e. in marriage. Not as S-C.

Line 4. מהר the 'dowry' is properly the price paid for a wife (cf. Gen. 34^{12} and often), here 5 shekels, no doubt the legal sum required to make the marriage valid. It was paid to the father, showing that he still had at least a legal *patria potestas*, although Mibṭaḥiah had been already married at least once (probably twice), must have been well over 30 years of age, and was able to conduct business in her own right. Anything given over and above the legal price was a present to the bride.

Line 5. על עליך 'it has come (עלל) to you', i.e. you have accepted the payment. וטב usually טיב, as in l. 15.

Line 6. הנעלת. Unfortunately there is no distinction in writing between the 1st and the 2nd persons. Freund and Jampel take it as the 2nd person, the father's present to the bride, not the bridegroom's gift. But the sum total in l. 14 shows that the presents were given by the same person who paid the 5 shekels, i.e. Asḥor. תכונה properly 'arrangement' or outfit, i.e. perhaps, to furnish the house. Cf. Nah. 2^{10}. שקלן II above the line, as often in this deed.

Line 7. חטב. In Prov. 7^{16} חטבות is translated by RV as 'striped cloths' (of the yarn of Egypt). In Talmud חוטבין are garments with a pattern or embroidered. Perhaps 'striped' is most likely here, but the meaning is uncertain.

Line 8. ידין dual of יד, Bab. *idu*, 'on both sides'. [ש]וה 'equal to', i. e. worth. It was a costly garment.

Line 9. שביט. A weaver's rod is שבט, whence the verb means to keep the rod closely pressed against the work, so that this should be 'closely-woven' stuff. It must have been specialized as a trade-term, and from its size can only have been some kind of shawl, as also לבש above. This was a cheaper article. ıĪ III III is probable here, as in l. 8, a stock size. The last unit is a long way from the rest, and one unit seems to be covered by a crease in the papyrus.

Line 10. נשחט. Cf. Jer. 9^{8}, שחוט (Ḳere for שוחט) explained by the Jewish commentators as = נמשך 'drawn out' (Ḳimḥi 'affilé'), and 2 Chron. 9^{15} זהב שחוט 'gold drawn out', i. e. beaten thin. Similarly in Talmud. Lagrange suggests 'avec franges'. The form is Niphal, therefore not Aramaic, but probably a trade-term derived from the language of Phoenician merchants (so Lidzbarski).

Line 12. תמ[חי], though it was difficult to guess, is not really doubtful. There are slight traces of חי. The papyrus is crushed here. It is no doubt a variant of Talm. תמחוי. There is no room for ו. ר II. The ר is badly made, like a כ. כפן ... II or possibly III, but as the price is 2 shekels, it was probably 1 shekel per cup. The prices are arranged in a descending scale.

Line 14. שקל a mistake for שקלן. חלרן ‍ב. There is a faint stroke after ב which might be a unit, but it is no doubt unintentional, as 21 ḥ. would not fit the sum on any reckoning. On the conclusions to be drawn from the sum of the items, see Introduction, p. xxii. In order to make up the total we must include the 5 shekels paid by Asḥor to Mahseiah. But the total must represent the whole of the payments in money (5 shekels) and goods (כל כספא ודמי נכסיא) made by one and the same person. Hence in ll. 6, 7 הנעלת must be 1st person 'I (Asḥor) gave'.

Line 15. The deed was drawn up in Asḥor's name. He therefore states the value of his own gifts, to make the most of them. He does not think it necessary to state the value of what he receives. נעבצן is quite unknown. Apparently a Niphal form, and so not Aramaic. If שוי is a 'bed' (cf. Arukh s.v. שוי i), the four נעבצן are very likely 4 feet.

Line 16. פק. Meaning unknown. The root פקק means either to 'split' or to 'stop up'. A 'hatchet'? Epstein suggests that it is for בק = בוקא or Persian بلك 'pitcher', cf. Heb. פך. He might compare בקבק, 'a flask'. סלק must be a noun describing the material, not as S-C. There is a slightly larger space than usual after it, which seems to indicate separation from what follows. But its meaning as a noun is unknown. כפן probably 'ladles' or 'bowls', not 'handles' as S-C. חצן, cf. חוצן 20[6] where it is associated with wood. I have translated it by 'ivory', cf. حضن. Nöldeke rejects this, and proposes 'palm-leaves', taking פרכם as a 'tray' or 'basket'. חקם, &c., above the line, being singular, must refer to פרכם (feminine ?) and mean 'containing'. Then ח is not for חלרן, since this series is not valued, nor a cipher for 8 (as Döller, Staerk) since letters are never so used in these texts, but must be a measure, as in 24[38]. שנן מיטאן, meaning quite unknown. The translation of שנן (root, 'to be sharp') as 'knife', is a mere guess of no value.

Line 20. יום. אחרן has been accidentally omitted.

Line 22. בערה, Hebrew. Borrowed as a technical term.

Line 23. שנאת, as in 9[8]. בראשה, 'is on her head', i. e. apparently 'she is responsible' for it. תתב from תוב, she shall return to the scales, or Haphel, she shall put back in its entirety. Not from יתב, as Nöldeke, 'sie setzt sich', and Jampel who compares Lev. 5[24] and translates 'sie soll als Hauptsumme das Scheidungsgeld auf die Wage legen'.

Line 24. \ווו ווו is more probable than \וו ווו because of the space. ר וו not for ר וו לי, as Staerk. Since ר וו = ½ a shekel she had to pay back the original מהר with 50 per cent. added. הנעלת and תתנפק (l. 25) are opposed. Freund and Jampel take הנעלת here and in l. 27 as 3rd person 'what she has received'. But it must refer to the same person as in l. 7, 'what I delivered to her she shall give up'.

Line 25. חם is certain from l. 28, but the precise meaning is unknown. Cf. Gen. 14[23]. Lidzbarski suggests 'radish' as something of small value. One would expect the meaning to be akin to that of חוט. The phrase means 'to the last shred'. לחאן probably two words, as in l. 29.

Line 26. ידין is clear. Probably a mere mistake.

Line 27. אבר[י]. If he divorced her, he forfeited the five shekels paid for her, but got back the presents. הנעלת is difficult. The writer seems to be confused about the persons. He is writing in Ashor's name, but speaks of him in the 3rd person in l. 26. Here he seems to revert to the 1st person, as above. Or can this be 3rd fem., 'she put (i. e. received) into her hand'?

Line 28. ביום חד וכ׳, a legal formula for 'all together'.

Line 29. לה is a sort of reflexive with תהך, cf. לֶךְ לְךָ. מִן לא seems the only possible reading—for בלא = the usual ולא.

Line 30. לתרכותה. This is a third case. She might divorce him, or he might divorce her in legal form, or he might eject her forcibly and illegally, in which case he would have to pay a heavy fine. Epstein thinks that תרך = נרש, the later term for divorce by a נט, but it surely implies an aggravation of what precedes. מן ביתה זי א׳ perhaps not merely a case of the anticipatory pronoun, but זי א׳ is added because ביתה might be *his* or *her* house, to make it quite clear.

Line 31. ויע[די] is better than ויע[מר] (as S-C) which is not found in these texts. דין must mean the legal obligation or provisions of the deed. As she is evidently regarded in this case as wrongly treated, it is reasonable to suppose that she would be freed from any further obligations. אבל. He reverts to the 1st person, though he has just used the 3rd (ינתן) in l. 30.

Line 32. Cf. Greek Pap. Tebtunis i, no. 104, l. 18: *καὶ μὴ ἐξέστω Φιλίσκῳ γυναῖκα ἄλλην ἐπαγαγέσθαι ἀλλὰ Ἀπολλωνίαν . . . μηδὲ τεκνοποιεῖσθαι ἐξ ἄλλης γυναικός . . . ἐὰν δέ τι τούτων ἐπιδειχθῇ ποιῶν . . . ἀποτισάτω . . . τὴν φερνήν.*

Line 33. אחרן, probably a mistake for אחרנן (so Nöldeke). We might read ב[ר] ואנתה, or אחרן may be plural of אחר as אחרה (l. 32) is its feminine (so Nöldeke) instead of אחרנה.

Line 35. [אהנ]תר is not very certain. It does not seem quite the suitable word, but an equivalent of הערת is wanted, and nothing else suggests itself. המו. It may perhaps be הערתהם, but the מ is made as in מלכא just below, and the following stroke should be ו.

Line 36. קבל ס[פר אחר]ן 'in accordance with any other deed', is erased, and has therefore been omitted in the translation.

Line 37. The scribe is the same as in nos. 10 and 13.

Line 38. פנוליה. Lagrange thinks this is the son of her former husband, who was probably dead. The next pair of names is very uncertain. S-C read Yezaniah b. Uriah, and Lagrange thinks this may be her former husband, which is very unlikely. Possibly ירניה or מחסיה for the first name.

Line 39. רעיבל ב̄ very uncertain. For the form cf. רעויה and נבורעי. The endorsement is lost. One would like to know what they called the document (ספר אנתו?).

No. 16.

An Appeal to a Higher Court. About 435 B.C.

The papyrus is so much broken that very little can be made out of it. The mention of year 31 requires a date in the reign of Artaxerxes I, since of the only three kings who reigned so long, Darius I is too early and Artaxerxes II is too late. A Nephayan (if that is the pronunciation) was רבחילא in 411 (see 30^{7}), but his father Waidrang was רבחילא in 416 (see 25^{2}) and was promoted to *fratarak* before 411. Nephayan here must therefore be a different person from Nephayan in no. 30: perhaps his grandfather. The 31st year of Artaxerxes I was 435 B.C. and the deed must have been drawn up then or soon after. It seems to be an appeal from the decision of a lower court to a higher authority, but all the details are obscure.

Sachau, plate 7. Ungnad, no. 7.

1 . . . . ע̄]ל א̄ . . ם [ועל בג]פרן בר [ושחי . . . .
2 זנה ח]קלא [דג]לן מהחסן לה מן שנת 𐡜 //// [עד ש]נת 𐡜𐡛 \ [ארתחשסש
3 אף] שאילת [קד]ם תר[וח ו]דינא ואמרת קדם דינ̄[א . . . .
4 חק]לא רדית ז̄[אנב]א̄ מנהן [לא] לקחת אלך דיני[א . . . .
לי
5 . . . ובעשק עביד ואמרת קדם תרוח ודי[נא . . . .
ומנכי |||ן דיני]א
6 . . מ]ן שנת 𐡜 //// עד שנת 𐡜𐡛 \ ובגפרן ונפין עלו לסון ולק . . .
7 . . דתביא זי נפין רב חילא זי סון ודיני מדנתא איך ל . . . .
8 א]נ̄ה קדם מראי שלחת לאמר בעשק עביד לי וכע[נת . . . .
9 שאל לתרוח ודינא ע[ל] דנה בעשק אל יתעבד לי ז̄ . . . .

[1] . . . . *to* Ar*s*ames (?) *and to Mega*phernes b. *WŠḤI* . . . . [2] *this fi*eld our *detach*ment owned from the 24th *year to* the 31st year of *Artaxerxes* . . . [3] *also* I was examined *bef*ore TR*WḤ and* the court, and I stated before the court . . . . [4] the *fi*eld I ploughed but the *produce* I did *not* receive from them. These judges . . . . [5] . . . and a wrong was done to me, and I stated before TRWḤ and the court . . . . [6] . . . from the year 24 to the year 31, and Megaphernes and Nephayan and Mannuki, the 3 judges, went up to Syene and to*ok with them* (?) . . . . [7] . . . the assessors (?) of Nephayan, commander of the garrison of Syene, and the judges of the province, how . . . . [8] I (?) before my lord have sent saying, 'A wrong was done to me,' and no*w* . . . . [9] ask TRWḤ and the court abo*ut* this, (and) let wrong not be done to me, and . . . .

Line 1. Some lines necessary to explain the case are lost at the beginning. א̄ . . ם, perhaps ארשם. פרן is clear. As it must be a name (since בר follows), and as בגפרן occurs in l. 6, the restoration is probable. [ושחי] restored from 22^{133}, dated 419. The beginning was perhaps to this effect: 'I brought an action before the ordinary court about a field to which I laid claim. Having failed to obtain justice, I now appeal to the highest authorities, to Arsames (?) and Megaphernes.'

Line 2. קלא is certain. As מחחסן is used elsewhere of holding property in land, חקלא is a probable restoration. [דג]לן is only a conjecture, but it fits the space. If it is right, it is interesting as showing that the דגל could hold property as a corporation. דבר as in l. 6.

Line 3. שאילת is no doubt a passive form. In later Aramaic אשתאל means to 'undergo examination' before a court, and hence to 'bring an action'. The meaning seems to be the same here. Cf. שאילא, 7^6. חר[ות] as l. 5. Either a title or (more probably) a name—but it is not found elsewhere.

Line 4. רדית, not ־את. If the dispute is about a field, it may mean 'plough', and the word before be חקלא. ו[אנב]א̄, a word for 'produce' is required. מנהן is the only possible reading. 'From them' (fem.) i.e. the other party. They must have been women. [לא]. There is a slight trace of ל. לקחת. The last letter is a badly made ת. אלך is certain. Ungnad's אית is impossible. דיני[א] might be דינא, but אלך requires the plural.

Line 5. וכעשק. The proper meaning of עשק is 'unfairness' in withholding from a person his due. It therefore suits the restoration proposed in l. 4. The word occurs in ll. 8, 9 also. The כ is difficult. It might be for כי (cf. Phoenican ז for זי), 'and that a wrong was done'. But Seidel is probably right in taking it as otiose, cf. בעמלא, 40^2, כחסן, $7^{5,8,9}$. It would then be originally a modifying particle (like *que non* for *je crois que non*) which afterwards lost its force. No doubt a popular idiom.

Line 6. II[I דיני]א very doubtful. The first stroke is too long, and there is hardly room for דיני. ולק . ., perhaps ולק[חו עמהם].

Line 7. דתכיא from דת (OP *dāta*), 'lawyers', 'assessors'? There is a slight trace of something before it—פ or ב or מ. איך. It is difficult to see what the construction can be.

Line 8. [א]נ̄ה or זנה or דנה (cf. l. 9). מראי is the high official addressed. Elsewhere it generally means Arsames. וכע[נת] or וכען or וכעת.

Line 9. ו̄ . . . Perhaps 'and to my companions' (in the *degel*). This is the end of the text.

No. 17.

Relating to Supplies for the Garrison (?). 428 B.C.

A strip of papyrus written on both sides. Lines 1–4 are on the recto, 5–7 on the verso. It is so much injured that parts of the facsimile are illegible, and I have accordingly adopted in most cases the reading of

Sachau and Ungnad, who had the original before them. The date is certain. The king is Artaxerxes I (since II would be too late), and his 37th year is 428 B.C.

It is a letter addressed to a high official (no doubt Arsames) and perhaps relates to the accounts for the collection and distribution of corn (as rations) cf. no. 24.

Sachau, plate 5. Ungnad, no. 5.

[אל מראן]
1 ארש]ם עבדיך אחמניש וכנותה בגדן וכנותה וספרי מדינתא שלם מראן
אלהיא [ישאלו
2 שגיא ב]כל עדן וכעת לן שלמת על כל מנתא לם זי יהבנה במדינתא אתר
זי ב . . . .
3 . . . מפרש זן זן ירח בירח הוו שלחן עלי אף נשתונא כתיב יהיב לן כעת . . . .
4 . . . . ונשתח . . . .
5 . . . . מראן ארשם . . . . . . [עבר]יך אחמניש וכנותה
אזדכריא ב . . . .
6 . . . . זי נפרע חרוץ וכנותה ספרי מדינ[תא
כל ||| לחיא
7 . . . עלים סיגעבש אזדכרא כנתהם ב ר/// /// /// למרחשן שנת
ד ר/// /// / ארתחשס[ש]
לותהם

[1] *To our lord Arsa*mes, your servants Achaemenes (?) and his colleagues, Bigdan (?) and his colleagues, and the notaries of the province; the welfare of our lord may the gods *seek* [2] *abundantly at* all times. And now you have paid us for all the contribution assuredly which we gave in the province at (?) the place which is . . . [3] . . . plainly set forth, each item month by month they were sending to me. Also a written document was given to us. Now . . . [4] . . . . and we will . . . [5] . . . . our lord Arsames . . . . . your *servant*s Achaemenes (?) and his colleagues the recorders in . . . . [6] . . . . which we pay. Ḥaruẓ and his colleagues the notaries of *the* province, all 3 villains (?), [7] . . . the servant (?) of SYN'BŠ the recorder, their colleague, on the 19th of Marḥeshwan in the 37th year of Artaxerx*es*, to them.

Line 1. Probably the words אל מראן stood above this, cf. 21[1]. ארש]ם] is likely. It occurs in l. 5 (Ungnad, doubtfully). אחמניש here and in l. 5 is very uncertain. כנותה as in Ezra 5[6] (RV 'companions'), and frequently in these texts. בגדן very uncertain. There is a stroke which would fit a ג, but Ungnad does not print it. Cf. בגתן, Esther 2[21]. Compounded with OP *baga*, 'god'? ישאלו וכ׳ the regular formula in letters, but sometimes in the singular. 'May (the) god(s) inquire after your health', i. e. be careful of it, on the analogy of the ordinary greeting of one man to another (מה שלמך).

Line 2. על כל מנחא 'for every piece'? or perhaps = Heb. על מנת כל 'in every respect'. יהבנה is Sachau's reading. אתר זי 'the place in which', i. e. 'where'?

Line 3. מפרש, cf. Ezra 4^{18} &c. 'Exactly'? as Sachau, or 'separately'. זן זן 'thing by thing', i. e. each several thing. נשתונא, Ezra 4^{18} &c., cf. Pers. نوشتن.

Line 4. ונשתח (my reading) not ונשתונא apparently.

Line 5. אזדכריא. A Persian compound of אזדא 'information', and *kar*, 'making'.

Line 6. זי נפרע (my reading). The ר is more like ס. It cannot govern חרוין. כל III לחיא (my reading), is very doubtful. Added as an afterthought below the line. Cf. 30^{7}. חרוין = חרוט is Egyptian, which may account for the abusive epithet.

Line 7. עלים 'servant'? or part of a longer word. סינעבש very doubtful. A name is wanted, but a compound of Sin is unlikely (6^{10}!) because of the י (Ungnad). למרחשון probably so. Ungnad reads למחרשון as a scribal error. לחם = לותהם seems to be the only way of reading it, but the sense is not clear, and לות does not occur in these texts. In Ezra there is מן־לות־.

No. 18.

End of a Marriage Contract. About 425 B. C.

As to the date there is very little evidence. If Ya'uḥan here is the same person as in no. 10, she was a נשן (unmarried girl?) in 456 B. C. She now appears to have been married and to have a marriageable daughter, so that the date of this deed cannot be much earlier than 430 or 425 B. C. The scribe here is the son of the man who wrote nos. 10, 13, 15 (456–441), and therefore presumably rather later. The document appears to be part of a marriage contract, like no. 15, with provision for the case of a divorce (שנאה in l. 1), though the precise terms are not clear. It seems that Ya'uḥan (a widow?) had made over to her daughter Sallua, on the latter's marriage (with Hoshaiah?) certain money and effects as dowry, and Ya'uḥan here renounces all right to reclaim them in case of Sallua's divorce. But other combinations are possible.

Sachau, plate 33. Ungnad, no. 36.

1 . . . ךּ . . בּ . . . . מש]לך בר [או]רי דין שנאה ולא ת[כה]ל יהוחן ברת
[משלך תאמר לה]

[א]לה זנה

2 ולסלוא ברתה כזי נכסיא וכספא זי כתיבן בספרא ברחמן יהבת לכם כען צבית

3 אהנצל הם הן תאמר כזת חיבה הי לא ישתמע לה כתב מעוזיה בר נתן בר ענניה

4 ספרא זנה כפם הושעיה [וי]הוחן ושהדיא בנו שהד חרמנתן בר ביתאלנתן
בר צחא

5 שהד חגי בר פנוליה שהד יאוש בר [אז]ניה שהד ביתאלנתן בר יהונתן

[1] . . . . *Meshu*llak b. *U*ri a deed of divorce. And Ya'uḥan daughter of *Meshullak* shall have no *right to say to him* [2] and to Sallua her daughter, As I gave these goods and the money which are set forth in this deed, as a free gift to you, now I desire [3] to take them away. If she says so, she is liable, no heed shall be paid to her. Ma'uziah b. Nathan b. Ananiah wrote [4] this deed at the direction of Hoshaiah *and Ya'*uḥan, and the witnesses hereto: Witness, Ḥeremnathan b. Bethelnathan b. Ẓeḥo. [5] Witness, Haggai b. Penuliah. Witness, Yeosh b. *A*zaniah. Witness, Bethelnathan b. Jonathan.

Line 1. Ungnad reads the marks at the beginning as numerals. לך[is fairly certain. The downward stroke from the ל is accidental. The restoration is from 22^{68}. In 10^{2} Ya'uḥan is daughter of Meshullak, but how he comes in at this point is not evident. דין is certain, not כסף (as Sachau). The tail of the י is an accidental mark in the papyrus, and the head of it is broken. It must mean a sentence or act of divorce. ולא תכהל certain, though only the lower parts of the letters remain. [משלך] restored from 10^{2}. [תאמר] is restored to correspond to l. 3, the usual formula being 'she shall not say . . . if she says so . . .' [לה] 'to him' or 'to X' is wanted since 'and to S' follows. There does not seem to be room for a name. I take 'him' to be the husband of Sallua.

Line 2. ולסלוא. Other forms of the name are סלוה and סלואה. ברתה. If לה is the husband of S, this must be 'her (Ya'uḥan's) daughter'. If it is 'his daughter' לה must be S's father. ברחמן as in 43^{3}, 'as a free gift', 'out of the affection which I bear to her'. לכם, i.e. to S and her husband.

Line 3. כזת. The ז is badly formed, and זת (= זאת) does not occur elsewhere in these texts, but it can hardly be anything else. חיבה not the usual formula. ישתמע impersonally. 'It (the claim) shall not be heard as regards her'.

Line 4. הושעיה. It is difficult to see how he is concerned, unless he is the husband of S, and this is their marriage deed. Then he and Ya'uḥan would be the parties to the deed, as in no. 15 Asḥor and Mahseiah negotiate the marriage of Mibṭaḥiah. (But no. 15 is written at the direction of Asḥor only.) Since it is the mother who gives away her daughter, she must be a widow, otherwise the father would have done it. If Hoshaiah were the father, there would be no need to say so much of Ya'uḥan the mother. Ḥeremnathan and Bethelnathan are compounded with the god-names חרם and ביתאל, just as יהונתן with יהו in l. 5. See Introduction, p. x. These names only occur here. The grandfather has an Egyptian name.

Line 5. יאוש ב׳ [אז]ניה as in 12[8].

No. 19.

List of Names. About 420 B.C.

A Meshullam b. Shemaiah (l. 5) is mentioned in 22[119], and a son of Nathan b. Hodaviah (l. 10) in 22[127]. Possibly l. 4 is the same as in 22[116]. It seems therefore as if the two lists have some connexion. No. 22 is dated 419 B.C. In 20[2] there is a Menahem b. Meshullam (as in l. 7) under date 420 B.C. This list may therefore probably be dated 420 ±.

Sachau, plate 23. Ungnad, no. 23.

1 . . . .
2 בעדיה בר אֿ . . .
3 אושע בר או[ריה ?]
4 וֿכֿין בר שלם בר . . .
5 מש[ל]ם בר שמעי[ה]
6 שמעיה בר שלם
7 מנחם בר משל[ם]
8 חגי בר יזני[ה]
9 אגרי בר אש . . .
10 נתן בר הודויה

[1] . . . . [2] Ba'adiah b. A . . . . [3] Oshea' b. *Uriah* (?). [4] WKYN b. Shallum b. . . . [5] Meshullam b. Shemaiah. [6] Shemaiah b. Shallum. [7] Menahem b. Meshull*am*. [8] Haggai b. Jezaniah. [9] Agiri b. Ash . . . [10] Nathan b. Hodaviah.

Line 1. Only slight traces remain.

Line 3. [. . .]או. Only אוריה and אושע are possible. The former is more likely, as father and son rarely bear the same name in these texts.

Line 4. וכין very uncertain. It might be ובכן, but neither is known to me as a name. Ungnad and Sachau מתן.

Line 9. אגרי. Ungnad compares Bab. *Agiri*. Sachau compares *Agur*. For the father's name Sachau suggests אשבל. A כ would be possible.

No. 20.

Settlement of a Claim. 420 B.C.

The papyrus has a bad break where it was bent at one third of its breadth, and the latter part is not very easy to read. On the whole, however, the text is fairly certain.

Menahem and Ananiah, sons of Meshullam (cf. 19[7]), had sued Yedoniah and Mahseiah (cf. 25[3], 28[2]), sons of Asḥor and Mibṭaḥiah (cf. no. 15), concerning certain property which had been deposited (as a pledge or loan?) with Asḥor by their grandfather, Shelomem, and which had not been restored. They have now been satisfied (by payment?) and hereby resign all further claim on the sons of Asḥor.

The date is the 4th year of Darius, who must be Darius II, and the year is therefore 420 B.C. Mibṭaḥiah was married to Asḥor in no. 15, which was dated, partly on the evidence of this deed, about 440 B.C. Her elder son can hardly have been much under 20 years of age when he became a party to this action. Asḥor had evidently died in the meantime, otherwise the action would have been taken against him, not against his sons. So too Shelomem and Meshullam must have died, otherwise one or other of them would have brought the action. This corroborates the date of no. 1 (494 B.C.), where Shelomem b. Azariah is a witness. He must have been a young man then, since he lived to transact business with Asḥor, and the interval of seventy-four years between no. 1 and this deed is not too long for three generations.

The death of Asḥor probably took place just before this action, which was necessary to settle up his affairs. Similarly the division of slaves in no. 28 was no doubt consequent on the death of Mibṭaḥiah.

Sayce and Cowley, H.

בירח אלול הו פא[ני] שנת IIII\ דריהויש מלכא אדין ביב בירתא אמר
מנחם ועַנניה כל [II בני] משלם בר שלומם יהודין זי יב בירתא לדגל ארנגבו
לידניה ומחסיה כל II בני אסחור בר צחא מן מבטחיה ברת מחסיה יהודין
לוכם רגלא לאמר [אנחנ]ה רשינכם בדין נפא קדם דמנדין פרתרך וידרנג
רב חילא לאמר אי[תי] נכסיא לבשי קמר וכתן מאני נחש ופרזל מאני עק

6 והוצן עבור ואחרן ורשין לאמר אסחור אבוכם לקח מן שלומם בר עזריה אף

7 אמר איתי זי בפק[דון] הפקדו והו החסן ולא התיב לה ומנכן רשינכם

8 אחר שאילתם ואנת ידניה ומחסיה בני אסחור הוטבתם לבבן באלך נכסיא

9 וטיב לבבן בנו מן [יומ]א זנה עד עלם אנה מנחם ועنניה רחיקן אנחנה מנך

10 מן יומא זנה עד עלם ל[א] נכהל אנחנה ובנין ובנתן ואחין ואיש זילן קריב ובעל

11 קריה לא יכהלון ירשו[נכ]ם אנת ידניה ומחסיה דין ודבב ולא יכהלון ירשון
לבניכם ·

12 ואחיכם ואיש לכם [ביש]ם נכסן וכסף עבור ואחרן זי שלומם בר עזריה
והן אנחנה

13 ובנין ובנתן ואיש זי[לן] ובני שלומם בר עזריה ירשונכם וירשון לבניכם
ובנתכם

14 ואיש זילכם ה[י] ירש[ת] דין עלא ינתן לכם או לבניכם ולמן זי ירשון אביגרנא

15 זי כסף כרשן עשרה ב[אבנ]י מלכא כסף ר // לכרש \ והו אפם רחיק מן
אלה נכסיא זי

16 רשין עליהם ולא דין ולא ד[בב] כתב מעוזיה בר נתן ספרא זנה כפם
מנחם ועنניה כל II

17 בני משלם בר שלומם שה[ד מ]נחם בר נדול גדול בר ב־כיה מנחם בר עזריה

18 שהד הודויה בר זכור [בר] אושעיה

Endorsement.

19 ספר זי כתב מנחם ועنניה כל [II] בני מנחם בר שלומם

20 [לידני]ה ומחסיה כל II בני אסחור בר צחא

[1] In the month of Elul, that is Pa*yni*, 4th year of Darius the king at that time in Yeb the fortress, said [2] Menahem and Ananiah bo*th sons of* Meshullam b. Shelomem, Jews of Yeb the fortress, of the detachment of Iddinnabu, [3] to Yedoniah and Mahseiah, both sons of Ashor b. Zeḥo by Mibṭahiah daughter of Mahseiah, Jews [4] of the same detachment, as follows: *We* sued you in the court of NPA before Damandin the governor (and) Waidrang [5] the commander of the garrison, saying: There *are* goods, garments of wool and cotton, vessels of bronze and iron, vessels of wood [6] and ivory, corn, &c., and we pleaded saying: Ashor your father received (these) from Shelomem b. Azariah, and also [7] said, 'They are on dep*osit*'. They were deposited, but he kept possession and did not return (them) to him, and therefore we sue you. [8] Then you were examined, and you Yedoniah and Mahseiah, sons of Ashor, satisfied us concerning these goods, [9] and we were satisfied therewith. From this *day* for ever I Menahem and Ananiah, we renounce all claim on you. [10] From this day for ever we shall have no power, and our sons and our daughters and our brothers and any man related to us or a freeman of [11] the city shall have no power to bring *against you*, Yedoniah and Mahseiah, suit or process, nor shall they have the power

to sue your sons [12] or your brothers or any one of yours *on account* of goods and money, corn, &c., belonging to Shelomem b. Azariah. If we [13] or our sons or our daughters or any one of *ours*, or the sons of Shelomem b. Azariah, sue you or sue your sons or your daughters [14] or any one of yours, or whoever shall sue about it, he shall pay you or your sons, or whomsoever they sue, a fine [15] of the sum of ten kerashin, royal *weight*, at the rate of 2 R to 1 karash, and he assuredly has no claim on these goods [16] about which we sued, and no suit or *process* (can lie). Ma'uziah b. Nathan wrote this deed at the direction of Menahem and Ananiah both [17] sons of Meshullam b. Shelomem. Wit*ness*, *Me*nahem b. Gadol. Gadol b. Berechiah. Menahem b. Azariah. [18] Witness, Hodaviah b. Zaccur *b*. Oshaiah. (Endorsement.) [19] Deed which Menahem and Ananiah bo*th* sons of Menahem b. Shelomem wrote [20] *for Yedoni*ah and Mahseiah both sons of Ashor b. Ẓeḥo.

Line 1. The day of the month is not given, which is unusual. The Egyptian month may be פא[ני] or פא[פי]. From the calculations of Mr. Knobel and Dr. Fotheringham it seems that Payni suits the chronology best. So also Gutesmann.

Line 2. [בני ‖] restored from l. 3. ארננבו is Babylonian.

Line 4. זכם as in 9^{2}. The sons of Ashor here belong to the *degel* of Iddinnabu, but in no. 28 to that of Warizath (?). In no. 15 Ashor himself (as an Egyptian ?) is not assigned to any *degel*. Mibṭaḥiah, one would suppose, belonged to her father's *degel*, i.e. either Warizath or Haumadata. נפא, cf. 7^{4} where it seems to be a place-name. Not נֹף Memphis, see Nöldeke, Clermont-Ganneau, Pritsch. Nor can it be OP *napā*, even if that could have the meaning of 'family', as has been suggested. The רבחילא seems to have held his court (and had his headquarters) at Syene. The דין נפא was a superior court since the *fratarak* presided over it. דמנדין must be a name (so Pritsch, Andreas), not as S–C. Clermont-Ganneau suggests 'tribunal' or 'judge', &c. Lagrange thinks the phrase = מן קדם דין. פרתרך as in 30^{5}, &c. From OP *fratara* = 'prior', 'superior', and so 'governor'. It cannot be dependent on וידרנג (quasi 'lieutenant' of W), because that would imply a lower rank than W, whereas in 30^{5} W has become *fratarak*, and his son is רבחילא (30^{7}). Hence *fratarak* is not followed by ביב or בסון. He governed the district or province, while the רבחילא commanded only the garrison of Syene (including Elephantine). A ו has been omitted before וידרנג. So Pritsch; Lagrange doubtfully.

Line 5. איתי . . , ו״ 'there are goods and we sued', i.e. concerning certain goods we sued. Cf. 14^{4}, also a builder's stock.

Line 6. וחוצן, Nöldeke 'palm-leaves'. Jampel compares Ps. 129^{7}, Neh. 5^{13}, and takes it as clothing. Cf. on 15^{16}. ורשין is on the broken place, but is fairly certain. לקח. The omission of the object is awkward.

Line 7. The construction is very awkward. איתי זי seems to mean 'they are things which are . . .' The following ב requires a noun, and בפקדון is most likely. הפקדו is Lidzbarski's suggestion. S–C read 'זפק. If a Hophal is admissible it gives a sense, but the form is not found, I believe, elsewhere in these texts.

Line 8. שאילתם passive as in 16[3].

Line 9. רחיקן 'we withdraw from you', i.e. renounce all claims. מנך an oversight for מנכם.

Line 13. After ובנתכם there is a faint א which has been erased. If the document were a forgery this would be evidence that it was written by an Arab who used the dual suffix كما—referring to two persons.

Line 14. וזי as elsewhere for ומן זי. Probably subject, not object, of ירש[ון], which I restore as plural, as at the end of the line, in spite of ינתן singular. The writer is confused by his own verbiage. עלא adverbially, cf. בגו. אביגרנא or ־דנא. A Persian term for 'fine', as in 25[15], 28[10], but the etymology is not clear.

Line 15. אפם, not אחר as S-C. רחיק too much obscured to read, but it is the word required. אלה is more probable than אלך (S-C).

Line 16. The same scribe as in no. 25.

Line 19. The second מנחם is a mistake for משלם.

No. 21.

Order to keep the (Passover and) Feast of Unleavened Bread. 419 B.C.

See Barth in *OLZ* 1912, 10, and Ed. Meyer in *Sitzb. Berl. Akad.* 1911, p. 1026.

This is one of the most interesting and important of these texts. See Introduction, p. xvi.

The date is the 5th year of Darius. This must be Darius II, since Yedoniah, who is addressed evidently as head of the community, holds the same position in no. 30 (408 B.C.). The year is therefore 419 B.C.

It is a letter from Hananiah, whose mission must have been official and important, since his arrival in Egypt is mentioned as a well-known event in 38[7]. Unfortunately the papyrus is very imperfect, half of the lines 4–10 being lost, but enough remains to show that it contains a direction to keep the festival of (Passover? and) Unleavened bread, and gives instructions for doing so. What is still more remarkable is that this direction is *based on the authority of Darius himself.* The question then arises, was this community, which possessed a temple and offered sacrifice to Ya'u, ignorant of the greatest of Jewish national festivals? Had they never celebrated it before? Was it a new institution? What had the Persian king to do with it? Something has already been said on these points in the Introduction, p. xvi+. A few remarks may be added here.

In the first place, we have no evidence that the Passover before this date was a regular annual ceremony. In the earliest documents (as estimated by the majority of critics) it is the seven days of Unleavened bread on which stress is laid. A national Passover-feast is unknown to J and E. The earliest mention of it is in Deut. 16, where it is closely related to the feast of Unleavened bread. Moreover in 2 Kings 23^{22} it is expressly stated of Josiah's Passover (which is usually believed to be closely connected with the ordinance in Deut.) that such a celebration had never been held כימי השפטים . . . וכל ימי מלכי ישראל וג׳ '*in* the days of the Judges . . . and all the days of the kings'. If then the Passover, as a national (but not necessarily an annual) institution, was introduced only in 622 B.C., it is not surprising that this colony, which was probably (already or) soon afterwards established in Egypt, should either know nothing of it, or should regard it as intended only for residents in Palestine, to be celebrated at Jerusalem, which indeed is the natural meaning of Deut. 16^{6}. No doubt the national festival was founded on primitive practices of some kind, but that is a totally different question. It is true that in the present broken condition of the papyrus the word Passover does not occur, but I think there is reason to believe that it was originally mentioned (see note below) and that the directions given here agree with Deut. 16 in connecting the Passover and Unleavened bread. If not, and if the papyrus refers only to the feast of Unleavened bread, then it is still remarkable that directions were necessary for the keeping of so old and, one would think, so well-established a festival.

In either case the explanation may be found perhaps in the rabbinical saying quoted in the Introduction, p. xix. That 'Ezra gave the Law a second time' is not a paradox but a statement of historical fact. Whatever parts of the Pentateuch were in existence before the fifth century B.C., it cannot be held that its provisions had any great influence on the people in general. The earlier parts of the O.T. and the prophets, if read without prejudice, seem to me to show quite the reverse. In fact the kings were too much occupied with politics and other mundane matters to enforce a ceremonial law, even if they had the desire to do so, and the times of the Judges were too anarchic to admit of it. Josiah's great effort is described as exceptional. Any law which is not enforced, soon becomes a dead letter, and Josiah's institution came to nothing, while the exile must have involved the further neglect of everything of the nature of national festivals. It was Ezra who made modern Judaism, by instituting (or re-instituting) the ceremonial law and formulating regulations for the national festivals. The books of Ezra and Nehemiah show this as clearly as the earlier literature shows the lack of them. The reason why he was able to enforce the Law and thus prevent its falling (again?) into neglect, is that he had the support of the Persian king. Why this was so, what caused the Persian kings to take so much interest in the Jews, whether it was part of a general policy of religious tolerance or was due to special circumstances, must remain matters of speculation. The fact at any rate is evident from what we are told of Cyrus (e. g. in Isaiah 45[1+]), Cambyses in pap. 30[13.14], and Darius here. What has hitherto seemed incredible is that they should have concerned themselves with details of ceremonial, as in the letter of Artaxerxes in Ezra 7, but the present papyrus (and the style of other letters in this collection) removes all reason for doubting the genuineness of the Persian letters in Ezra. [See further Ed. Meyer, *Die Entstehung des Judentums*, and his *Papyrusfund.*] Whether the instructions as to the manner of keeping the festival come directly from the king, or are issued by Hananiah on his own authority, depends mainly on the meaning of שליח in l. 3, where see note. As to Hananiah, there is no evidence for identifying him with any person of that name mentioned in the book of Nehemiah. His arrival in Egypt (38[7]) seems to have led to trouble. Was this due to his stirring up religious zeal or national feeling in the colony and encouraging animal sacrifices which were resented by the Egyptians? And was this the cause of the destruction of the temple soon after (no. 30)?

The papyrus is written on both sides, ll. 1–7 on the obverse, ll. 8–11 on the reverse—an insignificant document for so important a communication.

Sachau, plate 6. Ungnad, no. 6.

1 אל אח]י
2 יד]ניה וכנותה ח]ילא י]הודיא אחוכם חננ[יה] שלם אחי אלהיא [ישאלו
3 וכעת שנתא זא שנת //\ /\ דריוהוש מלכא מן מלכא שליח על ארש]ם לאמר
4 בירח תעובי יהוי פסח לחילא יהוד]יא כעת אנתם בן מנו ארב[עת עשר
5 יומן לירח ניסן ופסחא עב]דו ומן יום ר ///\ \ עד יום ב \ ל[ניסן
6 שבעת יומן זי פטירן אנתם] דכין הוו ואזדהרו עבידה א[לתעבדו

7 ביום ר/// \/ וביום ⅃ \ אף שכר א]ל תשתו וכל מנדעם זי חמיר א[יתי בה
8 אלתאכלו מן יום ר/// \/ מן]מערב שמשא עד יום ⅃ \ לניס[ן שבעת
9 יומן אל יתחזי בכם אל תהנ]עלו בתוניכם והחתמו בין יומי[א אלה
10 כן יתעבד כזי אמר דריוהוש מל]כא

Address. 11 [אל] אחי ידניה וכנותה חילא יהודיא אחוכם חנני[ה

[1] *To* my *brethren*, [2] *Yedo*niah and his colleagues the Jewish gar*rison*, your brother Hanan*iah*. The welfare of my brethren may the gods *seek*. [3] Now this year, the 5th year of King Darius, word was sent from the king to Ars*ames, saying:* [4] *In the month of Tybi* (?) *let there be a Passover for the Jew*ish *garrison*. Now you accordingly count fo*urteen* [5] *days of the month Nisan and keep the Passover*, and from the 15th day to the 21st day of *Nisan* [6] (*are*) *seven days of Unleavened bread*. Be clean and take heed. *Do no* work [7] *on the 15th day and on the 21st day. Also* drink no *beer*, and anything at all *in* which *there is* leaven [8] *do not eat, from the 15th day from* sunset till the 21st day of Ni*san, seven* [9] *days, let it not be seen among you*; *do not bri*ng (it) into your dwellings, but seal (it) up during *those* days. [10] *Let this be done as Darius* the *King commanded.* (Address.) [11] To my brethren Yedoniah and his colleagues the Jewish garrison, your brother Hanan*iah*.

Line 1. There are traces of letters which may be restored from l. 11.

Line 2 is also made more certain by l. 11. כנותה are generally mentioned by name. To put חילא יהודיא in apposition to it strikes me as slightly contemptuous or condescending on the part of the great man. Another mark of his importance perhaps is that he calls himself simply Hananiah, without further description, just as Arsames does in 26^1. אלהיא is plural, though used by a Jew to Jews. It had perhaps become stereotyped in use, and had ceased to be consciously regarded as plural, as was the case with Hebrew אלהים. Not a pl. majestatis. At the end we must restore, according to the regular formula, either ישאלו or ישאלו בכל עדן. The length of the lines can only be determined by the amount required to complete the sense.

Line 3. זא fem. as in 30^{17}. The following date is parenthetical. It is not 'this year is the 5th year', but 'this year (viz. the 5th year)'. דריוהוש. The later spelling. שליח. Arnold takes this as 'I being sent', and thinks the instructions are all given on Hananiah's own authority. He compares Ezra 7^{14}. This is not so. שליח is impersonal, 'orders were sent', as in 26^6, 'about which orders were sent from me', cf. 26^4 ישתלח in the same sense. Ezra 7^{14} is to be taken in the same way, 'orders were sent from the King' (not as RV), otherwise both there and here a pronoun would be required. Then if an order was sent it must be recited in what immediately follows, i.e. it was the Persian king who decreed (without specifying details) that the festival should take place in due form, and words to that effect must have stood in the lost part of l. 4. [לאמר] or לם is needed after שליח to introduce the decree in l. 4.

Line 4. If the above view is right, the first half of the line contained the king's decree. It may be objected that there is not room, but cf. Waidrang's order for the destruction of the temple in $30^{7 \cdot 8}$, consisting of only five words. There is no need for anything more than such a short and peremptory command: 'in the month Tybi let there be a Passover (or a festival) for the Jewish garrison'. תעובי. Dr. Fotheringham tells me that in this year Tybi 1 = Nisan 10. [לחילא יהוד]יא. There is a trace of ד, and the restoration (so Sachau; Ungnad יהודיא) is probable. This cannot be part of Hananiah's own words. He has already used חילא יהודיא in l. 2. He would not have repeated it, but would have said 'you'. It must therefore be part of the king's message. כעת evidently begins Hananiah's own comment or addition, and (like כן) is explanatory of something which preceded. The king's message would not plunge thus *in medias res* without saying what it was all about, and if it were an *oratio obliqua* אנתם would not be used. כן 'therefore', 'in accordance with this command just stated'.

Line 5. [עב]דו. If right, this suggests פסחא before it, as on the ostrakon in *PSBA* 1915, p. 222, תעבדן פסחא 'that she may prepare the Passover'. This is of course a conjecture, but it is probable, and makes the text consistent. The word פסחא could not occur anywhere after this point. ל[ניסן]. The mention of the month is necessary. Probably not ל[ירח ניסן], which would be too long.

Line 6. In the first half of the line something is wanted to explain the significance of the seven days. The proposed restoration is merely conjectural. The prohibition of leaven cannot have occurred here, since it appears in l. 7. דכין is a complete word, as there is no sign of any letter before it, therefore not שרכין, as Perles. The ־ין shows that it comes from a ל״ה (ל״י) stem. Hence I take it as = זכין 'clean'. [א[לתעבדו is necessary.

Line 7. The beginning ought to mention the first and last days, since work was never forbidden on all the seven days (Barth). [א]ל חשתו cannot refer to wine, which was ordered to be drunk at the Passover, and was never forbidden during the days of Unleavened bread. Barth (with others) is certainly right in taking it to refer to beer, a specially Egyptian drink, which in Mishna Pesaḥim 3^1 is forbidden, because it was made of fermented grain, and so partook of the nature of leaven. This is therefore a special prohibition necessary for Jews living in Egypt, and there is nothing corresponding to it in Exod. or Deut. The word used for beer in the Mishna is זיתום (ζῦθος). A Greek word is unlikely here, and nothing else is obvious. I have supplied שכר because that is used in the Talmud of a drink not classed as wine, but it may have been an Egyptian word. [א]יתי בה] is Sachau's restoration. [א]לתאכלו] would be better, but then it would be difficult to restore the next line.

Line 8. [מן יום ד׳ III I\] is required by עד יום כ׳ I.

Line 9. [אל יתחזי] I have restored from Deut. 16[4]. The mention of dwellings implies the later בריקה, the searching out and removal of leaven. [אלתהנ]עלו. There is a trace of נ, not ועלו as Ungnad, who evidently thinks of Deut. 16[7], 'go into your dwellings'. But that was *after* eating the Passover, and is unsuitable here. They were to go into their dwellings and put blood on the door-posts as a protection against the destroying angel (in Egypt). It had nothing to do with the feast of Unleavened bread with which this part of the document is especially concerned. The Passover is treated (in l. 5) only as a preliminary to it. Reading תהנעלו, the absence of a pronoun in the accusative is admissible in a series of prohibitions like this. Barth would restore וכל מנדעם זי חמיר אל..., but these words would hardly be repeated from l. 7. וחתמו. The ח is uncertain. It might almost be a ס. The sense would be the same, 'seal it up', i.e. put it away out of sight.

Line 10 ends in the middle. A possible א remains and a trace of ב. Something of the kind restored is wanted to wind up the message.

No. 22.

Names of Contributors to Temple Funds.

419 B.C.

A very broad sheet of papyrus, containing now 7 columns of Aramaic and the longitudinal half of a column of Demotic. On the reverse are 3 lines.

It is very much damaged, especially col. 1 and the lower parts of the other columns.

It contains a list of names of persons who contributed 2 shekels each to the God Ya'u, as stated in l. 1. The purpose of the subscription is not further explained, but clearly it must have been for the expenses of the temple. Col. 7 begins with a statement of the total so far, and its apportionment, on which see note.

As to the date: no king is named, and Epstein therefore takes the 5th year to be the 5th year of the revolt from Persia, which would be about 400 B.C., and believes the money to be intended for the temple at Jerusalem. But we have no evidence that during the revolt dates were expressed in this way. In the only dated document of that period (no. 35) the year of Amyrtaeus is given. As to no. 11, see notes. Nor do we know (and it is not probable after the events of no. 30) that the Jewish colony ever identified themselves so completely with the inimical Egyptians as against the friendly Persian government, that they would have adopted almost at once an era of 'freedom' (cf. the Bar Kokhba coins) or whatever it may have been called. As to the money being destined for Jerusalem there is again no evidence, and the allocation of it in col. 7 makes this highly improbable.

It is more likely that the 5th year here is the same as the 5th year in no. 21, and that the list belongs, like many other of these texts, to the reign of Darius II (so Seidel). Its date will then be 419 B.C. The reason of the omission of the king's name perhaps is that the document is not of an official or legal character, but contains merely internal accounts of Yedoniah's office. Up to the end of col. 6 the subscriptions are for the month Phamenoth, and the list was no doubt kept in the office to receive additions as the money was paid. The style of the writing, which is rather cursive and hasty, agrees with this view. In such a document it is natural that the name of the king should be taken for granted. It was a temporary record, not for permanent use, nor intended for reference in the far future.

The contributions are probably connected with Hananiah's mission in some way. Perhaps his (re-)institution of (Passover and) Unleavened bread was part of a religious revival, and the money was wanted for sacrifices. It may in that case have led to the hostility which caused the destruction of the temple. Or of course it may have been a customary contribution, like the half-shekel at Jerusalem. The suggestion that the money was for re-building the temple (cf. nos. 32, 33), and that the date is therefore after 408 B.C., carries no weight. You cannot build a temple on a half-crown subscription.

There are several traces of palimpsest, as though the papyrus had been cleaned and used again at intervals.

Sachau, plates 17–20. Ungnad, no 19.

ב //\ לפמנחתף שנת ///\ זנה שמהת חילא יהודיא זי יהב כסף ליהו 1
אלהא לגבר ל[ג]בר כסף [ש //]

Col. 1.

2 משׁ[למ]ת ב[ר]ת גמר[י]ה בר מחסיה כסף ש //
3 זכור [בר הודוי]ה בר זכור כסף ש //
4 שׁרי[ה בר]ת הושע בר חרמן כסף ש //
5 — כל //[/ . . . .]
6 הוש[ע בר בית]אלנורי הו כסף ש // ל[ה]
7 הוש[עיה בר נתן] בר הושעיה בר חגני[ה כסף ש // לה]
8 נבו[. . . . . . .]ה כסף ש // לה
9 . . . . נני [בר] כחל כסף ש // לה
10 . . . . בר יהו[. . . כסף] ש // לה
11 . . . . בר נה[בת ברת מח]סה [כסף ש /]| לה
12 נ]חן בר ענני ב[ר] . . . .
13 . . . . [ב]רת זברי[ה]
14 . . . .
15 . . . . . . ב]רת פלול[יה] . . .
16 . . . . ברת . . . .
17 . . . . ב[ר] . . . .
18 . . . . ברת . . . .
19 כל מאת שנדן
20 מאת נבועקב שלום בר מנח[ם]

Col. 2.

21 משלם בר שמוח כ ש // לה
22 פלטי בר מיכה כ ש // לה
23 מלכיה בר יתום בר הדדנורי [כ] ש // לה
24 ד שלמיה בר ישוב כ ש /[/ ל]ה
25 נדול בר משלם בר מבטחי[ה כ] ש /[/] לה
26 מנחם בר חצול הו בר שמע[יה כ ש // לה]
27 סיטך בר משלם הו כ ש // לה
28 גדול בר שמוח הו כ ש // לה
29 משלם בר חגי בר הצול כ ש // לה
30 הצול בר חגי בר הצול כ ש // לה
31 כל [מאת . . . .]|
32 . . . . ש //
33 . . . . כ ש // . .
34 . . . .
35 . . . . /.

36 . . . .

37 . . . . כ ש //

38 . . . .

Col. 3.

39 שלם בר הודו [כ ש]//

40 חורי בר ונה [כ ש]//

41 שמוע בר שלם [כ ש]//

42 מתן בר ידנ[יה כ ש]//

43 אז[ריה בר . . . . כ ש]//

44 עננ[י בר . . . .]

45 זכ[. . . . . ש]//

46 ענני [. . . . .]

47 הוש[ע] בר נתון [כ ש//]

48 ד [. . . .] בר [. . . . . כ ש]//

49 [. . . .] בר נ[. . . . כ] ש//

50 [. . . . . כ ש/]/

51 [. . . .] בר [. . . . . .] בר ישביה . . .

52 [. . . . . כ] ש//

53 [. . . . . כ ש/]/

54 . . . .

55 [. . . . . ש]//

56 [. . . . . .] הושע כ ש//

57 [. . . . . .] יהוטל כ [ש//]

58 [. . . . . . . ע]נני כ ש//

59 [. . . . .] ישביה . . .

60 . . . .

Col. 4.

61 הושע בר סגרי כ ש//

62 מנחם בר מתן כ ש//

63 נתון בר חגי כ ש//

64 חגי בר מיכא כ ש//

65 מחסה בר אורי כ ש//

66 שלום בר זכריא כ ש//

67 מנחם בר זכריא כ ש//

68 דד משלך בר אורי כ ש//

69 פמת בר סגרי כ ש//

70 ענני בר מעווי כ ש //

71 [הו]שע בר מנחם כ ש //

72 חגי בר הוריא כ ש //

73 [מנ]חם בר אורי בר משלך כ ש //

74 . . . .

75 . . . . כ ש //

76 . . . . מתן כ ש //

77 [. . . . ב]ר מתן כ ש //

78 פ[נול]יא בר מנחם בר פוסי כ ש //

79 חו[רי] בר מנחם [בר] פוסי כ ש //

80 פלוליה בר [הו]שע כ ש //

81 מנחמת ברת ע[נני] בר אסתח כ ש //

82 משלמת ברת [. . .]ה כ ש // אחת מחת וש

Col. 5.

83 מפתח ברת טסהז כ ש //

84 יהושמע ברת נתן כ ש //

85 שבית ברת חורי בר שלם כ ש //

86 רעיא ברת נרי כ ש //

87 יהושמע ברת משלם כ ש //

88 מפתח ברת שלם כ ש //

89 יחמול ברת פלטי בר יאוש כ ש //

90 אביהי ברת אושע כ ש //

91 נהבת ברת מחסה כ ש //

92 יהוחן ברת יגדל כ ש //

93 משלמת ברת צפליא כ ש //

94 . . . .

95 מנ[ח]מת ברת [. . . . כ ש /]/

96 נהבת ברת ז[. . . כ] ש //

97 יחמול ברת [של]ם כ ש //

98 יהושמע ברת הושע בר זכור כ ש //

99 יהושמע ברת חגי כ ש //

100 אב[יה]י ברת נתון כ ש //

Col. 6.

101 יהוחן ברת גדליה כ ש //

102 סלוה ברת נרי כ ש //

103 יהוטל ברת יסלח כ ש

104 אבעשר ברת הושע כ ש //

105 יהועלי ברת עמניה כ ש //

106 מפתח ברת צפליה כ ש //

107 נהבת ברת זכור כ ש //

108 𐡜𐡜𐡜𐡜 — מנחמת ברת ידניה בר ענתי כ ש //

109 משלם בר מעוזי כ ש //

110 משלמת ברת פנוליה כ ש //

111 נתון בר פלליה בר נתון כ ש //

112 הצול ברת הודויה כ ש //

113 . . . . נתן כ [ש //]

114 . . . . ז]כריה . . . . . ש //

115 . . . . בר נתן בר . . . ה כ ש //

116 . . . . בר שלם ב[ר . . . .]ה כ ש //

117 [יה]ושמע ברת קון כ ש //

118 רעויה בר אורי כ ש //

119 𐡜𐡜𐡜𐡜𐡛 — משלם בר שמעיה כ ש //

Col. 7.

120 כספא זי קם יומא הו ביד

121 ידניה בר גמריה בירח פמנחתף

122 כסף כרשן 𐡜𐡛\ שקלן /// /// //

123 בנו ליהו כ 𐡛// ש /// ///

124 לאשמביתאל כרשן /// ///\

125 לענתביתאל כסף כרשן 𐡛//

126 מיכיה בר יהושמע כ ש //

127 אושע בר נתן בר הודויה כ ש //

128 אחיו בר נתן בר ענני כ ש //

129 עזריה בר הצול כ ש //

130 ישביה בר ברכי[ה כ ש] //

131 . . . . //

132 . . . . ה ברת כי . . כ ש //

Reverse.

133 בנפרן בר ושחי כ ש // לאנרם

134 ושחי בר זדמר כ ש // לה

135 חני בר מפטחיה כ ש // לטב //\

Col. i.

[1] On the 3rd of Phamenoth, 5th year. This is (a list of) the names of the Jewish garrison who gave money for Ya'u the God, man by man the sum of 2 *shekels:* [2]—Meshu*llem*eth da*ugh*ter of Gemar*i*ah b. Mahseiah, the sum of 2 sh. [3]—Zaccur *b. Hodavi*ah b. Zaccur, the sum of 2 sh. [4]—Serai*ah daught*er of Hoshea b. Ḥarman, the sum of 2 sh. [5]—All 3 . . . . [6]—Hosh*ea b. Beth*elnuri, he (gave (?)) the sum of 2 sh. for himself (?). [7]—Hosha*iah b. Nathan* b. Hoshaiah b. Hanani*ah the sum of 2 sh. for himself* (?). [8]—Nabu . . . . *b.* . . . . ah, the sum of 2 sh. for himself (?). [9] . . . . . . nani *b.* KTL, the sum of 2 sh. for himself (?). [10] . . . . . b. Ya'u . . . . *the sum of* 2 sh. for himself (?). [11] . . . . . b. Ne*hebeth daughter of Mah*seh, *the sum of* 2 *sh.* for himself (?). [12] Nathan b. Anani b. . . . . . . [13] . . . . . i *d*aughter of Zebadi*ah* . . . . [14] . . . . [15] . . . . . *d*aughter of Pelul*iah* . . . . [16] . . . . . . daughter of . . . . . [17] . . . . . . i b. . . . . . [18] . . . . .daughter of . . . . . [19] *All of* the company of Siniddin. [20] The company of Nabu'aḳab:—Shallum b. Mena*hem* . . . .

Col. ii.

[21]—Meshullam b. Samuaḥ, sum of 2 sh. for himself (?). [22]—Palti b. Michah, sum of 2 sh. for himself (?). [23]—Malchiah b. Yathom b. Hadadnuri, sum of 2 sh. for himself (?). [24] 20—Shelemiah b. Jashub, sum of 2 sh. *for* himself (?). [25]—Gadol b. Meshullam b. Mibtaḥi*ah, sum of* 2 sh. for himself (?). [26]—Menahem b. Haẓul, that (is) the son of Shema*iah, sum of* 2 *sh. for himself* (?). [27]—Simak b. Meshullam, he (gave) the sum of 2 sh. for himself (?). [28]—Gadol b. Samuaḥ, he (gave) the sum of 2 sh. for himself (?). [29]—Meshullam b. Haggai b. Haẓul, sum of 2 sh. for himself (?). [30]—Haẓul b. Haggai b. Haẓul, sum of 2 sh. for himself (?). [31] All of *the company of* . . . . . . u. [32] . . . . 2 sh. [33] . . . . sum of 2 sh. [34] . . . . [35] . . . . [36] . . . . [37] . . . . sum of 2 sh. [38] . . . .

Col. iii.

[39]—Shillem b. Hodav *sum of* 2 *sh.* [40]—Hori b. VNH *sum of* 2 *sh.* [41]—Shamua' b. Shillem *sum of* 2 *sh.* [42]—Mattan b. Yedon*iah, sum of* 2 *sh.* [43]—*Uriah b.* . . . . . ., *sum of* 2 *sh.* [44]—Anan*i b.* . . . . . . [45]—Zac . . . . 2 [46]—Anani . . . . [47]—Hosh*ea* b. Nathun *sum of* 2 *sh.* [48] 20— . . . . . b. . . . . 2 [49] . . . . . b. N . . . . 2 sh. [50] . . . . 2 *sh.* [51] . . . . b . . . . b. Joshibiah . . . . [52] . . . . 2 sh. [53] . . . . 2 *sh.* [54] . . . . [55] . . . . 2 *sh.* [56] . . . . . Hoshea, sum of 2 sh. [57] . . . . . Ya'uṭal, sum of 2 *sh.* [58] . . . . . . *A*nani, sum of 2 sh. [59] . . . . Joshibiah . . . [60] . . . .

Col. iv.

[61]—Hoshea b. SGRI, sum of 2 sh. [62]—Menahem b. Mattan, sum of 2 sh. [63]—Nathun b. Haggai, sum of 2 sh. [64]—Haggai b. Micha, sum of 2 sh. [65]—Maḥseh b. Uri, sum of 2 sh. [66]—Shallum b. Zecharia,

sum of 2 sh. [67]—Menahem b. Zecharia, sum of 2 sh. [68] 40—Meshullak b. Uri, sum of 2 sh. [69]—Pamut b. SGRI, sum of 2 sh. [70]—Anani b. Ma'uzi, sum of 2 sh. [71]—*Ho*shea b. Menahem, sum of 2 sh. [72]—Haggai b. Huria, sum of 2 sh. [73]—*Mena*hem b. Uri b. Meshullak, sum of 2 sh. [74] . . . . [75] . . . . sum of 2 sh. [76] . . . . . Mattan, sum of 2 sh. [77] . . . . . b. Mattan, sum of 2 sh. [78] Pe*nul*iah b. Menahem b. Posai, sum of 2 sh. [79]—Hor*i* b. Menahem *b.* Posai, sum of 2 sh. [80]—Peluliah b. *Ho*shea, sum of 2 sh. [81]—Menaḥemeth daughter of A*nani* b. 'STḤ, sum of 2 sh. [82]—Meshullemeth daughter of . . . . ah, sum of 2 sh. Sister of Mahath and S . . . (?).

Col. v.

[83]—Mephatteaḥ daughter of ṬSTZ, sum of 2 sh. [84]—Ya'ushama' daughter of Nathan, sum of 2 sh. [85]—Shabith daughter of Ḥori b. Shillem, sum of 2 sh. [86]—Re'ia daughter of Neri, sum of 2 sh. [87]—Ya'ushama' daughter of Meshullam, sum of 2 sh. [88] 60—Mephatteaḥ daughter of Shillem, sum of 2 sh. [89]—Yaḥmol daughter of Palti b. Yeosh, sum of 2 sh. [90]—Abihi daughter of Oshea, sum of 2 sh. [91]—Nehebeth daughter of Maḥseh, sum of 2 sh. [92]—Ya'uḥan daughter of Yigdal, sum of 2 sh. [93]—Meshullemeth daughter of Ẓephalia, sum of 2 sh. [94] . . . . [95] Mena*ḥe*meth daughter of . . . . . *sum of* 2 sh. [96] Nehebeth daughter of Z . . . *sum of* 2 sh. [97] Yaḥmol daughter of *Shill*em, sum of 2 sh. [98] 70—Ya'ushama' daughter of Hoshea b. Zaccur, sum of 2 sh. [99]—Ya'ushama' daughter of Haggai, sum of 2 sh. [100] Ab*ih*i daughter of Nathun, sum of 2 sh.

Col. vi.

[101]—Ya'uḥan daughter of Gedaliah, sum of 2 sh. [102]—Salluah daughter of Neri, sum of 2 sh. [103]—Ya'uṭal daughter of Yislaḥ, sum of 2 sh. [104]—Ab'osher daughter of Hoshea, sum of 2 sh. [105]—Ya'u'alai daughter of Immanuiah, sum of 2 sh. [106]—Mephatteaḥ daughter of Ẓephaliah, sum of 2 sh. [107]—Nehebeth daughter of Zaccur, sum of 2 sh. [108] 80—Menaḥemeth daughter of Yedoniah b. 'Anathi, sum of 2 sh. [109]—Meshullam b. Ma'uzi, sum of 2 sh. [110]—Meshullemeth daughter of Penuliaḥ, sum of 2 sh. [111]—Nathun b. Pelaliah b. Nathun, sum of 2 sh. [112]—Haẓul daughter of Hodaviah, sum of 2 sh. [113]— . . . . Nathan, sum of 2 *sh.* [114] . . . . *Ze*badiah . . . . 2 sh. [115]— . . . . . b. Nathan b. . . . . h, sum of 2 sh. [116]— . . . . . b. Shillem b. . . . . h, sum of 2 sh. [117]—*Ya'u*shama' daughter of Ḳon, sum of 2 sh. [118]—Re'uiah b. Uri, sum of 2 sh. [119] 90—Meshullam b. Shemaiah, sum of 2 sh.

Col. vii.

[120] The money which was paid on that day into the hand of [121] Yedoniah b. Gemariah in the month of Phamenoth, (was) [122] the sum of 31 kerashin 8 shekels, [123] of which 12 k 6 sh. for Ya'u, [124] 7 kerashin for Ishumbethel, [125] the sum of 12 kerashin for 'Anathbethel. [126]—Micaiah b. Ya'uyishma', sum of 2 sh. [127]—Oshea' b. Nathan b. Hodaviah, sum of 2 sh. [128]—Ahio b. Nathan b. Anani, sum of 2 sh. [129]—Azariah

b. Hazul, sum of 2 sh. ^{130}—Joshibiah b. Berech*iah*, *sum of 2 sh.* ^{131} . . . . 2 . . ^{132}— . . . . h daughter of Ki . . . ., sum of 2 sh.

(Reverse.)

^{133}—Megaphernes b. VŠḤI, sum of 2 sh. for ’NDM (?). ^{134}—VŠḤI b. ZDMR, sum of 2 sh. for himself (?). ^{135}—Haggai b. Miphṭaḥiah, sum of 2 sh. for . . . (?).

Line 1 extends across the top of cols. 1 and 2. זנה שמהת, a careless construction, literally ‘this (document) is (a list of) the names’. חילא. The garrison was co-extensive with the colony. Many of the names are feminine. זי יהב loosely used for ‘quorum quisque dedit’. Grammatically the antecedent is חילא. ליהו, but see below on ll. 123+. ש // restored from what follows. There is perhaps a trace of ש.

Line 2. The stroke at the beginning marks off the separate items, as frequently in accounts, cf. no. 81.

Line 3. ה[הודוי], cf. 20^{18} (420 B.C.). A man was often named after his grandfather.

Line 4. שרי[ה] is hardly enough to fill the space. The name (as masc.) is biblical.

Line 5. כל //[/], so Ungnad, but it might be a ש (e. g. כל שקלן /// ///), or even a מ (כל מאת . . .), cf. l. 9.

Line 6. הו and לה (restored from l. 8+) must denote some special modification of the entry. For הו cf. ll. 26–8, not in any other complete line. This line begins a new section which is distinguished by the use of לה in ll. 6–11, the other lines being incomplete. The next section (ll. 20–30) also has לה, otherwise only l. 134. It may mean ‘for him’, i. e. for Ya’u, or ‘for himself’, cf. לטב /// in l. 135, which is equally obscure, or it may be some note that the money has been paid or has not been paid. It is always at the end of the line.

Line 7. הוש[עיה ב׳ נתן] is supplied from 40^{5}. הושעיה alone would not fill the space, and another short name is required. חגי[ה] doubtful. Ungnad צפניה.

Line 8 and the following lines are too much broken for restoration. נבו (Ungnad) is very doubtful. There seems to be a space after it, which excludes נבו[כדרי] or נבו[נתן].

Line 9. כחל doubtful. An impossible name.

Line 11. Cf. l. 91. In l. 25 a man is distinguished by his mother's name.

Line 12. There are traces of [נ]תן. Cf. 8^{32}, and below, l. 128.

Line 14. Perhaps there was no name here—which would make the total right in l. 24.

Line 19. מאת apparently = *centuria*, a subdivision (?) of the *degel*. שנדן = Sin-iddin is probably right. We should expect ס, but cf. שנחאריב Aḥiḳar 3, &c., and שנזרבן Nerab 1[1]. The line below marks the close of the section.

Line 20 the beginning of a new section, continued in the next column.

Line 21. From this point כ is written for כסף.

Line 22. מ̄יכה, a badly written מ, which looks like two letters.

Line 24. ישׁ̄וב (Ungnad) rather than ישוב (Sachau, for ישוביה). The 𐡜 in the margin gives the total number of persons up to this point.

Line 27. סימך an unknown name. Ungnad suggests a mistake for יסמך; cf. סמכיהו, 1 Chron. 26[7].

Line 31 another summation, like l. 19, closing the section.

Line 38. Faint traces of a line.

Line 39. שִׁלֵּם (Ungnad), not שַׁלֻּם, which would be written plene. הודו shortened from הודויה, for which there is not room.

Line 40. חו̇רי, cf. l. 85. Egyptian? The ו is badly written, and ר may be ד. ונה, Ungnad compares וניה, Ezra 10[36].

Line 42. מתן for מתניה, Ezra 10[37].

Line 43. Ungnad reads אק, but there is no name beginning so.

Line 45. Either זכור or זכריה—probably the latter, as there is a faint trace of a possible ר. There were three names in this line.

Line 47. Cf. 33[5].

Line 48. The 20 in the margin is difficult. There is a 𐡜 at l. 24. If this were a continuation of the same reckoning it ought to be 𐡜𐡜, and some of the broken lines must have had no names. It is more probably a new total of a list beginning at l. 32 (since l. 31 ends a section). In that case three lines are lost at the end of col. 2. No line is lost at the top of col. 3. Then col. 2 was one line longer than col. 1, and the detached fragment should be moved lower down. Without seeing the original papyrus it is impossible to know whether this can have been so.

Line 57. יהוטל not necessarily masc. as Ungnad says. He compares אביטל, חמיטל in O.T. In l. 103 it is fem. See note on l. 11. The name means 'Ya'u is a protection', cf. בטלה זי אהורמזד often in Behistun.

Line 61. ה̄ושע. The ה like that in l. 84. It might possibly be אושע.

Line 68. The total 𐡜𐡜 here and afterwards is correct.

Line 69. פ̄מת, Egyptian = Παμύθης, is Ungnad's suggestion. Cf. 72[4].

Line 72. ח̄ני. The name must be short. The י is probable, and there are traces of חנ. הוריא carelessly for אוריה.

Line 73. משל̄ך, cf. l. 68.

Line 78. פ̄[נול]יא or פ[לול]יא, cf. l. 80. Ungnad suggests פלטיא. For the other names cf. 12[7].

Line 79. ח̄[רי]ו. Ungnad's חנ[י] is hardly possible. Cf. l. 40.

Line 81. ע[נני] a conjecture to fit the space. אסחח Egyptian, compound of Isis?

Line 82. אחת וכ׳. Sachau takes this as a new entry, and reads אחת מחת כי״ש //. But as Ungnad remarks, the name would not be omitted, and this would make the total (in l. 88) wrong. Seidel compares Phoenician למחת in an inscription in the Louvre, of which the meaning is obscure. [Usually taken as 'exact' or 'standard' money, but that is a mere guess. It might go with the clause following and be = למען, cf. perhaps (?) Assyr. *ana muḫḫi.*] אחת here can only be 'sister', and מחת can only be a proper name. The next letter looks as though it were joined on (מחתו). The two strokes may be a ש, as Sachau and Ungnad ('sister of M and S'), or the numeral //. Perhaps the former is better.

Line 83. מפחח very strange, but supported by ll. 88, 106. טפח̄ו. The חו is written over an erasure.

Line 85. שבית, cf. שבחית fem. and שבתי masc. in no. 81.

Line 86. נר̄י for נריה—but the ר is like a ו.

Line 88. מפחח, cf. l. 83. The scribe wrote מחח, then rubbed out the מ and wrote a פ, adding a מ in the margin. This shows that the oblique initial stroke was added after the line was written—perhaps as the entries were checked off, or to show that the money was paid.

Line 89. יח̄מול, cf. l. 97.

Line 93. צפליא, cf. l. 106. Seidel and Lidzbarski think = צפניה.

Line 96. . . . ז̄ might be part of e. g. a נ. In l. 107 נהבת ברת זכור occurs. The same person would hardly be named twice.

Line 98. The marginal number (70) was added after the line was written. It overlaps into the text and covers the oblique stroke. Note that from l. 81 to l. 108 the contributors are all women.

Line 103. יסלח over an erasure.

Line 114. [ז]ב̄ריה. Ungnad [צ]פניה.

Line 117. קון short for קוניה.

Line 120. Here begins the total of receipts so far. קם 'stood', i.e. was received. יומא הו, i. e. the 3rd of Phamenoth, cf. l. 1.

Line 121. Yedoniah the head of the community, as in no. 30.

Line 122. The arithmetic is not very satisfactory. Since 1 karash = 10 shekels (Introduction, p. xxiii), 31 k. 8 sh. = 318 sh. representing the contributions of 159 persons at 2 sh. each. As the list now stands, the first numeration (to l. 30) makes 26 persons, the second (to l. 119) makes 91 : total 117 persons. We thus require 42 more persons (or 42 lines at least), making two more columns. These can only have stood at the beginning. Further the total of 31 k. 8 sh. does not agree with the sums allocated, which amount to 31 k. 6 sh. only. Two shekels are therefore not accounted for.

Line 123. בנו as often in accounts. Lit. 'in it are 12 k.' &c., i.e. it is divided into 12 k. &c. The most difficult point about the document is the allocation of the money. The heading says it was for Ya'u, but here only 12 k. 6 sh. are assigned to Ya'u out of 31 k. 8 sh. The rest is divided between what seem to be two other deities. Were they then regarded as other manifestations of Ya'u? See Introduction, p. x.

Line 126 after a blank space, begins a supplementary list.

Line 129. עזריה over an erasure, and uncertain.

Line 130. ישביה rather than ישעיה (Ungnad). ברכי[ה] doubtful. Ungnad בנאי, which is no name. There is a trace of ה.

Reverse, three lines.

Line 133. בנפרן. Why was a Persian contributing? ושחי probably also Persian. לאנדם. The א is strangely formed and uncertain. The word is unintelligible. It would seem to indicate the destination of the money, cf. לה above.

Line 134. זרמר. The מ is badly formed, like כנ. The name should be Persian, or Babylonian (Zeri-Nannar?).

Line 135. לטב //\ probable, but inexplicable. Ungnad's לטביה is impossible.

No. 23.

List of Names. Probably about 420 B. C.

Another list of names, for what purpose is unknown.

It is undated, but put here because the writing is very like that of no. 22 (and no. 19), and some of the names appear in both. See notes below. Its date is therefore probably about 420 B. C.

As l. 8 is marked 10 in the margin, two lines must be lost at the top. There is nothing to show whether anything is lost at the end. Another 10 on the left-hand side belongs to another column, now lost.

Sachau, plate 23. Ungnad, no. 22.

1 אחיו בר נתן

2 נתן בר מעוזיה

חור בר בֿניה
מחסה בר יהוטל
חנן בר פחנם
שלום בר ח . . .
פלטי בר מֿתֿן
ר כשי בר עזור ר
פטחנם בר חורי
רעויה בר זכריה
מנחם בר מתן
פחנם בר זכור
חגי בר מיכיה
דֿידי בר אורי בר מחסה
שוא בר זכריה

[1] Ahio b. Nathan. [2] Nathan b. Ma'uziah. [3] Hur b. Benaiah (?). [4] Mahseh b. Ya'uṭal. [5] Ḥanan b. Pekhnum. [6] Shallum b. H . . . . [7] Palṭi b. Mattan (?). [8] 10 Kushi b. Azzur. [9] Petekhnum b. Hori. [10] Re'uiah b. Zechariah. [11] Menahem b. Mattan. [12] Pekhnum b. Zaccur. [13] Haggai b. Micaiah. [14] Didi (?) b. Uri b. Mahṣeh. [15] Sheva b. Zechariah.

Line 1. Cf. 22^{128} (419 B.C.), and 25^{19} (416 B.C.).

Line 2. On the principle that a man often bears the name of his grandfather, this may be the son (or father) of Ma'uziah b. Nathan in 20^{16} (420 B.C.), cf. also 33^{2} (407 B.C.).

Line 3. בֿניה, so Ungnad. Seidel compares 22^{40} ונה = וניה = בניה (?). The name בניה is possible, or פריה, and there is a mark above the line which suggests פנוליה, with the letters written close together.

Line 5. פחנם, Egyptian, as in l. 12, but the other name in each case is Jewish.

Line 7. מֿתן. The מ is very uncertain. Sachau reads נבתן, and it is certainly more like נב, but no such name exists. His suggestion that it is for נבונתן is not very probable. Even the ת is doubtful. It looks more like a י with an accidental stroke below.

Line 11. Cf. 22^{62}.

Line 13. Cf. 22^{64}.

Line 14. דֿידי. The first letter seems to be a correction. There is no name דידי (or רירי). Sachau suggests that it is for ידידיה.

Line 15. שוא, cf. 1 Chron. 2^{49}.

No. 24.

Account of Corn supplied. Probably 419 B.C.

Fragments of a document in three columns, containing a list of names of persons in receipt of rations as members of the garrison of Syene, with a note of the amount received by each. It is related to no. 2 in character, though not of the same date (see below), and may indeed be a report like that promised in 2[11] (נכתן דין, see note there). Cf. also no. 17 (ten years earlier) which refers to some such statement of accounts. It thus differs entirely from no. 22. As Sachau points out, there is nothing specially Jewish about it. It is another proof that Aramaic was used not only in dealing with Jews, but was the official language of the provincial governments in the Persian empire. The decipherment is very difficult as the names are mostly foreign, and the papyrus is much torn.

As to the date: l. 34 mentions the 4th year, and if the restoration of l. 35 is accepted, we may conclude that the list was drawn up in the 5th year. From the resemblance to no. 2 it is tempting to take these as years of Xerxes, which would make the date 481 B.C., but the writing (especially of col. 1) is so much later in style than that of no. 2, that it seems necessary to put it, with the majority of these texts, in the reign of Darius II. It will then belong to the same year as no. 22, viz. 419 B.C.

Sachau, plates 21, 22. Ungnad, no. 20.

Col. 1.

1 [ש] פ[ט]מ[ת בר א]שמן שא\

2 ש זביס . בר נבושלו שא\

3 ש חני בר שמעי[ה] שא\

4 ש אשמ[ן בר א]פ[ע שא]\

5 ש פטסי בר זפרות [שא]\

6 ש־צחא [בר] צפר. . לה שא\ הו

7 כ ש שמו[ח . . . .] שא\ ר\\

8 ש חור . . . .

9 ש . . . .

10 ש . . . . . שה . . . . . //

11 ש . . . . נתן ש[א\]

12 ש . . . . אחלבני [שא\]

13 ש ח[ור ב]ר נורשוש שא\

14 ש ש[מש]גרי בר בלבן שא\

15 ש ורדֿ בר זותי
16 ב ש חו[ר] בר יעולן שא | ר ||
17 ש שֿ . . . בר אביהו שא |
18 ש . . . . . פחרזֿ שא |

. . . יהיב
. . . מדי]נת נא

Col. 2. 19 . . . . . קֿנגו א . . זֿ . . . פבי שא | הו
20 . . . .
21 . . . . לד
22 . . . עג . . . פ . שא\
23 . . . שא
24 . . . . .
25 . . . . בר פטנתןֿ שא\
26 . . . נֿכל בר אֿורי שא |

27 כ]ל נפש דדר///\ בנו
28 כל נפש //] לחר שא | ר// לשא ///
29 כל נפש] ד// לחר שא | לשא ד//
30 כל נ]פש דר לחר שא[|| ר || ל]שא דדדר/// //
31 כ]ל נפקתא יתֿ . . .
32 ש]א | לד

. . . צחא בר
. . . ח
. . . מ

Col. 3. 33 כל נפק[תא זי י]היב לחילא סונכניא [מן יום . . .
34 הו י[ום ד לירח מ]חיר שנת ///\ עד יום
35 ד למ[חיר שנת /// \] זי יהיב במכל . . .
36 היתי [. . . . . מן] מדינת נא ביד ונפר
37 . . . . בר בר אֿחֿ ועדרי בר אֿו . .
38 שֿ[ערן א ול]ף ///\ לדד /// /// ג/ן הֿ /// /
39 ומן [עֿ]בֿור [ת]שטרס פתפא זי יהב לה[ילא
40 מֿן אלֿףֿ ר/// /// [/]/ן
41 נֿ]רנא ול[ף //] לדדר// ג | ח . . .

42 וי׳ [. . . . . . י]היב פתף לחילא [. . . . . מן
43 תש[טרס א א]לף /// //// 𐡝𐡜𐡜𐡜𐡛
44 . . . . מחיר שנת
45 . . . . א ומן א
46 . . . . 𐡝𐡜𐡜𐡛/// ///
. . . לחילא ה . . .
. . . היתי . . .

Col. i.

[1] *Ration of* Peṭemut (?) b. Išmn, barley ardab 1. [2] Ration of Zbis. b. Nebushalliv, barley ardab 1. [3] Ration of Haggai b. Shemaiah, barley ardab 1. [4] Ration of Išmn b. Ap', barley ardab 1. [5] Ration of Petisi b. Zaphruth, barley ardab 1. [6] Ration of —Zeḥo *b.* Zphr . . for him barley ardab 1 . . . (?). [7] K. Ration of Samuaḥ . . . . . . barley ardab 1 and 2 quarters. [8] Ration of Ḥor . . . . . . [9] Ration of . . . . [10] Ration of —. . . . . 2 (?). [11] Ration of . . . . Nathan, barley ardab 1. [12] Ration of . . . . Aḥlbni, *barley ardab 1.* [13] Ration of Hur b. Nurshavash, barley ardab 1. [14] Ration of Shamashgiriya b. Belbani, barley ardab 1. [15] Ration of Vrd b. Zuthi. [16] K. Ration of Hur. b. Y'ulu, barley ardab 1 and 2 quarters. [17] Ration of . . . . . b. Abihu, barley ardab 1. [18] Ration of . . . . . . phri, barley ardab 1.

Col. ii.

[19] . . . . barley ardab 1 . . . (?). [20] . . . . [21] . . . . 100. [22] . . . . barley ardab 1. [23] . . . . barley ardab. [24] . . . . [25] . . . . . b. Pṭntu, barley ardab 1. [26] . . . nkl b. Uri, barley ardab 1.

[27] . . . . *To*tal persons 54, including [28] *total persons 2* at $1\frac{1}{2}$ ardabs of barley each, = barley ardabs 3. [29] *total persons* 22 at 1 ardab of barley each, = barley ardabs 22. [30] *total per*sons 30 at $2\frac{1}{2}$ ardabs of barley each, = barley ardabs 75. [31] . . . *to*tal output a*mounting to* [32] . . . . barley ardabs 100.

Col. iii.

[33] Total out*put of what was de*livered to the garrison of Syene from the . . . [34] that is the *20th day of the month Meḥ*ir in the 4th year, to the [35] 20th of Me*ḥir in the 5th year.* What was delivered as food . . . which [36] . . . . . brought *from* the district of Thebes by the hand of Onophris, [37] . . . . b. Br'vh, and 'Edri b. A . . . [38] *Barley ardabs 1446*, g 2, h 4.

[39] And of corn (?) of Tšṭrs, the ration which was given out to the gar*rison* [40] from (?) 1019. [41] . . . . . 1252, g 1, h . . .

[42] And what . . . . . was given as a ration to the garrison . . . . from [43] Tšṭrs, *ardabs* 1690.

[44] . . . . Meḥir, year . . . . [45] . . . . and from . . . [46] . . . . . xx76 . . . .

Line 1. The ש at the beginning is restored because it stands before each line of this column. Sachau suggests that it is for שקל, as elsewhere, but then what is its meaning? It is more likely to be some word for 'portion', 'ration', like שיעור. [ח]מ[ט]פ, cf. פמח 22^{69}. Egyptian. [א]שמן last letter very doubtful, as in l. 4. Hardly אשמש. שאו \. Judging from no. 2 this must be for שערן ארדב \, the allowance of the man named, for how long? Sachau and Ungnad take it for *še'u* ($\frac{1}{180}$ of a shekel), which is unlikely.

Line 2. נבושלו, cf. 2^8.

Line 3. חני is certain. Not חפי as Sachau. It is a narrow נ as in l. 14.

Line 4. [א]פ[ע] quite uncertain. It must be a very short name, cf. 53^6.

Line 5. זפרות uncertain. Sachau חרוין, but ח is impossible.

Line 6. The oblique stroke as in l. 10. Cf. no. 22. . . צפר uncertain. Sachau . . חור which is possible. לה and הו as in no. 22.

Line 7. The כ is taken by Sachau for כסף, but the list has nothing to do with payments in money. Here and in l. 16 are the only two cases in which the ration is שאו \ רו \\\, which may be a mere coincidence, but in any case the meaning of כ is obscure.

Line 12. אחלבני uncertain. Sachau reads א חלקי[ה], but it is difficult to see what א can belong to, since the preceding word ought to be בר. What Sachau reads as ק is the same combination as in בלבן, l. 14.

Line 13. ח[ור] or . . ח. It must be a short name.

Line 14. ש[מש]גרי is Ungnad's suggestion, but the second ש is hardly possible.

Line 16. יעולן or יעולו (Sachau).

Line 17. אביהו more probably than אבי הו, since this הו (l. 6) comes at the end of the line.

Col. ii.

Lines 19–26 are too much broken to be restored.

Line 25. פטנחן. The last letter may be anything. Egyptian.

Lines 27–32 sum up the account so far. As the total number of persons to this point is 54, about half the names are lost. This cannot be the whole חילא, cf. no. 22.

Line 28. One would naturally restore נברן ||, but that the strange expression כל נפש followed by a numeral is used in l. 30. The two persons are those marked with כ in lines 7 and 16. I take ר as רבעתא. Therefore 2 persons at $1\frac{1}{2}$ each = 3.

Line 30. If 30 persons get 75, each must have $2\frac{1}{2}$. Hence we may restore שא[|| ר ||]. Cf. 2^7 where נ || = ר || here.

Line 31. . . . ית must be some word for 'amount to'. Thus:

	2	at $1\frac{1}{2}$	= 3
	22	at 1	= 22
	30	at $2\frac{1}{2}$	= 75
Total	54	get	100

Col. iii.

The left-hand fragment seems to have been set too much to the left. Probably l. 40 reads continuously, and if so there is less to be supplied in the other lines than Sachau shows.

Line 33. נפקתא זי יהיב if right, is a clumsy expression for 'expenses, namely, what was paid'. סונכניא, cf. סונכנן 33^6, 'Syenians'. Sachau explains it as a Persian formation in *-kan*, which is then inflected as Aramaic. The form שושנכיא 'of Susa', in Ezra 4^9, is scarcely parallel, unless that be a mistake for שושנכניא. At the end something is missing, for there is a faint trace of a letter, and some words are wanted to connect with the next line. Judging from the ordinary formula in contracts, [הו י[ום in l. 34 implies a parallel date here containing the name of the Jewish month. This makes the line rather long, for in l. 34 there seems to be nothing after עד יום. However, the lines vary very much in length in this document. If the Jewish month was mentioned here, it points to the conclusion that the 'Syenian garrison' was the same as, or part of, the חילא יהודיא, and that these accounts relate to the Jewish colony. The עד in l. 34 implies a מן somewhere before, and it can only come here. As to the Jewish month, Dr. Fotheringham tells me that in year 4 of Darius the 20th of Meḥir would coincide with the 19th of Iyyar, and in year 5 with the 30th of Iyyar.

Line 34. [י[ום ב is restored from l. 35 for reasons given in the note there. עד יום. The line might end with ב־ לאיר הו יום, but probably the date was expressed singly the second time. Similarly ירח is omitted before מחיר in l. 35.

Line 35. \/ /// שנת is restored here for several reasons. The two broken names of months, one ending in ־חיר and the other beginning with מ־, seem likely to be both מחיר, which could only recur at an interval of a year (or years). The mention of 'year 4' in l. 34 suggests that the account ran into another year. The large, though uncertain, totals imply a long period. In Greek papyri of the second century B.C. the ration (σιτώνιον) of corn seems to have been 1 artaba of corn per man per month, together with a cash payment in lieu of more corn. See e.g. Kenyon, *Greek Papyri in the British Museum*, p. 55. Probably it was about the same at the date of this papyrus. It appears, therefore, that down to l. 26 we have a list of men receiving the monthly ration, some getting the minimum of 1 ardab (שאו), others more. Ll. 27–32 then give the summary for the *month*. Col. 3 gives the totals for the year. זי begins a fresh entry. There is a space before it. The preceding lines were the heading. במכל. Sachau is no doubt right in taking this for במאכל, cf. למכר 32[2]. Epstein cft. מכילתא, &c. and translates 'by measure'. Some words are wanted after it to connect with the next line. Does it mean σιτώνιον as distinct from ὀψώνιον, the money payment?

Line 36. חיתי. If I am right in bringing the fragments closer together, there is room for about 7 letters in the gap, i. e. a name of five letters and מן. נא No, i. e. Thebes.

Line 37. בר is written twice, so that one of them must be part of the name. אוה. The name is improbable, as also בראוה would be.

Line 38. ש[ערן] is most likely from the slight traces remaining. It cannot be שקלן. The ף may be part of כסף or אלף. We then require either שקלן or ארדבן. If ח at the end is for חלרן, the line should refer to money and we might restore ש[ערי ש אל]ף. If it is a measure we may read ש[ערן א | ל]ף. In either case אלף, which is unfortunately less likely than כסף. I do not feel satisfied about the line. |/נ as in 2[7] = ||ר. Epstein suggests Talm. נריוא = סאה. //// ח. The ח is not well formed, but can hardly be anything else. Cf. l. 41. Epstein suggests חלק.

Line 39. [ע]בור very uncertain. [ת]שטרס as in 27[9], the Egyptian name of the 'southern province'. פתפא must be a popular word for 'ration' (so Lidzbarski), formed from פת? יהב probably only a mistake for יהיב.

Line 40. Ungnad reads מן אלון, but cannot explain it. אלוך = Ass. *alluku* 'palace' is improbable. אלף ־ is the most likely. Then there are no hundreds, and the other fragment must join on here, the line reading continuously, but the meaning is obscure.

Line 41. [גו]רנא perhaps, as in 27[5], but the ו is doubtful. A letter is wanted before it, perhaps ל, hardly מן. ל[ף]| as in the Behistun text for אלף. Cf. 30[28] ולף = 31[27] אלף.

Line 42. At the end מן is wanted to govern תשטרס in l. 43.

Lines 44–46 are too much broken to be restored. They apparently state a total for the year—from Meḥir in one year to Meḥir in the next.

No. 25.

Renunciation of Claim. 416 B. C.

The papyrus is in an almost perfect state of preservation.

The date, which is given twice, is the 8th (Egyptian 9th) year of Darius (II) = 416 B. C.

The document is a deed of renunciation or conveyance, similar to several others, no. 6, no. 8, no. 13. The parties are connected through Mibṭaḥiah. Yedoniah b. Hoshaiah was the nephew of Jezaniah, her first husband (see no. 9), whose house is the matter in dispute. Yedoniah b. Nathan and Mahseiah are her sons by her third marriage. They have already appeared in 20[3] as her sons by Asḥor, so that either he bore both names, or he had changed his name from Asḥor to Nathan between 421 and 416. As to the claim of Yedoniah and Mahseiah on the house, if it was not by purchase or arrangement, it probably came about as follows: Mibṭaḥiah had no children by her first marriage, since by 9[7] they would have inherited the property. She was divorced and afterwards married Asḥor-Nathan (see no. 15) about 440 B.C. and her property was united to his. When Jezaniah died, his house should have gone to his children by Mibṭaḥiah, but as there were no children and as no provision was made for that event in no. 9, her two sons by Asḥor now claim this house after her death. On the other hand, since Jezaniah died without issue, his brother Hoshaiah may have had or thought he had (we do not know what the law may have been) some title to the property, perhaps under some provision of the will of their father Uriah, and after Hoshaiah's death his son would claim. Much of course remains obscure. We do not know for instance what was the rule of inheritance in case of a provision becoming void, or in case of intestacy—nor whether real property passed in a special way.

The following table shows the relations of the people concerned :

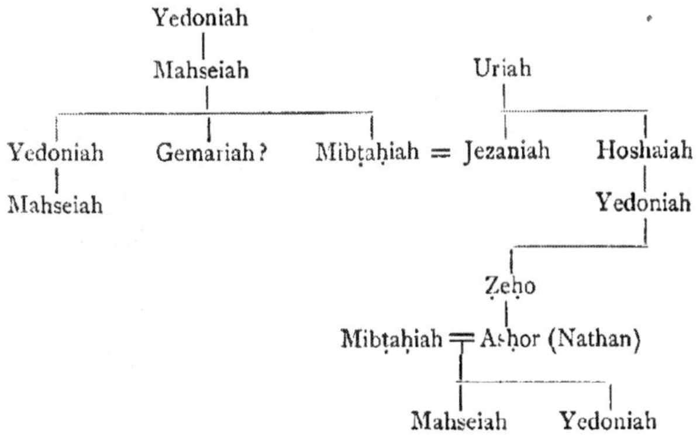

Sayce and Cowley, J.

1 ב /// לכסלו שנת /// /// |/ הו יום ⌐// לתחות שנת /// /// /// |// דריוהוש
מלכא אדין ביב

2 בירתא אמר ידניה בר הושעיה בר אוריה ארמי זי יב בירתא קדם וידרנג
רב חילא

3 זי סון לידניה בר נתן ומחסיה בר נתן אחוה אמהם מבטחיה ברת מחסיה
בר ידניה קדם

4 ודרנג רב חילא זי סון לאמר. רחקת מנכם מן בית יזניה בר אוריה הא תחומוהי

5 עליה בית הושע בר אוריה דבק לה תחתיה לה בית הצול בר זכריה דבק לה

6 בתחתיה ומנעלא כוין פתיחן תמה מועה שמיש לה אגורא זי יהו אלהא וארח

7 מלכא בניהם מערב שמיש לה בית מבטחיה ברת מחסיה זי יהב לה מחסיה אבוה

8 דבק לה זך ביתא זי תחומוהי כתיבן מנעל זילכם הן אנת ידניה ומחסיה כל ||/

9 בני נתן עד עלם וזי בניך אחריכם, ולמן זי רחמתן תנתנונה לא אכהל אנה
ידניה ובני,

10 ואנתה ואיש לי, לא אכהל אגרנכם דין ודבב. אפלא נכהל נרשה לבר וברה לכם

11 אח ואחת אנתה ואיש לכם, או גבר זי תזבנון לה ביתא זך או זי ברחמן
תנתן לה,

12 בשמי אנה ידניה ובשם בני ואנתה ואיש לי והן אנה ידניה רשיתכם ורשכם

13 בר לי וברה אנתה ואיש בשמי ובשם בני, שטר מן בר וברה זי יזניה בר אוריה,

14 וירשון לבר וברה ואנתה ואיש לכם או נברן זי תזבנון לה או זי ברחמן
תנתנו לה

15 ביתא זך וזי ירשכם דין ינתן לכם אבינרנא זי כסף כרשן עשרת הו
כרשן ⌐ כסף

16 ר || לכרש | באבני מלכא וביתא אפם זילכם עד עלם וזי בניכם אחריכם שטר מן

17 בנן זי יזן בר אוריה ולא דין, כתב מעוזיה בר נתן כפם ידניה בר הושע ושהדיא

18 בגו מנחם בר שלום מחסיה בר ידניה מנחם בר גדו[ל] בר בעדיה ידניה
בר משלם

19 יסלח בר גדול גדול בר ברכיה יזניה בר פנוליה אחיו בר נתן

Endorsement.

20 ספר מרחק זי כתב ידניה בר הושע על בית יזניה בר אוריה

21 לידניה בר נתן ומחסיה אחוהי כל ||

[1] On the 3rd of Chisleu, year 8, that is the 12th day of Thoth, year 9 of Darius the king at that date in Yeb [2] the fortress said Yedoniah b. Hoshaiah b. Uriah, Aramaean of Yeb the fortress, before Widrang commander of the garrison [3] of Syene, to Yedoniah b. Nathan and Mahseiah

b. Nathan, his brother, their mother being Mibṭaḥiah daughter of Mahseiah b. Yedoniah, before [4] Widrang commander of the garrison of Syene, as follows: I withdraw (my claim) against you on the house of Jezaniah b. Uriah. These are its boundaries: [5] at the upper end, the house of Hosea b. Uriah adjoins it; at the lower end of it, the house of Haẓul b. Zechariah adjoins it; [6] at the lower end and above, there are open windows; on the east of it, is the temple of the God Ya'u, and the highway [7] of the king between them; on the west of it, the house of Mibṭaḥiah daughter of Mahseiah, which Mahseiah her father gave her, [8] adjoins it. This house, whose boundaries are described above, is yours, Yedoniah and Mahseiah both [9] sons of Nathan, for ever, and your children's after you. To whom you will, you may give it. I shall have no power, I Yedoniah, or my sons [10] or female or male dependant of mine, I shall have no power to set in motion suit or process against you, nor shall we have power to sue son or daughter of yours, [11] brother or sister, female or male dependant of yours, or any man to whom you may sell this house, or to whom you may give it as a gift, [12] on behalf of myself, Yedoniah, or on behalf of my sons or dependants female or male. If I, Yedoniah, sue you, or you are sued by [13] a son of mine or daughter or female or male dependant, on my behalf or on behalf of my sons, (or any one) except a son or daughter of Jezaniah b. Uriah, [14] or (if) they sue son or daughter, or female or male dependant of yours, or a man to whom you may sell or to whom you may give as a gift [15] this house, or whoever shall bring a claim against you, shall pay you a fine of the sum of ten kerashin, that is 10 kerashin at the rate of [16] 2 R to 1 karash by royal weight, and the house is assured to you for ever and to your sons after you, failing [17] any sons of Jezan b. Uriah, without question. Ma'uziah b. Nathan wrote (this deed) at the direction of Yedoniah b. Hosea and the witnesses, [18] including Menahem b. Shallum: Mahseiah b. Yedoniah: Menahem b. Gado*l* b. Ba'adiah: Yedoniah b. Meshullam: [19] Yislaḥ b. Gadol: Gadol b. Berechiah: Jezaniah b. Penuliah: Ahio b. Nathan. (Endorsement.) [20] Deed of renunciation, which Yedoniah b. Hosea wrote concerning the house of Jezaniah b. Uriah, [21] for Yedoniah b. Nathan and Mahseiah his brother, both of them.

Line 1. The year is given first as 8, then as 9. The second numeral is certainly 9, for the units are always arranged in threes, so that the faint trace in the middle is to be read as a unit obscured by a crease in the papyrus. The Egyptian year began with Thoth, and did not coincide with the Jewish year beginning with Nisan. This synchronism is important.

Line 2. וידרנג as in $20^{4.5}$ (420 B.C.). Here it is the lower court over which he presides. In no. 20 he sat with the *fratarak* in the higher court of Nepha. Note that he was commander in Syene, and held a court in Yeb. No *degel* is mentioned, perhaps because the case was taken before the commander and not before the head of the *degel*.

Line 3. אחוה a mistake for אחוהי. אמהם an unusual addition, no doubt because it was really Mibṭaḥiah's property. If Ashor-Nathan was dead, there would be an additional reason for giving her name as a further means of identification.

Line 4. ודרננ, &c. repeated by mistake (?). רחקת lit. 'I withdrew from you (and) from the house', cf. 6^{22} and often. יזניה called יזן in 8^{6} and below, l. 17.

Line 5. עליה 'at the south end', as elsewhere, see the plan in note on 5^{4}. הצול (S-C הפּגוּל) is now certain, as the name occurs elsewhere. His father owned the house in 5^{5}.

Line 6. כוין פתיחן. It is difficult to see how there could be 'ancient lights' if דבק has its usual meaning to 'adjoin'. They must have looked on to the high road at either end of the frontage. אגורא as in 13^{14}. It was the temple, see no. 30. ארח מלכא. Cf. Révillout, *La propriété*, pp. 168, 322, &c.

Line 7. בניחם a mistake for ביניהם. יהב לה in no. 8.

Line 8. מנעל a mistake for מנעלא as in l. 6.

Line 9. בניך a mistake for בניכם.

Line 10. ואנתה ואיש, cf. $8^{10.11}$. The formula differs slightly from that used in other (and earlier) deeds. The persons are named in a receding scale of contiguity, and in pairs; son and daughter, brother and sister (l. 11), so that אנתה can hardly be 'wife' (as S-C). She would naturally come after her husband and before the children. The words are again a pair, and איש 'husband' is impossible, as a man is speaking. Translate therefore '(any) woman or man depending on me'.

Line 11. ברחמֿן 'in friendship', not ־מָן as Staerk. תנתון a mistake for תנתנון cf. תנתנו in l. 14.

Line 13. שטר מן as in l. 16. It corresponds to לחן elsewhere, e.g. in 8^{11}, and should mean 'except' as commonly in Syriac. The proviso is not very clear however. Jezaniah must have been dead by now, perhaps recently deceased, and hence the action. He cannot have had children by Mibṭaḥiah, because they would surely have had a prior claim to their cousin Yedoniah. (This was not the house which Mahseiah gave her in no. 8.) If he had been divorced from Mibṭaḥiah, that would account for his being alive at the time of her subsequent marriage (15^{38} ?), and might also be a reason for presuming (in law) a doubt whether he had other issue. In that case the clause would mean 'if any representative of mine, except my cousin (if any), should sue you'. Yedoniah b. Hoshaiah then admits the claim of Jezaniah's children (if any), who could not be liable to a fine for trying to establish it, if they came forward. There may of course have been a son of Jezaniah who had gone away and not been heard of.

Line 14. נברן a mistake for נבר. תנתנו should be תנתנון.

Line 15. ירשכם a mistake (?) for ירשנכם. ינתן not אנתן as S-C. אבינרנא as in 20[14].

Lines 16, 17. שטר מן as in l. 13 'unless any sons of J. come forward'. Note בנן זי ינן indefinite 'any sons' not בני ינן 'the (known) sons' as e. g. in l. 9 בני נתן.

Line 17. מעוזיה also wrote nos. 18, 20. His father wrote nos. 10, 13.

Line 18. מנחם ב' גדול and l. 19 גדול ב' ברכיה as in 20[7].

Line 19. אחיו ב' נתן brother of the scribe?

No. 26.

Order to Repair a Boat. 412 B.C.

A large sheet of papyrus, extra broad, as befitted its official character. Lines 17–28 are on the reverse.

It is dated in the 12th year of Darius (see note on l. 28) = 412 B.C. This is one of the most difficult of the texts, partly owing to the broken condition of ll. 1–6, which makes the precise nature of the orders uncertain, but still more because of the many technical terms and foreign words of which the meaning is unknown. It relates to the repairing (not building, see note on l. 1) of a Nile-boat used by certain boatmen in Government employment, and full details are given as to the work to be done on it. The procedure seems to be as follows: the men in charge of the boat reported to Mithradates (their foreman ?) through Psamsineith, one of their number, that the boat was in need of repair. Mithradates reported to Arsames, who sent an order to Waḥprimaḥi, an Egyptian apparently holding some local office. This is the purport of ll. 1–3. The order (ll. 3–6) is that whereas a specification of the necessary repairs had been required (from Psamsineith?) and sent to the Treasury officials, these should now inspect the boat and do the repairs if necessary. Ll. 6–9 state that they did inspect it, found the specification correct, and that the chief of the ship's carpenters considered the repairs necessary. The specification is then recited (ll. 10–22). This part is full of technical terms. In ll. 22, 23 Arsames orders Waḥprimaḥi to have the work carried out accordingly. Much is obscure, but this seems on the whole to make the text consistent.

All the persons mentioned bear non-Jewish names, except 'Anani l. 23.

Aramaic is thus used in a communication from the Persian governor to an Egyptian official.

For special treatment of the text see Torczyner in *OLZ* 1912, p. 397, and Holma in *Öfversigt af Finska Vetenskaps-Societetens Förhandlingar* 1915, B, no. 5.

Sachau, plates 8 and 9. Ungnad, no. 8.

1 מן ארשם על והפרעמחי וכעת בלא[ה ספינתא זי פסמסנית וכנותה נופתיא זי כרכיא כזי שלח]

2 עלין מתרדת נופתא לם כן אמר פסמסנ[ית . . . . , נופתיא זי]

3 כרכיא כן אמרו ספינתא זי מהחסנן א[נח]נה עדן הוה אופשרה למע[בר על זנה שלחת לם אשרנ

4 יתנגד ע[לת]בלא וישתלח על המדכריא זי גנזא המו עם פרמנכר[יא שמשלך וכנותה ספינתא זך]

5 י]חוו ואופכרתה יעבדו וישתלח זרניך זי .וה אשרנא הגרונה ואחרן [והמדכריא אשרנא כלא]

6 ינתנו ולעבק אופשרה יתעבד ואחרן זי מני שליח עליהם עלונה שלחו ו[כן אמרו עבדיהם על]

7 חלא זי לקבל בירתא ב[גו כרכ]יה מתרדת נופתא החוין ספינתא נחוי זי ביד פסמסנית ו . . .

8 כלתרין נופתא זי כרכיא נגידה עלתבלא ואנחנה החוין לשמשלך וכנותה פרמנכריא שמו [כר]

9 כנופי סנן נגריא ספיתכן וכן אמרו עדן הוה אופ[שרה] ל[מע]בר זנה אשרנא זי אפיתי אופשרה

10 למעבד עקי ארז ואר חדתן טף אמן עשרה שים [ל]בטק אמן תמנין בפשכן תלתה בנו סננן אמן עשרה

11 ותרין שף עשרה וחמשה [חד לא]מן עשרן סעבל אמן שבען חנן לבטנא תלתה קלעם לקומתא חד

12 עקי חלא אמן שתן פחטמוני לפערער חד לאמן תרין אפסי תחת חלא חמשה מסמרי נחש ופרזל

13 מאתין עקי ארז לובר חסין תמים אמן עשרן כלא יהיתה חליפתהם לובר ותבירן עלנגזא עזלי

14 כתן עבין כרשן מאה ותמנין רקען כרשן מאתין וחמשן עקי ארז חדתן חגן תרין לחד אמן חמשה

15 פשכן תלתה בפשכן תלתה לח[ל]א מסמרי נחש מאה וחמשן לחד פשכן תלתה מאתין שבען וחמשה

16 לחד צבען עשרה כל מסמרין ארבעמאה עשרן וחמשה טסן זי נחש אמן
עשרן מסמריהם מאתין

Reverse.

17 עקי ארז לובר רשות מצן בנכר חד מנן עשרה כלא הוספה כברי כרשן
עשרה ולהנדונה זרניך כרשן מאה

18 ויהוספון על עקיא זי יתיהב על טף בארבא לחד פשכן תלתה חפוש ועל
פתיא ועביא צבען תרין ועל

19 שים בארכא לחד פשכן תלתה חפוש ועל פתיא צבען תרין ועל שף וחנניא
בארכא לחד פשך חד ועל

20 סעבל עקי חלא דרי תמים בארכא לחד פשכן תלתה חפוש ועל פתיא צבע
חד עזלי כתנא רקעתא

21 ורניכא כבריתא במתקלת פרס יתיהב ישתלח לם אשרנא זנה יתיהב עליד
שמו בר כנופי סנן

22 נגריא ספיתכן לעינין אופשר ספינתא זך ולעבק יעבד כזי שים טעם כעת
ארשם כן אמר אנת עבד

23 לקבל זנה זי המרכריא אמרן כזי שים טעם ענני ספרא בעל [טע]ם
. נבועקב כתב

24 וחפרימחי . . . . . ית . ה לתובה בל . . ל . . . . תה . .
ח . . . .

25 כזי שים טעם . . . . . ל כתב . . . . . (blank)

26 (Demotic)

27 מן ארשם זי ב . Address.

28 נבועקב ספרא ב ־ ||\ [ל]טבת שנת ־ || דריו[הוש מלכא]

[1] From Arsames to Waḥprimaḥi: Now *the boat of Psamsineith and his colleagues the boatmen of the fortifications is* worn out *as reported* [2] to us by Mithradates the boatman as follows: Thus says Psamsin*eith* . . . . *the boatmen of* [3] the fortifications say thus: The boat of which we have charge, it is time to do its repairs. *Thereupon I sent word as follows: Let the specification* [4] be drawn up ac*cur*ately and sent to the accountants of the treasury. They with *the* commander*s Shemsillek and his colleagues* are to inspect *this boat* [5] and make a report on it (?), and let the arsenic (?) which is required (?) by the specification, paint (?) and the rest be sent, *and let the accountants* give *all the materials* [6] and let its repairs be done immediately, and the rest about which word was sent to them from me. Thereupon they sent and *thus said their messengers: On* [7] the beach which is in front of the fortress, be*tween* its *fortification*s Mithradates the boatman showed us the boat. We report that by Psamsineith and . . . . ., [8] both boatmen of the fortifications, it is described accurately, and we have reported to Shemsillek and his colleagues the commanders, (and) Shemau *b.* [9] Kenufi, head of the carpenters, of SPYT, and they said

thus: It is time to *make its repairs*. This is the specification which [is required (?)] immediately to do its repairs: [10] Cedar and cypress (?) wood, new, (each) plank 10 cubits . . . . 80 cubits by 3 hand-breadths, among them ribs (?) of 12 cubits; [11] yards (?) 15, each of 20 cubits; a S'BL, 70 cubits; cabins (?) for the hold (?) 3; a sail (?) for the mast (?), 1; [12] planks for the ḤL of 60 cubits; a PIṬMUNI for the P'R'R, 1 of 2 cubits; APSI under the ḤL, 5; nails of bronze and iron, [13] 200; planks of cedar, seasoned (?), strong, TMHS, 20 cubits; the equivalent of all of it, both sound (?) and broken, he is to bring to the treasury; sails (?) of [14] cotton, thick, 180 kerashin; awnings (?), 250 kerashin; planks of cedar, new; 2 ḤNN, each 5 cubits [15] 3 hands by 3 hands; for the ḤL, nails of bronze, 150, each 3 hands, 275, [16] each 10 finger-breadths; total nails, 425; plates of bronze, 20 cubits; nails for them, 200; [17] planks of cedar, seasoned (?), Egyptian (?) government, 1 talent 10 minae in all; add (?) sulphur, 10 kerashin, and arsenic for the painting (?), 100 kerashin; [18] and they shall add to the planks which are (?) supplied, to the boards in length each 3 hands clear (?), and to the breadth and thickness 2 fingers; and to [19] the SIM, in length each 3 hands clear (?), and to the breadth 2 fingers; and to the planed boards (?) and ḤNN in length each 1 hand; and to [20] the S'BL, the wood for the ḤL, the rows of TMHS, in length each 3 hands clear (?), and to the breadth 1 finger. The sails (?) of cotton, the awning (?), [21] the arsenic, the sulphur, are to be supplied by Persian weight. Let word be sent that these materials are to be delivered to Shemau b. Kenufi, head of [22] the carpenters, of SPYT, for the purpose of the repair of this boat, and let him do (it) at once, according to the order issued. Now Arsames says as follows: You are to act [23] in accordance with this which the accountants say, according to the order issued. 'Anani, the secretary, drafted the order. Nabu'akab wrote (it). [24] Waḥprimaḥi . . . . [25] according to the order issued . . . . wrote . . . [26] . . . . [27] From Arsames, which he . . . . [28] Nabu'akab *wrote* the document on the 13th of Tebeth, in the 12th year of Dar*ius the king* . . . .

Line 1. A curt beginning, as from a great man to a subordinate. בלא], Epstein cft. Dan. 6^{15}, and reads בלא [ישים], but the phrase there is שם בל (not בלא). The lost words must have stated the case. This word is more probably the verb בלא 'to be worn out', generally used of clothes and such like, but also applicable to a boat. The boat was in charge of the נופתיא זי כרביא (l. 3), and Psamsineith was one of them (ll. 7, 8). As he makes the report in l. 2, it is probable that he was mentioned here. For the name cf. Lieblein, *Dict. des noms propres hiérog.*, no. 1216. נופתיא זי כרביא from l. 8, where see note.

Line 2. לם must introduce a report of Mithradates: 'M. sent saying, thus says P.'. It cannot be 'for thus says M., P. . . .' Psamsineith alone speaks, since אמר is singular, and he does not include himself with the other boatmen (so that we cannot continue with אנחנה) because אמרו

(l. 3) is in the 3rd person. Hence some phrase must have followed such as 'the boat service is interrupted, for'. נופתיא זי from l. 8, is necessary.

Line 3. כרכיא, see on l. 8. מהחסנן 'having charge of' under Government, not 'owning', since it was to be repaired by Government. Elsewhere the word is used of holding land, and perhaps means to hold on lease, or by a grant, not as freehold. עדן הוה is abrupt and strange, but can only mean 'it is time to'. No doubt a translation of the Egyptian idiom *sp pw*, introducing a request &c. אופשרה an unknown word. From the context it can only mean 'its repairs'. In line 22 the construct form אופשר occurs, so that ה־ must be the pronominal affix. It has been assumed that the word is Persian, but no satisfactory explanation of it as such has been given. I cannot help feeling that it is connected with the Talmudic אפשר, the origin of which is also obscure. למע[בר] as in l. 10. The missing words must have stated that Arsames gave an order (as in l. 4). He is not giving it here, because in l. 6 (שלחו) he says that it was carried out. Hence some such words as here supplied are necessary. [אשרנא], see on l. 5.

Line 4. יתנגד. The subject cannot be the boat, which is always ספינתא feminine. Therefore not 'let it be towed', nor 'let it be carpentered' (יתנגר). Whatever it was, it had to be sent to the Treasury. They would hardly send the boat bodily. We should expect 'a statement of the cost', and hence I have ventured to supply אשרנא in the sense of 'specification', taking יתנגד in the sense of the passive of Hebrew הִגִּיד 'declare', 'state'. ע[לת]בלא, so Perles, as in l. 8, and Epstein, in the sense of '(towed) by a rope'. This is unlikely, as noted above. If תבלא here and in l. 8 can mean a 'measuring line' (Heb. חֶבֶל) the phrase would mean 'according to measure', i. e. 'accurately'. Ungnad's ע[ם] בלא 'with care' is unlikely. המרכריא, or המר׳. Perles thinks = אמרכל (Targums). It must be one of the many Persian titles, compounded with *-kar*, 'make', and treated as Aramaic. The meaning of המר־ is unknown. Cf. הדבריא in Daniel, where the מ has been assimilated (hence הד׳ not המר׳ here), and the second part is *-bar*, 'bearing', or the ב is a corruption of כ (due to the similarity of Heb. דבר), and the word is the same as here. In connexion with the Treasury it must mean the men who do the accounts, 'clerks'. המו begins a new sentence, without a conjunction. פרמנכריא as in l. 8. From Persian *farmān* and *kar*, 'those who make (or give) orders'. The words supplied are from l. 8.

Line 5. יחוו (Epstein יחון) is probably right. Ungnad אחרן. The

Haphel of חוה, and the Pael (or Haphel with ה dropped) are common in the sense of 'cause to see', 'show'. The Peal, which should mean 'see', is not found in BA, but perhaps occurs in these papyri. Here 'inspect'. אופכרתה another unknown word. ז̊ר̊ניך very uncertain. The first letter is like a badly made ע, the second is obliterated, the rest is probable (not ־מך as Ungnad). I have restored it because in l. 17 it occurs, as here, in connexion with הנדונה. See notes there. זי. ה̊ז̊. Ungnad חוה, but this is doubtful, and gives no sense, unless we could translate 'which was (mentioned in) the specification. אשרנא as in ll. 9, 21 and 30^{11}. Cf. Ezra $5^{3.9}$. The meaning of the word in all these places is as uncertain as its origin. In Ezra $5^{3.9}$ the LXX have *χορηγία*, but in the parallel passage (1 Esdr. 6^{4}) *στέγην καὶ τἆλλα πάντα*, and in verse 10 + *ἐθεμελιοῦτε*, which represents the Masoretic tradition אֻשַּׁיָּא. In 30^{11} 'outfit', 'decoration', 'detail' would be suitable. Here it seems to mean the description of the outfit, so that I have ventured to use the word 'specification'. But the meaning of this much-discussed term is not settled. הנדונה as in l 17. No doubt a Persian word, perhaps compounded with *han-* = *ham-*. The 'caulking'? In modern Persian اندودن means 'to plaster'. 'Painting'? Holma compares Persian اندام (Arab. هنذام) a 'limb', but also a 'fitting together', and so 'decoration'. Cf. הַדָּמִין in Daniel 2^{5} &c. The addition of ואחרן shows that we have here an enumeration of materials. זי (Ungnad) following it, is not probable. Torczyner reads באחרן, which he takes as beginning a new sentence (like אחר) 'then', and compares Dan. 4^{5}. [אשרנא] is doubtful. Something is wanted like 'all the materials'.

Line 6. לעבק as in l. 22 and $42^{7.8.13}$, in all which places the meaning 'at once', 'speedily' is suitable. In Aḥiḳar 103 עבק is perhaps a verb, see note there. ואחרן זי, Torczyner 'und nachdem'. על זנה, Heb. על־זה 'thereupon', continues the narrative by explaining that the preliminary order was carried out by the officials. שלחו is therefore a narrative perfect, not imperative. [כן]ו̊ seems best to fit the remaining traces of letters. Hence אמרו is probable, and serves to introduce the 1st persons in l. 7. About nine more letters are wanting, which should contain something to govern ח̄לא in l. 7.

Line 7. ח̄לא can hardly be anything else. In l. 12 it denotes some part of the boat. The ordinary meaning 'sand' is suitable enough here. It was outside the town, and must mean the sand on the river-bank, on which the boat was moored. They sent to inspect it. ב[נו] looks more likely than בין or ביד. [כרכ]יה, doubtful, but there is a trace of the tail of the second כ. If it is right, כרך will mean the outer fortifications of the town, running down to the river. נחוי asyndeton, as often, especially in official style. The form is Pael, or contracted Haphel, 'we report'. ...ו. The lower parts of the letters are left, but I cannot identify the name, which was probably Egyptian.

Line 8. נופתיא זי כרכיא not 'boatmen of the towns', which would be pointless. נופת is Persian, 'boatman'. If כרך is rightly explained above as 'fort', i.e. the outer fortifications of the בירתא of Syene (but Epstein thinks 'rafts'), then these men were employed by the Government to convey things by river from one point of the fortifications to another, or to bring supplies from elsewhere to the forts. They were therefore important, as an Army Service Corps, for maintaining communications. In no. 2 (and no. 3) it was Espemet (elsewhere described as a 'sailor of the difficult waters') who brought the corn &c. (to Syene? by river?) and delivered it to Hosea and his partner, who distributed it to the garrison. He no doubt belonged to this service. נגירה must refer back to יתנגר (l. 4), and if the explanation there is right, this will be a passive participle agreeing with ספינתא, 'it is described'. החוין 'we showed' or 'reported', not as in l. 7, 'he showed us'. שמו, see Spiegelberg, Hauswaldt Papyri. בנופי, Lieblein, *op. cit.* no. 770.

Line 9. ספיתכן, explained by Sachau as a derivative of ספינה, with נ assimilated, and the Persian suffix *-k*, afterwards inflected as Aramaic, hence 'belonging to ships'. Cf. שושנכיא in Ezra, 'belonging to Susa'. But this would require the emphatic form נגריא ספיתכיא, for 'ship's carpenters'. Epstein suggests that it is formed from the name of the nome Sape, like סונכן, 67, 3^1, cf. 33^6, 24^{33}, but in the singular. In his later article, however, he gives this up, and proposes ספינ̄תכן 'your ship', As ספינתא is used so often in this text, it is unlikely that we should have the form ספית־ (which is not a mistake, cf. l. 22), and as the only other use of ־כן is with a place-name, it is better to take ספית־ as a place-name. It will then refer to Shemau, 'the chief of the carpenters, a man of SPYT', a place otherwise unknown (Egyptian *spt* = nome). זנה אשרנא. The account of the inspection being finished, this begins the specification of the repairs as stated by Arsames (i.e. from his office), down to l. 22. 'This is what is to be done ... now (l. 22) do it'. אפיתי. The Ass. *appitti*, 'immediately', naturally suggests itself, cf. לעבק, ll. 6, 22. So Torczyner. (Seidel אף איתי, meaning?). But the construction is difficult if אופשרה has the same meaning as before. If it could mean 'it is fitting' (Talm. אפשר), then אשרנא would be governed by למעבד, which is not very probable.

Line 10. Here begins the specification as sanctioned by Arsames.

אר (or אד) must be some kind of wood. Ungnad suggests Bab. *eru*, a kind of cedar (cf. *erinu*). טף, Bab. *ṭappu*, a 'plank'. (Perles says *duppu*, 'tablet', cf. טפסר.) The Coptic топ is 'keel'. [ל]בטק. The tail of ב remains. There is room for one letter before it, and only ל is possible. Bab. *batḳu* means 'injury', 'broken part', cf. Ezek. $27^{9.27}$, ברק. If בטק can be connected with these, שים might be 'put', but in l. 19 it must be a noun. The 80 cubits 3 hand-breadths must be the measurement of the broken part (?). The planks were to be 10 cubits long, and sufficient in number to cover 80 cubits. בגו, as often, 'among (them)'. סנגן, if it has anything to do with סנן might mean beams to keep the planks in place, but 12 cubits seems rather long for 'ribs'. Holma suggests 'rudders'.

Line 11. שף would naturally be taken as part of שוף, but in l. 19 it is a noun. Holma thinks it is אסקופא 'threshold', then 'yard' of a ship. [חד ל]אמן. There are traces of ח and room for ל. For the construction, cf. 2^{8}, ... לשערן // נכרן. סעבל, not בעבל (as Ungnad). Egyptian? חנן. Ungnad quotes Bab. *ḫinnu*, part of a ship. It must be plural here (חִנִּן for חננן). In l. 19 we have חנניא with the נ resolved, as in עממיא. Holma proposes 'cabins', and compares Jonah 1^{5}, Krauss. *Talm. Archäologie* ii, p. 341. But this would be unsuitable in a specification. You would have to state the materials required to make them. Egyptian *ḥn* means 'rowing' &c., which again does not suit the context. בטנא, the 'belly' of the boat, i.e. the 'hold'. קלעם another unknown word. קומתא the 'upright', i.e. the mast? Ungnad an 'erection'. Holma a 'cabin' on deck.

Line 12. חלא must be some part of the boat, since something is to be under it, therefore not as in l. 7, nor the name of a wood (as Ungnad). עקי חלא perhaps 'planks *for* the 'ח'. פחטמוני and פערער, Egyptian; *pḫ* is 'deck', and *pḥ* is 'hinder part'. אפסי is plural. Holma cft. Heb. אפסין (Ass. *apšû*, 'rope'), but why construct state?

Line 13. לובר as compared with חרתן (l. 10) suggests Bab. *labiru* 'old', i.e. seasoned, but the ו is difficult. תמים unknown. יהיתה. Haphel of אתה 'bring'. The subject is 'one', 'they', indefinite. חליפתהם. Perles cft. Bab. *ḫalapu*, to 'cover with metal', to 'plate'. This does not suit the context. Can it mean 'the exchange' of it, its equivalent or value? Holma 'what is left over'. Sprengling 'calkage', suggesting that it is the origin of *calafatare*, *calfeutrer*. תבירן the 'broken pieces'. עולי, the root means to 'spin'. The phrase should mean 'spun cotton'. It was a very large quantity. Sails? or nets?

Line 14. כרשן apparently the value. רקען something spread out, 'awnings'. Holma cft. Heb. ריקוע 'plating' (or 'awnings'). Cf. l. 20.

Line 15. לח[ל]א again a part of the boat, as in l. 12, not a wood.

Line 16. טמן copper-plates for the bottom or other parts of the boat.

Line 17. רשות (or דשות) can only mean 'authority' &c. in Aramaic. (Holma, 'strong'.) Is מצן a mistake for מצרן? The two words might then conceivably mean 'government of Egypt', i.e. from Egyptian stores. Holma cites Bab. *miṣṣu*, a kind of wood. כנכר וכ׳. 1 talent 10 minae is apparently the cost of materials mentioned so far, to which is to be added the cost of the sulphur and arsenic. כלא in apposition to עקי ארז וכ׳, ends the clause. הוספה imperative with ה־ cohortative? This suffix, common in Hebrew, does not occur in BA, nor in these papyri (?) elsewhere. כברי. What was it for? הנדונה, as in l. 5, is probably 'painting', for which arsenic would be used. זרניך 'arsenic' in Talmud and Syriac, is usually taken as a loan-word from Greek (so Ungnad), and this has been used as an argument against the authenticity of these papyri, since a Greek word would hardly be found in Egypt so early as 412 B.C. (The objection is not convincing, since trade with Greece flourished long before this, and the material was very commonly used. Cf. סתתר = στάτηρ.) But the reverse is probably the case. There is no apparent reason why yellow orpiment (*auripigmentum*) should be called the 'masculine' substance, ἀρσενικόν, in Greek. (First in Aristotle. Note, not ἀῤῥενικόν, except by a scribal correction in Theophrastus.) The Greek is more likely to be due to a popular etymology of a foreign trade-word. In Arabic it is زرنيخ. (In a late Coptic papyrus Mr. Winstedt has pointed out to me **пассарпнщ пⲁⲗⲗⲁⲥⲫⲁⲣ** = الزرنيخ الاصفر = 'yellow-arsenic', and **пассарпнщ пкоккос** = 'red arsenic'.) It is not found, I think, in old Egyptian. In Persian it is زرنى or, influenced by Arabic, زرنيخ. From its occurrence here זרניך may well be a Persian word from زر 'gold', the *-n-* being formative ('golden' substance), and the *-k* the suffix common later in Pahlavi. On the other hand, Dr. Langdon quotes Sumerian *urudu za-ri-in* = Bab. *zarinnu*, a colouring (copper-like) substance used to dye wool. The form *zariniku* does not occur, but would be correct, with *-k-*, as a loan-word from Sumerian. *Za-ri-in* is found as early as 2500 B.C., and is, he considers, a good Sumerian compound.

Line 18. יהוספון i.e. something extra is to be allowed on the measurements. חפשׁ should mean 'freed', 'exempt'. Construction? The translation 'clear', 'fully' is only a guess.

Line 19. שׁים must be a noun here, governed by על, and similarly in l. 10. Meaning? שף must have some special meaning, not merely 'smoothed plank'. Cf. l. 11. חנניא a plural from חַן. Cf. עממיא from עַם.

Line 20. דרי 'rows', i.e. 'boards'? of חמים. Holma thinks 'old', Ass. *dûru*. רקעתא, st. emph. Hence רקען, l. 14, is feminine.

Line 22. לעינין seems to be לְעִנְיָן. The first י may be a mistake. אנת עבד is addressed to Waḥprimaḥi, who was to see that the orders were transmitted to Shemau, and that he carried them out.

Line 23. המרכריא. It was therefore the Treasury officials who drew up the order ending with כזי שים ט׳ in l. 22. ענני was apparently chief secretary to Arsames. Perhaps the same as in $38^{4,10,11}$, who was a great person, since he is not further described. Hardly the same as in 30^{19} = 31^{18}, nor the father of the scribe in 10^{20} &c. בעל [טע]ם 'author of the order'. He drew it up for approval by Arsames, and it was copied by a clerk. The words ענני . . . טעם seem to be in a different hand, therefore a signature. נבועקב כתב. If this means that he was the copying clerk, it is strange, as the hand is again different. Perhaps it means 'countersigned by N.' as Arnold, *Journ. Bib. Lit.* 1912, p. 25. Hardly the same man as in 22^{20} (or 12^{11}?).

Line 24 is evidently written by Waḥprimaḥi himself. He was an Egyptian, and wrote Aramaic so badly that no single word, except his name, is certain. The latter part of the line too is faded. As the letter was addressed to him, this line and the next must have been added after receipt.

Line 26, after a blank space, contains remnants of demotic writing. Sprengling reads Sobk . . . (part of a name) and *baris* (so also Spiegelberg), which Herodotus says is the Egyptian word for a Nile-boat.

Line 27. Part of the address is lost. After ב is a stroke which looks like פ.

Line 28. ספרא may be 'the scribe', but as 'Anani was so called in l. 23, perhaps it is 'the document', and כתב is to be supplied in l. 27. \//⌐ ב Ungnad reads \//⌐ ב, and takes ⌐ for ⊐, but it is only a badly made ⌐. שנת ⌐ון. The units are doubtful. I accept them on Ungnad's authority, as they may be clearer on the original.

No. 27.

Petition to Arsames (?). About 410 B.C.

This papyrus was first published by Euting in the *Mémoires présentés . . . à l'Académie des Inscriptions*, vol. xi, Paris, 1903. It belongs to the

Strasbourg Library, for which it was bought in 1898–9 from a dealer at Luxor. It consists of one strip (not three fragments, as Ungnad says) 63 cm. long by 7·3 broad. The writing on the recto runs lengthwise, and is divided into two columns. On Euting's facsimile there are slight traces of another column preceding them, but this is uncertain. The upper and lower edges are broken, so that the columns are not continuous. There is writing also on the verso, beginning at the right-hand end of the strip and runningacro ss it at right angles to that on the recto. From Euting's facsimile it seems that no line is lost at the top or bottom of the verso, but all the lines are incomplete at the beginning and end. The writing on the verso differs in character from that on the recto, but this may be only because it is written the wrong way of the papyrus—not necessarily by a different hand. The document refers to events in the 14th year of Darius (II), i. e. 411 B.C., and one may reasonably assume that it was written in that year or shortly after. In the light of texts discovered since, these events appear to be connected with the troubles narrated in no. 30, and the papyrus is a (draft of a) letter (to the satrap Bigvai ? or Arsames ?) complaining of the action of the Egyptian priests and the governor Waidrang. There can be no doubt that it emanates, like the rest of these texts, from the Jewish colony (or garrison) at Elephantine. In the lost beginning the writers must have stated their case. They then affirm their loyalty, and instance other illegal acts committed by their enemies, of which they say evidence can be obtained from the police. In spite of their good behaviour, their enemies have prevented them from offering sacrifices to Ya'u, and have plundered (or destroyed) their temple. They end by petitioning for protection, and that the damage may be made good. This seems to make the document consistent and intelligible. Unfortunately a line, or more, is lost at the beginning and therefore also at the top of column 2. Nothing, however, seems to be lost at the lower edge, so that the text was originally continuous from l. 10 to the verso. It ought not to be difficult to restore the verso, but as we do not know the original width of the strip, and as the reading of the verso is in parts uncertain, we cannot determine the length of the lines on the verso. It is therefore not claimed that the restorations are anything more than a rough approximation, or that they do more than indicate the connexion of the text. On the whole, while this petition is clearly connected with no. 30 and several phrases are common to both, I have placed it earlier because no. 30 (written in 408) received an answer (no. 32), so that another petition in these terms would be unnecessary. This may indeed have been the earlier letter mentioned in 30[18]. It is strange that so important an event as the destruction of the temple should not have been more explicitly described. There may, however, have been another column, in which it was narrated. At any rate the temple was destroyed in 411, and this petition cannot have been written except in or after that year—therefore between 411 and 408. It does not appear to have met with any success, and in 408 consequently another attempt (no. 30) was made.

The person addressed is called מראן, a high title applied to Bigvai in no. 30. Ungnad suggests that it here denotes Arsames, the governor of Egypt. The fact that he is named in l. 2 is not a serious objection. The use of the 3rd person is merely due to formality.

The facsimile in Euting's original publication is not very legible, but is helpful in some points. That of Sachau is excellent.

Sachau, plate 75. Ungnad, no. 2[a].

1 . . . נ]תנגן אֿנחֿנה . בין דג[ל]ן זי מצריא מרדו אנחנה מנטרתן לא שבקן
2 ומנדעם מחבל [לא] אשתכח לן בשנת ר//// דריוהוש [מל]כא כזי מראן
ארשם
3 אזל על מלכא זנה דושכרתא זי כמריא זי חנוב אלה[א עבד]ו ביב בירתא
4 המונית עם וידרנג זי פרתרך תנה הוה כסף ונכסן יהבו לה איתי קצת
5 מן גורנא זי מלכא זי ביב בירתא נדשו ושור חד בנֿ[ו ב]מנציעת בירת יב
6 וכען שורא זך בנה במנציעת בירתא איתי באר חדה זי בניה Col. 2.
7 בנ[ו בי]רתא ומין לא חסרה להשקיא חילא כזי הן הנדיז יהוון
8 בב[רא ז]ך מיא שתין כמריא זי חנוב אלך ברא זך סכרו הן אזד
9 יתעבד מן דיניא תיפתיא גושכיא זי ממנין במדינת תשטרס
10 יתי[דע] למראן לקבל זנה זי אנחנה אמרן אף פרישן אנחנה
11 מן מחבל ז]ךֿ בחֿסֿניא זי ביב ב[ירתא הוו Reverse.
12 . . . . . כֿ]ן אנחנה דֿכֿין אֿ[ף מנדעם
13 מחבל כזנ]ה לא אשתכח ל[ן ולא שבקן
14 לן כמר]יא להיתיה מנ[חה ולבונת
15 ועלוה] למעבד תמה ליהו א[לה שמיא
16 . . . . אֿרֿ זה . . . . .
17 . . . . . .]להן אתרודן חדֿה [עבדו תמה
18 ושירית] אשרנא לקחו לנפש[הום כלא
טב
19 וכעת ה]ן על מראן שגיא עש[קא יזדכר

זי לן עבי]ר אנחנה מן חילא [יהודיא
הן על מ]ראן טב יתשים [טעם כזנה
זי אמרן] אנחנה הן על מ[ראן טב ישתלח
לם אל ינ]גנן למנדעמתא זי א[יתי לן
ומדבח]א זי לן זי נדשו ל[מבניה

[1] . . . we should be injured (?). When (?) detachments of the Egyptians rebelled, we did not leave our posts, [2] and *no*thing disloyal was found in us. In the 14th year of *Ki*ng Darius, when our lord Arsames [3] went away to the king, this is the crime which the priests of the god Khnub *committ*ed in the fortress of Yeb [4] in concert with Waidrang who was governor here, after giving him money and valuables: there is a part [5] of the king's stores which is in the fortress of Yeb, (this) they wrecked, and *they* built a wall *in* the midst of the fortress of Yeb . . . . [6] Now this wall is built in the midst of the fortress. There is a well which is built [7] with*in* the *for*tress, and it never lacks water to supply the garrison, so that (?) if it is supervised (?) they would be [8] (able to get) water to drink in *this* we*ll*. Those priests of Khnub stopped up this well. If inquiry [9] be made of the magistrates, officers (and) police who are set over the province of TŠṬRS [10] it will be made *known* to your lordship in accordance with what we say. Moreover we are innocent [11] *of this damage* to the stores which *were* in *the* for*tress of* Yeb [12] . . . . . thus we are free from blame, and *anything* [13] *harmful of this kind* has not been found in *us*, *but* the *priests will not allow* [14] *us* to bring meal-*offering and incense* [15] *and sacrifice* to offer there to Ya'u the *God of heaven* [16] . . . . [17] . . . . . but *they made there* a fire (?) [18] *and the rest of* the fittings they took for *them*selves, *all of it*. [19] *Now if* it please your lordship, *let the* inj*ury be* very much *remembered* [20] *which was done to us*, us of the *Jewish* garrison. [21] *If it* please *your lor*dship let an *order* be given *according to* [22] *what* we *state*. If it *please your* lor*dship, let word be sent* [23] *that they shall not in*jure anything which *is ours* [24] *and* to *build* the *altar* of ours which they destroyed.

Line 1. A word of three or two letters is lost at the beginning. תנגן is clear. On Euting's facsimile there is a very slight trace of נ before it. If it is part of the verb נגן the tense is strange, and the usual sense of נגינה ('striking' a musical instrument) is unsuitable here. In l. 23 נגנן . . seems to be part of the same verb. I suggest that the root originally had the sense of 'striking' in general (restricted in Hebrew usually to striking a musical instrument), and that this could be extended to mean 'inflicting an injury'. Cf. Ps. 77^7, נגינתי, 'my affliction' I remember, and try to account for it, ('song' is pointless). In the titles of Pss. 4, 6, 54, 55, 61, 67, 76, Hab. 3^{10}, בנגינות is perhaps 'concerning (or, in) afflictions'. So Job 30^9 &c., נגינתם, the object of their injurious remarks, 'slander'. The word is not found in the cognate languages, but cf. the kindred roots נכח, נגע, נגף. אנחֿנה very doubtful. The trace of the first letter might be a ל, cf. the construction in l. 23. בין. There is the down-stroke of a letter before it which may belong to a ק or a ו (?). A conjunction 'when' is wanted. דג[ל]ן. The ל is almost entirely lost. On Euting's facsimile the trace remaining looks more like ע, but בין רגען זי for 'during the moments when' is hardly possible. If דגלן is right it would appear that the Egyptians as well as the Jews were divided into companies.

Line 2. ומנדעם מחבל וכ׳, cf. Dan. 6^{24}. כזי מראן ארשם וכ׳ as in $30^{4.5}$.

Line 3. דושכרתא a Persian word.

Line 4. המונית as in 30^{6}, a Persian word, probably adverbial 'in league with', not a noun governed by עבדו, as Ungnad seems to take it. וידרנג is here *fratarak*, as in 30^{5}, where his son is רב חילא. Hence *fratarak* is the higher title. In nos. 20^{4} (420 B.C.) and 25^{2} (416 B.C.) he was only רב חילא, and so must have been promoted in the interval. איתי seems to cause an unnecessary asyndeton, 'there is a part . . . they destroyed (it)'. The construction is probably borrowed from Persian, cf. the Behistun inscr. i. 13 end, *didā Nisāya nāma . . . avadašim avājanam*, '(there is) a province N. by name . . . there I killed him', and very frequently. איתי may therefore be neglected in translation, like ית which is perhaps derived from it.

Line 5. גורנא. Euting and Ungnad יורנא, but י is improbable, and gives no sense. It was no doubt a store of supplies for the troops. Cf. הֿסֿניא in l. 11. בנ[ו]. Ungnad בנ[ה]. But there is hardly room for ה, which has a long side-stroke in this hand. A ו seems most probable, but it might possibly be בנ[ין] 'we built', to protect the granary, which would be a meritorious act, and (l. 6) 'the wall is still to be seen'.

Line 6. בנה passive participle masculine. The feminine would be בניה. איתי begins a fresh charge.

Line 7. חסרה feminine, agreeing with באר. כזי הן הנדיז is very difficult. Ungnad takes כזי as 'so that' (?). The double conjunction is strange. At any rate הן הנדיז must form a subordinate clause by itself, since יהוון is wanted for the apodosis. Therefore הנדיז must express a verbal idea. The noun הנדז occurs in 13^{4}, where see note. Here literally 'if it was measured', i. e. if it was fairly shared. (Or is הנ הנד׳ a dittography?) Andreas takes it to mean a 'heap'—'if (there were) a heap (of them)', i. e. if they were very numerous—an odd expression. Nöldeke translates 'einberufen', and so Smend.

Line 8. בב[רא] restored from ברא זך farther on. אזר Persian, as אזרא, Dan. $2^{5.8}$, where it is taken as 'statement', 'information'. Here rather 'verification', i. e. inquiry.

Line 9. תיפתיא = תפתיא, Dan. $3^{2.3}$ ('sheriffs'), and thus confirms the reading and vocalization there. The exact meaning of the title is uncertain. גושכיא a Persian title from *gūš*, 'to hear', *gauša*, 'ear'. Cf. τὰ βασιλέως ὦτα, Xen. Cyrop. viii. 2, 10, and Hdt. i. 114, ὀφθαλμὸς βασιλέος, the king's informers, police. תשטרם, cf. 24^{39}, and Spiegelberg in Euting's article.

Line 10. פריין. If the sentence continues in l. 11, the meaning will be 'separated from', and so innocent of. Cf. the use of רחיק in 14^{11}, and often. Note the frequent use of אנחנה, 'they have done all this, whereas *we* are innocent'.

Line 11. The verso begins here. בחסניא. The ח has a very unusual form. Cf. גורנא, l. 5.

Line 12. [כ]ן. What Ungnad takes for a ל is really the tail of the ך in l. 11. דכין uncertain. The כ is short. The word occurs in 21^{6}. א[ף]. The traces of א are doubtful.

Line 13. [כזנ]ה. The ה cannot be the termination of a feminine noun, which would be subject to אשתכח, masculine. We may restore מחבל from l. 2, or באיש. [שבקן לן] as in 30^{23}.

Line 14. [כמר]יא as in l. 3. Ungnad [מצ]ריא, which may be right. מנ[חה]. The remains of ח are clear, and מנחה gives the clue to the passage. Cf. 30^{21} for the order.

Line 15. א[לה שמיא] as in $30^{27.28}$, or it might be אלהא and some short word joining on the next line.

Line 16 is hopelessly lost.

Line 17. אתרודן. Perhaps a compound of Persian *atar*, 'fire'. The temple was burned, cf. 30^{12}, but the two statements do not agree exactly. חדה is more probable than Ungnad's חנה. It is used merely like the indefinite article.

Line 18. [ושיריה] from 30^{11}. אשרנא must be taken in a wide sense. In 30^{11} it is the woodwork of the building, which was burned. Here it must include the sacred vessels, which were stolen. [כלא] is probable. Not עבדו, as Ungnad, which is not wanted here as it is in 30^{13}.

Line 19. Having finished their statement they now come to their petition. The frequent repetition of 'if it please your lordship' shows that the person addressed must have been of exalted rank. For the phrase cf. Ezra 5^{17}, וכען הן על מלכא טב. שגיא must go with the next clause, not with טב. It is adverbial, as in Aḥiḳar 51 &c. [עש[קא as in $16^{8,9}$. But the restoration is only approximate. Ungnad's [עש[ת is not very convincing. 'Think very much' is a strange expression, and I doubt if they would use an imperative in this humble petition. But cf. 30^{23}.

Line 20. Euting and Ungnad read the first letter as ע, but it is more like ד, ר, or ב. אנחנה in apposition to לן as in 6^{8} &c.

Line 23. נ[ינ]נון, cf. note on נתננן, l. 1.

No. 28.

Assignment of Slaves. 411 B.C.

Very well preserved. Hardly any letter is really doubtful.

The date is double (as in no. 25), the 13th year in the Jewish reckoning, the 14th in the Egyptian, of Darius II = 412–411 B.C.

Mibṭaḥiah was dead, recently no doubt, and Mahseiah and Yedoniah, her two sons by Nathan (= Asḥor) now proceed to divide her slaves between them. There were two lads, brothers, one of whom went to each of the sons, and their mother and a young child, about whom they are to make an agreement later, i. e. when the boy is old enough. The child therefore was not to be separated from his mother before a certain age, though it does not appear who was to have charge of them in the meantime. As the slaves bear Egyptian names, it is evident that Jews could own Egyptian slaves.

The only difficulty in the document is as to the marking on the slaves, see note on l. 4.

Sayce and Cowley, K.

1 ב כ ///\ לשבט שנת ־||| הו יום ||| ||| ||\ לחתחור שנת ־///\ דריהוש
מלכא ביב בירתא

2 אמר מחסיה בר נתן \ ידניה בר נתן \ כל |\ ארמין זי סון לדגל ו[ריז]ת
לאמר אנחנה אשתוין

3 בחדה ופלגן עלין עבדיה זי מבטחיה אמן. והא, זנה חלקא זי מטאך בחלק,
אנת ידניה

4 פטוסירי שמה אמה תבא עבד יוד \ שנית על ידה בימן שניתת מקרא
ארמית כזנה ·

5 למבטחיה, והא זנה חלקא זי מטאני בחלק, אנה מחסיה בלא שמה אמה תבא
עבד יוד \

6 שנית על ידה, בימן שניתת מקרא ארמית כזנה: למבטחיה אנת ידניה שליט בפטוסירי

7 עבדא זך זי מטאך בחלק, מן יומא זנה ועד עלם ובניך אחריך ולמן זי צבית תנתן לא אכהל

8 אנה מחסיה בר וברה לי אח ואחה לי ואנש זילי, דיןן למרשה עליך ועל בניך עלדבר פטוסירי,

9 שמה עבדא זי מטאך בחלק. הן רשינך דינא עלא, אנחנה מחסיה ובני או נרשה לבר

10 וברה לך ולאנש זילך עלדבר פטוסירי עבדא זך זי מטאך בחלק, אחר ננתן לך אבינדנא כסף

11 צריף, כרשן עשרה במתקלת מלכא, ורחיקן אנחנה מנך ומן בניך מן דין עלדבר פטוסירי זך

12 זי מטאך בחלק, לך יהוה, וזי בניך אחריך, ולמן זי צבית תנתן ולא דין, אף איתי תבא

13 שמה אמהם זי עלימיא אלה, ולילו ברה זי לא עד נפלג עלין כזי [ע]דן יהוה נפלג המו,

14 עלין, ונכר חלקה נהחסן, וספר פלגנן נכתב בינין, ולא דין, כתב נבותבלתי בר נבוזראבן

15 ספרא זנה ביב בירתא כפם מחסיה וידניה אחותי שהדיא בנו מנחם בר גדול

16 שהד חנן בר חני שהד נתן בר יהואור שהד שלם בר נתן

Endorsement.

17 ספר פלגן עבד, פטוסירי, כתב מחסיה בר נתן לידניה בר נתן אחוהי

[1] On the 24th of Shebaṭ, year 13, that is the 9th day of Athyr, year 14 of Darius the king in the fortress of Yeb, [2] said Mahseiah b. Nathan (and) Yedoniah b. Nathan, in all 2, Aramaeans of Syene, of the detachment of Wa*ri*zath, as follows: We have agreed [3] together and have divided between us the slaves of Mibṭaḥiah our mother, and note, this is the share which comes to you as a share—you, Yedoniah—, [4] Peṭosiri by name, whose mother is Tebo, a slave. A yod is marked on his arm at the right of a marking in the Aramaic language, thus, [5] 'Mibṭaḥiah's'. Note also, this is the share which comes to me as a share—me, Mahseiah—, Belo by name, whose mother is Tebo, a slave. A yod [6] is marked on his arm at the right of a marking in the Aramaic language thus, 'Mibṭaḥiah's'. You, Yedoniah, are master of Peṭosiri, [7] this slave, who has come to you as a share, from this day for ever, and your children after you, and to whom you will you may give (him). I shall have no power, [8] I Mahseiah, son or daughter of mine, brother or sister of mine, or any dependant of mine, to move the court against you or against your children in the matter of Peṭosiri [9] by name, the slave who has come to you as a share. If we move the court against you in the matter, we Mahseiah or my

children, or (if) we sue son [10] or daughter of yours or dependant of yours in the matter of Peṭosiri this slave who has come to you as a share, then we will pay to you a fine of standard [11] money ten kerashin, royal weight, and we renounce all claim against you and your children as regards this Peṭosiri [12] who has come to you as a share. He belongs to you and your children after you, and to whom you will you may give (him) without question. Also as to Tebo [13] by name, the mother of these lads, and Lilu her son, whom we do not yet divide between us, when it is *time* we will divide them [14] between us, and we will each take possession of his share, and we will write a deed of our partition between us, and (there shall be) no dispute. Nabutukulti b. Nabu-zira-ibni wrote [15] this deed in the fortress of Yeb at the direction of Mahseiah and Yedoniah his brother. Witnesses thereto: Menahem b. Gadol; [16] Witness Hanan b. Haggai; Witness Nathan b. Ya'u'or; Witness Shallum b. Nathan. (Endorsement.) [17] Deed of assignment of a slave, Peṭosiri. Written by Mahseiah b. Nathan for Yedoniah b. Nathan his brother.

Line 2. Mahseiah, named after his grandfather, Mibṭaḥiah's father. נתן = Asḥor, see note on 15^{2}, and cf. especially 20^{3} with 25^{3}. The \ is not a mark of punctuation, but the cypher 'one', which may be omitted in translation. Its use here is derived from the practice of putting it after names in lists or accounts, for the purpose of adding more easily. The total in such cases is preceded by כל. So here, the precise translation would be 'Mahseiah b. N. (1 man), Yedoniah b. N. (1 man), total 2 men'. Hence no 'and'. ו[ריז]ת is probable, though not certain. The restoration has been questioned because the דגל וריזת occurs in no. 5, which is sixty years earlier, but as we do not know on what grounds these names were attached to the *degalin*, it is useless to speculate about possibilities. If the name is that of the commander, this must be another man of the same name.

Line 4. פטוסירי, cf. the ostrakon in CIS 138 A. 4. יוד \. There is no doubt as to the reading either here or in l. 5, but the meaning is very uncertain. The practice of tattooing slaves is mentioned in Ostr. M (verso), published by Sayce and Cowley, but why should these be marked with a yod? It may be assumed that it was an Aramaic yod, the smallest letter in the alphabet, not the Phoenician letter, which is larger. It was therefore not very well suited for a distinguishing mark. If the letter is meant (i.e. if they really used this name for it at this time) the only way of translating is as given above (from Clermont-Ganneau). It cannot be the initial of Yedoniah, because it is also used on Mahseiah's slave. Whatever it meant, the mark was למבטחיה י. The \ is again a 'one', not as S-C. Stenning suggests that it is for יְרֵת, thus changing the mark into '(belonging to) the heir of M.'

Clermont-Ganneau takes it as the initial of some verb (in the future) meaning to 'annul'. Guillaume proposes יהו (improbable) or ירת. If by any possibility יור could be descriptive of the kind of slave, the sentence would be simple, '1 yod slave, marked &c.' But I see no hope of explaining it so. שניח, a passive participle from a root שנת (not as S-C), because of the noun שניתת. The meaning 'marked' (in Ostr. M. כתב) is required by the context, though the root is not found elsewhere. There is a late Hebrew word שנתות, for the marks on vessels for measuring, usually explained as tooth-like marks (from שן), which would not account for the ת. In Assyrian *šintu* is said to mean markings on animals. ידה, properly the arm, or rather the whole limb including both arm and hand, and so to be taken here. Similarly רגל is the whole limb, leg and foot together. If it was necessary to distinguish the hand or foot specially, a word like כף was added, cf. פס ידא, Dan. 5[5], and in mod. Arabic كف يد (Clermont-Ganneau orally). בימן must go with what follows (so Clermont-Ganneau). שניתת a ḳaṭîl-form from שנת. מקרא is 'reading'. We should regard it from the other point of view as 'writing'.

Line 8. דינן must be 'judges'. Usually דין, which may mean either 'judge', or 'law-suit'. אנש only here and in l. 10. Usually איש.

Line 9. דינא, similarly 'the judge'. עלא adverbially for 'about him'.

Line 10. אבינדנא (or ־רנא) as in 20[14], 25[15].

Line 11. כסף צריף probably = the usual לעשרתא ‖ ר as the standard. במתקלת מ׳ = the usual באבני מ׳. מן דין. The מ is almost certain. It is dependent on רחיקן by a confusion of two constructions, 'we withdraw from you as regards litigation', and 'we withdraw from litigation as regards you'.

Line 12. וי a loose parallel to לך. It should be ולבניך. איתי, cf. 27[4], where also it is not required by the construction.

Line 13. עד = Heb. עוד. ערן, cf. on 26[3].

Line 16. יהואור more probably than יהואדר (as S-C). A variant of אוריה. Cf. 1[2], יההאור (fem.).

No. 29.

Contract for a Loan. About 409 B.C.

Fragments only.

The date is between the 15th and 19th years of Darius II, probably the 16th year, i.e. 409 B.C.

It relates to a debt, part of the price of a house (?), due from the son of Hosea to Yislaḥ. The text is too much broken for restoration, and perhaps the pieces are not correctly put together. Hence the details are uncertain. It resembles no. 35 in some respects.

Sachau, plate 15. Ungnad, no. 15.

1 בי]רת מסורע שנת ר-/// //[/ ד]ריוהוש מלכא ביב בירתא [אמר נתן בר] הושע ארמי זי
2 סון לדגל נבוכדרי ליס[לח] בר גדול ארמי זי סון לדגל [. . . . . לא]מר איתי לך עלי
3 כסף כר[ש חד שקלן ארבעה . . . . .]תרי במנין /// //[. זי הוו] עלי מן קצת כסף
4 דמי בית מ̅נ̅[. . . . . ע̅]ל̅ם̅ אמר אנה נ[ת̅ן אשלם] לך בכספא זנה
5 כרש חד̅ ארבעה עד נ̅ד̅ן̅ . . . . . ירח פחנס שנת [ר-/// /// | דר]יוהוש מלכא
6 בין ירח[א זנ]ה והן בכספא זנה כרש חד שקלן ארב[עה לא ש]למת יהבת לך
7 . . מנא . . . . .

[1] In the month of Mesore, year 16 (?) of Darius the king, in Yeb the fortress *said Nathan* (?) *b.* Hosea, Aramaean of [2] Syene, of the detachment of Nabukudurri, to Yis*laḥ* b. Gadol, Aramaean of Syene, of the detachment of . . . . . *as fol*lows: There is to your credit against me [3] the sum of *one* kar*ash, four shekels the balance* (?) *of* 5 (?) minae *which were* due from me as part of the amount [4] of the value of the house (?) of M . . . . I Na*than* declare *that I will pay* you this sum, [5] one karash, four, by . . . . . the month of Paḥons, year *17 of Dar*ius the king [6] . . . . . . and if I *do not p*ay (and) give you this sum of one karash fo*ur* shekels [7] . . . .

The end is lost. It probably contained provisions similar to those in No. 11.

Line 1. שנת ר- /// ///. Five strokes certainly. Judging from the space required for the name יסלח in l. 2, there were probably six. [נתן] is supplied from נ[תן] l. 4. A ידניה ב׳ הושעיה was a party to no. 25, when Yislaḥ b. Gadol was a witness, in 416 B.C.

Line 2. נבוכדרי as in 35^{2} and also in 7^{3} (461 B.C.). Cf. note on 28^{2}. איתי לך עלי 'you have a claim against me for', cf. 35^{3}.

Line 3. כרש חד וכ׳ restored from l. 6. [ ]תרי. Sachau suggests [כת]תרי from 35^{4}, but that would require a numeral after it. במנין must be 'minae', but ב is strange. קצת as in 35^{4}. Sachau takes it as 'total', and so Ungnad, who cft. Neh. 7^{70}—but מקצת there means 'a part'. In 27^{4} קצת מן must mean 'part of', as in other Aramaic. Apparently (Nathan) b. Hosea had bought a house with another person, and part

(1 karash 4 shekels) of his share (5 minae) of the price was still owing to the vendor Yislaḥ b. Gadol.

Line 4. בית̄. The ח and letters after it are very uncertain. [ע]לם̄ uncertain. Possibly the lower fragments here are not in place, and this may account for the long tail of ר in אמר. נ[תן]. There is a trace of ת, and of ם in אשלם. Cf. 35^4.

Line 5. כ׳ חד ארבעה. No doubt שקלן was omitted by accident, but it may have been the popular usage '1 karash 4'. עד as in 35^6 denotes the time limit. Then . . . נר ought to denote the day of the month, or some such detail. The letters are clear. שנת[ ]. The number is quite uncertain—17?

Line 6. בין ירח[א] 'within this month'? It is so difficult that I think the fragment must be out of place. יהבת, no ו as one would expect, cf. 35^7.

Line 7. . . . מנא . . If the fragment is out of place these letters do not belong here.

No. 30.

Petition to the Governor of Judaea. 408 B.C.

This is in many ways the most important text of the series.

It is a fine papyrus, with ll. 1–17 on the recto and ll. 18–30 on the verso. It is in excellent condition, hardly a letter being really doubtful, and although there are some difficulties, the meaning is as a rule clear. The date (l. 30) is the 17th year of Darius II = 408 B.C.

It is a (draft or copy of a) letter from Yedoniah, who thus appears to be the chief priest (see below) and head of the community at Yeb, to Bigvai the Persian viceroy of Judaea. It describes a plot (to which allusion has already been made in no. 27) between the Egyptians and the Persian governor Waidrang for the destruction of the temple, which took place three years before the date of writing. Incidentally the temple is described, and some historical facts are mentioned. Finally Bigvai is asked to give orders for its re-building. Cf. no. 27.

The larger questions raised by this document have been discussed in the general introduction. It is only necessary here to say something of the persons with whom this letter is concerned. (See Sachau, p. 4+, and Ed. Meyer, *Papyrusfund*, p. 70+).

On the form of the name בגוהי, see *JRAS* 1920, p. 179. It is only a variant (and later form) of בגוי (Neh. 7^7, &c.), which is Graecized as Βαγώας. (The persons are of course not the same.) Josephus (Ant. xi, 7) mentions together a viceroy Bagoses and a High Priest Ἰωάννης at about this date, and we are forced to conclude that they are the same persons as the בגוהי and יוחנן of this letter. It is true that his account lacks precision, and that his materials for the history of the period seem to have been scanty. He could no longer draw upon Nehemiah. Since Bigvai was viceroy in 408, it is evident that Nehemiah was either dead or superseded by him at that date. Hence the 'two and thirtieth year of Artaxerxes' (Neh. 13^{6}) must refer to Artaxerxes I and be the year 433 B.C. We thus obtain a fixed point in the history of Nehemiah.

The Bagoses of Josephus has generally been identified with the minister Bagoas under Artaxerxes III (358–337), mentioned by Diodorus Siculus (xvi, 47). But the name was common, and since Bigvai here was in office in 408, the two persons cannot be identical. Josephus describes his Bagoses as ὁ στρατηγὸς τοῦ Ἀρταξέρξου, which of course might refer to any one of the three kings of that name. A various reading is τοῦ ἄλλου Ἀ. Whether or not that can mean 'alterius Artaxerxis' 'the 2nd A.' is not of great importance. It is evident that if Bagoses-Bigvai was governor of Judaea in 408, under Darius II, the only Artaxerxes under whom he can have served was Artaxerxes II (404–358). What is meant precisely by στρατηγὸς is not so clear. After being governor of Judaea under Darius II, he may have gone on active service under Artaxerxes II, but it is not impossible that Josephus confused him with the Bagoas who was a military commander under Artaxerxes III, and hence described him as στρατηγός. He was capable of such things. Bigvai was therefore a successor (immediate ?) of Nehemiah as פחת יהוד.

The Johanan who was contemporary with him as High Priest, is mentioned in the list in Neh. $12^{22.23}$, a later addition to the book, hardly due to Nehemiah himself. Of this Johanan (Ἰωάννης) we have a short account in Josephus (Ant. xi, 7). He was on no good terms with Bagoas, who intended to turn him out of office and install his brother Jeshua in his stead. In consequence Johanan killed Jeshua in the Temple. It would appear from Josephus that this took place in the reign of Artaxerxes, and therefore some years after the date of this letter. If, however, Johanan and Bigvai were already on bad terms, we can understand why Johanan is not associated with Bigvai in the answer to the letter (no. 32). Moreover Bigvai would see no objection to the existence of the temple at Elephantine, while Johanan would officially condemn it.

The mention of Sanballat (l. 29) is more difficult. Nehemiah speaks of him (for no doubt he is the same person) frequently as a bitter opponent. Cf. especially Neh. $3^{33.34}$. Though he does not give him the title of פחת שמרין (as here) it is evident that Sanballat was in some sort of authority in Samaria, and there is no reason why he should not have been still in office in 408. This is implied by the expression 'sons of S. governor of S.'. If he had been dead the phrase would have been 'sons of S. who was (formerly) governor of S.' (זי פחת שמ' הוה), as Sachau remarks. So far this letter is not inconsistent with Nehemiah. Again, according to Neh. 13[28] a son of Joiada, i. e. a brother of Johanan, had married a daughter of Sanballat, and had apparently been expelled from Jerusalem. This also is not inconsistent with other facts. Now if we turn to Josephus we find that he diverges from Nehemiah, and seems to have telescoped the history. He says that Sanballat was sent to Samaria by Darius, which might be correct if he meant Darius II. But he definitely calls him 'Darius the last king' (Ant. xi, 7, 2 τελευταίου, not 'former'). He thus confuses Darius II with Darius III, and puts the events nearly 100 years too late. Then he makes the daughter of Sanballat marry Manasseh, a brother of Jaddua (and therefore a son, not a brother, of Johanan) and brings him into relation with Alexander the Great after the defeat of Darius III at the battle of Issus (333 B.C.). It has always been difficult to reconcile Josephus' narrative with other facts. If Sanballat was governor of Samaria in 408, and had grown-up sons then, he must have been at least 40 years old, and it is hardly possible that he should have lived 76 years longer—for Josephus makes him die in 332 (Ant. xi, 8, 4). The view that there were two Sanballats, each governor of Samaria and each with a daughter who married a brother of a High Priest at Jerusalem, is a solution too desperate to be entertained. We are therefore forced to conclude that while Nehemiah's contemporary account is consistent with other historical facts, Josephus has gone astray by confusing the two kings Darius and the two officials Bigvai, and then has filled in his history largely by imagination. Events may have happened somewhat as he says, but not when he says, and the result does not give us a high opinion of his trustworthiness as an historian.

The fact that the Jews of Elephantine applied also to Delaiah and Shelemiah at Samaria and mention this to the authorities at Jerusalem, shows that (at any rate as far as they knew) no religious schism had as yet taken place. Both names occur in Nehemiah, and it is not impossible that they denote the same persons as here. They are not said here to be resident at Samaria, and they may have been at Jerusalem in the time of Nehemiah, but of this there is no evidence. After the building of the temple at Shechem it would probably have been impossible.

Yedoniah, who sends the letter, is clearly the head of the community.

Sachau thinks he was not a priest because of the phrase (l. 1) 'Y. and his assessors the priests'. To me the phrase seems to imply exactly the contrary, as if it were 'Y. and the other priests with him', i. e. כהניא is in apposition to both ידניה and כנותה. It is not 'Y. and the priests his assessors'. He is no doubt the same as Yedoniah b. Gemariah in 22[121], since the money there subscribed for the temple would most naturally be paid to the representative of the congregation, and as it was for the use of the temple, he would probably be the head priest. Moreover we have no evidence in these documents that the colony was under an ethnarch (as Sachau), appointed either by themselves or by the government. Nor is it likely. They brought their actions at law before the *fratarak*, or more directly (as soldiers) before the רבחילא, in all civil matters. On the other hand for religious purposes they had priests, and must have had a chief priest, who would be the natural representative of the religious community when acting together as such. The present petition is treated as a religious matter, and Yedoniah therefore has charge of it. The priests his assessors formed with him what would have been in later times the בית דין or ecclesiastical court.

A question which naturally presents itself is, why, if this letter was sent to Jerusalem, was it found in the ruins of Elephantine 2314 years afterwards? The answer seems to be that it was not the letter actually sent, but either a draft or a copy. The former is suggested by the large number of corrections (words inserted above the line, and erasures) and by the appearance of the writing, which is hasty and uncouth, much more so than in most of the other documents. Indeed if the style were not so straightforward and the words so familiar, one would often be in doubt as to the reading. No. 31 is another draft, differing only in detail, but fragmentary, and it is probable that no. 27 is a draft of an earlier petition. No. 31 helps in the elucidation of no. 30, and also shows that the scribe was not very accurate. We may well suppose that the serious step of appealing to the governor of Jerusalem, over the head of Arsames, was not taken without careful consideration, and that a copy (or the corrected draft) of the letter would be kept as a record.

Incidentally the letter seems to show that Bigvai was superior in rank to Arsames, or that they approached him as having more sympathy with the Jews.

Sachau, plate 1, 2. Ungnad, no. 1.

1 אל מראן בגוהי פחת יהוד עבדיך ידניה וכנותה כהניא זי ביב בירתא שלם

2 מראן אלה שמיא ישאל שגיא בכל עדן ולרחמן ישימנך קדם דריוהוש מלכא

3 ובני ביתא יַתִּיר מן זי כען חד אלף וחין אריכן ינתן לך וחדה ושריר הוי בכל עדן

4 כען עבדך ידניה וכנותה כן אמרן בירח תמוז שנת ר//// דריוהוש מלכא כזי ארשם

5 נפק ואזל על מלכא כמריא זי חנוב זי ביב בירתא המונית עם וידרנג זי פרתרך תנה

6 הוה לם אגורא זי יהו אלהא זי ביב בירתא יהעדו מן תמה אחר וידרנג זך

7 לחיא אגרת שלח על נפין ברה זי רבחיל הוה בסון בירתא לאמר אגורא זי ביב

8 בירתא ינדשו אחר נפין דבר מצריא עם חילא אחרנן אתו לבירת יב עם תליהם

9 עלו באגורא זך נדשוהי עד ארעא ועמודיא זי אבנא זי הוו תמה תברו אף הוה תרען

10 זי אבן \/// בנין פסילה זי אבן זי הוו באגורא זך נדשו ודשיהם קימו וציריהם

11 זי דששיא אלך נחש ומטלל עקהן ארז כלא זי עם שירית אשרנא ואחרן זי תמה

12 הוה כלא באשה שרפו ומזרקיא זי זהבא וכספ ומנדעמתא זי הוה באגורא זך כלא לקחו

13 ולנפשהום עבדו ומן יומי מלך מצרין אבהין בנו אגורא זך ביב בירתא וכזי כנבוזי על למצר

14 אגורא זך בנה השכח ואגורי אלהי מצרין כל מגרו ואיש מנדעם באגורא זך לא חבל

15 וכזי כזנה עביד אנחנה עם נשין ובנין שקקן לבשן הוין וצימין ומצלין ליהו מרא שמיא

16 זי החוין בוידרנג זך כלביא הנפקו כבלא מן רגלוהי וכל נכסין זי קנה אבדו וכל גברין

17 זי בעו באיש לאגורא זך כל קטילו וחזין בהום אף קדמת זנה בעדן זי זא באיש

18 עביד לן אגרה שלחן מראן ועל יהוחנן כהנא רבא וכנותה כהניא זי בירושלם ועל אוסתן אחוה

19 זי ענני וחרי יהודיא אגרה חדה לא שלחו עלין אף מן ירח תמוז שנת \///ר דריהוש מלכא

20 ועזנה יומא אנחנה שקקן לבשן וצימין נשיא זילן כארמלה עבידין משח לא משחן

21 וחמר לא שתין אף מן זכי ועד יום שנת \/// ///ר דריהוש מלכא מנחה ולבו[נ]ה ועלוה

22 לא עבדו באגורא זך כען עבדיך ידניה וכנותה ויהודיא כל בעלי יב כן אמרן

23 הן על מראן טב אתעשת על אגורא זך למבנה בזילא שבקן לן למבניה חזי בעלי

זי

24 טבתך ורחמיך תנה במצרין אגרה מנך ישתלח עליהום על אגורא זי יהו אלהא

25 למבניה ביב בירתא לקבל זי בנה הוה קדמין ומחתא ולבונתא ועלותא יקרבון

26 על מדבחא זי יהו אלהא בשמך ונצלה עליך בכל עדן אנחנה ונשין ובנין ויהודיא

27 כל זי תנה הן כן עבדו עד זי אגורא זך יתבנה וצדקה יהוה לך קדם יהו אלה

28 שמיא מן גבר זי יקרבלה עלוה ודבחן דמן כדמי כסף כנכרין ולף ועל זהב
על זנה

בשמן

29 שלחן הודען אף כלא מליא באגרה חדה שלחן על דליה ושלמיה בני סנאבלט
ח
פת שמרין

כלא

30 אף בזנה זי עביד לן ארשם לא ידע ב כ למרחשון שנת ר/// ///\
דריהוש מלכא

[1] To our lord Bigvai, governor of Judaea, your servants Yedoniah and his colleagues, the priests who are in Yeb the fortress. The health [2] of your lordship may the God of Heaven seek after exceedingly at all times, and give you favour before Darius the king [3] and the princes of the palace more than now a thousand times, and may he grant you long life, and may you be happy and prosperous at all times. [4] Now your servant Yedoniah and his colleagues depose as follows: In the month of Tammuz in the 14th year of Darius the king, when Arsames [5] departed and went to the king, the priests of the god Khnub, who is in the fortress of Yeb, (were) in league with Waidrang who was governor here, [6] saying: The temple of Ya'u the God, which is in the fortress of Yeb let them remove from there. Then that Waidrang, [7] the reprobate, sent a letter to his son Nephayan who was commander of the garrison in the fortress of Syene saying: The temple which is in Yeb [8] the fortress let them destroy. Then Nephayan led out the Egyptians with the other forces. They came to the fortress of Yeb with their weapons, [9] they entered that temple, they destroyed it to the ground, and the pillars of stone which were there they broke. Also it happened, 5 gate-ways [10] of stone, built with hewn blocks of stone, which were in that temple they destroyed, and their doors they lifted off (?), and the hinges [11] of those doors were bronze, and the roof of cedar wood, all of it with the rest of the furniture and other things which were there, [12] all of it they burnt with fire, and the basons of gold and silver and everything that was in that temple, all of it, they took [13] and made their own. Already in the days of the kings of Egypt our fathers had built that temple in the fortress of Yeb, and when Cambyses came into Egypt [14] he found that temple built, and the temples of the gods of Egypt all *of them* they overthrew, but no one did any harm to that temple. [15] When this was done, we with our wives and our children put on sack-cloth and fasted and prayed to Ya'u the Lord of Heaven, [16] who let us see (our desire) upon that Waidrang. The dogs tore off the anklet from his legs, and all the riches he had gained were

destroyed, and all the men [17] who had sought to do evil to that temple, all *of them*, were killed and we saw (our desire) upon them. Also before this, at the time when this evil [18] was done to us, we sent a letter *to* your lordship and to Johanan the high priest and his colleagues the priests who are in Jerusalem, and to Ostanes the brother [19] of 'Anani, and the nobles of the Jews. They have not sent any letter to us. Also since the month of Tammuz in the 14th year of Darius the king [20] till this day we wear sack-cloth and fast. Our wives are made widow-like, we do not anoint ourselves with oil [21] and we drink no wine. Also from that (time) till (the present) day in the 17th year of Darius the king, neither meal-offering, incense, nor sacrifice [22] do they offer in that temple. Now your servants Yedoniah and his colleagues and the Jews, all *of them* inhabitants of Yeb, say as follows: [23] If it seem good to your lordship, take thought for that temple to build (it), since they do not allow us to build it. Look upon your [24] well-wishers and friends who are here in Egypt, (and) let a letter be sent from you to them concerning the temple of the God Ya'u [25] to build it in the fortress of Yeb as it was built before, and they shall offer the meal-offering and incense and sacrifice [26] on the altar of the God Ya'u on your behalf, and we will pray for you at all times, we, our wives, our children, and the Jews, [27] all who are here, if they do so that that temple be re-built, and it shall be a merit to you before Ya'u the God of [28] Heaven more than a man who offers to him sacrifice and burnt-offerings worth as much as the sum of a thousand talents. As to gold, about this [29] we have sent (and) given instructions. Also the whole matter we have set forth in a letter in our name to Delaiah and Shelemiah the sons of Sanballat governor of Samaria. [30] Also of all this which was done to us Arsames knew nothing. On the 20th of Marḥeshwan the 17th year of Darius the king.

Line 1. There are traces of a line above, which has been washed off. מראן is the highest title (under the king) used in these texts. פחת יהוד does not occur in the O.T., but פחת יהודה in Hag. 1^1, &c., and פחת יהודיא in Ezra 6^7. יהוד = Judaea commonly in Daniel.

Line 2. אלה ש' ישאל, cf. on 17^1. אלה שמיא often in Ezra and Nehemiah.

Line 3. בני ביתא are the people of the palace, the king's entourage, which had so much influence with him. חד אלף, cf. חד שבעה Dan. 3^{19}. חדה ושריר as in 62^2. הוי the imperative is awkward.

Line 4. There is an erasure (one letter) after אמרן. כזי ארשם נפק as in $27^{2.3}$. It was evidently an important event and his absence may have given the opportunity for this attack. He seems to have been back in Egypt when no. 32 was written.

Line 5. כמריא, cf. 27^3. Correctly used as in the O.T. for priests of a foreign god. המונית as in 27^4, which combines the readings of this passage and 31^5. Here, as in 27^4, it must be an adverb, and a verb is wanted, which was probably forgotten by the writer because the sentence was long. It would be quite in order if he had written אמרין instead of לם in l. 6. In 31[5] the word is not used, and the construction is simple.

Line 6. יהעדו with indefinite subject, 'let them destroy'. אחר a mere conjunction 'then' or 'so'.

Line 7. לחיא has been much discussed. It seems to be a term of reproach, and a participle from לחה a root frequent in these texts. Cf. e.g. Aḥiḳar 138 where גבר לחה is a man who does not honour his parents, and l. 139 לחיתי 'my misfortune'. In the inscription of Nerab 1[10] מות לחה is a 'miserable death' (or the 'death of a wicked man'). It is difficult to find a word to cover all the uses. Here it seems to be almost parenthetical, 'this W. (the villain)' as the later Jews would add ימח שמו. It is strange that it should be used in a formal document, and even stranger in the answer (32[6]), where there was not the same excuse for strong feeling. A title would be more in place, but the suggestion that it is for לוחיא 'tabellarius' is impossible. נפין Nepāyān (Sachau) must have succeeded his father as רבחילא after 416. His head-quarters were at Syene, whereas the *fratarak* was in Yeb (תמה l. 5). אגורא a very important building 'the temple in Y.', but 31[7] adds זי יהו אלהא.

Line 8. ינדשו corresponds to יהעדו in l. 6. It occurs in 27[5.24] and in 31 and 32. Probably = Heb. נתש. אחרנן plural, agrees in sense with חילא, if there is no scribal error. תליהם Sachau cft. Gen. 27[3] (LXX φαρέτρα, Onḳ. 'sword'). It does not occur elsewhere. No. 31[8] has זניהם, and the meaning of both must be 'weapons' in a very general sense.

Line 9. Note the asyndeta, common in Aramaic, but perhaps also used here for greater vividness. הוה Sachau takes this as introducing the sentence, like Hebrew ויהי, and this is no doubt simplest. But cf. the use of איתי 27[4], &c., which is perhaps similar. תרען are 'gate-ways' of solid stone.

Line 10. בנין may be a participle, but more probably the noun 'a construction of'. דשיהם 'doors' as in Targum. In l. 11 דשיא. קימו so Hoonacker (p. 41, note e). Sachau קימן, but ן always has a projection at the top. The ו is carelessly written. The expression is strange 'they stood the doors up', i.e. leaned them against the wall to burn them, or 'lifted' them off their hinges? Barth's suggestion קיםן 'wood' is impossible. A confusion of ם with מ would be easy in some later kinds of square Hebrew, but is impossible in this writing. Moreover as עק is used in the next line, a different word would hardly be used here, especially as it does not occur elsewhere in these texts. Finally קיסא means rough, unworked wood, sticks, &c., quite unsuitable in this context.

Line 11. דששיא (an erasure of one letter before it). The singular must have dagesh (רשׁא) which is resolved in the plural, as in עממיא and (l. 15) שקקן. נחש, the material in apposition to צירידם, as probably בנין in l. 10. עקהן, so Sachau, as in 31^{10}, an impossible form. Ungnad cft. שמהן (= שמות, but שמהת 22^{1}) אבהן (= אבות), but these are feminine forms, whereas עק is masculine, with plural עקן (עקיא, &c.). The ן looks like a mere blot here, and may have been erroneously copied in 31^{10}. כלא זי. The זי is not wanted, or תמה הוה is omitted. ואחרן. Torczyner 'und zuletzt alles was dort war', but it is more probably used loosely for 'other (things)' 'the rest'.

Line 12. וכסף a mistake for וכספא. מנדעמתא 'anything', i.e. everything. כלא note the repetition (3 times in 2 lines) to emphasize the completeness of the destruction.

Line 13. מן 'beginning from' i.e. already in. מלך a mistake for מלכי (so 31^{12}). אבהין a strange form, but confirmed by 31^{13}. We should expect אבהתן. למצרין. The ין is added above the line because there was not room. Cf. ll. 12, 17, 18, &c. Cambyses came into Egypt in 525.

Line 14. השכח as in 31^{13}. A final ה was written and erased. באגורא is the complement to חבל 'did harm to this temple' and מנדעם is adverbial 'in anything'—not 'harmed anything in this temple'.

Line 15. עביד as in 31^{14}, not עבדו as Sachau and Ungnad. צימין a mistake for צימן? So l. 20. מרא שמיא as Dan. 5^{23}.

Line 16. החוין Haphel (in 31^{15} חוינא Pael) 'caused us to see', Heb. הראנו, of seeing vengeance inflicted on an enemy. Cf. חזין l. 17. כלביא וכ׳ a very difficult phrase. הנפקו is 'took out', which Hoonacker explains as an inversion 'they took out the chains from his feet' for 'his feet from the chains', cf. Heb. גֻּלָּה. With רגלוהי the meaning of כבלא must be a ring worn as an ornament, though its later meaning is usually 'fetter'. No. 31^{15} כבלוהי. It has been proposed to take כלביא as 'dog-like', a term of abuse applied to Waidrang, which is improbable. The phrase has not yet been satisfactorily explained.

Line 17. כל. 31^{16} כלא. זא feminine as in 21^{3}.

Line 18. עביד ought to be fem. See on ll. 24, 27. אגרה as in l. 19 for the usual אגרת, a loan-word from Bab. *egirtu*. (But cf. ἄγγαρος, from Persian.) It is a secondary form developed in Aramaic when the consciousness of its origin was beginning to be lost. Cf. perhaps דנה for דנת in 10^{23}. The letter may have been no. 27. Then מראן there is

Bigvai. מראן, cf. 31^{17}. על is omitted by mistake. אוֹסתן is confirmed by 31^{18}.

Line 19. ענני an important person, since Ostanes is described as his brother, not as son of any one. He seems to be settled at Jerusalem, and therefore is hardly the same as the secretary Anani in 26^{23}. Whether he is the Anani of 1 Chron. 3^{24} there is nothing to show. דריהוש, and in l. 21, probably only a mistake for דריוהוש 31^{19}.

Line 20. ועזנה corrected by a ר above the line, suggests that in popular pronunciation the ר was assimilated to the ז. Cf. עדבר 45^{3} for על ד׳ and Dan. 4^{14} עד־דברת (Epstein). בארמלה one would expect the plural. עבידין. A mistake for the feminine (due to the masc. form of נשיא?). משחין. The י is blotted. If it is to be read, it is a mistake for משחן as 31^{20}.

Line 21. זכי is certain, but must be a mistake. It is the form used in addressing a female, and in any case מן זך could not mean 'from that time'. In 31^{20}, מן זך עדנא. ועד. Note the ע, which shows how the tail developed. ועד יום very awkward. Either we want ועד יומא זנה זי (Ungnad), or perhaps ועד יומי. ועלוה (= Heb. עולה) does not occur in BA, but may be inferred from the plural עלון (sing. עלתא later) which is found in Ezra as well as מנחה.

Line 22. עבדו. The ו is probable though the lower parts of the letters are effaced. The passage is defective also in 31^{21}. We should expect עבדן. יהודיא used like ישראל in late Hebrew for an ordinary member of the community who is not a כהן or a חכם. כל, in 31^{22} כלא. אמרין. The ין is blundered. 31^{22} אמרן correctly. It is a participle.

Line 23. למבנה probably a mistake for למבניה. שבקן. The subject is 'the Egyptians'. 'They do not leave us alone to build it', i. e. do not allow us. חזי is confirmed by 31^{23}. Not an interjection (as Ungnad), but 'look upon your friends', parallel to אתעשת על אגורא. Cf. e. g. ראה עניי, Ps. $25^{18,19}$.

Line 24. ישתלח should be fem. Cf. יהוה l. 27. Ungnad compares the old Babylonian usage.

Line 25. ומחתא a mistake for ומנחתא. יקרבון is written over an erasure of a word beginning with יה. 31^{25} נקרב. 'They will offer' (future) not 'let them offer', jussive, which would be יקרבו.

Line 26. There is a spot of ink after יהו, which one is tempted to take for the beginning of a ה, but it is more likely to be a false start for אלהא. With נצלה עליך cf. Ezra 6^{10} (Jampel).

Line 27. כל in 31^{26} again כלא. עבדו perhaps a mistake for עבדת 'si ita feceris'. In 31^{26} תעבד 'si ita facies'. עד זי 'until', i. e. so that. וצדקה not ו of the apodosis, as Ungnad. The *if*-clause goes with what precedes, and this begins a new sentence. צדקה, a righteous or meritorious act (because conferring a benefit). One wonders what Bigvai understood by it. Cf. Deut. 24^{13}.

Line 28. מן, as first shown by Bruston, is comparative, 'more than', but the sentence is clumsy in spite of Sachau's illustrations. דמן כדמי 'in value like the value of' is surely a mistake, and דמן should be omitted, as in 31^{27}. ולף = אלף as in 31^{27}, and often. ועל זהב וכ׳. Epstein makes על a noun meaning a large amount, and cft. עליתא, e.g. in Baba B. 133^{b}, but the meaning there is uncertain, and there is no evidence for על in that sense. Also 31^{27} omits ו which makes it impossible. Clearly the reference is to the bakhshish, which they would of course expect to pay, but about which it would be polite to write as little as possible. That Bigvai was not above such considerations we see from Jos. Ant. xi, 7, 1, where he is said to have exacted 50 shekels for every lamb sacrificed. This seems to have been after the murder of Jeshua, and therefore after the date of this letter, so that there can hardly be an allusion to it here. The mention of the value of the sacrifices however is strange.

Line 29. שלחן הודען probably asyndeton, 'we have sent, we have made known', and אף begins a new sentence. Hoonacker translates 'nous avons instruit notre envoyé'. This would be excellent, but 'messenger' would certainly be שליח. It may be a mistake for that. The parallel passage in no. 31 is lost. Cf. Ezra 4^{14} (Jampel). דליה ושלמיה. Both names occur in Nehemiah (6^{10}, 13^{3}), but there is no evidence for identifying the persons, nor for assuming that these lived at Jerusalem. A Delaiah occurs (once only) in the Samaritan list of High Priests, possibly about this date. (See Cowley, *Samaritan Liturgy*, p. xx, note 1.) סנאבלט, in Nehemiah סנבלט. Cf. סנחריב = סנאחריב. The name is Babylonian, though his sons' names are Jewish. פחת = σατράπης, the title used by Josephus. He is never called so by Nehemiah. שמרין as in Ezra $4^{10,17}$, where it is the name of the city or district (Heb. שמרון), and so probably here. The Samaritans still use שמרין as a gentilic name for themselves (Heb. שמרונים).

Line 30. בלא in 30^{29} comes before זי, better. עביד לן as in l. 18, 'done to us'. ארשם לא ידע because he was away at the time (ll. 4, 5). They do not wish to accuse him to his superior. It might be dangerous. ב though not certain, is probable.

The many mistakes, solecisms and corrections in this text, and the frequent Hebraisms here and elsewhere, give the impression that the writer was not really at home with Aramaic as a means of expressing himself. Although no Hebrew document is found in this collection, it is not impossible that these Jews commonly spoke Hebrew among themselves. They would be compelled to use Aramaic in business transactions, as the language of the Government, and as long as composition was confined to legal documents, with their familiar set phrases, they could manage it well enough. But they came to regard it as the natural vehicle for literary expression, letters, &c., and when they went outside the legal formulae, the task was beyond their powers. They no doubt understood it, since they had Aḥiḳar and the Behistun inscription in Aramaic translations (not made by the Jews of Yeb). It may have been necessary to use Aramaic in writing to Bigvai, and of course Johanan would be quite familiar with it.

The question of the use of the two languages by the Jews is of some importance, though the conclusions reached by Naville do not seem to be justified.

No. 31.

A Duplicate of No. 30. *Same date.*

A fragment of a duplicate of no. 30, perhaps copied from it.

It has been torn lengthwise down the middle, so that the ends of all the lines are missing. The writing, though not good, is better than that of no. 30, and it has fewer mistakes. In some places it helps to elucidate no. 30. The lines have not been completed in the transcript here, since that would be merely repeating the other copy.

Ll. 27–29 are on the verso.

The date is the same as that of no. 30, viz. 408 B.C.

Sachau, plate 3. Ungnad, no. 3.

1 אל מ[ראן בגוהי פחת יהוד עבדיך ידניה וכנות]ה כה[ניא
2 אלה [שמיא י]שאל בכל עדן לרחמן י[שי]מ[נך קדם ד]ריוהוש [
3 אריכן ינתן לך וחדה ושריר הוי בכל עדן כעת עב[ד]ך ידניה [
4 שנת ר///\ דריוהוש מלכא כזי ארשם נפק ואזל [על] מלכא [
5 בירתא כסף ונכסין יהבו לוידרנג פרתרכא זי תנה הוה ל[ם
אחר
6 יהעדו מן תמה וידרנג זך לחיא אגרת שלח על נ[פי]ן ברה זי
7 זי יהו אלהא זי ביב בירתא ינדשו אחר נפין זך דבר מצר[יא
8 זניהום עלו באגורא זך נדשוהי עד ארעא ועמודיא זי א[בנא

9 תרען רברבן /// // בנין פסלה זי אבן זי הוו בא[גו]רא זך [

10 אלך נחש ומטלל אנורא זך כלא עקהן זי ארז עם ש[ירית

11 באשתא שרפו ומזרקיא זי זהבא וזי כספא ו[מנד]עמתא [

12 עבדו ומן יום מלכי מצרין אבהין בנו אגורא זך ביב [

13 זך בנה השכח ואגורי אלה[י] מצריא [כ]ל[א מגרו] ואיש מנ[דעם

14 עביד אנהנה עם כשין ובנין שקקן לבשן הוין צ[ימין

15 חוינא בוידרנג זך כלביא הנפקו כבלוהי מן רגלוהי וכ[ל

16 בעה באיש לאגורא זך כלא קטילו וחזין בהום אף [

17 לן אגרה על זנה של[..] שלחן על מראן א[ף] על יהוחנן [

18 ועל אוסתן אחוהי זי ענני וחרי יהוד אנ[רה] חדה [

19 שנת ר///\ דריוהוש מלכא ועד זנה יומא אנחנה שקק[ן

20 משח לא משחן וחמר לא שתין [אף מ]ן זך ע[דנ]א ועד ז[נה

21 מנחה לבונה ועלוה לא עבדו באגורא זך כען [

22 ויהודיא כלא בעלי יב כן אמרן הן על מר[א]ן טב א[תעשת

23 שבקן לן למבניה חזי בעלי טבתך ורחמיך זי תנה [

24 על אגורא זי יהו אלהא למבניה ביב בירתא לקבל [

25 ועלותא נקרב על מדבחא זי יהו אלהא בשמך ונצ[לה

26 ויהודיא כלא זי תנה הן כן תעבד זי עד אגורא זך ית[בנה

27 שמיא מן גבר זי יקרב לה עלוה ודבחן דמי כסף כנכרן אלף על [

28 מליא אגרה חדה בשמן שלחן על דליה ושלמיה ב[ני

29 כלא זי עביד לן ארשם לא ידע ב ד למרחשון שנת ר/// [///\

[1] To *our* lord *Bigvai, governor of Judaea, your servants Yedoniah and* his *colleagues the* priests . . . [2] God of *Heaven* seek after at all times. May he *give you* favour *before D*arius . . . [3] May he grant you long *life*, and may you be happy and prosperous at all times. Now your serv*ant* Yedoniah . . . [4] Year 14 of Darius the king, when Arsames departed and went *to* the king . . . [5] The fortress. They gave money and valuables to Waidrang the governor who was here, sa*ying* . . . [6] let them remove from there. Then that Waidrang, the reprobate, sent a letter to his son Ne*pha*yan, who . . . [7] of Ya'u the God, which is in the fortress of Yeb, let them destroy. Then that Nephayan led out *the* Egypt*ians* . . . [8] their weapons. They went into that temple. They destroyed it to the ground, and the pillars of s*tone* . . . [9] 5 great gateways, built of hewn stone, which were in that te*mp*le . . . [10] those, of bronze, and the roof of that temple, all of it, of cedar wood, with the res*t* . . . [11] they burnt with fire, and the basons of gold and of silver and *every*thing . . . [12] they made. Already in the day of the kings of Egypt our fathers had built that temple in Yeb . . . [13] He found that built, and the temples of the gods of the Egyptians all *of them they overthrew*, but

no one did any . . . [14] was done, we with our wives and our children have been wearing sack-cloth, fa*sting* . . . [15] let us see (our desire) on that Waidrang. The dogs tore off his anklets from his legs and a*ll* . . . [16] sought to do evil to that temple, all of them, were killed and we saw (our desire) upon them. Also . . . [17] to us, we sent a letter about this . . . to your lordship a*nd* to Johanan . . . [18] and to Ostanes the brother of 'Anani, and the nobles of Judaea. A let*ter* . . . [19] Year 14 of King Darius till this day we *wear* sack-c*loth* . . . [20] we do not anoint ourselves with oil and we drink no wine. *Also fro*m that *tim*e till t*his* . . . [21] meal-offering, incense nor sacrifice do they offer in that temple. Now . . . [22] and the Jews all of them, citizens of Yeb, say as follows: If it seem good to your lords*hi*p, t*ake thought* . . . [23] allow us to build it. Look upon your well-wishers and friends who are here . . . [24] concerning the temple of the God Ya'u to build it in the fortress of Yeb as . . . [25] and the sacrifice we will offer on the altar of the God Ya'u on your behalf, and we will p*ray* . . . [26] and all the Jews who are here, if you do so that that temple be *re-built* . . . [27] Heaven, more than a man who offers to him sacrifice and burnt-offerings worth the sum of a thousand talents. As to . . . [28] matter, we have sent a letter in our name to Delaiah and Shelemiah the *sons of* . . . [29] all that was done to us Arsames knew nothing. On the 20th of Marḥeshwan the 17th year . . .

Line 2. לרחמן. No ו before it. The text must have been shorter than in 30^{3}, probably omitting יתיר מן זי כען חד אלף.

Line 5. The word המונית (30^{5}) is not used here, and the sentence is simpler.

Line 8. זניהום = תליהם (30^{8}) of which it shows the meaning.

Line 9. רברבן. 30^{10} has זי אבן which is not wanted, since it occurs just afterwards, and is probably a mistake. פסלה. In 30^{10} פסילה is more correct.

Line 10. עקהן is quite clear here. Copied from 30^{11} in error? The unnecessary זי before עם is omitted.

Line 11, end. זי is probable. Sachau ל, but the mark is too low, and is unintentional.

Line 12. יום. In 30^{13} better יומי. מלכי is better than מלך 30^{13}.

Line 13. There is room for כלא which would be right.

Line 15. חוינא Pael = החוין 30^{16}. After כלביא the next word begins on a slightly different level, which looks as though the writer was conscious of beginning a new clause. If so כלביא must qualify what went before. Cf. note on 30^{16}.

Line 16. בעה shows that כל גבר preceded—a mistake, since the sentence goes on with a plural. 30^{16} correctly גברן and בעו.

Line 17. . . של perhaps שלחן repeated by mistake, but it looks more like שלנך.

Line 18. יהור Judaea, in 30^{19} יהוריא.

Line 19. דריוהוש correctly. 30^{19} דריהוש, which thus seems to be a mere mistake.

Line 20. משחן correctly, for the doubtful משחין in 30^{20}. זך ערנא better than זכי 30^{21}. At the end a trace of ז probably. זנה is better than יום 30^{21}.

Line 21. עברו is not more certain here than in 30^{22}.

Line 22. אמרן correctly. 30^{22} אמרין is a mistake.

Line 25. נקרב, in 30^{25} יקרבון.

Line 26. הן כן. There seems to be a slight additional space before this, as though it began a new sentence. חעבר is better than עברו 30^{27}. זי עד a mistake for עד זי.

Line 27. דמי more correctly than 30^{28}.

Line 28. אגרה = באגרה 30^{29}. Perhaps the construction was different, e.g. 'concerning all this we sent a letter'.

Line 29. כלא better here than as in 30^{30}. ב ב is certain here.

No. 32.

Answer to No. 30. *About* 408 B. C.

Complete, but carelessly written. The lines vary in length and are irregularly spaced.

This is the answer to the petition in 30, 31. Though not dated, we may assume that it was brought back by the messenger in 408. Apparently the answer was given verbally and this is a note of it made by the messenger. The first three lines are crowded together and parts of them look as though written at a different time from the rest. Judging from this impression, one would say that the text originally began with l. 2:

זכרן לם יהוי לך במצרין
על בית מדבחא זי אלה

i.e. with the actual message. Then the writer felt that something was wanted to show from whom the message came, and he added l. 1 with a thicker pen, and the words projecting at the end of l. 2 and beginning of l. 3. This would account for the repetition of זכרן, which is otherwise unnecessary. The report is not a formal answer, for no titles are given to Bigvai and Delaiah, and it is not addressed to any one. It is not composed by a skilled scribe, for the contents are ill-balanced: ll. 5–7 are unnecessarily full, and the really important part, rather clumsily expressed, occupies only ll. 8–11.

Sachau, plate 4. Ungnad, no. 3.

זכרן זי בגוהי ודליה אמרו
לי זכרן לם יהוי לך במצרין למםר
קדםארשם עלבית מדבחא זי אלה
שמיא זי ביב בירתא בנה
הוה מן קדמן קדם כנבוזי
זי וידרנג להיא זך נדש
בשנת ר///\ דריוהוש מלכא
למבניה באתרה כזי הוה לקדמן
ומנחתא ולבונתא יקרבון על
מדבחא זך לקבל זי לקדמין
הוה מתעבד

[1] Memorandum from Bigvai and Delaiah. They said [2] to me: Let it be an instruction to you in Egypt to say [3] to Arsames about the altar-house of the God of [4] Heaven, which was built in the fortress of Yeb [5] formerly, before Cambyses, [6] which Waidrang, that reprobate, destroyed [7] in the 14th year of Darius the king, [8] to rebuild it in its place as it was before, [9] and they may offer the meal-offering and incense upon [10] that altar as formerly [11] was done.

Line 1. זכרן 'a record' (cf. Ezra 6[2]) or perhaps a 'thing to be remembered', as it seems to have meant in l. 2 if that was the original beginning. The זי is 'of', not 'which'. That would be זי אמרו לי בגוהי וכ'.

Line 2. לי is by the thicker pen, projects beyond the line, and is smudged as though something were erased. לם here only a strengthening particle, as in Aḥiḳar 2, 13, 20 &c., not 'saying'. יהוי the jussive form, 'let it be a thing to be remembered, to say', i.e. remember to say. למםר no doubt for למאמר, for which more commonly לאמר. Something has been erased, and the unusual form is perhaps due to his having originally written לם קדם. Then he erased קדם and wrote מר. He probably intended to write לאמר.

Line 3. קדם ארשם project into the margin, and were clearly added later. There are traces of על under (אר)שם. The order is to be given to Arsames, who thus appears to have had no power (or will) to build the temple on his own authority. He must also have been inferior in rank to Bigvai. One would have expected something more formal than this rather off-hand verbal instruction. בית מדבחא. It is not clear why he uses this expression instead of אגורא. Epstein takes it as 'house of sacrifice'. After אלה he had begun to write שמיא and then erased it.

Line 5. מן קדמן 'from of old', i. e. long ago.

Line 6. לחיא as in 30[17], an odd word to use in a document of this kind, but all the passage (ll. 5–7) seems unnecessary. Between this line and the next there is extra space, but nothing is missing.

Line 8. למבניה. The construction, depending on למאמר, is very loose. He had apparently forgotten what his main verb was.

Line 9. Note that עלותא is omitted—no doubt intentionally. It is generally supposed that the animal sacrifices had offended the Egyptians, and that this was sufficient to make Bigvai discountenance them, apart from any view which the priests at Jerusalem might hold, and with which Bigvai might or might not sympathize. But as Ed. Meyer points out (*Papyrusfund*, p. 88), the Egyptians did themselves sacrifice certain animals, and he thinks that the prohibition was due to the Zoroastrian view that fire was profaned by contact with dead bodies. יקרבון i. e. so that they may offer. The word is written over an erasure. Perhaps the passive was originally written. It was a longer word, since a ן is visible at the end.

Line 11. מתעבד. I have translated 'done' for want of a better term. It is really a cult-word, עבד meaning to perform a religious act.

No. 33.

A further Petition, connected with No. 30. *About* 407 B.C.

Much injured on the left-hand side, and the ends of the last four lines entirely lost.

It is a letter from five prominent men of the colony at Yeb, relating to the rebuilding of the temple, and may therefore be dated at about the same time as nos. 30–32. Like them, it is no doubt a draft, or a copy kept for reference, since there is no address or signature. The writing is excellent, and certainly not by the same hand as no. 32, as Sachau says.

The mention of the bakhshish in ll. 13, 14 suggests that it was sent to Bigvai (cf. 30[28]), who is denoted by מראן in ll. 7, 12, 13, but it is quite possible that they had to bribe more than one official. This may have been a private letter sent (על זהב 30[28]) with no. 30, or it may have been sent after receipt of the answer (no. 32) as Ed. Meyer thinks. Unfortunately the broken lines at the end do not show very clearly what they want to say about the question of the sacrifices.

Sachau, plate 4. Ungnad, no. 4.

עבדיך ידניה בר ג[מריה] ישמה ا
מעוזי בר נתן ישמה [ا]
שמעיה בר חגי ישמה ا
הושע בר יתום שמה ا
הושע בר נתון שמה ا כל גברן ااا اا
סונכנן זי ביב בירתא [מ]ה[חס]נן
כן אמרן הן מראן [ירח]מן
ואגורא זי יהו אלהא זי[לן יתבנה
ביב בירתא כזי קד[מן בנ]ה הוה
וקן תור ענז מקלו [ל]א יתעבד תמה
להן לבונה מנחה [ונסך . . .
ומראן אודים יעב[ד עלונה אחר
ננתן על בית מראן כ[סף . . . . ואף
שערן ארדבן אל[ף

[1] Your servants Yedoniah b. *Gemariah* by name, 1. [2] Ma'uzi b. Nathan by name, 1. [3] Shemaiah b. Haggai by name, 1. [4] Hosea b. Yathom by name, 1. [5] Hosea b. Nathun by name, 1: total 5 men, [6] Syenians who *hold property* in the fortress of Yeb, [7] say as follows: If your lordship is *favourable* [8] and the temple of Ya'u the God which *we had* (?) *be rebuilt* (?) [9] in the fortress of Yeb as it was form*erly built*, [10] and sheep, oxen (and) goats are *not* offered as burnt-sacrifice there, [11] but incense, meal-offering *and drink-offering only*, [12] and (if) your lordship giv*es* orders *to that effect, then* [13] we will pay to your lordship's house the *sum of* . . . . *and also* [14] a thous*and* ardabs of barley.

Line 1. [מריה]ג. There is a trace of מ. This is no doubt the same Yedoniah as in 22^{121} and 30^{1}. Cf. the names in 34^{5}.

Line 2. מעוזי = מעוזיה 18^{3}, 20^{16}.

Line 6. סונכנן a Persian formation from סון, declined as Aramaic. They belonged to Syene, i. e. to *degalin* stationed there, but held property in Elephantine. [מ]ה[חס]נן is very probable.

Line 7. [ירח]מן. The מן is probable. Some word of this kind is wanted after הן מראן, cf. 27^{19} &c. On the form cf. אשבקן Aḥiḳar 82 (not 'pity *us*').

Line 8. זי[לן יתבנה] perhaps. Epstein's proposal זי ישמיא יתבנה is too long, and the phrase is always אלה שמיא not אלהא זי ש׳.

Line 9. [בנ]ה is right, and קד[מן] is necessary. The stroke before הוה belongs to the line above, therefore not יהוה.

Line 10. וקן. The ו means 'on the understanding that'. קן תור. At first sight one would take these as 'birds and dove'. (So Bondi who compares the use of קן in Mishna.) But as ענז is added קן is probably for עאן = צאן, and תור is 'ox'. מקלו. The form is strange (from √קלה). It is no doubt borrowed from Bab. *maḳlu(tu)*, 'burnt-sacrifice'.

Line 11. Animal sacrifice was not to be offered, whether out of consideration for Persian or Egyptian feeling, but incense and meal-offerings were unobjectionable. מנחה, without ו, may imply a third term—perhaps נסך 'drink-offering' (but cf. l. 10). There is a trace possibly of the ך, and of another word.

Line 12 seems to be still part of the long protasis, introduced by הן in l. 7, 'and if you give orders accordingly'. אוריס not a name (as Ungnad), which would not fit in. Ed. Meyer proposes Persian *avadaesa*, which he translates 'information'. It must be something of the kind, an official term for 'edict'. It is quite uncertain how much is lost at the end of the line, but something (אחר or אנחנה) is wanted to introduce the apodosis in l. 13.

Line 13. Ungnad reads נתן, but that is only used in the future, and the נ is never assimilated. The strange character at the beginning is really נכ, rendered illegible by the crack in the papyrus. כ[סף] probably. The amount is quite lost. At the end ואף is wanted as there is no conjunction with שערן (l. 14).

No. 34.

A Letter. Probably about 407 B.C.

Fragment of the end of a letter.

Though little can be made out consecutively, it certainly relates to some violence done to Yedoniah and his colleagues, some of whom are the same as in no. 33. As no mention is made of this in the preceding texts, the fragment would seem to be later than those. The statement that houses were entered and goods taken, indicates a renewal of the pogrom described in no. 30. It is perhaps not too rash to conclude that it took place after the receipt of Bigvai's answer (no. 32) and was due to some action taken by the Jews in the way of preparations for the rebuilding of the temple. The date would then be in or soon after 407 B.C. There is no evidence to show that the temple ever was re-built, and the series of documents stops very soon after this, as far as we can judge. Egypt was getting into a very unsettled state, and apparently threw off the Persian yoke in or about 404 B.C. (cf. no. 35). It may well be that the Egyptians took the opportunity of the prevailing unrest to get rid of the Jewish garrison, and began by making away with (or killing ?) the chief men of the colony.

The writing is unskilful. Perhaps it is not an official document but a private letter. It may have been sent from some other place, e.g. Thebes, to Yeb.

Sachau, plate 15. Ungnad, no. 16.

1 . . . . כוש

2 . . . . הנום הא זנה שמהת נשיא זי א[שתכחו

3 בבבא בנא ואתחדו א[סירן רמי אתת הודו אסרשות אתת הושע פלול אתת יסלח רעיא [. . . . .]

4 צביא ברת משלם יכולא אחתה הא שמהת גבריא זי אשתכחו בבבא בנא ואתחד[ו אסירן]

5 ידניא בר גמריה הושע בר יתום הושע בר נתום חגי אחוהי אחיו בר מח[סיה . . . . .]

6 בתיא זי עלו בהן ביב ונכסיא זי לקחו אתבו אם על מריהם להן דכרו למרא[. . . בסף]

7 כרשן / לי ד עוד טעם לא עד יהוי להן תנה שלם ביתך ובניך עד אלהיא יחוונ[א בהן]

1, 2 . . . . khnum, now these are the names of the women who were *found* 3 *at the gate in Thebes* (?) *and were taken pri*soners: Rami, wife of Hodav, Asirshuth, wife of Hosea, Pelul, wife of Yislaḥ, Re'ia . . . . . . 4 Zebia, daughter of Meshullam, Yekhola her sister. These are the names of the men who were found at the gate in Thebes (?) and *were* taken *prisoners:* 5 Yedonia b. Gemariah, Hosea b. Yathom, Hosea b. Nathum, Haggai his brother, Ahio b. M*ahseiah* (?). *They have left* (?) 6 the houses which they had entered in Yeb, and the property which they had taken they have restored indeed to the owners of it, but they mentioned (?) to his lordship *the sum of* 7 120 kerashin. Moreover they will have no further authority here. Peace be to your house and your children till the gods let *us* see (our desire) *upon them.*

Line 1. Only the lower parts of a few letters remain, which cannot be re-constructed.

Line 2. חנום. The marks preceding it may be פט. The name Petehnum occurs in 23[9]. זנה שמהת as in 22[1]. א[שתכחו] and the beginning of l. 3 may be perhaps so restored from l. 4.

Line 3. [א]סירן is more probable than to assume a name סירן (Ungnad). רמי a short form of רמיה, as הודו of הודויה. אסרשות

compounded with Osiris. Hosea had married an Egyptian. פלול cf. פלוליה.

Line 4. צביא very doubtful. Cf. צבי. משלם. There is very little space for ל, but we can hardly read anything else. יבולא doubtful. Ungnad קולא. Sachau כרולא. בנא 'in No', i.e. Thebes? So Epstein, but he afterwards suggests it is for בנה, and thinks it is the gate in the wall mentioned in 27^{6}, but the word is too common to serve as a clue. Why were they found in (or at) the gate anywhere? בב no doubt means here the 'gateway' which served as a court of justice, and may also have contained a prison (cf. e.g. Aḥiḳar 23). But it is not evident what had happened to them. אתחר[ו], as Epstein, for אתאחרו, is possible. Cf. למסר 32^{2}, במכל 24^{35}. Sachau אתחר[בו] 'were killed'. Arnold אתחר[פו] 'were insulted'.

Line 5. The same persons as in $33^{1.4.5}$. נתום for נתון, influenced by יתום just before. מח[סיה] very doubtful. The second letter is unrecognizable. After the name a word is wanted to govern בתיא in l. 6, e.g. 'they left' or 'they made good'.

Line 6. זי עלו בהן. Sachau 'which they entered with them', i.e. into which they brought them (the women). This is impossible, for עלו requires ב before the place entered (cf. e.g. 30^{9}). He takes בהן as being necessarily the feminine pronoun. The only possible translation is 'the houses into which they entered', and בהן must be = BA בְּהוֹן, masc. (cf. מנהן 16^{4}) as בהם = בהום. It is strange that both forms should occur in the same text, but the change from ם to ן, which prevailed in all branches of Aramaic, must have begun at some time. This letter shows signs of being written informally, which might account for what was perhaps at first a vulgarism. That the distinction between final ם and ן was not very clearly marked at this date is illustrated by נתום for נתון in l. 5. The ם (in the pronoun) was however the earlier, and not merely due to Hebrew influence, since it is found at Senjirli (e.g. Bar-rekub, ll. 18, 19). In 82^{11} בהן is perhaps masculine. The feminine does not occur, I think, in these texts. אתבו can only be Aphel of תוב, although an Aphel is not found elsewhere in these texts. (Ithpe'el for Hithp. does occur). Perhaps it is another instance of a late form in this letter. אם not as in Hebrew (as Ungnad). Others take it as a mistake for הם, which would be simplest. The reading is certain, and, if right, may be the same as the אם in 13^{11}. If so, it is probably a distinct particle, and not, as explained there, a mistake for אפם. מריהם for מראיהם = בעליהם 'the owners of them'. דכרו not דברו (as Ungnad). Epstein cft. ذكرب = 'rem tribuit', and so 'paid', but I do not know this meaning.

It is strange to have ד׳ instead of ז׳, cf. זכרן $32^{1 \cdot 2}$, יזכרני Aḥiḳar 53, but also דכר 'male' $15^{17 \cdot 20}$ דכי &c. The sense is quite obscure—'reminded'? . . . למרא. The restoration ־יהם is possible, but the two spellings so near together are unlikely. Possibly למראן, another case of bribing the governor. [כסף] is wanted before כרשן, l. 7.

Line 7. עוד וכ׳ is very difficult. The clause seems to end with חנה, the succeeding words being the final salutation. The עד after לא is for עוד (written fully when it stands alone) and לחן (like בהן l. 6) is 'to them'. טעם properly 'edict' or 'order'. Here 'authority'? 'power to act'? יחוונ[א] Pael or syncopated Haphel, cf. החוין 30^{16}. The suffix should be ן, but there is a slight trace of א, perhaps another approach to the forms of BA; cf. 31^{15} חוינא.

This is the end of the letter, as the rest of the papyrus is blank.

No. 35.

Contract for a Loan. About 400 B.C.

Very much broken. The largest fragment, containing the beginning, can be fairly well restored. The small fragments cannot be put together. The text must have been long, since the small pieces mention other matters besides the debt of 2 shekels. They must belong to the latter part of the document, after a gap.

Before ll. 1, 3, 5, 10 a thick line is drawn half across the page. The meaning of this is not evident.

This is the latest of the *dated* documents, if (as no doubt is the case) Amyrtaeus is the man who rebelled against Persia shortly before 400 B.C. There was indeed an earlier Amyrtaeus who rebelled under Artaxerxes I, but he only succeeded in establishing himself temporarily in the north, and there are perhaps other indications of the later date (see notes). The later Amyrtaeus cannot have been reigning as early as 408 (at least in Yeb) since we have documents of that year dated in the reign of Darius. Ungnad is therefore probably right in putting the 5th year at about 400 B.C.

This seems to be a case arising out of a marriage settlement, and the parties appear to have been husband and wife—perhaps divorced. The man owes the woman 2 shekels, which he promises to pay by a certain date. The large fragment seems to end with the customary promise not to make further claims, but the formulae must have differed from those used elsewhere. Hence some of the restoration is uncertain.

Sachau, plate 34. Ungnad, no. 37.

1 ב כ֗/ [לפמנ]חתף שנת /// // אמורטיס מלכא אדין
2 אמר [מנחם] בר [של]ום ארמי זי יב ברתא לדגל נבוכדרי
3 לסלו[אה] ברת ס[מ]וח לאמר איתי לכי עלי כסף ש׳ //
4 הו [כס]ף֗ סתתרי / מן קצת כספא ונכסיא זי עלספר
5 אנתותכי אנה מנחם אנתננה ואשלמנלכי עד
6 כ֗ ד לפרמתי שנת /// // אמו[רט]יס מלכא [הן ל]א
7 [שלמת] ויהבת לכי כספא זנה [ש]קלן // [הו] סתתר[י /]
8 [עד יומא] זנה זי מנעל כתיב [ומ]טא ב[/ לפ]חנס
9 [יעקף] כספכי [זנה] כסף שק[לן //] הו כס[ף סתת]רי /
10 [ואנתננלכי] א[נת] כלואה [כספ]כי וא[. . . כס]פכי
11 . . . . . . כל ע֗ד [הן ר]שתכ[י ורשת] לב[ר

f.	e.	d.	c.	b.
. . . .	. . . .	תנק	ין	תֿמֿ ח
כֿם ש	בֿגו	דין א	שערן	זנה כי
. . ע .		ל כל	שקלן ///	שה לא
. .		א	. לסגן	ידֿ
			כספ	א
			מנ	

[1] On the 21st (?) *of Phamen*oth, year 5 of Amyrtaeus the king at that time [2] said *Menahem* b. *Shal*om, Aramaean of Yeb the fortress, of the detachment of Nabukudurri, [3] to Sallu*a* daughter of Sa*m*uah, as follows: You have a claim on me for the sum of 2 shekels, [4] that is the *sum* of 1 stater, being part of the money and goods which are (prescribed) in the deed [5] of your marriage. I, Menahem, will give it and pay you in full by [6] the 30th of Pharmuthi, year 5 of King Amy*rt*aeus. *If* I have *not* [7] *paid off* and given to you this sum of 2 *she*kels, *that is* 1 stater [8] *by the* said *day* which is written above, *and it c*ome to *the 1st* (?) *of* Pa*ḥ*ons, [9] *this* your money, the sum of 2 shek*els* that is the su*m of* 1 *sta*ter, *shall be doubled* (?), [10] *and I will give you*, Sallua, your *money* and . . . . . your *money* [11] . . . . *if* I *s*ue you *or sue your* son . . . .

Line 1. כ֗/ב. There may have been another unit, i.e. 22 or even 23. אדין goes with the preceding (Ungnad), not the following words.

Line 2. [מנחם] is certain from l. 5. Of his father's name ום is certain, so that we may identify him with Menahem b. Shalom in 25[18] (416–7 B.C.) and 44[1] (undated). ארמי זי יב is unusual. Cf. 7[2], where the man also belonged to the degel of Nabukudurri, but he only held property in Yeb, and 25^{2}, where Menahem was a witness. For whatever reason, Aramaeans are usually 'of Syene' and Jews 'of Yeb'. See Introduction, p. viii. On the persistence of the name of the degel (461 to *c.* 400) see note on 28^{2}. The system of the degel remained in spite of the revolt. ברתא for בירתא, a mistake?

Line 3. ס[מ]וח. The missing letter *may* be מ, from the trace remaining, but no such name is known. Cf. שמוח $22^{21,28}$.

Line 4. סתתרי = στατήρ. The first occurrence of a Greek word in these texts. Due to the revolt? מן קצת as in 29^{3}, 'part of' (Heb. מקצת). קצת does not mean 'total' (as Ungnad).

Line 5. ספר אנתותכי is her kethubha, cf. 14^{4}. ואשלמן another instance of the energetic imperfect without pronominal suffix, as pointed out by Seidel, cf. 8^{10} and Aḥiḳar 82.

Line 6. בי״ר לפרמותי. This was the next month after Phamenoth, so that he engages to pay within five weeks.

Line 8. ב[/ לפ]חנס the next month after Pharmuthi. We might restore ב[ירח פ]חנס. The ב after מטא is strange, but it must be the preposition. Elsewhere ל or על. For the tense, cf. 10^{7}.

Line 9. [יעקף] a mere guess, from 11^{8}, where see note.

Lines 10, 11 are much broken and the restoration is uncertain. [ואנתנולכי] cf. ואשלמולכי l. 5. וא[. . . We should expect ומרבית as in no. 11, but there is no obvious word.

Line 11. ער (Ungnad). The ר is doubtful, and the connexion more so. כל might be part of יכל, but that would require an imperfect after it, not רשת, which seems to be the reading.

Of the small fragments, *c* refers to some transaction, later in the deed, relating to barley and a sum of 3 shekels.

In *e*, בנו [ושהריא] suggests the end of the deed. The lower part of the fragment is blank, so that probably this came at the end of the line and the witnesses' names were written at the side as in no. 11.

No. 36.

Part of a Marriage Contract. No date.

Fragments only. No name or date. It is not certain that the small pieces belong to the same document as the large fragment. The writing seems to be by a different hand.

This is undoubtedly part of a marriage contract like no. 15, and deals with the gifts to the bride. The mention of clothing and a bronze cup and bowl, here as in no. 15, suggests that these were customary gifts.

K 2

Sachau, plate 10. Ungnad, no. 9.

1 חדרת ⁊/ כ̄ן ש
2 אמן ///\/ פשכן ///\ ב //\ ופשכן ///\ דמי כסף שקלן //\ מ̄ . . . ט̄/
חדרתה̄ אמן
3 ///\/// ב ///\ וזרת דמי כסף שקלן ///\ חלרן ד̄ מ̄ . . טה / חדרתה
זיקמר דמי כסף
4 חלרן ⁊ כף | זי נחש דמי כסף חלרן ⁊///\/ זלוע | זי נחש . . . . . .

b.

בכסף שקלן || זל . .
ד̄מי

[ד]מוהי כסף כ ||
שקלן /// ///\\

c.

ולה̄ ור̄ב
ל א

[1] new, 11 (?) . . . . [2] 5 cubits 4 hands by 3 (cubits) and 4 hands, worth the sum of 3 shekels; 1 . . . new, 7 cubits [3] by 4 and a span, worth the sum of 4 shekels 20 ḥallurin; 1 . . . new, of wool, worth the sum of [4] 10 ḥallurin; 1 cup of bronze worth the sum of 15 (?) ḥallurin; 1 bowl of bronze . . . .

Line 2. ט̄ . . . מ̄. Perhaps the same as the equally illegible word in l. 3, but written by mistake without the ה. It must be some kind of shawl, as in no. 15, but שבים cannot be read. חדרתה̄. Ungnad and Sachau חדת זי, but it is difficult to read the marks so, and measurements are never preceded by זי. The ה is rather far from the ת—perhaps it was partly erased.

Line 3. וזרת not חדת (Ungnad), which does not need to be repeated. טה . . מ̄. Only the ה is certain.

Line 4. כף as 15[16], or כס as 15[12] followed as here by זלוע.

Of the smaller fragments, Sachau puts together the two parts of *b* and reads them consecutively, but '2 shekels whose value is 2 k.' is impossible. He reads זי, but it is . . זל, an incomplete word, so that there was a space between the pieces. In the other line ד̄מי is not on the same level as שקלן, so that perhaps the pieces are not consecutive. From the texture of the papyrus they seem to be so. *c* is unimportant.

No. 37.

A Letter.

A well-written piece, but the ends of all the lines are lost, and it is difficult to establish their connexion. Letters were generally written in long lines, and much may therefore be lost.

No year is mentioned. Yedoniah, to whom the letter is addressed, is no doubt the same person as in 30[1], so that the date must be not far from

410 B.C., but there is nothing to indicate it more exactly. The letter reports to the heads of the community some cause of complaint against the Egyptians, in which Arsames had given a decision. The details are quite obscure. It was sent to Yeb from some other place, possibly Thebes (see on l. 6).

Sachau, plate 11. Ungnad, no. 10.

1 אל מראי ידניה מעוזיה אוריה וחילא עבדכ[ם . . . . שלם מראי אלהיא]
2 ישאלו בכל עדן שלם לן תנה כענת בכל יום זי [
3 הו קבל פתיפרסן חד זוך הו קבל פתיפרס א[חרן
4 איתי לן בזי מצריא שחד להן יהבן ומן זי[
5 ומצריא קדם ארשם להן גנבית עבדן אף [
6 מרינת נא וכן אמרן מזדיזן הו פקיד למרינא [
7 נרחל בזי זעירן אנחנה בזו כען הא סברת[
קדמן
8 הן לו גלין אנפין על ארשם לכן לא כזנה הו[ה
9 יאמר מלין קדם ארשם פיכן מהשדך אנפין [
10 תשכחון דבש תקם חתילן חבלן משבי צל שפ[

Reverse.

11 מלין לבתכם אתה פסו בר מנכי למנפי וה[
12 ופתפרסא ויהב לי כסף סתתרן ר // והדה מנה[
13 חורי יהב לי כזי בלוהי על כדא אמר תירי בו[
14 בצות מלכא וכלין להן ונזק ארשם וכפר צה[א
15 וחורי זי כלו ביום /// /// לפאפי מטו אגרתא [על מרינת נא ואנחנה
16 נעבר מלה

(Address.)

17 אל מראי יאדניה מעוזיה [אוריה

[1] To my lords Yedoniah, Ma'uziah, Uriah and the army, your servant . . . . . *The welfare of my lords may the gods* [2] seek at all times. It is well with us here. Now every day of . . . . [3] he received rations (?). One pay-day (?) he received an *extra* ration . . . . . . [4] is ours, because the Egyptians give them a bribe, and since . . . . . [5] of the Egyptians before Arsames, but act dishonestly. Also . . . . [6] the province of Thebes, and say thus: It is a Mazdaean who is set over (the) province . . . . . [7] we fear robbery because we are few. Now behold, I thought . . . . . . [8] if we had appeared before Arsames previously. But it was not so . . . . [9] He will speak words before Arsames, he pacified us, appeasing our anger . . . . [10] You will find ? ? [11] full of wrath against you. Pasu b. Mannuki came to Memphis, and . . . . . . [12] and the ration; and he gave

me the sum of 12 staters, and one . . . . . . [13] Hori gave me, since they had withheld it on account of the pitcher. Tirib . . . said . . . . . [14] by order of the king, and we withheld (it) from them. So he gave damages against Arsames and pardoned Zeho . . . . [15] and Hori, what they had withheld. On the 6th day of Paophi the letters came *to the province of Thebes, and we* [16] will do the thing.

[17] To my lords Yedoniah, Ma'uziah, *Uriah* . . . . . .

Line 1. The words restored are part of the usual formula. Before them the name of the writer must have stood, either X or X bar Y. The line therefore contained 44 or 53 letters approximately.

Line 2. זי the relative? or זי[וך] as in l. 3?

Line 3. פתיפרסן plural, therefore not connected with חד, but the end of a clause. Zend *paitifrasa* means 'judgement', 'retribution', hence 'payment'? Lidzbarski 'rations', from פת and פרס? In 11^{6} פרס is 'pay'. זיוך perhaps Persian. From the context it seems to be a technical term for 'pay-day'.

Line 4. להן 'to them' as in 34^{6}. זמן Ungnad דמן, but the phrase is always דמי not דמן זי, and the letter is more like a ז. It is difficult to see how the line is to be completed. Perhaps [. . . ומן זי[וכא זנה לא.

Line 5. להן 'but'. גנבית adverbial from גנב, 'thievishly'.

Line 6. מדינת נא not 'our province', which would be מדינתן, but the 'province of No' i.e. Thebes. מזדיזן is good Persian for a 'worshipper of (Aura)mazda'.

Line 7. בזז goes with the preceding words, since כען always begins a new sentence. It must be object of נרחל, though the order is strange. סברת. Sachau and Ungnad כברג, but the ס is fairly certain. It must therefore be part of the common Aramaic verb סבר.

Line 8. קדמן adverbial, for לקדמן (Sachau). Then לכן may(?) be 'but'.

Line 9. פיסן in 40^{2} seems to be a name, and so perhaps here. Asyndeton is common.

Line 10. תשכחון Haphel with ה omitted. The rest of the line is unintelligible, though the reading is certain and the words are well-known. תקם if from קום, would be singular, though a plural verb preceded. חתילן if from חתל (Heb. 'twist') suggests that חבלן are 'ropes'. משכי צל. The י may be only a false start of the צ. 'Drawing out shade' and 'extending protection' make equally little sense.

Lines 11–17 are on the reverse.

Line 11. מלין לבתכם. From Ezek. 16^{30} and no. 41^{4} it would seem that מלין is 'full'. With לבת Baneth cft. Ass. *libbâtu* 'wrath'. It can hardly be for לבית־ in both places.

Line 12. סתתרן as in $35^{4.7.9}$, a late text. The stater was 2 shekels.

וחדה כינה not 'one mina' as Sachau, nor 'one of them', since both mina and stater are masculine. Perhaps Heb. מָנָה 'portion'.

Line 13. כלוהי from כלא, frequent in legal documents, 'to prevent someone from getting his rights'. כרא 'jug' or 'pitcher', part of the matter in dispute. Sachau prefers to read כרא (i.e כֹּר) and Ungnad cft. Bab. *kurru*. תירי בו[. Perhaps a name, like Τιρίβαζος, &c., but it is not certain that בו (not בר) belongs to it.

Line 14. בצות for the later בצואת. ונזק must begin a new sentence (not as Sachau), since there is an extra space before it. It is a strange word to be applied to so great a man as Arsames, if he is the object. 'Gave damages against' is only a conjecture. Sachau's explanation of נזק does not seem possible. צחֿ[א]. The ח is not very certain. Ẓeḥo and Ḥor are associated as servants of 'Anani in 38[4].

Line 15. מטו masculine, with a feminine subject.

Line 16. מלה like Heb. דבר a 'thing'.

Line 17. יארניה quite clearly, for 'יד' in l. 1.

No. 38.

A Letter of recommendation.

A letter from Ma'uziah at Abydos to the heads of the community at Yeb, stating that he had been helped by Ẓeḥo and Ḥor who are now going to Yeb and deserve to be well treated.

The papyrus is written on both sides (ll. 9–12 on the reverse) and is much broken. It is not dated, but see on l. 3.

Sachau, plate 12. Ungnad, no. 11.

1 אל מראי ידניה אוריה וכהניא זי יהו אלהא מֿתן בר ישביה ונריה בר[

2 עבדך מעוזיה שלם מרא[י אלה שמיא ישאל שגיא בכל עדן ו]לרחמן תהוֿ קֿדֿםֿ

3 אלה שמיא וכעת כזי וידרנג רב חילא מטא לאבוט אסרני עלדבר אבנצרף ! זי

4 השכחו גניב ביד רכליא על אחרן צחא וחור עלימי ענני אשתדרו עם וידרנג

5 וחרנופי בטלל אלהֿ שמיא עד שזבוני כען הא אתין תמה עליכם אנתם חזו עליהם

חור

6 מה צבו ומלה זי צחא יבעה מנכם אנתם קמו קבלהם כן כזי מלה באישה

7 לא יהשכחון לכם לכם יהֿיֿ . . . . חנום הו עלין מן זי חנניה במצרין עד כען

8 ומה זי תעבדון לחור ל[תריה]ם עבדו [אנ]תם חור עלים חנניה אנהם זולו מן בתין

Reverse.

9 נכסן ולקֿבל זי ידכם מה ימֿנֿהֿ הבו זֿיֿ לי חסרןֿ חֿדֿ לכם בזך שלח אנה עליכם הו

10 אמר לי שלח אגרת קדמת [הנל]ו חסרן א שים שים אחרוהי בבית ענני זי תעברון

11 לה לא יתכסון מן ענני

12 אל מראי ידניה אוריה [ו]כהניא ויהודיא זי חי[לא] מעוזיה בר צחא

[1] To my lords Yedoniah, Uriah and the priests of the God Ya'u, Mattan b. Joshibiah and Neriah b. . . . . [2] your servant Ma'uziah. The welfare of my lords *may the God of heaven seek abundantly at all times, and* may you be favoured before [3] the God of heaven. And now, when Waidrang, commander of the army, came to Abydos, he imprisoned me because of a precious(?) stone which [4] they found stolen in the hand(s) of the dealers. Afterwards Zeḥo and Ḥor, the servants of 'Anani, used their influence with Waidrang [5] and Ḥornufi, with the help of the God of heaven, until they got me freed. Now behold, they are coming there to you. Look after them [6] as to what they want, and in the matter which Zeḥo (and Ḥor) asks of you, help them. So when they find no fault [7] in you, *they will acknowledge* to you *that* Khnum is against us from the time that Hananiah was in Egypt till now. [8] And what you do for Ḥor, do for *both of them*. Ḥor is a servant of Hananiah. Sell(?) from our houses [9] goods, and according to your ability pay what he assesses. Whatever is lacking to me makes no difference to you. On this account I am sending word to you. He [10] said to me: Send a letter first(?). If there is anything wanting, the amount is fixed for it in the house of 'Anani. What you do [11] for him will not be hidden from 'Anani. [12] To my lords Yedoniah, Uriah *and* the priests, and the Jews of *the army*, Ma'uziah b. Zeḥo(?).

Line 1. The names are fairly certain, though only the upper half of the letters remains. The name of the father of Neriah is lost, and it does not occur elsewhere.

Line 2. עבדך a slip for עבדכם. He was really thinking only of Yedoniah. The restoration is the common formula. תהוו. Sachau reads הוו, which would be difficult. The ת is practically certain. Note the horn at the top. There is hardly room for וו, and it is possible that the scribe wrote תהו (by mistake?). It is not תהוון, being jussive. קדם very indistinct, but no doubt right.

Line 3. אלה שמיא not אלהיא as elsewhere. Because he was writing to the priests? רב חילא. Therefore before 411 B.C. when Waidrang held the higher office of *fratarak* (30^5). לאבוט, so that the commander of Syene had jurisdiction over Abydos. אבנצרף, as one word, can hardly mean anything but a precious stone, though the expression is strange. צרף implies 'refining' and is correctly used of silver. A testing stone (lapis lydius) would hardly be valuable enough. The ו is only equivalent to the indefinite article, like חד elsewhere.

Line 4. על אחרן cf. Aḥiḳar 133. עלימי ע׳ not 'slaves', since they were in a position to reason with Waidrang, but subordinate officials, 'secretaries'. 'Anani was a man of high position, since he is mentioned as well known. Perhaps the same as in 26^{23}, the secretary of Arsames. איתחררו cf. Dan. 6^{15}. Properly 'wrestle', 'struggle'.

Line 5. חרנופי Egyptian. בטלל cf. בטלה זי in Behistun frequently. חזו עליהם 'look upon' in a friendly sense, cf. 41^{6}.

Line 6. קמו קבלהם also in a friendly sense, 'rise up before them', i.e. meet them half-way, not as Sachau 'withstand them'.

Line 7 must contain the apodosis to the sentence beginning with כזי. The second לכם is not a dittography (as Ungnad), but begins the apodosis. It must then be followed by a verb, not a title (as Ungnad). The verb is illegible and possibly something was written above the line. If לכם is 'to you' the verb should be 'they will admit' or 'ils vous donneront raison'. It is possible, however, that we should read לכמ[ריא] and supply something like 'they will attribute it to'. Evidently there was some trouble between the Jews and the priests of Ḥnub, as in no. 30, and Zeḥo and Ḥor were coming to inquire into it. The writer wishes to warn Yedoniah that it is important to make a good impression on them. It is tempting to read לכמ[רי היכלא זי] חנום but then there is no verb, and זי does not seem probable. As to Hananiah, cf. 21^{2}. His mission to Egypt was an important event. As suggested above (introduction to no. 21), it was perhaps his institution of animal sacrifice in connexion with the Passover, which caused trouble with the Egyptians: Ḥnub was hostile to the Jews from that time (419 B.C.).

Line 8. ל . . . . ם. Perhaps ל[תריה]ם. עלים. If this is the same Ḥor, he was apparently employed both by 'Anani and Hananiah. The latter, though a Jew, was a Persian official. זולו perhaps 'remove', cf. Arab. زال. They were to hide their valuables for safety. Or 'sell' as Seidel and Barth, cf. Is. 46^{6}?

The sense of the next two lines is obscure.

Line 9. The beginning is nearly obliterated. This is Sachau's reading, which is probably right. נכסן 'goods', indefinite, any there may be. ידכם 'your ability'. One would expect בידכם. יִמנה is probable. Sachau's זי חסרן is impossible. הבו. Sachau's ומה is impossible. זי (Sachau) very uncertain. One would expect הן 'if'. לי is more probable than לא (Sachau). חסרן perhaps. It looks like חסרה. Can it mean 'whatever loss there is to me, does not matter to you? חד (Sachau) very doubtful. שלח as elsewhere, 'I send word'. חו. It is not clear who is meant.

Line 10. קרמת. This seems to be the only possible reading, but the form is obscure. [הנל]ן is purely conjectural. Meaning 'if you cannot pay in full'? שימא is probable. It apparently means 'an account is kept'. אחרותי. Sachau cft. 9^4, 13^7.

Line 11. לה i.e. for Hor. יתכסן. I think the meaning must be as translated, but the verb ought to be singular. Perhaps it is an error due to the preceding תעבדון.

Line 12. זי חי[לא] and the rest is very much obliterated. The more usual phrase is זי ביב, but the ח is probable. מעויה may be supplied from l. 2. The rest is as read by Sachau, but cf. 33^2, &c., which would suggest בר נתן, and perhaps this might be read here. There are traces of something above the line.

No. 39.

Two fragments of the beginning of a letter.

Only the greetings remain. The address is written on the back. There is no date.

Sachau, plate 13. Ungnad, no. 12.

1 אל מראתי שלוה עבדכי הושע ש[לם] אלהיא כל ישאלו שלמכי בכל עדן שלם

2 מראי מנחם שלם מראתי אביהי ש[לם בר]ה וברתה שלם תחנום ויהוישמע שלם

3 משלמת שלם חצול שלם . . . . ן זי עליכי שלם כלכליה ובעת הושרתי

4 . . . . אמר לי יאוש לאמר הבה בזהב

5 אל מרא[תי שלוה] עבדכי . . . . .

[1] To my lady Selava, your servant Hosea gr*eeting*. May the gods all seek your welfare at all times. Greeting to [2] my lord Menahem. Greeting to my lady Abihi. Gr*eeting to* her *son* and her daughter. Greeting to Tekhnum and Ya'uyishma'. Greeting to [3] Meshullemeth. Greeting to Hazul. Greeting to . . . . which are upon you. Greeting to all of them. And now, you have ratified [4] . . . . Ye'osh said to me as follows: Pay (?) in gold (?) . . . .
[5] To *my* lady *Selava*, your servant *Hosea* . . . . .

Line 1. שלוה only here. Perhaps the same as סלוה, &c., elsewhere. Feminine of שלו (סלין) 'quail'? עבדכי. This is only a polite form. He was not a slave. ש[לם] is probable from the next line. There is a space after it.

Line 2. [בר]ה seems to be required by וברתה.

Line 3. זי עליכי is fairly certain. I cannot guess what it means, nor how the lacuna is to be filled. כלכליה must mean 'everybody'. The ה is uncertain and the form anyhow is strange, perhaps popular. הושרתי can only be 2nd pers. fem. Haphel of ישר. Cf. S-C, M a 6, 8 where it is taken in the sense of 'ratify' a document.

Line 4. The beginning is lost. אמר לי יאוש. Only the tops of the letters remain, but the reading is tolerably certain. הבה בזהב very uncertain. Cf. 42[6].

No. 40.

Fragments of a letter.

No date. Address on the back.

Sachau, plate 13. Ungnad, no. 13.

1 אל אחי פלטי אחוך הושע[ה שלם אחי אל]ה שמיא [י]שאל בכל עדן שלם שוא ובנוהי שלם אב[. . . .

2 שמעת בעמלא זי עמלת כזי . . . . אזלת אנה וצחא בר פחה אמרן לפיסן וא[

3 ושלח אגרה עלדברכן לצא[. . . . . ע]ל ינקיא עליך לבבי שריק כל זי יהבה[

4 מעוזיה מלה זילך תהשלח על . . . .

5 אל אחי פל[טי בר יאו]ש אחוך הושעיה בר נתן

[1] To my brother Piltai, your brother Hoshai*ah*. *The welfare of my brother may the Go*d of heaven seek at all times. Greeting to Sheva and his children. Greeting to Ab . . . [2] I have heard of the trouble which you took when . . . . . . I went. I and Zeḥo b. Peḥa spoke to Paisan (?) and . . . . [3] and he sent a letter about it to Zeḥo (?) . . . . . . concerning the children. About you my heart is distressed (?). All that he gave . . . . [4] Ma'uziah. Your matter you should send to . . . .

[5] To my brother Pil*tai b. Yeo*sh, your brother Hoshaiah b. Nathan.

Line 1. . . . , אב. Perhaps אב[יהי] or אב[א].

Line 2. בעמלא. Seidel explains the ב as otiose, cf. 16[3]. If so, it may be a mark of familiar style. כזי rather than בזי as Sachau. אזלת, so Sachau. פיסן seems to be a name here, but cf. 37[9]. . . . ,וא. Sachau , , ואמ. Seidel ואר[שם].

Line 3. עלדברכן as one word, cf. מנכן. . . לצא. Sachau reads
ל
חצא and takes it for לצחא. עליך with what precedes ('to you') or with what follows ('concerning you'). שריק = פריק 'empty'?

Line 4. מעויה fairly certain. מלה 'matter' (דבר) as in 37[16]. תהשלח more probable than ־ק (Sachau) if על follows.

Line 5. [יאו]ש seems to be the only possible name. אחוך. Sachau thinks they were step-brothers, but אח is only a polite form of address to an equal, cf. 21[2.11] and frequently.

No. 41.

Fragments of a letter.

Chiefly containing complaints that the writer has not heard from the addressee. Undated. The beginning of every line except the first, is lost. Ll. 6–9 are on the reverse.

Sachau, plate 14. Ungnad, no. 14.

1 אל אחי צח[א ובנוהי אחוכם . . . . . שלם אחי אלה]יא כלא ישא[לו] שגי בב[ל ערן . . . . . .

2 ות . . . . כן מטאת עלי שלמך שמעת שגיא חדית שמעת

3 . . . . זי הוה י[א]תה עליך הוית אשלח שלמך כען

4 . . . . לא אמרו [לי] מנכן הוית מלא לבתך קדם דלה

5 . . . . ת מן סון אגרת חדה בשלמך לא שלחת עלי

Reverse.

6 . . . . חזי על עלימיא וביתי כזי תעבר לביתך

7 . . . . רחיק מנה מ[ן] זי יעבד לעינוהי שלמך וטעמך

8 . . . . בשלם

9 אל [אחי צחא בר פחה ובנוהי . . . . בר ה[. . . . א]חוכם

[1] To my brothers Zeḥo *and his sons* (?), *your brother* . . . . . *the welfare of my brother* may the *gods* all seek abundantly at a*ll times* . . . . . [2] And . . . . *whenever a letter* came to me I heard of your welfare, I rejoiced abundantly. I heard [3] . . . . who used to *come* to you, I used to send a greeting to you. Now [4] . . . . they did not tell me. Consequently I was full of wrath against you before Dallah [5] . . . . *after* I *came* from Syene you did not send a letter to me about your welfare [6] . . . . look after the servants and my house

as you would do for your own house. [7] . . . . abstaining from what he would do in his presence. News of yourself, and your wishes [8] *send to me* . . . . in peace. [9] To *my brothers Ẓeḥo b. Peḥa and his sons* . . . . . b. H . . . . your *bro*ther.

Line 1. [א]צח is probable. Since the pronouns in the following lines are always singular, it would be supposed that Ẓeḥo was the only person addressed, but in l. 9 we have אחוכם implying more than one person. The only explanation I can suggest is to supply ובנוהי. The end of this line is lost.

Line 2. מטאת. The subject is no doubt אגרת.

Line 3. ה̄ח̄[א]ת̄ is probable from the traces remaining. The construction הוה יאתה seems to mean كان يجي 'he used to come', and so הוית אשלח, but it does not occur in BA, and only rarely in the papyri. A popular use?

Line 4. מלא לבחך cf. 37^{11}. רלה a name? Cf. דליה, דלוי, ידלה.

Line 5. ה̄. Part of אולת or a similar verb? חדה the indefinite article, cf. 30^{19}.

Line 6. חזי על as in 38^{5}. The meaning here is clear.

Line 7. מנה מ[ן]. For the double מן, cf. 28^{11}. If the construction is the same here, מן זי יעבד must be 'from that which he does'. מן cannot be for מה as Sachau seems to take it. The space after לעינוהי shows that it ends the sentence.

Line 9. It is difficult to reconstruct the address. פחה is only conjectured from 40^{2}. אחוכם implies more than one person addressed. The name of the writer must have preceded it.

No. 42.

A Letter.

Two fragments, very much injured. Apparently a business letter, but the details are quite obscure. Perhaps connected with no. 38. It was dated (in l. 14), which is unusual in letters, but the year is lost, and there is no other indication of date. Ll. 12–15 are on the reverse.

Sachau, plate 16. Ungnad, no. 17.

1 [אל אחי . . .]ו̄ם אחוך ה[וש]ע שלם ו.ברת שניא מ̄ר̄.ה̄ת ל[ך בכל
עדן ובעת

2 [אנחנה קדם פי]ס̄ן̄ דינא וע[לימ]ה שלמן כסף כרשן ד וכרש . . . .

3 . . . . ב]ידי[ך] זי ה[ו י]נ̄ת̄ן כ[סף צ̄ריף] כרשן /// // כע[

4 עמך על זי [ינ]תן לך כסף [כרש]ן ///// וכתב להם ספר עליהם והן לא [ינתנון כל] בכ[פא

5 ברבא ולא [יאמר]ו לך לאמ[ר] הב ערבן זבן ביתא זי זכור וביתא זי אשנ . . . הן לא זבנו

6 המו בעי א[י]ש זי יזבן ביתא [ר]בא זי הודו והבה לה בכספא זי יקו[ם] עלוהי וכזי

7 אגרתא זא [ת]מטא עליך אל תקום חת מנפי לעבק הן השכחת כסף [ח]ת לעבק

8 והן לא השכחת אפם חת [לע]בק אזל על ביתאלתדן וינתן לך כתון שטטן ואסה ן

9 כתון י.חה ן זי קמר פעפס ן סרבלק ן . . . . צבע ול . . . . קטא פרא כ //////

10 כתן ו [ש]חיק וכזי ינתן המו לך שלח עלי והן לא יהב המו לך [ש]לח עלי כען

11 הן נחת אנת למנפי אל תשבק לאשנ . כזי זבן הב לי כנדר זך לא כ . . .

Reverse.

12 כזי יהנעלו המו יהודיא קדם [ארשם . . . ל . . . . ן . . . . [רח]קת [מ]ני . . .

13 מליהם אל תקום חת לעבק ולעבק הנחתלי כתון ו בידך על[מנפי] . . . . כ . . .

14 לי . ני ע[לוהי] כתב ב ד /// ///ן לתעובי ה[ו ניס]ן [ש]נת . .

15 א[ל אחי . . . וס בר] חג[י אחוך הושע]

[1] *To my brother* . . . . us, your brother H*osh*ea, greeting and . . . exceedingly be . . . upon *you at all times. Now* [2] *we in the presence of Pai*san (?) the judge and his *servant* have paid the sum of 10 kerashin, and a karash *remains* [3] . . . . *in your* hands, that h*e should* give (?) 5 kerashin *pure silver.* Now . . . . . [4] with you, as to his giving you the sum of 5 *kerash*in; and write for them a deed concerning them; and if they do not *give you all* the money [5] at interest (?), and do not *speak* to you saying, 'Give security', buy the house of Zaccur and the house of AŠN . . . If they do not sell [6] them, seek out a man who will buy the big house of Hodav and give it to him for (?) the money at which it is valued. When [7] this letter reaches you, do not delay, come down (to) Memphis at once. If you have found money, come down at once. [8] And if you have not found (it), still come down *at o*nce. Go to Betheltaddan and he will give you a striped coat of WASA, [9] a . . . coat of wool, a P'PS, a cloak of . . . dyed, and . . . . 6 kerashin. [10] An old coat. And when he gives them to you, send to me. And if he does not give them to you, send to me. Now [11] if you come down

to Memphis, do not leave (anything) to AŠN . . when he has sold. Give me according to this . . . . not . . . [12] when the Jews bring them before *Arsames* . . . . *say* . . . . you *ren*ounce your claim *on* me . . . *and after* [13] their words do not delay, come down at once and at once bring down to me a coat in your hand to *Memphis* . . . *as* [14] he wrote to me (?) . . . a*bout it*. On the 27th of Tybi, *that is Nisan*, year . . . .

[15] To *my brother* . . . *us b*. Haggai, *your brother Hoshea.*

Line 1. מ is clear, and before it probably ו. After שלם is another word of greeting connected by ו. Sachau proposes וחררת, Ungnad ושדרת. The first letter is more like ב than anything else. Possibly ורחמת (cf. 9[7]) with a very bad מ. After שגיא a verb (?) illegible. The restoration here and in l. 2 is very uncertain.

Line 2. סן is doubtful. Seidel suggests פיסן, as in 37[9] (?) and 40[2]. וכרש at the end, not וברשן as Ungnad.

Line 3. ה[ו י]נתן very doubtful. The connexion would be difficult. [צריף]. There are traces which may belong to צ and פ.

Line 5. Ungnad suggests 'at interest'. In no. 11 the word is מרבית. [יאמר]ו seems, on the analogy of other passages, to be required by לאמר which follows. זבן. The nature of the suggested transaction is not clear. It may be Peal 'buy' or Pael 'sell'. . . . אשנ as in l. 11. An Egyptian name?

Line 6. והבה must be 'and give it'. בכספא '*for* the price'. יקו[ם] if right (and nothing else seems probable), shows the amount missing between the two fragments. 'The price which stands (*or* is set) upon it', i. e. its market value.

Line 7. זא fem. as in 21[3], 30[17]. [ת]מטא. Ungnad 'ימ', but there is room for the more correct ת. תקום 'stand still', i. e. delay. חת can only be the imperative of נחת, but one would expect a preposition after it. לעבק as in 26[6] &c. Cf. note on Aḥiḳar 103. הן with the perfect in the sense of a future perfect.

Line 8. אפם as in 5[8] &c., but here retaining more of the sense of אף, 'nevertheless'. ביתאלתדן not 'the house of Ilutaddan' but 'to Bethel-taddan'. There is no division. Cf. Bethelnathan 18[5] &c. It is formed with the god-name Bethel, but with the verb in the Babylonian form. שטמן must be descriptive of the garment, but the word is not found elsewhere. It is probably another instance of a plural with dagesh resolved, like עטמיא, חנניא, שקקן. The singular would then be שט(א) 'line' &c., and the garment a coat with lines or stripes. Cf. חטב 15[7]. ואסת̄ך. So Ungnad. The meaning is unknown. The ו is part of the word, since the items here are not connected by 'and'. It is no doubt a further description of the coat.

Line 9. פעפם is more probable than Ungnad's פעקם. Perhaps an Egyptian name for some sort of garment. כרבלק cf. סרבל in Daniel, with the Persian final *k*. It is usually taken to mean 'trousers'. Andreas 'cloak'. צבע very uncertain. Cf. 15^8. ...ול or ...פל. קטא פרא unintelligible here.

Line 10. כתן apparently the same as כתון ll. 8, 9. [ש]חיק 'rubbed' 'worn out' is better than Ungnad's כחיק. [ש]לח. Seidel [אפם ש]לח as in l. 8. But if the reading of l. 6 is right there would be room only for ש.

Line 11. נחת a participle rather than for נחתת. אנת Ungnad אנתן, but his ן is only a dark fibre in the papyrus. The reading and translation of the latter part of the line are very uncertain. כנדר. Only the tops of the letters remain, and seem to read so. It cannot be נדר a 'vow', nor can we read כנכר.

Lines 12–15 are on the reverse.

Line 12. [ארשם] possibly fits the traces remaining, but this and the rest of the line are very uncertain. [רח]קת is a likely word, if a law-suit was in question. [מ]ני. Ungnad זי. Something must then have followed to govern מליהם l. 13.

Line 13. על[מנפי] seems to fit the traces. The addressee was urged to go there in l. 7. As the letter was found at Elephantine he probably was then there.

Line 14. Beginning very uncertain. כתב ends the sentence with a space after it. The date following is that of the letter. After לתעובי traces perhaps of ה and ן. After שנת the numeral (ר ?) is obliterated, and the king's name if it was ever written.

Line 15 not being shown on the facsimile, I have restored it from Ungnad's reading.

No. 43.

A deed of gift or exchange.

Very fragmentary. Most of l. 1 is lost, and the first halves of ll. 5–12. Some of the lacunae can be filled with certainty as the formulae are known, but much is doubtful.

The date is lost.

Sachau, plate 33. Ungnad, no. 35.

1 [ביום ר] ////// לפא[פי הו . . . שנת . . . . מלכא אדין ביב אמרת מפטחיה ברת גמריה יהודי]

2 זי יב בירתא לדגלה א[רמית] לאסורי ברת גמ[רי]ה אחתה והמנה למ[מ]ר אנה] מפטחיה

3 יהבת לכי כסף שקלן /// /// הו שתה באבני מלכא כסף ר̄ // לכרש \
אנה מפטחיה יהבת לכי ברחמת̄

4 לקבל סבול [זי יהבתי לי ורח]קת מנכ[י] מן יומא זנה ועד עלם לא אכהל
ארשנכ[י] דין [ו]דבב בשם

5 [כספא זנה זי יהבת לכי וספרא כתבת עלא ו]ל[א י]כהל בר לי וברהלי
אח ואחהלי קריב ורחיק

6 [ירשנכי דין ודבב זי ירשנכי בשם כספא זנה זי] יהבת לכי ינתן לכי אבינן[ד]
כסף כרשן // [כ]פם אמרת

7 [אנה מפטחיה אף איתי פתפא לי מן בית מלכא אנה מפ]טחיה זי הוה בידכי
יהבתהי לי וטיב לבבי

8 [בגו מן יומא זנה ועד עלם רחקת מנכי מן כס]פא זנה ופתפא זי הוה לי
מן בית מלכא ולא אכהל

9 [ארשנכי דין ודבב אנה מפטחיה . . . . . . בר]לי וברה לי הנגית והנבנ̄א
זי ל[י בש]ם כספא זנה

10 [זי כתיב מנעל ופתפא זי הוה לי מן בית מלכא וכל זי][לי] זי ירשנכי בשם
כספא זנה ופת[פא זי כת]יב מנעל

11 [ינתן לכי כסף כרשן // כתב . . . . . בר . . . .] ספרא זנה כפם מפטחיה
ברת גמריה ושהדיא בנו

12 [שהד . . . . . בר . . . . . שהד . . . . . בר] פדיה שהד מנכי בר ספעמרא

13 ספר מרחק זי כתבת מפטחיה ברת גמריה לאסורי] אחתה

[1] *On the* 25th *day* of Pa*ophi that is . . . . year . . . of king . . . . at that time in Yeb, said Miphṭaḥia daughter of Gemariah, a Jew* [2] of Yeb the fortress, according to her company an *Aramaean*, to Asori daughter of Gem*ar*iah, her sister and partner (?), say*ing: I* Miphṭaḥia [3] give to you the sum of 6 (that is, six) shekels, royal weight, of the standard of 2 R to 1 karash. I, Miphṭaḥia, give (it) to you as a gift [4] in consideration of the support *which you gave me and* I *renounce all claim* on you from this day for ever. I have no power to institute against you suit or process in the matter of [5] *this money which I give you and have written a deed about it and* no son or daughter of mine, brother or sister of mine, relative or stranger, shall have power [6] *to institute against you suit or process. Whoever shall sue you on account of this money which* I give to you shall pay to you a fine of 2 kerashin, as I have said [7] *I, Miphṭaḥia. Also there is the allowance from the treasury to me, Miph*ṭaḥia, which was in your possession. You have given it to me, and my heart is content [8] *therewith. From this day forth for ever I renounce all claim on you regarding* this money and the allowance which was (made) to me from the treasury, and I have no power [9] *to institute against you suit or process,*

I, Miphṭaḥia . . . . or son or daughter of mine, compatriot or partner of mine *concerning* this money [10] *which is stated above and the allowance which was (made) to me from the treasury and all that* is mine. Whoever shall sue you in the matter of this money and the allo*wance which is stat*ed above [11] *shall pay you the sum of 2 kerashin. X b. Y wrote* this deed at the direction of Miphṭaḥia daughter of Gemariah and the witnesses hereto. [12] *Witness X b. Y; witness Z b.* Pedaiah; witness Mannuki b. SP'MRA.

Endorsement. [13] *Deed of renunciation which Miphṭaḥia daughter of Gemariah wrote for Asori* her sister.

Line 1. Only *// ///* are certain. ברת גמריה as in l. 11. Cf. אחתה in l. 2. She was probably a niece of Mibṭaḥiah daughter of Mahseiah.

Line 2. לדגלה. Epstein takes this as a name (cf. דגליהו), but such a name does not occur and would not fit the usual formula. It is probably the common word דגל 'her (*or* his?) company', but the expression is unusual. א[רמית] a doubtful conjecture. If it is right, her father was a Jew of Yeb, but she had been drafted (owing to marriage or otherwise) into a company which was reckoned as Aramaean. See Introduction, p. viii. Epstein proposes א[חת], but the double description is improbable apart from other objections. לאסורי. Epstein בלאסורי 'D. wife of Belusuri'. There is a mark (a blot?) before the ל but it can hardly be a ב. והמנה probable, but the word is unknown. Perhaps a compound of OP *ham-* 'partner'? or 'twin'? לממ[ר] as in 32^{2}, not the usual לאמר. [אנה]. Something more is wanted to fill the space, though the writing is large.

Line 3. *//*ר. The ר is reduced to a mere spot. It is restored here as being the usual formula. Epstein *//* ז, which is not found elsewhere. From here the writing becomes smaller. ברחמת is more probable than ־מן (Ungnad). Read ־מת?

Line 4. סבול. Seidel cft. Aḥiḳar 48, and translates 'in return for food'. Perhaps it has a more general sense 'support'.

Line 5. The restoration is common form, and so in l. 6. ספרא as in 13^{9} or ספר as in 13^{3}.

Line 6. [כ]פם. The כ is lost, but there is room for it, and it is no doubt to be read. Seidel thinks פם = אפם, as אם = אפם in 13^{11}.

Line 7. The פתפא mentioned in l. 8 must have been introduced here, but the restoration is not certain. It is doubtful if אנה מפטחיה could stand so far from לי.

Line 8. The restoration is not certain. Rather more is wanted. פתפא cf. $24^{39.42}$. It must be some sort of government allowance. בית מלכא 'the treasury'. In 11^{6} אוצרא.

Line 9. The restoration is no doubt right as far as it goes, but more is wanted to fill the space. הנגית והנבגא (Ungnad והנבקא) = קריב ורחיק elsewhere. Probably Persian. Sachau suggests *hamgaêlha* 'fellow-countryman'. For הנבגא Epstein cites Mandaic האמבאגא 'competitor', Syr. ܗܩܒܠܐ ?

Line 10. The restoration is probable.

Line 12. ספעמרא (or ־דא). There is no doubt about the reading, but a letter may be lost at the end. Egyptian?

Line 13. The endorsement is lost, except the last word.

No. 44.

An affidavit.

Fragments, recording, if the restoration is mainly correct, an oath taken in a law-court. This view depends on the restoration of מו[מאה] in l. 1 and the explanation of ימא in l. 2. Apparently Pamisi and Espemeṭ (?) had possession of an ass. Menahem b. Shallum here declares that half (the value) of it belongs to him, that Pamisi claimed that half and asserted that he had given a he-ass for it. Menahem states that he has not received anything, money or value, for his half. The difficulty is that in l. 7 Pamisi is called 'your father', i. e. father of Meshullam, to whom the oath is addressed. But in l. 2 Meshullam is called the son of Nathan. It may be another case of a man bearing an Egyptian as well as a Jewish name. If so, it appears that Meshullam, inheriting from his father, laid claim to half the ass, and the father being dead and no evidence forthcoming of his payment, Menahem took an oath in support of his rights. Much depends on the amount of space to be allowed between the right-hand fragment and the rest. On the whole the restoration of ll. 1–3 seems probable and this would settle the position of the fragments. There is no date, and no room for one. Sachau points out that a Menahem b. Shallum is a witness in 25^{18} (416 B.C.).

On the margin are two transverse lines of writing, much faded, which do not belong to this document.

Sachau, plate 32. Ungnad, no. 33.

מו[מאה זי] מנחם בר שלום בר
הו[דויה זי] ימא למשלם בר נתן
בי̊[הו אלה]א̊ במסגדא ובענתיהו
ו̊[אמר לה] לאמר אתנא זי ביד
פ[מסי ואספ]מט זי אנת רשה לי
ע[ליה הא] פלגה זילי הו צדיק

א̅[ף אמר לה]חסנותה פמסי אבוך
ל̊[ם] יהב לי חמר חלף פלגה
ו̅לא [יהב] לי כסף ודמי כסף חלף
[פלגה]

[1] *Oath of* Menahem b. Shallum b. [2] Ho*daviah which* he swore to Meshullam b. Nathan [3] by *Ya'u* the *God*, by the temple and by 'Anathya'u, [4] and *spoke to him* saying: The she-ass which is in the possession of [5] Pa*misi and Espe*met, a*bout* which you sue me, [6] *behold*, the half of it which is mine is legal(ly mine). [7] *But* Pamisi your father *claimed*(?) *to* own it [8] sa*ying that* he gave me a he-ass in exchange for half of it. [9] But he did not *give* me either money or value in exchange for [10] *the half of it*.

Line 1. Epstein proposes to begin with מ[חיר], but there is no parallel for so expressing a date. For the oath cf. 14^{4} seqq.

Line 2. הו[דויה], or הו[שע], but cf. 22^{39}.

Line 3. ב̊י̊[הו]. As the grandfather is named in ll. 1, 2, we might read בר here, followed by a name, but it is difficult to see what the construction could then be. Epstein proposes בר הודו, thus making the parties cousins, and cft. 22^{127}, 19^{10}. [אלה]א̅. The א is strange, but probable. במסגדא properly 'the place of worship', like مسجد a 'mosque' (used even of the temple at Jerusalem). ענתיהו cf. ענתביתאל in 22^{125}. The man evidently did swear by 'Anathya'u, whatever be restored before it, and this was therefore the name of a god, presumably a sort of consort of Ya'u.

Line 5. פ[מסי] is conjectured from l. 7. [ואספ]מט. The מ is fairly certain, and the termination is so uncommon that we may reasonably restore the name from 4^{7}, cf. 6^{10}, 8^{7}.

Line 6. פלגה וכ' lit. 'the half of it, which is mine, is just', i.e. half of it is legally mine.

Line 7. [לה]חסנותה infin. Haphel, cf. 15^{30} לתרכותה. Then the construction requires a verb preceding it. Perhaps אמר (?) in the sense of 'thought to' 'claimed to'. פמסי אבוך. There is no doubt about the reading, and it can only mean 'P. your father', so that Meshullam's father was named both Pamisi and Nathan (l. 2), as Asḥor in 15 and 20 is Nathan in 25 and 28. It is strange to find both names used in one document.

Line 8. ל̊[ם]. There is no room for more, if the space is rightly estimated.

Line 9. דמי כסף 'the equivalent of money' i. e. valuables.

Line 10. There is a trace of the first letter, but there can have been only one word, as the rest of the line is blank.

No. 45.

A contract.

Fragment, incomplete on all sides, of an agreement concerning fish. It seems that X had accused Mahseiah of robbing or cheating him about some fish. Mahseiah was required by the court to swear (cf. no. 44) that he had not cheated. X now undertakes to pay for the fish in money or grain of the same value, under a penalty if he fails to do so. The details are not clear.

The date is lost, but the king was probably Artaxerxes, and if the scribe was the same as in 10[20], the deed was written about 450 B. C.

Sachau, plate 32. Ungnad, no. 34.

1 [ב . . . ל . . . . הו ניס]ן שנת[. . . ארתחשסש מ]ל[כ]א בס[ון] בירתא
אמר . . .]
2 [בר . . . לדגל ארתבנ]ו למחסיה בר שיבה ארמי זי סון [בירתא . . .
3 [לאמר אנה רשיתך] עדבר נונין לאמר חמצת מ[נ]י ושא[ילת קדם
4 [דיניא וטענו מומא]ה לך ביהו אלהא כזי נונן לא חמ[צת מני
5 [. . . . .] אתוב או עבורא זנה דמי נוניך [. . .
6 [. . . . .] לך כל נוניך או דמיהם זי תמא[. . .
7 [. . . . .] לך הן לא יהבת לך בין יו[מ . . .
שערן
8 [. . . . . אנתן לך אבינדנ]א קב ׀ לפרס ׀ כל ירחן ושנן[. . .
9 [. . . . . כתב נתן בר] ענני ספרא [זנה] ב[סו]ן בירת[א כפם
10 . . . .

[1] *On the . . . of . . . that is Nisan*, year . . . of *Artaxerxes* the *king*, in S*yene* the fortress, *said* . . . [2] *b. . . . of the company of Artaban*u to Mahseiah b. ŠYBA, Aramaean of Syene *the fortress*, [3] *as follows: I sued you* concerning fish, saying, you defrauded me, and *I was* exam*ined before* [4] *the judges and they imposed an oat*h on you by the God Ya'u, that *you did* not de*fraud me* of fish. [5] . . . . I come back, or this corn, the value of your fish . . . . . . [6] . . . . to you all your fish, or the value of them, which you (?) . . . . . [7] . . . . to you, if I do not pay to you within . . . da*ys* . . . . [8] . . . . . *I will pay you a fin*e of 1 kab of barley for each portion every month and year . . . . [9] . . . . . *Nathan b.* 'Anani *wrote this* deed in *Sy*ene *the* fortress *at the dictation of* [10] . . . .

Line 1 is mostly obliterated, but enough is legible to show that it contained a date in the usual form. The first legible marks are probably ־ן rather than ־ני or ־פי, and the month-name is likely to be Jewish, though not necessarily Nisan. ארתחשסש is required by the space.

Line 2. [...]ן suggests the *degel* of Artabanu or Iddinnabu. שיבה an unknown name. At the end it is not clear how the lacuna is to be filled.

Line 3. רשיתך. Something of the kind is wanted, and this is the natural word. ערבר if not a mistake, is a popular form of עלדבר cf. Dan. 4[14]. חמצת cf. Heb. חָמוֹץ, &c., from a root meaning to 'act harshly' or 'unjustly'. If מני is right it must mean 'took away wrongfully'. מ[נ]ך. There is a trace of נ. The shape of י is peculiar, but cf. the י in יהבת l. 7. ... ושא can only be ושאילת, cf. 16[3], 20[8]. Then the subsequent phrase, or something like it, is necessary.

Line 4. [מומא]ה a word for 'oath', or 'swear' is required by ביהו. The form of the phrase is not quite satisfactory. In 6[6] we have טענוך לי מומאה 'they imposed on you an oath to me'. Cf. 8[24]. This can hardly be read here, because the oath seems always to be required of an accused person to substantiate his innocence, not of the accuser to support his charge. Here לך is the accused, Mahseiah, and טענוך = טענו לך. נונן. In line 3 נונין, so that both forms could be used. חמ[צת] is necessary to rebut the charge in l. 3.

Line 5. אחוב is certain, but it is difficult to restore the context. עבורא זנה. It does not seem to have been mentioned before, so that perhaps זנה implies that it was there in court.

Line 6. ... תמא. The reading is certain. It cannot be for חמה. It looks like a verb in the 2nd person imperfect, 'which you . . .', but there is no obvious way of completing it.

Line 7. The usual formula introducing the penalty for non-payment. בין יו[ם . .]. Probably a numeral followed, 'within *x* days'.

Line 8. [אביגרנ]א cf. 20[14], &c. פרס 'allowance' or 'ration'? The arrangement is not clear, nor is the meaning of כל ירחן ושנן 'every month and year'.

Line 9. The name of the scribe is restored from 10[20], but it might be Ma'uziah b. Nathan b. 'Anani as in 18[3] (about 425 B.C.).

Line 10 which should give the names of both parties, is lost, as well as the names of the witnesses.

No. 46.

A conveyance.

Fragments containing the beginnings of some lines of a conveyance of property (a house?) from Shelomem b. Hodaviah to his wife Abihi, or from some one else to Abihi wife of Shelomem.

The date is lost, and the names give no clue. The writing is unusual.

Sachau, plate 31. Ungnad, no. 32.

וקנינה זי . . .
שלומם בר שנית . . .
אית לה עם . . .
. . . והי ו . . .
. . . ל . . . א . . .
בעל קריה וב[על . . .
לאם לא שליט . . .
וזי יקום לתרכ[ותה מן ביתא זנה זי יהב שלומם
לאביהי אנתתה [ינתן לה אבינדן כסף כרשן ///‎ //
באבני מלכא כ[סף ר // לעשרתא וביתא אפם בית
אנתתה זי שלו[מם בר הודויה זי יהב לה ולא דין
שהדיא זכור ב[ר . . . שהד . . . בר . . . שהד
משלך בר הושעי[ה שהד . . . בר . . . שהד . . . בר . . .
שהד גדול בר הו[. . . שהד . . . בר . . . שהד . . . בר . . .
כל ||| ||| |/ כ[תב . . . בר . . . ספרא זנה כפם אביהי
ושלומם בר הוד[ויה בעלה

[1] and his property, which . . . [2] Shelomem b. ŠNYTH . . . [3] he has with . . . [4] . . . his . . . . s, and . . . [5] . . . . [6] citizen, or . . . [7] but (?) he has no power . . . [8] and whoever shall arise to dr*ive her away from this house which Shelomem gave* [9] to Abihi his wife *shall pay her a fine of 5 kerashin* [10] by royal weight, of the st*andard of 2* R *to the ten and the house is truly the house of Abihi* [11] the wife of Shelo*mem b. Hodaviah which he gave her, and no suit* (*shall lie*). [12] Witnesses: Zaccur b. . . . [13] Meshullak b. Hoshaiah . . . [14] Witness, Gadol b. Ho . . . [15] Total 8. *X b. Y wrote this deed for Abihi* [16] and Shelomem b. Hoda*viah her husband.*

Line 1. זי is probably the relative.

Line 2. שנית. Only ש is certain. The נ might be פ (as Ungnad). The י is probable. No combination makes a name. This Shelomem is apparently not one of the contracting parties, since the party Shelomem has a different father in l. 16.

Line 3. אית for איתי as also in 54[4]. עם. The ע is very small and badly made, but can hardly be anything else. There is no sign of any letter immediately following ם.

Line 4. והי . . The pronoun? (e.g. בנוהי).

Line 5. The tails of other letters are visible, but the words cannot be restored.

Line 6. וב[על דגל] perhaps.

Line 7. לאם. Sachau suggests that it may mean 'people', which is impossible. Cf. 9^{6}, a similar proviso in a similar document. It ought to mean להן. Perhaps for לם? שליט. The ט is very strange, but it cannot be anything else. A pronoun אנת or הו must have followed.

Line 8. לתרכ[ותה] or ־תך, is well restored by Sachau from 15^{30}. Hence the property must have been either a house or land, and 'her' or 'you' must be the wife, Abihi.

Line 10 belongs to the clause stating the penalty.

Line 13 &c. The name-groups do not occur elsewhere.

Line 14. הו[דויה] or הו[שעיה], and so perhaps a brother of either Meshullak or Shelomem.

Line 15. The statement of the number of witnesses is unusual.

Line 16. הוד[ויה]. The ד is not clear, but it can hardly be anything else.

No. 47.

Fragments of a conveyance. No name or date.

Sachau, plate 35. Ungnad, no. 38.

1 . . . . זי בניך מן . . .
2 . . . . בר וברה לך קדם סגן ומרא ל . . .
3 . . . . יהבת לך אנתן לך כסף כרשן . . .
4 . . . . . . בדין ודבב בשם בי[תא . . .
5 . . . . שאלת . . . .
6 . . . . נח . . . .
7 אכל אקבל עליך קדם סגן ומ[רא . . . .
8 ויהבת לך אף לא אכל אמר אנת . . .

[1] . . . . of your sons by . . . . . [2] . . . . . . son or daughter of yours, before a magistrate or (my) lord to . . . . . [3] . . . . . . I have given to you, I will pay you the sum of . . . kerashin . . . . [4] . . . . suit or process on account of *this* h*ouse* . . . . [5] . . . . you (*or* I) asked (?) . . . .

[6] . . . . [7] I shall have *no* power to complain against you before a magistrate or (my) lo*rd* . . . . [8] and have given to you. Moreover I shall have *no* power to say: You . . . . .

Line 1. מן 'by' followed by the name of the mother.

Line 2. In 10^{18} we have סגן ודין. Elsewhere מרא, applied to Arsames, seems to be the proper title of the Persian satrap.

Line 3. יהבת. Ungnad and Sachau אמרת, but the reading is not really doubtful. The sentence originally was 'if I claim back anything which I have given *you*, I will pay &c.', or something similar.

Line 4. בדין וד׳. So Ungnad. Only the tail of the ב (?) is visible. The phrase does not occur elsewhere, and the construction is not clear.

It is quite uncertain how much space is to be allowed between the two fragments, and in fact one would not take the second fragment (from its appearance) to belong to the same papyrus as the first, but for the use of the unusual phrase סגן ומ[רא] in l. 7 as in l. 2.

Line 6. . . . נת . . . not אנחן.

No. 48.

Small fragments of perhaps a marriage contract. No date.

Sachau, plate 35. Ungnad, no. 39.

1 בר זכור ס . . .
2 מןכל כספא זי כתיב מן עלא ולא א . . .
3 ברתך למלקחה לאנתו אנתן למחסיה . . .

[1] b. Zaccur . . . . [2] of all the money (?) which is set forth above, and *I shall* not *be able* . . . [3] your daughter to take her in marriage, I will pay to Mahseiah . . .

Line 1. . . . ס is doubtful. Seidel conjectures ס[ונכן] 'of Syene'.

Line 2. כספא can hardly be right, nor can Ungnad's נכסיא. A plural would not be followed so closely by כתיב singular. The rest of the line must have been '. . . if I wish another wife than your daughter', which would make it rather long. Cf. 15^{31}.

Line 3. למחסיה apparently the father of the bride, who was not old enough to act for herself as in no. 15. One wonders whether she can have been the much-married Mibṭaḥiah again, who was a daughter of Mahseiah. If so it was her first marriage, but cf. note on 8^{2}.

No. 49.

Fragment of a contract, or of a deed relating to a claim.

The beginning, containing the date, is entirely lost.

The writing is very unusual, probably by an unpractised hand. Note the badly made ט, כ, ח, ו, while י and ר are of a good, early form. There are also mis-spellings: see notes.

Sachau, plate 38. Ungnad, no. 45.

אמר סמכי בר ששי לשלמם בר גלגל לא[מר . . .
אמר לך אחלי עליך כסף וחטן ושערן . . .
[ו]כל מדעם זי יחיה בה איש ולשל[. . .
לך וברה י[ש]ל[ח ע]ליכם מדעם מכל ז . . .
. . . א . . . . שהדיא בג[ו . . .

[1] Said Semaki b. Shashai to Shelomem b. Galgul as *follows*: . . . [2] said to you, I have against you (a claim for) money and wheat and barley . . . [3] *and* anything whereby a man may live, and to *send* . . . [4] to you, and his son shall *send* to you some food . . . [5] . . . . *the* witness*es* here*to* . . .

Line 1. סמכי ב׳ ששי. Ungnad cft. סמכיהו (1 Chron. 26^{7}) and ששי (Ezra 10^{40}). לשלמם fairly certain, for לשלומם. גלגל Ungnad cft. גלגול 10^{21}.

Line 2. אמר 3rd person, referring to the claim of a third party. אחלי if right, is for אית(י) לי, 'there is to me', cf. 35^{3}. חטן for חנטן, with נ assimilated as in Hebrew.

Line 3. [ו]כל. The כ is quite certain. As this writer makes his ו very large (see וברה l. 4), nothing more is required to fill the space. מדעם as in l. 4, for מנדעם elsewhere. ולשל . . . The letters missing cannot be ־מם. Perhaps ולשלחה.

Line 4. לך, not לכל as Ungnad. What he takes for the final ל is really the tail of כ in the line above. י[ש]ל[ח]. The ש is very uncertain, but nothing else seems likely. [ע]ליכם is the most probable restoration. Note the plural. מכל for מאכל rather than for מן כל. Cf. לממר 32^{2}.

Line 5. שהדיא. The יא is very doubtful.

No. 50.

Fragments, perhaps of a legal document. The lines are here numbered consecutively, but their true position is quite uncertain. As to the general sense, nothing is clear, and there is nothing to identify the date 'year 13'.

Sachau, plate 38. Ungnad, no. 47.

. . . .
. . . כתב [בפ]חנם . . .
. . . [פ]מנחתף שנת 𐡛/II . . .
. . . בעה עליך גבריא ד . . .

5 . . . . . . גבריא זי אתבציו עד . . . שנ]ת . . .

6 . . . . יקמו באוצרא בית נחמ . . .

7 . . . |/ מ . . . כנופי . . .

8 . . . . מ . . .

9 . . . כ̄כרן ולף ש / . . .

10 . . . מר̄ . . .

11 . . . נ̄את ח̄כ . . .

12 . . . . . . ל ש̄ . . .

13 . . . . . . ן ///\ . . .

14 . . . . . למנתן . . .

15 . . . ⌐/// /// . . .

[1] . . . . [2] . . . wrote *in Pa*ḥons . . . [3] . . . *Pha*menoth, year 13 (?) . . . [4] . . . suborned against you the men . . . [5] . . . . . . the men who were sought out, till . . .-year . . . [6] . . . . they stand in the treasury. The house of N . . . [7] . . . 2 . . . Kenufi . . . [8] . . . . . . [9] . . . 1 thousand talents, . . . shekels . . . [10–12] . . . . [13] . . . . . . 4 . . . [14] . . . . . . to give . . . [15] . . . . 16 . . .

Line 1. Nothing legible.

Line 2. [בפ]חנס is Ungnad's suggestion.

Line 3. ||/ might be עד.

Line 4. בעה על' 'sought' i.e. incited or suborned against you.

Line 5. אתבציו if right, can only mean 'were sought out'.

Line 6. Construction not clear. . . . נחמ a name?

Line 7. כנופי as in 26[9,21].

Line 9. כ̄כרן not certain. Cf. 30[28] כנכרין ולף. ולף as often, for one thousand.

The rest contains nothing worthy of note.

No. 51.

Fragment containing the right-hand side of a column of names, apparently none of them Jewish. The names of the fathers seem not to have been given.

Line 1 was the beginning of the column, since l. 10 is numbered ⌐ in the margin. A mark on the right, near l. 6, suggests that originally there was at least one other column.

Sachau, plate 23. Ungnad, no. 24.

. . .

בתוהי

. . בו .

פחי

וחישתב

ארתבנו

. . דרג

. . איסכ

פרנם

בגבחש

פרניש

זבמן

פרתפרן

אשירת

[4] Pahi? [5] VHŠTB. Artabanus. [7] Dargman? [8] 'ISK . . . [9] PRNM. [10] Bagabukhsha 10. [11] PRNIŠ. [12] ZBMN. [13] Phrataphernes. [14] Ashyadata.

Line 1 contains no complete letter.

Line 3. . . בו. Ungnad בר.

Line 4. פחי cf. 14^2. Egyptian, though the rest, when they can be recognized, are Persian names.

Line 5. . . וחשתב a compound of Persian *vakhš*?

Line 7. . . דרג Dargman? 8^{23} &c.

Line 8. Cf. אסכישו 2^{10}.

Line 10. בגבחש Persian Bagabukhša, Μεγάβυζος.

Line 13. Cf. 5^{17}. Ungnad פרתנן.

Line 14. אשירת Persian Ašyadata (Ungnad).

No. 52.

Fragments of two parallel columns containing chiefly names.

No date. At the beginning of some lines in col. 2 are marks, of unknown meaning. Ungnad thinks they may indicate fractions.

The writing is unusual.

Sachau, plate 24. Ungnad, no. 25.

Col. i.

1 . . . ו
2 . . . הו
3 . . . ד
4 . . . בקע
5 . . . ונשפט
6 . . . יצעקו
7 . . ש]פט על
8 . . . דיה זי [א]חדת

Col. ii.

9 יאשיה בר . . .
10 . . . בר זכר]יה
11 . עדש הש . . .
12 שמעיה בר . . .
13 הושעיה בר [צפ]ניה
14 יאוניה בר [שפ]טיה
15 זכריה בר [זב]דיה
16 משלם בר [יא]זניה
17 יאוניה [בר] חלקיה

Col. i.

1–4 . . . . . 5 . . . and we judge 6 . . . they complain 7 . . . *ju*dge concerning 8 . . . . . . which you (or I) received.

Col. ii.

9 Josiah (?) b. . . . 10 . . . b. Zechar*iah*
11 . . . 12 Shemaiah b. . . . 13 Hoshaiah b. *Zepha*niah 14 Jaazaniah b. *Shepha*tiah 15 Zechariah b. *Zeba*diah 16 Meshullam b. *Jaa*zaniah 17 Jaazaniah *b.* Hilkiah.

Lines 5–8 look like part of a letter.

Line 8. זי. Ungnad ה, but it stands alone.

Line 9. יאשיה. The ש is very doubtful.

Line 14. יאוניה. Ungnad יאציה, which is not known as a name. Cf. the צ in l. 6.

Line 15. [זב]דיה might of course be [זב]ריה.

Line 16. משלם. The ם is strange, but can hardly be anything else.

No. 53.

Fragment containing part of a column of names.

Lines 8 and 11 have been erased, or perhaps the papyrus is palimpsest. Before l. 9 (on the reverse) there are marks of perhaps a line erased. No date.

Sachau, plate 74. Ungnad, no. 26.

1 . . . . בר . . .
2 פטיסי בר נתין
3 חגי̄ בר בארי
4 פסו בר כ̄שי
5 —. נ̄חחנום בר חנמו
6 אשמכדרי בר אפע̄
7 חור בר אס̄כשית
8 . . . . . .

Reverse.

9 אש̄מרם בר נבונד .
10 פסו בר מנכי
11 . . . .

1 . . . . . . b. . . . 2 Peṭisi b. Nethin. 3 Haggai b. Beeri. 4 Pasu b. KŠI. 5 . nḥ-ḥnum b. Ḥnomo. 6 Išum-kudurri b. AP'. 7 Ḥor b. ASKŠITH. 8 . . . .

Reverse.

9 Išum-ram b. Nabunad(in ?) 10 Pasu b. Mannuki. 11 . . . . . .

Line 1. Ungnad בר נתן, which does not seem possible.

Line 2. The son has an Egyptian name, the father's is Jewish. נתין. The proper Aramaic form of נְתוּן used elsewhere.

Line 5. Ungnad and Sachau מנחחנום, but מ is doubtful. Not ענח'. The line at the side is perhaps ר.

Line 6. אפע̄ or אפט.

Line 7. Cf. 51^8.

Line 9. נבונד. A final ן does not seem possible.

No. 54.

Fragment containing two imperfect letters, one on the recto and one on the verso. They are in different hands, both unskilled, the recto being the more so. Evidently both refer to the same matter, but their relation is puzzling. Sachau and Ungnad think that one side is the answer to the other. If so, the reverse would seem to have been written first, note l. 15, שלחו לנב׳ and l. 2 שלחת לנב׳. This, however, does not suit l. 10 מראי and l. 1 עבד־, if the words are used literally, but perhaps they are only formal and Sachau's view is best. The letters cannot be by two writers to the same person, note l. 4 לך and l. 11 לי.

On the recto a line is written vertically at either side. Something is lost at the end, but probably not much at the side of the verso.

Sachau, plate 36. Ungnad, no. 40.

עבדכם [ויש]חי
הא שלחת
לנבונתן
הן אית לך
חמרן ־
ישבקון המו
אף לך . . .
right-hand side. . . . די תנה בנוה[י] שנא
left-hand side. . . . ע]בדך נשזבנ[הי

Reverse.

מן ע]קבנבו שלם מראי
שגיא] בעת הן לי חמרן ־
. . . א זילכם י . . .
. . . נו נבונתן בצבו
. . . למה[ך] מן קדם רבחילא
. . . שלחו לנבונתן וישבק

[1] Your servant *WŠḤI*. [2] Behold, I have sent [3] to Nabunathan (saying): [4] If you have [5] 10 asses [6] they will give them up (?),[7] also to you . . . [8] . . . here his sons exceedingly. [9] . . . your servant (?), we will rescue him.

Reverse.

[10] *From* 'Aḳabnabu, greeting to my lords [11] *exceedingly*. Now if I have 10 asses, [12] . . . . . . yours (?) . . . [13] . . . . . . Nabunathan . . . [14] . . . . . . to go (?) from the commander. [15] . . . . . . send to Nabunathan and he will give up . . . . . .

Line 1. עבד[כם]. The tails remaining can hardly represent anything but ־כם. On the other hand this does not agree with לך (clearly) in l. 4. [ויש]חי only a conjecture, but חי is probable. Cf. 22[133,134].

Line 2. הא. The א has an archaic form.

Line 4. אית is certain. Ungnad אחת. For איתי. Cf. 46[3]. לך. The ך is archaic.

Line 5. חמרן ד־ is certain. The numeral is not quite clear, but is corroborated by l. 11. There is nothing more in the line.

Line 6. ישבקון. For the ו cf. l. 3 לנבונתן. It is not a ר, as Ungnad. 'They will leave them alone' i. e. lay no claim to them? המו probable, with ה above the line.

Line 7. All uncertain.

Line 8 vertically on the right-hand side. ־די is the end of a word. בְּנוֹה[י] fairly certain. Not כ־ (as Ungnad), cf. the ך in l. 4.

Line 9. Vertically on the left-hand side. [ע]בדך̄. The ך is doubtful. The following mark is not א (as Ungnad), but the ו projecting from l. 6. נשוב̄נ[הי. The ב is strange. There are traces of ־הי, which is suitable if this is the verb שוב.

Line 10, on the verso, begins the other letter. [ע]ק̄ב̄נבו is Ungnad's reading. There is a mark after it which may be unintentional. Before it probably מן, which would fix the amount lost at the beginnings of the lines. מראי plural? Cf. שלחו in l. 15 if that is imperative.

Line 11. שניא fits the space as determined by l. 10.

Line 12. ז̄ילכם̄ uncertain. There seems to be an א above the line, but Ungnad reads זילכי. The last letter may be a ם as in קדם l. 14. This would be suitable if מראי is plural, but ־כי fem. could not refer to מראי masc. After it Ungnad reads ה שנת . . ., but this is very doubtful.

Line 13. בצ̄בו̄ faint and uncertain. Ungnad באבו, and Sachau conjectures באבו[ט] 'in Abydos', but the א would be impossible in this hand.

Line 14. למה[ך] is Sachau's conjecture. There is no sign of the ך.

After l. 15 the rest is lost.

No. 55.

Fragment, as Ungnad thinks, of an inventory incomplete on both sides. It may, however, be part of a letter. If so, it would seem to begin on the reverse, cf. no. 54. This depends on the amount lost. A line may be wanting at the beginning, but there does not seem to be much missing at the sides. There is no date.

Sachau, plate 36. Ungnad, no. 41.

Obverse.

ותפסח ⸌

ויהבלי

3 זכריה כרש

4 . . . . \ זי

5 אמרת ל . . .

6 יהב לגדוך

Reverse.

7 ביתאלנד[ן]

8 מישאן \ זי

9 . בו . וחת .

10 . . . נתן

11 וכרבלה \

12 צצנן \\

Obverse.

[1] and I TPSH [2] and Zechariah gave me [3] (I) karash. [4] . . . I . . . which [5] I said to . . . [6] he gave to GDVK (?)

Reverse.

[7] Bethelnad*in* [8] I MŠ'N of [9] *Abydos* (?) and go down (to) *Syene* (?) [10] . . . give. [11] and I hat. [12] 2 . . .

Line I. ותפסה apparently a noun. The ו shows that it cannot begin the document.

Line 4. \ זי. Ungnad זה. It is uncertain whether anything followed זי.

Line 5. . ל hardly לי, as Ungnad.

Line 6. All quite uncertain. There is no name like גדוך.

Line 7. ביתאלנד[ן] not נתן- as Ungnad. A Babylonian form. Cf. $18^{4,5}$.

Line 8. מישאן as in 15^{16a}. Meaning unknown.

Line 9. . בו. Read אבוט Abydos? An א is hardly possible. וחת cf. 42^{7}. If it is a verb, the stroke following cannot be \. Perhaps ס[ון]?

Line 10. נתן or כתן?

Line 11. כרבלה (not כר' 42^{9}) 'a hat' as in Dan. 3^{21}. A Persian, not a Jewish, garment.

Line 12. צצנן. So Ungnad, but the second צ is like the א in l. 8. Sachau thinks it is =צנצנת.

No. 56.

Fragment of the beginning of a letter, with part of the address on the back. No date.

Sachau, plate 37. Ungnad, no. 44.

1 . . . . אלהיא ישאלו שלמך בכל עדן וכעת . . .

2 . . . ת בר יח . . אזל לסון ועבד ליהו . . .

3 . . . . י אזיבו [ב]ר ברכיא הו . . .

Reverse.

4 [אל אחי . . . בר] גדול אח[ו]ך יסלח בר נתן

[1] . . . may the gods seek after your welfare at all times: and now . . . [2] . . . -t b. . . . went to Syene and made for Ya'u- . . . [3] . . . . . . Azibu b. Berechiah . . .

Reverse.

[4] *To my brother* . . . *b.* Gadol, your brother Yislaḥ b. Nathan.

Line 1. A variety of the usual formula, as in no. 39. It no doubt began אל אחי . . . בר גדול אחוך יסלח בר נתן, so that quite half the line is lost at the beginning, and probably something at the end.

Line 2. The names are quite uncertain. Not יח[מול] which is fem. in 22^{89}. ליהו . . . probably, as Ungnad suggests, part of a compound name.

Line 3. אזיבו rather than אאבו (as Ungnad). Cf. אזבי 1 Chron. 11^{37}? ברכיא popular for -כיה, cf. ידניא 14^{2}. Ungnad takes it as 'knees'.

No. 57.

Fragments of a letter. No date. The readings are mostly as in Ungnad, the facsimile being indistinct.

Sachau, plate 38. Ungnad, no. 46.

1 . . . . שלם ליתנא שלם . . .

2 . . . כ]רבלן // לחם נמ . . .

3 . . . . י . . . הו . . .

4 . . . . שלמכם . . .

5 . . . . תי . . .

6 . . . . בת לא . . .

7 . . . במיא זי . . .

8 . . . . . . שלם . . .

9 . . . . . . ערן . . .

10 . . . .

[1] . . . Greeting to Yathna; greeting to . . . . [2] 2 hats . . . . [3] . . . . . .
[4] . . . . . . your welfare . . .
[5] . . . . . [6] . . . . . [7] . . . like the waters of . . . [8] . . . . . . greeting . . .
[9] . . . . . . time . . . [10] . . . .

Line 2. לחֿםֿ. The ם is more like ין, but חין does not occur.
Line 7. כֿמֿיא probable. Ungnad only יא . .
Line 8. Ungnad adds פ—very doubtful.

No. 58.

Fragment. The recto (l. 3) contains what may be part of the address of a letter. The verso (ll. 1, 2), in an unskilful hand, contains two lines imperfect at the beginning (and at the end?) There is no sign of anything above or below them. The letters are rather wide apart, but there are no spaces between words. Sachau thinks it may be Hebrew, but after dividing it in various ways, I have failed to extract any meaning from it, either as Hebrew or Aramaic. Perhaps it is best to regard it as a learner's writing exercise, bearing no relation to the recto. It was written on an old scrap of papyrus torn from a letter, and already bearing the words in l. 3.

Sachau, plate 37. Ungnad, no. 43.

1 . . . מאֿלהיכלישלמכישלם . . .
2 . . . שלמכלכליפֿרקֿנֿישלם . . .
3 . . . בר . . . . בר שבתי

Of lines 1 and 2 the meaning is uncertain. Line 3 . . . b. Shabbethai.

Line 2. פֿרקֿנֿי. The ק might be a ת, and the נ a כ.
Line 3. Ungnad reads עמרי after the first בר.

No. 59.

The top left-hand corner of a document in demotic Egyptian. The Aramaic endorsement shows it to be an affidavit, if the two sides are related.

Sachau, plate 39. Ungnad, no. 49.

Recto, a demotic document.

Verso. ספר מומה זי כתב חמן . .

Verso, endorsement: Deed of an affidavit, which Ḥaman wrote . . .

ס׳ מוכיה cf. 44[1].

חמן seems to be a complete name, but it does not occur again in these papyri. The traces of letters after it do not belong to it.

No. 60.

A Greek letter.

Fragments, of which the larger contains part of a letter in Greek to 'king Ptolemy'. On one of the small fragments are traces of Aramaic writing, but nothing can be read with certainty. The date is said (judging from the writing) to be early in the third century B. C.

The text was published in F. Preisigke's *Sammelbuch griech. Urkunden* i (1915) no. 5111, from which the reading here is taken. It is clearly the beginning of a letter reporting some attack by Ethiopians (on Elephantine or Syene?) which the writer helped to repel.

Sachau, plate 39. Ungnad, no. 48.

βα]σιλεῖ πτολεμαίωι χαίρειν περταῖος ἀρνού[φιος
]φ . . . . κατέβησαν αἰθίοπες κα[ὶ ἐ]πολιόρκ[ησαν
]φρακτεύω ἐγὼ καὶ δύο ἀδελφοὶ στ[αθμὸν (?)
]σ . ν ἐπὶ βοήθειαν καὶ ἀνείλομεν[

[1] To king Ptolemy, greeting. Pertaeus, son of Arnu*phis* . . . [2] . . . . Ethiopians came down and besieged . . . [3] . . . . I . . . and my two brothers . . . [4] . . . . to help and we destroyed . . .

Line 3. . . . *φρακτεύω*. The *φ* is doubtful, as well as the meaning. If it is a verb, the present tense seems unsuitable. *στ[αθμόν]* does not seem a very happy conjecture.

No. 61.

An inventory.

On the reverse of a papyrus of the Behistun inscription. There are two columns, of which the first contains part of the end of the inscription (see p. 253) and the other contains this list or inventory. The date is lost. The reading is particularly difficult, owing to the broken and discoloured state of the papyrus. The text here differs a good deal from that of Ungnad and Sachau.

Sachau, plate 55, col. 2. Ungnad, no. 67, ii.

[ז]כרן כסין זי נח[ש]
חנן בר חני ליד[
כסין זי נח[ש] בל[

כם כסף חד

בילוף /// .

. . . . ⥲

בילוף . . . . לג

. זי ס[תת]רין //

רכ . . למאכל ///

זכרן ענ̄י אח

מנכ[י ב]ר ענניה

ביום [/ לא]דר שנת . . .

כסין . . כסף (?) ש ד /

כס כסף \

יקמ[ון] ש / . . .

ז . . . . ///

ולף (?) . . // /// \

ככ /// . . . /

. . . .

[1] Memorandum: cups of bronze . . . [2] Hanan b. Haggai . . . [3] cups of bronze 21 . . . [4] cup of silver, one . . . [5–7] . . . . [8] of 2 *staters* . . . [9] . . . to eat, 3 . . .
[10] Memorandum: 'Ani . . . [11] Mannuki *b.* 'Ananiah [12] on day *1 of A*dar, year . . . [13] cups . . . the sum of 21 shekels [14] cup of silver, 1: [15] *they* are worth shekels . . . [16–19] . . . .

Line 1. זכרן 'memorandum' as in $32^{1.2}$.

Line 5. בילוף is probable, as in l. 7, or אלוף. Meaning?

After l. 9 there is a blank space, and a horizontal stroke.

Line 10 begins a new list. ענ̄י or ענני a name?

Line 12 contained a date which was no doubt nearly that of writing. דר is fairly certain. Sachau [א]פף Epiphi, and one would expect an Egyptian month.

Line 13. After כסין probably a numeral. כסף is only a conjecture, but it is better than Ungnad's פרן.

Line 15. יקמ[ון] 'are valued at'? Cf. 15^{16a}. ש̄ or /// as Ungnad.

After l. 19 the papyrus is blank.

The following (nos. 62–68) are for the most part groups of small disconnected scraps. The reading of them as printed by Sachau has been revised with the facsimiles and a few passages have been restored, but in the absence of context it is not possible to make much out of them. They do not admit of connected translation, but points of interest are treated in the commentary.

No. 62.

No. 1. The verso of a Behistun fragment.
Probably accounts, like no. 61. Beginnings of lines only.

Sachau, plate 56 (reverse). Ungnad, no. 68 E.

No. 1.

1 חנ]ן
2 +
3 מית נבועקב בר]
4 זכרן חנן בר עזרי]ה
5 ל . . . עלדבר פת]
6 לא . שז באן]
7 . . . . כסף

No. 3.

1 ק .
2 ול .
3 בה .
4 בח .
5 / זבן .
6 / ל .
7 בח .

Nos. 2, 4, 8, 9 Behistun fragments.
Nos. 5–7, 10–20 unimportant.

Line 2 a mark of division, not like that in Aḥiḳar. Perhaps only a horizontal stroke crossed through.

Line 3. נבועקב cf. $26^{23.28}$ and 22^{20} where it is preceded by מאת (centuria) which may perhaps be read or intended here. The father's name is not mentioned in either passage.

Line 4. זכרן as in $61^{1.10}$. The / here and in l. 5 (in Ungnad) does not belong to the line.

No. 3. The verso of a Behistun fragment (ll. 18–28). Unimportant.

No. 63.

On the back of a Behistun fragment (ll. 1–15).

Accounts or inventory, like no. 61, in two columns. Beginnings of ll. 1–7 lost. Ends of ll. 8–16 lost.

Sachau, plate 53 (reverse). Ungnad, no. 69.

Col. i.

1 . . / שנת [ר]/// [//] כסף . . בא לת[

2 . . . / /// תויא אנתת אחרטים ש פ [/]//\

blank.

3 . . . כך ברת זכ[ור . . .]בך פ // סאן ///\

4 . . . ל שלמת ש . . .

5 . . . פ ׀

blank.

6 . . . א אליהויש[מע] בר . . עבי בר

7 . . . א

Col. ii.

8 זכור בר . . . י שנת /// ///[

9 עזריה לחנא נגרא תנ[

blank.

10 זכרן על מנחם בר שלום [

11 ארך אמן /// כ //   ב . [

12 זכרן על עז[ר]יה לחנא זי[

13 תנין ע.א ע . . נא רבא זי . . [

blank.

14 זכרן קניא זי הפשר ול . . . [

15 [פנו]ליה בר אושע באפף שנת ר///[

16 . . . יהב ל . . רין בירח מסורע [

Line 1. The numeral as restored is fairly certain, cf. l. 15 which is probably the same or the next year.

Line 2. תויא. Ungnad cft. Θαυής in Greek papyri. אחרטים. Ungnad cft. Aḫarṭiše. ש no doubt for שקלן. פ not for כסף, as Ungnad. It must be some term defining שקלן.

Line 3. כך . . . may be ח . . . There is a נהכת ברת זכור in 22[107].

Line 6. אליהויש[מע] might be אליהו ///, but there are faint traces of מע. The name occurs elsewhere, but the father is not mentioned.

Line 8. /// /// שנת is against what was said on l. 1.

Line 9. Nothing between עזריה and לחנא. It is merely a large ה. לחנא as in l. 12 seems to be some term descriptive of Azariah. In Aḥikar 83 לחנת the ל is a preposition.

Line 10. על (as in l. 12) after זכרן, is unusual. For the name cf. 44^1.

Line 11. // כ is written. Probably meant for // ב as usual in measurements. Then a blank before a new entry.

Line 12. זֿיֿ or [נג[רא as in l. 9.

Line 13. תנין can only mean 'secondly', referring to Azariah, who was previously mentioned in l. 9. ע.א Ungnad עקא improbable. It may be כספיא written close together.

Line 14. קֿניא cf. קניה in 1^2, the 27th year of Darius, and 5^2, the 15th year of Xerxes. הפשר. In Hebrew the Hiphil means 'to come to an agreement'. In later Aramaic the Pael means to 'settle' an obligation, so that the Aphel (not used) might mean the same 'to pay'. On an ostrakon (Sayce and Cowley M, ll. 5, 6, 8) the word הושר is used in a somewhat similar sense. It is tempting to identify the two words, but ו seems clear there, and פ here.

Line 15. פנו]ליה] is only conjectural. The papyrus is creased. The name occurs elsewhere, but the father is not mentioned. Date perhaps as in l. 1.

No. 64.

Fragments 1–16 belong to Behistun.

Sachau, plate 57. Ungnad, no. 70 B.

No. 17.	]כריא	No. 18.	מ]לכא שערן[
	נ]לאדן		]סֿנתן על[.
	blank.		
	. . . צֿרֿמלך[	No. 19.	[. הקימת[
	]יירח		]ם אנה ה[ו
No. 20.	]השיארש[	No. 21.	. . [. ליֿ[
	]שלח עליך[		]בטל . [ ]באו[
	ל]סֿיון שנת[		
	שנ]ת אחרה ה[	No. 22.	]תֿ[
	מן]מצרין אמ[.		]בֿיֿן[
	]אֿ במה[		
	[. . שנֿתֿ[		

No. 23.
[מן כבש]
[נכת ח]

No. 24.
[שנת]
[כרת]

No. 25.
[ש]
[ה פילל ? . .]

No. 26.
[א זי לקאן] [אבוט]
[אמר בכרס] [לקל ישרא ?

No. 27.
א]יתי כ[
אש]למנך[

No. 28.
[תא ז]
[ידין]
[ש בן ה]

No. 29.
גבר]יא זי אסירן[
ח]שיא[ר]ש מלבא[

No. 17, l. 1. Perhaps [פרמנ]כריא as in 26[4]. l. 2. Sachau suggests a name [נרג]לאדן. Note the form of the א. l. 3. צרמלך . . . a name. l. 4. יירח is clear. Sachau בירח.

No. 18. From a contract. l. 1. Sachau restores [באבני מ]לכא. l. 2. Sachau [ל]מנתן. The remains of מ are doubtful.

No. 19. Cf. Aḥiḳar 44, 46.

No. 20. From a letter of the reign of Xerxes, i. e. before 465 B.C. l. 3. [ל]סיון only slight traces remain. Probably to be read so. l. 5. [מן]. The tail of a letter quite close to מצרין can only be ן or ת.

No. 21, l. 2. Sachau suggests בטלה, and refers the fragment to Behistun.

No. 22. Unimportant.

No. 23. From the Aḥiḳar proverbs?

No. 24. From a contract?

No. 25. Unimportant.

No. 26. Something seems to be written between the lines. פכרס perhaps a name.

Nos. 27, 28. From contracts.

No. 29. From a letter or list of prisoners in the time of Xerxes, i. e. before 465 B.C. Cf. no. 34.

No. 65.

Eighteen fragments of legal documents, &c.

Sachau, plate 58. Ungnad, no. 71.

No. 1.
[ומרביתה]
[בכספא זנה]
[תור מאן ז]

No. 2.
[גדול ב]ר
[ידניה בר]

No. 3.
אמר מת̅ן בר יש[
לזכם דגלא[
הוה לחתסנ . [

No. 4.
]שלם אחי בכל
]שלם כעת
לאחת ה̅
]את זי ח̅

No. 5.
//]/ /// /// לירח ה[
]ברת אשין ארמי[ן

No. 6.
] מלכא [
]כ̅א בי[ב

No. 7.
]כת . . . . ב̅אתו[
]. כס[ף כ]רשן המשה[
ב̅ר̅ תחנו̅ם ספרא [זנ]ה̅
demotic.
]זכרי ב[ר . . .]אל
]בית [

No. 8.
]י̅שאלונני̅[
]ספרא זנה[

No. 9.
]מל[
]ה̅ו̅[
נ]ת̅ו̅[

No. 10.
]ד [
]כרשן י̅ [

No. 11.
demotic ?
]שהד פטפ̅[
א]חמנש . [

No. 12.
ז]נ̅ה̅[
]כ̅תי[ב

No. 13.
]תרכנה[
]ירח ת̅[

No. 14.
]בר̅י̅[
]צ̅פנ̅[
כ]ס̅פא ז[נה
]כ̅י̅ לא[
] . . פ̅ר̅א̅[

No. 15.
נשכעד[רי
blank.

No. 16.
] /// [
] ? מר̅[
] ? ? פן[

No. 17.
]עליה[

No. 18.
ס]פרא[
]הודויה ב[ר
blank.

No. 2. The end of a document or column. Perhaps from a list of names.

No. 3 begins with the second line of a document. מתן בר יש[ביה] cf. 38^1. להחסנ[ותה] Sachau.

No. 4. Beginning of a letter.

No. 5. From the first two lines of a contract. ח . . . Ungnad suggests Ḥoiak, the Egyptian month (כיחך in 72^{18}). ארמי[ן] probably.

No. 6. From a contract.

No. 7. From a contract to which no. 11 also belongs. They are combined thus:

[כת . . . באתו]
[כס[ף כ]רשן חמשה]
כתב . . . .] בר תחנום ספרא [זנ]ה [כפם . . . ושהדיא בגו

demotic.

[שהד פטפ[. . . בר . . . שהר] זברי ב[ר . .]אל
א]חמניש [. . . . .] בית [. . .

l. 1. hardly באתו[ר]. l. 3. Clearly the end of the body of the contract, giving the scribe's name. But תחנום is feminine. l. 4 in demotic. No doubt a witness. Griffith reads on no. 7, 'H-e[-'r-ṭy-s] i. e. Ah[arṭais]. Cf. אחרטים 63^{2}. The demotic on no. 11 is uncertain. l. 5. Witnesses' names in their own handwriting. . . . פטפ. Possibly פטסי. At any rate an Egyptian name. l. 6. [א]חמניש cf. 17^{1}. But there is a trace of a letter (ה?) after ש, which is against this reading.

No. 8. Sachau thinks this may belong to nos. 7, 9, 11–13, but I doubt if they are all in the same hand. ישאלונני. The י is very unusual in form.

No. 9. תנו, perhaps . . ינתנו or תנתננה.

No. 10. Unimportant.

No. 11. See under no. 7.

Nos. 12, 13. Unimportant.

No. 14. The writing is unusual. Note צ (if so). The א is late.

No. 15. נשכעד[רי]. Sachau. Witness's name at the end of a deed. Cf. 2^{19}, 3^{23}.

No. 16. Unusual writing. Reading quite uncertain.

No. 17. Unimportant.

No. 18. End of a deed. Cf. 10^{22}.

No. 66.

Sixteen fragments of legal and similar documents.

Sachau, plate 59. Ungnad, no. 72.

No. 1.

זנה ש[מחת גבריא]
[ה בר פטנתר שמ[ה
[גבריא זי ש[מהתהם כתיבן מנעל
[גברן מנן יה]
קד]ם בנבווי ל .]

blank.

No. 2.

[מת]
[א בר ת]
[כתיב]
[ו ברב .]
[. . .]

blank.

No. 3.
]ימה לך [
]בין נהת[
lost.
]ין יה[

No. 4.
blank
]לח זי מ[
]לרגל[
]שערן [
] אנת [

No. 5.
]י א[
]ו פי[
] . תהמ[
[אסר .]
]בתל[

No. 6.
]בגרת בר[
בי]ב בירתא[
מן יומי מ]לך מצר[ין

No. 7.
מ]לי דבק לה[
]ה בב ב[יתא
]אתרפרת[

No. 8.
זך כרשן / [
ענני ספרא זנ[ה
אזניה ענג[י
blank.

No. 9.
]שלם עבדך[
]וקצרתי[

No. 10.
]לונפר[
]ליזניה[

No. 11.
]מנכם ומן ב[

No. 12.
]מנתי[
]י אבוטים [
]ם דמי[
]ם כ . זיל[
[ל]

No. 13.
]תחומוה[י

No. 14.
[/// ב]
]ה לה בית[
מרח]ק ביתא / זי כ[תב
. . . .

No. 15.
. . . . . .
[.א א . מן מ[וע]א למערב]
]/// ע . . . . .

No. 16.
]תנתנון לה בשנ[ת
]לכם הן ג . . .

No. 1. From a list of names, perhaps in a letter. l. 1. [זנה ש]מחת as in 22[1], 34[1]. l. 2. An Egyptian name. l. 4. כנבוזי as in 30[13], 32[5]. This is the last line of a column, followed by a blank.

Sachau suggests that nos. 1–3, 5, 6, 9–11, 16 all belong to the same document. The writing of nos. 1, 2, 6 seems to be by the same hand, but it is not possible to arrange them together with any certainty.

The document may relate to the destruction of the temple at Yeb (no. 30 &c.), and was perhaps a petition to the Persian governor, recounting the names of the men responsible for the destruction, and praying for their punishment and for the restoration of the temple. The foreign names in fragments 1 and 6 agree with this, and the mention of Cambyses and the (native) king of Egypt imply a reference to the history of the temple, as in no. 30.

No. 2 is probably part of the same as no. 1. The blank space shows the relative position of the lines. They are not continuous, but that is not surprising, if they were as long as in no. 30.

No. 3. Not by the same hand as no. 1. In l. 3 the surface has flaked off.

No. 4. From the beginning of a contract relating to barley.

No. 5. Probably not by the same hand as no. 1.

No. 6. See on no. 1. בגדת Persian Bagadata (Theodorus). In 3^{24} he has an Egyptian (?) father. The context is the same as in 30^{13}—the city of Yeb, the king of Egypt, Cambyses.

No. 7. Subject obscure. The name is Persian. Probably not אתרפרן.

No. 8. From the end of a deed. נתן בר ענני wrote 10^{20}. אזניה cf. 12^{8}, 18^{5}. The י has two strokes, but the writing is rough, and it may be so.

No. 9. From the beginning of a letter.

No. 10. לונפר 'to Onophris' (Sachau).

No. 11. Unimportant.

No. 12. אסוטים apparently an Egyptian name. Not אחרטים as above.

No. 13. Perhaps from a lease or conveyance, as in 6^{7}.

No. 14. Possibly part of the same as no. 13. Cf. 6^{22}.

No. 15. From a similar document, giving measurements of a house as in $8^{4.5}$. למערב is certain, and confirms כין כ[וע]א. Sachau and Ungnad read למעבד, and ascribe the fragment to Behistun.

No. 16. From a contract. . . . נ no doubt is part of נרי (Sachau).

No. 67.

Eighteen fragments of legal documents, &c.

Sachau, plate 60. Ungnad, no. 73.

No. 1.]לתעובי ש[נת
]ארדנבו ל[

No. 2. ם] ב /// // לפ[
]השלחת ל[
.]שה[

No. 3.
]ביה ארמי סונכן לרגל[
]גריתך בדין [
]יתומה וסלואה [

No. 4.
]לאדר הו[
]קון ארמי זי[
. . . . . .

No. 5.
]וטיב לבב[
]רחקת מנך מן י[ומא זנה
]איש לי יגרנך ד[ין
. זי . . . . . .

No 6.
]ן בר פס[
]כם בר כט[
]בר אני[
]ור [

No. 7.
]י כל
ל]זה מראי
ל]אית

No. 8
ירח ירח פק[
אל אחי מ[

No. 9.
]שנ[
]סתתרי / . [

No. 10.
]וש /// / זי מרבי[תא
]שנת ⅃ /// /// // לדר[יוהוש

No. 11.
א]ושע [
[שלם]

No. 12.
אחרי יהוי [
. . . .

No 13.
]מר חטה // [
]בשמש ⅃ / . [
]י נע[
]אר[
]תרנ
]נא ח[

No. 14.
]תי[
]ת לאסר[
]אמר . [
[. נלך מ[
]ם תשי ש[
blank.

No. 15.
]ך יהו
]גדל אח[

No. 16.
]שקלן //[
]כספא ינתן[

No. 17.
]צחא . [

No. 18.
]ויקהונה[
. . . . . .

No. 1. From the beginning of a contract. ארדנבו Babylonian name, probably of the *degel*, cf 20^2.

No. 2. Unusual hand. From a contract? The date ('on the 5th of P . . .') is not that of the deed, as there are traces of a previous line.

No 3. סונכן 'a man of Syene'. Cf. 24^{33}, 33^6. Yethoma and Selu'a are sisters in $1^{1,2}$, to which this may refer.

No. 4. From the beginning of a contract. קון if right and a complete name, cf. 22^{117}.

No. 5. Common form in contracts.

No. 6. Reading uncertain. The hand is like that of some of the ostraka. Perhaps a list of names.

No. 7. Ends of lines, of a letter?

No. 8. From a contract. Unusual hand.

No. 9. 'One stater', cf. 37[12] &c.

No. 10. From a contract. מרבי]תא] (Sachau) is doubtful. The date, which is fairly certain, is no doubt of Darius II (406 B.C.).

No. 11. Perhaps from a letter.

No. 12. Unusual hand. Otherwise unimportant.

No. 13. Reading and meaning uncertain. The ח and ט have unusual forms. Cf. no. 2.

No. 14. Meaning uncertain. From a contract?

No. 15. From the beginning of a letter?

No. 16. From a contract.

No. 17. Unimportant.

No. 18. Note the imperf. of לקח without ל.

No. 68.

Twelve fragments of legal documents, letters and accounts. Mostly with writing on both sides.

Sachau, plate 61. Ungnad, no. 74.

No. 1. Obv.	מ]כם ומנן . . . . .]שלם אחוך תקותיא שלם [blank.	Rev.	. . . . . . שלם יהוה] על . . . . . ל
No. 2. Obv.	]שׁ̄ מלכא אדין ב]יב]זי ליה̄]]ת עמכי למ]	Rev.	blank. ב]רת זכור
No. 3. Obv.	]י פ .]]בּ̄א אל]]עד תחזה]]לבשך ולא]]לת פתום	Rev.	blank.]לך̄ כל ר] [. ל . .] [. . ח]
No. 4. Obv.	]אדין ביב אמרת מבט] שׁ̄	Rev.	]זי כתבת מפטחיה ב]רת

No. 5. Obv.
]ה עבדת[
]כרש בזרען זיל[
blank.

Rev.
]כו[
]במלן ל . . זנה[
] . ר //
blank.

No. 6. Obv.
]א יהיבא [
מ]דינתא[

Rev.
]לי אזב[
]סב אמש[
] . שמל[

No. 7. Obv.
]בך[
]קי בת[
] . תאל א[
]תאלה[

Rev.
blank.

No. 8. Obv.
]סתרי אחוכי[
]ובניה שלם [

Rev.]אחתי כ[תרי

No. 9. Obv.]נתן עד[

Rev. מרא[י

No. 10. Obv.
]פרד . ונת[
]עם זי תנ[תן
] ערבן חסין [

Rev.
י]הוישמע בר [
] . ברך בר [
] . נבושדר[

No. 11. Obv.
ב /// לתעובי[
זכרן חמר[ן
באֿרעא . [
ב /// לתעובי אמ[
כל[

Rev.
] . ל . . . . המרן |
]מרינת נא

No. 12. Obv.
עבדיך[
בין[
ארת[
בלבנ[
כל ד[
כל ד[

Rev. כפ[ר]א זי לבהתא אנתתה . [

No. 1. From a letter. תקותיא is strange. תקוה is known as a name. Reverse mostly obliterated.

No. 2. From a contract. If ש is right (as Sachau) it might belong to Xerxes, Artaxerxes, or Darius. One of the parties was a woman (as shown by עמכי), and according to the endorsement, a daughter of Zaccur.

No. 3. Obscure.

No. 4. From a contract. The name is evidently [מבטח]יה, which is spelt מפט' in the endorsement. There is nothing to show whether this was the notorious daughter of Mahseiah.

No. 5. From a letter or contract?

No. 6. Unimportant.

No. 7. Obscure. In ll. 3 and 4 ביתאל?

No. 8. From a letter to סחרי from her brother. The name may be short for סחריאל, which is known.

No. 9. From a letter?

No. 10. From a contract? ערבן, if right, = Heb. ערבון. Reverse, names (of witnesses?). Sachau's נבושדר is probable.

No. 11. Accounts, cf. 61. Beginnings of lines. l. 2. חמר[ן] a name(?). Or חמרן as in $54^{5.11}$? l. 4. The date is added in the margin. l. 5. כל introducing a total. Rev. l. 1. חמרן or חמרן as obv. l. 2. l. 2. מדינת נא as in 24^{36} 'district of Thebes'. Not 'our city' (as Sachau).

No. 12. Beginnings of lines from a report. l. 3. . . ארת a Persian name. Reverse, endorsement, as in contracts, but written at right angles to the obverse. The name is uncertain.

The following (nos. 69–78) have been already published in the CIS. They are all fragmentary and very difficult to interpret. They are reprinted here for the sake of completeness because they evidently belong to the same period and class as the documents from Elephantine. Moreover the discovery of the better preserved texts has thrown light on some points which were previously obscure. As they have been carefully edited in the CIS a full commentary is unnecessary here. Only divergences from the views taken there will be noted.

No. 69.

Six fragments, not all belonging to the same document. B is certainly in a different hand from the rest.

Ungnad suggests that they are part of a story. They may, however, belong to a letter or petition or report narrating one of the many troublesome incidents in the history of the colony. The reading throughout is very uncertain and the fragments are too much broken to admit of translation. They were first published by Lepsius in his *Denkmäler*, vol. xii, pl. 124, and afterwards in CIS ii, 1, 149. From the character of the writing it seems that they belong to the same period as the rest of these texts, and that they probably came from Elephantine.

Fragment A is in two columns.

Sachau, plate 51. Ungnad, no. 64. CIS. ii, 1, no. 149, plate xix.

A

י]החוה יו[	. . . .
אחר] מלל על פטנפחתף[	]בין .
]כן אמר אחרו[	. . . . .
א . . . . ואסרוהי ו[	]שמש
לא שבקוהי עד כנ[	]א . חטרן בי
א	. . . .
. . . . . .	. . . . . פחת
כלל . . נתו בבב הנ[	]שבו ביבולי
נס.לת חתמובי צליח[	]נתכי זי
ב . . ח יהיב לתחות[	]פתירות ברי לי
נהי.ש קסתר /// ויםלל על[	]אמחות בר . . . תה זי
זי לא באגר יהבת לה אף נתנת[	]אלהא
לוששן וכנותה [	]שבק . . . . ל . . . .

B	D	C	F
המו כן אמ[רו	א]מחו[ת	שלם לבר[	. . . .
שימו לה[	ר // ח[	ה במנ[	. . . .
גנוא א[	ש ש ד[		//// ל[
עביד[	תרא א . . ד[		// ל[
זר	תנה[		

E

ד[

חמר ברא זי[

לי[

A, col. ii.

[1] he will show . . . [2] *then* he spoke to Petenefḥotep . . . [3] . . . thus he said, They seized . . . [4] . . . and imprisoned him and . . [5] they did not let him go till . . . [6] . . . . [7] . . . . [8] . . . . in the gate? of [9] . . . [10] . . . given to Thoth . . . [11] . . . . . . 3 and he will speak to . . . [12] which I did not give to him as payment; also I gave . . . [13] to WŠŠN and his companions.

The rest does not admit of translation.

Col. ii, l. 4. וֹאסרוהי (Ungnad) seems the only way of making a word of it, but the וא is very doubtful. l. 8. כלל very uncertain. Hardly מלל. l. 10. לתחות. The Egyptian god Thoth rather than the month. l. 11. \\// probable Ungnad ש. l. 13 לושׂשן a name 'to W.'

No. 70.

Beginning of a letter Cf. 30[1] and often.

CIS. ii, 1, no. 144, plate xv.

אל מראי מתרוהשת עבדך פחים שׂ[לם

חיא חדה ושרירא מראי יהוי ית[יר

[1] To my lord Mithravahisht, your servant Pahim, *greeting* . [2] Living, happy and prosperous may my lord be *exceedingly* . . .

Line 1. מתרוהשת a Persian name. 'Mithra is best'. שׂ[לם]. There is a trace of the ש. The line was probably long, and continued שלם מראי אלה שמיא ישאל בכל עדן.

Line 2. חיא with חדה ושרירא is best taken as in CIS 'vivus', but the emphatic forms are strange. מראי not vocative, but subject of יהוי. יהוי is jussive, not a mere by-form of יהוה ית[יר] cf. 30[3]. The ת is certain, not ק.

No. 71.

Two fragments, perhaps belonging to the same text, which no doubt was a story. Apparently Bar Puneš had done some meritorious service for which he was suitably rewarded by the king.

CIS. ii, 1, no. 145, plate xvi.

A. Recto.

	ולא ימלא ב[טנ]הם לה[ם
	איש כיבי אבהיהם[
]ין	קרמתהם עד יבנון קר[
]ע	וביומן אחרנן יאכל[
]והי	צדקה לאבוהי ויזב[ן
]תך	ויתקלנהי בלבה ויקטל איש ל[
]אישה	מראה וישרה איש בני מראה[
	לחם ויתכנשון אלהי מצרין[
	. . . . . שנן 𐡁𐡁 \\// פח[

A. Verso.

10 . . . .]לבני על תסהדא זי מלכא ושמ[ע
11 . . . . . .] בר פונש הו אחר ענה מלכא[
12 . . . . . .] בר פונש מליא זי מלכא אמר ו[ענה
13 . . . . . ק]טלת המו תהך בחרב חילך וח[
14]ו יחלף זך ושביא זי שבית בזא שנתא[
15]באלך ונרמיך לא יחתון שאול וטללך[
16 בר פונ]ש על אלפי מלכא ו . . . . . במנצ[חן

B. Recto.

17]מלכא וזעק ומשח[
18]ונה זי קרה[
19 ת]תלנהי כן כזי עבדת לבנוה[י
20]לולא באתר ימ[א] קטל[תהי
21]שעתרם בתמאי ומנח[ם
22 ו]ך תהך ותשתה[
23]ה עם אלהן ולחש עזור[
24]צב . ב . . [וביומן] אחרנן[

B. Verso.

25] זי ינתן לה אבוהי[
26 יתבנ]שו אלהי מצרין [זי
27 מצ]רין ויהוון[
28]מה ותאבד צדקתא ואי[
29]סו ואתנפק איש[
30]ש עלדבר כספה כשר[
31]פגרה לקברה [ול
32]ויאמרון לה ויעני[
33]נתה כפלג . . . תלך ול[

[1] And he shall not fill their be*lly* with br*ead* . . . [2] every man the sufferings of their fathers . . . [3] before them until they should build a ci*ty* (?) . . . [4] And in after days he shall eat . . . [5] righteousness to his father, and shall sell . . . [6] And he shall weigh it in his heart (?) and one shall kill . . . [7] his lord, and one shall set free the sons of his lord . . . [8] bread, and the gods of Egypt shall be assembled . . . [9] . . . . 44 years . . .

[10] . . . . . . to my sons concerning the testimony (?) of the king and he heard . . . [11] . . . . . . it was Bar Puneš. Then the king answered . . .

[12] . . . . . . Bar Puneš the words which the king said and *he answered* . . . [13] . . . . . . thou hast killed them, thou shalt go with the sword of thy troops, and . . . [14] . . . he shall make up for (?) this, and the prisoners whom thou hast captured this year . . . [15] . . . in these, and thy bones shall not go down to the grave, nor thy spirit . . . [16] . . . *Bar Puneš* over the hosts of the king, and *set him* among the offi*cers* . . .
[17] . . . the king, and he cried out and measured (?) . . . [18] . . . this which happened . . . [19] . . . *thou* shalt hang him. Thus as thou didst to his sons . . . [20] . . . unless (?) in a place by the sea *thou* hast killed *him* [21] . . . ? ? ? [22] . . . *th*is, thou shalt go and drink . . . [23] . . . with (the) gods, and he whispered, help . . . [24] . . . . . . *and in* after *days* . . .
[25] . . . which his father shall give him . . . [26] . . . the gods of Egypt *shall be assem*bled, *who* . . . [27] . . . *E*gypt, and they shall be . . . [28] . . . and righteousness shall perish . . . [29] . . . and the man was taken out . . . [30] . . . on account of his money . . . [31] . . . his body to its grave, and . . . [32] . . . and they shall speak to him and he shall answer . . . [33] . . . . . . for half . . . .

Line 2. כיבי. One would expect כאבי, if it means 'pains'. אבהיהם is more probable than אלהיהם. Cf. אבהין 'our fathers' 30^{13}.

Line 3. קדמתהם. CIS קימיהם, but the spaces are too large for י. Cf. קדמתך 'before you' Aḥiḳar 101. . . קר CIS קר[יה].

Line 4. וביומן את'. Cf. Aḥiḳar 39, 52 &c.

Line 6. בלבה. The ב is more like a ד.

Line 7. וישרה may mean 'set free' (CIS) but? Above the line are the letters בב, faint, palimpsest?

Line 10. חסהדא CIS 'testimonium', but the root is always written with ש in these texts. The ר might be a ב.

Line 11. הו belongs to what precedes, and אחר begins a new sentence, as e. g. in Aḥiḳar *passim*.

Line 13. בחרב חילך CIS 'with the sword of thy strength'. Perhaps rather 'with the sword of thy troops' i. e. with thy armed forces, addressed to the king.

Line 14. יהלף very uncertain. זך CIS לך. בוא שנתא cf. 21^{3}.

Line 15. יחתון with an accusative as in 42^{7}, but in 42^{11} with ל. שאול is certain. It does not occur elsewhere in these texts. טללך thy shadow i. e. thy spirit or soul.

Line 16. אלפי more likely 'thousands' than 'officers', as CIS. במנצ[חן]. CIS takes it as a name. The restoration adopted here would be suitable, if the word is possible in Aramaic.

Line 17. ומשה fairly certain. Perhaps 'measured' cf. 9^{4}, rather than 'anointed'.

Line 18. קרה (CIS קרא by a slip), no doubt 'happened'.

Line 19. כן בני probably begins a new sentence.

Line 20. לולא CIS 'nisi' as later. But לו 'if' in these texts seems to occur only in the compound הן לו. Perhaps it is a noun. The lost letter preceding it looks like ש. Or is it הן לו לא?]ימ[א] קטל is more probable than CIS ים יקטל. באתר ימא like Heb. במדינת הים 'a place by the sea'.

Line 21. שעתרם. So CIS. The ר is more like ם, but ב is possible.

Line 22. ותשתה. The second ת is fairly certain. CIS ותשלה.

Line 24. ־נן are clear, and אחר probable, which suggests וביומן before it.

Line 26. יתכנ[שו] as in l. 8. זי printed as certain in CIS, is not visible on the facsimile.

Line 29. סו . . . CIS בו . . .

Line 30. עלדבר כספה. CIS עלך בר כבוה ו[י], but the names are not known. Reading very uncertain.

Line 31. פנרה doubtful. CIS [יב]רבון is hardly possible. לקברה (or לקבלה). Probably a noun rather than infin. Pael. ול . . . printed as certain in CIS, is not visible on the facsimile.

Line 32. זיעני CIS צערי, but נ is more probable than ר.

Line 33. חלך not a Hebraism for תהך, which is used in l. 22.

No. 72.

Fragment, written on both sides, containing accounts for wine, evidently referring to a private household rather than to a trade.

There are parts of two columns on either side, but the right-hand column in each case is nearly all lost. The lines were short, and each as a rule contained a single complete entry.

CIS does not say where the papyrus was found. It may not have come from Elephantine. The writing is not like that of the other documents, and is perhaps somewhat later, but as it is no doubt the work of a man who was not a professional scribe, it is not easy to judge.

CIS. ii, 1, no. 146, plate xvii.

1	]פאפי זי מתיהב	נפקתה בירח פאפי
2		ב \ לפאפי לשרתא חמר צידן קלבי \ מצרין[
3	]מצרין קלבי \	ב // לפאפי לשרתא מצרין קלול \ קלבין //
4	מצר]ין קלול \ קלבין //	היב לצחא בר פמת חמר מצרין מאנן /// //[
5		בנו קלולן // קלבין /// עליך זער שר
6		]ב.ל עליך קדם עחר מ[צר]ין קלול \
7		]מצרין קלול \
8		]ל.לא מצרין קלבי \

]ז̈ בצ . . מצרין קלול \

]לישרתא חמר צידן קלבי \ מצרין[

]בר פחה מצרין קלול \

]ל[שרתא מצרין ק]לול \

B.

ב ד /// לשרתא קלול \ קלבי \

ב ד ///\ לבנדו \ קלבין ||

לנקיה קדם אפתו אלהא רבא קלבי \

קדם
לנקיה אסי אלהתא קלבי \

]תנה   לשרתא חמר צידן קלבי \

]\   ב ד /// // לכיתך זי הו יום לנדר לשרתא קלולן ||

]קלבי \   ב ד /// /// קדם א[

עליך אנדומא[

]\   ב ד ||| ||| || ל[

]י \   ב ד ||| ||| ||| ל[

]פצתא   עחרנפי לה[

לשרתא[

ל[

A. Col. i.

[1] . . . Paophi, which was given out [2] . . . .
[3] . . . *wine of* Egypt, ḳelbi 1. [4] . . . *wine of Egy*pt, ḳelul 1, ḳelbi 2.

Col. ii.

[1] Expenses in the month of Paophi: [2] On the 1st of Paophi for dinner, wine of Sidon, ḳelbi 1, Egypt(ian) . . . [3] On the 2nd of Paophi for dinner, Egypt(ian), ḳelul 1, ḳelbi 2 [4] Given to Zeḥo b. Pamuth, wine of Egypt 5 bottles [5] containing ḳelul 2, ḳelbi 3, for you . . . [6] . . . . . . for you before 'Aḥor, *Egy*pt(ian), ḳelul 1. [7] . . . . . . Egypt(ian), ḳelul 1. [8] . . . . Egypt(ian), ḳelbi 1. [9] . . . . Egypt(ian), ḳelul 1. [10] . . . . . . for dinner, wine of Sidon, ḳelbi 1, Egypt(ian) . . . [11] . . . . . . b. Peḥa, Egypt(ian), ḳelul 1. [12] . . . . . . for *dinner, Egypt(ian), ḳe*lul 1.

B. Col. i, nothing important.

Col. ii.

[13] On the 23rd for dinner, ḳelul 1, ḳelbi 1. [14] On the 24th to Bagadeva (?) 1, ḳelbi 2. [15] For a purification before Apuaitu, the great god, ḳelbi 1. [16] For a purification before Isis the goddess, ḳelbi 1. [17] For dinner, wine of Sidon, ḳelbi 1. [18] On the 25th of Khoiak, which was the day of a vow, for dinner, ḳelul 2. [19] On the 26th before . . . [20] For you . . . [21] On the 28th for *dinner* . . . [22] On the 29th for *dinner* . . . [23] Aḥornufi . . . [24] For dinner . . . [25] For . . .

Line 1. מתיהב more probably than מחכתב (CIS). The end is blotted. As it is at the end of the line, the sentence must have continued in l. 2, probably with ביד 'given into the hand of'. נפקתה translated 'expenses' is rather 'what was served out'.

Line 2. לשרתא perhaps as CIS 'pro prandio'. צירן. We have corroboration of the large trade in Syrian wine in the numerous jar-handles bearing Phoenician names published by Sachau on pl. 69 sqq. קלבי only found in this papyrus.

Line 4. היב if not a mistake, must be a popular form for יהיב.

Line 5. בנו as elsewhere frequently. CIS בנף, but the use of בנו was unknown at the time. The end of the line is quite unintelligible.

Line 6. The first word looks like כבל or כפל (?). עליך 'on your account' i.e. for the master to whom the return is made. עחר CIS the Egyptian god. If so, it was an offering, and Egyptian wine was used. But this is doubtful.

Line 8. CIS בלילא.

Line 11. פחה as a name occurs in 40^2.

Reverse.

Line 14. לבנרו (not ־רן) a Persian name compounded with *baga*? CIS לבנור.

Line 15. אפתו must be a god-name.

Line 16. אסי not very clear, but must be so. אלההתא CIS רבתי would not be used in this Aramaic. The last letter is almost certainly א. The first letter is probably א, and there is room for לה, though it is hardly legible. Cf. אלההה 14^5.

Line 17. תנה is certain. Not as CIS.

Line 20. אנדומא CIS אנוומי. Very uncertain.

Lines 21, 22. Supply probably ל[שרתא].

Line 23. פצתא rather than פינתא (CIS). Meaning?

No. 73.

Fragments of accounts, perhaps by one hand, put together without regard to their original position. Owing to their lack of connexion they present little of interest except the names, which, however, are not always legible. They are all Egyptian, so that the use of Aramaic is remarkable, unless the steward was a foreigner (Jew?).

CIS. ii, 1, no. 147, plate xviii.

1	]עלן בנפא נפיא	⌴ פש]
2	ע]לימא הו	כל

3 בגרום רא̄ ///// 𐡜𐡜𐡜 𐡝 /|///|// לף ///𐡜
4 יהי]ב לענחחפי בר פטאסי לס̄ . . ל̄ טפש
5 . . . . //𐡘//𐡘// 𐡝 𐡜 𐡛 ⊔ לע.לן
6 ס̄ו בכל רעי 𐡛
7 נ]פקת נפשה . . ליד יהעברו ב . . .
8 יהיב לתבא ברת מ̄ . . . . . בנפ̈א
9 ל]ענחבס בר פטאסי לי ולברלי ולך̄ .
10 . . ב ליטחפימו בר שנוט . . . //
11 לפ̄טחרפחרט בר פט . . . בך ו̄התוכדוא̄
12 ⊔ לנפטסבק 𐡛//𐡘 פש
13 רעי לפמסא בר שחפימו רעי |𐡝 𐡜 /// //
14 נפקת מדינתא
15 של ⊔ לפטחנם רעי 𐡜𐡜𐡜
16 ⊔ לאחרחיב בר חפימו 𐡜𐡜𐡜
17 כל רעי //|//|/| 𐡝 𐡛 /// /

[1] ? ? ? [2] He is the servant. [3] 23885 . . . [4] *Give*n to 'Anḥḥapi b. Peṭisi . . . [5] . . . 850 [6] . . . in all 10 re'i. [7] Personal expenses: . . . will be done . . . [8] Given to Tebo daughter of . . . . . . [9] *To* 'Anḥḥabis b. Peṭisi. To me and to my son and to . . . (?) [10] To Šaḥpimu b. Šenuṭ . . . 2. [11] To Peteḥarpoḥraṭ b. Peṭ . . . . . . [12] ⊔ to Neftisobḳu . . . 13 . . . [13] re'i. To Pemeso b. Šaḥpimu, 125 re'i. [14] Town expenses: [15] ⊔ to Peṭeḥnum 60 re'i. [16] ⊔ to Aḥreḥib b. Ḥapimu 60. [17] Total re'i 814.

Line 1. עלך̄, cf. עלנה 78[1]. I do not know the word. בנפא cf. l. 8. It looks like בנפנא. CIS 'ratio corporum viritim'.

Line 2. [ע]לי̄מא probable. CIS only מ. הו. A side-stroke is missing. Hence CIS גו.

Line 3. לף for אלף as in the Behistun text.

Line 7. 'Expenses for himself' (ipse, the master) i.e. personal expenses.

Line 9. לי וכ׳ very faint and uncertain.

Line 10. שנוט probable. CIS חרום.

Line 11. לפטח׳. The פ is really a נ.

Line 12. לנפ׳ or ל לפט׳.

Line 15. לפטחנם possible, but it is more like לפטחום as CIS.

No. 74.

Fragment of a list of names, all probably Egyptian.

CIS. no. 148, plate xv.

1 פטי בר פחפי פלגה ת.קא

2 פסמשך בר פ[מ]ת בר נעצב בנ . . .

3 פמן בר בנ[ת] . . .

4 סמתו בר ענחמת

5 הדיו בר פטאסי

6 חנס בר פטאסי

[1] Peṭi b. Paḥapi, his half is . . . [2] Pasmašak b. Pa*mu*th b. Ne'eẓab, in . . . [3] Pamen b. Ban*it* . . . [4] Smitu b. 'Anḥmuth. [5] Hadiu b. Peṭisi. [6] Ḥons b. Peṭisi.

Line 1. ת.קא CIS תזחא, but the ז might be ד, ר or פ. The ק is more probable than ח, cf. the ח in ll. 4, 6.

Line 2. פ[מ]ת. A מ is the most likely letter to fill the space. Cf. 72[4]. נעצב CIS נטצב, neither very probable names.

Line 4. The final ח is partly visible.

Line 5. הדיו. CIS cft. הודו, but? פטאסי. Traces of סי are visible.

No. 75.

Fragment, very difficult. It can hardly be taken as in CIS.

The stroke after l. 5, and the summing up with כל are both characteristic of accounts. The reading of אשלן is certain (l. 5), and if this has its ordinary meaning, the papyrus would seem to contain an inventory of a plantation.

CIS. ii, 1, no. 150, plate xx.

1 רבתכה במרע קרק[ע . . .

2 וחנמיא קרבתא . . .

3 אהבתה במרע ק[רקע

4 פקרקפתח קר[בתא

5 כל אשלן דל . . .

6 תני אמת . . .

7 רבתכה אשל[ן . . .

8 אחותה הי . . .

9 כ]ל [אש]ל[ן . . .

Translation quite uncertain.

Line 1. רבתכה as in l. 7. CIS 'domina tua', but the suffix never has this form in the papyri. It can hardly be a Hebraism. במרע as in l. 3, where it might be במסע. Hardly במוע 'east', or = מֵרק 'narrow'? קרק]ע. CIS קרם is hardly possible. It might be . . קרת.

Line 2. וחנמיא a name? for חנמיה cf. חנמאל Jer. 32[7] &c. Or cf. חנמל ('frost'?) in Ps. 78[47].

Line 3. אהבתה so CIS. The second letter is not like ה, and the ב is more like ם.

Line 4. פקר׳ an Egyptian name compounded with פתח.

Line 6. תני perhaps like תוב 'again', beginning a new series.

Line 9 probably as l. 5 'total, tamarisks . . .'

No. 76.

Fragment of a report of legal proceedings. Very little can be read with certainty on the facsimile, so that the text is for the most part that of CIS.

CIS. ii, 1, no. 151, plates xx and xxi.

1 . . . חותם עד כמו . . . למי ר ־// וכן אמר . . ך צחא זך . . .

עביד

2 . . . ר וכנותה הנש . . . . . ל . . . . . ברת צחא זך . . .

3 . . . ה צחא זך לי[ד]ניה ביום ־[לפ]אוני כעת . . .

4 . . . . תן על משאלת . . . . . . ל . עם . . .

[1] . . . seal, till . . . 12 R and thus they (?) said *to* you: this Zeḥo . . . *before* [2] . . . and his colleagues . . . was done to . . . daughter (?) of this Zeḥo . . . [3] . . . this Zeḥo to Yedoniah (?) on the 10th day *of Pa*ūni, now . . . [4] . . . *will* give, on the petition of . . . . . .

Line 1. ר ־// וכן אמר restored from pl. xxi. Possibly it was אמרו לך, in which case there may have been another name after צחא זך. At the end perhaps קדם.

Line 2. ר . . . the end of a name. ברת very doubtful.

Line 3. לי[ד]ניה. It is doubtful if ד would fill the space. [לפ]אוני. As וני is clear, this is more probable than לפאפי (CIS), but the name does not occur for certain elsewhere.

Line 4. תן . . . part of נתן.

No. 77.

Small fragment of the beginning of a letter.

CIS. ii, 1, no. 152, plate xx.

1 שלם מראי . . .
2 עלים חד תמ]ה . . .

Reverse.

3 . . . חנה על . . .

[1] The welfare of my lord . . . [2] A servant there . . .

Line 1. מראי is certain. Not רבא as CIS.
Line 2. עלים probable, though the ע has an unusual form.
Line 3 apparently the address.

No. 78.

Fragment of accounts, very difficult to read on the facsimile.

CIS. ii, 1, no. 153, plates xx and xxi.

Obverse.

1 עלנה בי]רח . . .
2 בגו
3 כסף ש \\// \\// . . .
4 דמי ולף ⊣⊣ /
5 כל כסף ש[ק]לן \\\\ . . . .
6 כל כסף כרש . . .

[1] Accounts in the *month* . . . [2] including [3] the sum of 6 shekels . . . [4] the value of 1111 . . . [5] total money, shekels 2 . . . [6] total money, karash . . .

Line 1. עלנה cf. 73[1], but the reading in both places is uncertain. It must mean 'accounts'.

Line 2. בגו is now certain.

Line 4. דמי is probable, but does not seem suitable.

Line 5. ש[ק]לן is more probable than the CIS reading.

Line 6. כרש (or plural) is no doubt right. The word was not known to CIS.

The reverse is illegible.

No. 79.

Fragment found at Elephantine near the site of the temple. It is not included in Sachau's volume. As there is no facsimile the text is printed here as in Ungnad's edition.

Cf. also De Vogüé in *Répertoire*, 246; Clermont-Ganneau in *Recueil* vi, p. 246; Lidzbarski, *Ephemeris* ii, p. 217.

It seems to be part of an inventory or specification. Cf. no. 26.

Ungnad, no. 89.

1 . . . . .

2 בנו חדה אמן ־// פתי אמה / דורה פ[ש]כן [///]/ . . .

3 בנו לוח אחרה אמן /// /// /// ופלג פתי אמה / דור[ה . . .

4 לוח [א]חרה אמן /// // פתי א[מה /] דורה פש[כן . . .

[1] . . . . [2] including one of 12 cubits, one cubit wide, 4 (?) hands thick (?) . . . [3] including another board of 9 cubits and a half, 1 cubit wide, . . . thick (?) . . . [4] another board of 5 cubits, 1 cubit wide, . . . hands thick (?)

Line 1 is illegible.

Line 2. דורה must be a third dimension, 'thickness'. Ungnad cft. דורא 'circumference'. This cannot be the exact sense here since the object was 1 cubit wide. The thing is no doubt a לוח, whatever that is (as in ll. 3, 4), not a single plank, but a flat surface of some kind.

No. 80.

Fragment found with no. 79. The writing is on both sides. There is no facsimile, so that I have adopted here the readings of Clermont-Ganneau (*Recueil* vi, p. 246), as printed by Ungnad. See also De Vogüé, *Répertoire* 247; Lidzbarski, *Ephemeris* ii. p. 219. The text is too fragmentary to give any connected sense. It seems to be a report of some incident concerning the garrison from which legal proceedings resulted.

Ungnad, no. 90.

1 על ב . . .

2 א[מ]רו . . . . . חו פנ[ה . . .

3 . . להם ו[ר]בי מאותהם . . .

4 חרבה חי[ל] לא איתי . . .

5 חילא [זנה] הוו מחס[נן . . .

6 אף בען ביר[ת]א זא חי[ל . . .

Reverse.

7 כען כן א̄[מר] מתרדת . . .

8 אנתם דיניא אמרו ל . . .

9 ינתן [ל]מר̄יא

[1] To B . . . [2] they said . . . [3] . . . to them, and their centurions . . . [4] his sword, there is no force . . . [5] this force, they were holders of . . . [6] Now also this fortress (?) . . .

[7] Now thus *says* Mithradates . . . [8] you, judges, say to . . . [9] he will give to my lord (?)

Line 3. ו[ר]כי מאו' no doubt 'heads of their hundreds' i.e. centurions as Ungnad suggests. Cf. מאת נ' 22[20] &c.

Line 5. מחם[נן] for מהחכנן, is not very convincing.

Line 8. אמרו imperative.

Line 9. [ל]מר̄יא read למראי? There was probably something after it.

The next three papyri are later than those from Elephantine.

No. 81.

This was published in *PSBA*, 1907, p. 260, with facsimiles. The papyrus was bought by Sayce, with other fragments, from a dealer at Luxor who believed them to have come from Ḳus. It was given by Sayce to the Bodleian Library where it is referenced as MS. Aram. a. 1 (P). It consists of two long strips about 20 × 2½ inches (and some fragments). The writing is on both sides and is divided into 10 columns running down the width of the papyrus. Originally no doubt the two fragments were united along the long edge and the columns were continuous across both. Probably something is lost between the fragments (i.e. in the middle of each column) but hardly anything at the top or bottom. The document evidently began with l. 1. The columns are not always kept distinct, but sometimes run into one another where the lines are long. The lines often slope, so that the beginning or end is occasionally lost. These two defects make the decipherment more than usually difficult. The difficulty is further increased by the unskilful writing, by the broken condition of the papyrus, by the condensed and disconnected nature of the entries, by the abbreviations and by apparent inconsistencies of the writer.

No date is given, but the many Greek names suggest the Ptolemaic period, and this is corroborated by the character of the writing, which shows a much later stage of development than that of the Elephantine documents. It is unlikely, however, that Aramaic survived, even in individual cases, long after the time of Alexander, and we shall perhaps not be far wrong in assuming a date about 300 B. C.

With regard to particular letters, א, ב, ה, ל, ש have practically arrived at the ordinary square shape נ has much the same form as in the Elephantine documents: ד and ר are still indistinguishable: ז is difficult to distinguish from the unit \. כ and נ when medial, have the tail bent, but when final, it is straight · in מ the right-hand stroke turns round, thus approximating to the square form ס shows the most pronounced change, being sometimes nearly joined below, as in the square form ק only requires a longer tail to give it the square form: ת much as at Elephantine, but the left-hand stroke is shorter.

The text consists of accounts, not of a household (like no 72), but apparently of a business of some kind. Many entries seem to relate to wine, others perhaps to money-lending, but the precise meaning of most of them is obscure.

A peculiarity of this document is the way of writing the numerals. In a series of units the last one or two or three are written sloping against the preceding stroke, e g. \\\///, but almost \\\// In the *PSBA*, not having found this arrangement before, I printed it as \\\// &c., and took it to represent a fraction, e. g. $3\frac{3}{4}$ It is, however, simply a way of writing 6, &c (/// /// at Elephantine), due perhaps rather to a personal fancy of the writer than to a later method. This value is proved by the ratio regularly preserved (where the reading is certain) between the number of לגן and the number of ר. Thus in l. 62 \\\ בר \\\/// לגן, '6 bottles at (i e. costing?) 3 R'. Whatever the meaning is, it will be found that 2 bottles always correspond to 1 R, if the units are read as here suggested.

Another obscure combination is פ\מ. This must in some way mean one half Cf ll 96–98, where (if 2 bottles = 1 R) 5 bottles should be valued (?) at $2\frac{1}{2}$ R, 3 bottles at $1\frac{1}{2}$ R, and 1 bottle at $\frac{1}{2}$ R As a mere conjecture I suggest that פ may be for פלג and that מ may be for מוסף 'added' (the perfect Hophal occurs in Dan. 4^{33}) or some such word The whole will then be equivalent to $+\frac{1}{2}$. (פליג ‎|‎ מוסף?).

The ר here, as elsewhere, is for רבע 'quarter' (of a shekel) This is shown by l. 94 where 9 bottles should at the same rate be valued at $4\frac{1}{2}$ R and the text has 'at 1 sh(ekel) + $\frac{1}{2}$ (R)'. Therefore 1 shekel = 4 R or quarters.

Col. a.

1 חשבן ענביא זי כתבת . . . . אבהי
2 שלמצין נצבתא זי זבדיה חנטן ס \ ר \
3 שבתית ברת עבדיה חנטן ס \ ק /// ///\ \ פ
4 ארסין . . . . חנטן א ר \\
5 בב ארס[ין] שטר \ א . . .
6 . . . .
7 . . . . . . [גר]בן . . זילי ר/// ///\\\
8 [מן שמ]עון גרבן // יחנן כהנא גרב \
9 מן שבתי ישיב גרבן \\ מן נתן \ גרב \
10 מן חני דיפרס גרבין \\
11 תבא ברת חניה ביתא— א \\\ א \ על . .
12 . . . . א ומן ס.גרה
13 . . . .

Col. b.

14 שטריא ביד יונתן ואנה
15 סלק לאפנא שמעון בר חגי
16 בב שמתי שטר \ בחמראן דד
17 בב שמעון שטר \ בברשן ר \\
18 ש /// ///\\
19 בב שמעון שטר \ [בזח]; ///\ ←
20 [בב שמעו]; [ש]טר \ בחלרין ///\ מדלא
21 וירחין ר \\ מדלא
22 עבדיהו זכור שטר \ בוזן \ ←ד
23 בב עבדיהו זכור שטר \ בחנטן א ר
24 שבתי חני תתן שטר \ בביתה
25 בב שבתי חני שטר \ בחנטן א ד //\\
26 בידה שט[ר] \ יחנן בר דלוי ע . . .
27 בזוזן \ ←

Col. c.

28 ביד [יו]נתן חנטא [זי ?] יחיי בר ..בניה
29 ביד יונתן רביסה ///\\\ זי חמרין
30 תפלה זי בכסף ר נחתן \\ זי כסף

ביד נתן וזיכא זי משלם בר עזגר ב״ש \\
וזיכא זילי בידה וזיכא רבא זילנא בידה
רבא בידה ה־זולא בידה כה . . ה שפיר[ה]
בידה . . . . זא זי ידניה . . .
בי[דה . . .

. . . . חנטן א\\\ ר \
[ביד]ה חרשא זי נחש נכרם, ברת חגיה . .
בידה חרשא זילנא במצי . . א

ב

חמרא זי יהבו יתלי שנתא זא של . . . בהגא
בטמאסן ד \ חל גרבין \\ הג . . .
דלוי זערא גן בדד \\\/// חל \ . . . .
במידלה אביתי גרבן \\\
עבדיהו פחס גרבין \\\/// חל \
מהני זוזן \ ר

Col. d.

זי . . חת לטבה ה . . .
ד . . \/// היד ח \ . . .
לח . . צען רבה // . . . .
צען [רב]ה \\\/// פא . . .
. . . . חלא חד קרה . . .
. . . . ינ . יה \\/// ב . . .
. . . . קסר . . .

Col. e.

תא ו
נח
ת
זי

הרגלתי בש
דדד \\// ר \
א ש
ש

verso, Col. f.

. . . . . ארבעיא באפנא
כ״ כא \ בש \ ר \\ שאר ש \

62 נכים לגן \\\/// בר \\\ שאר כ̄ \ פ

63 בב נכים לגן \\\/// בר \\\ שאר \

64 אפלגים יתן כא \ פ בש \\ ר \

65 יניא לגן \\ \\ בר \\

66 יניא לגן . . . .

67 . . . . בר \

68 . . . . [ל]גן \\\/// בר \\\

69 אנה לגן \\

70 נ̄תן נרבי לג \ במ\פ

71 יניא לגן \\\ בר \ מ\פ '

72 בב נכים לגן \\\/// בר \\\

73 יניא לג . . .

Col. g.

74 נבם לגן \\\/// בר \\\

75 יניא לגן \/// בר \\

76 בב נכים לגן \\\/// בר \\\

77 שאר ר \\

78 יהודה לגן \\ בר \

79 בב נכים לג \ מ\פ

80 יניא לגן \\ בר̄ \

81 יניא כא\פ ב̄ . . .

82 . . . . . ב̄ . . . . ר \

83 בנרב חמשת . .

84 יסדרס לגן \\ בר \

85 פ̄רס כא \ בש \ ר \\

86 הרגלתי פלג בר \\\

87 לסמקם לגן /// /\\\ בר \\\ מ\פ

88 כסתם לגן \\//// בר \\\

89 דפרוס לגן \/// בר \\

90 אביתי נתין . . . . ב̄ר̄ \\\

Col. h.

91 אבית̄י ב̄ . . . . . .

92 יסדרס לגן \/// . בר \\

93 יניא לגן \\\/// בר \\\

94 בכים לגן /// \\\/// בש \ מ\פ

95 יוניא לגן \\ בר \
96 יהודה לגן |///\ בר \\ מ\פ
97 יניא לגן \\\ בר \ מ\פ
98 רחבל לג\ במ\פ
99 עבדי ישב ל . . . .

100 . . . . . . [לגן] ///\ בר \\
101 ינ[יא] לגן //[/\] בר \\
102 פתפי לגן ///\ בר \\
103 פתו לגן /// /// בר \\\
104 יוניא לגן ///\ בר \\
105 זפרה לגן \\ בר \
מ ///\\\
106 ב פתו כאן \\ בש \\\ שאר
107 ארמים לגן /// [ב]ר \ מ\כ
108 . . . .

Col. i.

109 בבית ישיב יקל . לעתיד ///\\
110 בביתנא סלעתין \\ בראמן \\ פתחן
111 נחשיא זי יהבו על תמריא זי פחי
112 שנתא זא במכס כרשן ///\\\\\ ש //\
113 בב פתו לגן /// ///\\ בש \
114 בב פתו לגן \\ בר \\ erased { לגן /// ///\\ בש\
115 אביתי לבתנא . . . ערביא לגן //\ בר . .

116 . . . . כ . . . .
117 . . . . [לגן] ///\ בר \\

Col. k

118 . . . שאר תכ . . . . היבא
119 בזילי נכים דמי חמר . .
120 ש \\\ .
121 . . . פה נכים ח . . .
122 ד י לתחות
123 ד (erasure) א
124 זוזן ד ///\ ר \

125 . . . . . .
126 ססרתס [לגן] \\\ בר \ מ\פ

127 אנה לגן ר \\ ⸍שבתי חניה לגן ///\
בר \\

128 בב אנה לגן ///\

129 בב אנה לגן /// ///

130 בש \ בב אנה לגן ///\\\

131 בר \\ ⸍נכים כא \ ש \ בר [\\ ש]אר ר \\
ר \\

132 בר \\ ⸍יהורה לגן ר \\ ב̄[ש \\]\ שאר ר \\\

133 בר \\ בב [אנה] לגן ///\

Col. l.

134 \\ בחנ[ט]ן ס \

135 ||| מ \

136 \\\ בחנטן ס \

137 ר \\ מ \

138 \\ עד

[1] Account of the produce which Abihi wrote . . . [2] (daughter of) Shelamẓin: the farm of Zebadiah, wheat 1 seah 1 quarter. [3] Shabtith daughter of Obadiah, wheat 1 seah, 7 . . . 1 half(?) [4] Arsin . . . . . . wheat, 12 ardabs. [5] . . . Ars*in* 1 bond . . . [6] . . . .

[7] . . . . . . flagons . . . mine, 9. [8] *From Sim*eon 2 flagons. Johanan the priest 1 flagon. [9] From Shabbethai (daughter of) Yashib 2 flagons from Nathun (?) 1 flagon. [10] From Haggai (son of) Diaphoros, two flagons.

[11] Tabo daughter of Ḥaniah, the house. Ardabs 3 . . . [12], [13] . . . . . .

[14] The bonds in the hand of Jonathan and me: [15] Simeon b. Haggai came up to . . . [16] . . . ŠMTI, 1 bond for 40 she-asses. [17] . . . Simeon, 1 bond for 12 kerashin [18] 8 shekels. [19] . . . Simeon, 1 bond for 400 zuzin.

[20] . . . *Simeo*n, 1 bond for 4 hallurin . . . [21] and 12 months . . . [22] Obadiah (son of) Zaccur, 1 bond for 120 zuzin. [23] . . . Obadiah (son of) Zaccur, 1 bond for 10 ardabs of wheat. [24] Shabbethai (daughter of) Haggai will give 1 bond on her house. [25] . . . Shabbethai (daughter of) Haggai, 1 bond for 24 ardabs of wheat. [26] In her hand is 1 bond of Johanan b. Dallui . . . [27] for 100 zuzin.

[28] In the hand of *Jo*nathan, the wheat of(?) Yaḥya b. . . beniah. [29] In the hand of Jonathan . . . 6 of asses. [30] A phylactery (?) of silver, 10; 2 trays of silver. [31] In the hand of Nathan, the . . . of Meshullam b. 'Azgad for 2 shekels. [32] My . . . in his hand; our large . . . in his hand. [33] The large one in his hand, and the small (?) one in his hand; a beautiful . . . [34] in his hand. The . . . of Yedoniah . . . [35] in *his hand.*

[36] . . . . . . wheat 2 ardabs 1 quarter. [37] *In* his *hand* the . . . of bronze. NKRS, daughter of Ḥaniah . . . [38] In his hand our . . . . . . [39] The wine which they gave shall be kept back (?) this year. ŠL . . . the priest

[40] in ṬMASU 21 . . . 2 flagons . . . [41] Dallui junior, a garden for 46, 1 ḥallur (?) . . . [42] . . . Abithi 3 flagons. [43] Obadiah . . . 6 flagons, 1 ḥallur (?) [44] Profit (?) 100 zuzin.

[45] which he *brought* down to Thebes (?) . . . [46] . . . . . . [47] To Ḥ . . he lent 2 plates . . . [48] he *lent* 6 plates . . . [49–51] . . . . . .

[52–55] . . . . . .

[56] Hargalti for . . . shekels . . . [57] 64, 1 quarter . . . [58], [59] . . . . . .

[60] . . . . . . the forty in . . . [61] K 10, 1 ka at 1 shekel 2 quarters, remainder 1 shekel. [62] Nikias 6 bottles at 3 quarters, remainder $\frac{1}{2}$ k. [63] . . . Nikias 6 bottles at 3 quarters, remainder 1. [64] Apollonius will pay $\frac{1}{2}$ ka at 2 shekels 1 quarter. [65] Yania 4 bottles at 2 quarters. [66] Yania . . . bottles . . .

[67] . . . . . . at 1 quarter. [68] . . . 6 *bo*ttles at 3 quarters. [69] Self 2 bottles. [70] Nathan. We will lend 1 bottle at $\frac{1}{2}$. [71] Yania, 3 bottles at 1$\frac{1}{2}$ quarters. [72] . . . Nikias, 6 bottles at 3 quarters. [73] Yania, . . . bottle . . .

[74] NBS, 6 bottles at 3 quarters. [75] Yania, 4 bottles at 2 quarters. [76] . . . Nikias, 6 bottles at 3 quarters. [77] Remainder, 2 quarters. [78] Judah, 2 bottles at 1 quarter. [79] . . . Nikias, 1 bottle, $\frac{1}{2}$. [80] Yania, 2 bottles at 1 quarter. [81] Yania, $\frac{1}{2}$ ka at . . .

[82] . . . . . . 1 quarter. [83] Per flagon five . . . [84] Isidoros, 2 bottles at 1 quarter. [85] Poros, 1 ka at 1 shekel 2 quarters. [86] Hargalti, a half at 3 quarters. [87] Lysimakhos, 7 bottles at 3$\frac{1}{2}$ quarters. [88] Kostos, 6 bottles at 3 quarters. [89] Diaphoros, 4 bottles at 2 quarters. [90] Abithi (son of) Nathin, 6 *bottles* at 3 quarters.

[91] Abithi . . . . . . [92] Isidoros, 4 bottles at 2 quarters. [93] Yania, 6 bottles at 3 quarters. [94] Bakkhias, 9 bottles at 1 shekel $\frac{1}{2}$ (a quarter). [95] Yonia, 2 bottles at 1 quarter. [96] Judah, 5 bottles at 2$\frac{1}{2}$ quarters. [97] Yania, 3 bottles at 1$\frac{1}{2}$ quarters. [98] Reḥabel, 1 bottle at $\frac{1}{2}$ (a quarter). [99] Obadiah (son of) Yashub . . .

[100] . . . . . . 4 *bottles* at 2 quarters. [101] Yan*ia*, 4 bottles at 2 quarters. [102] PTPI, 4 bottles at 2 quarters. [103] PTU, 6 bottles at 3 quarters. [104] Yonia, 4 bottles at 2 quarters. [105] ZPRH, 2 bottles at 1 quarter. [106] For (?) PTU, 2 ka at 3 shekels, remainder 6 M. [107] Armais, 3 bottles at 1$\frac{1}{2}$ quarters. [108] . . . . . .

[109] In the house of Yashib . . . 5 . . . [110] In our house . . . 2 . . . 2 . . . open. [111] Bronze-bands which they put on the date-palms of Peḥi. [112] This year for tax 7 kerashin 3 shekels. [113] . . . PTU, 8 bottles at 1 shekel. [114] . . . PTU, 2 bottles at 2 (?) quarters. 8 bottles at 1 shekel. [115] Abithi to our house (?) . . . 'RBIA, 3 bottles at *1$\frac{1}{2}$* quarters.

[116] . . . . . . [117] . . . . 4 *bottles* at 2 quarters.

[118] . . . remainder . . . . . . [119] For mine, Nikias value of wine [120] 3 shekels. [121] . . . Nikias . . . [122] 30th of Thoth. [123] . . . . . . [124] 24 zuzin 1 quarter.

[125] . . . . . . [126] Sostratos, 3 *bottles* at $1\frac{1}{2}$ quarters. [127] Self, 12 bottles. Shabbethai (son of) Ḥaniah, 3 bottles at 2 quarters. [128] . . . Self, 4 bottles. [129] . . . Self, 6 bottles [130] at 1 shekel . . . Self, 6 bottles [131] at *2* quarters. Nikias 1 ka 1 shekel, at *2* quarters, *re*mainder 2 quarters [132] at 2 quarters. Judah, 12 bottles at *3 shekels* 2 quarters remainder 3 quarters [133] at 2 quarters . . . *Self*, 4 bottles.

[134] . . . 2 for wheat 1 seah. [135] . . . . . . [136] . . . 3 for wheat 1 seah. [137, 138] . . . . . .

Line 1. ענביא is more probable than ענקא (*PSBA*) 'Fruits' meaning 'produce' in general. אבהי for אביהי elsewhere, a feminine name.

Line 2. שלמצין a feminine? name. Cf. שלמצה Salome, in Midrash and Talmud, said to be for שלם ציון. She may be the mother (or father) of Abihi, ברת being omitted as בר is elsewhere in this document. נצבתא 'plantation' i.e. field or farm. ם for מאה.

Line 3. זר very doubtful. It does not correspond to any other entry. פ \ 'one half' should have מ as elsewhere.

Line 4. ארסין as l. 5. Sayce suggests Arsinoë.

Line 5. בב Sayce 'on account of', perhaps for בבית. It generally occurs where a name is repeated.

Line 7. [גר]בן large bottles. Probably of wine.

Line 9. ישיב a name. The בר[ת] is omitted. After נתן the \ is unintelligible, and perhaps is not to be so read. It may be נתון.

Line 10. דיפרס Diaphoros. בר omitted. גרבין perhaps a dual form (Sayce), or a mere caprice as גרבן is used before with \\.

Line 11. ביתא reading and meaning uncertain. The rest of the line is also unintelligible.

Line 12. גרה . ם a name?

Line 15. לאפנא Sayce, 'to our side' (לפנינו) i.e. joined our partnership (?).

Line 16. חמראן, 'she-asses' with א to distinguish it from the masculine? The ב־ no doubt means 'concerning'.

Line 19. ↤ is probably the same as the sign for 100, often used in the Behistun text. Perhaps originally for מ[אה].

Line 20. מדלא in later Aramaic should mean 'property', which does not seem suitable here or in l. 21.

Line 22. זוזן must be very small coins since the number is so large—hardly a quarter of a shekel.

Line 24. תתן if right is for תנתן.

Line 29. רכיכה (or רכ'). Possibly a name. In any case the numeral after it is difficult to explain.

Line 30. תפלה. Can it be used in the ordinary sense, a 'phylactery' in a silver case? The numeral is again difficult, unless it means the value, 10 shekels (?), and similarly in l. 29.

Line 31. ווכא a quite unknown word. Sayce suggests that it is Persian, but there seem to be no traces of Persian in this document.

Line 33. ווֹלא 'cheap' (Sayce), but the reading is very doubtful.

Line 34. זא or שׂא, probably the end of a noun. ?חרשא as in ll. 37, 38.

Line 37. חרשא some unknown article made of bronze. נכרס. The final letter might be another ס. Greek or Egyptian?

Line 39. יתלי is probable. 'Shall be held in suspense' i.e. not used, or not reckoned in the account?

Line 40. בטמאסו. The last letter seems to belong to this name (?).

Line 41. דלוי. Name? as elsewhere. Sayce suggests 'bucket', but the form (for דלי) is difficult.

Line 42. במירלה cf. מרלא ll. 20, 21. It may be related to דלוי.

Line 43. פחם is used of 'stirring' wine, i.e. causing it to ferment?

Line 44. מהני perhaps 'profit' from הני.

Line 45. לטבה. Sayce 'to Thebes'.

Line 47. רבה 'lent at interest'.

Line 56. הרגלתי as in l. 86, where it should be a name.

Line 62. כ \ פ is fairly certain, not מ \ פ.

Line 65. יניא probably like the common form ינאי, for יוחנן. In ll. 95, 104 יוניא. It can hardly be 'the Greek'.

Line 74. נבם perhaps badly written for נכם = נכים.

Line 78. יהודה. The name does not occur in the Elephantine texts.

Line 83. After חמשת something is wanted. There is not room for more than one letter, or two.

Line 86. פלג i.e. half a ka, as the price shows.

Line 98. רחבל perhaps for רחבאל, cf. רחביה 1 Chron. 23^{17} &c. Names in -el are not found in the Elephantine texts.

Lines 102. פתפי 103. פתו apparently names.

Line 109. לעתיך (and in l. 110). A connexion with √לעי seems unsuitable.

Line 110. בראמן apparently to be so read, but the א is strange. A plural is required.

Line 114 is erased, being no doubt an erroneous repetition of l. 113.

Line 115. לבתנא for לביתנא? ערבזא or ער׳, apparently a name.

Line 126. ססרתס. Sayce suggests perhaps Sostratos.

Line 130. בש \. If this refers to l. 129 the proportion is unusual. It should be בר ///, and so in l. 131.

No. 82.

Fragments of a legal document, bought by Prof. Sayce in Egypt and given by him to the Bodleian Library (MS. Aram. e. 2 (P)). It was published in *PSBA*, 1915, p. 217, with a facsimile.

The writing is similar to that of no. 81, and the date is therefore probably about the same, early in the 3rd century B.C. As it is an official document it would not have been written in Aramaic, one would suppose, much after 300 B.C.

Unfortunately it is too fragmentary to admit of a continuous translation. Probably nothing is missing before l. 1, or only part of a line which may have contained the address, e.g. 'to our lord X'. The beginnings and ends of all the lines are lost, and several words are illegible, so that the details are quite obscure. As far as it can be made out, the general sense seems to be that three litigants were concerned with the division of certain property, including a house. One of them was perhaps executor and had handed over part of the estate to the 'heads of the congregation', who were now to distribute it. If the reading עבדיך is right in l. 1, the document is a report of proceedings by the judges to some higher official. The 'judges' are probably officers of state, but the 'heads of the congregation' must be Jewish elders who were recognized by them. The place of the action may have been Abydos or טבה (Thebes?), where there must have been a Jewish settlement at this date. The name Abydos occurs in 38[3].

1 . . . . ועבדיך דיניא זי בא[בוט] . . .
2 [בר ד]לוי דליה בר ח[גי] שבעה בר עבדיה[ו] . . . .
3 . . . בית זומי בטבה בירתא אחה חזי . . .
4 . . . . . . זי שוק פ . . י אנתן אחרה . . .
5 . . . . שלמת עלראשי עד[תא] . . .
6 . . . . יתקדם ביה ושהדו עלכלנבס[ן] . . .
7 . . . א ואחריא לקבל חלקן /// כען דו . . . .
8 . . . . פהו ולא הוה בי מלא ויתנון ל . . . .
9 . . . . . תה להן לא . . . בר . . . ויתנון ה[לק] . . . .
10 . . . [חל]קן /// זי תורה לפלטה אחתה ל . . . .
11 . . . ליהא תרין זי בהן יאתה שלי . . . .
12 . . . אבהון ישר חלק . . . .
13 . . . קמינא לא[בוט] . . . .
14 . . . הם עלוי . . . .

[1] . . . . . . and your servants the judges who are in A*bydos* . . . [2] *son of Da*llui, Delaiah b. Ha*ggai*, Shib'a b. Obadiah . . . [3] . . . the house of Zomi in the city of Thebes, H . . . came . . . [4] . . . . . . of the street (?) . . . I will give. Afterwards . . .

[5] . . . . . . I paid to the heads of the con*gregation* . . . [6] . . . let him come before him; and they gave evidence as to all goods . . . [7] . . . and other things in 3 parts. Now . . . [8] . . . . and it was not a complete house (?), and they shall give to . . . [9] . . . . . . but to A . . . son of . . . and they shall give a p*art* . . . [10] . . . 3 *pa*rts of a Tora to PLṬA his sister to . . . [11] . . . . . . two which he shall bring . . .

[12] . . . Abbahun, correct division . . .

[13] . . . before us to A*bydos* . . . [14] . . . . . .

Line 1. The remains of letters at the beginning have not been deciphered. At the end a place-name is wanted, as in l. 13, and א[בוט] seems the most likely, but it is only a conjecture.

Line 2. [ד]לוי as on an ostrakon, Sachau pl. 68, $2^{1.3.5}$, which may be of about the same date. שבעה cf. O.T. שבע. The ה is more like ם. These were no doubt the three persons interested. Cf. l. 7.

Line 3. זומי uncertain. Cf. זומא in Mishna. בטבה must be the name of a town. Sayce suggests Thebes as in 81^{45}. חזי . . or חני . . must be part of a name, but its relation to the transaction is not clear.

Line 4. שוק very doubtful. There are traces of another line between ll. 4 and 5.

Line 5. עד[תא]. The ד is doubtful, and therefore the restoration is uncertain, but it is probable. The word occurs in 15^{22}, and is correct for the Jewish community.

Line 6. ביה for בה (?) is unusual. 'Before him'? עלבלנכם[ן] followed by ואחריא l. 7, cf. 20^{12}. But the reading here is uncertain.

Line 7. לקבל '(divided it) according to' i.e. into 'three parts' for the three litigants.

Line 8. הוה very uncertain. What 'a full house' means I cannot guess. ויתנון is clear, for וינתנון at Elephantine.

Line 10. תורה is certain, and the three parts (+ 2 in l. 11) suggest חמשה חומשי תורה. The word does not occur in the Elephantine papyri, where there is no allusion to the Law. Or is it תור 'her ox'? It was evidently a valuable possession. How פלטה was concerned with it is not clear.

Line 11. תרין ז' or תריהום? בהן יאתה 'come with' i.e. bring them.

Line 12 probably the last line, ratifying the apportionment. אבהון a name. Cf. אבהו, אבון.

Lines 13, 14. It is quite uncertain where this fragment belongs.

No. 83.

A fragment with writing on both sides, in the Harrow School Museum. It is not dated. The recto, containing a column of accounts, is in a fairly early hand, probably before 400 B.C. The verso, containing a list of names and a few lines of accounts, is more roughly written and probably nearly as late as 300 B.C. That the papyrus should have been used again after such an interval is strange, but not impossible, especially as the verso shows signs of being palimpsest.

The verso is very much faded in parts, and on both sides the reading is uncertain owing to the lack of context and the few opportunities of comparison.

ב \/// לתעבי
מטא צחא מנפי
ב \// // מן פטאס[י
חלפן א[ד] /// //
ב /// |// אד /// //
ב /// \/// אד /// /[/]
[ב] /// /// // אד [/// //]
ב /// /// |// אד [/// //]
בר אד /// //
בר| אד /// //
בר/| אד /// //
בר//| אד //| /|
בר\/// אד /// //
[ב]ר//| // אד /// //
בר//| //| אד /// //
בר/// [\/// אד ///] //
בר/// /// || [אד] /// //
[בר] //| //| /[//] אד /// //

Reverse.

סוקן /// /// //
. . . רן ///
בעלי פתורא
צחא \
פטנתר \

24 פסו ∖
25 צחא ∖
26 ישם ∖
27 פי ∖

28 נפקה . צמי
29 על מירי‍תא ככרן ///
30 עלים צחא כל ∖ . .

[1] On the 4th of Tybi [2] Ẓeḥo came to Memphis. [3] On the 5th from Petisis [4] on our account 25 ardabs. [5] On the 6th 25 ardabs. [6] On the 7th 25 ardabs. [7] *On* the 8th *25* ardabs. [8] On the 9th *25* ardabs. [9] On the 10th 25 ardabs. [10] On the 11th 25 ardabs. [11] On the 12th 25 ardabs. [12] On the 13th 25 ardabs. [13] On the 14th 25 ardabs. [14] *On* the 15th 25 ardabs. [15] On the 16th 25 ardabs. [16] On the 17th *25 ardabs.* [17] On the 18th 25 *ardabs.* [18] *On the 19*th 25 ardabs.

Reverse.

[19] . . . 8. [20] . . . 3.

[21] Money-lenders: [22] Ẓeḥo 1 [23] Petnether 1 [24] Pasu 1 [25] Ẓeḥo 1 [26] YŠM 1 [27] Pi 1

[28] Expenditure . . . [29] For the inheritance (?) 3 talents. [30] The servant of Ẓeḥo, each . . .

Line 2. מנפי very faint, but probable if מטא does not require ל. Cf. 42^7 חת מנפי if that really means 'go down *to* M.'

Line 4. חלפן probably. חלרן would not make sense. Cf. חלף in 44^8. א no doubt for ארדבן.

Lines 5–18 simply enumerate the days from the 6th to the 19th, on each of which 25 ardabs were received or given out.

Line 19. סוקן. I cannot guess what word this is.

Line 21. At the side are three strokes belonging to a previous column. פתורא the 'table' of a money-changer?

Lines 22–27. The names are all Egyptian. For the ∖ after each cf. 33^{1-4}.

Line 26. ישם quite uncertain.

Line 28. צמי . not עצמי, and there is no obvious word.

Line 29. מירי‍תא apparently so to be read. 'Inheritance'? ככרן at Elephantine כנכרן.

The Story of Aḥiḳar.

Eleven sheets of papyrus, all more or less fragmentary, three of them with double columns.

They contain an Aramaic version of the well-known story of Aḥiḳar, followed by a collection of proverbs, similar to, but not the same as, those found in later versions. Lines 1–78, the narrative, are practically continuous, but the story is not finished. As to the remainder, the proverbs being disconnected, or only occasionally related in subject, it is impossible to say whether the sheets of papyrus are continuous.

There is no date, but from the appearance of the writing we may safely conclude that it belongs, like the majority of these documents, to the latter part of the fifth century B.C.

The story, and this version of it in particular, is interesting for the following reasons among others:

(1) The hero is mentioned by name in the book of Tobit.

(2) There seem to be references to the story in various books of the Old and New Testaments.

(3) Hitherto it has been known only in later (post-Christian) forms.

(4) The papyrus shows that the original work goes back at least as far as the fifth century B.C. and probably earlier.

(5) It is thus the earliest specimen of wisdom-literature outside the Old Testament and cuneiform texts.

The general questions relating to the story and its transmission, may be studied in English in '*The Story of Aḥiḳar* . . . by Conybeare, Rendel Harris and A. S. Lewis', 2nd ed. Cambridge, 1913 (here quoted as 'Story') and in Charles' *Apocrypha and Pseudepigrapha*, vol. ii, Oxford, 1913 (here quoted as 'Charles') p. 715+, by the same editors, together with the works mentioned there. It is only proposed here to deal with the Aramaic text found in these papyri and with the questions specially connected with it.

Owing to the broken state of the papyri their reading and interpretation alike are often uncertain. A large number of articles dealing with the text have added something to its elucidation, but much still remains to be done. For the present purpose the suggestions of the following scholars, as being the most worthy of attention, have been carefully considered:

Baneth, *OLZ*, 1914, 248, 295, 348.

Epstein, *ZATW*, 1912, p. 128; 1913, pp. 222, 310; *OLZ*, 1916, 204.

Grimme, *OLZ*, 1911, 529.

Lidzbarski, *Ephemeris III* (1912), p. 253.

Ed. Meyer, *Papyrusfund*, p. 102.

Montgomery, *OLZ*, 1912, 535. *Expository Times*, 24 (1913), p. 428.

Nöldeke, *ZDMG*, 67, p. 766. 'Untersuch. zum Achiqar-Roman' in *Abh. der Gött. Ges.* 14, 4 (1913).

Perles, *OLZ*, 1911, 497; 1912, 54.

Seidel, *ZAW*, 1912, p. 292.

Smend, *ThLZ*, 1912, 387.

Strack, *ZDMG*, 1911, p. 826.

Stummer, *OLZ*, 1914, 252; 1915, 103. *Der kritische Wert* . . . Münster, 1914.

Torczyner, *OLZ*, 1912, 397.

Wensinck, *OLZ*, 1912, 49.

The Aramaic is not (as assumed in Charles, p. 720) the original of the book. There are indeed few Hebraisms in it, and although it was found in a Jewish colony, the story shows no sign of Jewish origin. It is not derived from Hebrew sources[1] and there is no reason why we should expect it to be so. The Jews were not the only literary people of the time. The fact that Tobit refers to it as a well-known story, does not prove that it was known to the author as being a piece of native Jewish literature. Its fame was much more widely spread. At the time when these papyri were written, Egypt was, and had been for a century, under Persian rule, and as we see from other documents, the Persian government officially used Aramaic in the provinces. The language was therefore well-known at headquarters, qualified translators must have been employed (as earlier by Assurbanipal), and it is reasonable to suppose that texts other than purely official documents would gradually be made known abroad through this medium. It is true we know little enough of Aramaic in the fifth century B.C., and nothing at all of its literary narrative style, but one cannot read a few paragraphs of Old Persian (such as Darius' inscription at Behistun) without being struck by the general similarity in style of the Aramaic narrative of Aḥiḳar. It is always unsafe to trust to an abstract estimate of style, but when, as here, inherent probability points to the same conclusion, the argument deserves consideration. Moreover there are a few definite signs that the Aramaic is under Persian influence. The name of Assyria is written אתור (as later in the Targums), not אשור as in the Sinjirli inscriptions. This is not because the papyrus is 300 years later than the Sinjirli texts but because it follows the Persian form Athura[2]. A peculiarity of the Aḥiḳar text is

[1] The resemblance of phrases, e.g. in 2 Sam. $16^{11.19.23}$ and 18^{18} (אין לי בן) to expressions used in Aḥiḳar, is due to mere coincidence.

[2] This was first suggested to me by Prof. Sayce.

the constant use of שמה after a person's name, as in line 1 אחיקר שמה 'a man named Aḥiḳar'. This is not found in ordinary Aramaic[1], but is a common idiom in Old Persian as Behistun ii, 6 Vidarna nāma 'a man named Vidarna'. The use of אחר again, as an almost redundant conjunction, is exactly parallel to the OP pasāva 'afterwards' used in the same way.

The Aramaic then is a translation from Persian or made under Persian influence, but Persian was probably not the original language of the story. The Persians were not, at the beginning, a literary people, although they made great efforts to become so after their conquest of Babylon. It was part of their enlightened policy. Now Clement of Alexandria (*Stromata* i, 15, 69, ed. Stählin, Lpz., 1906) says that the Greek philosopher Democritus of Abdera borrowed from Babylonian moral sayings[2] and incorporated with his own compositions a translation of the στήλη of Akikaros[3], who no doubt is Aḥiḳar. It is true that Clement goes on to say that Democritus, who prided himself on his travels, claimed to have visited Babylon, *Persia* and Egypt and to have sat at the feet of the magi and priests (τοῖς τε μάγοις καὶ τοῖς ἱερεῦσι μαθητεύων), so that he might have borrowed from a Persian text or even from the present Aramaic, since his travels must have taken place[4] when this papyrus was already in existence. But Clement was evidently following a trustworthy authority and would not have associated Aḥiḳar with Babylonian writings if he had meant Persian. The debt of the Greeks to Babylon as well as to Egypt and even to India in matters of physical science and philosophy is acknowledged, and need not be emphasized here. Moreover the view that the story came from a Babylonian source agrees with other indications. Though it bears a Persian colouring over its Aramaic dress, its body is clearly Babylonian. The kings Senacherib and Esarhaddon are in the right order (not reversed, as in the later versions) and their names are more correct in form than in the OT, the names Nadin and Nabusumiskun are purely Babylonian, so is the use of אלהים (pl. = *ilâni*) and שמש as a god (neither of them Persian), while the frequent mention of

[1] Though it occurs in other documents of this collection, where it is also due to Persian influence.

[2] Δημόκριτος γὰρ τοὺς Βαβυλωνίους λόγους ἠθικοὺς [αὑτοῦ?] πεποίηται· λέγεται γὰρ τὴν Ἀκικάρου στήλην ἑρμηνευθεῖσαν τοῖς ἰδίοις συντάξαι συγγράμμασι. The first sentence, which is not very clear, is quoted by Eusebius in *Praep. Evang.* x. 4. Diogenes Laertius v, 50 mentions a work Περὶ τῶν ἐν Βαβυλῶνι ἱερῶν γραμμάτων, edited by Theophrastus. Cf. also *Strabo* xvi, p. 762, παρὰ δὲ τοῖς Βοσπορηνοῖς Ἀχαίκαρον.

[3] See Story, p. xli +, for a discussion of the statement and reasons for accepting it.

[4] He lived from 460 to 361 B.C.

Assyria would be quite unsuitable in a Persian composition. There would have been no need to put the story back into Assyrian times, since the incidents related might just as well have occurred under a Persian despot. We know that the Babylonians did possess λόγους ἠθικούς, gnomic or 'wisdom'-literature, in the form of proverbs,[1] some of which are similar in character to the proverbs of Aḥiḳar, and like them are collected under the name of a particular person. It appears then much more reasonable to suppose that the Aḥiḳar story and proverbs were originally composed in Babylonian, than to assume that the original was Persian, since we have no knowledge of the existence of any such literature among the Persians in or about 500 B.C. The composition must go at least as far back as that and may be even older.[2]

With regard to the word στήλη, used by Clement, there has been some unnecessary discussion. Of course no one writes a long series of proverbs on a *pillar*, or at least it would be very unusual to do so. They would be written (in Babylonia) on a tablet or tablets of clay, which might be of any size up to, say, 10 inches long. It is unlikely that Clement had ever seen a cuneiform tablet, and if his authority implied that the proverbs of Akikaros were inscribed on some hard substance, he might reasonably take it for granted that they were inscribed in the only way he knew, namely like a Greek inscription on a column. Therefore στήλη need only represent 'tablet', and does not imply any special distinction. The very strangeness of the word corroborates the story.

The Aramaic papyrus must be dated some time before 400 B.C., say about 430. The supposed Babylonian original cannot be earlier than 668, in the form from which the Aramaic is translated, although the story may be based on an earlier fact or legend. We have no definite proof, but some indications, of a more precise date. It is natural to suggest the time of Assurbanipal[3] (successor of Esarhaddon), the great patron of learning, at whose direction countless texts of all kinds were re-copied, and new works composed. Probable as this date is, however, there are reasons against it. In reading the Aramaic text attentively (and assuming that it represents the Babylonian original faithfully) one cannot help feeling that the historical setting is vague.[4] Esarhaddon is not

[1] See Langdon in *PSBA* 1916, p. 105+ and the references there. Also in *AJSL* 1912, p. 217.

[2] But not earlier than 668 (Esarhaddon's death) if that king's name belonged to the original story.

[3] Cf. his complaint of the ingratitude of his brother, in Rogers, *History of Babylonia* ii, p. 447, which might have suggested the Aḥiḳar story.

[4] So Ed. Meyer, Papyrusfund, p. 120+.

a living portrait: he has become a conventional figure. More definite is the fact that nowhere is either Nineveh or Babylon named—at least in the fragments preserved. The king nearly always has the title 'king of Assyria', and we cannot suppose that his capital would not sometimes be mentioned if its greatness was still a memory.[1] Nineveh was destroyed, and with it 'the kingdom of Assyria, all of it' just before 600 B.C. How long would it take to obscure the features of history and to make Assyria a suitable setting for an old-world story? Suppose we allow 50 years from the fall of Nineveh,[2] and allow something over a century for the story to become popular and to be translated from Babylonian into (Persian? and thence into) Aramaic. We are then brought to about the same date as Sachau for the original composition, about 550 (Sachau says 550–450), only that we hold it to have been first written in Babylonian. Whether it was translated first into Persian and thence into Aramaic, or directly from Babylonian into Aramaic, cannot be decided and is of no great importance. The Aramaic translation was made not later (perhaps earlier) than 450, by a scholar who, if he did not make it from Persian, was familiar with the Persian language and accustomed to translating from Persian, and whose Aramaic was strongly influenced by Persian. The existing papyrus is not his first draft, as is shown by the blanks in it. The copyist worked on a text which was already old and injured. He experienced the same difficulties as we have; sometimes he could not read his text and sometimes he did not understand it.

It must have been this or a similar Aramaic version which the author of Tobit knew, for there is nowhere any sign of the existence of an early Hebrew translation.[3] Nor is there any reason why there should have been one. Aramaic was perfectly well understood by the Jews in the last centuries B.C., was in fact more a vernacular than Hebrew. If an Aramaic version of it already existed, as we see it certainly did, there would be no need to translate a piece of purely popular literature into Hebrew.

Before the recovery of this Aramaic text, the story was known in

[1] Cf. e.g. the frequent mention of Babylon in the book of Daniel.

[2] Events moved rapidly at that time. In 550 the greatness of Egypt under Necho and Hophra was recent enough to account for its appearance in the story, if it was original—see below. In Tobit 14^{15} (Sinaitic text) Aḥiḳar is associated with the fall of Nineveh, so that this may have been mentioned in the original form of the story.

[3] Whether or not the book of Tobit was originally written in Hebrew does not concern us here. At any rate the version published by Neubauer (*The Book of Tobit*, Oxford, 1878) is merely a mediaeval Jewish production. The name of Aḥiḳar is there spelt אקיקר.

several later versions and appears in the Arabian Nights and even in India. As long ago as 1880 it was pointed out by Hoffmann [1] that the name of the hero is mentioned in the book of Tobit (1^{22}, 14^{10}, &c.). There are two possible ways of accounting for this fact: either the story already existed before the book of Tobit and was well known, or it was compiled in order to justify the reference in Tobit, just as the histories of the more obscure apostles were composed in the early church. The former, which in any case would seem the more probable, is now shown to be true, since the papyrus is two or three centuries earlier than Tobit.[2] A comparison between this early text and the later versions is rendered more difficult by the broken state of the papyri. The book, if it may be called so, is divided into two main parts, the narrative proper and the proverbs. Whether the two parts were originally distinct and whether the narrative was only used as a setting for the proverbs, we need not now inquire. In the later versions these two parts are subdivided into four: (1) the introduction, down to the adoption of Nadin; (2) the maxims by which he was educated; (3) the rest of the narrative, including Nadin's treachery, the restoration of Aḥiḳar and the episode in Egypt; (4) the maxims by which Nadin was punished. Our Aramaic text is, as would be expected, much simpler in the narrative part than the later versions. We have the beginning, and the first 4 fragments (=5 columns) are continuous, bringing the story down to the point at which Nabusumiskun reports to the king that he has killed Aḥiḳar. There seems therefore to be no place for the educative series of proverbs, which should begin at l. 9, in the middle of a continuous piece. The rest of the narrative is lost, so that we cannot tell whether it contained the Egyptian episode or not. So far as it goes, the narrative is on the same lines as in the later versions. If it continued on those lines, something is wanted to account for the rehabilitation of Aḥiḳar, and this may have been supplied by the Egyptian episode, though perhaps in a much less elaborate form.[3] On the other hand the ending may have been more abrupt and arbitrary, especially if the story was only intended as a prop for the proverbs. It must have ended happily, otherwise there would be no point in the scheme by which Aḥiḳar's life was saved. In

[1] In *Auszüge aus syrischen Erzählungen . . . in Abhandlungen für d. Kunde d. Morgenlands*, vol. 8.

[2] Which is supposed to have been written *c.* 230 B.C. See Simpson in Charles, *Apocrypha*.

[3] The incidents in this episode strike me as being too modern in character for a Babylonian story. At any rate I do not recall anything quite like them in cuneiform literature.

any case the whole of the narrative must have come first. Then follow the proverbs. They must have belonged to the story, because some of them clearly refer to Nadin's conduct, but they differ so much from the series in the later versions, that we have little help in determining their order where the papyrus is not continuous. Pap. 55 (line 79) does indeed start with a few lines corresponding roughly to a group early in the Syriac second series. Otherwise there is only occasional agreement with any of the later versions. The original collection formed a nucleus which was increased, diminished or varied according to the taste of subsequent editors. Collections of proverbs, including fables, were a favourite form of literature among the Semitic (and other) peoples. They were often compiled as representing the teaching of some particular wise man, and were put forth under his name. Thus the Babylonian collection mentioned above is ascribed to a person whose name is broken, we have the Hebrew collection of Ben Sira, and in the OT the book attributed to Solomon (Prov. 1^{1}, 10^{1}) with which are incorporated (perhaps the sayings of the wise 24^{23}) the proverbs of Solomon which Hezekiah's scribes copied out, 25^{1} (העתיקו 'translated' or 'transliterated'?), the words of Agur 30^{1}, and the words of king Lemuel 31^{1}. (The last for instance would form an exact parallel to the Aḥiḳar text if some one had prefixed to them an edifying story to explain why his mother taught him). Many of these sayings must have been constantly quoted conversationally, and have become part of the current wisdom of the world. But from their very popularity they tend to be modified—improved or distorted, simplified or obscured—and would soon lose all memory of their original ownership. Then arises another wise man, *qui prend son bien où il le trouve*, and with his own work incorporates, consciously or unconsciously, popular sayings (and often more than one form of the same maxim) without any intention of plagiarizing. Or he takes some well-known book of maxims and improves it. In this way has 'wisdom'-literature grown, and thus we may account for the differences between the proverbs of the Aramaic Aḥiḳar and those of the later versions, as well as for the elements which it has in common with Ben Sira, the book of Proverbs, or with similar works. In fact there is no reason why, if Aḥiḳar had been current in his circle, the compiler of the book of Proverbs should not have included parts of it in his work, just as he included the 'words of Agur', which are no more Jewish in spirit than Aḥiḳar. They are just worldly wisdom. Later Hebrew works, such as the *Derekh Ereẓ zuṭa*, generally have a definitely Jewish (but not necessarily religious) colouring. In the following notes no attempt is made to trace the proverbs in other literature. That would involve a much more extensive commentary. My object has been to contribute something to the establishment of the text and its meaning, without which the larger questions cannot be satisfactorily discussed.

The use of the sign ⳩ to mark the end of a proverb is not found in the narrative part, nor in any other of these papyri. It may be an archaic א, for אחר (?), but cf the sign ⳩ used in the 'Logia' to mark off sayings, Grenfell and Hunt, *Oxyrh Pap* iv, pl. 1. This may be held to indicate that the proverbs formed a distinct document, but probably the sign was only used in such disconnected compositions.

In trying to restore the text certain points must be taken into account The papyrus was written in columns which were not all of the same width. The text of the narrative was written continuously, with division of words but without leaving blank spaces If the original width of the column can be ascertained, we can estimate approximately the number of letters missing in a lacuna. The width of the column, however, is not maintained with the same mathematical precision as e g in a well-written Greek or Hebrew biblical MS. Thus the width of the first column seems to be shown by line 10, where the completion at the end may be taken as certain, cf. 30^{12}. But if it is right, the line must have been shorter by 3 or 4 letters than e g. l 13 where the restoration at the end is equally certain. Within such limits, however, the width of the column is a useful guide. The style is so simple and the repetition of set phrases is so frequent that in many cases a lacuna can be filled with great probability, while in some the context compels a particular restoration

None of these helps are found in the proverbs, where restoration is consequently very difficult. There we often have half a line, or less, left blank, so that the width of the column is no sure guide These blanks occur also in the version of the Behistun inscription and no doubt represent passages which the scribe could not read in his exemplar and so simply left them out. There are no recurrent phrases, and in literature of this kind there is no telling what the author will say next. It is the unexpected which makes the proverb The later versions seldom help. There is therefore much room for subjective reconstruction, with little result that can be called satisfactory.

THE WORDS OF AḤIḲAR

Col. i. Sachau, plate 40.

1 אלה מ]לי אחיקר שמה ספר חכים ומהיר זי חכם לברה [. . .
2 כזי] אמר ברא לם יהוה לי קדמת מל[ו]הי [רב]ה אחיקר וי[עט אתור כלה הוה
3 וצב]ית עזקתה זי שנחאריב מלך אתו[ר ואמר אנ]ה לם בנן ל[א לי ועל עטתי
4 ומלי הוה שנחאריב מלך אתור א[חר מית שנ]חאריב מ[לך אתור וקם שמה
5 אסרחארן ברה והוה מלך באתור חל[ף שנחאריב א]בוהי בֿ[ארין אמרת
6 שב [אנה ומן] ל[י יהוה] לבר אחר[י ל . . . . . מ]ותה [ומן יהוה
7 ל[ספר וצבית עזקת]ה לאס[רחארן מלכא כזי אנה הוית לשנחאריב
8 מלך] אתור אחר אנ[ה אחיקר לקחת נדן שמה] ברה [זי אחתי ורביתה
9 וחכמתה וטבתא הֿ[שגית ו]ה[קימתה בב]ב היכלא עמ[י קדם מלכא בגו
10 סגדוהי קרבתה קדם אסרחארן מלך אתור וחכמה מ[נדעמתא
11 ז]י שאלה אחר רחמה אסרחארן מלך אתור ואמר חין ש[גיאן לאחיקר יהוו
12 ס]פרא חכימא יעט אתור כלה זי הקים לברה ולא בר [לה בר אח]תה
13 כזי כן אמר מלך את]ור גהנת וסגד[ת] לם אחיקר קדם אסרח[ארן מלך] אתור
14 וליומן אחרנן אנה א]חיקר כזי ח[ז]ית אנפי אסרחארן מלך אתור טבן ענית
15 ואמרת קדם מלכ]א אנ[ה פלחת לשנח]אריב מלכא אבוך [ז]י מלך הו[ה קדמיך
16 . . . .[וכעת הא

Col. ii. Sachau, plate 41.

17 שב אנה לא אכהל למפלח בבב היכלא [ולמעבד לך עבידתי
18 ה]א נדן שמה ברי רבא והו יחלף לי ספר [ויעט אתור כלה והו
19 צבי]ת עזקה יהוה לך אף חכמתי וע[טתי חכמתה ענה אסרחארן יה[ו]ה
20 מל]ך אתור ואמר לי כותא לם [ברך ספר ויעט וצבית עזקה לי
21 יהוה] חלפיך עבידתך הו יעבד [לי אחר אנה אחיקר כזי שמעת
22 מלתא י]היבא אזלת לי לביתי [ושלה הוית בביתי וברי זנה
23 זי רבי]ת והקימת בבב היכלא [קדם אסרחארן מלך אתור בגו
24 סגדוה]י אמרת הו טבתא יבע[ה עלי לקבלזי עבדת לה אחר
25 בר אח]תי זי אנה רבית עשת על[י באישתא אף אמר בלבבה
26 לם [כאלה מ]ל[ן] אכל א[מר אחיקר זך שבא זי צבית עזקה הוה
27 לשנחא[רי]ב מלכא אבוך [הו חבל מתא עליך כי יעט וספר
28 חכים הו ועל עטתה ומל[והי הות אתור כלה אחר אסרחאדן

29 שגיא ירגש מלן שמע [כאלה זי אנה אמר לה ויקטל אחיקר אחר
30 כזי ברי זי לא ברי בדא [עלי כדבחא זא . . . .
31 ל . . . . .

Col. iii. Sachau, plate 42.

32 באדין התמלא חמא אס]רחאדן מלך אתור ואמר
33 יאתי לי נבוסמסכן ח]ד מן רבי אבי זי לחם אבי
34 אכל אמר מלכא אחיקר] תבעה אתר זי אנת תהשכח
35 ותקטלנהי] הגלו [את]יק[ר] זך שבא ספר חכים
36 ויעט כל אתו]ר למה הו יחבל מתא עלין אחר כזי
37 כן אמר מלך א]תור מני עמה גברן // אחרנן למחזה איך
38 יתעבד אזל נב]וסמסכן זך רביא רכב ב[ס]וסה חד קלי[ל
39 ונבריא אלך] עמה אחר לי[ו]מן אחרנן תלתה לם
40 הו עם גברן א]חרנן זי עמה ה̄[זני] ואנה מהלך בין כרמיא
41 וכזי חזני נב]וסמסכן רביא [זך קרב]תא בזע כתונה הילל
42 ואמר אנת הו] ספרא חכימא ובעל עטתא טבתא זי גבר
43 צדיק הוה וע]ל עטתה ומלוהי הות אתור כלא ירעך
44 ברא זי רבי]ת זי הקימת בתרע היכלא הו חבלך ותובא
45 באישא הו קר]בתא דחלת לם אחיקר ענית ואמרת לנבוסמ[סכן
46 רביא זך אף] אנה הו אחיקר זי קדמן שזבך מן קטל זכי
47 כזי שנחאריב] אבוהי זי אסרחאדן זנה מלכא חמר עליך
48 למקטלך קרב]תא יבלתך לביתא זילי תמה הוית מסבל לך

Col. iv. Sachau, plate 43, col. 1.

49 כאיש עם אחוהי והצפנתך מנה אמרת קטלתה עד זי לעד[ן א]חרן וליומן אחרנן
50 שגיאן קרבתך קדם סנחאריב מלכא והעדית חטאיך קדמוהי ובאיש[תא]
51 לא עבד לך אף שגיא סנחאריב מלכא רחמני עלזי החיתך ולא קטלתך כען אנת
52 לקבלזי אנה עבדת לך כן אפו עבד לי אל תקטלני בלני לביתך ע[ד] ליומן אחרנן
53 אסרחאדן מלכא רחמן הו כמנדע על אחרן יזכרני ועטתי יבעה א[חר] אנת
54 תקר]בני עלוהי ויהחיני אחר [ענה] נבוסמסכן רביא ואמר לי אל תדחל לם
55 תח]יי אחיקר אבוה זי אתור כלה זי על עטתה סנחאריב מלכא וחיל אתור

56 כלא הוו] קרבתא נבוסמסכן רביא אמר לכנותה גבריא אלך תרין זי עמה

57 אנתם הצי]תו לם א[ף הקשי]ב[ו] עלי ואנה אמר לכם עטתא [זילי] ועטה טבה הי

58 שגיא] א[חר ענו גבריא] אלך תרין ואמרו ל[ה אנת] ל[ם א]מר לן נבוסמסכן רביא

59 זי [אנת] א[מר ואנחנה נשמע]נך קרבתא [ענה נבוסמסכן ר]ביא ואמר להם שמעו לי

60 לם זנה [אחי]קר רב [וצבית עז]קה זי אסרחאדן [מלכא ה]ו ועל עטתה ומלוהי

61 חיל [אתו]ר כלא הוו אנחנה אל נקטלנהי [זכי עלים חד] סריס זילי אנתן לכם

62 יתקטל בי[ן] טוריא [אל]ה תרין חלף אחיקר זנה וכז[י ישתמיע ג]ברן אחרנן מלכא [יש]לח

63 א]חרין פגרה זי אחיקר זנה למחזה אחר [יחזון פגר]ה זי סריסא [זנ]ה עלימא זילי

Col. v. Sachau, plate 43, col. 2.

64 עדזי על אחרן אסרחאדן [מלכא יזכר אחיקר ועטתה יבעה ויבאש

65 עלוהי ולבב אסרחאר[ן מלכא יתוב עלי ויאמר לרבוהי וסגרוהי

66 נבכן אנה אנתן לכם כמס[פר הלא הן לו תשכחון אחיקר ועטתא זנה

67 טיבת על כנותה אלך ת[רין גבריא ענו ואמרו לנבוסמסכן רביא

68 עבד לקבלזי אנת עשת [אל נקטלנהי ותנתן לן עלימא

69 זך סריסא חלף אחיקר [זנה הו יתקטל בין טוריא אלך תרין

70 בזך עדנא אשתמיע במ[דינת אתור לם אחיקר ספרא זי אסרחאדן

71 מלכא קטיל אהר נבוס[מסכן רביא זך יבלני לביתה והצפנני אף

72 הוה מסבל לי תמה כ[איש עם אחוהי ואמר לי . . . . לחם ומין

73 יסתבלון קדם מראי ה[ן . . . .

74 סבל שגיא ונכסן שפ[יען יהב לי אחר נבוסמסכן זך רביא

75 אזל על אסרחאדן מל[כא ואמר לה לקבלזי אמרת לי כן עבדת

76 אולת השכחת לאחיק[ר זך וקטלתה וכזי שמע זנה אסרחאדן

77 מלכא שאל לגבריא ת[רין זי מני עם נבוסמסכן ואמרו כן הוה כזי

78 אמר א[די]ן עד אסרחא[דן מלכא . . . .

Col. vi. Sachau, plate 44.

79 מ[ה] חסין הו מן חמר נער ב[ג]תא

80 ברא זי יתאלף ויתסר ויתשים ארחא ברגלו[הי . . .

81 אל תהחשך ברך מן חטר הן לו לא תכהל תהנצלנ[הי מן באישתא
82 הן אמחאנך ברי לא תמות והן אשבקן על לבבך [לא תחיה
83 מחאה לעלים כא[יה] לחנת אף לכל עבדיך אל[פנא ✱ איש זי
84 קנה עבד פר[יך ו]אמה גנבה פ[חד] הו [הנעל לביתה ו . . .
85 שם אבוהי וזרעה בשם שרחותה ✱ עקרבא [יהשכח ?
86 לחם ולא י[אכ]ל [עד י]חיה וע[ל]והי טב מן זי יט[עמנהי
87 ל[. . . .] עבדת [. . . . .]רם אילתא שגיאת מסמ[. . . .
88 אריא יהוה מסמה לאילא בסתר סוידא והו [. . .
89 ודמה יאשד ובשרה יאכל הא כן פגעהם זי [אנש]א ✱ מ . . . אריה . . .
90 שבק חמר ולא יסבלנהי ינשא בות מן כנתה [וינ]שא מ[וב]לא זי לא זי̇לה
91 וטעון גמלא יטעננהי ✱ חמרא רב[ן] לאתנא [מן ר]חמתה וצנפריא [ג . . .
92 תרתין מלן שפירה וזי תלתא רחימה לשמש ש[תה] חמרא ויניקנהי ב̇ב̇ש
חכמה [?
93 וישמע מלה ולא יהחוה ✱ הא זנה יקיר [קדם] שמש וזי ישתה חמרא
ולא [יניקנהי
94 וחכמתה אבדה [ו . . . . נד] מן חזה ✱ . . שמת[. . . . . .]ינו
עממא [חכמתהם] אלהיא ה[. . .

Col. vii. Sachau, plate 45.

95 אף לאלהן יקירה הי ע[ד לע]ל[מן לה] מלכותא בש[מי]ן שימה הי כי בעל
קדשן נשא[ה
96 ב[רי] אל ת[ב]ט יתרא עד תחוה [כל מ]לה
97 זי] תאתה על בלך כוי בכל אתר [עיני]הם ואדניהם ל[הן] פמך אשתמר
לך אל יהוה טרפי[ך
98 מן כל מנטרה טר פמך ו[על] זי ש[מעת] הוקר לבב כי צנפר הי מלה
ומשלחה גבר לא ל[קח
99 מ[.]י אחדי פמך אחרי כן הנפק [לאחו]ך בעדרה כי עזיז ארב פם מן ארב
מלחם
100 אל תכבה מלת מלך רפאה תהוי [לאחו]ך רכיך ממלל מלך שרק ועזיז הו
מן סכין פמ[ין
101 חזי קדמתך מנדעם קשה [על א]נפי מ[לך] אלתקום זעיר כצפה מן ברק אנת
אשתמר לך
102 אלית[וג]הי עלא[מ]ריך ותהך [ב]לא ביומיך
לך
103 קדמ]ת מלך הן פקיד אשה יקדה הי עבק עבדה[י א]לתהן שק עליך
ותכסה כפיך [כי

104 א]ף מלת מלך בחמר לבבא ✱ [למ]ה ישפטון עקן עם אשה בשר עם סבין איש עם [מלך

105 טעמת אף זעררתא מררתא ו[טעמ]א חסין ולא איתי זי [מ]ריר מן ענוה רכיך לשן מ[לך

106 ועלעי תגין יתבר כמותא זי [ל]א מתחזה ✱ בשניא בנן לבבך אליחדה ובזעריהם [אלתבהת

107 מלך ברחמן אף קלה גבה ה[ו] מן הו זי יקום קדמוהי להן זי אל עמה

108 שפיר מלך למחזה בשמש ויקיר הדרה לדרכי ארקא בנית[א]

109 מאן טב כס[ה] מלה בלבבה ו[הו זי] תביר הנפקה ברא

110 אריא אזל קרב לש[למה לחמרא] ל[ם] שלם יהוי לך ענה חמרא ואמר לאריא

Col. viii. Sachau, plate 46.

111 נשאית חלא וטענת מלח ולא איתי זי יקיר מן [זפתא?

112 נשאית תבן ונסבת פרן ולא ולא איתי זי קליל מן תותב

113 חרב תדלה מין שפין בין רעין טבן

114 איש זעיר וירבה מלוהי מסרסרן לעלא מנה כי מפתח פמה מע[ל]ה

115 אלהן והן רחים אלהן הו ישימון טב בחנכה למאמר

116 שניאן [כ]וכב[י שמיא זי] שמהתהם לא ידע איש הא כן אנשא לא ידע איש

117 אריה [לא אי]תי בימא על כן יקראון לקפא לבא

118 נמרא פגע לענזא והי עריה ענה נמרא ואמר לענזא אתי ואכסנכי משכי [ענת

119 ענזא ואמרת לנמרא למה לי נסיכי גלדי אל תלקחן מני כי לא [ישא]ל

120 שלם טביא להן למונק דמה ✱ רבא אזל על אמ[ריא] . . . . . . א . . .

121 אשתק ענו אמרי[א] ואמרו לה שא לך זי ת[נ]שא מנן אנחנה א[מריך

122 כי לא בידי אנ[ש]א מ[נש]א רגלהם ומנחתותהם מן בלע[די אלהן] ל[כן . . .

123 כי לא בידיך מ[נש]א רגלך [ו]למנחתותה ✱ הן נפקה טבה מן פם א[נשא טב

124 והן לחיה תנפק [מן] פמהם אלהן ילחון להם ✱ הן עיני אלהן על אנ[שא

125 איש מצלח עקן בחשובא ולא חזה באיש גנב זי שתר בי וישת[מר?

Col. ix. Sachau, plate 47, col. 1.

126 אלתדרג ק]שתך ואל תהרכב חטך לצדיק למה אלהיא יסגה בעדרה ויהתיבנהי עליך

127 . . . . אנת יה ברי הכצר כל כציר ועבד כל עבידה אדין תאכל ותשבע ותנתן לבניך

128 הן דר]גת קשתך והרכבת חטך לצדיק מנך חטא מן אלהן הד

129 . . . אנת יה ברי זף דגנא וחנטתא זי תאכל ותשבע ותנתן לבניך עמך

130 ו]פתא יקירתא ומן גבר לחה אלתזף א[ף הן] תזף זפתא שלין לנפשך אלתשים עד

131 ו]פתא [תשלם זפת]א חליה כ[זי חס]יר ומשלמותה ממלא [ב]י

132 כל זי תשמע תבחננ]הי בארניך כי חן גבר הימנותה [כי] שנאתה כרבת שפותה

133 עלק]רמן כרסאא לכדבא [. .]ט ועלא[חרן יה]נשנון כדבתה וירוקן באנפוהי

134 מכדב גזיר קדלהכבחולה תימנה זי [תחבא ?] לאנפין כאיש זי יעבד לחיתא

135 ומן אלהן לא נפקת ✱

136 אלתמאס] זי בערבך ואל תרגג לכביר זי ימנע מנך

137 אלתרבי] חיל ואל תהשנא לבבא

138 זי] לא יתרום בשם אבוהי ובשם אמה אלירנח שמ[ש עלוהי] כי גבר לחה הו

139 מני] נפקת לחיתי ועם מן אצדק ✱ בר בטני הנשש ביתי [? ומ]ה אמר לנבריא

140 ה]ות לי שהר חמס ומן אפו צדקני ✱ מן ביתי נפקת חמת[א] עם מן אקשה ואעפה

141 רז]יך אלתגלי קדם [רח]מיך [ו]אליקל שמך קדמיהם

Col. x. Sachau, plate 47, col. 2.

142 עם זי רם מנך אלתעבר בנ[צוי ?

143 עם זי אצי[ל] ועזיז מנך [אלתשפט כי ילקח

144 מן מנתך [ועל]זילה [יהוסף ?

145 הא כן איש זעיר ועם [איש רב ישפט

146 אלתהעדי מנך חכמתא ו[. . .

147 אל תסתכל כביר [וא]ל ירעך ח[כמתך

148 אל תחלי ואל[יבלע]וך אלתמר [ואלירקוך

149 הן צבה אנת ברי זי תהוה [רם השפל נפשך קדם אלהא

150 זי יהשפל לאיש רם (?) ו[ירים לאיש שפל

151 מה ילוטון ש[פו]ת [אנ]שא ל[א ילוטון אלהן

152 טב כבש . . .

153 נפשך אלירחם . . .

154 ירפון המו להן זי אל עמה . . .

155 יהשחתון ידי ואל פמי ואל . . .

156 יאפך אל פם אפכא וינסח לשנ[ה

157 עי]נין טבן אל יאכמו ואדנין [טבן אל יסתתמו ופם טב ירחם

158 כשיטא ויאמרנה

Col. xi. Sachau, plate 48, col. 1.

159 איש [שפ]יר מרדה ולבבה טב כק[שת]ה חסינה זי מת[נגרה] בג[בר] איתי

160 הן לא י]עמד איש עם אלהן ומה יתנטר עלאון נוה

161 . . . מן . . שי בטן וזי לה אלעמה מן יהו[ה ד]אנהי

162 . . נה . . . . ו אנשא ועממא עברו בהם ולא שבקו המו ולבבהם [פתיח ?]

163 לא ידע] איש מה בלבב כנתה וכזי [יח]זה גבר טב לגבר ל[חה יזהר לה

164 לא] ילוה עמה ב[ארחא] ובעל אנר לא יהוה לה גבר טב [ע]ם ג[בר לח]ה

165 סנ]יא שדר לרמנ[א] לם סניא לרמנא מה טב שג[יא] כבי[ך לזי נ]גע [באנ]ביך

166 . . ענ]ה [רמנ]א ואמר לסניא אנת כל[ך] כבן עם זי נגע בך

167 צדיק אנשא בעדרה כלנטתוהי הוין

168 בית] רשיען ביום רוח תתחלל ובשהינן יצעון תרעיה כי בזיזת

169 צדיק המו] + עיני זי נטלת עליך ולבבי זי יהבת לך בחכמה

170 מאסת וי]הבת שמי בשרחו[תא]

171 הן יאחדן רשיעא בכנפי לבשך שבק בידה אחר אדני לשמש הו

172 י]לקח זילה וינתן לך

Col. xii. Sachau, plate 48, col. 2.

173 הקימני אלבצדיק עמך ל[מה

174 ימותון שאני ולא בחרבי[

175 שבקתך בסתר ארזא וסח[רת ?

176 שבקת לרחמיך והוקרת [שנאי

177 רתא גבר זילא ידע מה י[

178 חכים ממלל כי מפתח פם ס[

179 אתנ[והי ש[

180 בא[

. . . . . .

184 . . . . . נ]פלת ססא בערב[

185 . . . . מיא[

186 .ב. ח נחשא נפלת ססא[

187 נפשי לא תרע ארחה עלבן [י

188 כפן יהחלה מררותא [ו]צהוה[

189 ישתבע כעם מן לחם ותתרוה [נפש עניה מן חמר

190 אנשא . . . . . חלא . . . א

Col. xiii. Sachau, plate 49.

(*a*)

191 חר דרך קשתה והרכב [חט]ה ולא[

192 הן יפקד לך מראך מין למנטר[(*b*)

193 למשבק זהב בידך + אלת[ב מ ? פ ?

194 . . . א ולא יפשר קרב עלי ואל יאמר לך ר[חי]ק מני

195 . . שה ולא יע[. .] לה

196 [עבד זי ברג]לה ארח ו[הו גנ]ב לא י[ת]קנה

197 . . . ד + . . ביתה עמה [נפק]ת [א]שה מ[ן אנ]פין

198 [זי אלהא +] . . . . . למ[ראה] . . קש ברינה כזי עבד לחי[תא] ל[מ]ראה

199 . . . ת מראה . . . . אבא הויה + צנפריא . . . . . . און על .

200 . . . ה וי . . . . . איש לחה זי יהנשג כ . . .

201 . . . ד כזי [י]שלחנ[ך] למה תשתנה באנפוהי

202 . . . ה דמו . . . . אנפוהי עלדבר זי

203 .. מכרא . . . . [ק]דמיך בחין קדם

204 . . . ם חד לערדה [ארכב] עליך ואנ[ה] אסבלנך

205 לך יהו]י סבוליך וכסתך ואנה רכביך לא אחזה

206 בין בש]ר ובין שאני בזק אל ינעל ברגלי

207 הן + אליאמר עתירא בעתרי הדיר אנה

(*c*)	(*d*)
197* ד +	רע את
198* למ	תישנא
199* ת מראה	
200* ה ו	

Col. xiv. Sachau, plate 50.

208 A אלתה]חוי לערבי ימא ולצידני כ[רא] B כי עבירתהם פרישה

209 . . . חמרא הו זי יטעמנהי ומ[. . הו י[כ]טרנהי

210 . . . ד אמיר מית שאני וענת ו[לא י]דע זי [י]אתה מן אחרוהי

211 . . . ינסח ורם מן גלדי + רג . . בבותא הן . נ . מן . . בלך

212 . . . כן הי . ל . . . . להן ז . . .

213 . . . . עויר עינין . . .

214 . . . . יאתה . . . . B . . . . . לה . . .

215 . . . . עינין . . . . D . . . . מיא . .

216 . . . . עויל וחרש ארנין ל . . . . C . . . הי וה . נ . . בנן . . .

217 . . . . מן בטן ידע ברחרן ולא מ[ן] . . . אן . . . .

218 . . . אל יקנה איש לא ב[ע]ולה C זי . . . . . א וג . . . E לטב

219 . . . מתקנה ג[רה] כגרה ואנת[ה] H . . ש . . G . . . . F כב . . .

220 . . . . . נה . . . . . . ית . . . . . . יא כלא . . . . ך עלו . . .

221 . . . מה . . . מה . . מן . . . . . H . גנב G . . . F ה . . .

222 . . . זנה בית רעה נשק באשה

223 . . . . . רחמן . . מן בעל עד

Col. i.

[1] *These are the wo*rds of one named Aḥiḳar, a wise and ready scribe, who taught his son . . . [2] *For* he said, 'Surely he shall be a son to me'. Before *his* words Aḥiḳar *had become gre*at and *had been counsellor of all Assyria* [3] *and bea*rer of the seal of Senacherib king of Assyria, *and he said: I* indeed *had no* sons *and on my counsel* [4] and words Senacherib king of Assyria used to (rely). *Then Sen*acherib k*ing of Assyria died and there arose* [5] his son named Esarhaddon and became king in Assyria inst*ead of Senacherib his f*ather. At *that time I said* [6] '*I am* old *and who shall be* to *me* a son after *me to . . . ? and who shall be* [7] *scribe and bearer of the sea*l to Esarhaddon *the king, as I was to Senacherib,* [8] *king of* Assyria?' Then I, *Aḥiḳar, took Nadin, as he was called,* the son *of my sister, and brought him up,* [9] and taught him and *showed great* kindness (to him), *and set him in the ga*te of the palace with *me before the king among* [10] his courtiers. I brought him before Esarhaddon king of Assyria, and he told him wh*atever* [11] he asked him. Then Esarhaddon king of Assyria loved him and said '*Long* life *be to Aḥiḳar,* [12] the wise scribe, counsellor of all Assyria, who set up as his son, when *he had* no son, *the son of his sis*ter.' [13] When the king of Assyria had thus spoken, I bowed down and made obeisance, I Aḥiḳar, before Esarh*addon king of* Assyria. [14] *And in after days I,* Aḥiḳar, when I saw the face of Esarhaddon king of Assyria favourable, I answered [15] *and said before the king,* 'I *served Senach*erib the king your father who was king *before you* [16] . . . . *and now behold*

Col. ii.

[17] I am old. I cannot work in the gate of the palace *and do my service to you.* [18] *Beh*old, my son, Nadin by name, is full-grown. Let him take my place as scribe *and counsellor of all Assyria, and* let him [19] be seal-*bear*er to you. My wisdom also and my coun*sel I have taught him.' Then answered Esarhaddon* [20] *ki*ng of Assyria and said to me, 'So indeed it shall *be. Your son shall be scribe and seal-bearer to me* [21] in your stead. He shall do your service *for me.' Then I, Aḥiḳar, when I heard* [22] *the promise g*iven, went away to my house *and was resting in my house. And this my son* [23] *whom* I had *brought up* and set in the gate of the palace *before Esarhaddon, king of Assyria, among* [24] *his*

courtiers, I thought, 'He will see*k my* good *in return for that which I have done for him*'. *Then* [25] *the son of* my *sister* whom I had brought up, imagined against *me evil and said in his heart*, [26] 'Surely *such words as these* can I *say*, "*This Aḥiḳar, the old man, who was seal-bearer* [27] to Senacherib the king your father *has corrupted the land against you, for he is a counsellor and* a skilful [28] *scribe* and by his counsel and wor*ds all Assyria was* (*guided*)." *Then Esarhaddon* [29] will be greatly troubled when he hears words *like these which I shall speak to him, and will kill Aḥiḳar.*' *Then* [30] when my son who was not my son, had devised *this falsehood against me* . . . . . [31] . . . .

Col. iii.

[32] *Then was E*sarhaddon king of Assyria *filled with rage* and said, [33] '*Let there come to me Nabusumiskun* one of the officers of my father, who *ate* the bread of my father.' [34] *The king said*, 'You are to seek *Aḥiḳar* (in) a place which you shall find [35] *and kill him.* Even if this Aḥiḳar, the old man, is a skilful scribe [36] *and counsellor of all Assy*ria, why should he corrupt the land against us?' Then when [37] *the king of Assy*ria *had thus spoken*, he appointed with him 2 other men to see how [38] *it would be done.* This *Nab*usumiskun the officer *went away* riding on a swift horse of his, [39] *and those men* with him. Then after three more days indeed [40] *he, with o*ther *men* who were with him, *saw me* while I was walking among the vineyards. [41] *And when this Nab*usumiskun the officer *saw me the*n he rent his clothes, lamenting, [42] *and said*, '*Are you he*, the skilful scribe, giver of good counsel, who [43] *was a righteous* man *and by* whose counsel and words all Assyria was (guided)? [44] *The son whom you brought up*, whom you set in the gate of the palace, has injured you (?); he has ruined you, and [45] an *evil* return *is it*.' *Th*en I, Aḥiḳar, indeed was afraid. I answered and said to Nabusum*iskun* [46] *the officer*, '(*Yes, and*) *also* I am that Aḥiḳar who formerly saved you from an undeserved death [47] *when Senacherib* the father of this Esarhaddon, the king, was angry with you [48] *to kill you. The*n I took you to my house. There I was supporting you

Col. iv.

[49] as a man (deals) with his brother, and I hid you from him. I said, "I have killed him", until in after time and many days [50] after, I brought you before king Senacherib and took away your offences before him, and he did you no evil. [51] Moreover king Senacherib was well pleased with me that I had kept you alive and had not killed you. Now [52] according as I did to you, so do also to me. Do not kill me. Take me to your house un*til* other days. [53] King Esarhaddon is kind as any man (?). Hereafter he will remember me and desire my counsel. Th*en* you [54] *shall brin*g me to him and he shall let me live.' Then *answered* Nabusumiskun the officer and said to me, 'Fear not. Surely [55] *you shall l*ive, Aḥiḳar, father of all Assyria, by whose counsel king Senacherib and *all* the army of Assyria [56] were (guided).' Then Nabusumiskun the officer said to his companions, those two men who were with him, [57] 'He*arken*, indeed, a*nd liste*n to me, and I will tell you *my* counsel,

and it is a good counsel [58] *exceedingly*.' Th*en answered* those two *men* and said to *him*, 'Tell us indeed, Nabusumiskun the officer, [59] what *you* th*ink, and we will listen* to you.' Then *answered Nabusumiskun the* officer and said to them, 'Hear me, [60] indeed this *Ahi*ḳar was a great man *and bearer of the se*al to *king* Esarhaddon, and by his counsel and words [61] all the army of *Assy*ria were (guided). Let us not kill him *undeservedly*. *A slave*, a eunuch of mine, I will give to you. [62] Let him be killed between *the*se two mountains instead of this Aḥiḳar, and whe*n it is heard*, the king *will* send other *m*en [63] after us to see the body of this Aḥiḳar. Then *they will see the body* of *thi*s eunuch my slave,

Col. v.

[64] until afterwards Esarhaddon *the king remembers Aḥiḳar and desires his counsel, and grieves* [65] over him, and the heart of Esarhadd*on the king shall turn to me and he shall say to his officers and courtiers,* [66] "I will give you riches as the num*ber of the sand if you find Aḥiḳar*."' *And this counsel* [67] seemed good to his companions, those t*wo men*. *They answered and said to Nabusumiskun, the officer*, [68] 'Do according as you think. *Let us not kill him, but you shall give us* that *slave*, [69] the eunuch, instead of Aḥiḳar *here*. *He shall be killed between these two mountains*.' [70] At that time it was reported in the co*untry of Assyria, saying*, '*Aḥiḳar the scribe of Esarhaddon* [71] the king is killed.' Then Nabusu*miskun, that officer, took me to his house and hid me, also* [72] he sustained me there as *a man* (*deals*) *with his brother, and said to me* . . . '*Bread and water* [73] shall be carried to my lord' . . . [74] abundant sustenance (?) and (other) things in pl*enty*. *Then Nabusumiskun, that officer*, [75] went to Esarhaddon the k*ing and said to him*, '*According as you commanded me, so have I done*. [76] I went and found *that* Aḥiḳar *and killed him*.' *And when* king *Esarhaddon* [77] heard this he asked the t*wo* men *whom he had appointed with Nabusumiskun and they said*, '*So it was, as* [78] he says.' Th*en* as long as *king* Esarha*ddon* . . . . .

Col. vi.

[79] What is stronger than wine foaming in the p*ress*? [80] The son who is trained and taught, and on *whose* feet the fetter is put *shall prosper*. [81] Withhold not thy son from the rod, if thou canst not keep *him from wickedness*. [82] If I smite thee, my son, thou wilt not die, and if I leave (thee) to thine own heart *thou wilt not live*. [83] A blow for a slave, rebuke for a maid, and for all thy servants dis*cipline*. *A man who* [84] buys a lic*entious* slave (or) a thievish maid *brings* an*xiety into his house, and disgraces* [85] the name of his father and his offspring with the reputation of his wantonness. The scorpion *finds* [86] bread and does not *eat* in order that *he may* live, but it is too good for him to t*aste*. [87] . . . . . . thou hast done . . . . . . the blood of the hind . . . [88] The lion devours (?) the hart in the secrecy of (his) den (?), and he . . . [89] and will shed his blood and eat his flesh: so is the contact of *men*. Fr*om fear of* the lion [90] the ass left *his burden* and will not carry it. He shall bear shame before his fellow *and shall be*ar a b*ur*den which is not *his*, [91] and shall

be laden with a camel's load. The ass made obeisance to the she-ass from love of her, and the birds . . . [92] Two things are a merit (?), and of three there is pleasure to Shamash: *one who drinks* wine and gives it (to others), one who restrains (?) wisdom . . . [93] and he hears a word and does not reveal (it). Behold, this is precious *before* Shamash. But one who drinks wine and does not *give it to others* [94] and his wisdom goes astray . . . . . who sees? . . . Thou hast placed . . . . . the peoples their wisdom the gods . . .

Col. vii.

[95] Even to gods is it precious, *to it* for *ever* belongs the kingdom, in *heaven* it is treasured up, for the lord of holiness has exalted *it*. [96] My son, do not chatter overmuch till thou reveal *every word* [97] *which* comes into thy mind, for in every place are their *eyes* and their ears; *but* keep watch over thy mouth, let it not be *thy* destruction (?). [98] More than all watchfulness watch thy mouth, and *over* what *thou hearest* harden thy heart, for a word is (like) a bird, and when he has sent it forth a man does not *recapture it* (?). [99] *Count* the secrets of thy mouth, afterwards bring forth (advice) to thy *brother* for his help, for stronger is the ambush of the mouth than the ambush of fighting. [100] Suppress not the word of a king: let it be a healing to thy *brother*. Soft is the speech of a king, (but) it is sharper and stronger than a *two*-edged knife. [101] Behold before thee something hard: *in presence* of a *king* delay not. Swifter is his anger than lightning. Do thou take heed to thyself. [102] Let him not *show* it at thy *words*, that thou go away before thy time. [103] *In presence* of a king, if (a thing) is commanded thee, it is a burning fire; hasten, do it; do not put sackcloth upon thee and hide thy hands, *for* [104] also the word of a king is with wrath of heart. *Why* should wood strive with fire, flesh with a knife, a man with *a king*? [105] I have tasted even the bitter sloe, and the *taste* was strong, but there is nothing which is more bitter than poverty. Soft is the tongue of a *king* [106] but it breaks the ribs of a dragon, like death which is not seen. In a multitude of children let not thy heart exult, and in the lack of them *be not thou ashamed*. [107] A king is like the merciful (?): even his voice is high: who is he that can stand before him, except one who is like (?) him? [108] Glorious is a king to see, like Shamash, and precious is his sovereignty to those who walk on the earth in tranquillity. [109] A good vessel hides a thing within itself, but *one that* is broken lets it go forth. [110] The lion went near to *greet the ass* saying, 'Peace be to thee'. The ass answered and said to the lion . . . . . .

Col. viii.

[111] I have lifted sand and carried salt, and there is nothing which is heavier than *debt*. [112] I have lifted chaff and taken up crumbs, and there is nothing which is lighter than (to be) a sojourner. [113] A sword will trouble calm waters whether they be bad (or) good. [114] A little man when he multiplies his words, they fly away (?) above him, for the opening of his mouth . . . [115] gods, and if he were beloved of (the) gods they would put something good in his palate to speak. [116] Many

are the sta*rs of heaven whose* names man knows not: so man knows not men. [117] There *is no* lion in the sea, therefore they call the . . . . lion (?). [118] The leopard met the goat and she was cold. The leopard answered and said to the goat, 'Come, and I will cover thee with my hide.' [119] The goat *answered* and said to the leopard, 'What hast thou to do with me, my lord? Take not my skin from me.' For *he does* not [120] salute the kid except to suck its blood. The master (?) went to the sh*eep* . . . . . [121] I will be silent. The sheep answered and said to him, 'Take for thyself what thou wilt *take* from us. We are *thy shee*p.' [122] For it is not in the power of men to *lift* up their foot and to put them down with*out* (*the*) *gods*. [123] For it is not in thy power to *lift* thy foot and to put it down. If there goes forth good from the mouth of *men, it is well,* [124] and if a curse shall go forth *from* their mouth, (the) gods will curse them. If the eyes of (the) gods are over m*en* [125] a man cuts (?) wood in the dark and does not see, like a thief who breaks into (?) a house and es*capes* (?).

Col. ix.

[126] *Bend not* thy bow and shoot not thy arrow at the righteous, lest God come to his help and turn it back upon thee. [127] . . . . . do thou, O my son, gather every harvest, and do every work, then thou shalt eat and be filled and give to thy children. [128] *If* thou hast *ben*t thy bow and shot thy arrow at one who is more righteous than thou, it is a sin in the sight of God. [129] . . . . . do thou, O my son, borrow corn and wheat that thou mayest eat and be filled and give to thy children with thee. [130] A heavy loan and from a wicked man, borrow not, an*d if* thou borrow take no rest to thy soul till [131] *thou pay back* the loan. *A loan* is pleasant w*hen there is ne*ed, but the paying of it is the filling of a house. [132] *All that thou hearest thou mayest try* by thy ears, for the beauty of a man is his faithfulness, *for* his hatefulness is the lying of his lips. [133] *At fi*rst the throne is *set* up for the liar, but at l*ast* his lies *shall* find (him) out, and they shall spit in his face. [134] A liar has his neck cut, like a maiden of the south (?) who *hides* (?) (her) face, like a man who makes a curse [135] which came not forth from (the) gods. [136] *Despise not* that which is in thy lot, and covet not some great thing which is withheld from thee. [137] *Increase not* riches, and lead not (thy) heart astray. [138] *He who* is not proud of (?) the name of his father and the name of his mother, let not the *sun* shine *upon him,* for he is an evil man. [139] *From myself* has my curse gone forth, and with whom shall I be justified? The son of my body has spied out (?) my house, *and what* can I say to strangers? [140] *There w*as a cruel witness against me, and who then has justified me? From my own house went forth wrath, with whom shall I strive and toil? [141] Thy *secr*ets reveal not before thy *frie*nds, that thy name be not lightly esteemed before them.

Col. x.

[142] With one that is higher than thou, do not go (?) to qu*arrelling* (?). [143] With one that is a noble (?) and stronger than thou, *contend not, for he will take* [144] of thy portion *and will add it to* his own. [145] Behold,

so is a little man who *contends* with *a great man.* [146] Remove not wisdom from thee, and . . . . [147] Be not over crafty, *and let not thy wisdom* be extinguished. [148] Be not sweet lest they *swallow* thee up. Be not bitter, *lest they spit thee out.* [149] If thou, my son, wouldst be *exalted, humble thyself before God* [150] who humbles the lofty man and *exalts the humble man.* [151] How can the *lips* of *men* curse *when* (*the*) *gods curse not?* [152] Better is he that restrains . . . [153] Let not thy soul love . . . . [154] heal them, except one who is like him. [155] My hands shall destroy, and . . . . [156] God (?) shall turn back the mouth of the unjust (?) and shall tear out *his* tongue. [157] Good *eyes* shall not be darkened and *good* ears *shall not be stopped, and a good mouth will love* [158] the truth and speak it.

Col. xi.

[159] A man *exc*ellent in character and whose heart is good is like a strong b*ow* which is *bent* by a str*ong man.* [160] *If* a man stand *not* with (the) gods, how shall he be saved by (?) his own strength? [161] . . . . belly and that which is like it, who shall be judging him (?)? [162] . . . . men, and peoples pass over them and do not leave them, and their heart is . . . . [163] A man *knows not* what is in the heart of his fellow, and when a good man *sees* an *evil* man *he will beware of him,* [164] he will *not* accompany him on *a journey,* and will not hire him—a good man with *an evil man.* [165] The *bramb*le sent to *the* pomegranate saying, 'Bramble to Pomegranate, what is the good of *thy ma*ny thorns *to him who tou*ches thy *fruit?*' [166] . . . . the *pomegranate answer*ed and said to the bramble, 'Thou art all thorns to him who touches thee.' [167] The righteous among men, all who meet him are for his help (?). [168] *The house of* wicked men in the day of storm shall be destroyed (?), and in calm (?) its gates shall fall (?), for the spoiling of [169] *the righteous are they.* My eyes which I lifted up on thee and my heart which I gave thee in wisdom, [170] *thou hast despised and* hast turned my name into wanton*ness.* [171] If the wicked take hold of the skirts of thy garment, leave (it) in his hand. Then approach (?) Shamash. He [172] *will* take his and give it to thee.

Col. xii.

[173] God set me up as a righteous man with thee, w*hy* . . . . [174] My enemies shall die, but not by my sword . . . . [175] I left thee in a hiding-place of cedar, and *thou hast* gon*e about* . . . [176] Thou hast left thy friends and hast honoured *my enemies.* [177] Pity (?) a man who knows not what he . . . [178] A wise man speaks, for the opening of the mouth of . . . [179-183] . . . . [184] . . . the moth fell into . . . [185] . . . . [186] Into a house (?) of bronze the moth fell . . . [187] My soul knows not its path, therefore . . . [188] Hunger sweetens that which is bitter *and* thirst . . . [189] Let him that is vexed be satisfied with bread, and *the soul of the poor* be sated with wine. [190] Men . . . . . .

Col. xiii.

[191] One bent his bow and shot his arrow, and it did not . . . . [192] If thy lord entrust to thee water to keep . . . [193] to leave gold in thy hand. Do

not . . . [194] . . . . . . come near to me, and let him not say, 'Be far from me'. [195] . . . . [196] . . . . . . *a slave on whose foot* is a fetter and *who is a thief* should not *be* bought. [197] . . . . . . his house with him, a fire *went forth* from *before* [198] *God. He who accuses his lord shall be entr*apped in his law-suit, as if he uttered a curse on his lord. [199] . . . . . . his lord . . . . . . The birds . . . [200] . . . . . . an evil man who overtakes . . . [201] . . . . . . thee when he send*s thee*, why shouldst thou be changed in his sight? [202] . . . . . . his sight because [203] . . . . . . before thee tested before [204] . . . . . . one to the wild ass '*Let me ride* upon thee and I will feed thee.' [205] . . . . . . *keep for thyself* thy feeding and thy saddle, but I will not see thy riding. [206] . . . . . . *between flesh* and shoe let him not put a pebble into my foot. [207] . . . . . . Let not the rich man say, 'In my riches I am glorious'.

Col. xiv.

[208] *Do not* show to an Arab the sea or to a Sidonian the desert, for their work is different (?). [209] He who treads out the wine is he who should taste it, and he who . . . he should guard it. [210] . . . . . . and *I* know *not* what *will* come after it. [211] . . . he shall tear out, and blood from my skin . . . . . . [212] . . . . [213] . . . . . . blind in the eyes . . . [214] . . . . . . he shall come . . . [215] . . . . . . eyes . . . [216] . . . a child and a deaf man, ears . . . [217] . . . from the belly one (?) knows a noble person, and not from . . . [218] . . . let not a man buy either a married woman . . . [219] *let* a ma*id be* bought as a maid, and a wife . . . [220] . . . . [221] . . . . . . thief . . . [222] . . . this, the house of his neighbour caught (?) fire . . . [223] . . . merciful . . . owner . . .

Line 1 is clearly the beginning. The first words are probably אלה מלי (so Baneth), cf. Prov. 24^{23} and דברי Prov. 30^{1}, 31^{1}. Nöldeke proposes מתלי (cf. Prov. 1^{1}), which would imply that the narrative is merely an introduction to the maxims. שמה 'by name', a Persian idiom frequent in this text, but also occurring in the other papyri, cf. e.g. 33^{1-5}. ספר ח' ומהיר not only a scribe but a learned man. In Hebrew cf. Ezra 7^{6}. The end of the line is difficult to restore, and none of the suggestions are convincing. The remains of the letter after לברה are not a ו or ז but part of ת or מ. One would expect some word to show that he was not really a son.

Line 2. [כזי] only a guess to fit the space. It will depend on the restoration of l. 1. יהוה a future, not precative (יהוי). מל[ו]הי. The הי are practically certain. The phrase seems to mean 'before this narrative begins'. [רב]ה 'had become great', more probable than ענה (Baneth). It continues in the 3rd person with occasional quotations in the 1st person. The composition of these first lines is difficult, and one cannot be sure where the 1st person takes up the story.

Line 3. [וצב]ית Epstein? Perles צבת. The י is certain, and there is part of the foot of ב, so that there is no doubt about the word. It is

Bab. *ṣâbit*, 'bearer' of the seal. עזקתה cf. Dan. 6^{18}. [אנ]ה is practically certain. The end seems to be required by ומלי in l. 4. Note the Persian form אתור and the Assyrian שְׁנַחֲאֵרִיב.

Line 4. מלי not מלא (as Sachau? and Ungnad). To take as 'full' (of years) seems impossible. הוה . . . על i.e. relied upon. Cf. l. 43.

Line 5. אֲסַרְחַאדֹּן (Ungnad) the Assyrian form. ב[ארין]. The ב is doubtful, and the restoration uncertain. The line is long because שמה is written above ברה.

Line 6 is too much broken to be restored with any certainty, and so too l. 7. Baneth proposes 'I took my sister's son, Nadin by name, . . .' but it seems too soon to introduce the adoption of Nadin, which ought to come just before line 9. The vacant space may have had something like 'to do my service', cf. ll. 17, 21, but I cannot fill it up satisfactorily. The ל is probable.

Line 8. The account of the adoption seems to come in most naturally here, beginning with אחר.

Line 9. After וטבתא a verb is wanted, and the tail of a ח is visible, but ה[שנית] is not a very convincing conjecture. [ו]ה[קימתה] וכ' from l. 23. עמ[י]. Epstein עמר (joined with the preceding words), but this verb is rarely (if ever) found (l. 160) in the papyri. At the end the king must be mentioned to account for סגרוהי '*his* courtiers' in l. 10.

Line 10. קרבתה i.e. I brought him specially to the notice of the king. מ[נרעמתא] is no doubt right, cf. 30^{12}.

Line 11. ש[ניאן] is probably right, with חין. If the fragment on the left is rightly placed, יהוו is probable, for there are traces of הו on it. The 3rd person (therefore a name לאחיקר), not לך, is required by הקים in l. 12. But the restoration is rather long.

Line 13. The first letters remaining must belong to [את]ור which implies מלך preceding. Therefore the king's remarks ended with l. 12, and the beginning of l. 13 must be the protasis of a new sentence of which the apodosis begins with נחנת.

Line 14. [וליומן אחרנן] cf. ll. 39, 49. At the end, nothing after ענית.

Line 15. [ואמרת] is required after ענית. אנ[ה] must begin Aḥikar's statement of his case which is continued in l. 17. [פלחת] from l. 17, but it does not quite fill the space.

Line 16. Only slight traces remain. It must have formed the transition to l. 17.

Line 17. (Pl. 41.) At least half of this column is lost. בב is Babylonian for Aramaic תרע as in l. 44. The restoration of the end is not by any means certain. Cf. l. 21.

Line 18. נדן is a short form of some Assyrian name like Assur-nadin-apli (Ungnad). רבא. The following ו shows that it is not an adjective, but a verb (so Baneth) 'is grown up', cf. Dan. 4^{19}, though one would expect רבה, as in l. 2. יחלף וכ' must mean 'he shall succeed me as scribe', Arab. خلف, cf. Mesha inscr. l. 6 (Ungnad). The restoration is probably right, as עזקה l. 19 shows that the regular formula was used.

Line 19, beginning as l. 3. The restoration of the end must be right. וע[נתי] is the only possible word, and ענה אס' is required by the beginning of l. 20. The only word which is doubtful is חכמתה, but nothing better suggests itself.

Line 20. כותא is not a title (as Sachau), nor is it connected with 'Meskin Kanti' applied to Nabusumiskun in the Syriac and Arabic versions, see Story, p. 112, n. 1, and p. xxxv. It is simply an adverb 'so' formed from כות 'like'. יה[וה] is above the line, which is consequently long. The end is from ll. 2 and 3. For ברך perhaps read הו.

Line 21. הלפיך 'instead of you' begins a new sentence. The end is probable if the beginning of l. 22 is right.

Line 22. [י]היבא, as Nöldeke, seems the only possible completion. לי ethical dative, as often with a verb of motion. ושלה הוית בביתי from Dan. 4^1, is only a guess. וברי זנה is required by l. 23.

Line 24. [סגדוה]י there is perhaps a trace of ה. Nöldeke and Lidzbarski propose [בר]י, but it cannot be ר, and more is needed to fill the space. אמרת 'I said to myself' i.e. I thought. יבע[ה עלי] seems probable as the contrast to עשת על[י] in l. 25. The rest is only a guess, cf. l. 52.

Line 25. [בר אח]תי is certain. The trace of ח is fairly clear. [באישתא] is required as the opposite to טבתא in l. 24. The rest depends on the way in which l. 26 is filled up.

Line 26. Epstein and Nöldeke propose [קרצי] אכל 'he maligned', continuing עשת עלי in l. 25. Then l. 26 might begin למ[לכא]. But there is a trace of ל before אכל, leaving room for a narrow letter like ן, and מלן is suggested by l. 29. If this is read, אכל must be 'I can', and אמר (future) is required after it. Then the 'words' followed, as shown by l. 27, addressed to the king.

Line 27. The restoration is partly from l. 36, which should repeat the terms of the accusation. [ספר] is required by חכים in l. 28. He was able to stir up the country against the king because he had won its confidence by his wisdom.

Line 28. ועל ע' ומ' [הות] cf. ll. 4, 43, 55.

Line 29. ירגש 'will be enraged', still part of the statement of Nadin's contemplated plan, which must end in this line. שמע. For the construction cf. רכב in l. 38. Something is wanted to define מלן, not אלך, nor a relative clause, since either of these would require מליא. I have proposed כאלה here and in l. 26 'words to this effect', because Nadin need not be rehearsing the exact terms of his slander, but the trace of a letter after שמע is certainly more like ז. Perhaps after all the relative did follow, rather incorrectly, and כאלה should be omitted.

Line 30. ברא וכ'. So Epstein. It might of course be ברא[חתי] written together as being one idea, like רבחילא—'my son who was not my son (but) the son of my sister'. The rest of this and the next line must have described how he went to the king and made his charge, but there is nothing to guide us in restoring the lacuna.

Plate 42. This column is fairly complete on the left-hand side. The amount lost on the right is shown by l. 37 where the restoration is almost certain. After the short line 43 the lines are slightly longer, and there is a good deal of difference in length throughout the column.

Line 32. Restored from Dan. 3^{19}. But perhaps we should read שניא רגש from l. 29. Baneth proposes ענה before [אם]רחארן, which would require something else at the beginning.

Line 33 has been much discussed. It has been assumed that Aḥiḳar is speaking, and that therefore אבי is Aḥiḳar's father. But the words are clearly spoken by the king, and אבי is Senacherib, for ואמר l. 32 must be 'he (Esarhaddon) said'. רבי is pl. constr. of רביא, used frequently of Nabusumiskun, the Assyr. *rabû* (Ungnad) 'a great man', 'officer', not 'youth', 'page' as Baneth. From ll. 46–50 it appears that Nabusumiskun had been in the service of Senacherib, and must have been a person of some age and dignity. Nabusumiskun must have been mentioned by name before l. 38 where his name first appears in the extant text, and there seems to be no other place than this. [ח]ר. There are traces of ח.

Line 34 must begin with אבל, or אבלו. Then, since the line goes on in the 2nd person (אנת), something (אמר) is required to introduce the change. The words to be restored after אבל are very uncertain, but it seems necessary that Aḥiḳar should be mentioned by name in the command. The connexion of ll. 33–36 is however very difficult. חבעה. Baneth takes this from חבע 'seek him wherever . . .', but that late formation can hardly be assumed here. Though the phrase is difficult, it may be 'thou shalt seek (בעה) Aḥiḳar in a place which thou shalt find' i.e. find a suitable place and then fall upon him there. Not 'seek him wherever (אחר זי) thou shalt find him', which would be זי תהשכחה (בה). Or the object of תהשכח may have begun l. 35, forming some phrase implying that he was to be killed, without the use of the direct term קטל, e.g. עִלָּה (or עלוהי) תהשכח לה, cf. Dan. 6^5. Then אתר זי would be 'where' as in Ezra 6^3.

Line 35 may begin with ותקטלנהי or with some phrase like that suggested above. The name of Aḥiḳar can hardly have stood here as object to תהשכח, since it is used just afterwards. תנלו (Epstein, Nöldeke) is no doubt right. 'If he is wise, why does he . . . ?' i.e. he may be very clever, but he shall not . . . The line is very short.

Line 36. The first ר is fairly certain. It is too broad for ו, as Nöldeke (ולמה). מתא Assyr. *mâtu*, does not occur elsewhere in these papyri nor in BA, though it is common later. [Restored in Beh., ll. 16, 17.]

Line 37. עמה i.e. with Nabusumiskun, so that he must have been mentioned before (cf. l. 33). למחוה more probable in this context than לם חזה, cf. l. 63.

Line 38. The beginning should be '(how) the order would be carried out'. Perhaps יעבר or יתֿעבר. [אזל] or ואזל is wanted, taking רכב as a participle. [נב]וסמסכן. Ungnad points out that a person of this name was a high official under Senacherib. Perhaps the story had an historical foundation. רביא he was חד מן רבי שנ' (l. 33). בסוסה חד 'on a horse of his', not feminine. A distinguished officer would not have ridden a mare. קלי[ל] 'light' i. e. swift.

Line 39. The restoration is certain. It is a short line. -ל 'after the lapse of'.

Line 40. The lacuna in the middle is difficult. Some word is wanted like 'met', 'found me'. The letter before it is taken as פ by Nöldeke and Epstein, who complete it as פ[נעו]. But this would require a complement פגעו לי (cf. l. 118) for which there is not room. If פנעני were possible (?) the space might perhaps (?) allow of it. Then the line would have to begin הו עם גברן. But the letter may be part of a ח, not פ at all. Then the reading ח[זוני] or ח[זני] would be obvious.

Line 41. The construction depends on the restoration of the middle of the line. Baneth's קרבתא is almost certain from the remains of the letters. It occurs in ll. 56, 59, where the obvious meaning 'battles' is clearly unsuitable. Baneth makes it an adverb from קרב ('near') meaning 'soon', 'then', used like אחר. For the form he compares עלא, ברא, כותא (l. 20). Such an adverb is not otherwise known, but it would certainly fit these passages. If it is read here, it must begin the apodosis, and the first part of the line must contain the protasis, somewhat as restored. [חזני]. For the form cf. גרבי 14[9], רשכם 25[12]. הילל perf. Haphel of ילל, asyndeton.

Line 42. The restoration at the beginning is certain, since it must correspond to אנה הו in l. 46.

Line 43. [צדיק] is only a guess. Some word of the kind is required. If הות is used like הוו in l. 61 ('was dependent on'), the sentence ends with בלא. Of the next word, which should begin a new sentence, only ך is certain, and י is probable. The second letter is ב or ד or ר, the third may be ע (or ד, ר?). Nöldeke, Epstein יבעך. If ך is the pronoun, the verb cannot be future as that would require ־נך. If it is radical ידרך or יברך are the only possibilities, and neither gives a sense. Of roots beginning with י only ידע is possible, and that gives no sense. I suggest ירע as a collateral form of רעע, 'has injured thee', but it is not satisfactory. If the broken י could be disregarded ברך would be simple.

Line 44. [זי רבי]ת is necessary. The first word depends on the reading of l. 43. תרע the proper Aramaic, for which בב is used in ll. 9, 23. ותובא has been much discussed. Epstein proposes ותובא [תב לתיובא דחלתא ר]בתא, but that is impossible and is in any case too long. Baneth makes it an adverb = תוב (as in 1[7], 9[12]) = 'moreover', see note on l. 41 for the form. It is probably only a noun from תוב and means 'recompense'.

Line 45. [קר]בתא is Baneth's conjecture, and is probable, but it would make his תובא impossible, for two adverbs of nearly the same meaning could not come so close together. Otherwise we might restore [באישא הי תו]בתא 'the return is an evil return', but two consecutive asyndeta דחלת . . . ענית would then be difficult.

Line 46. [רביא] is the regular title of Nab., cf. ll. 54, 56, &c. Some particle is wanted with the sense 'Yes, and also (it is I who)'. Neither אף nor לם is quite satisfactory. קטל זכי no doubt means an 'innocent (i.e. unmerited) death'.

Line 48. [קרב]תא is again Baneth's reading, and it certainly suits the context. Or we might read [למעבד באיש]תא cf. ll. 50, 51. מסבל 'supporting' (with food, &c.) as elsewhere in these texts.

Plate 43 contains parts of two columns. Col. i evidently follows on pl. 42, and col. ii must follow col. i. Col. i is broad and well preserved in the earlier part.

Line 50. סנחאריב with ס as in ll. 51, 55, more correctly. The spelling with ש is due to the Assyrian confusion of ס and ש (Ungnad).

Line 52. אפו a mere strengthening of אף, cf. אפם 5[8] &c. In both forms the addition is probably the pronoun, which has lost its proper meaning. בלני imperat. of יבל. ע[ד] ליומן not עד זי לי (Ungnad), for which there is hardly room. The next line begins a new sentence.

Line 53. כמנדע. Torczyner 'bekanntlich', which does not seem probable. Can it mean 'any one', 'a person'? כמנדע על אח' would then be equivalent to כאיש עם אחוהי l. 49. על אחרן however may be 'afterwards' (so Torczyner) as in l. 64, cf. Dan. 4[5]. א[חר] probably, or א[רין].

Line 55. [תח]יי is no doubt right. Epstein and Nöldeke propose [אב]יי = 'patricius'. Baneth [אנת] יי for יה = 'oh'. לם rather demands a verb here.

Line 56. [כלא הוו] as in l. 61. There are traces of א and the final ו. קרבתא 'then' (Baneth) is simplest. Ungnad takes it as 'battles' and supplies עבדן הוו.

Line 57. אנתם fits the space better than הוו (זי עמה). The words following are fairly certain. עלי not עא (Ungnad) which is not a word, and there is a blank space before it. The ל and י have been run together.

Line 58. נבריא is certain, and ענו is required before it. Of אחר part of the ח remains. Of שגיא there is a trace of א. Epstein ואמרו לי is unsuitable.

Line 59. The beginning is Baneth's restoration. From the traces of letters remaining זי אנת אמר is almost certain. It appears to mean 'what you think', which is strange just after אמר in its ordinary sense. קרבתא as in l. 56. The next words are necessary.

Line 60. [וצבית] is probably right, cf. l. 3. Nöldeke proposes רב[חילא ועז[קה. [מלכא ה]ו. The words must have been written wide apart to fill the space, but there is hardly room for [מלך אתור ה]ו.

Line 61. הוו. The meaning 'were dependent on' is necessary here. It is plural agreeing in sense with חיל. Before סרים Nöldeke supplies עלים, but the trace of a letter is more like ד than ם, and rather more is required to fill the space. [זכי] from l. 46, is wanted as a reason for not killing him.

Line 62. יחקטל is written above the line. בי[ן] is more probable than בג[ו] as Ungnad. [אל]ה so Nöldeke, Lidzbarski. The expression is strange. ישתמיע from l. 70. Baneth וכז[י על אחרן] which is less satisfactory.

Line 63. [א]חרין is fairly certain. 'After us'? (as Baneth). Nöldeke, Epstein [א]חרין. Then פגרה must be the object of למחזה, which is awkward. [זנ]ה above the line.

Plate 43, col ii. Less than half the width of the column is preserved, containing the beginnings of the lines.

Line 64. The restoration is from l 53 [ויבאש] is from Dan 6[15], 'it shall be evil upon him', i. e he will regret it.

Line 65. The restoration is of course only a conjectural approximation.

Line 66. כמס[פר] seems to be the only possible word, and this requires something like חלא after it The rest of the line must contain the end of the speech, and the resumption of the narrative with a subject to טיבת in l 67.

Line 67. Restoration probably right It thus gives the length of the lines in this column.

Line 68. Restored from l. 61, but the line is short.

Line 69. Restored from l 62, but again the line is short.

Line 70 An abrupt transition אשתמיע for השתמע. The reading is clear. Noldeke completes the line במ[תא כלא לם] and the rest much as here but rather too long.

Line 71. Restored from ll 48, 49, to which this passage is evidently related

Line 72 must contain a direct statement by Nab. to introduce יסתבלון—not a command, which would require יסתבלו כ[איש] Ungnad reads כע[ ] and Epstein כע[בריא זי]. But כא is certain.

Line 73. מראי 'my lord', i e you, Aḥikar. ה[ן] is rather more probable than ה[ם] The line is difficult to restore.

Line 74. סבל. Seidel takes it as a noun = 'food' cf סבול 43[4]. It might however be a verb '(bread, &c.) he brought' נכסן not 'Schatze' (as Ungnad) which would have been of no use to him, nor 'goods', but in a weakened sense, 'things', i. e. necessaries The restoration is fairly certain.

Line 77. Restored from l. 37.

Line 78 does not admit of restoration. This is the end of the narrative part.

Plate 44 begins the proverbs.

Lines 80–85 are the same group as in the Syriac 22–26

Line 79. At first sight one would compare no 8 in the Syriac So Nöldeke, who restores ב[י]תא and takes חמר נער as 'braying ass'. But this gives no construction. Baneth ב[ו]תא as in l. 90 'what is stronger . . .? The burden', but this meaning for בות is quite uncertain. Wensinck ב[בי]תא, for which there is not room. חמר נער may also mean 'fermenting wine' (Perles) and this allows of the simple restoration

ב[ג]תא. It is true this is a Hebraism, for גת is not found in Targum (though it is in Syriac) but there are other Hebraisms in this text—or are they common Semitic? The proverb must then have been '(there are various strong things but) what is stronger than wine foaming in the press?' Alluding to the intoxicating effect of new wine. There is nothing after ב[ג]תא in this line.

Line 80. יתסר more probably from אסר than from יסר. The א is dropped as in למּמר (perhaps) and למּכל, and in later Aramaic. 'Is restrained'. ארחא must mean a 'fetter' or something similar. In Onḳelos it (or אריתא) translates Heb. מוט, which is elsewhere used as a symbol of oppression. It must refer here to some form of punishment by tying the legs to a bar, or the stocks. The end must have been 'shall prosper in later life', or something of the kind. Cf. Syr. 22, Arm. 14 and Arabic.

Line 81. הן לו = אִלּוּ. Cf. Prov. 23^{14} (משאול תציל). 'If you cannot keep him out of mischief, then beat him.' Cf. Syr. 22.

Line 82. Cf. Prov. 23^{13}. The occurrence of the same idea in two consecutive lines in both places cannot be accidental. אשבקן. Seidel cft. יחיתן Hab. 2^{17} and concludes that, with ן־ *energicum*, the pronominal suffix may be omitted, if the sense is clear. Marti rejects this, but it seems probable, cf. 35^{5}, &c. At the end something short is wanted, like 'thou wilt not prosper'. Cf. Armenian 14.

Line 83. מחאה a noun (Nöldeke, Wensinck). כא[יה] so Nöldeke, cf. Syr. ܟܠܐ. Baneth and Sachau כא[סר], which is possible from the traces remaining, but does not give a very good sense. ה is more probable at the end. לחנת. The ל must be the preposition, therefore not 'concubine' as in BA. The meaning 'maid-servant' is required here for חנת, cf. Sayce and Cowley, Ostr. M b 1. אַל[פנא]. A noun is required as before. There is a trace of פ, cf. יתאלף in l. 80. Cf. again Syr. 22. At the end something is wanted to introduce l. 84. If ll. 92–94 give the approximate width of the column, several words would be required here, since the line must apparently have read straight on.

Line 84. פר[ין] is better than פר[יר] (as Epstein). אמה גנבה is certain, but a conjunction is necessary, either ו of which there is no trace, or או for which there is no room. פ[חד] uncertain, and not very suitable. הו. The ה is almost certain. After it Ungnad reads ל, but the upper stroke is really the tail of the ך in l. 83. We might read either הו הנ[על] or הנ[על]. At the end a connexion with l. 85 is wanted. The lines all seem to be short before l. 89, so that either the column was narrower above than below, or the fragment attached to it from l. 89 onwards does not really belong there. Cf. l. 170 and Syr. 24, Arab. 25.

Line 86. The form of this proverb is very uncertain. It seems to mean that the scorpion refuses bread because he cannot appreciate it, his natural food being insects and vermin. לחם ולא י[אכ]ל is probable. There is not room for יאכלנהי. The next word is very doubtful. There is a mark of a ל (but not high enough), but כל חיה ('he will not eat anything living') is unsuitable, because that is just what he does eat. Perhaps it is ע(ד) יחיה.

Line 87 is too much broken to restore. מסמ[ה] perhaps, as in l. 88.

Line 88. מסמה Mr. Hayes (privately) suggests Arab. شمّ to 'scent', which would be suitable, but the participle (Pael) would be מסמם. The ה must be radical, so that we should have to assume a form סמה = סם. סורא or סוירא no doubt means 'lair' or something similar, but the word is unknown. Epstein's comparisons for this word and מסמה are unconvincing.

Line 89. At the ends of ll. 89–94 Sachau joins on another fragment. It does not seem certain that it belongs here, nor how much is lost between the two pieces. It makes these lines much longer than the rest. After זי Ungnad supplies [אילתא וארי]א, which is pointless. Nöldeke 'of the weak with the strong'. Seidel [בני אנש]א which is possible, but too long if the following lines are rightly restored. The traces of the next word (נת, מ?) are quite uncertain. It might be 'for fear of'. At the end perhaps a word for 'burden'.

Line 90. Seidel 'he who neglects an ass and does not feed it', taking סבל as in l. 74. בות Baneth takes to mean 'burden'. Seidel and Epstein think it = 'shame' and cfnt. Ps. 15^3. [וינ]שא Epstein [זי יהנ]שא 'whom he makes to bear a burden'. Baneth [זי יסבלנהי וינ]שא and at the end וילא זיל[ה עם זילה] i.e. a double burden. All very uncertain and obscure.

Line 91. רכן 'bowed to' (Epstein) is more probable with ל than רכב (Ungnad). [מן ר]חמתה. Some trace of מ. What the birds have to do with it one cannot guess. Perhaps the fragment is not in place. The proverb must end with the line, since l. 92 begins a new sentence.

Line 92. שפירה Nöldeke thinks a mistake for שפירן. As it stands it can only be a noun 'an ornament'. רחימה similarly 'a pleasure'. שמש the Babylonian god (Smend), the judge of right and wrong. ע[תה] so Seidel, Nöldeke, Grimme. Cf. l. 93. ויניקנהי. Seidel adduces a root ناق to 'vomit' which is unknown to me (? ناف 'drink to excess'), and such a proceeding could hardly be pleasing even to Shamash.

Obviously it must be connected with ינק 'gives it (to others) to drink', but the form is difficult. Strack cft. *Mishna Aboda Z.* ii, 1 חניק, cf. Exod. 2⁹. A root נוק would be a regular parallel to ינק. כבש חכמה Ungnad says = Heb. כָּבַשׁ but does not say how he would translate it. It is כבשׁ 'he who keeps (his) wisdom to himself' (as Nöldeke), or possibly even, as a contrast to אבדה in l. 94 'keeps it under control' and does not let it go astray through drunkenness. The line may have ended here, though something is wanted to balance the clause. Then וישמע וכ' is the third thing pleasing—the sociable wine-drinker, the modest wise man, and the discreet confidant. This form of numerical maxim is common in Jewish 'wisdom'.

Line 93. וישמע is apparently not in the same construction as ויניקנהי l. 92, but is used loosely in the sense of 'and one who hears'. יקיר must mean 'precious', and this clause sums up the preceding proverb. [קדם] a trace of ם remains. וזי must begin the converse statement, 'but he who'. ישתה. The ה is not very probable. [יניקנהי] seems likely, but it makes the line long.

Line 94. מן ח' [ו . . . . נר] Ungnad ו—ק.ר מתחזה. After the mark of division (doubtful) Baneth restores מן שמין . . . עממא חכמתהם 'from heaven the nations (receive) their wisdom; the gods give it'. For the end Ungnad and Nöldeke suggest חכמתה מן אלהיא הי. All very obscure.

Plate 45.

Line 95 seems to refer to wisdom. If so, it is probably the continuation of l. 94. ע[ד לע]ל[מן לה], so Baneth. בש[מי]ן so Sachau, Baneth (cf. l. 94), &c.

Line 96 might be read אל ת[לו]ט יומא (as Ungnad) 'curse not the day till thou see (the night?)'. There is perhaps a trace of ל. But can לוט take an accusative? The usual word for 'curse' in these papyri is לחי. If ת[ב]ט as a jussive form is possible, and the blank space may be disregarded, it forms a good connexion with l. 97. יתרא adverbial, cf. the forms עלא, בותא, קרבתא. תחוה for תהחוה. It cannot be read תחזה as Nöldeke and Seidel. [כל מ]לה is required for l. 97. The rest of the line is blank, which is strange, if it reads straight on. The scribe must have omitted something illegible, but ought to have left the blank at the beginning instead of the end of the line.

Line 97. [זי] is most probable. The sentence cannot have begun thus, with a feminine verb. ל[הן]. So Epstein (?). Ungnad, Nöldeke לות. Baneth לצר. Seidel לם. פמך a nom. pendens 'but as to thy mouth, take heed'. טרפי[ך] is very difficult. It ought to mean 'ruining thee', but it is a strange word to use, and in the plural.

Line 98. ש[מעת] is Grimme's restoration. הוקר lit. 'make heavy a (i. e. thy) heart upon (i. e. with regard to) what thou hearest' משלחה. Noldeke and Grimme take this as passive. It may equally well be active. ל[קח] (Grimme) is not very satisfactory 'does not catch it (again)'. Epstein proposes ל[בב] 'a man without heart (i. e. sense)'

Line 99. מ[.]י. There is no obvious word. מני 'count' would not fill the space. The י might be א. אחדי (or אחרי), cf. perhaps Syr. אוחרתא, 'secrets', parallel to ארב 'ambush' (so Montgomery). Baneth would omit it. הנפק (Baneth) is certain. There is no suffix. After it there is just room for [לאחו]ך but the actual word is quite conjectural. בעררה cf. l. 126. מלחם a mistake for מלחמה, a Hebraism

Line 100. חכבה, in later Aramaic 'extinguish', here, more generally, 'suppress'. Epstein and Noldeke תכטה (cf. Syr. קטא), but this gives no good sense. After רפאה there is perhaps room for הי [לאחו]ך is quite conjectural, but a repetition of the word restored in l. 99 would be natural in this style The rest of the line is a separate proverb. שרק is 'smooth' (Noldeke, Epstein). Halévy 'sharp' (cft. شرق) and so Baneth (cft. 40^3) סכין פמ[ין] is Baneth's very probable conjecture.

Line 101. [על א]נפי is probably right. Seidel [קדם א]נפי is unlikely, and too long. תקום cf. 42^7 and the sense of l. 103. בצפה probably = קצפה (Seidel, Stummer). Perles כצ[ר]ה, but there are traces of פ. זעיר with 'anger', must mean 'swift' or 'sharp', but it is difficult to account for such a meaning. Stummer suggests 'fearful' and cft. ذعر.

Line 102. יח[ונ]הי seems the only possible form—Pael as in l. 96, instead of Haphel as elsewhere—'let him (the king) not show it (anger)'. א[מ]ריך is more probable than אבדיך 'to them that destroy thee' (Epstein). The rest of the line is blank.

Line 103. [קדמ]ת fits the space. Epstein [. . מל]ת. פקיר i. e. if any order is given. לך is added above the line. הי fem. is attracted to the gender of אשה, but (עבד)הי is correct as a masc. suffix There is a trace of the י, therefore not עבדה (*pace* Noldeke). עבק. The ב is badly formed, but can be nothing else. Cf לעבק in $26^{6,9\ 22}$, $42^{7,8,13}$. Epstein cft. Heb חבק, Syr עפק, 'embrace', 'seize', grasp it and do it i. e. do it promptly. Noldeke and Perles compare Targ. אבע (for Heb. מהרה) 'hasten'. There is no doubt about the meaning in the papyri. [א]לתהן שק. The reading is certain. Epstein, Noldeke, Baneth take it as תהנשק 'do not kindle (it) upon thee', but this does not give a satisfactory sense in connexion with 'and hide thy hands'. I cannot help thinking that we have a scribal error here. 'Hiding the hands' suggests that שק is 'sackcloth'. It is clearly separated from חתן. If so, חתן may be a mistake for תנתן, which might easily occur in this writing if the original was not clear, and the meaning is 'do not put sackcloth upon thee and hide thy hands', i. e. do not go into mourning about it and pretend you cannot do it. ותכסה is certain, not ותכוה as Baneth to suit the reading תהנשק. At the end perhaps כי to connect l. 104.

Line 104. בחמר (cf. l. 47) rather than בחמר. [מלך] is suggested by the preceding proverbs. They are grouped more or less according to subject. Perles supplies אלהא and cft. Job 9^2, 25^4, Is. 10^{15}, 45^9.

Line 105. זעררתא (Epstein, Nöldeke) is certain, cf. زعرور. מררתא must be an adjective, not a noun (as Wensinck). ו[מעמ]א is probable, since the א is fairly certain, rather than ו[אכל]ת or ו[בלע]ת as Nöldeke. Then חסין must be 'strong' though it is not the word we should expect. Nöldeke, Perles 'lettuces' to suit ו[אכל]ת. מ[לך] cf. l. 100. Seidel's מן משחא (cft. Prov. 5^3, 25^{15}, Ps. 55^{22}) is too long.

Line 106. [אלתבהת] or a similar verb, is required.

Line 107. כרחמן. Grimme 'like the merciful' i.e. God, but this hardly suits the general tenor of the proverbs. Seidel takes the כ as otiose, and cft. 16^5. זי אל עמה as in ll. 154, 161, a very difficult phrase. Nöldeke and Seidel 'he with whom God is'. But the usual word is אלה or אלהיא, not אל (? l. 173). Grimme takes it as = Hebr. אשר לעמתו 'one who is his equal'. In l. 161 אלעמה is written as one word, which would imply that אל is the preposition, but the translation is less suitable to that passage. The line ends here.

Line 108. כשמש may be either 'like Shamash' or 'like the sun'. בניח[א]. There is only room for one letter, and this restoration of Nöldeke's is probably right: law-abiding persons will uphold the dignity of their king. Epstein proposes בני ח[לוף] (Prov. 31^8), but there is not room. Though there is a slight space before ח, it must go with בני, since there is no word of two letters beginning with ח which would be suitable. The rest of the line is blank.

Line 109. כמ[ה]. Perhaps כ[סי] fits the space better. ו[הו זי] is almost certain. Baneth ו[זי הו] does not fit the traces of letters so well. Perles ו[מאן] would not fit at all. The line ends with ברא.

Line 110. Nöldeke fills the lacuna with לש[לם חמר אמר] ל[ה], but there is hardly room, and we should moreover expect חמרא (cf. l. 118) for which the space is still less adequate. חמר(א) is required by חמרא farther on, and perhaps we may read as printed. For this use of לם cf. $26^{2.21}$, 10^{13}, and especially l. 165 below (if so to be read) where

לם seems to be fully equivalent to לאמר. שלם. The last stroke is simply part of ם. It is not necessary to read the impossible שלף (Sachau) or שלו (Ungnad). The answer of the ass is unfortunately lost, since clearly none of the other fragments join on to this—unless it were l. 79, where see note.

Plate 46.

Line 111. At the end there are traces of two letters, which do not fit Stummer's מגלה or מגרה 'exile'. They may be פת, which suggests ופתא—not the word we should expect. Cf. Syriac no. 45.

Line 112. Cf. Syriac no. 46 and the passage of Ben Sira quoted in Baba B. 98b (ולא מצאתי קל מסובין וכ'). פרן perhaps plural of פר from √פרר, cf. פרור, 'crumbs'. Epstein cft. פארי 'bran' as parallel to סובין in the quotation from Ben Sira. ולא is repeated by mistake. The first is partly erased. תותב is simply the Hebrew תושב 'settler', and there is no need to make it an abstract noun as Grimme and Stummer. It is parallel to אֹרֵחַ 'traveller', 'visitor' in the Ben Sira passage. קליל 'light' i.e. contemptible.

Line 113. רעין Ungnad 'friends', Nöldeke 'shepherds', neither of which gives much point. The combination with טבן suggests that it may be a Hebraism, and the phrase a mistake for בין רעין בין טבן 'whether they be bad or good'. This might have a meaning. The rest of the line is blank.

Line 114 is very difficult. ירבה must govern מלוהי, and to multiply words is a reproach, cf. ll. 96, 97 &c., and Eccles. 10[14]. מסרסרן apparently agrees with מלוהי. Its connexion with עלא suggests that it is for מסלסלן (so I. Löw) cf. שרשרה for שלשלת, and Midr. Ber. R., § 91 סלסליה תרוממך. Baneth 'they fly away'. מע[ל]ה is suggested by the traces remaining. Baneth מע[ר]ה. The meaning of the line is obscure.

Line 115. אלהן is probable. רחים אלהן 'beloved of the gods' (Nöldeke, Epstein). למאמר is probable, though the א is badly made.

Line 116. The restoration may be regarded as certain. Perles omits זי.

Line 117. אריה collective (Ungnad). [לא אי]תי is quite certain from the traces remaining. לקפא is the only possible reading. Epstein suggests the meaning 'flood' and לבא = לביא—they call a flood 'lion' because it is thrown out of the sea, and therefore is not in it. But this is too far-fetched. Another suggestion is that קפא = قُفَّة 'boat', which makes the meaning no clearer. The root קפה means to float on the top of the water or to congeal, so that the noun might mean 'scum'. לבא seems to be = לביא. But the meaning is quite obscure.

Line 118. עריה 'cold' (Grimme). ענזא is the emphatic form. At the end ענת is required, but it makes the line rather long.

Line 119. נסיכי 'my lord' is certain. Sachau and others כסיכי, but the form is impossible. Then למה לי must be a complete phrase: 'why (do you say that) to me' or 'what have I to do with you'. תלקחן is not for תלקחנה (Sachau) but simply the energetic form governing גלדי. [ישא]ל (Epstein, Nöldeke), not תשאל (2nd person) as there is no trace of the tail of ת. Hence כי introduces a comment on the answer of the goat.

Line 120. טביא 'kid' by an oversight for ענזא. רבא is doubtful. Sachau reads דבא 'the bear', followed by others. Nöldeke prefers to take it for דאבא (דיבא = זאב) 'the wolf'. The sequel however seems rather to require a human person here. אמ[ריא] is probable here and in the next line. For the lacuna Baneth suggests '... lamb[s and said, give me one of you]', and takes אשתק (l. 121) as 'I shall be content'. This would be suitable, though it is difficult to see how the Aramaic would express it. The trace of a letter at the end seems to belong to an א, with a space before it—hence beginning a new word.

Line 121. אשתק can only be 'I am (will be) silent'. Perles proposes דבא שתק, but nothing seems to be lost at the beginning. ת[נ]שא is certainly right (as Baneth), not ת[ב]עה as Ungnad, nor תבעא as Sachau. א[מריך]. The א is probable.

Line 122. אנ[ש]א (Baneth) is no doubt right. Cf. Gen. 41^{44}. ומנהחותהם is incorrect if רגלהם is singular, but it is a natural *constructio ad sensum*. Nöldeke assumes a mistake for רגליהם. [אלהן] ל[בן]. There are traces of ן (or ך) and of כ (not לא as Epstein). Then we must either supply a verb like 'we know' or suppose that כי (l. 123) is a mistake due to the line above it, or that l. 123 is a repetition of the proverb in another form.

Line 123. א[נשא] is a conjecture, but probable. There is not room for much to complete the sentence, and טב is likely to have been repeated, as √לחה in l. 124.

Line 124. לחיה probably 'curse' here; elsewhere 'evil'.

Line 125 is very obscure. If God looks after men, a man may chop wood in the dark without harm to himself. This is strange enough, but why is he like a burglar? מצלח עקן. Grimme 'passes through a wood'. Sachau 'causes trees to grow'. But to 'split' wood is an accepted meaning in Aramaic, and the other suggestions do not make the passage more intelligible. After כאיש a זי is deleted. שחר. Sachau says = סתר. Nöldeke, Epstein 'breaks into'. Perles cft. 1 Sam. 5^9, where יִשָּׂתְרוּ seems to mean 'burst out', of tumours (but the

Jewish commentators connect it with סתר). He also compares Bab. *Šulturu* and Ezra 5^{12}, where סתר (شتر) is clearly 'destroy'. בי (not בנ) for בית as in 9^{3}. ‎[וישת[מר]‎ is more probable perhaps than ‎[וישת[ר]‎.
Either the text is wrong, or some words are used in an unknown sense.

Plate 47 is in two columns, of which the first is fairly well preserved, but the lines are very unequal in length, and the beginnings of all of them are broken off.

Line 126. Noldeke restores ‎[ברי אל תנגד ק]שתך‎ There is not room for ברי. The natural word would be תנגד, but in l 191 we have דרך, as in Hebrew, and in l. 128, a root ending in נ. This suggests דרג, a collateral form of דרך. As the same word was probably used here and in l. 128, I have restored תדרג. There is no trace of the ק It may have been written, as in l. 128, at a distance from the ש. For the general sense cf. Pss 11^{2}, $64^{4\,5}$. למה 'lest'. Cf. Ezra 4^{22} (Ungnad). יסגה (Pael) as in Talmud 'goes' (Noldeke, Perles, Grimme) The verb is singular with אלהיא plural, but perhaps this is only a mistake (so Perles) for אלהא, and not as in Hebrew. בעדרה cf. Exod. 18^{4}, Deut. 33^{26}, Ps. 146^{5}.

Line 127. Probably four or three letters are lost at the beginning. If it were Hebrew, we should supply לעולם, but there is no obvious word. הכצר is usually taken for הקצר 'gather harvest' (Grimme 'labour'). Cf. l. 101 כצפה for קצפה. Ungnad suggests as an alternative قصد 'to aim at' For the end Strack cft. Deut. 6^{11}, $8^{10\,12}$, 11^{15}

Line 128 is parallel to l. 126, as l. 129 to l 127. ‎[הן דר]גת‎. Noldeke דרכת, but נ is clear. Halévy and Pognon ‎[הן נ]גת‎ for נגדת. לצדיק מנך must go together 'one more righteous than thou'. חטא probably 'sin', with a play of words. Grimme 'arrow'. מן אלהן is difficult for 'as regards, in the sight of, God'. הר (or הר) must be a slip for הו. Grimme proposes to read הריא 'from thee is the arrow, from God is the direction' But after הר the papyrus is intact and blank. We should expect 'the arrow will be turned back upon thee by God'.

Line 129. For the beginning cf. l. 127. זף רגנא (Epstein, Noldeke, Halévy, Grimme) is right. Sachau and Ungnad זפרגנא, which Lidzbarski says means a 'quince', but he does not explain the construction זף is imperative of יזף 'borrow' as in l. 130.

Line 130. לחה (Epstein) is probable from the traces remaining Cf l 138. ‎[אף הן]‎א Noldeke, Epstein. שלין, not שליו (as Strack). It must be a plural abstract of שליא, cf. سلوان (Noldeke).

Line 131. The restorations are by Noldeke and Epstein. They add

זי at the beginning, but I doubt if there is room. [חשלם] is probably right, but there is no trace of it. ממלא [ב]י Epstein 'payment of it fills the house', which gives no sense, and is grammatically incorrect, as the subject is feminine, but perhaps not impossible in these texts. Nöldeke better 'the filling of a house'. The point is not obvious. Can it mean that the payment of a debt is liable to take everything you have in your house? Baneth, mistake for מלא. [ב]י cf. on l. 125. There is a trace of the ב. The line ends here.

Line 132. [כל] is probable, as there is a trace of ל. There is room for the restored words, but they are not very convincing. Baneth's איש מכרב אלחשמענהי is less suitable, and does not include the ל. [כי] שנאחה. There is a trace of כ. It looks like an alternative to what precedes, cf. ll. 122, 123. שנ׳ 'Hässlichkeit' i.e. 'ugliness'.

Line 133. [ק]רמן is certain, and there is just room for על. Baneth cft. על א[חרן] further on. ..זט (or ..אט) must be the predicate. No satisfactory restoration has been proposed. [יה]נשגון (not שגרן as Sachau &c.) = Heb. ישׂיגו 'overtake'. The object is omitted as probably in l. 82. Or 'they shall overtake (i.e. find out) his lies'. ירוקן from רקק, either for ירוּקן, or a mistake for ירקן.

Line 134. Probably nothing before מכרב. גזיר קדלה. Perhaps we should divide קדל הך. Baneth cft. Ekha R. 12 (?) תביר קדל. On the analogy of Heb. ערף implying strength, it may mean his strength is broken, he fails in his object. But why like a maiden? תימנה Epstein thinks is from ימא, but it must be an adjective (Nöldeke). In Ezek. 21[2] דרך ת׳ may be 'the southern way'. Perhaps this is 'a southern maiden', though one would expect a gentilic form. זי is probably right. Then there is room for a verb of four letters. לאנפין. The ל introduces the object. We should expect '*her* face'. The idea may be that the liar wears a mask, but is unsuccessful in his devices, like one who curses wrongfully. לחיתא is a curse, not an oath (as Epstein).

Line 135. A mark at the beginning looks as if the scribe wrote זי (or א) and erased it. ומן is quite clear. Note that the sign ⳾ comes at the end of a proverb, not at the beginning of a new one. The rest of the line is blank.

Line 136. [אלתמאס] or something equivalent is required. יְמְנַע passive (Nöldeke). The rest of the line is blank.

Line 137. [אלתרבי] is only conjectural. Cf. e.g. Deut. 8[13.14], Ezek. 28[5], Ps. 62[11]. But [אלתהוי ד]חיל would be possible. חיל. There is an א at the end, which is erased. תהשנא as Heb. שׂנה. Ungnad aptly compares Sirach 8[2] (Heb.). The rest of the line is blank.

Line 138. [זי] Nöldeke and Epstein. יִתְרְנָם Nöldeke, or for יתרומם. No doubt 'prides himself upon'. שמ[ש עלוהי]. There is perhaps room for this. 'Let not Shamash rise upon him' i.e. be favourable to him. Nöldeke and Epstein שמ[שה] כי, but the space requires more letters, and 'his sun' is not very suitable. The suggestion שמ[ה . .] is not very probable. ידנח would then mean 'be illustrious', which is possible in Syriac, but hardly at this date. The verb suggests שמש.

Line 139. מני is probable from the traces. 'From me went forth', i.e. was due to myself, so that I cannot demand satisfaction (אצדק) from any one else. הנשׂשׂ a Haphel (Seidel) with the meaning of Pael 'to feel', 'spy out'. Ungnad takes the ה as interrogative, which is hardly possible. [ומ]ה אֵמַר (Seidel) is possible, but not certain. 'What can I say' being parallel to the preceding clause. Ungnad's ענה fits neither the space nor the sense nor the remains of letters. It would also require ואמר. Grimme ואנה אמר gives no sense. Some word for 'evil' would be suitable, taking אמר as 3rd person.

Line 140. [ה]וה he, i.e. my son, was. Nöldeke [מן ביתי ה]וה but there is not room. שהד חמם 'a malicious witness'. Ungnad cft. Exod. 23^{1} (where it is associated, as here, with false reports) and Ps. 35^{11}. חמת[א] עם. Nöldeke ועם, but there is scarcely room. עפה an alternative form of יעף 'with whom shall I strive and weary myself?', i.e. why should I weary myself by striving? So Strack who cft. עפי in Targ. Prov. 21^{25}. Seidel cft. عنا iii, and Job 9^{4}. Ungnad misreads it as אפעה.

Line 141. [רז]יך fits the space. Nöldeke, 'my son, thy secrets'. Seidel חטאיך. [ו]אליקל is required, but there is no trace of the ו. The latter part of the line is blank.

Plate 47, col. ii. The lines were probably shorter than in col. i, but only the beginnings remain. A stroke after ll. 142, 144, 145, 146 seems to divide the proverbs. Few sentences can be completed satisfactorily.

Line 142. בנ[צוי]. The צ is probable. From נצה 'to quarrel'.

Line 143. אצי[ל]. Nöldeke rejects this, but the א is probable. It might possibly be כ, and Perles suggests כציר (for קציר) but does not explain it. [אלחשפט]. Cf. l. 104, and Arab. no. 38.

Line 144. מנתך. From מנה 'weigh', Arab. يوزن وزنك. The traces following seem only to fit ועל. [יהוסף] possibly.

Line 145. [איש וכ'] is only a conjecture.

Line 147. תסתכל 'be crafty'. Seidel cft. Eccles. $7^{16,17}$. ידעך 'be extinguished' (Ungnad) seems to be the only explanation. Or ? ירעך cf. l. 43. The ה following is fairly certain. The masc. verb with a fem. subject following is not impossible. Cf. l. 153.

Line 148. חחלי. The ח is badly formed and damaged. Sachau and Ungnad תרלי or תבלי which give no sense. Cf. Arm. no. 8. [יבלע]וך fairly certain. There are traces of ב and ע. Not יבלעונך because jussive 'let them not swallow'. The end is restored from the Armenian.

Line 150. רם suits the context, but a longer word is required.

Line 151. ש[פו]ת [אנ]שא (Nöldeke, Epstein) is probably right. For the end cf. ll. 134, 135.

Line 152 was perhaps something like Prov. 16^{32}.

Line 153. נפשך fem. is apparently subject of ירחם masc.

Line 154. The sentence must have begun in l. 153. זי אל עמה as in l. 107, cf. l. 161.

Line 155. The beginning of the sentence, containing the object, must have been in l. 154. For the masc. verb cf. on l. 153. אל must be the preposition. The meaning is obscure.

Line 156. יאפך for יהפך, so Nöldeke who takes אל as 'God' and אפכא as a participle. 'God overturns the mouth of the perverse'. If אל is a preposition, it will be 'he shall turn retribution to the mouth . . .'

Line 157. יאכמו 'be blackened' i. e. darkened. Cf. كمد. Masc. again as in l. 153. The restoration is probable, though merely conjectural.

Line 158. כשיטא perhaps (as elsewhere כ for ק) = קשיטא 'truth'. יאמרנה seems to require פם in l. 157, after eyes and ears. The rest of the line is blank.

Plate 48, col. i. The lines are again very unequal in length.

Line 159. Probably nothing before איש. [שפ]יר. Another suggestion is חסיר, but the trace remaining favours פ rather than ס. מדרה = מְדָּה, with dagesh resolved, or rather with the double ד not yet represented by ר. Ungnad proposes מדרה 'his dwelling', which is less suitable. For the form cf. עממיא, שקקן, &c. בק[שת]ה. Nöldeke objects that this would require חסינתא, and proposes בקריה, but the remnants point to ש rather than ר and the space would not be filled by רי. Reading בקשתה we can only suppose that it is a mistake for בקשת, which is more suitable. זי מת . . . . is fairly certain. In l. 128 דרג seemed to be used of the bow. Either that or נגד may be supplied here. איתי after the participle is unusual.

Line 160. [י]עמר if it is used in this Aramaic. Ungnad [י]שתמר is impossible. The long stroke before מ is accidental, and the letter is ע. 'Stand with' = on the side of. ומה. Apodosis introduced by ו. אין as in Hebrew? But על is difficult for 'by means of', 'trusting upon'. נוה or possibly נופ[ה], not נפ[הם] (as Baneth). 'His own strength'.

Line 161. The first letter visible is מ (probably). Perhaps the word before it is a participle 'he who guards himself against'. Epstein assumes too much space at the beginning, and reads מן [כב]שי 'secrets'. Ungnad [אנ]שי. זי לה אלעמה (Epstein's לא is impossible), cf. ll. 107, 154. The fact that אל is written as one word with עמה suggests that it is the preposition. Also the addition of לה here makes the translation 'to whom God is with him' impossible. Hence אלעמה = לְעִמּהּ, as Grimme, is more probable. יחו[ה ד]אנתי, Nöldeke וה[טר]אני 'overthrow him' is impossible. The ו is certain but ה after it is doubtful. The ד is quite uncertain. Epstein proposes באנתי, which he takes as 'in his strength'. A participle דאן is doubtful. In Ezra 7[25] דאנין is Kethibh, דיינין Ḳere.

Line 162 is very difficult and the restoration quite uncertain. עממא must be plural (so Nöldeke). Elsewhere עממיא. [פתיח] (meaning?) appears best to fit the remaining traces. ולבבהם. There is a trace of the ם.

Line 163. [לא ידע] gives a suitable meaning. [יזהר לה] or something similar is required if the sentence ends with the line. Baneth proposes בארחא continuing the sentence in l. 164.

Line 164. ילוה (Epstein) is certain. ב[ארחא] (Baneth) is merely conjectural. אגר either 'roof' (cf. 5[4]) 'he will not be a co-tenant with him', or 'wages', 'he will not employ him'. The epexegetical noun-clause at the end is strange.

Line 165. [כנ]יא. There is not room for more at the beginning. לם is probable. The small fragment ought to be slightly bent upwards. There is not room for [ש]לם (Nöldeke, Epstein) as well as the א of לרמנ[א]. מה טַב Nöldeke 'why'. Or perhaps 'what is the good of?' שנ[יא]. Ungnad שנ[יא]ן, but the ן is very doubtful. שניא is a noun, 'the multitude of', as in l. 106. [לזי] as Sachau. Ungnad עם זי from l. 166, but there is hardly room. [באנ]ביך seems to be required, but there is hardly room.

Line 166. At the beginning there is space for about two letters—not אחר.

Line 167. צדיק אנשא (Nöldeke, Epstein) is certain. 'The righteous among men'. Seidel צדיק אלהא 'as for the righteous, God is his help'. בעדרה as in l. 126. נטחוהי. Nöldeke cft. نطح (to butt!) and Pal. Syr. נטח, Aphel 'to touch' (and so Strack), 'all who meet him are for his help'. Grimme 'all who smite him perish' (هوى). הוין participle of הוה? We should expect the future. Perhaps it is to be read otherwise, or the whole passage may be corrupt. The rest of the line is blank.

Line 168. [בית] seems to be required by תרעיה. תתחלל. Perles cft. Jer. 23^{13} (with Targ.) 'is profaned' i.e. destroyed. ובשהינן parallel to ביום רוח or the antithesis of it. From √שהה it might mean 'in tranquillity' but form? יצען Pael of יצע? 'they spread' i.e. cast down? Nöldeke cft. صفا 'fall'. בזיה apparently 'plunder' or 'prey'.

Line 169. The restoration is merely conjectural, and not very convincing. The rest of the line seems to belong to the series of reproachful sayings, at the end of the later versions.

Line 170. Beginning conjectural, but something of the kind is necessary. 'Set my name in wantonness' i.e. disgraced it by wantonness. The rest of the line is blank.

Line 171. יאחרן the energetic form (Nöldeke). ארני cf. دنا and Syr. רנא. Perhaps 'approach' (Nöldeke, Smend). לשמש הו the Babylonian god of justice. It is written לשמ שהו by an accident.

Line 172. The fragment containing זי is upside down in the facsimile. After לך the line is blank.

Plate 48, col. ii. The left-hand side of the column is lost, and the lower half is too fragmentary for restoration. There is no evidence of the length of the lines, unless the restoration of l. 189 is right.

Line 173. אל perhaps 'God' though it is joined to בצדיק. בצדיק 'as a righteous man', ב circumstantiae. Nöldeke 'by means of a righteous man', i.e. Nabusumiskun. The line may have ended 'why hast thou plotted against me?' It would then belong to the second series of sayings.

Line 174. שאני a mistake (Sachau) for שנאי. In l. 206 it must be a different word. The line may have ended 'for God will avenge me'.

Line 175. סתר 'a secret place' (cf. Ps. 91^{1}) hence 'abode', 'home'. וסח[רת]. Baneth cft. Deut. $32^{10,11}$.

Line 176 goes with l. 175, as the side-stroke indicates. והוקרת, so Nöldeke, who reads שנאיך, as Halévy. Baneth takes it as 'hardened [thy heart]', and רחמיך as 'piety'.

Line 177. רתא perhaps 'pity', cf. Samaritan Aramaic ארתי, or 'admonish' as Syriac (Aphel).

Line 178. . . . ס Löw proposes ס[פק] 'is enough'.

Lines 179–183. No word is certain.

Line 184. Meaning obscure. Apparently related to l. 186.

Line 186. ב . ת. Sachau's בבית is improbable. It is more like דברת. Nöldeke translates 'into a house of bronze', an unlikely expression.

Line 187. נפישי is most likely from the traces remaining. תרע (or תרען) may be 2nd or 3rd person fem. ארחתה rather than יהא (Ungnad).

Line 188. Cf. Prov. 27^{7}.
Line 189. Cf. Prov. $31^{6,7}$.

Plate 49. Four fragments. No line is complete.

Line 191. דרך. In ll. 126–8 דרג appears to be used. There is a stroke after this line (cf. above, ll. 173–188). As this always starts from the first letter, there was nothing before חד.

Line 192. Halévy completes 'and if you keep it, your master may leave', &c., and so Nöldeke. Perhaps rather 'keep it with care, so that afterwards he may be willing to leave'; cf. l. 103.

Line 193. למשבק. The מ is badly formed, but can be nothing else. According to Sachau's arrangement the end of this line is the beginning of the second fragment.

Line 194. Cf. Syr. nos. 31, 32, Prov. 25^{7}.

Line 196. ארח cf. l. 80.

Line 197. The small fragment *c* may belong here. ביתה is fairly certain.

Line 198. קש . . . Baneth restores [לא יצדק איש קדם ש]מש. If the small fragment belongs here, the line might be 'he who brings an accusation against his master, shall be entrapped (some part of יקש, a Hebraism) in his law-suit . . .'

Line 199. אבא הויה. Baneth suggests דאבא and cft. Syr. no. 36.

Line 201. Seidel begins with לך 'go', but the first letter seems to have a tail, therefore not ל. The line must have been something like l. 192.

Line 203. מכרא if = מכר, it ought to be מנכר(א) (Ungnad). בחין probably from בחן 'test'.

Line 204. The restorations are by Seidel and Baneth. The proposals for the beginning are not convincing. לערדה more probably than לעררה (as in l. 126).

Line 205. י[לך יהו]י Seidel. The root סבל here and in l. 204 probably means 'support (with food, &c.)'. If so, כסתך is probably not 'fodder' (Ungnad) כִּסְתָא, but 'cushion' (i.e. saddle) Heb. כֶּסֶת. רכביך 'thy riding upon me'. אחזה is clear. Baneth 'I will not accept thy saddle'. But the phrase is so strange that there must be some mistake.

Line 206. שאני. Perles cft. Bab. šênu 'shoe' and so Nöldeke and Halévy. If so, [בין בש]ר is no doubt right.

Plate 50. One large and seven small fragments. Little can be read on the facsimile. The arrangement adopted here is uncertain, as the text is too much broken to give a sense.

Line 208 seems to mean 'do not set a man to a task for which he is unsuited'. פרישׂה is not very probable.

Line 209. חמרא (Baneth) is fairly certain. Supply before it perhaps 'he who makes'. ... ומ. Baneth ומין, but a participle is wanted.

Line 210. First half very uncertain, and the sense obscure.

Line 211. ורם (or ודם). Sachau נדם which Seidel takes as 'piece'.

Line 216. עויל 'a child'? חריש 'a dumb person', infant?

Line 217. ברחרן if right, may = Heb. בר חורים, as Sachau.

Line 218. Cf. perhaps l. 84, but the reading is very uncertain. בֿ[ע]ולה. Seidel בזילה 'with his own money'.

Line 219. נרה perhaps as restored in Mesha l. 16 'maid'. At the end possibly כב[הולה].

Line 222. Epstein נשקה אישה.

The Behistun Inscription.

This great trilingual inscription is famous as having formed the basis of the decipherment[1] of cuneiform writing. If any confirmation of that decipherment were still required, it would be supplied by the Aramaic version found in these papyri—the earliest specimen we possess (other than cuneiform) of a Semitic translation of any text. The inscription itself was carved by order of Darius the son of Hystaspes on the face of an almost inaccessible rock on the road from Babylon to Ecbatana (Hamadan), in the early part of his reign, probably not later than 510 B.C., to commemorate the means by which he consolidated his power.[2] Such a record however, splendid as it was, could not by itself spread the fame of his exploits, for, though travellers by the road were no doubt numerous, the *inscription* was too far off to be read by them. Darius therefore caused copies and translations to be made and sent to various parts of his dominions. To these an allusion seems to be made at the end of the inscription, in a passage which is best preserved, but difficult to understand[3] in the Susian or Elamite version.[4] 'By the grace of Auramazda I made inscriptions in another manner (?) . . . which had

[1] See A. J. Booth, *The Discovery and Decipherment of the Trilingual Cuneiform Inscr.* (1902) for a full account, and R. W. Rogers, *Hist. of Babylonia and Assyria* (1915), p. 83, &c.

[2] King and Thompson, *The Sculptures and Inscription of Darius* . . . (London, 1907).

[3] Only what is certain is given here. It is unnecessary to discuss it.

[4] There are traces of it also in the Persian. See King and Thompson.

not been done before . . . and it was written . . . and I sent those inscriptions into all lands and the people [read them]'. A fragment of one such copy, in cuneiform Babylonian on stone, was found recently at Babylon,[1] and fragments of an Aramaic version are contained in these papyri—a material more suitable for sending 'into all lands'. The papyri seem to represent at least two copies of the version. So important a piece of work was no doubt done officially by the great king's own scribes,[2] and sent out to the chief men of the provinces, who would preserve the record and make it known by public reading to their people or by publishing copies of it.

Although the language of Darius was Persian, it is probable that for state purposes Babylonian continued to be used in the capital, and that the Babylonian part of the Behistun inscription is to be regarded as the official text. It alone gives the number of killed and of prisoners taken—an important part of the record. For international purposes Aramaic was used, and it is natural that the official Aramaic version should follow the official Babylonian text. Sachau (p. 185) considers that the correspondence between the two is very close and literal, while Ed. Meyer[3] regards the Aramaic as a free translation. Both are partly right. The Aramaic gives the numbers of killed and prisoners, and otherwise where it corresponds to the Babylonian it is generally very close—the same words and phrases being regularly rendered in the same way, sometimes without regard to differences of idiom, as is the manner of ancient translators. But the papyri are too much broken to warrant our saying that this is always the case. Indeed in some of the lacunae it does not seem possible to restore any Aramaic which will translate the Babylonian exactly. Moreover the fragment (p. 266, plate 56, 4) of a second copy does not entirely agree with the first. The same seems to be true of the fragment of a Babylonian copy found at Babylon (see above), for Weissbach notes that there is not always room for the standing phrases 'Auramazda helped me: under the protection of A.', &c. He suggests that the mention of Auramazda was purposely omitted as unacceptable to Babylonians, and that where the words *ina ṣilli* (=בטלה) occur, they may have been followed by the name of a Babylonian divinity (Nabu or Marduk) or by *ilâni rabûte*. It seems then that the copies distributed either were intentionally adapted to their readers, or that they unintentionally diverged from the original. It is curious that the Babylonian

[1] See *Veröffentlichungen d. Deutschen Orient-Gesellschaft* iv. p. 24+.
[2] See introduction to Aḥiḳar above, p. 205.
[3] *Papyrusfund*, p. 101.

fragment corresponds to parts of the Aramaic version where the original on the rock is defaced—a fact which may interest any one who still doubts the genuineness of these papyri.

The Aramaic version was no doubt made soon after the great inscription was engraved. The present fragments, however, represent a later copy. This is conclusively shown by the blank spaces which occur at irregular intervals and which indicate omissions. Thus e. g. between ll. 22 and 23, the other copy (of which pl. 56, 4 is a fragment) originally contained the omitted passage. The official Aramaic copy, sent out by Darius say about 510 B. C. must therefore have become worn out in the course of years, but these Jews of Elephantine, being a literary people, thought it worth while to re-copy the document and to preserve it as an historical record. On the whole they did the work carefully, but the exemplar was already illegible in parts, and this may account for some of the divergences from the Babylonian text. They made some mistakes too, and where the writing was hopelessly obliterated, they did not attempt to restore it, but left a blank space to be filled up when the Babylonian original, after lying dead for 2,000 years, was brought to life again. This is corroborated by the character of the writing, which is the same as that of most of the other documents in this collection and would naturally be dated about 420 B. C.—about 80 or 90 years after the document originally sent by Darius.

The papyri are unfortunately very much broken. Not a single line is complete, and one piece (ll. 50–63) is so much defaced as to be almost illegible, at least on the facsimile. Thanks to the frequent use of set phrases and to the close relation of the two languages, it is often possible to restore the Aramaic with certainty, especially where it is evidently following the Babylonian text. But owing to the divergences mentioned above, and also to the fact that the Babylonian text is itself sometimes defective, restoration is not always possible. (In ll. 50–63 I have done little more than copy down Ungnad's readings.) These defects are less regrettable here than in the Aḥiḳar text, since for practical purposes we already possess the Babylonian text, supplemented by the Susian (or Elamite) and Persian versions, and no conjectural emendation could supply us with a new historical fact. The interest of the Aramaic, fragmentary though it is, consists in its being an early translation, in the evidence it gives of the relation of Babylon to the provinces, and in its confirmation of the decipherment of cuneiform.

THE BEHISTUN INSCRIPTION

Col. i. Sachau, plate 52.

1 קטלו בהם /]// /// // ר ד /// //// וחין אחדו [. .] ר /// /// בתרתי
רגליא מרדיא אתכנש[ו אזלו

2 לערקה זי דדרש] למעבד קרב [א]חר עבדו קרבא [ב]תגר שמה ברתא
בארמנ אהורמזד סעד[ני בטלה זי

3 אהורמזד חילא זי]לי קטלו למרדיא ב ר/// /// // לאיר עבדו קרב קטלו
בהם /// //לף ד ד [/// ///

4 רגליא מרדיא א]תכנשו אזלו לערק[ה] זי דדרש למעבד קרב אחר עבדו
קרב בהיו [שמה

5 ברתא בארמנ אהור]מזד סעדני בטלה זי אהו[רמזד] חילא זילי למר[ד]יא
[ק]טלו ב/// /// //[/ לסיון

6 עבדו קרב קטלו ב]הם ////ו ר ד[ד]ד ר// וחין אחד[ו . . . .] ר //
אחר דדרש מנ[דעם ל]א עביד מכת[ר לי בארמנ

7 דריהוש מלכא כן אמר] והומס [ש]מה עילמי פרסי [לארמנ] ש[לחת]
אמרת אזל ח[יל]א זך מרדיא [זי לא

8 ישמעו לי קטל המו] אחר והומס אזל לארמנ לממטה מר[די]א אתכ[נ]שו
אזל[ו לערקה זי] וה[ומס למעבד

9 קרב אחר עבדו קרבא] קטל בהם ||לף ד ר///\

10 בתרתי רגליא מר]דיא אתכנשו א[ז]לו לערקה זי והמוס למעבד קרב [ע]בדו
קרבא [ב ד ר] לאיר עב[דו קרבא

11 קטלו בהם //לף ד ד] //// // [ו]חין אחדו /לף /// // ר ד ד ד ר /// //[/ //]
אחר וה[ומ]ס מנדעם [לא עבד מ]כתר לי [בארמנ

12 דריהוש מלכא כן אמר אחר אנה מן בב]ל [נפק]ת אזלמ[די] לממטה [ל]מדי
בכנדור שמה במד[י פרו]רת זך ע[ם

13 חילא אחה למעבד קרב עבדן קרבא] אהור]מ[זד ס]עדנ[י] בט[ל]ה זי אהורמזד
חילא זי [פרורת ק]טלת ב[ד /// //

14 למרחשון (?) עבדן קרבא קטלת בהם ...] //// //[וחין] אחדת | ר /// /// //לף
ר[. . . אחר פרורת זך

15 . . . . . . אחר שלחת] חי[לא

* * * * *

Col. ii. Sachau, plate 54, col. 1.

16 דריהוש מלכא כן אמר אחר מתא] לי הות זנה זי בפרתו עברת
17 דריהוש מלכא כן אמר מתא מרדו] שמה מרגו מלך עליהם עבדו
18 פרדא שמה אחר שלחת ודרש שמה פ]חתא [זי בחתר]י אמרת אזל [ק]טל
19 לחילא מרדיא אחר דדרש עבד קר]בא עם מ[רגו]יא אהורמזד סעדני
20 בטלה זי אהורמזד קטלו למרדיא] אלף בד[/// לבס]לו עבדו קרב
21 קטלו בהם דדר /// //לף // לדד /// והין אחרו] /// ///לף /// /// ///
ל[ד]דדר //

22 דריהוש מלכא כן אמר איש חד ויז]דת שמה פרסי יתב בפרס [אמר
23 אנה ברזי ברה זי כרש אחר חילא פרסיא] כמסת זי בבתיא באלוך זי ב[ר]ת[א
24 מרדו עלוהי אזלו הו מלך הוה בפר]ס אחר אנה חילא זי בפרס זעיר
25 זי לא מרדו וחילא זי מרי זי עמי הו]ה שלחת ארתורזי שמה פרסי
26 בראשהום שלחת אחר חילא זי] פרס ומד[י] עמי אז[לו] אחר ארתו[רזי
27 עם חילא לרחא שמה בפרס אזל אחר ויזד]ת [זך] זי אמ[ר] אנה ב[ר]זי
[את]ה [ע]ם
28 חילא למעבד קרב עבדו קרבא] אהורמזד סעדני בטלה זי אה[ורמזד
29 חילא זי לי קבלו לחילא זי ויזדת בר// לאיר] עבדו קרבא [ק]טלו בהם
/// ל /// . .
30 והין אחדו . . . אחר אזל ויזדת זך עם] חילא זעי[רא] רכבי סוסין קד[ם
31 לפישיורא שמה ברתא אחר עם חילא א]תה לערקה [זי] ארתורזי למעבד
32 קרב עבדו קרבא קטל חילא זי לי] חיל[א זי ויזד]ת בירח ת[שרי ?

Plate 56[3].

18* . . . . שמ]ה
19* אֿ אחר ד[
20* חילא זי ל[י
21* /// //לף // רל ד[
21a* ה]ות זנה זי אנה[
22* אמ[ר] וידזת ש[מה
23* בר]ה זי כ[ר]ש אחר [ה
24* ע]לוהי אזלו הו מ[לך
25* מר]דו וחילא זי מרי[
26*]ם שלחת וש[
27*]לא [ל]רח[א] שמה[
28* . . . . . ק[ר]ב זק[

Sachau, p. 203, no. 7.

19† מ]רג[ויא
20† ///
21† ל]ף

Col. iii. Sachau, plate 54, col. 2.

33 עבדו קרבא קטלו בה[ם . . . וחין אחדו . . .
34 ויזדת אחדו וחרא זי ע[מה הוה אחדו דריהוש מלכא כן אמר אחר
35 שמת ר̄ . . קטיליא וח[רא זי עמה הוה צלבת בהודיזיא (?) שמה בפרס
36 דדר// זנה זי אנה בפרס [עבדת

37 דריהוש מלכא כן אמר ו[יזדת זך זי אמר אנה ברזי חילא להרוחתי
38 שלח ואיש חד בראשהו[ם לערקה זי ויונא שמה עבדי פרסי פחתא
39 זי בהרוחתי לם אזלו ל[ויונה ולחילא זי לדריהוש מלכא שמעו
40 קטלו חילא זי ויזדת [לערקה זי ויונא אזלו למעבד קרב עבדו קרבא
41 אהורמזד סעדני [בטלה זי אהורמזד חילא זילי קטלו למרדיא קטלו
42 בהם [//]V ל[ף /]/// ↩דדדר[. . וחין אחדו . . . בר/// לטבה
43 עבדו קרב אהורמזד ס[עדני בטלה זי אהורמזד חילא זילי קטלו לחילא זי
44 מרדיא קטלו בהם ///[. . . וחין אחדו . . . אחר אזל
45 גברא זך זי רב הוה [עליהם עם חילא זעירא רכבי סוסין אתה
46 ע]רק אר[ש]ד [בר]תא במ[דינת הרוחתי אחר אזל ויונא עם חילא לערקה
47 למעבד קרב עב]ד קר[בא אחדה וחרא זי עמה הוה קטל נפחר קטיליא
48 וחיא זי חי]לי קטלו [ואחדו . . . דריהוש מלכא כן אמר אחר מתא לי הות
49 זנה זי בהרו]חתי עבד[ת דריהוש מלכא כן אמר . . .

* * * * * *

Plate 56[8].

46*]חיל[
47*]נפחר ק[
48*]אחר מת[
blank

Col. iv. Sachau, plate 55, col. 1.

50 דריהוש מלכא כן אמר אנ]ת מלך זי אחרי תהוה איש זי יכדב
51 . . . .]מן כדבן שגיאן אזהר ע̄ . . . זי יכדב
52 . . . .]הודע איך זי עביד אנת [ואיך ?] הלכתך
53 . . . . א]נת יאמר שמע זי פרתר יאמר (?)
54 . . . .]בר זי מ̄סבב יעבד זך חזי אף קדמתך
55 . . . .]טובך אימניש תהוה ורבליך על ילדן (?)
56 . . . .]חרא ת . . . כדבתא נ̄ . . . [ז]י י . . .
57 . . . . ז]נה . . . לא תהצפן . . .
58 . . . . ש]נא ויומיך יארכון וה[ן תהצפן

59 דריהוש מלכא כן אמר אלה גבר]יא זי קמן עמי הוו ע[ד] אנה [קטלת] לנ[ו]מ[ת]

60 וך מגוש זי אמר אנה ברזי המו] שגיא [עמי] אתנצחו

61 וינדפרנה שמה בר ויספרה] פר̄[סי גוברוה] בר מרדני(?)

62 פרסי . . . . פר]סי מ . . . . מנא ברה(?)

63 . . . . א סבל . . . . .

Plate 56[8].

62* פרס[י

63* ל

64 בר

Transcription of the corresponding parts of Bab. [i. e. the Babylonian text of the Behistun inscription], taken from King and Thompson, *The Sculptures and Inscription of Darius* . . . p. 177. The numbers in parentheses (50, &c.) indicate the lines of the cuneiform text. These have been divided so as to show their correspondence to the lines of the Aramaic version, indicated in the margin. Passages in italics, bracketed, are as supplied by the editors from the other versions. The fragment mentioned above (p. 249) begins in l. 10.

1. (50) . . . . arki nikrutu ipḫurunimma ittalku'

2. ana tarṣi Dadaršu ana epišu taḫaza arki itepšu' ṣaltum (51) [*ina alu Tigra šumšu ina Uraštu Urimizda issi dannu ina ṣilli ša Urimizda uḳu attûa idduku ana nikrutu*

3. *agašunu ûmu 18 (KAM) ša Airu itepu*]šu ṣalti idduku' ina libbišunu 546 u balṭutu

3 *a*. uṣṣabbitunu 520 arki ina šanitum

4. ḫarrâni nikrûtu (52) [*ipḫurunimma ittalku' ana tarṣi Dadaršu ana epišu taḫaza arki itepšu' ṣaltum ina Uyama šumšu ina Urašṭu*

5. *Urimizda issi dannu*] ina ṣilli ša Urimizda uḳu attûa ana nikrutu idduku ûmu 9 (KAM) ša Simânu

6. itepšu ṣaltu (53) [. . . . . *arki Dadaršu amatu la epuš idaggalu paniya*

6 *a*. *adi muḫḫi ša anaku allaku ana Madâ*]

7. Dariyamuš šarru kiâm iḳabbi Umissi šumšu gallâ Parsâ ana Urašṭu (54) [*altapar umma emuḳu nikrutu ša la iššimmu'inni dûkušunûtu arki*

8. *Umissi ittalak ana Urašṭu ana*] kašadu nikrutu ipḫurunimma ittalku' ana tarṣi Umissu ana epeš taḫaza

9. arki itepšu ṣaltu (55) [*ina Izala ina Aššur Urimizda issi dannu*

ina ṣilli ša Urimizda uḳu attûa ana nikrutu idduku ûmu 15 (KAM) ša Ṭebêtu itepšu ṣal]ti idduku ina libbišunu 2024

10. ina šaniti ḫarrâni nikrutu ipḫurunimma illiku' ana tarṣi Umissi ana epiš taḫaza (56) [*arki itepšu ṣaltu ina Utiyâri ina Urašṭu Urimizda issi dannu ina ṣilli ša Urimizda uḳu attûa*] ana nikrutu idduku ûmu 30 (KAM) ša Airu itepšu ṣaltum

11. idduku ina libbišunu 2045 u balṭutu uṣṣabbitu 1558 (57) [*arki Umissi amatu la epuš idaggalu paniya*

11 *a. adi muḫḫi ša anaku ana Madâ alliki*

12. *Dariyamuš šarru kiâm iḳabbi arki anaku ultu Bâbilu uṣam*]ma attalak ana Madâ ana kašadi ana Madâ ina Kundur šumšu ina Madâ (58) [*ina libbi ana muḫḫiya Parumartiš agašu ša iḳabbu umma anaku šar Madâ itti*

13. *uḳu ittalak ana epišu taḫaza arki nitepuš ṣaltu*] Uramizda issi dannu ina ṣilli ša Uramizda uḳu ša Parumartiš (59) [*adduku ûmu 25*

14. *ša .... nitepuš ṣaltu arki Parumartiš agašu*

15. *itti uḳu*] iṣi eliya ša sisê iḫliḳma illikma ina Raga' šumšu ina Madâ arki anaku uḳu (60) [*altapar ana muḫḫišunu Parumartiš agašu* ......

* * * *

16. (68) [*Dariyamuš šarru kiâm iḳabbi arki mâtu ana attûa tatur agâ ša anaku ina Partû epušu*]

17. Dariyamuš šarru kiâm iḳabbi mâtu Margu' šumšu takkirannima

18. ištên amêlu Parada' šumšu (69) [*Margumâ ina ḳaḳḳadišunu arki Dadaršu šumšu gallâ Parsâ paḫâtu ša Baḫtar altapar umma alikma dûku*

19. *ana uḳu nikrutu ša la išimmu*]'inni arki Dadaršu ittalak itti uḳu itepšu ṣaltum itti Margumâ (70) [*Uramazda issi dannu*

20. *ina ṣilli ša Uramazda uḳu attûa idduku ana nikrutu agašunu ûmu 23 ša Kislimu itepšu ṣaltum*]

21. idduku ina libbišunu 55243 u balṭutu uṣṣabbit 6572

21 *a.* Dariyamuš šarru (71) [*kiâm iḳabbi arki mâtu ana attûa tatur agâ ša anaku ina Baḫtar epušu*

22. *Dariyamuš šarru kiâm iḳabbi ištên amêlu Umizdatu šumšu ina Tar*]ma' ina Iutiya šumšu ina Parsu ašib šû itbamma ina Parsu iḳabbi ana uḳu (72) [*umma*

23 *anaku Barziya marušu ša Kuraš arki uḳu ša Parsu mala ina alluka' ša Iutiya* ......

24. *ittekrû' lapaniya ana muḫḫišu ittalku' šû ana šarru*] ina Parsu [*ittur*] Dariyamuš šarru kiâm iḳabbi arki anaku uḳu ša Parsumi iṣi

25. (73) [.......... *Artamarziya šumšu gallâ Parsâ*

26. *ina ḳaḳḳadišunu altapar*] uḳu ša Parsu ittiya ittalku' ana Madâ arki Artamarziya

27. itti uḳu (74) [*ana Parsu ittalak ana Parsu ana kašadu ina Rakha šumšu ina Parsu Umizdatu agašu ša iḳabbu umma anaku Barziya itti*

28. *uḳu ittalak ana tarṣi*] Artamarzi ana epiš taḫaza itepšu ṣaltum Uramazda issi dannu ina ṣilli ša Uramazda

29. (75) [*uḳu attûa idduku ana uḳu ša Umizdati ûmu 12* (*KAM*) *ša Airu itepšu ṣaltum*]

30. arki Umizdatum agašu itti uḳu iṣi eliya ša sisê iḫlikma

31. ana (76) [*Piši'ḫumadu illik ultu libbi šû itti uḳu ittalak ana tarṣi Artamarziya ana epiš*

32. *taḫaza ina Parga šadû šumšu itepšu ṣaltum*] Uramazda issi dannu ina ṣilli ša Uramazda uḳu attûa idduku ana uḳu ša Umizdati (77) [*ûmu 5* (*KAM*) *ša* . . .

33. *itepšu ṣaltum*

34. *Umizdatu agašu u mâr-bânûti ša ittišu ṣubbutu'*] Dariyamuš šarru kiâm iḳabbi arki anaku

35. Umizdatu agašû u mâr-bânûti ša ittišu gabbi ina zakipi (78) [*ina Uma* . . . *šumšu ina Parsu altakan*

36. *Dariyamuš šarru kiâm iḳabbi agâ ša*] anaku ina Parsu epušu

37. Dariyamuš šarru kiâm iḳabbi Umizdatu agašû ša iḳbû (79) [*umma anaku Barziya uḳu ana Aruḫatti*

38. *išpur ištên amêlu ina ḳaḳḳadišunu iltapar ana tarṣi Umimana' šumšu gallâ*] Parsâ paḫâtu

39. ša Aruḫatti umma alkama Umimana' duku' u ana (80) [*uḳu ša ana Dariyamuš šarru išimmu'*

40. *arki uḳu ša Umizdatum išpuru illiku' ana tarṣi Umimana' ana epiš taḫaza ina Kâpišaka*]na itepšu ṣaltu

41. Uramazda issi dannu ina ṣilli ša Uramazda uḳu (81) [*attûa idduku ana uḳu nikrutu*

42. *ûmu 13* (*KAM*) *ša Ṭebêtu*

43. *itepšu ṣaltum arki ina šanitum ḫarrâni nikrûtu ipḫurunimma ittalku' ana tarṣi Umimana' ana epiš taḫaza ina Gandutava*] itti [*nikrûtu*] itepšu ṣaltum Uramizda issi dannu ina ṣilli ša Uramazda (82) [*uḳu attûa idduku ana uḳu*

44. *nikrutu ûmu 7* (*KAM*) *ša Addaru itepšu ṣaltum* . . . .] arki

45. amêlu agašû ša ina eli uḳu rabû ša Umizdatum išpuru itti uḳu iṣi eliya (83) [*ša sisê iḫliḳma*

46. *ana Aršada šumšu ina Aruḫatti illik arki Umimana' itti uḳu* . . . . .] šašu ina libbi

47. iṣṣabatsu idduksu u mâr-bânûti ša ittišu idduk napḫar dîku

48. u baltu ša uḳu (84) [. . . . . *Dariyamuš šarru kiâm iḳabbi arki mâtu ana attûa tatur*

49. *agâ ša anaku*] ina Aruḫatti epušu Dariyamuš šarru kiâm iḳabbi adi muḫḫi ša anaku ina Parsu u Madâ (85) [*aturu* . . .

* * * *

50. (105) . . . . [*Dariya*]muš [*šarru*] kiâm iḳabbi mannu atta šarru ša belâ arkiya amêlu ša uparraṣu

51. u parkâni (106) la ta[. . . . . . *Dariyamuš šarru kiâm iḳabbi*

52. . . .] kî narû šuatu tammari u ṣalmânu agannutu

53–57.

58. (107) . . . ka u na . . ka lušam'id ûmêka [*lur*]rik Uramazda lurabbiš (108) u' mi[*mma*] ša . . . . nutum nikâ la tanakkû . . . . . . Uramazda lirur (109) u zêru]*ka* . . .

59. *Dariyamuš šarru kiâm iḳabbi agannutu*] ṣâbê . . . . ittiya ituru' adi muḫḫi ša anaku ana Gumâti agašû

60. (110) Magušu a[*duku ša iḳabbu umma anaku Barziya* . . . .

61. . . . .]šu šumšu apilšu ša Misparu' Parsâ Umitlana' šumšu apilšu ša Suḫra' Parsâ (111) Gubaru' šumšu apilšu ša Mard[*u* . . . *šumšu*

62. *Parsâ* . . . . . . *šumšu apilšu ša* . . . . . . *Parsâ*] Magabudišu šumšu apilšu ša Za'tu'a Parsâ Ardimaniš šumšu apilšu ša Umaḫku

63. (112) Parsâ . . . . ṣâbê agannutu lu mâdu suddid.

(*end of Bab.*)

Col. i.

[1] *They killed of them* 827 and took alive . . . 06. A second time the rebels gathered together. *They went* [2] *to meet Dadarshish* to join battle. Then they joined battle at the fortress called Tigra, in Armenia. Auramazda helped *me; by the protection of* [3] *Auramazda* my *army* slew the rebels. On the 18th of Iyyar they joined battle. They slew of them 504*6*.

[4] *Again the rebels g*athered together. They went to meet Dadarshish to join battle. Then they joined battle at Huyav *as it is called,* [5] *the fortress in Armenia. Aura*mazda helped me; by the protection of Au*ramazda* my army slew the rebels. On the 9th of *Sivan* [6] *they joined battle. They killed of* them 472 and took alive ...02. Then Dadarshish did no*thing* (further), waiti*ng for me in Armenia.*

[7] *Thus says Darius the king,* One Vaumisa by name, my servant, a Persian, *to Armenia I sent.* I said, 'Go, that *army*, the rebels *who do not* [8] *obey me, slay them.*' Then Vaumisa went to Armenia. On (his) arriving (there) the rebels gathered together. They went *to meet* Vau*misa*

to join [9] *battle. Then they joined battle.* He killed of them 2034. [10] *A second time* the *rebels* gathered together. They went to meet Vaumisa to join battle. They joined battle. *On the 30th* of Iyyar they *joined battle.* [11] They killed of them 2045 *and* took alive 1578. Then Va*umisa did no*thing, waiting for me *in Armenia.*

[12] *Thus says Darius the king, Then* I *went out from Babylon* and went to *Media.* On arriving in Media at a (city) named Kundur in Media that *Phraortes with* [13] *the army came to join battle. We joined battle. Auramazda helped me,* by the protection of Auramazda I slew the army of *Phraortes.* On *the 25th* [14] *of Marheshwan* (?) *we joined battle. I killed of them* ...5 *and alive* I took 108010. *Then that Phraortes* [15] . . . *Then I sent the* ar*my* . . .

Col. ii.

[16] *Thus says Darius the king, Then the country* was mine. This is what I did in Parthia. [17] *Thus says Darius the king. The country* called Margiana *rebelled.* As king over them they made [18] *one Frada by name. Then I sent* (*the man*) *named Dadarshish,* governor *of Bactria.* I said, 'Go, kill [19] *the army, the rebels.' Then Dadarshish joined bat*tle with the Margians. Auramazda helped me. [20] *By the protection of Auramazda they killed* those *rebels.* On the *23rd of Chis*leu they joined battle. [21] *They killed of them 55243, and took alive* 6972.

[22] *Thus says king Darius, A certain man, Vayaz*data by name, a Persian, dwelt in Persia. *He said,* [23] *I am Smerdis, the son of Cyrus. Then the Persian army,* as many as (?) were in the houses in the neighbourhood (?) of the for*tress,* [24] *rebelled. They went over to him. He became king in Per*sia. Then I sent the army, which was small, in Persia, [25] *which had not rebelled, and the army of Media which was with me.* Artavarzi by name, a Persian, [26] *I sent at the head of them. Then the army of* Persia and Media went with me. Then Artavar*zi* [27] *with the army went to the place called Rakha in Persia. Then that Vayazda*ta, who said, I am Smerdis, *came* (?) with [28] *the army to join battle. They joined battle.* Auramazda helped me, by the protection of A*uramazda* [29] *my army killed the army of Vayazdata. On the 12th of Iyyar* they joined battle. They killed of them 303... [30] *and took alive . . . Then that Vayazdata went with* a small force of cavalry be*fore* [31] *the fortress called Paishiyau-vada. Then, with his army, he* came to meet Artavarzi to join [32] *battle. They joined battle. My army killed the* army *of Vayazda*ta. In the month *Tishri* (?)

Col. iii.

[33] they joined battle. They killed of th*em . . . and took alive . . .* [34] they took Vayazdata, and the nobles who were wi*th him they* (*also*) *took. Thus says king Darius, Then* [35] I put 10... to death, and the no*bles who were with him I crucified at a place called Uvadaicaya in Persia* [36] 52 (of them). This is what I *did* in Persia.

[37] Thus says king Darius, *That* Vay*azdata, who said, I am Smerdis,* had sent *an army to Arachosia* [38] and a certain man at the head of

them *to meet my servant named Vivana, a Persian, the governor* [39] of Arachosia, saying, Go to *Vivana, and the army which obeys king Darius* [40] kill (them) The army of Vayazdata *went to meet Vivana to join battle. They joined battle* [41] Auramazda helped me. *By the protection of Auramazda my army killed the rebels They killed* [42] of them 4570... *and took alive .. On the 13th of Tebeth* [43] they joined battle Auramazda hel*ped me. By the protection of Auramazda my army killed the army of* [44] the rebels. They killed of them 3... *and took alive .. .. Then fled* [45] that man who was in command *over them with a small force of cavalry and went* [46] towards (?) Arshada the *fort*ress in the pro*vince of Arachosia. Then Vivana went with the army to meet him* [47] *to join battle He join*ed bat*tle He took him, and killed the nobles who were with him The total of the killed* [48] *and prisoners whom my* army killed *and took, was .. Thus says king Darius, Then the country was mine.* [49] *This is what I* did *in Ar*achosia. *Thus says king Darius . .*

* * *

Col. iv.

[50] *Thus says king Darius, Th*ou, O king, who shalt be after me, any man who lies [51] . ... . against liars, who are many, I warn (thee) .. . He who lies [52] . . make known how it was done Do thou .. .. thy going (?). [53] . . . he says, Hear what PRTR says [54] .... see also before thee. [55] .... [56] . . .... lies .... [57] ..... this .. *if* thou hide not . . [58] .. .. increase, and thy days be long; but *if thou hide*

[59] *Thus says king Darius, These are the men* who stood on my side till I *had killed that* Gaum*ata* [60] *the Magian, who said, 'I am Smerdis'. They* were especially distinguished *in my sight* [61] *Indaphernes, by name, son of Vayaspara* a Pers*ian* · *Gaubaruva* son of Mardonius (?) [62] *a Persian a Per*sian [63] . . .

Plate 52, containing the recto of the papyrus. For the verso (pl. 53), which has nothing to do with Behistun, see no. 63

The restorations are translated from the Babylonian text (Bab.), and will not be discussed where they are quite satisfactory. All the lines in this part of Bab. are defective at the beginning.

Line 1 = Bab. l. 50. The numbers of killed and prisoners are missing in Bab. The first numeral here must be /// since units are always arranged in threes The number of prisoners cannot be restored. רגליא is taken by Sachau as דגליא the rebel 'troops', and consequently בתרתי as 'a second time'. But e.g. in l. 8, where the phrase is similar, we have מרדיא, not דגליא מ׳, and nowhere else in this version is דגליא

used in this sense. It would be חילא as in l. 7. The phrase elsewhere in Bab. is *ina šanitum ḫarrâni* 'in a second campaign', though *ina šanitum* alone would be usual for 'a second time' (בתרתי). Perhaps the expression בתרתי רגליא means 'a second time', properly 'twice', cf. שלש רגלים in Exod. 23[14], &c.

Line 2. לערקה restored from l. 4, q. v. ברתא for בירתא as in l. 23? and 35[2]. [סעד[ני as often. Hence Bab. is *issidaunu* not *issi daunu*.

Line 3 קטלו *constructio ad sensum*, if חילא is rightly restored as subject, cf. l. 48. למרדיא. The ל might be used simply to mark the object, to avoid misunderstanding, but really it represents Bab. *ana* in the phrase *idduku ana nikrûtu*. Cf. also l. 5. The number of killed here does not agree with the number in Bab. but the latter may be a mistake for 5046 (so Ungnad). Then the number of prisoners may also be incorrect. The space between ll. 3 and 4 ought to have contained the words אחר בתרתי (or more) וחין אחדו /// // ... Bab. has *ina šanitum ḫarrâni*, though it ought to be 'in a 3rd campaign'. Either it is a mistake, or it means 'in another campaign'.

Line 4. זי [לערק[ה = later Aram. לאורע 'to meet', 'against' (Seidel and Ungnad), cf. לערעה in the fragment on pl. 57, no. 3, l. 6, and יעריעך Sirac. 13[7]. בהיו. The name, which is preserved in the Elamite version (Uiyama), must be הַיָו (Ungnad).

Line 5. [ברתא] supplied as in l. 2, but it is doubtful whether there is room. למרדיא cf. on l. 3.

Line 6. The numbers are lost in Bab. עביד a slip for עבד. The scribe perhaps intended to erase י. [מכח[ר cf. l. 11, &c. Ungnad cft. Job 36[2] (כַּתַּר). [בארדט] is probable in Pers. but is omitted in El. The space between ll. 6 and 7 should have contained the words עד זי אנה למדי אולת.

Line 7. עילמי is a mistake for עלימי (Ungnad). זך is not in Bab.

Line 8. I have restored שמעו, as the plural seems to be used with חילא. [קטל המו] (or ־הום) = Bab. *dûkušunûtu*. Cf. 28[13]. לממטה = Bab. *ana kašadu* 'on arrival'. It is a literal translation, not (as Ungnad) a mistake for לממטיה, and not an Aramaic idiom.

Line 9 a short line, left blank after the numerals. It is an interesting example of omission due to homoeoteleuton. The scribe wrote עבדו קרבא (*itepšu ṣaltu*) and then continued from the second עבדו קרבא, thus omitting all the passage which is now illegible in Bab. (Another fact which may interest those who doubt the genuineness of the papyri). The missing passage, restored from P. and El., is 'in Izalâ in Assyria. Auramazda was a strong helper. By the protection of A. my army fell upon the rebels. On the 15th day of Ṭebet they had joined battle'. He was copying of course from an Aramaic exemplar (not from the original inscription) and the omission must therefore be due to a mere oversight קטל. The subject is apparently והומם 2034. Bab 2024.

Line 10 omits (before the date) 'in Utiyari in Armenia. Auramazda was a strong helper. By the protection of A. my army fell upon the rebels'. והמום (for והומם). At this point the Babylonian fragment (see pp 249, 250) begins. It supplies some phrases lost in Bab.

Line 11. The prisoners are 157[8] probably Bab. 1558. [בארדט] in P. and El., but not in the Bab. fragment Between ll 11 and 12 supply (as between ll 6 and 7) עד זי אנה למדי אזלת

Line 12. [אזלמ[די if so to be restored, must be a mistake for אזלת למדי (so Ungnad), or אזל a participle 'going', cf. Aḥikar l 38 רכב. [פרו]רת זך Bab. (with the fragment) adds 'who spoke saying, I am king of Media There seems to be no room for this here.

Line 13. The Aramaic is again rather shorter than Bab.

Line 14 The name of the month is lost in Bab. The Persian has Adukaniš, perhaps = Marḥeshwan There seems to be no room in Bab for the number of killed and prisoners.

Line 15 quite uncertain

Plate 54 in two columns, very much injured In col. i the beginnings of the lines are lost, in col. ii the ends The length of the lines is shown by l. 17, where the beginning is certain, following the end of l 16 The Aramaic is shorter than Bab. A literal translation would make some of the lines of the right length (about 65 letters) but not all In col i there is a blank space at the top Some lines correspond to the Bab fragment, others agree with the fragments on pl. 56, nos. 3 (but this is a different recension) and 7.

Line 16. כיתא cf. l. 48* and Ahikar l 36.

Line 17 If מרגו is right, it must have changed places with מרדו, an error due to the similarity of the two words

Line 18 was evidently much shorter than Bab of which (as restored by K and T from P. and El) the full equivalent would be איש חד פרדא שמה מרגוי אחר שלחת דדרש שמה עבדי כרסי פחתא . . . The restoration here is only a conjectural selection. [בחתר]י The י is certain. Fragment 3 of plate 56 begins here (a 2nd copy)

Line 19. [לחילא] = *ana uku.* The line is again short. It should be

לחילא מרדיא זי לא שמעו לי אחר אזל דדרש עם חילא עבדו קרבא . . .

The Babylonian fragment begins in this line, and also no. 7 of plate 56, from a third (?) copy.

Line 20. There is not room for חילא זילי (as in Bab. fragment) before קטלו.

Line 21. Prisoners 6,972 as in Bab. fragment, but Bab. has 6,572. The space between ll. 21 and 22 should contain the words [דריהוש מלכא כן אמר אחר מתא לי ה]ות זנה זי אנה [בבחתרי עבדת]. The unbracketed words are found in fragment 3 of plate 56, which must belong to a different recension, since the relative positions of the remaining words would not fit this recension.

Line 22, after שמה, omits 'in Tarava in Iutiya by name' (by homoeoteleuton?) and inserts פרסי. At the end there is room for either מרד or אמר, but not (if l. 23 is rightly restored) for 'he rebelled in Persia, he spoke to the army saying', as Bab. [וין]דת is very uncertain. The fragment of the other copy, however, has וידזת which is merely a mistake for ויזדת. The letters here may be זדת, with the ד crowded in rather above the line.

Line 23. בבתיא (Ungnad) is the most probable reading. Perhaps it is a scribal correction of ביותיא 'in Iutiya'. אלוך is the same word as in Bab. fragment *alluk* 'barracks'? זי ב[ר]ת[א] very doubtful. Bab. fragment has a sign which is probably the beginning of *Iutiya*. In Bab. the passage is lost.

Line 24. [מרדו] cannot have stood in l. 23 and is therefore necessary here. The next words are restored from the fragment. The first legible letter is probably ם rather than [אמ]ר. If so, the phrase 'Darius the king says thus' is omitted. In Bab. the end of the line is uncertain. K and T read *uku ša Parsumi iṣi*. Weissbach objects to the form *Parsumi* and reads *Parsu miṣi*. Certainly *iṣi* would be expected here = זעיר.

Line 25. Beginning restored from P. and El. supported by the fragment. זי מדי as in the fragment, not זי במדי as זי בפרס in l. 24. פרסי is apparently the last word of the line, therefore no room for עבדי.

Line 26. [בראשהום שלחת] cf. l. 38 and the fragment, where also the ש of ריש is certain, though I cannot guess at the word. ומדי is strangely written. It may be a mistake for למדי (as Bab.), or the meaning may be 'the army of Persia and Media (which was) with me, went away' i. e. to Artawarzi—a better sense than Bab., though עמי is awkward.

Line 27. The restoration is based on the fragment, but it makes the line rather long. At the end אזל עם or אתה עם (cf. l. 31) is wanted, but neither fits the space. The ה is doubtful.

Line 28 is shorter than Bab. Either למעבד קרב or עבדו קרבא was omitted, or לערקה זי ארתורזי. If the last is omitted the line is about the right length.

Line 29. Bab is broken here. It seems to have omitted the numbers of killed and prisoners.

Line 30. Ungnad reads זי after זעי[רא]. At the end קר (or קד) suggests קד[ם], preposition or verb? It does not occur elsewhere in this version (but קדמתך l. 54).

Line 31. לפישיודא is only a guess at the Aramaic form of the name.

Line 32. So far as the remaining letters can be pieced together, this line differs almost entirely from Bab. ת[שרי] or ת[מוז] (Ungnad). The name of the month is lost in Bab. The Persian has Garmapada, and so El.

Pl. 54, col. ii. The ends of all the lines are lost. Judging from l. 34, where the restoration is probably right, the lines were of about the same length as those of col. i. A small fragment (pl. 56, no. 8) of another copy, supplements ll. 46–48.

Line 33. Bab. must have omitted either the number of killed &c. or the mention of the capture of Vayazdata.

Line 34. חרא collective, 'the nobility'. I have restored the verb in the singular, but it is quite as likely to have been plural.

Line 35 is difficult to restore as the phraseology is unusual. שמת is probable. The marks after it may be a numeral, but hardly המו, as Sachau and Ungnad. וח[רא] restored from Bab. Sachau וח[ייא], which would require a different restoration. I do not know whether צלבת would be the word used here, or בזקיפא (depending on שמת) as in Bab. בהודיזיא. The form of the name is quite uncertain.

Line 36. The numeral is in an unusual position if it refers to חרא or חייא. Bab. is broken here. K and T restore 'Darius the king says thus', which cannot have stood in the Aramaic. The latter part of the line I have left blank since nothing further is wanted here (according to Bab.) nor in the blank space following.

Line 38. ואיש חד בר׳ is parenthetical 'with a man over them'. ויזנא. The form of the name is conjectural.

Line 39. ולחילא. The ל is restored to agree with Bab. *ana* [uku].

Line 40. We should expect אחר חילא (Bab. *arki*), but the reading is clear. ויודח (so) a mistake for ויזדת. The name of the place ([Kapišaka]na) seems to have been mentioned in Bab., but there is not room for it here.

Line 42. The passage is broken in Bab., but there appears to be no room for the numbers. The date is restored from P. and El.

Line 43. Much of Bab. is omitted here (again owing to homoeoteleuton) after עברו קרב. As restored by K and T from P. and El. it would have had 'then in a second campaign the rebels assembled and went against Vivana to give battle. In Gandutava they joined battle with the rebels'.

Line 44. Bab. is broken, and the numbers (if stated) are lost. At the end אזל, or, if that is read at the end of l. 45, perhaps נפק.

Line 45 must be shorter than Bab. I have conjecturally omitted 'whom Vayazdata sent'.

Line 46. [ע]רק if correct, cannot be 'fled' (as Ungnad), which would require a preposition. It is perhaps used with a place-name as לערקה זי with persons, 'towards'. במ[דינת] might be במ[תא], as Ungnad. חילא may perhaps be read on the fragment (pl. 56, no. 8) which begins here.

Line 47. If [עב]ד קר[בא] is right, the beginning as restored seems necessary, and the passage must have differed somewhat from Bab. [נפחר] is restored from the fragment, where it is certain. It is a purely Babylonian word, which would not be expected here since כל would do perfectly well, and is commonly used to sum up elsewhere.

Line 48. קטלו· is clear, and therefore ואחדו is required. In Bab. the passage is broken. For the position of the numeral after ואחדו cf. l. 36. [אחר מתא] restored from the fragment, which must belong to a copy similar to this because the words fit into the right relative positions, but not part of this copy apparently. There is a broad blank space after l. 48*, which no doubt marks the end of a column.

Line 49. There is hardly room for אנה after זנה זי as in l. 36. After עבד[ת] the line may of course have been left blank, and the fragment might then have fitted here.

Plate 55 has two columns, of which col. ii (see above, no. 61) is not connected with the inscription. Col. i seems to be the end of the inscription. It is so much damaged, and the facsimile is so difficult to read, that I have simply adopted Ungnad's transcription for the most part.

Line 50 begins 'thou who shalt be king after me', but the succeeding lines do not correspond to either of the two passages in Bab. where this address occurs. On the whole it is best to equate l. 50 with Bab. l. 105, since ll. 57+ seem to agree to some extent with Bab. ll. 107+.

Line 51. שגיאן. The adverb שגיא is wanted. אזהר (?). Sachau 'I warn', rather than for אזדהר (21^6). The end is quite uncertain.

Line 52. עביד for עבד? as in l 6 הלכתך is obscure. It cannot be the Jewish הלכה.

Line 53. [א]נת. Ungnad's ־נך is perhaps right פרתר a name? Or cf פרתרך (Pers *fratara*). יאמר Can this, in either place, be Bab. 'see'? Bab. has *nâtu šuatu tammari*, but פרתר cannot be read פתכר (Pers *patikara*) 'image'.

Line 54 מ̄סבב more probable than מסכן (Ungnad)

Line 55. אימניש. The name of the king of Elam is so written elsewhere in the inscription It can hardly be a name here.

Line 56. . . . ת. Ungnad תקאם, meaning?

Line 57 ת̄הצ̄פן is fairly certain: 'hide' i e prevent the record from being known.

Line 58. [והן תהצפן] is no doubt to be restored Ungnad prints it as though he read it. The blank space after l 58 should contain the curse which follows in Bab.

Line 59 apparently corresponds to Bab. l 109, giving the list of Darius's generals קמן (or קמין?) is fairly certain. Ungnad קרון, and so Sachau in the text, but קמון in the index.

Line 60 The end of the line is blank according to Ungnad

Line 61 The restoration is purely conjectural מרדני is Sachau's suggestion. The small fragment on pl 56, no. 8. reverse, perhaps corresponds to some part of ll. 62+. The obverse of it has been noted as agreeing with ll. 46+.

The following are fragments of a copy or copies of the version of the inscription

Sachau, plate 56[1] obv.

1 [וי לן לקיחת וך א]נה

2 [נכסיהום ובתיהום]

3]זנה אנה עבדת אנה[

4]ת בטללה ז[י] אהו[רמזד

Bab. line 24 (end):

Darijamuš šarru kiâm ikabbi šarrûtu ša lapani

[25] [*zêruni itekmu ina aš*]rišu ultazziz anaku etepušu bîtâti ša ilâni ša Gumâtu agašû Magušu ibbulu anaku

[26] [. . .] ša Gumâtu agašû Magušu ikimmušunutu anaku uku ina ašrišu ultazziz Parsu Madâ

[27] [*u mâtâti šanitima ša itekmu ana šašu ina ašrišu anaku ultazziz kî ša ûmê pani*] ina ṣilli ša Urimizda aga anaku etepuš anaku uptekid adi muḫḫi ša bîtu attunu ina ašrišu

[28] [*ultazziz* . . . . . .] anaku ina ṣilli ša Urimizda libbû ša Gumâtu agašû Magušu bîtu attunu la iššu.

Sachau, plate 56[2].

Obv.

1 [. עבד]
2 א[ז]לו למע[בר
3 [וחין]
4 מר[גויא]
5 [בפר]ס
6 חי[לא ז]י
7 [א ב]
8 [זי עמ]

Rev.

///
הבת

Bab. line 36 + is as follows:

. . . ûmu 26 (KAM) ša kislimu ṣeltu [*nitepuš Dariyamuš šarru ki*]âm iḳabbi arki anaku ana Bâbilu attalak ana Bâbilu la kašadu ina Zazannu šumšu ša kišâd Purattu

[37] [*Nidintubel agašû*] ša iḳabbu umma anaku Nabukudurriuṣur [*itti uḳu ittalak ana tar.ia ana epiš taḫaza*] arki ṣeltu nitepušu Urimizda issi dannu ina ṣilli ša Urimizda uḳu ša Nidintubel [38] [*adduku* . . . . . .] ṣalti nitepušu ûmu [*2 (KAM) ša Ṭebêtu*]

Sachau, plate 56[4].

Obv.

1 [א וח]
2 קטלו חילא זי[לי לח]ילא זי
3 [𐡛 𐡔 𐡔 𐡓 /// ///]
4 אה[ורמזד חילא זי]לי
5 ח]ין אחדו /// 𐡛 [
6 [עיב

Rev.

1 . . ן לן]
2 אהורמזד יב
3 אהורמזד יק[
4 דריהוש]

Sachau, plate 56^{3}.

Obv.	Rev.
]חילא [	1 . . .
]קן [	2]שא[
ב]טלה[	3]יבר[
	4]י[

Plate 56^{6} Obv.	Rev.
]ב /[	1 . .
]קט[ל	2]רד[

Plate 56^{7} Obv.	Rev.
See under ll. 19–21.	]תת[
	]ה [

Plate 56^{8} Obv.	Rev.
See under ll. 46–48.	See under ll. 61 +.

Plate 56^{9} Obv.	Rev.
illegible.	]נ [

Plate 56^{10} Obv. illegible.	Rev.
	]ש ׀ ר[

Plate 56^{11} Obv.	Rev.
]מי[	]מזר[

Plate 56^{12} Obv. and rev. illegible.

Plate 56^{13} Obv.	Rev.
חיל]א זי[	// [
קר]בא[	/// [
	/// [
	/// [

Plate 56^{14} Obv.	Rev.
]חי[	nothing certain.
]מרת[	
]לא [	
]ל [	
אה]ור[מזד	

Plate 56^{15} Obv. | Rev.
]// ///| | blank.

Plate 56^{16} Obv. | Rev.
]לי לן[| nothing certain.

Plate 56^{17} Obv. | Rev.
ו]יחי[| nothing certain.

Plate 56^{18} Obv.]פרתן[| Rev.
]פרתו[| nothing certain.

Plate 56^{19} Obv. | Rev.
]אלין[| blank.

Plate 56^{20} both sides uncertain.

Plate 56, containing twenty fragments:

No. 1. Obverse, corresponding to Bab. ll. 24–28. Line 1, at the beginning restore מלכותא as Sachau. לקיחת is passive. Line 2. נכסיהום וכ׳ should refer to the property of the people, not of the gods, and corresponds to some words lost in Bab. l. 26. Line 3 = the end of Bab. l. 27. Line 4 = part of Bab. l. 28. בטללה is probable. Double ל = ל, cf. מרדה Aḥiḳar l. 159. But the first ל may only be part of a large ט. The word would then be בטלה, as usual. The Aramaic was apparently shorter than Bab. There does not seem to be room for a translation of all the end of Bab. l. 26, and the beginning of l. 27, unless the Aramaic lines were of exceptional length. This was not the case, judging by the amount to be covered by Aram. ll. 3 and 4.

The reverse is not Behistun, see no. 62.

No. 2, obverse. Ungnad cft. Bab. l. 36+ on the ground that in l. 5 בפר[ת] is the Euphrates which is only mentioned there. Sachau takes it as בפרתו, and connects it with l. 18+ above. The fragment does not fit either place, and may belong to a different recension. Line 4. [מר]גויא so Sachau, cf. ll. 17, 19. There is a trace of ר. Line 5. בפר[ס] more likely than בפר[ת]. Line 7. Perhaps [קרב]א ב with a date. Line 8. עמ[י] probably.

Reverse, unimportant.

No. 3, obverse, see under ll. 18–28.

Reverse probably not Behistun. See no. 62.

No. 4, obverse. Line 3. Cf. the last numerals in l. 11. The next line however does not fit that passage.

Reverse also Behistun The other copies are not written on the back. Sachau suggests that it belongs to the end, containing the curses.

Nos 5, 6 unimportant.

No. 7 see under ll. 19–21 Reverse unimportant

No 8, obverse, see under ll. 46–48 Reverse, see under l 61 +.

Nos. 9–12 unimportant.

No. 13, obverse Behistun Reverse, probably accounts.

No. 14 Sachau's reading. Only the last three lines are legible on the facsimile.

Nos 15–20 unimportant

Sachau, plate 57.

No 1.
[חיל]א
ש[מען לי]
במד[יא רבה]

No 2.
[ה]
ה[ם ///]
[נד̄נ]

No. 3.
ב[מרו שמ]ה
אהו[רמזד ח]ילא
ו[לף /// ///]
ע[ברי]
דריה[ויש מלכא]
[לערעה זי]
אהור[מזד סעדני]
blank.

No. 4.
מנד[עם לא ע]בד
space.
א[תכנש]ו
[אי̄ש̄]

Nos 5 and 6 nothing legible.

No. 7.
ד[דרש א]זל
[למעבד]
בטלה זי אהורמ[זד
blank

No. 8. . . .
אח̄[ר

No 9 ור̄

No. 10. illegible.

No 11. blank.
[/// ר /]
[ו]

No 12 [///]

No. 13. בפרת

No 14
[מ̄]
דד[ריש]

No 15.
פ[רסי]
[א]

No 16 . . .
[. ר]

Plate 57, twenty-nine fragments, of which nos. 1–16 are Behistun.

No. 1. Line 2. Sachau conjectures [לא מישת]מען, but ת is not possible. ש is possible, but doubtful. Line 3. Perhaps במרדיא and not as Bab. רבה is certain. Not [רבח[ילא] (as Sachau). Darius would hardly have recognized any רבחילא but himself.

No. 2. Line 3. נד̊נ̊ perhaps part of נדנתבל, and therefore belonging to Bab. l. 37.

No. 3. Line 3. [ו]לף quite uncertain. Line 4. [ע]ברי not מדי (as Ungnad), if the fragment belongs to Bab. ll. 46–50; see below. Line 6. לערעה if correct, is for לערקה elsewhere. Line 7 was the end of a column. See further on, no. 7.

No. 4. Cf. l. 6 after which there is also a space. The fragment does not, however, fit that or any other context apparently.

Nos. 5, 6 unimportant.

No. 7. למעבד. Note the form of the ב with its long rounded tail. The blank shows that this was the end of a column. Sachau suggests that nos. 3 and 7 (Ungnad, 1, 3, 4, 7) go together. Certainly the last line of no. 7 is the natural continuation of the last line of no. 3, and the blanks correspond. The two fragments then seem to precede pl. 52 and to correspond to part of Bab. ll. 46–50. No. 1 seems to come before them. Nos. 1, 3, 7 may be restored somewhat thus:

. . . . [חילא זי פרס

ומדי זי עמי זעיר הוה אחר אנה] חיל[א שלחת למדי והודרנה שמה בראשהום

אמרת איל לחילא זי מדי זי לא ש]מען לי [קטלהם (?) אחר הודרנה אזל

למדי עבד

קרב ב]מרו שמ[ה איש זי במד]יא רבה [לא עמד (?) אהורמזד סעדני בטלה

זי אהו]רמזד ח[ילא זילי קטלו למרדיא אלה ב ׳׳׳ ׳׳׳׳ לטבת עבדו קרבא

קטלו ו]לף ׳׳׳ ׳׳׳[. . . וחין אחדו . . . . . . דריהויש מלכא כן אמר דדרש

שמה ע]ברי [ארדטי לארדט שלחת אמרת חילא מרדיא זי לא שמען לי

קטלהם (?)

דריה]וש מלכא [כן אמר אחר ד]דרש א[זל לארדט לממטה אתכנשו מרדיא

אזלו] לערעה זי [דדרש] למעבד [קרב אחר עבדו קרבא בזוז שמה בארדט

אהור]מזד סעדני בטלה זי אהורמ[זד חילא זילי קטלו למרדיא אלה

The details may not be all correct, but this seems to fit the three fragments. As elsewhere, the Aramaic is shorter than Bab., e. g. it omits the latter part of Bab. l. 47. (If no. 4 comes in here, it must belong to another copy). On the other hand it gives the number of killed and prisoners, which Bab. must have omitted (There is a break in Bab l. 47, but not room for the numbers) The text then continues, without a break, as in Aram. l. 1, the beginning of a new column, so that it and these three fragments may all belong to the same copy

Nos. 8–12 unimportant

No 13. בפרת 'on the Euphrates' or בפרת[ו] 'in Parthia'.

No. 14 belongs to the account of Dadaršiš.

Nos. 15, 16 unimportant.

Nos. 17–29 not Behistun See above, no 64

INDEX

א = ארדב 24^{1} &c. $81^{4.5}$ &c. 83^{4} &c.

אב = יב 9^{2}.

אב month Ab 14^{1}.

אב father: אבי Aḥ. 33.33. אבוך 44^{7} Aḥ. 15.27. אבוהי $71^{5\cdot 25}$ Aḥ. 5.47.85.138. אבוה 25^{7} Aḥ. 55. אבוכם 20^{6}. אבהין (our fathers) 30^{13} 31^{12}. אבהיהם 71^{2}.

אבד: אבדו 30^{16}. יאבד 15^{27}. תאבד (3rd fem.) 71^{28}. אבדה Aḥ. 94.

אבה pr. n. 6^{16}.

אבהון pr. n.? 82^{12}.

אבהי pr. n. 81^{1}.

אבוט Abydos 38^{3} 64, 26? [$82^{1\cdot 13}$].

אביגרן (or ־דן) a fine 43^{6} [46^{9}]. אביגרנא 20^{14} 25^{15} 28^{10} [45^{8}].

אביהו pr. n. 2^{20} 24^{17}.

אביהי pr. n. 39^{2} $46^{9[15]}$.

אביהי ברת אושע 22^{90}.

אביהי ברת נתון 22^{100}.

אביתי pr. n. $81^{42.91.115}$.

אביתי ברת נתין 81^{99}.

אבן stone 15^{16} $30^{10\cdot 10}$ 31^{9}. אבן צרף 38^{3}. אבנא 30^{9}[31^{8}]. weight: באבני מלכא 5^{7} 6^{14} $8^{14\cdot 21}$ 9^{15} 10^{4} 14^{10} $15^{5\cdot 6\cdot 9\cdot 10\cdot 14\cdot 31\cdot 36}$ 20^{15} 25^{16} 43^{3} 46^{10}. באבני פתח 11^{2}.

אבעשר ברת הושע 22^{104}.

אגור ב׳ אחיו 10^{22}.

אגורא temple 13^{14} 25^{6} $30^{6\cdot 7\cdot 9\cdot 10\cdot 12\cdot 14\cdot 17\cdot 22-24\cdot 27}$ $31^{8-10\cdot 12\cdot 16\cdot 21\cdot 24\cdot 26}$ 33^{8}. אגורי 30^{14} 31^{13}.

אגר (or אגד) portico? 5^{4}. אגרא $5^{4\cdot 5\cdot 6\cdot 7\cdot 10\cdot 10\cdot 20}$.

אגר wages 69^{12} Aḥ. 164.

אגרה a letter $30^{18\cdot 19\cdot 24\cdot 29}$ $31^{17\cdot 18\cdot 23}$ 40^{3}. אגרת 30^{7} 31^{6} 38^{10} 41^{5}. אגרתא 42^{7}, pl. אגְרָתא 37^{15}.

אגרי ב׳ אש . . . 19^{9}.

אר see אד.

ארן 14^{4} 20^{1} 25^{1} 35^{1} [43^{1}] 68, 2, 4 Aḥ. [5.32.78] 127.

אדן ear: אדנין Aḥ. 157.216. אדניך Aḥ. 132. אדניהם Aḥ. 97.

אדני? Aḥ. 171.

אדננבו pr. n. (of a *degel*) 20^{2} 67, 1.

אדר month Adar 61^{12} 67, 4.

אהורמזד Auramazda. Beh. 2[3]5.5[13]13.19[20]28.28.41[41]43[43], pp. 265, 266, 269.

או $5^{6\cdot 8\cdot 9}$ $8^{18\cdot 20\cdot 26\cdot 26}$ $9^{8\cdot 13}$ $15^{17\cdot 20[22]26}$ 20^{14} $25^{11\cdot 11\cdot 14\cdot 14}$ 28^{9} $45^{5\cdot 6}$.

אודים 33^{12}.

אוה pr. n. 24^{37}.

און Aḥ. 160.

אוסתן pr. n. 30^{13} 31^{18}.

אופכרתה 26^{5}.

אופישר 26^{22}. אופישרה $26^{3.6[9]10}$.

אוצרא 2^{12} [2^{14} 3^{16}] 11^{6} 50^{6}.

אורי pr. n. [18^{1}] $22^{65.68.118}$ 24^{26}.

אורי ב׳ מחסה 23^{14}.

אורי ב׳ משלך 22^{73}.

אוריה pr. n. 6^{9} 8^{7} 9^{2} 15^{38} [19^{3} 22^{43}] $25^{2.4.6.13.17.20}$ $37^{1[17]}$ $38^{1.12}$.

אושע pr. n. 12^{2} 13^{14} 22^{30} 63^{15} 67, 11.

אושע ב׳ או[ריה] 19^{3}.

אושע ב׳ גלגול 10^{21}.

אושע ב׳ הודו 12^{4}.

אושע ב׳ יתום 12^{3}.

אושע ב׳ נתן ב׳ הודויה 22^{127}.

אושעיה pr. n. 20^{18}.

אזד 27^{8}.

אזדכרא 17^{7}. אזדכריא 17^{5}.

אזיבו ב׳ ברכיא 56^{3}.

אזל 27^{3} 30^{5} 31^{4} 56^{2} Aḥ. [38]75. 110.120 Beh. 8.12 ?[27.30.40.44. 46]. אזלת (1st sing.) 40^{2} Aḥ. 22.76. אזלו Beh. [1]4.8.10. 24*.26. אזל (imperat.) 42^{8} Beh. 7.18. אזלו Beh. 39.

אזניה pr. n. 12^{8} [18^{5}] 66, 8.

אח 1^{5} 5^{8} $6^{13.13}$ 8^{10} 13^{10} 25^{11} 28^{8} 43^{5}. אחי [56^{1}] 65, 4. 67, 8. אחוך $40^{1.5}$ $42^{1[15]}$ 56^{4} 68, 1 [Aḥ. 99. 100]. אחוכי 68, 8. אחוהי 25^{21} $28^{16.17}$ 30^{18} 31^{18} 34^{5} Aḥ. 49 [72]. אחוה for אחוהי 25^{3}. אחוכם $21^{2.11}$ $41^{[1]9}$. אחי $21^{[1]2.11}$ $40^{1[1]5}$ $41^{1[1.9]}$ [$42^{1.15}$]. אחין 20^{10}. אחיכם 20^{12}.

אחה sister 1^{5} 5^{8} $6^{13.13}$ 8^{10} 13^{10} 25^{11} 28^{6} 43^{5}. אחת 22^{82} 65, 4. אחתי 68, 8 [Aḥ. 8.25]. אחתה (her s.) 1^{2} 34^{4} $43^{2.13}$ 82^{10}: (his s.) [Aḥ. 12]. אחותה 75^{8}.

אחד take אחֲדָה [Beh. 47] אחדת (?) 52^{8} (1st sing.) Beh. 14. אחדו 69^{3} Beh. 4.6.11[21.30.33]34[34. 42.44.48], p. 266. יאחדן Aḥ. 171. למאחד 2^{17} [3^{19}]. אתחדו $34^{[3]4}$.

אחדי secrets? Aḥ. 99.

אחיאב ב׳ גמריה $2^{2.18}$ [2^{22} 3^{2}].

אחיו pr. n. 5^{15} 6^{18} 10^{22} 11^{16}.

אחיו ב׳ מ[חסיה] 34^{5}.

אחיו ב׳ נתן 23^{1} 25^{19}.

אחיו ב׳ נתן ב׳ ענני 22^{128}.

אחיו ב׳ פלטיה 10^{22}.

אחיקר pr. n. Aḥ. 1.2[8.11]13. 14 [21.26.29.34]35.45.46.55.60.62. 63[64.66]69[70]76.

אחלבני pr. n. 24^{12}.

אחמנש pr. n. $17^{1.5}$ 65, 11.

אחר afterwards: 9^{8} 13^{5} 20^{8} 28^{10} $30^{6.8}$ $31^{6.7}$ [33^{12}] [69^{2}] 71^{11} Aḥ. [4]8. 11 [21.24][28.29] 36.39 [53] 54 [58]63.71[74]171 Beh. 2.4.6.8. [9]11[12.14–16.18.19.23]24[26] 26[27.30.31.34.44.46.48]. אחרי כן Aḥ. 99. after: אחַרֵי 67, 12 Aḥ. 6 Beh. 50. אחריך 9^{13} $28^{7.12}$. אחריכי $8^{9.15}$ 13^{8}. אחרוהי 9^{4} 13^{7} 38^{10} Aḥ. 210. אחרין Aḥ. 63. אחריכם 9^{8} $25^{9.16}$ על אחרן Aḥ. 53.64[133]. other? fem. אחרה 15^{32} 64, 20. $79^{3.4}$ 82^{4}

אחריא אחרן (pl. ?) 15^{33}. 82^{7}.

אחרן other 1^{4} $5^{6\cdot8}$ $8^{11\cdot16\cdot18\cdot20\cdot26}$ $9^{8\cdot13}$ $13^{9\cdot11}$ $15^{10[17]22\cdot26[36]}$ $20^{6\cdot12}$ $26^{5\cdot6}$ 30^{11} [37^{8}] 38^{1} Aḥ. 49. אחרנא [9^{11}]. אחרנן $8^{10\cdot19}$ $9^{7\cdot9}$ 15^{32} 30^{8} $71^{4\cdot24}$ Aḥ. [14]37.39.40.49.52.62.

אחרחיב ב׳ הפימו 73^{16}.

אחרטיכ pr. n. 63^{2}.

אטר pr. n. 13^{3} Ezra 2^{16}.

אין 16^{7} Aḥ. 37 Beh. [52 ?] איך זי Beh. 52.

אילא Aḥ. 88. אילחא Aḥ. 87.

אימניע ?? Beh. 55.

. . . איסכ pr. n. 51^{8}.

איר month Iyyar Beh. 3, 10. [29].

איש man $8^{11\cdot12\cdot16}$ $20^{10\cdot12\cdot13\cdot14}$ 25^{10-11} 30^{14} 31^{18} 42^{6} 49^{3} 67, 5. $71^{6\cdot7\cdot29}$ Aḥ. 49 [72.83] 104.114.116.116.125. 125.134.145[145]150[150]159. 160.163.200.218 Beh. [22]38. 50.

איח for איתי ? 46^{3} 54^{4} 67, 7 ?

אית 8^{23} 9^{3} $15^{19\cdot32\cdot33}$ $20^{5\cdot7}$ [21^{7}] $27^{4\cdot6[23]}$ 28^{12} 29^{2} 35^{3} 37^{4} [43^{7}] 64, 27 Aḥ. 159. לא איתי 8^{10} $15^{18\cdot21}$ 80^{4} Aḥ. 105.111.112[117].

איתן ב׳ אבר 6^{16}.

אכל eat: Aḥ. [34]. יאכל 71^{4}? Aḥ. [86] 89. תאכל Aḥ. 127. 129. תאכלו [21^{8}]. למאכל 61^{9}.

אכב : יאכמו Aḥ. 157.

אל to [17^{3} $21^{1\cdot11}$] 30^{1} [31^{1}] $37^{1\cdot17}$ $38^{1\cdot12}$ $39^{1\cdot5}$ $40^{1\cdot5}$ $41^{1\cdot9}$ [$42^{1\cdot15}$ 56^{4}] 63^{6}? 67, 8.70^{1} Aḥ. 155 ? זי אל עמה Aḥ. 107.154.161.

אל not [21^{6-9} 27^{23}] $42^{7\cdot11\cdot18}$ Aḥ. 52. 54.61[68]81.96.97.100–103.106. 106.119[126]126.130[136]136. [137]137.138.141–143.146–148. 153.157[157]193.194.206–208. 218.

אל God Aḥ. 156? 173?

אלה God: 13^{14}. אלה שמיא [27^{15}] $30^{2\cdot27}$ 31^{2} 32^{3} $38^{[2]3\cdot5}$ 40^{1}. אלהא 2^{10} 3^{17} 6^{4} 7^{8} 22^{1} 25^{6} 27^{8} $30^{5\cdot6\cdot24\cdot26}$ $31^{7\cdot24\cdot25}$ 33^{8} 38^{1} [44^{3}] 45^{4} 69^{12} 72^{15} Aḥ. [149.198]. אלהן our god 7^{6}. אלהן gods 71^{23}? Aḥ. 95.115.115[122]124.124.128. 135[151]160. אלהי 30^{14} 31^{13} $71^{8.26}$. אלהיא 13^{15} 17^{1} 21^{2} 34^{7} [37^{1}] 39^{1} [41^{1}] 56^{1} Aḥ. 94.126?

אלהתה goddess 14^{5}. אלהתא 72^{16}.

אלה these, see זנה.

אלוך Beh. 23.

אלול month Elul 5^{1} 20^{1}.

אלך these, see זך.

אלף teach. יתאלף Aḥ. 80. אלפנא [Aḥ. 83].

אלף a thousand $24^{40\cdot43}$ 31^{27} [33^{14}]. אלפי 71^{16}. ולף see לף.

אם = אפם 13^{11} 34^{5}.

אם mother: אמה $28^{4\cdot5}$ Aḥ. 138. אמן (our m.) 28^{3}. אמהם 25^{3} 28^{13}.

אמה maidservant: 10^{10} Aḥ. 84.

אמה cubit: 79^{2-4}, pl. אמן $8^{4\cdot5}$ 9^{4} $15^{8\cdot9\cdot11}$ $26^{10-14\cdot16}$ $36^{2\cdot2}$ 63^{11} 79^{2-4}.

אמורטים Amyrtaeus $35^{1\cdot6}$.

אמחות pr. n.? 69^{11} 69 D.

אמן : הימנותה Aḥ. 132.

אמר sheep: אמריא Aḥ. [120] 121. אמריך [Aḥ. 121].

אמר say: 2^{3} 5^{1} 6^{2} 7^{2} 8^{1} 9^{1} 13^{1} 14^{1} 15^{2} 20$^{1.7}$ [21^{15}] 25^{2} 26$^{2.22}$ 28^{2} [29^{1}] 35^{2} 37^{13} 38^{10} 39^{4} [44$^{4.7}$ 45^{1}] 49$^{1.2}$ 64, 26. 65^{8} 69^{8} 71^{12} 76^{1} 80^{7} Aḥ. 2[3]11[13]20[25]32[34.37.42] 54.56.59[72.75]78.110.118.166 Beh. [7.12.16.17.22.22]27.34.37 [37.48–50.59.60]. אמרת 3rd fem. 1^{1} 10^{2} [43^{1}] 55^{6} 68, 4 Aḥ. 119. אמרת (1st sing.) 9^{5} 16$^{3.6}$ 43^{6} Aḥ. [5.15]24.45.49 Beh. 7.18. אמרת (2nd sing.) [Aḥ. 75]. אמרו 26$^{3[5]9}$ 32^{1} 41^{4} 80$^{2.8}$ Aḥ. 58 [67.77]121. אמרן 1st pl. 40^{2}. יאמר 15^{27} 37^{9} Aḥ. [65]194.207 Beh. 53.53? יאמרנה Aḥ. 158. תאמר (3rd fem.) 18$^{[1]8}$ 15^{23}. אמר 1st sing. 5^{12} 8^{20} 9^{14} 10^{11} 15$^{31.33}$ 47^{8} Aḥ. [26.29]57.139. יאמרו [42^{5}] יאמרון 71^{32}. נמר? 1st pl. [1^{6}]. אמר imperat. Aḥ. 58. אמר ptcp. 29^{4} [Aḥ. 59], pl. אמרן 26^{23} 27$^{10.22}$ 30^{4} 31^{22} 33^{7} 37^{6} 69 B? ־ין 30^{22}. אמיר? Aḥ. 210? למאמר Aḥ. 115. לממר 32^{2} [43^{2}]. לאמר 2^{3} 5$^{3.12}$ 6^{4} [7$^{4-8}$] 8^{3} 9^{3} 10^{3} [11^{1}] 13^{2} 15^{3} 16^{8} 20$^{4-6}$ [21^{3}] 25^{4} 28^{2} [29^{2}] 30^{7} 35^{3} 39^{4} 42^{5} 44^{4} 45$^{[3]3}$ [49^{1}]. אמריך thy words Aḥ. 102.

אן where (or לְהאן) 15$^{25.29}$.

אנבא [16^{4}]. אנביך [Aḥ. 165]. לאנדם? 22^{133}. אנדומא? 72^{20}.

אנה ego: 5$^{3.11}$ 6$^{5.7.8.12}$ 7$^{7[10]}$ 8$^{3.8.17.18.21.25}$ 9$^{3.5.14}$ 13$^{2.5.8-10.12.12}$ 14$^{9.11}$ 15$^{2.4}$ [16^{8}] 20^{9} 25$^{9.12.12}$ 28$^{5.8}$ 29^{4} 35^{5} 38^{9} 40^{2} 43$^{[2]3[7.7.9]}$ [45^{3}] 64, 19. 81$^{14.69.127-130[133]}$ Aḥ. [3.6–8.14.15]17[21] 25[29]40.46.52.57.66.204.205. 207 Beh. [12]21 a*[23]24.27.36 [37]59[60], p. 265, 3. אנחן 1$^{2.5}$. אנחנה 2$^{9.13.15}$ 20$^{[4]9.10.12}$ 26$^{3.8}$ 27$^{1.10.10.12.20.22}$ 28$^{2.9.11}$ 30$^{15.20.26}$ 31$^{14.19}$ 37$^{7[15]}$ [42^{2}] Aḥ. 59.61.121.

אנף : אנפי 15^{19} Aḥ. 14.101. אנפין [Aḥ. 197]. לאנפין? Aḥ. 134. אנפוהי Aḥ. 133.201.202. אנפין (our face) 37$^{8.9}$.

אנש 28$^{8.10}$. אנשא Aḥ. [89]116. 122[123.124.151.162.167.190].

אנת thou: 2$^{[9.12]16.17}$ [3^{19}] 5$^{11.14}$ 6$^{4.18.15}$ [7^{4}] 9$^{8.10-12}$ 10$^{8.16}$ 20$^{8.11}$ 25^{8} 26^{22} 28$^{3.6}$ [35^{10}] 42^{11} 44^{5} 47^{8} 66, 4 Aḥ. 34[42]51.53.58[59]68.101. 127.129.149.166 Beh. [50]52 [53]. אנתי fem. 8$^{9.11.12.26}$ 14^{7}. אנתם 21$^{4[6]}$ 38$^{5.6[8]8}$ 80^{5} [Aḥ. 57].

אנתה wife, woman: 8^{10} 15$^{32.33}$ 25$^{10-14}$ Aḥ. 219. אנתתא 7^{9}. אנתת 63^{2}. אתת 34$^{3.3.3}$. אנתתי 7^{5} 15$^{4[27]}$. אנתתך 6^{4} 9$^{4.6}$. אנתתה 15^{18} 46$^{9.11}$ 68, 12.

אנתו marriage: 14^{4} 15^{3} 48^{3}. אנתותבי 35^{5}.

אסודת ב׳ יהנתן 2^{21}.

אסוטים pr. n. 66, 12.

אסורי ברת גמריה $43^{2[18]}$.

אסחור ב׳ צחא $15^{2.17.19.21.21.23.24.26.30[37]}$ $20^{3.6.8.20}$.

אסי god-name 72^{16}.

אסבישו pr. n. 2^{19}.

אסבשית pr. n. 53^{7}.

אסמישד pr. n. 3^{24}.

אספמט pr. n. [$2^{2.22}$ 3^{3}] 4^{7} [44^{5}].

אספמת ב׳ פפטעונית 6^{10} 8^{7}.

אסר: אסרני 38^{3}. יתסר Aḥ. 80? אסירן prisoners: $34^{3[4]}$ 64, 29. אסרוהי 69^{4}.

אסרוך ב׳ פלטי? 13^{15}.

אסרחארן Esarhaddon: Aḥ. 5[7], 10, 11, 13, 14 [19.23.28]32.47.53. 60.64.65[70]75[76]78.

אסרשות pr. n. 34^{3}.

אסתח pr. n. 22^{81}.

אף also: $4^{2.3}$ 6^{7} 7^{10} $8^{18.23}$ 10^{10} $13^{11.13}$ [16^{3}] 17^{3} 20^{6} [21^{7}] 25^{10} $27^{10[12]}$ 28^{12} $30^{9.17.19.21.29.30}$ $31^{16.17}$ [33^{13}] 37^{5} [43^{7}.44^{7}] 47^{8} 54^{7} 69^{12} 80^{6} Aḥ. 19 [25.46]51[57.71]83.95[104]105. 107[130] Beh. 54.

אפו Aḥ. 52.140.

אפיתי? 26^{9}.

אפך? יאפך Aḥ. 156. אפכא Aḥ. 156.

אפל? אפלת 1st sing. pf. 13^{4}.

אפלנים pr. n. 81^{64}.

אפם surely: $5^{8.11}$ 6^{15} $8^{15.22}$ 20^{15} 25^{16} 42^{8} [46^{10}].

אפנא? $81^{15.60}$.

אפסי? 26^{12}.

אפע pr. n. [24^{4}] 53^{6}.

אפף month Epiphi 1^{1} 15^{1} 63^{15}.

אפתו god-name 72^{15}.

אציל Aḥ. 143.

אר (or אד) name of a wood: 26^{10}.

ארב Aḥ. 99.99.

ארבעה 10^{4} $29^{[3]5.6}$. ארבעיא 81^{60}. ארבעת עשר [21^{4}]. ארבעמאה 26^{16}.

ארדב 2^{4} 3^{8}. ארדבן $2^{4.5[6]7.8}$ 3^{5} 33^{14}.

ארדיכל 14^{2}. ארדכל 15^{2}.

ארוסתמר pr. n. 6^{21}.

ארז $26^{10.13.14.17}$ 30^{11} 31^{10}. ארזא Aḥ. 175.

ארח fetter: Aḥ. 196. ארחא Aḥ. 80.

ארח road: 25^{6}. ארחא [Aḥ. 164]. ארחה Aḥ. 187.

אריא Aḥ. 88.110.110. אריה Aḥ. 89.117.

ארייישא ב׳ ארוסתמר 6^{21}.

ארך: יארכון Beh. 58. אריכן ptcp. 30^{3} 31^{3}.

ארך length: $15^{8.9.11}$ 63^{11}. ארכא $26^{18.19.19.20}$. ארכה (its l.) 8^{4}.

ארמי $5^{2.2}$ 7^{2} $13^{2.3}$ 15^{2} 25^{2} $29^{1.2}$ 35^{2} 45^{2} 67, 3, 4. fem. ארמית [43^{2}]. ארמין 28^{2} 65, 5? ארמיא 14^{3}. ארמית in Aramaic $28^{4.6}$.

ארמים pr. n. 81^{107}.

ארמלה 30^{20}.

ארסין pr. n. $81^{4.5}$.

ארעא 5^{5} 6^{16} 15^{19} 30^{9} 31^{8} 68, 11.

ארק 6^{7} $8^{3.8}$ 9^{3} [13^{15}]. ארקא $6^{5-7.12-15}$ $8^{11.12.16.19.24}$ $9^{5.8.14}$ Aḥ. 108.

ארדט pl. n. Beh. 2.[5–7]8.11.

ארשד pl. n. Beh. 46.

ארשם pr. n. $17^{[1]5}$ 21^{3} $26^{1.22.27}$ 27^{2} $30^{4.30}$ $31^{4.20}$ 32^{3} $37^{5.8.9.14}$ [42^{12}].

ארתבנו 51^{6}: name of a *degel* 6^{8} [45^{2}].

ארתורזי pr. n. Beh. 25.26.31.

ארתחשסש Artaxerxes 6^{2} 7^{1} 8^{1} 9^{1} 10^{1} 13^{1} 14^{1} [15^{1} 16^{2}] 17^{7} [45^{1}].

ארתפרן pr. n. 5^{17} [7^{2}].

אשר: יאשר Aḥ. 89.

אשה fire: 30^{12} Aḥ. 103.104[197] 222. אשתא 31^{11}.

אשירת pr. n. 51^{14}.

אשין pr. n. 65, 5.

אשל: אשלן $75^{6\cdot7[8]}$.

אשמביתאל god-name 22^{124}.

אשמכדרי ב׳ אפע 53^{6}.

[א]שמן pr. n. 24^{1}.

אשמן ב׳ אפע? 24^{4}.

אשמרם ב׳ נבונד 53^{9}.

אשנ.. pr. n. $42^{5\cdot11}$.

אשרנא $26^{[3]5[6]9\cdot21}$ 27^{18} 30^{11}.

את = אית? 49^{2}.

אתה come: 37^{11} 82^{3} Beh. [13.31. 45]. אתית 1st sing. 5^{3} (+עליך) 15^{3} (+ביתך). אתו 30^{8}. אתין ptcp. 38^{5}. יאתה [41^{3}] 82^{11} Aḥ. [33]. תאתה (3rd sing.) Aḥ. 97.210.214. אתי imperat. Aḥ. 118. היתי $24^{30\cdot48}$. יהיתה 26^{13}. להיתיה 27^{14}.

אתור Assyria: Aḥ. [2] 3–5, 8, 10–14[18]20[23.28]32[36]37.43.55. 55[61.70].

אתנא 44^{4} Aḥ. 91.

אתעדרי ב׳... 2^{20}.

אתר 17^{2} 71^{20} Aḥ. 34.97. אתרא 13^{19}. אתרה 6^{2} 32^{8}.

אתרודן 27^{17}.

אתרופרן name of a *degel* 6^{9}.

אחרלי (or מתרלי?) pr. n. 5^{16} 13^{18}

אתרפרת pr. n.? 66, 7.

ב = בב? 81^{106}.

־ב: ביום 1^{1} &c. || ||| ||| בך &c. 3^{1} &c. בגו 2^{9} 4^{4} 5^{13} 8^{28} $9^{6\cdot17}$ 10^{21} 13^{17} 14^{12} $15^{6\cdot15\cdot37}$ 18^{4} 20^{9} 22^{123} 24^{27} 25^{18} $26^{10[7]}$ 27^{7} 28^{15} 35 e $43^{[8]11}$ 49^{5} 72^{5} 78^{2} $79^{2\cdot3}$ Aḥ. [9.23]. בוי 37^{7}. בבי? 13^{17}. בידי = בכפי? 3^{21}. ביה 82^{6}. בהום 31^{16}. בהן $34^{6[7]}$ 82^{11}. בלא [Aḥ. 102].

באר 27^{6}. ב[רא] $27^{8\cdot8}$.

בארי pr. n. 53^{8}.

באש: יבאש [Aḥ. 64]. באיש 30^{17} 31^{16}. באישא [Aḥ. 45]. באישה 38^{6}. באישתא 30^{17} [Aḥ. 25.50. 81].

בב = דבב 13^{19}.

בב? $81^{5\cdot16\cdot17\cdot19[20]23\cdot25\cdot63\cdot72\cdot76\cdot79\cdot113\cdot114\cdot128-130\cdot133}$.

בב gate: 66, 7. 69^{8}? Aḥ. [9]17.23. בבא $34^{3\cdot4}$.

בבל pl. n. [Beh. 12].

בבליא 6^{19}.

בגבחש pr. n. 51^{10}.

בגרו pr. n. 72^{14}.

בגרן pr. n. 17^{1}?

בגרת pr. n. 66, 6.

בגרת ב׳ אסמשר [3^{24}].

בגדת ב׳ נבוכדרי 5^{18}.

בגוהי pr. n. 30^{1} [31^{1}] 32^{1}.

בגפרן pr. n. $16^{[1]6}$.

בגפרן ב׳ ושחי 22^{133}
בדא Aḥ 30.
בהמיתה ? 9^{5}.
בהת: תבהת (2nd sing.) [Aḥ. 106].
בות Ah 90.
בזז. בזיזת Ah 168. בזז prey? 37^{7}
בזע Ah 41.
בזק Ah. 206.
בחן: תבחננהי [Ah 132] ? בחין Aḥ 203
בחתרי pl. n. [Beh 18].
בטא · תבט (2nd sing jussive ?) [Ah 96].
בטן Ah 161 217 בטנא 26^{11} בטני Ah 139. בטנהם [71^{1}]
לבטק 26^{10}.
? בילוף 61^{57}.
בין between · 5^{13} $7^{8\,10}$ 21^{9} 29^{6} 45^{7} Ah 40.62[69]113[206]206 בינין $5^{13\,14}$ 28^{14}. בניהם (= בי׳) 13^{14} 25^{7}.
בירתא (see also ברתא). [2^{1}] $6^{3\,4\,17}$ $7^{2[3]}$ $8^{2\,28}$ 9^{16} $10^{2\,3}$ $14^{2\,12}$ 20^{12} 25^{22} 26^{7} $27^{3\,5-7[11]}$ $28^{1\,15}$ 29^{1} $30^{1\,5-8\,13\,25}$ $31^{5\,7\,24}$ 32^{4} $33^{6\,9}$ 43^{2} $45^{1[2]9}$ 66, 6. 80^{6} 82^{3}. בירת 6^{3} 13^{4} 27^{5} 30^{8}.
ביתא $5^{3\,4}$ $8^{8\,15\,22\,27}$ $9^{3\,4\,6\,11\,12}$ $13^{2\,6\,7\,9\,13\,15}$ $25^{8\,11\,15\,16}$ 30^{3} $42^{3\,5\,6}$ [$46^{8\,10}$ 17^{1} 66, 7, 14. 81^{11}] Ah 48. בית $5^{5\,13}$ 6^{8-10} $8^{3\,5\,6\,6\,7\,7}$ $13^{11\,13\,14}$ $25^{4\,3\,5\,7\,20}$ [29^{4}] 33^{13} 38^{10} [46^{10}] 56^{6} 66, 14 81^{109} 82^{3} Ah [168]222 בית מדבחא 32^{3} בית מלכא $2^{12\,14\,16}$ [3^{13}] $43^{[7]8[10]}$ בי 8^{37} 9^{3} 82^{8} Ah 125 [131] בי זי לבנן [2^{16}] 3^{18} 10^{9} ביתי $5^{5\,5}$ 6^{8} $7^{[1]5}$ 41^{6} Ah 22[22]139.140. ביתך $7^{8\,9}$ 15^{3} 34^{7} 41^{6} Ah. 52 ביתכי $8^{15\,22}$ ביתה $15^{18\,30}$ Aḥ.[71 84]197. בִיתַה 81^{24} ביתנא 81^{110} ? בתנא 81^{115} בתיא 34^{6} Beh. 23 בתין (our houses) 38^{8}. בתיהום p. 263, 2.
ביתאלנדן pr. n 55^{7}
[בית]אלנורי pr. n. 22^{6}.
ביתאלנתן ב׳ יהונתן 18^{5}
ביתאלנתן ב׳ צחא 18^{4}
ביתאלעקב ב׳ עבר 12^{9}
ביתאלתדן pr. n. 42^{8}.
ביתאלתקם pr. n. $2^{6\,10}$.
בכים pr. n. 81^{94}
בל mind בלך Ah 97.
בלא pr. n. 28^{5}.
בלא be worn out: 3rd fem. בלא[ת] or ptcp. fem. בלא[ה] 26^{1}.
? בלבו pr. n. 24^{14}
מן בלעדי [Ah 122].
בלע: יבלעון [Ah. 148]
בנה build 5^{20}. בנית 2nd sing. 9^{12} בנו 3rd pl. [27^{5}] 30^{13} 31^{12} תבנה 2nd sing. fut 9^{8} יבנון 71^{3} בני imperat. fem. 8^{19} 9^{5}. למבנה $5^{5\,6\,9\,11}$ 9^{14} 30^{23}. למבניה [27^{24}] $30^{23\,25}$ $31^{23\,21}$ 32^{8} בנה ptcp pass. 27^{6} $30^{14\,26}$ 31^{13} 32^{4} [33^{9}] בניה fem 27^{6}. יתבנה 30^{27} [31^{26} 33^{9}]
בנויא the building: 9^{12}
בנין construction · 30^{10} 31^{9}
בניה pr. n 23^{3}.

בנת? pr. n. 74^{3}.

בנתריש ב׳ רחמרע 5^{19}.

בעריה pr. n. 19^{2} 25^{18}.

בעה 31^{16} 50^{4}. בעו 30^{17}. יבעה 38^{6} Aḥ. 24.53[64]. תבעה Aḥ. 34. בעי imperat 42^{6}.

בעולה? Aḥ. 218.

בעל [46^{6}] Aḥ. 223. בעל אגר Aḥ. 164. ב׳ רגל 5^{9} 13^{10}. ב׳ טעם 26^{23}. ב׳ עטתא Aḥ. 42. ב׳ קרישן Aḥ. 95. ב׳ קריה 5^{9} 13^{10} 20^{10} 46^{6}. בעלי (my husband) 15^{23}. בעלבי 8^{7}. בעלה 15$^{4.21}$ [46^{16}]. בעלי טבחך 30^{23} 31^{23}. בעלי יב 30^{22} 31^{22}. בעלי פתורא 83^{21}.

בצי: אתבציו 50^{6}.

בר son: 1$^{5.9-11}$ 2$^{2.2[2]19-21}$ 3$^{[2]22.23[24]}$ 5$^{2.2.8.9.15-19}$ 6$^{2.3.8-10.12.13.16-22}$ 7$^{2[3]}$ 8$^{2.5-7.10.12.23.26.28-35}$ 9$^{2.2.16-21[22]}$ 10$^{2.20-22.24}$ 11$^{1.12-16}$ 12$^{1-9.11}$ 13$^{1.3.13-15.17-21}$ 14$^{2.2.7.9.11-13}$ 15$^{2.17.20.37-39}$ 16^{1} 19$^{2-10}$ 20$^{2.3.6.12.13.16-20}$ 23$^{1-15}$ 25$^{2-5.10.13.14.17-21}$ 28$^{2.8.9.14-17}$ 33$^{1-5}$ 34$^{5.5.5.5}$ 35^{2} 37^{11} 38$^{1.1.12}$ 40$^{2[5]5}$ 41$^{[9]9}$ [42^{15}] 43$^{5[9]11.12}$ 44$^{1.2}$ 45$^{[2]2[9]}$ 46$^{2.11-16}$ 48^{1} 49$^{1.1}$ 52$^{9-17}$ 53$^{1-10}$ 56$^{2-4}$ 58$^{3.3}$ 61$^{2.11}$ 62, 1. 63$^{6.6.8.10.15}$ 65, 2. 66. 1, 6. 67, 6. 68, 10. 69^{10} 71$^{11.12[16]}$ 72$^{4.11}$ 73$^{4.9-11.13.16}$ 74$^{1-6}$ 81$^{15.26.28.31}$ 82$^{[2]2.2}$ Aḥ. 6.12[12.25]139 Beh. [61]61. ברחרן Aḥ. 217. ברא 69 E? Aḥ. 2[44]80. ברי Aḥ. 18[22] 30.30.82[96]127.129.149. ברלי 6^{12}&c. 73^{9}. ברך 6^{5} 68, 10. Aḥ. [20]81. ברלך 6^{13}. ברה 30^{7} 31^{6} 49^{4} Aḥ. 1.5.12 Beh. [23] 62? ברה 28^{13} [39^{2}] Aḥ. 8. בנן plur. 15$^{32.32.33}$ 25^{17} Aḥ. 3.106. בני 20$^{[2]3.8.13.17.19.20}$ 25^{9} 30^{29} [31^{28}] 71^{7}. בני ביתא 30^{3}. בני 10^{15} 13^{8} 14^{9} 25$^{9.12.13}$ 28^{9} 71^{10}. בניך 9$^{7.9.12}$ 10^{8} 28$^{7.8.11.12}$ 34^{7} 47^{1} Aḥ. 127.129; for בניכם 25^{5}. בניכי 8$^{9.11.13.15}$ 13^{7}. בנוהי 40^{1} [41$^{1.9}$] 54^{8} 71^{15} בניה 15^{34} 68, 8. בנין (our sons) 20$^{10.13}$ 30$^{15.26}$ 31^{14}. בניכם 20$^{11.13.14}$ 25^{16}.

ברה daughter: 1^{5} 5^{8} 6$^{12.13}$ 8$^{10.12}$ 14^{8} 25$^{10.12.13.14}$ 28$^{8.10}$ 43$^{5.9}$ 47^{2} 63^{3}. בראלי 14^{9}. ברת 1$^{1.2}$ 8^{35} 10$^{2.2.3}$ 14^{2} 20^{3} 25$^{3.7}$ 18^{1} 22^{2} &c. 35^{3} 43$^{[1]2.11[13]}$ 64, 24. 65, 5. 68, 2, 4 73^{8} 81$^{3.11.37}$. ברתי 9$^{4.7.8}$ 13^{4}. ברתך 15$^{3.5[6]}$ 48^{2}. ברתה 8^{3} 13$^{2.21}$ 18^{2} 39^{2}. בנתן (our daughters) 20$^{10.13}$. בנתכם 20^{13}.

ברא desert: [Aḥ. 208].

ברא outside Aḥ. 109.

בראמן? 81^{10}.

ברברי ב׳ דרגי 13^{19}.

ברזי pr. n. Beh. [23]27[37.60].

ברכיא pr. n. 56^{3}.

ברכיה pr. n. 20^{17} 22^{130} 25^{19}.

ברק Aḥ. 101.

ברתא = בירתא 35^{2} Beh. 2[5.23.31.46].

בשר Aḥ. 104 [206]. בשרה Aḥ. 89.

בתולה Aḥ. 134.

ג (a measure) 2^{7} $24^{38\,41}$.
גבה Aḥ. 107.
גבר $13^{8\,11}$ 25^{11} 28^{14} 30^{28} 31^{27} Ah. 42. 98. 130 132 138 [159] 163. 163 164 [164] 177. לגבר לגבר 2^{7} 22^{1}. גברא Beh. 45. גברין plur 30^{16}. גברן $2^{[6\,7]\,7\,8}$ 3^{7} [12^{10}] 25^{14} 33^{5} 66, 1. Ah 37 [40] 62 גבריא 2^{13} 34^{4} $50^{4\,5}$ 64, 29 66, 1 Ah. [39] 56 [58 67] 77 [Beh 59].
גדוך ? 55^{6}.
גדול pr n. 20^{17} 25^{19} 28^{15} 29^{2} 56^{4} 65, 2.
גדול ב׳ אושע 13^{14}
גדול ב׳ בעדיה 25^{18}.
גדול ב׳ ברכיה 20^{17} 25^{13}
גדול ב׳ הו . . . 46^{14}
גדול ב׳ יגדל 6^{18}.
גדול ב׳ משלם ב׳ מבטחיה 22^{25}
גדול ב׳ שמוח 22^{28}.
גדליה pr n. 10^{22} 22^{101}.
גדליה ב׳ ענניה 6^{20}.
גהן: גהנת (1st sing.) Ah 13.
גו: בגו see ־ב; גוה Aḥ. 160.
גוברוה ב׳ מרדני [Beh. 61].
גומת pr. n. [Beh. 59].
גורנא 24^{41} 27^{5}.
גושביא 27^{9}.
גזר גזיר ptcp pass. Aḥ. 134.
גלגול pr n 10^{21}.
גלגל pr. n. 49^{1}.
גלד. גלדי Aḥ. 119.211.
גלי. גלין 1st pl 37^{8}. תגלי Aḥ. 141
גמא papyrus-reed: 15^{13}.
גמלא Ah 91
גמריה pr n. 2^{2} 22^{121} [33^{1}] 34^{5} $43^{[1]\,2\,11\,[18]}$.
גמריה ב׳ אחיו 6^{18} 11^{16}.
גמריה ב׳ מחסיה 8^{29} 9^{18} 22^{2}.
גן 81^{41}
גנב. גניב ptcp pass. 38^{4} גנב (adj.) Ah 125 [196]. גנבה Aḥ 84.221 ? גנבית 37^{5}.
גנזא $26^{4\,13}$ 69 B
גפא 73^{1}. גפיא 73^{18}.
גרב גרב $81^{8\,9\,83}$. גרבן $81^{7\,9\,42}$. גרבין $81^{10\,10\,43}$.
גרה Ah. [219] 219.
גרי. גרבי 14^{9}. גריתך 67, 3. גריתכי 14^{8}. יגרנך 6^{14} 67, 5 יגרנכי 1^{6} 13^{10} אגרנך 6^{12}! אגרנכי 14^{7}. אגרנכם 25^{10}. יגרונכי 1^{6} נגרכי 1^{4}.
גרמיך 71^{15}
גשש הגשש Haphel ? Ah 139
גתא [Aḥ. 79].

[ד]אנהי ? Aḥ. 161.
דבב law-suit: 6^{12} $8^{12\,14\,20\,22}$ $9^{13\,15}$ 13^{9} $14^{7\,9-11}$ $15^{26\,29}$ $20^{11\,16}$ 25^{10} $43^{4\,[6\,9]}$ 47^{4}
דבח דבחן 30^{28} 31^{27}. מדבחא [27^{24}] 30^{26} 31^{26} 32^{19} בית מדבחא 32^{3}.
דבק adjoin: 3rd fut. fem תדבק 5^{5}. דבק ptcp. 8^{6} $25^{5\,6\,8}$ 66, 7. דבקה ptcp. fem. 5^{4}.
דבר to lead 30^{8} 31^{7}.
דבר word. עלדבר $6^{6\,16}$ $28^{8\,10\,11}$ 71^{30}, and see על. עלדברה $6^{3\,8}$. עלדבר כן 40^{8}.

דבש? 37^{10}.
רגל $5^{2.3.9}$ $6^{3.4.9.10}$ 7^{13} 8^{2} 9^{2} $13^{2.10}$ 14^{3} 15^{2} 20^{2} 28^{2} $29^{2.2}$ 35^{2} [45^{2}] 66, 4. 67, 3. לדגלה 43^{2}. דגלן (our *degel*) 16^{2}. דגלא 9^{2} 20^{4} 65, 3. דגלן 27^{1}.
דגנא Aḥ. 129.
דדרש pr. n. Beh. [2]4.6[18.19].
דהב 10^{9}.
דוכל ב׳ אביהו (or רוכל) 2^{20}.
דומא pr. n. 14^{13}.
דורה 79^{2-4}.
דושכרתא 27^{3}.
דחל: דחלת 1st sing. Aḥ. 45. תדחל Aḥ. 54. נדחל 37^{7}.
די = זי: דילכי $13^{7.11.16}$.
דידי ב׳ אורי ב׳ מחסה 23^{14}.
דין law-suit, claim: [2^{17}] 6^{16} $8^{17.22.27}$ 10^{19} 18^{1} 20^{14} $25^{15.17}$ $28^{11.12.14}$ 35 d [46^{11}] 67, 3, 5. דין ודבב 6^{12} $8^{12.14.20.21}$ $9^{13.15}$ $13^{9.10}$ $14^{7.9-11}$ 15^{20} $20^{11.16}$ 25^{10} $43^{4[6-9]}$ 47^{4}. דינא 14^{3}. בדינה Aḥ. 198. דין ספרא 15^{31}; [report, account? 2^{11}]; law-court: 20^{4}. דינא 7^{7} 28^{9}; judge: 8^{13} $10^{13.19}$. דינא $16^{3.3.5.9}$ 42^{2}. דינן 28^{8}. דיני 1^{8} 16^{7} דיניא 6^{6} 8^{24} [$16^{4.6}$] 27^{9} [45^{4}] 80^{8} 82^{1}.
דיפרס pr. n. 81^{10}.
דכא this: 14^{6}. דכי 14^{9}.
דכי clean: דכין 21^{6} 27^{12}.
דכר remember: דכרו? 34^{6}.
דכר male: $15^{17.20}$.
דלה pr. n. = דליה? 41^{4}.
דלוי pr. n. $81^{26.41}$? 82^{2}.
דלח: תדלח Aḥ. 113.
דליה pr. n. 30^{29} 31^{28} 32^{1}.
דליה ב׳ חגי 82^{2}.
דם blood Aḥ. 87.211. דמה Aḥ. 89.120.
דמידת pr. n. 6^{6}.
דמן value: 30^{28}. דמי 13^{5} 15^{14} 29^{4} 30^{28} 31^{27} $36^{2.3.3.4}$ 36 b 44^{9} 45^{5} 66, 12? 78^{4} 81^{119}. דמוהי 13^{3} 36 b. דמיהם 45^{6}.
דמנדין pr. n. 20^{4}.
דנה = זנה 16^{9}.
דנה loan? 10^{23}.
דנח: ידנח Aḥ. 138.
דעך: ידעך Aḥ. 147.
דפרום pr. n. 81^{83}.
. . דרג pr. n. 51^{7}.
דרג (verb): דרגת (2nd. sing.) Aḥ. 128. תדרג [Aḥ. 126].
דרגא pr. n. 5^{18}.
דרגי pr. n. 13^{19}.
דרגמן ב׳ חרשין $6^{2.7.8.17[22]}$ $8^{5.23.26}$.
דרי planks? 26^{20}.
דריהוש Darius: $30^{19.21.30}$ Beh. [7.12. 16.17.22.34] 37[39.48–50.59], p. 266.
דריוהוש Darius: 20^{1} $21^{3[10]}$ 25^{1} 26^{28} 27^{2} 28^{1} $29^{1.5}$ $30^{2.4}$ $31^{2.4.19}$ 32^{7} [67, 10].
דריוש Darius: 1^{1}.
דרך (verb) Aḥ. 191. דרכי ptcp. Aḥ. 108.
דשש: דששיא 30^{11}. דשיהם 30^{10}.
דתניא 16^{7}.

הא voici: $6^{7.7}$ 13^{13} 25^{4} $28^{3.5}$ $34^{2.4}$ 37^{7} 38^{5} [44^{6}] 54^{2} Aḥ. [16.18]89. 93.116.145.

האן where: להאן זי 15^{25} (or לה אן זי as in 15^{29}).

הר = הו Aḥ. 128.

הדדנורי pr. n. 6^{19} 22^{23}.

הדיו ב׳ פטאסי 74^{5}.

הדר: הדיר Aḥ. 207. הררה Aḥ. 108.

הו $5^{1.12}$ $6^{1.14}$ $8^{1.14}$ $9^{[1]12}$ $10^{1.4}$ $13^{1.7.16}$ 14^{1} $15^{[1]21}$ $20^{1.7.15}$ 22^{6}&c. 24^{6} $25^{1.8.15}$ 28^{1} $35^{4[7]9}$ $37^{3.3.6}$ $38^{7.9}$ [$42^{3.14}$] $43^{[1]8}$ 44^{6} [45^{1}] 67, 4. 71^{11} 72^{18} 73^{2} Aḥ. 18[18]21.24[27]28.36[40.42]44. 46.53[60.69]79.84.88.100.107. 107[109]115.128(הר) 138.171 [196]209.209 [Beh.24]. Demonstrative 22^{120}.

הודו pr. n. 12^{4} 22^{39} 34^{3} 42^{6}.

הודויה pr. n. [1^{9}] 2^{2} [3^{2}] 19^{10} $22^{112.127}$ 44^{2} $46^{[11]16}$ 65, 18.

הודויה ב׳ גדליה 10^{22}.

[הודוי]ה ב׳ זכור 22^{3}.

הודויה ב׳ זכור ב׳ אושעיה 20^{18}.

הודיזיא pl. n. [Beh. 35].

הוה 8^{3} 10^{5} 15^{8-10} $26^{3.9}$ 27^{4} $30^{6.7.9.12.12.25}$ 31^{5} $32^{5.8.11}$ 33^{9} [37^{8}] 41^{3} $43^{7.8[10]}$ 65, 3. 82^{8} Aḥ.[2]4.5.15[26.43] 72[77]140 Beh. [24.25.34.35] 45[47]. הות 3rd fem. 6^{7} Aḥ. [28]43 Beh. 16.21a*[48]. הוית 1st sing. 13^{4} $41^{3.4}$ Aḥ. [7.22] 48. הוו 17^{8} $27^{[11]}$ $29^{[3]}$ $30^{9.10}$ 31^{9} 80^{5}? Aḥ. [56]60 Beh. 59. הוין 30^{15} 31^{11}. יהוה 8^{17} [9^{11}] $11^{5.9}$ $28^{12.13}$ 30^{27} 68, 1. Aḥ. 2[6.6]19[20.21] 88.97.161.164. יהוי [20^{4}] 32^{3} 34^{7} 67, 12. 70^{2} Aḥ. 110 [205]. תהוה 3rd fem. 11^{3}. תהוי id. Aḥ. 100. תהוה 2nd sing. Aḥ. 149 Beh. 50.55. אהוה 11^{7}. יהוון 27^{7} 71^{27}. יהוו [Aḥ. 11]. תהוו 38^{2}. הוי imperat. 30^{3} 31^{3}. הוו 21^{6}. הוין ptcp.? Aḥ. 167.

הום them: בהום 30^{17}.

הומרת name of a *degel* 8^{2} 9^{2}.

הוריא pr. n. 22^{72}.

הושע pr. n. $2^{18.22}$ [3^{21}] 5^{17} 6^{18} $22^{56[80]101}$ $25^{17.20}$ 29^{1} 34^{3} 39^{1} [$42^{1.15}$].

הושע ב׳ אוריה (= הושעיה) 25^{5}.

הושע ב׳ ביתאלנורי 22^{6}.

הושע ב׳ הודויה 1^{9} $2^{1.18.22}$ [3^{21}].

הושע ב׳ זכור 22^{98}.

הושע ב׳ חרמן 22^{4}.

הושע ב׳ יגדל 8^{34} [9^{22}].

הושע ב׳ יתום 33^{4} 34^{5}.

הושע ב׳ מנחם 22^{71}.

הושע ב׳ נתום 34^{5}.

הושע ב׳ נתון 33^{5} 22^{47}.

הושע ב׳ סגרי 22^{61}.

הושע ב׳ פטחנום 6^{17}.

הושע ב׳ פלליה 8^{30} 9^{17}.

הושע ב׳ רעויה 8^{33} 9^{21}.

הושעיה pr. n. 5^{19} 18^{4} 40^{1} 46^{13}.

הושעיה ב׳ אוריה 25^{2}.

הושעיה ב׳ חנניה 22^{7}.

הושעיה ב׳ נתן 40^{5}.

הוש[עיה ב׳ נתן] ב׳ הושעיה ב׳ חנניה 22^{7}.

הושעיה ב׳ צפניה 52^{13}.

הי 5^{4} 8^{25} 9^{9} 15$^{4.18}$ 18^{3} Aḥ. [45]57. 95.95.98.103.118.

היו pl. n. Beh. 4.

היכלא Aḥ. 9.17.23.44.

הילל Aḥ. 41.

הימנותה see אמן.

הלך : תהך 3rd fut. fem. 15$^{25.28}$; 2nd fut. 71$^{13.22}$ Aḥ. 102. אהך 8^{22}. יהכון 10^{19}. מהלך Aḥ. 40. למהך? 54^{14}. הלכתך? Beh. 52.

הם = הום 18^{3}.

המדכריא 26$^{4[6]28}$.

המו 9$^{7.10.13}$ 10^{15} 26^{4} 69 B. [Aḥ. 169] Beh. 60; as object 13^{5} 15^{35} 28^{13} 30^{9} 42$^{6.10.10.12}$ 54^{6} 71^{13} Aḥ. 154. 162 [Beh. 8].

המונית 27^{4} 30^{5}.

המנה 43^{2}.

הן if: [2^{18}] 5$^{7.8.13}$ 7^{10} 8$^{20.26}$ 9$^{8.10.13}$ 10$^{6.7.14.15}$ 11^{7} 14^{8} 15$^{[29]33.35}$ 18^{3} 20^{12} 25^{12} 27$^{7.8[19.21]22}$ 28^{9} 29^{6} 30$^{23.27}$ 31$^{22.26}$ 33^{7} [35$^{6.11}$] 42$^{4.5.7.8.10.11}$ 45^{7} 54$^{4.11}$ 66, 16 Aḥ. 82.82.103.115.123. 124.124[128.130]149[160]171. 192 [Beh. 58]; that? [7^{4}]; see also להן.

הנלו if: 37^{8} [38^{10}] Aḥ. 35[66]81.

הנבגא 43^{9}.

הנגית 43^{9}.

הנדונה 26$^{5.17}$.

הנרז 13^{4}. הנדיז (verb?) 27^{7}.

הני : מהני 81^{44}.

הצול pr. n. 22$^{26.29.30.129}$ 39^{3}.

הצול ברת הודויה 22^{112}.

הצול ב׳ זכריה 25^{5}.

הצול ב׳ חגי ב׳ הצול 22^{30}.

הצול ב׳ שמעיה 22^{26}.

הרגלתי pr. n. 81$^{56.86}$.

הרוחתי pl. n. Beh. [37]39[46.49].

ו־ and, passim.

ואסה 42^{8}.

וידרנג = ודרנג 25^{4}.

והומים pr. n. Beh. 7.8[8]10.11.

וזיבא 81$^{31.32.32}$.

וחפרעמחי pr. n. 26^{1}. וחפרימחי 26^{24}.

וחשתב pr. n. 51^{5}.

ויזדת = וידזת Beh. 22*.

וידרנג pr. n. 20^{4} 25^{2} 27^{4} 30$^{5.6.16}$ 31$^{5.6.15}$ 32^{6} 38$^{3.4}$.

ויזדת = ויודת Beh. 40.

ויונה pr. n. [Beh. 38–40.46].

ויזדת pr. n. Beh. [22.27.29.30.32] 34[37].

וינדפרנה ב׳ ויספרה [Beh. 61].

ויספרה pr. n. [Beh. 61].

ונה pr. n. 22^{40}.

ונפר pr. n. 24^{36} 66, 10.

ורד ב׳ זותי 24^{15}.

וריזת name of a *degel*: 5$^{2.3}$ 6$^{4.10}$ 13^{2} 14^{3} 15^{3} [28^{2}].

ושחי pr. n. [16^{1}?] 22^{133} [54^{1}].

ושחי ב׳ זרמר 22^{134}.

וששן pr. n.? 69^{13}.

ושתן pr. n. 14^{13}.

זא this (fem.) 21^{3} 30^{17} 42^{7} 71^{14} 80^{6} 81$^{39.112}$.

זברי pr. n. 65, 7.

זבדיה pr. n. $22^{13[14]}$ 52^{15} 81^{2}.

. . . זבים pr. n. 24^{2}.

זבמן pr. n. 51^{12}.

זבן buy : זבן יזבן 42^{6} 71^{5}? זבן (imperat.) 42^{5}. Pa. sell זבן 42^{11}. זבנו 42^{5}. תזבנון $25^{11,14}$. לזבנה 9^{6}.

זרמר pr. n. 22^{134} (or זרמור).

זהב (= דהב) 30^{28} 39^{4} Aḥ. 193. זהבא 30^{12} 31^{11}.

זהר : יזהר [Aḥ. 163]. אזדהרו imperat. 21^{8}. אזהר Beh. 51.

זוזן $81^{[19]22,27,44,124}$.

זוית 5^{5}. זויתה 5^{4}.

זול : זולו imperat. 38^{8}. זולא ? 81^{33}.

זומי pr. n. 82^{3}.

זון $10^{10,17}$.

זותי pr. n. 24^{15}.

זי (relative) $1^{3,3,6,6}$ $3^{12,14,15,20}$ $4^{4,8}$ $5^{4,4,5,10,10,12-14,20,20}$ $6^{2,3,5,8,14,16,22}$ $8^{9,11,12,17,19,23[25]}$ $9^{[2]3,10,12}$ $11^{3,4,6,7,9,10,16}$ $13^{3,4,6,9,10,12[12]}$ $14^{6,8,14}$ $15^{19,24,26,27,29,32}$ $20^{7,14,15,19}$ $25^{7,8,11,11,14,14,15,20}$ $28^{3,5,7,7,9,10,12,12,13}$ $30^{1,3,5-7,9-11,12,16-18,24,27,28,30}$ $31^{7,9,23,26,27,29}$ $32^{4,6,10}$ 33^{5} &c. בזי 30^{23} 37^{4}. כזי $6^{1,7}$ $8^{24,25}$ 13^{4} 27^{2} 28^{13} 40^{2}; see also כ־. לקבל זי 30^{25} 32^{10} Aḥ. 52. 68 [75]. מן זי $8^{9,19}$ $13^{8[16]}$ 20^{14} 25^{9} $28^{7,12}$. עד זי 30^{27}. זילי 5^{4} $6^{5,7}$ $8^{3,25}$ 9^{3} 13^{8} 28^{8} 43^{10} 44^{6} $81^{7,32,119}$ Aḥ. 48 [57]61.63 Beh. [3]5[29.32.41.43]. זילך $5^{3,4,6,11,12}$ 6^{15} [7^{9}] 9^{2} 28^{10} 40^{4}. זילכי 1^{7} 8^{12}. ויליכי 8^{19}. זילה 5^{10} 8^{26} Aḥ. [90]144. 172. זילכם 20^{14} $25^{8,16}$ 54^{12}.

זילנא זילן 3^{15} $20^{10[13]}$ 30^{20}. $81^{32,38}$.

זי (genitive particle) $2^{6,6}$ &c. 3^{18} $5^{2,2}$ 6^{11} &c.

זיוך 37^{3}.

זין : זניהום 31^{8}.

זך = זילך 5^{7}.

זך this : $5^{4-6,10,12,14}$ $6^{7,7,12-14,16}$ $8^{11,12,16,16,19,24,25,27,27}$ $9^{1,5,8,12,14}$ $13^{7,9,13,15}$ $25^{8,11,15}$ $26^{[4]22}$ $27^{6[8]8[11]}$ $28^{7,10,11}$ $30^{6,9,10,12-14,16,17,22,23,27}$ $31^{6-10,12,13,15,16,20,21,23}$ $32^{6,10}$ &c. בזך hereupon : 38^{9}.

זכי $1^{4,6}$ 30^{21}. זכם 9^{2} 20^{4} 65, 3. אלך 16^{4} 20^{8} 27^{8} 30^{11} 31^{10} 71^{15} Aḥ. [39]56.58.67[69] Beh. 20. אלכי $14^{5,8}$ 13^{6}.

זכור pr. n. $10^{2,24}$ 15^{38} $22^{3,98,107}$ 23^{12} 42^{5} 46^{12} 48^{1} $63^{3,8}$ 68, 2. $81^{22,23}$.

זכור ב׳ אושעיה 20^{18}.

זכור ב׳ אטר 13^{3}.

זכור ב׳ הודויה ב׳ זכור 22^{3}.

זכור ב׳ צפניה 8^{32} 9^{20}.

זכור ב׳ שלם 13^{20}.

זכי (= דכי) innocent : Aḥ. 46[61].

זכם that very, the same ; 9^{2} 20^{4} 65, 3.

זכר remember : יזכר [Aḥ. 64]. יזכרני Aḥ. 53. יזדכר [27^{10}]. זכרן memorandum : $32^{1,2}$ $61^{1,10}$ 62, 1. $63^{10,12,14}$ 68, 11.

זכריא pr. n. $22^{66,67}$.

זכריה pr. n. 5^{5} 11^{15} $23^{10,15}$ 25^{5} 52^{10} 55^{3}.

זכריה ב׳ זבדיה 52^{13}.

זכריה ב׳ משלם 8^{30} 9^{13}.

זכריה ב׳ נתן $8^{7.29}$ 9^{17}.

זלוע 15^{13} 36^{4}.

זן זן 17^{3}.

זנה $2^{[9]10,11}$ $3^{9[10]}$ 5^{16} 6^{17} $8^{9.18.22.29}$ $9^{14.16}$ $10^{9.12.14.14.15.16.19.20.20}$ 11^{16} $13^{5.7.12.17}$ $14^{7.11}$ $15^{4.31[37]}$ $18^{2.4}$ $20^{9.10.16}$ 22^{1} $26^{[3]5.21.23}$ $27^{3.10}$ $28^{3.5.7.15}$ $29^{4.6.6}$ $30^{17.20.28.30}$ $31^{17.19[20]}$ 34^{2} &c. כזנה [27^{21}] $28^{4.6}$ 30^{15} 37^{9}. זנך 8^{8} 9^{6}. אלה 2^{13} 7^{10} 13^{13} 18^{2} 20^{15} [21^{9}] 28^{19} [Aḥ. 1.62] Beh. 59. כאלה [Aḥ. 26.29].

זעק 71^{17}.

זער 72^{5}? בזעריהם Aḥ. 106. זעיר Aḥ. 101,114.145 Beh. 24. זעירא [Beh. 30.45]. זערא 81^{41}. זעירן 37^{7}.

זעררתא Aḥ. 105.

זפרה pr. n. 81^{105}.

זפרות pr. n. 24^{5}.

זרמד pr. n. 22^{134} (or זרמר).

זרניך $26^{[5]17}$. זרניכא 26^{21}.

זרע 13^{8}. זרעה Aḥ. 85. זרען 68, 5.

זרק: מזרקיא 30^{12} 31^{11}.

זרת 36^{3}.

זת = זאת? כזת 18^{3}.

ח abbreviation for? 15^{15} $24^{38.41}$.

חבא: תחבא (3rd sing.) [Aḥ. 134].

חבל 30^{14} [Aḥ. 27]. חבלך Aḥ. 44. יחבל Aḥ. 36. מחבל $27^{2[11.13]}$. חבלן? 37^{10}.

חגי pr. n. 12^{5} $22^{63.99}$ 28^{16} 33^{3} 42^{15} 61^{2} $81^{15.24.25}$ [82^{2}].

חגי ב׳ בארי 53^{3}.

חגי (ב׳) דיברם 81^{19}.

חגי ב׳ הוריא 22^{72}.

חגי ב׳ הצול $22^{29.30}$.

חגי ב׳ יוניה 19^{8}.

חגי ב׳ מיכא 22^{81} 23^{12}.

חגי ב׳ מפטחיה 22^{133}.

חגי ב׳ נחום 34^{3}.

חגי ב׳ נתון 12^{1}.

חגי ב׳ פנוליה 18^{5}.

חגי ב׳ שמעיה 24^{3}.

חד one: 10^{6} 15^{28} $26^{[11]11.12.17.19.20}$ 27^{5} $29^{[3]5.6}$ 37^{3} [38^{9}] 61^{4} 77^{2} 81^{49} Aḥ. [33] 38 [61] 191.204 Beh. [22] 38. חד אלף 30^{8}. חד כחד 10^{7}. לחד 24^{28-30} $26^{14-16.18-20}$. חדה 15^{28} $27^{6.17}$ $30^{19.23}$ $31^{18.28}$ 37^{12} 41^{5} 79^{2}. כחדה 28^{3}.

חדי: חדית 1st sing. 41^{2}. יחדה Aḥ. 106. חדה ptcp. 30^{3} 31^{3} 70^{2}.

חרת: 8^{15} 13^{12} $15^{7.9.16}$ 36^{1}. חרתה $36^{2.3}$. חרתן $26^{10.14}$.

חוב: נחוב 2^{15}. חיבה ptcp. fem. 18^{3}.

חוט $15^{25.28}$.

חוי Pa. חוינא (showed us) 31^{15}. תחוה 2nd pers. Aḥ. 96. יחוונ[א] 34^{7}. יחונהי? Aḥ. 102. נחוי 26^{7}. Ha. החוין (showed us) 30^{16}; (we showed) 26^{7}. יהחוה 69^{1} Aḥ. 93. תהחוי [Aḥ. 208].

חור pr. n. 23^{3} 24^{8} (?) $38^{4.6.8.8}$.

חור ב׳ אסכשית 53^{7}.

חור ב׳ יעולן 24^{16}.

חור? ב׳ נורישוש 24^{13}.

חורי pr. n. 23^{9} $37^{13.15}$.

חורי ב׳ ונה 22^{40}.

חו[רי] ב׳ מנחם ב׳ פוסי 22^{79}.

חורי ב׳ שלם 22^{85}.

חזי Ah. 94. חזני [Ah. 40.41]. חזית 1st pers. Ah. 14. חזין 30^{17} 31^{16}. יחזה [Ah. 163]. תחזה 68, 3. אחזה Ah. 205. יחזון [Ah. 63]. חזי imperat. 30^{23} 31^{23} 41^{6} Ah. 101 Beh. 54. חזו 38^{5}. חזה ptcp. Ah. 125. למחזה Ah. 37.63.108. יתחזי [21^{9}]. מתחזה Ah. 106. מחזי 15^{11}.

חטא sin: Ah. 128? חטאיך Ah. 50.

חטא arrow: חטך Ah. 126.128. חטֵה [Ah. 191].

חטב 15^{7}.

חטה wheat? 67, 13.

חטר Ah. 81. חטרן 69^{6}.

חיה: יחיה 49^{3} Ah. 86. תחיה (2nd sing.) [Ah. 82]. תחיי [Ah. 55]. Ha. החיתך Ah 51. יהחיני Ah. 54. חיא living 70^{2}. חין Beh. 1.6.11[14.21.30.33.42. 44], p. 266. חיא [Beh. 48]. חין life 30^{3} Ah. 11. חיַי $8^{3.8}$.

חילא [2^{10}] 20^{5} $21^{[2]4.11}$ 22^{1} $24^{33[39]42.47}$ $25^{2.4}$ $27^{7.20}$ 30^{8} 37^{1} [38^{12}] 80^{5} Beh.[3]5[7.13]13[15.19]20*23–32[37]39–41[43.45.46], pp. 266, 267. חיל אחור Ah. 55.61. חיל $80^{4.6}$ Ah. 137. חילי [Beh. 48]. חילך 71^{13}.

חכם Pa. Ah. 1. חכמתה 1st pers. Ah. 9 [19]. חכֵּמֵה Ah. 10. חכמָה Ah. 92.169. חכמתא Ah. 146. חכמתי Ah. 19. חכמתך [Ah. 147]. חכמתֵה Ah. 94. חכמתהם Ah. 94. חכים Ah. 1. 28.35.178. חכימא Ah. 12.42.

חל? 81^{40}; = חלר(ן) 81^{41} &c.

חלא sand 26^{7} Ah. [66]111.

חלא part of a boat $26^{12.12[15]20}$.

חלי: תחלי Ah. 148. Ha. יהחלה Ah. 188. חליה Ah. 131.

חלל: תתחלל Ah. 168.

חלף: יחלף 71^{14} Ah. 18.

חלף in exchange for: 1^{3} $9^{10.11}$ $13^{4.6}$ $44^{8.9}$ Ah. 5.62.69. חלפיך Ah. 21. חלפן 83^{4}.

חליפתהם? 26^{13}.

חלק $28^{3.5.7.9.10.12}$ $82^{[9]12}$. חלקא $28^{3.5}$. חלקה 28^{14}. חלקן $82^{7[10]}$.

חלקיה pr. n. 52^{17}.

חלר: חלרן $10^{5.6}$ $11^{2.4}$ 15^{14} $36^{3.4.4}$ 81^{20}.

חם? $15^{25.28}$.

חמא [Ah. 32]. חמתא Ah. 140.

חמן pr. n. 59.

חמם Ah. 140.

חמין: חמצת (2nd sing.) $45^{2[4]}$.

חמר was angry: 69 E? Ah. 47. חמר wrath Ah. 104.

חמר ass: 44^{8} Ah. 90. חמרא Ah. 91[110]110. חמרין 81^{29}. חמרן $54^{5.11}$ 68, 11. חמראן 81^{16}.

חמר wine: 30^{21} 31^{20} $72^{2.4.10.17}$ 81^{119}? Ah. 79[189]. חמרא 81^{20} Ah. 92.93.209.

חמיר leavened: 21^{7}.

חמישה $26^{12.14-16.11}$ 65, 7. חמשת 81^{88}. חמשן $26^{14.15}$.

חן Ah. 132.

חנוב god-name 27^{3,8} 30^{5}.

חנום god-name 13^{15} 34^{2}? 38^{7}.

חנט : חטן 49^{2}. חנטן 81$^{2-1.23.25.30.131.136}$. חנטתא Aḥ. 129. חנטא 81^{28}.

חגיה pr. n. 81$^{11.37.127}$.

חנך : חנכה Aḥ. 115.

חנמו pr. n. 53^{5}.

חנמיא? 75^{2}.

חנן 26$^{11.14}$ 62, 1? חנניא 26^{19}.

חנן ב׳ חגי 28^{16} 61^{2}.

חנן ב׳ עוריה 62, 1.

חנן ב׳ פחנם 23^{5}.

חנני pr. n. 2^{3}.

חנניה pr. n. 21$^{2.11}$ 22^{7} 38$^{7.8}$.

חנם ב׳ פטאסי 74^{6}.

חנת Aḥ. 83.

חסין? 68, 10.

חסן : Ha. החסן 20^{7}. נהחסן 28^{14}. החסנהי imperat. 8^{26}. החסנותה 44^{7} [65, 3]. מהחסן 7^{2} 8^{2} 16^{2}. מחס[נן] 80^{5}. מהחסנן [3^{3}] 26^{3} [33^{6}]. חסניא 27^{11}. כחסן 7$^{5.5.9[9]}$. חסין 26^{13} Aḥ. 79.105. חסינה Aḥ. 159.

חסר : חסרה ptcp. 27^{7}. חסרן 38$^{9.10}$. חסיר [Aḥ. 131].

חפוש? 26$^{18-20}$.

חפימו pr. n. 73^{16}.

חצן 15^{16}. חוצן 20^{6}.

חקלא [16$^{2.4}$].

חרא Beh. 34[35.47]. בר חרן Aḥ. 217. חרי 30^{19} 31^{18}.

חרב 71^{13} Aḥ. 113. בחרבי Aḥ. 174. חרבה 80^{4}.

חרוין pr. n. 17^{6}.

חרומי 6^{2}. חרומיא 8^{23}.

חרמביתאל god-name 7^{7}.

חרמן pr. n. 22^{4}.

חרמן ב׳ אושע 12^{2}.

חרמנתן ב׳ ביתאלנתן ב׳ צחא 18^{4}.

חרנופי pr. n. 38^{5}.

חרש deaf Aḥ. 216.

חרשא (זי נחש) 81$^{37.38}$.

חרשין pr. n. 6$^{2.22}$ 8$^{5.23}$.

חשבן 81^{3}.

חשיארש Xerxes 5^{1} 64, 20, 29.

חשירש Xerxes 2^{1}.

חשך restrain : Ha. תהחשך Aḥ. 81.

חשך : חשוכא darkness Aḥ. 125.

חתחור month Athyr 28^{1}.

חתילן? 37^{10}.

חתם : חתמו imperat. 21^{9}. חותם 76^{1}.

טבה pl. n.? 81^{45} 82^{3}.

טביא gazelle : Aḥ. 120.

טבת month Tebeth : 26^{28} [Beh. 42].

טוריא Aḥ. 62[69].

טיב : טיב לבב 2^{9} 14^{6} 15^{15} 20^{9} 43^{7} 67, 5. טב לבב 15^{5}. טיבת Aḥ. 67. טב 22^{135} 27$^{19.21[22]}$ 30^{23} 31^{22} Aḥ. 86.109.115[123]152[157] 159.163–5. טבה Aḥ. 57. 123. טבתא Aḥ. 9.24.42. טבתך 30^{24} 31^{23}. טבן Aḥ. 14. 113.157[157]. טובך? Beh. 55.

טלל : בטלל 38^{5}. בטללה p. 265, 4. בטלה זי Beh. [2]5.13[20]28[41. 43], pp. 267, 269. מטלל 30^{11} 31^{10}. טללך 71^{15}.

טלפחן $2^{4.6}$ $3^{5.6.8}$.

טמאכו ? 81^{40}.

טסן 26^{16}.

טסתן pr. n. 22^{83}.

טעם verb: טעמת 1st sing. Aḥ. 105. יטעמנהי Aḥ. [86]209. טעם noun 26^{23} 34^{7}. שים טעם $26^{22.23.25}$ 27^{21}. טעמא [Aḥ. 105]. טעמך 41^{7}.

טען: טענת 1st sing. Aḥ. 111. טענו [45^{4}]. טענוך 6^{6}. יטעננהי Aḥ. 91. טען Aḥ. 91. Pe'il טעינת 1st sing. 8^{24}.

טף $26^{10.18}$.

טרפי[ד] Aḥ. 97.

יאדניה pr. n. 37^{17}.

יאוש pr. n. 22^{89} 39^{4} [40^{5}].

יאוש ב׳ אזניה 12^{8} 18^{5}.

יאו[ש] ב׳ פנוליה 13^{13}.

[יא]זניה pr. n. 52^{16}.

יאוניה ב׳ חלקיה 52^{17}.

יאזניה ב׳ שפטיה 52^{14}.

יאשיה ב׳ . . . 52^{9}.

יב Elephantine: [2^{1} 3^{3}] $6^{3.3.4}$ $7^{1.2}$ 8^{2} $10^{2.3}$ $20^{1.2}$ $25^{1.2}$ $27^{3.5.5.11}$ $28^{1.15}$ 29^{1} $30^{1.5-7.8.13.22.25}$ $31^{7.12.22.24}$ 32^{4} $33^{6.9}$ 34^{6} 35^{2} $43^{[1]2}$ 65, 6? 66, 6. 68[2]4.

יבל: יבלתך 1st sing. Aḥ. 48. נבל 2^{9}. בלני imperat. Aḥ. 52[71]. למובל 2^{13}. מובלא Aḥ. [90].

יגדל pr. n. 6^{18} 8^{34} [9^{22}] 22^{92}.

יד: ביד 22^{120} 24^{36} 26^{7} 38^{4} 44^{4} $81^{14.28.29.31}$. עליד 26^{21}. בידך $10^{12.14.19.20}$ 42^{13} Aḥ. 193. בידכי $8^{18.22}$ 43^{7}. ידה $28^{4.6}$. בידה $81^{32-35.37}$ Aḥ. 171. בידה $15^{6.7.25.28}$ $81^{26.38}$. ידי? Aḥ. 155. ידן (our hand) $2^{3[9]13}$ $3^{4(14)}$. ידכם 38^{9}. ידין (dual) 15^{8}: for דין 15^{26}. בידיך [42^{3}] Aḥ. 123. בידי Aḥ. 122.

ידניא pr. n. 14^{2}.

ידניא ב׳ גמריה 34^{5}.

ידניה pr. n. 6^{3} $8^{2.31.35}$ $9^{2.19}$ 11^{14} $13^{2.21}$ $21^{2.11}$ 22^{42} $25^{3.18}$ $30^{1.4.22}$ $31^{[1]3}$ 37^{1} $38^{1.12}$ 65, 2. 76^{3} 81^{34}. ינדיה 5^{2}.

ידניה ב׳ אסחור ב׳ צחא $20^{3.8.11[20]}$.

ידניה ב׳ גמריה 22^{121} 33^{1} 34^{5} (ידניא).

ידניה ב׳ הושע $25^{17.20}$.

ידניה ב׳ הושעיה ב׳ אוריה $25^{2.9.12}$.

ידניה ב׳ מחסיה 8^{31} 9^{20}.

ידניה ב׳ משלם 25^{18}.

ידניה ב׳ נתן $25^{3.8.12.21}$ $28^{2.3.6.15.17}$.

ידניה ב׳ ענתי 22^{108}.

ידע 30^{30} 31^{29}. אדע? Aḥ. 210. תדע 3rd fem. Aḥ. 187. ידע ptcp. Aḥ. 116.116[163]177.217. Ha. הודען 1st plur. 30^{29}. הודע imperat. Beh. 52. יתידע [27^{10}].

יה particle of address. Aḥ. 127.129.

יהב $8^{25[35]}$ 13^{3} 22^{1} 24^{39} 25^{7} $37^{12.13}$ 42^{10} $44^{8(9)}$ [$46^{8.11}$] $55^{2.6}$ 63^{16} [Aḥ. 74]. יהבה ? 40^{8}. יהבת 3rd fem. 13^{4}. יהבת 2nd sing. $2^{8[9.12]}$ 3^{14} 5^{3} 10^{3} Aḥ. 170. יהבתי [43^{4}]. יהבתהי 43^{7}. יהבת 1st sing. $8^{3.13.20}$ $9^{3.14}$ $13^{2.5.6.9.12}$ 15^{4} 18^{2} 29^{6} 35^{7} $43^{3.3(5)6}$ 45^{7} $47^{3.8}$ 69^{12} Aḥ. 169. יהבתה $8^{8.25}$ $13^{4.7.16}$. יהבו 1^{3} 27^{4} 31^{5} $81^{38.111}$. יהבן $1^{2.6}$ 37^{4}. יהבנה 1^{5} 17^{2}. הב imperat.

$42^{5.11}$. הבי 8^{18}. הבה 39^{4} 42^{6}. הבהי 13^{15}. הבו 38^{9}. יהיב 17^{3} $24^{18a.33.56.42}$ 69^{10} $73^{[4]8}$. היב = יהיב ? 72^{4}. יהיבא 68, 6. Aḥ. 22. יתיהב $26^{18.21.21}$. מתיהב ? 72^{1}.

יהה = יהו 13^{14}.

יההאור ברת שלומם 1^{2}.

יההדרי pr. n. 11^{13}.

יהו Ya'u $6^{4.6.11}$ $22^{1.123}$ 25^{6} 27^{15} $30^{6.15.24.26.27}$ $31^{7.24.25}$ 33^{8} 38^{1} $45^{[3]4}$ 56^{2}.

יהואור pr. n. 28^{16}.

יהוד Judaea 30^{1} $31^{(1)18}$.

יהודה pr. n. $81^{78.96.132}$.

יהודי $6^{3.9.10}$ 8^{2} [9^{2}] 10^{3} $43^{[1]}$. יהודיא $21^{2[4]11}$ 22^{1} [27^{20}]. יהודין $20^{2.3}$. יהודיא $30^{19.22.26}$ $31^{22.26}$ 38^{12} 42^{12}.

יהוחן ברת יגדל 22^{92}.

יהוחן ברת גדליה 22^{101}.

יהוחן ברת משלך $10^{2.21.23}$ $18^{1.4}$?

יהוחנן pr. n. 30^{18} 31^{17}.

יהוטל pr n. 22^{57} 23^{4}.

יהוטל ברת יסלח 22^{103}.

יהוישמע pr. n. 22^{126} 39^{2} 63^{6} 68, 10.

יהונתן pr. n. 18^{5}.

יהועלי ברת עמניה 22^{105}.

יהושמע ברת הושע ב׳ זכור 22^{98}.

יהושמע ברת חגי 22^{99}.

יהושמע ברת משלם 22^{87}.

יהושמע ברת נתן 22^{84}.

יהושמע ברת קון 22^{117}.

יהנתן pr. n. 2^{21}.

יוד $28^{4.5}$.

יום $1^{1.4}$ $5^{1.6.8}$ [6^{1}] $8^{1.18.20.26}$ $9^{1.8.18}$ 10^{1} $11^{3.10}$ 13^{1} 14^{1} $15^{[1]17.20.22.26.28}$ $21^{5.5[7.7.8]8}$ $24^{[33.34]34}$ 25^{1} 28^{1} 30^{21} $37^{2.15}$ [43^{1}] 45^{7} ? 61^{12} 72^{18} 76^{3} Aḥ. 168 : for יומי 31^{12}. יומא 8^{9} 14^{7} 15^{4} $20^{9.10}$ 22^{120} 28^{7} 30^{20} 31^{19} [35^{9}] $43^{4[8]}$ [67, 5]. יומן [$21^{5.6.9}$] $71^{4[24]}$ Aḥ. [14]39.49.52. יומי 30^{13} [66, 6]. יומיך Aḥ. 102 Beh. 58. יומיא 21^{9}.

יוניא pr. n. $81^{56.104}$.

יונתן pr. n. $81^{14[28]29}$.

יזן : מוזנא 15^{24}.

יזן ב׳ אוריה 8^{6} 25^{17}.

יזניה pr. n. 15^{38} 19^{8} 66, 10.

יזניה ב׳ אוריה 6^{9} 9^{2} 15^{38} ? $25^{4.13.20}$.

יזניה ב׳ פגוליה 25^{19}.

יזף : תזף 2nd sing. Aḥ. 130.130. זף imperat. Aḥ. 129. זפתא a loan : Aḥ. [111]130.130.131 [131]. זפת 10^{3}.

יחיי ב׳ . . בניה 81^{28}.

יחמול ברת [של]ם 22^{97}.

יחמול ברת פלטי ב׳ יאוש 22^{89}.

יחנן pr. n. 81^{9}.

יחנן ב׳ דלוי 81^{26}.

יטב : Ha. הוטבת לבבי 2nd sing. 6^{11}. הוטבתם לבבן 20^{8}.

יבולא ברת משלם 34^{4}.

יכל see כהל.

ילד : תלד 3rd fem. 15^{33}.

ימא swear 44^{2}. ימאתלה 1st sing. 8^{24}. ימאת 2nd sing. $6^{[4]8.11}$. ימאתי $14^{5.8}$. למומא 6^{6}. מומאה oath 6^{5} $14^{4.6.9}$ [44^{1} 45^{4}]. מומא 8^{24}. מומה 59.

ימא sea : 71^{20} Aḥ. 117.208.

ימן right hand: $28^{4.6}$.
ינדיה = ידניה 5^{2}.
יניא pr. n.? $81^{65.66.71.73.75.80.81.93.97[101]}$.
ינק: למונק Aḥ. 120. Hiphil? יניקנהי Aḥ. 92[93]. ינקיא children: 40^{8}.
יסדרם pr. n. $81^{84.92}$.
יסלח pr. n. 22^{103} 34^{3}.
יסלח ב׳ גדול 25^{19} 29^{2}.
יסלח ב׳ נתן 56^{4}.
יסף: Ha. יהוסף [Aḥ. 144]. יהוספון 26^{18}. הוספה imperat.? 26^{17}.
יסר: Ithp. יתסר Aḥ. 80?
יעא: מועא west: 8^{4} 13^{14} 66, 15. מועא שמש 8^{6}. מועה שמש 25^{6}. למוע שמש 6^{8}.
יעולן pr. n. 24^{16}.
יעט: יעט advisor Aḥ. [2]12[18.20.27.36]. עטה advice: Aḥ. 57. עטתא Aḥ. 42.57.[66]. עטתי Aḥ. [3.19]53. עטתה Aḥ. 28.43.55.60[64].
יצע: יצעון? Aḥ. 168.
יקד: יקדה ptcp. Aḥ. 103.
יקר: Ha. הוקר imperat. Aḥ. 98. הוקרת 2nd sing. Aḥ. 176. יקיר Aḥ. 93.108.111. יקירה Aḥ. 95. יקירתא Aḥ. 130.
ירושלם Jerusalem: 30^{18}.
ירח 1^{1} 2^{7} $10^{1.5.6}$ $11^{4.8}$ 13^{1} 15^{1} 20^{1} $[21^{4.5}]$ $.2^{121}$ 24^{34} $29^{1.5}$ $30^{4.19}$ 63^{16} 65, 5, 13. 67, 8. 72^{1} $[78^{1}]$ Beh. 32. ירח לירח 11^{4} 17^{3}. ירח בירח 11^{9}. ירחא $11^{3.4}$ 29^{6}. ירחן 45^{8}. ירחין 81^{21}.
ירע? ירעך Aḥ. 43.
ירת; ירתנה 3rd fut. 15^{21}. מיריתא 83^{29}.
ישב? pr. n. 81^{99}.
ישביה pr. n. 7^{2} $22^{61.69}$ 38^{1}.
ישביה ב׳ ברכיה 22^{130}.
ישוב pr. n. 22^{24}.
ישיב pr. n.? $81^{9.109}$.
ישם? pr. n. 83^{26}.
ישעיה pr. n. 5^{16} 8^{33} 9^{21}.
ישר 82^{12}. Ha. הושרתי 2nd fem. 39^{3}.
יתב 6^{2} Beh. 22. תב imperat. 9^{6}. תותב visitor: Aḥ. 112.
יתום pr. n. 12^{3} 33^{4} 34^{5}.
יתום ב׳ הדרנורי 22^{23}.
יתומה pr. n. 1^{2} 67, 3.
יתמא pr. n. 11^{1}.
יתנא pr. n. 57^{1}.
יתר: יתיר 30^{3} $[70^{2}]$. יתרא adverb? Aḥ. 96.

כ = כרש 36 b 63^{11}? 81^{61}.
כ = כסף $22^{21-30.33.37.39}$ &c.
כ־ adverb, passim. כזי $6^{1.7}$ $8^{[illegible]}$ 18^{2} $[21^{10}]$ $26^{[1]22.23.25}$ $27^{2.7}$ $30^{[illegible]}$ 31^{4} 32^{8} 33^{9} 37^{13} $38^{3.6}$ 40^{2} $41^{[illegible]}$ $42^{6.10-12}$ 45^{4} 71^{19} Aḥ. [2.7.13]14[21]30.36[41.47]62[76.77]97[131]163.198.201. כזנה 27^{18} 30^{15} 37^{8} and see זנה. כחד 10^{7} and see חד. כחסן $7^{5.6.8[9]}$ and see חסן. כעמלא 40^{2}. כען $9^{[illegible]}$ 18^{2} 27^{6} $30^{3.4.22}$ 31^{21} 37^{7} 38^{5} $41^{[illegible]}$ $42^{3.10}$ $80^{6.7}$ 82^{7} Aḥ. 51. עד כען

38^{7}. כענת 4^{6} [16^{9}] 37^{2}.
בעשק 16$^{5.8.9}$ and see עשק. כעת
17^{3} 21^{4} 26$^{1.22}$ 31^{3} 38^{3} [42^{1}] 54^{11}
65, 4. 76^{3} [Aḥ. 16]. ובעת 17^{2}
21^{3} [27^{19}] 39^{3} 56^{1}. כפם 5^{15}
6^{17} 8^{28} 9^{16} 10^{21} 18^{4} 43$^{[6]11}$ [45^{9}
46^{15}] and see פם.
כא 81$^{61.64.81.85.131}$ pl. באן 81^{106}.
באיה reproof [Aḥ. 83].
כבה : תכבה 2nd sing. Aḥ. 100.
כבלא 30^{16}. כבלוהי 31^{15}.
כבו Aḥ. 166. בביך Aḥ. 165.
כבר : כביר Aḥ. 136.147.
כבריתא 26^{21}. כברי 26^{17}.
כבש ptcp. Aḥ. 92.152.
כדא 37^{13}.
כדב : יכדב Beh. 50.51. כדב ptcp.
8^{17}. כדבא Aḥ. 133. כדבן
Beh. 51. מכדב Aḥ. 134.
כדבתא [Aḥ. 30] Beh. 56. כדבת
Aḥ. 132. כדבתה Aḥ. 133.
כדו pr. n. 2^{20} [3^{22}].
כהל : יכהל 5^{8} 43^{5}. יכל 1^{5} 13^{11}.
תכהל 2nd sing. Aḥ. 81. 3rd
sing. [18^{1}]. אכהל 5$^{6.11}$ 6^{12} [7^{10}]
14^{7} 25$^{9.10}$ 28^{7} 43$^{4.8}$ Ah. 17.
אכל 10$^{11.12}$ 13^{8} 15$^{31.35}$ 47$^{7.8}$
Aḥ. 26. יכהלון 8^{15} 20$^{11.11}$.
יכלון 10^{18}. נכהל 20^{10} 25^{10}
נכל 1^{4}.
כהן : כהנא 30^{18} 81$^{8.39}$. כהניא 30$^{1.18}$
[31^{1}] 38$^{1.12}$.
כוין 25^{6}.
כוכבי [Aḥ. 116].
כותא thus: Aḥ. 20.
כי Aḥ. [27]95.98.99[103]114.119.
122.123.132[132]138[143]168.
178.208.
כיא ב׳ אסבישו pr. n. 2^{19}.
כיבי 71^{2}.
ביחך month-name 72^{16}.
כנכרן = ככרן 50^{3} 83^{29}.
כל 2$^{5[6.13.16]}$ 3^{6} 6$^{5.16}$ 10$^{9.10.17}$ 11$^{6.7}$ 12^{19}
14$^{4.11}$ 15$^{13.19.24.27}$ 17$^{2.2.6}$ 20$^{2.3.16.19.20}$
21^{7} 22$^{5.19.31}$ 24$^{27-31}$ 25$^{3.21}$ 26$^{8.16}$ 28^{2}
30$^{2.3.14.16.16.17.22.23.27}$ 31$^{2.3.15.26}$ 33^{5}
35^{11} 35 d 37$^{2.2}$ [38^{2}] 39$^{1.1}$ 40$^{1.3}$
41^{1} [42$^{1.4}$ 43^{10}] 45$^{6.8}$ 46^{13} 48^{2} 49^{3}
56^{1} 58^{2}? 65, 4. 67, 7. 68, 3, 11, 12.
73$^{2.6.17}$ 75$^{5.9}$ 78$^{5.5}$ 82^{6} 83^{30} Aḥ.
[36]83.96–98.127.127[132]167.
כלא 26$^{[5]13.17}$ 30$^{11.12.12.29.30}$ 31$^{10.13.16.}$
$^{22.26.29}$ 41^{1} Aḥ. 43[56]61. כלך
[Aḥ. 166]. כלה 15^{20} Aḥ. [2]
12[18.28]55. כלכליה 39^{3}.
כלא restrain: כליתך 5$^{7.13}$. כלו
37^{15}. יכלא 5$^{9.10}$. אכלאנך 5^{8}.
כלין ptcp. 37^{14}. כלוהי ? 37^{13}.
כלביא 30^{16} 31^{15}.
כלכליה see כל.
כמר 13^{15}. כמריא 27$^{3.8[14]}$ 30^{5}.
כן 21$^{4[10]}$ 26$^{2.3[6]9.22}$ [27^{12}] 30$^{4.22.27}$
31$^{22.26}$ 33^{7} 37^{6} 38^{6} 69, 3. 69 B. 71^{13}
76^{1} 80^{7} Aḥ. [13.37]52[75.77]89.
99.116.145 Beh. [7.12.16.17.22.
34]37[48–50.59]. מנכן 20^{7}
41^{4}. עלדברכן 40^{3}. על כן
Aḥ. 117.187.
כנבוזי Cambyses 30^{13} 32^{5} 66, 1.
כנדור pl. n. Beh. 12.

כנדר?? 42^{11}.

כנופי pr n $26^{9\ 21}$ 50^{7}.

כנכר 26^{17} כנכרן 30^{28} 31^{27}. ככרן 50^{9} 83^{29}.

כנף כנפֵי Aḥ 171.

כנש: אתכנשו Beh. 1.4 8 10, p. 269 יתכנשון 71^{8}. יתכנשו [71^{26}]

כנתא: כנתה Ah. 90.163. כנתהם 17^{7}. כנותה 6^{6} $17^{1\ 1\ 5\ 6}$ $21^{2\ 11}$ $26^{[1\ 4]8}$ $30^{1.4\ 18\ 22}$ [31^{1}] 69^{13} 76^{2}. Ah, 56 67.

כנתן spelt 10^{10}.

כם cup: $61^{4\ 14}$. כסן 15^{12}. כסין $61^{1\ 3\ 13}$.

כסה hide Ah. 109. תכסה 2nd sing, Aḥ 103. אכסנכי Aḥ 118 יתכסון 38^{11}.

כסלו month-name: 6^{1} 8^{1} [9^{1}] 10^{1} 13^{1} 25^{1} [Beh. 20].

כסף 1^{7} $2^{15\ 15}$ 3^{17} $5^{7\ 7}$ $6^{14\ 15}$ $8^{14\ 14\ 21\ 21}$ $9^{15.15}$ $10^{3\ 5.5\ 9\ 23}$ $11^{1-3\ 7}$ $13^{5\ 6\ 11}$ $14^{3\ 10}$ $15^{5-8\ 10-14.23\ 24\ 31\ 34.36}$ $20^{12\ 15\ 15}$ $22^{1\ 1\ 2}$ &c. $25^{15\ 15}$ 27^{4} 28^{10} $29^{3\ 3}$ $30^{12\ 28}$ $31^{5\ 27}$ [33^{13} 34^{6}] $35^{3[4]9\ 9}$ 36^{2-4} 36 b 37^{12} $42^{2-4\ 7}$ $43^{3\ 3\ 6[11]}$ $44^{9.9}$ $46^{[9\ 10]}$ 47^{3} 49^{2} $61^{4\ 13\ 14}$ 62, 1. 63^{1} 65, 7. $78^{3\ 5\ 6}$ $81^{30\ 30}$ כסף צריף 5^{7} [42^{3}]. כספא $5^{10\ 13}$ 10^{14-16} 15^{13} 18^{2} 22^{120} $29^{4\ 6}$ 31^{11} $35^{4\ 7}$ 42^{6} $43^{[5\ 6]8-10}$ 48^{2} 65, 1, 14 67, 16. כספך $10^{7.11.12.18}$ $11^{4.8.8}$ [42^{4}] כספכי $35^{9[10\ 10]}$. כספה 71^{30}.

כספי $13^{18\ 19}$.

כסת · כסתך Ah. 205

כסתם pr. n 81^{88}.

כעס Ah, 189

כף hand: 15^{28}. בכפי 3^{21}. בפיך Aḥ. 103.

כף bowl 36^{4}; plur. כפן 15^{16}.

כפן hunger Aḥ. 188

כפר 37^{14}.

כצפה Aḥ. 101.

כצר: Ha. imperat. הכצר Aḥ. 127. כציר Aḥ. 127.

כרא see כדא.

כרבלה 55^{11}. כרבלן 57^{2}.

כרך. כרכיא $26^{[1]3[7]8}$.

כרם כרמיא Aḥ. 40.

כרסא. כרסאא Ah 133. כרסאה 6^{4}.

כרש Cyrus [Beh. 23].

כרש 10 shekels. 15^{6} 20^{15} 25^{16} $29^{3\ 5\ 6}$ 42^{2} 43^{3} 55^{3} 78^{6}. כרשן 1^{7} 2^{15} 5^{7} 6^{14} $8^{14\ 21}$ 9^{15} $13^{6\ 11}$ 14^{10} $15^{8\ 14\ 31\ 34\ 36}$ 20^{15} $22^{122\ 124\ 125}$ $25^{15\ 15}$ $26^{14\ 14\ 17.17}$ 28^{11} 34^{7} $42^{2\ 3[4]}$ $43^{6[11]}$ 47^{3} [46^{9}] 65, 7, 10. 66, 8. 68, 5. $81^{17\ 112}$.

כשי pr. n 53^{4}

כשי ב' עזור 23^{8}.

כשיטא Ah. 158.

כתב · $2^{18\ 22}$ $3^{20\ 21}$ $5^{15\ 20}$ $6^{16\ 22}$ $8^{23\ 26\ 27}$ 9^{16} 10^{20} 11^{16} $13^{3[6]16\ 17}$ $14^{11\ 14}$ 15^{37} 18^{3} $20^{16.19}$ $25^{17\ 20}$ $26^{23\ 25}$ $28^{14\ 17}$ $42^{4\ 14}$ [43^{11}·45^{9} 46^{15}] 50^{2} 59 66, 14. כתבת (3rd fem) 10^{23} [43^{13}] 68, 4 rev 81^{1}. כתבת (1st sing) $9^{4\ 14}$ $13^{9\ 12}$ [43^{5}] כתבתה 8^{17} [13^{12}] תכתב (2nd sing) 11^{6}. נכתב 28^{14}. כתיב [2^{17}] $5^{10\ 13}$ 10^{8} 17^{3} 35^{8} [$43^{10\ 10}$]

48^{2} 66, 2. כתיבן $2^{11.13}$ 18^{2} 25^{8} [66, 1].
כתון $42^{8.9.13}$. כתונה (his coat) Aḥ. 41.
כתל? pr. n. 22^{3}.
כתן 20^{5} 26^{14} 42^{10}. כתנא 26^{20}.
כתר : מכתר Beh. 6.11.
כתש : כתשת 2nd sing. 7^{5}. 1st sing. 7^{9}.

ל- marking object of verb, 5^{9} $13^{2.8}$ $15^{3.27}$ &c. שנת . . . לדריוש 1^{1} &c. לי 3^{10} 4^{1} 5^{3} 6^{4} &c. לך $5^{7.13}$ $6^{13.14}$ &c. for לכי 13^{16}. לכי $1^{2.5.6.6}$ $8^{3.8.12}$ &c. לה $5^{9.10}$ $6^{9.10.11}$ &c. לה fem. 18^{9}. לן 1^{8} 27^{2} &c. לכם $20^{12.14}$ $25^{10.11.14.15}$ &c. $38^{7.7}$ Aḥ. 57. להם 42^{4} &c. להן 34^{7} 37^{14}. לירח || 1^{1} &c. לכן 37^{8} : = על כן? [Aḥ. 122]. למחר [1^{4}]. לעלא Aḥ. 114. לקבל 8^{27} 82^{7} and see קבל.
לא $1^{4.5}$ &c.
לאם 46^{7}.
לבא lion Aḥ. 117.
לבב Aḥ. 65.98.163. טיב לבב 67, 5. לבבא Aḥ. 104.137. טיב לבבי 40^{3} Aḥ. 169. לבבי 14^{5} 15^{15} 43^{7}. הוטבת לבבי 6^{12}. לבבך Aḥ. 82.106. טב לבבך 15^{5}. לבבה Aḥ. [25]109.159. לבה? 71^{3}. טיב לבבן 2^{9} 20^{9}. הוטבתם לבבן 20^{8}. לבבהם Aḥ. 162.
לבנן בי זי לבנן [2^{16}] 3^{18} 10^{9}.
לבונה [27^{14}] 30^{21} 31^{21} 33^{11}. לבונתא 30^{25} 32^{9}.
לביש : ptcp. לבישן $30^{15.20}$ 31^{14}. לביש garment $15^{7.10}$. לבשך 68, 3 Aḥ. 171. לבשי 20^{5}. לבוש garment 14^{4}.
לבתך 41^{4}. לבתכם 37^{11}.
לג $81^{70.79}$. לגן $81^{62.63.65.66}$ &c.
להן but 8^{11} $9^{6.7.9}$ 27^{17} 33^{11} 34^{6} $37^{4.5}$ 82^{9}? [Aḥ. 97]. except 13^{12} $15^{32.32.38}$ Aḥ. 107.120.154.212?
לו, only in הן לו Aḥ. 81.
לובר $26^{13.13.17}$.
לוה : ילוה Aḥ. 164.
לוח $79^{3.4}$.
לוחי ב׳ מנכי 14^{13}.
לוט : ילוטנן Aḥ. 151[151].
לותהם? 17^{7}.
לחי : ילחון Aḥ. 124. לחיא the accursed 30^{7} 31^{6} 32^{6}, pl. 17^{6}? לחיה a curse Aḥ. 124. לחיתא Aḥ. 134[198]. לחיתי Aḥ. 139. לחה wicked Aḥ. 130.138[163. 164]200.
לחם 57^{2} $71^{[1]8}$ Aḥ. 33[72]86.189.
לחנא $63^{9.12}$.
לחש 71^{23}.
לילו pr. n. 28^{13}.
לם $10^{11.13}$ 17^{2} $26^{2[3]21}$ [27^{23}] 30^{5} [31^{5}] 32^{2} [44^{8}] Aḥ. 2 3.13.20. 26.39.45.54.57[58]60[70.110] 165 Beh. 39.
למה Aḥ. 36[104]119.126[173]201.
לסמקם pr. n. 81^{87}.

? לעתיך 81^{109}. מלעתין 81^{110}.
לף = אלף [24$^{38.41}$ &c.] 30^{28} 50^{9} 61^{17} 73^{3} 78^{4} Beh. 3.9[11]11,14[21] 21.42.
לקח 20^{6} [Aḥ. 98 ? ptcp.]. לקחת (2nd sing.) 7^{6} 10^{13}. לקחת (1st) 7^{3} 16^{4} [Aḥ. 8]. לקחו 27^{18} 30^{12} 34^{6}. ילקח Aḥ. [143]172. תלקחן 2nd sing. Aḥ. 119. יקחונה 67, 18. לקיחת Beh. p. 265, 1. למלקח 9^{11} 10$^{9.17}$. למלקחה 9^{9} 48^{3}. יתלקח 8^{17}.
לשן Aḥ. 105. לשנה Aḥ. 156.

מ = ? 81^{106}.
מ\פ = half 81$^{70.71}$ &c.
מאה 26$^{14.15.17}$. מאתא centuria [2^{11}] 3^{11}. מאת 2^{8} 22$^{19.20[31]}$. מאתה 2$^{6.10(10)}$. מאתין 26$^{13-16}$. מאותהם 80^{3}.
מאן 65, 1. Aḥ. 109. מאנן 72^{4}. מאני 20$^{5.5}$.
מאס : מאסת 2nd sing. [Aḥ. 170]. תמאס [Aḥ. 136].
מבטח ברת מחסה 8^{36}.
מבטחיה pr. n. 22^{25} 68, 4.
מבטחיה ברת מחסיה 8^{2} 9$^{3.7.10.12}$ 14$^{2.14}$ 20^{3} 25$^{3.7}$ 28$^{3.5.6}$. *See also* מפטחיה, מטחיה, מבטח, מפתח.
מגוש [Beh. 60].
מגר : מגרו 30^{14} [31^{13}].
מרדר Aḥ. 159.
מדי Media Beh. [12]12.12[25]26.
מדינה : מדינא 37^{6}. מדינתא 17$^{1.2[6]}$ 68, 6. 73^{14}. מדנתא 16^{7}.
מדינת נא 24$^{18b.36}$ 37$^{6[16]}$ 68, 11 r. מדינת 27^{9} [Aḥ. 70 Beh. 46].
מדלא 81$^{20.21}$. במידלה 81^{42}.
מה 38$^{6.8.9}$ Aḥ. 79[139]151,160,163. 177. מה טב Aḥ. 165.
מהיר skilled, Aḥ. 1.
מהר price of a wife 15^{4}. מהרה 15^{27}.
מות die; מית 5^{8} 62^{3} Aḥ. [4]210. מיתת (1st sing.) 10^{14}. ימות 15^{17}. תמות (3rd fem.) 15^{20}. (2nd sing.) Ah. 82. ימותן Aḥ. 174. מות death : מותא Aḥ. 106. מותי 8$^{8.8}$.
מזדיון 37^{6}.
מחא : אמחאנך Aḥ. 82. מחאה Aḥ. 83.
מחיר month name 24$^{[34.35]44}$.
מחסה (= מחסיה) pr. n. 5$^{9.12.20}$ 8^{36} 22$^{11.91}$ 23^{14}.
מחסה ב׳ אורי 22^{65}.
מחסה ב׳ ידניה 5$^{9.12.20}$ 8$^{35.36}$.
מחסה ב׳ יהוטל 23^{4}.
מחסה ב׳ ישעיה 5^{16} 8^{33} 9^{21}.
מחסיה pr. n. 6^{22} 8$^{29.31}$ 9$^{18.20}$ 22^{2} [34^{5}] 48^{3}, and see מחסה.
מחסיה ב׳ אסחור ב׳ צחא 20$^{3.8.11.20}$.
מחסיה ב׳ ידניה 5^{2} 6^{3} 8$^{1.18.28}$ 9$^{1.5.16}$ 11^{14} 13$^{1.17.17.21}$ 14^{2} 15^{2} 20^{3} 25$^{3.7.7.18}$.
מחסיה ב׳ נתן 25$^{3.8.21}$ 28$^{2.5.8.9.15.17}$, and see מחסיה ב׳ אסחור.
מחסיה ב׳ שיבה 45^{2}.
מחר : למחר [1^{4}]. מ׳ או יום אחרן 5$^{6.8}$ 8$^{18.20.26}$ 9$^{8.13}$ 15$^{17.20.22.26}$.
מחת 22^{82}.

מטא 7^{7} 10^{7} 35^{8} 38^{3} 83^{2}. מטאך
$28^{3.7.9.10.12}$. מטאני 28^{5}. מטאה
14^{5}. מטאת (3rd fem.) 41^{2}.
ממת 10^{6}. מטתכי 1^{4}. מטו
37^{15}. לממטה Beh. 8.12.
תמטא (3rd fem.) 42^{7}.
מחסיה ברת מטחיה (= מבט') 14^{10}.
מיכא pr. n. 22^{64}.
מיכה pr. n. 22^{22}.
מיכיה pr. n. 23^{18}.
מיכיה ב' יהוישמע 22^{126}.
מין 27^{7} Aḥ. [72]113.192. מיא
6^{11} 8^{8} 27^{8}.
מכי pr. n. 1^{11}.
מכל = מאכל 24^{35} 49^{4}.
מכם 81^{112}.
מכרא? Aḥ. 203.
מלא to be full 41^{4}. ימלא 71^{1}.
התמלא [Aḥ. 32]. תתמלא (2nd
sing.) 2^{17} $10^{11.17}$. ממלא Aḥ.
131. מלא full 82^{8} pl. מלין 37^{11}.
מלה see under מלל.
מלח salt Aḥ. 111.
מלח sailor 6^{11} 8^{8}. מלחא $2^{[2]}$ 5^{13}.
מלחם (= מלחמה) Aḥ. 99.
מלך king 30^{18} 66,6 Aḥ. 3–5[8]10.
11.13–15[20.23]32[37]100.100
[101]103.104[104.105]107.108.
Beh. 17[24]50. מלכא $1^{1.3}$ $2^{[1]12.}$
$^{14.16}$ [3^{13}] $5^{1.7}$ $6^{2.15}$ 7^{1} $8^{1.14.21}$ $9^{1.15}$ $10^{2.4}$
13^{1} $14^{1.10}$ $15^{1.2.5.7.9.10.15.35.36}$ $20^{1.15}$
$21^{3.8.10}$ $25^{1.7.16}$ [26^{28}] $27^{2.3.5}$ $28^{1.11}$
$29^{1.5}$ $30^{2.4.5.19.21.30}$ $31^{4.4.19}$ 32^{7} $35^{1.6}$
37^{14} $43^{[1]3[7]8[10]}$ [45^{1}]46^{10} 64, 18,
29. 65, 6. 68, 2. $71^{10-12.16.17}$ Aḥ.
[7.9.15]15.27[34]47.50.51.53.
55.[60]62[64.65]71[75]77[78]
Beh. [7.12.16.17.22.34]37[39.
48–50.59], p. 269, 3. מלכי
31^{12}. מלבותא Aḥ. 95. מלוכתא
6^{1}.
מלכיה pr. n. 8^{31} 9^{19}.
מלכיה ב' זכריה 11^{15}.
מלכיה ב' ישביה $7^{2.7}$.
מלכיה ב' יתום ב' הדדנורי 22^{23}.
מלל 69^{2}. ימלל 69^{11}? ממלל
Aḥ. 100.178. מלה 37^{15} $38^{6.6}$
40^{4} Aḥ. 93[96]98.109. מלת מלך
Aḥ. 100.104. מלתא [Aḥ. 22].
מלין 37^{9}. מלן Aḥ. [26]29.92.
מלי [Aḥ. 1]. מלי Aḥ. 4
מלוהי Aḥ. [2. 28] 43.60.114.
מליהם 42^{13}. מליא 30^{29} 31^{28} 71^{12}.
מן pronoun Aḥ. [6.6]94? 107. 139.
140.140.161. מן זי $8^{9.19}$ $13^{8.16}$
20^{14} 25^{9} $28^{7.12}$ 37^{4}.
מן preposition $5^{5.5}$ 6^{15} $7^{5.9}$ $8^{4.4.9}$ $9^{7.9.12}$
$11^{6.6}$ 13^{8} $14^{6.11}$ $15^{4.18.21.25.28-30.35}$
$16^{2[6]}$ $20^{3.6.9.10.15}$ $21^{3.5[8.8]}$ $25^{4.13.16}$
$26^{1.27}$ $27^{5.9[11]20}$ $28^{7.11.11}$ 29^{3} $30^{3.6.13.}$
$^{16.19.21.28}$ $31^{6.12.15[20]27}$ 35^{4} $38^{7.8.11}$ 41^{5}
$43^{4[7]8[8.8.10]}$ [46^{8}] 47^{1} 48^{2} [54^{10}
66, 6], 11, 15. 67, 5. $81^{8-10.12}$ 83^{3}
Aḥ. 33.46.79.81[81]90[91]98–
101.105.111.112.122–[124].128.
130.135.140.144.189[189]197.
210.211.217[217]223. Beh.[12]
51. מני 10^{13} 26^{6} [42^{12} $45^{3.4}$]
Aḥ. 119[139]194. מנך $9^{8.11}$
20^{9} 28^{11} 30^{24} 67, 5. Aḥ. 128.136.

$142.143.146.$ מנכי 8^{19} 14^{6} $43^{4[8]}$. מנה 6^{8} $13^{7.16}$ 15^{36} 41^{7} Aḥ. 49.114. מנן 66, 1. 68, 1. Aḥ. 121. מנכם 25^{4} 38^{6} 66, 11. מנהם 5^{10}. מנהן 16^{4}. מן זי $4^{[4]8}$ 41^{7} Aḥ. 86. מנכן therefore 20^{7} 41^{4}. מנעל 25^{8} 35^{8} $43^{10[10]}$ [66, 1]. מנעלא [$2^{13.17}$] 3^{20} $5^{10.13}$ 25^{6} 48^{2}. מן קדם 54^{14}. מן קדמן 32^{5}. מן אחרוהי Aḥ. 210.

מנדע Aḥ. 53.

מנדעם 21^{7} $27^{2[12]}$ 30^{14} [31^{13}] Aḥ. 101 Beh. [6]11. מדעם $49^{3.4}$. מנדעמתא 27^{23} 30^{12} 31^{11} [Aḥ. 10].

מנה mina: מנן 26^{17}. מנין 29^{3}.

מנחה [27^{14}] 30^{21} 31^{21} 33^{11}. מנחתא 30^{25} 32^{9}.

מנחם pr. n. $22^{20.71}$ 39^{2}.

מנחם ב׳ אורי ב׳ משלך 22^{73}.

מנחם ב׳ גדול 20^{17}.

מנחם ב׳ גדול ב׳ בעדיה 25^{18} 28^{15}.

מנחם ב׳ הצול ב׳ שמעיה 22^{26}.

מנחם ב׳ זכור 15^{38}.

מנחם ב׳ זכריא 22^{67}.

מנחם ב׳ משלם ב׳ שלומם $20^{2.9.16.19}$.

מנחם ב׳ משלם 19^{7}.

מנחם ב׳ מתן 22^{62} 23^{11}.

מנחם ב׳ עזריה 20^{17}.

מנחם ב׳ פוסי 12^{7} $22^{78.79}$.

מנחם ב׳ שלום 25^{18} $35^{2.5}$ 44^{1} 63^{10}.

מנחם ב׳ שלומם (=משלם ב׳ ש׳) 20^{19}.

מנחמת pr. n. 22^{96}.

מנחמת ברת ע[נני] בר אסתח 22^{81}.

מנחמת ברת ידניה ב׳ ענתי 22^{108}.

מני count: imperat. מנו 21^{4}. ימנה [38^{9}]. Pa. appoint: מני Aḥ. 37[77]. ממנין 27^{9}. מנה share 37^{12}? מנתא $1^{3.3.4.6.7}$ 17^{2}. מנתי? 66, 12. מנתך Aḥ. 144. מנין number 2^{14} 3^{13}.

מנכי pr. n. 14^{13} 16^{6} 37^{11} 53^{10}.

מנכי ב׳ ספעמרא 43^{12}.

מנכי ב׳ ענניה 61^{11}.

מנע: ימנע passive Aḥ. 136.

מנפי Memphis 37^{11} $42^{7.11[13]}$ 83^{2}.

מנציעת $27^{5.6}$.

מסורע month-name 8^{1} [9^{1}] 13^{1} 29^{1} 63^{16}.

מסמרין *see* סמר.

(ב)מסת Beh. 23.

מעוזי pr. n. $22^{70.109}$.

מעוזי ב׳ נתן 33^{2}.

מעוזיה pr. n. 23^{2} $37^{1.17}$ 38^{2} 40^{4}.

מעוזיה ב׳ נתן ב׳ ענניה 18^{3} 20^{16} 25^{17}.

מעוזיה ב׳ צחא [38^{12}].

מעזיה ב׳ מלכיה 8^{30} 9^{19} (Neh. 10^{9}).

מעלה? Aḥ. 114.

מפטח ברת טשתז 22^{83}.

מפטח ברת צפליה 22^{106}.

מפטח ברת שלם 22^{88}.

מפטחיה pr. n. 22^{135}.

מפטחיה ברת גמריה $43^{[1]2.3.7[7.9]11[13]}$

מפטחיה ברת מחסיה $13^{2.4[21]}$ $15^{5.6.18.19.20.22.27.29.33-36}$.

מפטיח (=מבטחיה) $15^{3.32}$.

מצן (?) 26^{17}.

מצרין Egypt $30^{13.14.24}$ 31^{12} 32^{2} 38^{7} 64, 20. 66, 6. $71^{8.26[27]}$ $72^{2-4[6-12]}$ מצריא 27^{1} 30^{8} $31^{7.13}$ $37^{4.5}$.

מקלו 33^{10}.

מרא $47^{2[7]}$. מרא שמיא 30^{15}. מראי 16^{8} 37^{17} 38^{2} 39^{2} 54^{10} 67, 7. 68, 9. $70^{1.2}$ 77^{1} 80^{9} Aḥ. 73. מראך Aḥ. 192. מראה $71^{7.7}$ Aḥ. [198]198.199. מראן $17^{[1]1.5}$ $30^{1.2.18.23}$ $31^{[1]17.22}$ $33^{7.12.13}$ 34^{6}? $27^{2.10.19.21[22]}$. מראַי $37^{[1]}$ $38^{1.12}$. מריהם 34^{6}. מראתי $39^{1.2.5}$.

מרגו pl. n. Beh. 17. מרגויא [Beh. 19] p. 266.

מרד : מרדו 27^{1} Beh. 17 [24.25]. מרדיא Beh. 1.3[4]5.7.8[10.19. 20.41]44.

מרדני? pr. n. Beh. 61.

מרחשון month-name 17^{7} 30^{30} 31^{29} [Beh. 14?].

מרע? $75^{1.3}$.

מרר : תמר (2nd sing.) Aḥ. 148. מריר Aḥ. 105. מררתא Aḥ. 105. מררותא Aḥ. 188.

משאן 15^{16} 55^{8}.

משח anoint : משחן (perf.) 31^{20}. משחַן (perf.) 30^{20}. משח oil 30^{20} 31^{20}.

מׄשח measure 71^{17}? משחה measurement : משחת 9^{4}. משחתה 8^{4}.

משך : משכי 37^{10}? Aḥ. 118.

משלך pr. n. $10^{2.23}$ 22^{73}.

משלך ב׳ אורי $[18^{1.1}]$ 22^{68}.

משלך ב׳ הושעיה 46^{13}.

משלם pr. n. 8^{30} 9^{18} 19^{7} $22^{27.97}$ 25^{18}.

משלם ב׳ הושע 6^{18}.

משלם ב׳ זכור ב׳ אטר $10^{2.8.16.24}$ $13^{3.7}$.

משלם ב׳ חגי ב׳ הצול 22^{29}.

משלם ב׳ יאזניה 52^{16}.

משלם ב׳ מבטחיה 22^{25}.

מישלם ב׳ מעוזי 22^{109}.

משלם ב׳ נתן 44^{2}.

משלם ב׳ עזגד 81^{31}.

משלם ב׳ שלומם $20^{2.17}$ cf. מנחם ב׳ של׳.

משלם ב׳ שמוח 22^{21}.

משלם ב׳ שמעיה 19^{5} 22^{119}.

משלמת pr. n. 22^{82} 39^{3} 63^{4}.

משלמת ברת גמריה ב׳ מחסיה 22^{2}.

משלמת ברת פנוליה 22^{110}.

משלמת ברת צפליא 22^{93}.

מתא Aḥ. [27]36 [Beh. 16.17.48].

מתן pr. n. $22^{62.76.77}$ 23^{11}.

מתן ב׳ ירניה 22^{42}.

מתן ב׳ יש . . . 65, 3.

מתן ב׳ ישביה 38^{1}.

מתרדת pr. n. $26^{2.7}$ 80^{7}.

מתרוהשת pr. n. 70^{1}.

מתרלי (or אתרלי) pr. n. 5^{16}.

מתרסרה ב׳ מתרסרה 13^{18}.

נא pl. n. $24^{13\,b.36}$ $34^{3.4}$ $37^{8[15]}$ 68, 11.

נאהבת pr. n. 1^{4}.

נברא pr. n. 2^{21}.

נבוראבן pr. n. 8^{28} 9^{16} 28^{14}.

נבוכררי pr. n. 5^{18}. name of *degel* $[7^{3.4}]$ 29^{2} 35^{2}.

נבולי ב׳ דרגא 5^{18}.

. . נבונר pr. n. 53^{9}.

נבונתן pr. n. $14^{11.12}$ $54^{3.13.15}$.

נבוסמסכן pr. n. 6^{19} Aḥ. [33]38.41. 45.54.56.58[59.67]71[74.77].
נבועקב pr. n. 22^{20} $26^{23.28}$.
. . . נבועקב ב׳ 12^{11} 62, 1.
נבושרר pr. n. 68, 10?
נבורעי ב׳ ושהן 14^{13}.
נבורעי ב׳ נבונתן 14^{12}.
נבושלו pr. n. $2^{8[10]}$ 24^{2}.
נבותכלתי ב׳ נבוראבן 28^{14}.
נבז 11^{6}.
. . נבג pr. n. [2^{19}] 3^{23}.
נבם pr. n. 81^{74}.
נגר : נגידה 26^{8}. יתנגד 26^{4}. מתנגדה [Aḥ. 159].
נגן : [ינ]גנת 27^{23}. [נ]תנגן 27^{1}.
נגע Aḥ. 165.166.
נגרא 2^{3} 63^{9}. נגריא $26^{9.22}$.
נדן pr. n. 72^{18} Aḥ. [8]18.
(כ)נדר ? 42^{11}.
נריש 32^{8}. נדישו $27^{5.24}$ 30^{10}. נרשוהי 30^{9} 31^{8}. ינרשו 30^{8} 31^{7}.
נהבת pr. n. 22^{96}.
נהבת ברת זכור 22^{107}.
נהבת ברת מחסה $22^{[11]91}$.
נין : נונך 45^{4}. נונין 45^{3}. נוניך $45^{5.6}$.
נופהא $26^{2.7}$. נופתיא $26^{[1.2]8}$.
נוק = ינק : יניקנהי Aḥ. 92[93].
נורישריש pr. n. 24^{13}.
נזק 37^{14}.
נחש copper, bronze 10^{10} 14^{4} 15^{11-13} 20^{8} $26^{12.15.18}$ 30^{11} 31^{10} $36^{4.4}$ $61^{1.3}$ 81^{37}. נחשא Aḥ. 186. נחשיא 81^{111}.
נחת : נחת 42^{11}. יחתון 71^{15}. Ha. הנחת imperat. $42^{7.7.8.13}$. הנחת imperat. 42^{13}. מנחתותה infin. Aḥ. 123. מנחתותהם Aḥ. 122.
נחתן ? 81^{80}.
נטח : נטחותי ptcp. Aḥ. 167.
נטל : נטלת 1st sing. Aḥ. 169.
נטר : ינטרנהי Aḥ. 209. טר imperat. Aḥ. 98. מנטר infin. Aḥ. 192. יתנטר Aḥ. 160. מנטרה watchfulness Aḥ. 98. מנטרתן 27^{1}.
ניח[א] Aḥ. 108.
ניסן month-name $21^{[5.5]8}$ [42^{14} 45^{1}].
נכים pr. n. $81^{62.63.72.76.79.119.121.131}$.
נכסן $7^{5.9}$ 13^{5} 14^{4} 20^{12} 27^{4} 31^{5} 38^{3} 82^{6} Aḥ. 66.74. נכסין 30^{16}. נכסיא 13^{4} $14^{6.8}$ 15^{14} 18^{2} $20^{5.8.15}$ 34^{6} 35^{4}. נכסי 15^{35}. נכסיכי 13^{6}. נכסוהי $15^{19.30}$. נכסיה 15^{21}. נכסיהום p. 265, 2.
נבריא Aḥ. 139.
נברם. ברת חניה 81^{37}.
נמרא Aḥ. 118.118.119.
נסב : נסבת 1st sing. Aḥ. 112.
נסח : ינסח Aḥ. 156.211.
נסיך : נסיכי Aḥ. 119.
נסך 33^{11}.
נעבצן 15^{15}.
נעזב pr. n. 74^{2}.
נער Aḥ. 79.
נפא pl. n.? 7^{4} 20^{4}.
נפחר Beh. 47*.
נפטסבק pr. n. 73^{12}.
נפין pr. n. $16^{6.7}$ $30^{7.8}$ $31^{6.7}$.

נפל : נפלת (3rd fem.) Aḥ. 184.186.

נפק 30^{5} 31^{4}. נפקת (1st sing.) [Beh. 12]. נפקת (3rd fem.) Aḥ. 135. 139.140[197]. תנפק (3rd fem.) 9^{9} Aḥ. 124 (2nd sing.) 5^{12}. נפקה Aḥ. 123. למנפק 5^{14}. Ha. הנפקה Aḥ. 109. הנפקת (2nd sing.) 7^{5}. הנפקו 30^{16} 31^{15}. יהנפק 13^{11}. ינפק 13^{12}. תהנפק (3rd fem.) $15^{26.28}$. יהנפקון $8^{15.17}$. הנפק imperat. Aḥ. 99. הנפקי (imperat. fem.) 8^{27}. אתנפק 71^{29}? נפקה outgoings 83^{28}. נפקתא $24^{31.33}$. נפקתה 72^{1}. נפקת $73^{7.14}$.

נפ׳ש 24^{27-30} [Aḥ. 189]. נפשי Aḥ. 187. נפשך 7^{6} Aḥ. 130[149] 153. נפשה 13^{18} 73^{7}. נפשהום 27^{18} 30^{13}.

נצבתא 81^{2}.

נצוי ? [Aḥ. 142].

נצח : אתנצחו Beh. 60. מנצחן [71^{16}].

נצל : Ha. אהנצל 8^{18} 18^{3}. תהנצל (3rd fem.) 9^{10}. תהנצלנהי Aḥ. 81.

נקבה $15^{17.20}$.

נקיה $72^{15.16}$.

נקמן [7^{8}]. נקמיא [7^{10}].

נרי pr. n. $22^{86.102}$.

נריה pr. n. 12^{6} 38^{1}.

נ׳שא : נשאה Aḥ. 95. נשאית (1st sing.) Aḥ. 111.112. ינשא Aḥ. 90.[90]. תנשא (3rd fem.) Aḥ. 121. שא imperat. Aḥ. 121. מנשא [Aḥ. 122.123].

נ׳שג : יהנשג Aḥ. 200. יהנ׳שגון Aḥ. 133.

נשבעדרי pr. n. 65, 15.

נשבעדרי ב׳ נבג . . 2^{19} 3^{23}.

נשן women : נשיא 30^{20} 34^{2}. נ׳שין (our wives) $30^{15.26}$ 31^{14}.

נשן spinster ? 8^{2} 10^{2}.

נשק Aḥ. 222. תהנשק Aḥ. 103 (note).

נשתונא 17^{3}.

נתום pr. n. 34^{5}.

נתון pr. n. 12^{1} $22^{47.100.111}$ 33^{5}.

נתון ב׳ חגי 22^{53}.

נתון ב׳ פלליה ב׳ נתון 22^{111}.

נתין pr. n. 53^{2} 81^{90}.

נתן give. נתנת (2nd sing.) 3^{12} 11^{1} 69^{12}. ינתן 1^{6} 5^{10} 6^{14} 8^{13} 13^{11} 15^{30} 20^{14} 25^{15} 30^{3} 31^{3} $42^{3(4)8.10}$ $43^{6(11)}$ [46^{9}] 67, 16. 71^{25} 80^{9} Aḥ. 172. יתן 81^{64}. תנתן (2nd sing.) $28^{7.12}$ [68, 10] Aḥ. [68] 127.129. תתן (3rd sing.) 81^{24}. תנתנן (energ.) 8^{10}. תנתננה 13^{8}. אנתן $5^{7.13}$ 8^{21} 9^{15} 11^{4} 14^{10} $15^{34.36}$ [35^{10} 45^{8}] 47^{3} 48^{3} 82^{4} Aḥ. 61.66. אנתננה 35^{5}. ינתנון 11^{6}. יתנון $82^{8.9}$. ינתנו [2^{12}] 26^{6} [42^{4}]. תנתנון (2nd plur.) 66, 16. תנתנונה 25^{9}. תנתנו 25^{14}. תנתון 25^{11}. ננתן $2^{11(13)}$ 28^{10} 33^{13}. מנתן (infin.) $8^{16.19}$ 9^{6} 15^{3} 50^{14} 64,18. מנתנה 9^{9}.

נתן pr. n. $8^{7.29}$ 9^{17} 20^{16} $22^{84.113.115}$ 23^{1} 24^{11} $25^{3.3.9.17.19.21}$ $28^{2.2.16.17.17}$ 33^{2} 40^{5} 44^{2} 56^{4} $81^{9.31.70}$?

נתן ב׳ הודויה 19^{10} 22^{127}.

הושע [נתן ב׳] $29^{1[4]}$.

[נתן ב׳] הושעיה ב׳ חנני[ה] 22^{7}.

נתן ב׳ יהואדר 28^{16}.

נתן ב׳ מעוזיה 23^{2}.

נתן ב׳ נריה 12^{6}.

נתן ב׳ ענני 10^{20} $22^{12.128}$ [45^{9}].

נתן ב׳ ענניה 8^{32} 9^{20} 13^{17} 15^{37} 18^{3}.

נתר : אהנתר [15^{35}].

ס = סאה ? $81^{2.3.134.136}$.

סאה : סאן 63^{3}.

סבב : מסבב ? Beh. 54.

סבל Beh. 63. יסבלנהי Aḥ. 90. אסבלנך Aḥ. 204. מסבל Aḥ. 48.72. לסבול [2^{6}]. יסתבלון Aḥ. 73. סבל food Aḥ. 74. סבול 43^{4}. סבוליך Aḥ. 205.

סברת 37^{7}.

סגד : סגדת (1st sing.) Aḥ. 13. סגדוהי Aḥ. 10[24.65]. מסגדא 44^{3}.

סגה : יסגה Aḥ. 126.

סגן 35 c $47^{2.7}$. סגן ודין 8^{13} $10^{13.18}$. סגן נגריא $26^{9.21}$.

סגנן 26^{10}.

סגרי pr. n. $22^{81.69}$.

סהר = שהד ? : תסהדא 71^{10}.

סוירא (or ־רא) Aḥ. 88.

סון pl. n. 3^{9} $5^{2.2}$ 6^{17} 8^{28} 9^{16} $13^{2.3}$ $14^{2.3.3.12}$ 15^{2} $16^{6.7}$ $25^{3.4}$ 28^{2} $29^{2.2}$ 30^{7} 41^{5} $45^{1.2.9}$ 56^{2}. סונכן 33^{6} 67, 3. סונכניא 24^{33}.

סוס : סוסה Aḥ. 38. סוסין Beh. 30.

סחר : סחרת (2nd sing.) [Aḥ. 175].

סיון month-name 64, 20. [Beh. 5].

סימך ב׳ משלם 22^{27}.

סינסשר ב׳ נבוסמסכן 6^{19}.

סינעבש pr. n. 17^{7}.

סכין Aḥ. 100.104.

סכל : תסתכל Aḥ. 147.

סכר : סכרו 27^{8}.

סלוא pr. n. 18^{2}.

סלואה pr. n. 67, 3.

סלואה ברת סמוח ? $35^{3.10}$.

סלואה ברת קניה 1^{1}.

סלוה ברת נרי 22^{102}.

סלק 15^{16} 81^{15} ?

סמה : ptcp. מסמה Aḥ. [87]88.

ס[מ]וח pr. n. 35^{3}.

סמכי ב׳ ששי 49^{1}.

סמר : מסמרין 26^{16}. מסמרי $26^{12.15}$. מסמריהם 26^{16}.

סמתו ב׳ ענחמת 74^{4}.

סנאבלט pr. n. 30^{29}.

סנחאריב (see also שנ׳) Aḥ. 50.51.55.

סניא Aḥ. 165.165.166.

ססא Aḥ. 184.186.

ססרתס pr. n. 81^{126}.

סעבל $26^{11.20}$.

סעד : סעדני Beh. 2.5.13.19.28.41. [43], p. 269, 3.

ספ (= ספר) 13^{12}.

ספינה : ספינתא $26^{[1]3[4]7.22}$.

ספיתכן $26^{9.22}$.

ספעמרא pr. n. 43^{12}.

ספר writer Aḥ. 1[7]18[20.27]35. ספרא Aḥ. 12.42[70]. ספרי $2^{12.14}$ $17^{1.6}$.

ספר document 5^{20} 6^{22} $8^{16.23.26.35}$ 9^{4} 10^{25} $13^{3.11.21}$ $14^{4.14}$ [15^{36}] 20^{19} 25^{20} $28^{14.17}$ 35^{4} 42^{4} 43^{18} 59. ספרא $2^{21[22]}$ 3^{10} 5^{15} 6^{16} $8^{16.18.22.25.27.28}$ $9^{14.16}$ $10^{6.12.13.19.20}$ $11^{16.16}$ $13^{6.9.12.17}$ 14^{11} $15^{31[37]}$ $18^{2.4}$ 20^{10} $26^{23.28}$ 28^{15} $43^{[5]11}$ 45^{8}[46^{15}]65, 7, 8, 18. 66, 8. 68, 12. מספר number [Aḥ. 66].

סרבלק 42^{9}.

סרים Aḥ. 61. סריסא Aḥ. 63.69.

סרסר: מסרסרן Aḥ. 114.

סתי god-name [13^{15}] 14^{5}.

סתם: יסתתמו [Aḥ. 157].

סתר secret place Aḥ. 88.175.

סתרי pr. n. 68, 8.

סתתרי $35^{4.7[9]}$ 67, 9. סתתרן 37^{12}. סתתרין? 61^{8}.

עׄבר 56^{2} Aḥ. 51.198 [Beh. 11.19. 47]. עבדת (2nd sing.) 9^{10} 71^{19} Aḥ. 87? עבדתי (2nd fem.) 14^{6}. עבדת (1st sing.) 7^{6} 68, 5? Aḥ. [24]52[75] Beh. 16[36]49, p. 265. עבדו 4^{1} [$27^{3.17}$] $30^{13.22.27}$ $31^{12.21}$ Beh. 2.3.4[6.9.10]10.17. 20[28]29[32]33[40]43. עבדן (1st pl.) 14^{3} 37^{5} [Beh. 13.14]. יעבד 26^{22} [33^{12}] 41^{7} Aḥ. 21.134 Beh. 54. תעבד (2nd sing.) 31^{26} 41^{6}. יעבדו 26^{5}. תעבדו [jussive 21^{6}]. תעבדון $38^{6.10}$. נעבד 37^{16}. מעבד $26^{9[9]10}$ 27^{15} [Aḥ. 17] Beh. 2.4[8]10[13.28] 31^{1}[40.47], p. 269, 7. עבד (imperat.) 26^{22} Aḥ. 52.68.127. [י]עבדה Aḥ. 103. עבדו [21^{8}] 38^{8}. עביד (ptcp. pass.) 6^{5} $16^{5.8}$ [27^{20}] $30^{15.18.30}$ $31^{14.29}$ 69 B4 76^{2} Beh. 6.52 (=עבד). עבידין 30^{20}. יתעבד 16^{9} [21^{10}] 26^{8} 27^{9} 33^{10} [Aḥ. 38]. יתעבדו 73^{7}. מתעבד 32^{11}. עבידה work 21^{6} Aḥ. 127. עבידתא 9^{10}. עבידתך Aḥ. 21. עבידתי [Aḥ. 17] עבידתהם Aḥ. 208.

עבד servant 10^{18} $28^{4.5.17}$ Aḥ. 84[196]. עבדא $28^{7.9.10}$. עבדך 30^{4} [31^{3}] 38^{2} 54^{9} 66, 9. 70^{1}. עבדי [Beh. 38]. עבדכי $39^{1.5}$. עבדכם 37^{1} 54^{1}. עבדיה (her s.) 28^{3}. עבדיהם [26^{6}]. עבדיך $17^{1[5]}$ $30^{1.22}$ [32^{1}] 33^{1} 68, 12 82^{1}. Aḥ. 83.

ישב (ב׳) עבדי 81^{99}?

עבדיה pr. n. 81^{3}.

עבדיהו pr. n. 82^{2}.

זכור (ב׳) עבדיהו $81^{22.23}$.

פחם (ב׳) עבדיהו 81^{43}.

עבין 26^{14}. עביא 26^{18}.

עבק Aḥ. 103. לעבק $26^{6.22}$ $42^{7.7.8.13.13}$.

עבר: עברו Aḥ. 162. תעבר (2nd sing.) Aḥ. 142?

עבור corn 14^{4} $20^{6.12}$ 24^{30}. עבורא $2^{9[12.13]17}$ $3^{[9]12}$ 45^{5}.

עד preposition $5^{5.5.11}$ $8^{9.11}$ $11^{3.8.10}$ 13^{16} 14^{7} $15^{4.25.28}$ 16^{6} $20^{9.10}$ $21^{5.8}$ 24^{34} $25^{9.16}$ 28^{7} 29^{6} $30^{9.20.21}$ $31^{8.18.20}$ $35^{5[8]}$ 38^{7} $43^{4[8]}$ 50^{5} 76^{1} 81^{138}? Aḥ. 52.95. עד זי 30^{27} Aḥ. 49.64. זי עד (= עד זי) 31^{26}.

לא עד not yet 28[13]. no longer 34[7]. עד? 35[11]. עד conjunction 2[17] 10[11.17] 34[7] 38[5] 68, 3. 69[5] 71[3] Aḥ. 78[86]96.130. Beh. 59.

ערב: ערבך Aḥ. 136.

ערבר = עלרבר 45[3].

ערה 15[22.26]. עד[תא] 82[5].

ערי: יערי [15[31]] Ha. הערת (1st sing.) 15[35]. הערית (1st sing.) Aḥ. 50. תהערי (2nd sing.) Aḥ. 146. יהעדו 30[6] 31[6].

ערן 17[2] 26[8.9] 28[13] 30[2.3.17.26] 31[3] 37[2] [38[2]] 39[1] 40[1] [41[1] 42[1]] 56[1] 57[9] Aḥ. 49. ערנא 31[2[20]] Aḥ. 70.

ערר: בעררה Aḥ. 99.126.167.

עררי pr. n. 24[37].

עור 34[7].

עורנחר ב׳ דומא 14[19].

עויל Aḥ. 216.

עויר Aḥ. 213.

עזגר pr. n. 81[31].

עזור pr. n. 23[8].

עזז: עזיז Aḥ. 99.100.143.

עול: עולי כתן 26[18]. עולי כתנא 26[20].

עזקה Aḥ. 19[20.26]60. עזקתה Aḥ. 3[7].

עזר: עזור 71[25].

עזריה pr. n. [1[10]] 20[6.12.13.17] 62, 1. 63[9.12].

עזריה ב׳ הצול 22[129].

עחר god-name 72[6].

עחרנפי pr. n. 72[23].

עילמי = עלימי Beh. 7.

עין: עינין Aḥ. 157.213.215. עיני Aḥ. 124. עיני Aḥ. 169. עינוהי 41[7]. עיניהם [Aḥ. 97].

עינין matter, purpose 26[22].

עכר pr. n. 12[9].

על preposition 6[5.13.14] 7[7] 8[16.23.27] 11[6.16] 14[3.5.6] 15[19.28.29] 25[20] 26[8.18] &c. 27[3] &c. 28[4.6.8] 30[5.7.18.23.24.26.28.29] 31[6.17.22] 34[6] 35[4] 42[8.13] 69[2] 81[111] &c. Aḥ. 97 &c. על אחרן Aḥ. 53. 64[133]. עלדבר 6[5.6.8.16] 28[8.10.11] 38[3] 62, 1. 71[30]. Aḥ. 202. עלדברכן 40[3]. עלוי 42[4] 82[14] Aḥ. 51. על יד 26[21]. על ידן 2[8[9]13] 3[4.14]. על קדמן עלבן Aḥ. 117.187. [Aḥ. 133]. עלתבלא 26[[4]8]. עלי 7[[4]7] 11[2.9.9] 15[15] 17[3] 29[2.3] 35[5] 41[2.5] 42[10.10] Aḥ. [24]25[30]57[65] 194. עליך 5[3] 6[5.16] 10[13.18] 15[5] 28[8] 30[26] 40[3] 41[3] 42[7] 47[7] 49[2] 50[4] 64, 20. 72[5.6.20] Aḥ. [27]47.103. 169.204. עליכי 8[13.15.17] 13[11.14] 14[5] 39[3]. עלוהי 42[6[14]] Aḥ. 54. 65.86[138 Beh. 24]. עליה 8[24] [44[6]]. עלין 26[2] 28[3.13.14] 30[19] 38[7] Aḥ. 36. עליכם 38[5.9] 49[4]. עליהם 14[5.8] 20[16] 26[6] 38[5] 42[4] Beh. 17[45]. עליהום 30[24]. עלוי above 5[6.9]. עלויה 5[11]. מנעל 35[8] 43[10]. עליה upper part 5[4.5] 6[11] 8[4.5] 13[13] 25[5] 65, 17.

עלא above 5[5.11]. לעלא Aḥ. 114. מנעלא 3[20] 5[10.13] 25[6] 48[2]. עד עלא 5[5.11]. concerning it 13[5.10] 28[9] [43[5]].

עלוה sacrifice [27^{15}] $30^{21.26}$ $31^{21.27}$. עלותא 30^{25} 31^{25}.

עלל: על $15^{5.16}$ 30^{13}. עלת (2nd sing.) [7^{4}]. עלת (1st sing.) 7^{8}. עלו 16^{8} 30^{9} 31^{8} 34^{8}. Hanphel הנעלת (1st sing.) $15^{6.7.24.27}$. הנעל [Aḥ. 84]. ינעל? Aḥ. 206. יהנעלו 42^{12}. תהנעלו [21^{9}].

עלם (עד) $8^{9.11}$ 13^{16} 14^{7} 15^{4} $20^{9.10}$ $25^{9.16}$ 28^{7} $43^{4[8]}$. עד לעלמן [Aḥ. 95].

עלים 17^{7} 38^{6} 77^{2} 83^{30} Aḥ. [61].83. עלימא 73^{2} Aḥ. 63[68]. עלימה [42^{2}]. עלימי = עילמי Beh. 7. עלימיא 28^{13} 41^{6}. עלימַי 38^{4}.

עלן 73^{1}. עלנה 78^{1}.

עלע: עלעִי Aḥ. 106.

עם preposition 1^{4} 9^{6} 26^{4} 27^{4} $30^{5.8.8.11.15}$ $31^{10.14}$ 38^{4} 46^{3} 68, 10. 71^{23} Aḥ. [40]49[72.77]104.139. 140.142.143.145.160[164]166 Beh. [12]19[27.27.30.31.45.46]. עמי Beh. [25]26.59[60 Ah. 9]. עמך 42^{4} Aḥ. 129.173. עמכי 68, 2. עמה 8^{27} Aḥ. 37.39. 40.56.164.197. [Beh. 34.35. 47]. אלעמה Aḥ. 107.154. 161.

עם people: עממא Aḥ. 94.162.

עמד: יעמד Aḥ. 160.

עמודיא 30^{9} 31^{8}.

עמל: עמלת (2nd sing.) 40^{2}. עמלא 40^{2}.

עמניה pr. n. 22^{105}.

עמר $15^{7.10}$ cf. קמר.

ענביא 81^{1}.

ענה $71^{11[12]}$ Aḥ. [19.54.59]110.118 [166]. ענת (3rd fem.) [Aḥ. 118]. ענית (1st sing.) Aḥ. 14.45. ענת? Aḥ. 210. ענו Aḥ. [58.67]121. יענִי 71^{32}.

ענוה Aḥ. 105. עניה [Aḥ. 189].

ענזא Aḥ. 118.118.119. ענז 33^{10}.

ענחבס ב׳ פטאסי 73^{9}.

ענחנום ב׳ חנמו? 53^{5}.

ענחפי ב׳ פטאסי 73^{4}.

ענחמת pr. n. 74^{4}.

ענני pr. n. 10^{20} $22^{12.44.46[58]128}$ $26^{2?}$ 30^{13} 31^{18} $38^{4.10.11}$ 45^{9} 66, 8 (cf 61^{10}?).

ע[נני] ב׳ אסחת 22^{81}.

ענני ב׳ מעוזי 22^{70}.

ענניה pr. n. 6^{20} 8^{32} 9^{20} 13^{17} 15^{37} 18^{3} 61^{11}.

ענניה ב׳ משלם ב׳ שלומם $20^{2.9.16.19}$.

ענת see כ(ענת).

ענתביתאל god-name 22^{125}.

ענחי pr. n. 22^{108}.

ענתיהו god-name 44^{3}.

עפה: אעפה Aḥ. 140.

עק 20^{5}. עקן Aḥ. 104.125. עקיא 26^{18}. עקִי $26^{10.12-14.17.20}$. עקהן? 30^{11} 31^{10}.

עקבן ב׳ שמשנורי 11^{12}.

עקבנבו pr. n. 54^{10}.

עקף: יעקף 11^{8} [35^{9}].

עקרבא Aḥ. 85.

ערב mix: מערב 2^{5}. בערב? Aḥ. 184.

ערב west: מערב ל׳ 8^{7} 9^{3}. למערב

6^{9} 8^{3} 66, 15. מערב שמש 6^{9} 13^{15} 25^{7}. מערב שמשא sunset 21^{3}.
ערבי Arab Aḥ. 208.
ערביא pr. n.? 81^{115}.
ערבן $10^{9.13.17}$ 42^{5} 68, 10.
ערדה Aḥ. 204.
עריה Aḥ. 118.
ערע : לערעה p. 269, 3. Cf. ערק.
ערק [Beh. 46]. לערקה זי Beh. [2]4[8]10.31.38.40[46].
ערר : ? imperat. עורי (fem.) 8^{27}.
עשׁי : בעשק $16^{8.9}$. עשקא [27^{19}].
עשרי 8^{14} 20^{15} 25^{15} $26^{10.10.11.16.17.17}$ 28^{11}. עשרתא 6^{15} $8^{14.21}$ 9^{15} [46^{10}]. עשרן 6^{14} $26^{11.13.16.16}$.
עשת Aḥ. 25.68. אתעשת 30^{23} [31^{22}]. עשתא 8^{5} 9^{5}.
עת see (כ(עת.
עתד : imperat. עתד 9^{6}.
עתיק 8^{16}. עתק 13^{12}. עתיקא 13^{6}.
עתר : עתרי (my riches) Aḥ. 207. עתירא Aḥ. 207.
עתרשורי ב׳ נבוזראבן 8^{27} 9^{16}.

פ = ? $63^{2.3.5}$. פלג = ? $81^{3.63}$ &c.
פאני month-name [20^{1}]. ? פאוני 76^{3}.
פאפי month-name 2^{1} 7^{1} 37^{15} 43^{1} 72^{1-3}.
פגע Aḥ. 118. פגעהם (their meeting) Aḥ. 89.
פגר : פגרה 71^{31} Aḥ. 63[63].
פדיה pr. n. 43^{12}.
פונש (בר) pr. n. $71^{11.12(16)}$.
פוסי pr. n. 12^{7} $22^{73.79}$.
פחד [Aḥ. 84].
פחה pr. n. 40^{2} [41^{9}].
פחה governour : פחת יהוד 30^{1}[31^{1}]. פחת שמרין 30^{29}. פחתא [Beh. 18.38].
פחטמוני 26^{12}.
פחי pr. n. $14^{2.12}$ 51^{4} 81^{111}.
פחים pr. n. 70^{1}.
פחנם pr. n. 23^{5}.
פחנם ב׳ זכור 23^{12}.
פחנם month-name 5^{1} 14^{1} 29^{5} 35^{3} 50^{2}.
פחפי pr. n. 74^{1}.
פחרי pr. n. 24^{18}.
פטאסי pr. n. $73^{4.9}$ $74^{5.6}$ 83^{3}.
פטאסי ב׳ נבונתן 14^{11}.
פטוסירי pr. n. $28^{4.6.8.10.11.17}$.
פטחנום pr. n. 6^{17}. פטחנם 73^{15}.
פטחנם ב׳ חורי 23^{3}.
פטחרפחרט ב׳ פט . . . 73^{11}.
פטי ב׳ פחפי 74^{1}.
פטיסי ב׳ נתון 53^{2}.
פטירן [21^{6}].
פטמת pr. n. 24^{1}.
פטנפחתף pr. n. 69^{2}.
פטנתן pr. n. 24^{25}.
פטנתר pr. n. 66, 1. 83^{23}.
פטסי ב׳ זפרות 24^{6}.
פטפ . . pr. n. 65, 11.
פי pr. n. 83^{27}.
פיא ב׳ פחי $14^{1.9.12.14}$.
פים ? פיסן 37^{9} : pr. n.? 40^{2} [42^{2}].
פישורא pl. n. [Beh. 31].
פכרם pr. n.? 64, 26.

פלג divide: פלגן (1st pl.) 28^{3}. נפלג 28^{13}. פלג half $1^{2.3}$ 9^{11} 71^{33}? 79^{3} 81^{86}. פלגא $9^{11.12}$. פלגה $44^{6.8[10]}$ 74^{1}. פלגן division 28^{17}. פלגנן (our div.) 28^{14}.

פלול pr. n. 34^{3}.

פלוליה pr. n. 22^{15}.

פלוליה ב׳ הושע 22^{80}.

פלח: למפלח Aḥ. 17. פלחת (1st sing.) [Aḥ. 15].

פלטה pr. n. 82^{10}.

פלטו pr. n. 13^{15}.

פלטי pr. n. 40^{1}.

פלטי ב׳ יאוש 22^{89} [$40^{1.5}$].

פלטי ב׳ מיכה 22^{22}.

פלטי ב׳ מתן? 23^{7}.

פלטיה pr. n. 10^{22}.

פלטיה ב׳ אחיו 5^{15}.

פלליה pr. n. 8^{30} 9^{17}.

פלליה ב׳ נחון 22^{111}.

פם Aḥ. 99.123.156[157]178. על פם 2^{18} 11^{16}. כפם 5^{15} 6^{17} 8^{28} 9^{16} 10^{21} 13^{17} 14^{12} [15^{37}] 18^{4} 20^{16} 25^{17} 28^{15} $43^{[6]11}$ [45^{9} 46^{15}]. פמי Aḥ. 155. פמך Aḥ. 97–99. פמה Aḥ. 114. פמין [Aḥ. 100].

פמן ב׳ בֿנת.. 74^{3}.

פמנחתף month-name $22^{1.121}$ 35^{1} 50^{3}.

פמסא ב׳ שחפימו 73^{13}.

פמסי pr. n. $44^{[5]7}$.

פמת pr. n. 72^{4} 74^{2}.

פמֿת ב׳ נעצב 74^{2}.

פמת ב׳ סגרי 22^{63}.

פ[נול]יא ב׳ מנחם ב׳ פוסי 22^{78}.

פנוליה pr. n. 13^{18} 18^{5} 22^{110} 25^{19}.

פנוליה ב׳ אושע 63^{15}.

פנוליה ב׳ יוניה 15^{38}.

פסו pr. n. 37^{11} 83^{24}.

פסו ב׳ כשי 53^{4}.

פסו ב׳ מנכי 53^{10}.

פסח [21^{4}]. פסחא [21^{5}].

פסל: פסילה 30^{10}. פסלה 31^{9}.

פסמסנית pr. n. $26^{[1]2.7}$.

פסמשך ב׳ פמת 74^{2}.

פעפס 42^{9}.

פערער 26^{12}.

פפטעונית pr. n. [2^{2}] 5^{13} 6^{10} 8^{7}.

פק 15^{16}.

פקד: יפקד Aḥ. 192. פקיד 37^{6} Aḥ. 103. Hophal? הפקדו 20^{7}. פקדון [20^{7}].

פקרקפתה? pr. n. 75^{4}.

פרא 42^{9}.

פרדא pr. n. [Beh. 18].

פרורת pr. n. [Beh. 12–14].

פרזל 10^{10} 14^{4} 20^{5} 26^{12}.

פרכס 15^{16}.

פרמנכריא $26^{4.8}$.

פרמתי month-name 35^{4}.

פרן Aḥ. 112.

פרניש pr. n. 51^{11}.

פרנם pr. n. 51^{9}.

פרם pr. n. 81^{85}.

פרס share 45^{8}. פרסי 11^{6}. פרסן 2^{16}.

פרס Persia 26^{21} Beh. 22[24]24.26[27.35]36. פרסי Beh. 7.22.25[38.61.62.62]. פרסיא [Beh. 23].

פרע: נפרע? 17^{6}.

פרין : פריין [Aḥ. 84].

פרש : מפרש 17^{3}. פרישה Aḥ. 208. פרישן 27^{10}.

פרת : נפרת 14^{8}.

פרתו Parthia. Beh. 16.

פרתפרן pr. n. 51^{13}.

פרתפרן ב׳ ארתפרן 5^{17} [7^{8}].

פרתר pr. n. Beh. 53.

פרתרך 20^{4} 27^{4} 30^{5}. פרתרכא 31^{5}.

פשך 8^{4} 9^{4} 26^{19}. פשכן $26^{10.15.15.15.18-20}$ $36^{2.2}$ $79^{2.4}$.

פשר : הפשר 63^{14}.

פתו pr. n. $81^{103.106.113.114}$.

פתום? 68, 3.

פתורא 83^{21}.

פתח to open: פתיח [Aḥ. 162?]. פתיחן 25^{6}. למפתח 5^{14}. מפתח Aḥ. 114.178. פתחן 81^{110}.

פתח god-name 11^{2}: pr. n. 72^{11}.

פתי 8^{4} 79^{2-4}. פתיא 26^{18-20}.

פתיפרס 37^{3}. פתיפרסא 37^{12}. פתיפרסן 37^{3}.

פתירות pr. n.? 69^{10}.

פתך 24^{42}. פתפא 24^{39} $43^{[7]8[10.10]}$.

פתפי pr. n. 81^{102}.

צבו? 54^{13}.

צבי : צבית (3rd fem.) $15^{26.29}$. צבית (2nd sing.) 4^{4} $28^{7.12}$. צבית (1st sing.) 18^{2}. צבו 38^{6}. תצבין (2nd sing. energ.) 13^{16}. צבה (ptcp.) Aḥ. 149.

צביא ברת משלם 34^{4}.

צבית [Aḥ. 3.7.19.20.26.60].

צבע dyed 15^{8} 42^{9}.

צבע finger 26^{20}. צבען $26^{16.18.19}$.

צדק : צדקני Aḥ. 140. אצדק 8^{22} Aḥ. 139. יצדקון 10^{19}. צדקה 30^{27} 71^{5}. צדקתא 71^{28}. צדיק 44^{6} Aḥ. [43]126.128.167[169] 173.

צדק pr. n. 5^{2} 6^{8} 8^{6}.

צהי : צהוה Aḥ. 188.

צוי : צות? 37^{14}.

צום : צימין $30^{15.20}$ [31^{14}].

צות : הציתו [Aḥ. 57].

צחא pr. n. [15^{2}] 18^{4} $20^{3.20}$ $24^{32\ n.}$ 37^{14} $38^{4.6[12]}$ $41^{1[9]}$ 67, 17. 76^{1-8} $83^{2.22.25.30}$.

צחׄא ב׳ פמת 72^{4}.

צחא ב׳ פתח 40^{2} [41^{9}].

צחא ב׳ צפר . . 24^{6}.

צידן pl. n. $72^{2.10.17}$. צידני Sidonian. Aḥ. 208.

ציר : ציריהם 30^{10}.

צל 37^{10}.

צלב : צלבת (1st sing.) [Beh. 35].

צלח : מצלח Aḥ. 125.

צלי : Pa. נצלה 30^{26} [31^{25}]. מצלין 30^{15}.

צנפר Aḥ. 98. צנפריא Aḥ. 91.199.

צעה : יצעון Aḥ. 168.

צען $81^{47.48}$.

צעק : יצעקו 52^{6}.

צפליא pr. n. 22^{93}.

צפליה pr. n. 22^{106}.

צפן : Ha. הצפנני [Aḥ. 71]. הצפנתך Aḥ. 49. תהצפן (2nd sing.) Beh. 57 [58].

צפניה pr. n. 8^{32} 9^{20} [52^{13}].
צפניה ב׳ מבי 1^{11}.
צפר . . pr. n. 24^{6}.
צנן ? צננ 55^{12}.
צרף : אבנצרף 38^{3}. כסף צריף [2^{15}] 5^{7} 28^{11} [42^{3}].

קב : 45^{4}.
קבל complain : קבלת (1st sing.) 6^{6}. יקבל 8^{13}. אקבל 10^{12} 47^{7}. יקבלון 6^{16} 10^{18}.
קבל Pa. receive 37$^{3.3}$.
קבל preposition 15^{36}. קבלהם 38^{6}. לקבל 8^{27} 26$^{7.23}$ 27^{19} 30^{25} 31^{24} 32^{10} 38^{9} 43^{4} 82^{7} Aḥ. [24]52.68[75].
קבר : לקברה 71^{21}.
קדל : קדלה ? Aḥ. 134.
קדם before 2$^{[11]12.14}$ 6^{5} 8^{24} 10$^{13.18}$ 16$^{[3]3.5.8}$ 20^{4} 25$^{2.3}$ 30$^{2.27}$ 31^{2} 32$^{3.5}$ 37$^{5.9}$ 38^{2} 41^{4} 42$^{[2]12}$ [45^{3}] 47$^{2.7}$ 54^{14} [66, 1] 72$^{6.15.16.19}$ Aḥ.[9]10.13.[15.23] 50.73[93]141[149]203. Beh. 30. קדמיך Aḥ. [15]203. קדמוהי Aḥ. 50.107. קדמין (קדמן=?) 30^{25}. קדמיהם Aḥ. 141. קדמת 30^{17} 38^{10} Aḥ. 2[103]. קדמתך Aḥ. 101 Beh. 54. קדמתהם 71^{3}. לקדמן קדמן 33^{9} 37^{8} Aḥ. 46. עלקדמן 32$^{8.10}$. מן קדמן 32^{5}. [Aḥ. 133].
קדם verb : יתקדם 82^{6}.
קדש : קדשן Aḥ. 95.
קול : קלה Aḥ. 107.
קום : קם 22^{120} [Aḥ. 4]. יקום 15$^{26.29}$ 42^{6} 46^{8} Aḥ. 107. תקום (3rd fem.) 15^{22}. תקום (2nd sing.) 42$^{7.13}$ Aḥ. 101. תקם 15^{16} 37^{10}. קמו (imperat.) 38^{6}. קמן (ptcp.) Beh. 59. יקמו 53^{6}. יקמון 61^{15}. Pa. קימו 30^{10}. Ha. הקים Aḥ. 12. הקימני Aḥ. 173. הקימת (2nd sing.) 64, 19 ? Aḥ. 44. הקימת (1st sing.) Aḥ. 23. הקימתה [Aḥ. 9].
קומתא 26^{11}.
קון pr. n. 22^{117} 67, 4 ?
קוניה ב׳ צדק 5$^{2.8.11.15.20}$ 6^{8} 8^{6}.
קטא 42^{9}.
קטל Beh. 9[32.47]. קטלת (1st sing.) Beh. 13[14.59]. קטלתך Aḥ. 51. קטלתה Aḥ. 49[76]. קטלת (2nd sing.) 71^{13}. קטלתהי 71^{20}. קטלו Beh. [1]3.3.5[6. 11.20.21.29]29.33.40[41.41. 43]44.48. תקטלני (2nd sing.) Aḥ. 52. תקטלנהי (2nd sing.) [Aḥ. 35]. יקטל 71^{6} [Aḥ. 29]. נקטלנהי Aḥ. 61[68]. קטילו 30^{17} 31^{16}. למקטלך [Aḥ. 48]. קטל (imperat.) Beh. [8]18. קטיל Aḥ. 71. קטיליא Beh. 35[47]. יתקטל Aḥ. 62[69]. קטל death Aḥ. 46.
קלבי 72$^{2.3.8.10.13.15-17.19}$. קלבין 72$^{3-5.14}$.
קלל : יקל Aḥ. 141. קליל Aḥ. 38. 112.
קלול 72$^{3.4.6.7.9.11-13}$. קלולן 72$^{5.18}$.
קלעם 26^{11}.
קמינא ? 82^{13}.

קמר 20^{5} 36^{3} 42^{9} cf. עמר.

קן 33^{10}.

קנה 30^{16} Aḥ. 84. יקנה Aḥ. 218. יתקנה Aḥ. 196. מתקנה Aḥ. 219. קנין 14^{4}. קניני 15^{33}. קנינה $15^{19.22.30}$ 46^{1}.

קניא pr. n. 63^{14}.

קניה pr. n. 1^{2}.

קסתר? 69^{10}.

קפא Aḥ. 117.

קצר: קצרתי? 66, 9.

קצרי ב׳ יההדרי 11^{13}.

קצת 29^{3} 27^{4} 35^{4}.

קרא: קרית (2nd sing.) [7^{4}]. קרית (1st sing.) 7^{10}. אקרא $7^{7[10]}$. יקראון Aḥ. 117. מקרא $28^{4.6}$. מקריא 7^{6}.

קרב: קרב (imperat.) Aḥ. 194. קרב (ptcp.?) Aḥ. 110. Pa. קרבתך Aḥ. 50. קרבתה Aḥ. 10. יקרב 30^{28} 31^{27}. יקרבון 30^{23} 32^{9}. תקרבני (2nd sing.) [Aḥ. 54]. נקרב 31^{25}. קריב a relative 5^{9} $6^{12.13}$ 20^{10} 43^{5}. קרב id. 1^{5} 13^{10}. קרב battle Beh. 2–4[6.9]10[13]20[28.32.40]43[47]. קרבא Beh. 2[9]10[10.13.14.19.28]29[32]33[40.47]. קרבתא adv.? Beh. 56.59 Aḥ. [41.45.48] cf. $75^{2[4]}$.

קרה happen? 71^{18}.

קריה 5^{9} 13^{10} 20^{11} 46^{6}.

קרקע [$75^{1.2}$].

קשב: הקשיבו [Aḥ. 57].

קשט: Ha. הקשט 4^{3}.

קשי: אקשה Aḥ. 140. קשה adj. Aḥ. 101. קשיא 6^{11} 8^{8}.

קשת: קשתך Aḥ. 126.128. קשתה Aḥ. 159? 191

ר = רבעתא 6^{15} $8^{14.21}$ 9^{15} $15^{7.12-14.24}$ 20^{15} $24^{7.16.28}$ 25^{16} [46^{10}] 68, 5. 76^{1}? $81^{2.3}$ &c.

ראמן? 81^{110}.

ראש beginning 6^{1}. principal 11^{5}. רשא $10^{6.6}$. head ראשה 15^{23}. ראשהום Beh. [26]38. ראשׁי 82^{5}.

רב noun [2^{11}] Aḥ. 60 Beh. 45. רבא? Aḥ. 120. רב adj. [Aḥ. 145]. רבא 30^{18} 42^{6} 63^{13} 72^{15} $81^{32.33}$. רברבן 31^{9}. רבני [2^{11}] 3^{11}. רבחיל 30^{7}. רבחילא 1^{3} 16^{7} 20^{5} $25^{2.4}$ 38^{3} 54^{14}.

רבה verb Aḥ. 2. רבא Aḥ. 18. ירבה $10^{4.6}$ $11^{2.5}$. רבה ptcp. 11^{5}. Pa. $81^{47.48}$? רבית (1st sing.) Aḥ. [23]25. רביתה [Aḥ. 8]. רבית (2nd sing.) [Aḥ. 44]. ירבה Aḥ. 114. תרבי (2nd sing.) [Aḥ. 137]. נרבי 81^{76}. רבא interest? 42^{5}. מרבי 11^{7}. מרבית $11^{3.5}$. מרביתא $10^{6.6}$ 67, 10? מרביתה $10^{4.8.11.12.14-16.18}$ $11^{8.9}$ 65, 1.

רביא Aḥ. 38.41[46]54.56.58.59[67.71.74]. רבֵּי 80^{3} Aḥ. 33. רבותי [Aḥ. 65].

רבתכה? $75^{1.7}$.

רגג: תרגג (2nd sing.) Aḥ. 136.

רגל: רגלי Aḥ. 206. רגלך Aḥ. 123. רגלה [Aḥ. 196]. רגלהם Aḥ. 122. רגלוהי 30^{16} 31^{15} Aḥ. 80. רגליא? Beh. 1[4.10].

רגש: ירגש Aḥ. 29.

רדי: רדית (1st sing.) 16^{4}.

רוה: תתרוה (3rd fem.) Aḥ. 189.

רוח Aḥ. 168.

רוך pr. n. 1^{3}.

רוכל ב׳ אביהו (or דוכל) 2^{20}.

רום: ירים Aḥ. 150. יתרום? Aḥ. 138. רם Aḥ. 142[149] 150?

רזיך [Aḥ. 141].

רחא pl. n. Beh. 27*.

רחבל pr. n. 81^{98}.

רחם: רחמני Aḥ. 51. רחמה Aḥ. 11. רחמתי $8^{10.19}$ [13^{8}]. רחמתן 25^{9}. ירחם Aḥ. 153 [157]. ירחמן [33^{7}]. רחמן friendship 30^{2} 31^{2} 38^{2}. ברחמן 18^{2} $25^{11.14}$. רחמיך friends 30^{24} 31^{23} Aḥ. [141] 176. רחים Aḥ. 115. רחימה Aḥ. 92. רחמן Aḥ. 53.223. כרחמ Aḥ. 107. רחמת gift 9^{7} 43^{3}. רחמתה love of her Aḥ. 91.

רחמרע? pr. n. 5^{19} CIS 154, 7.

רחק: רחקת (1st sing.) $13^{7.16}$ 14^{6} 25^{4} $43^{[4.6]}$ 67, 5. (2nd sing.) [42^{12}]. רחיק stranger 1^{6} 5^{9} $6^{13.13}$ 13^{10} 43^{5}. removed 6^{15} 14^{11} 20^{15} 41^{7} [Aḥ. 194?] רחיקן 20^{9} 28^{11}. מרחק renunciation 6^{22} $8^{25.25}$ 14^{14} 15^{20} [43^{13} 66, 14].

רכב: ארכב [Aḥ. 204] ptcp. רכב Aḥ. 38. רכבי סוסין Beh. 30 [45]. רכביך Aḥ. 205. Ha. הרכב Aḥ. 191. הרכבה (2nd sing.) Aḥ. 128. תהרכב (2nd sing.) Aḥ. 126.

רכיך Aḥ. 100.105.

רכיסה? 81^{29}.

רכל: רכליא 38^{4}. רכליך? Beh. 55.

רכן [Aḥ. 91].

רמי pr. n. 34^{3}.

רמנא Aḥ. 165.165[166].

רע: רעה Aḥ. 222. רעין Aḥ. 113.

רעויה pr. n. 8^{33} 9^{21}.

רעויה ב׳ אורי 22^{118}.

רעויה ב׳ זכריה 23^{10}.

רעי $73^{6.13.13.15.17}$.

רעיא pr. n. 34^{3}.

רעיא ברת נרי 22^{96}.

רעיבל pr. n. 15^{39}.

רפא: ptcp. רפאה Aḥ. 100. ירפון Aḥ. 154.

רקע: רקען 26^{11}. רקעתא 26^{20}.

רקק: ירוקן Aḥ. 133. ירקון [Aḥ. 148].

רשא see ראש.

רשי 8^{24}. רשכם 25^{12}. רשת (1st sing.) [35^{11}]. רשתבי 35^{11}. רשיתך [45^{3}]. רשיתכם (1st sing.) 25^{12}. רשין $20^{6.16}$. רשינך 28^{9}. רשינכם $20^{4.7}$. ירשה 8^{26}. ירשנכי 8^{12} 13^{9} $43^{[5.6]10}$. ירשכם 25^{15}. ארשנך 9^{13}. ארשנכי 8^{20} $43^{4[9]}$.

ירשון 20$^{11.13.14.14}$ 25^{14}. ירשונכם 20$^{11.13}$. נרשה 25^{10} 28^{9}. ptcp. רשה 44^{5}. למרשה 28^{8}. רשות 26^{17}.

רשע : רשיעא Aḥ. 171. רשיען Aḥ. 168.

רתא Aḥ. 177.

ש׳ [2^{6}]. = שקל 11$^{2.3}$ 22$^{[1]2}$ &c. 35^{3} 50^{9} 61$^{13.15}$ 63^{2}? 69 D 78^{3} 81$^{18.31}$ &c. = ration 24$^{[1]2}$ &c. = שערן 24^{1} &c.

שאל Aḥ. 77. שאלה Aḥ. 11. שאלת? 47^{5}. שאילת (1st sing. pass.) 16^{3} [45^{3}]. שאילתם 20^{8}. ישאל 30^{2} 31^{2} [38^{2}] 40^{1} [Aḥ. 119]. ישאלו [17^{1} 18^{2}] 37^{2} 39^{1} 41^{1} 56^{1}. ישאלונני 65, 8. שְׁאַל imperat. 16^{9}. שאילא 7^{8}. משאלת 76^{4}.

שאול Sheol 71^{15}.

שאני (= שנאי?) Aḥ. 174.

שאני Aḥ. 206.210?

שאר : 81$^{61-63.77.106.118.131.132}$. ישתאר 11^{9}. שירית [27^{18}] 30^{11} [31^{10}].

שבט : שביט 15^{9}.

שבט month-name 28^{1}.

שבי capture : שבית (2nd sing.) 71^{14}. שביא captives 71^{14}.

שבית ברת חורי ב׳ שלם 22^{85}.

שבע be filled : שבעת (2nd sing.) Aḥ. 127.129. ישתבע Aḥ. 189.

שבע seven : שבען seventy 26$^{11.15}$. שבעת [21$^{6.8}$].

שבעה ב׳ עבדיהו 82^{2}.

שבק 69^{12}? Aḥ. 90. שבק (imperat.) Aḥ. 171. שבקת (2nd sing.) Aḥ. 176. שבקתך (1st sing.) Aḥ. 175. שבקו Aḥ. 162. שבקוהי 69^{5}. שבקן 27^{1}. ישבק 54^{15}. תשבק (2nd sing.) 42^{11}. אשבקן Aḥ. 82. ישבקן 54^{6}. למשבק Aḥ. 193. שבקן (ptcp.) [27^{13}] 30^{23} 31^{23}.

שבתי pr. n. 58^{3}.

שבתי (ברת) חגי 81$^{24.26}$.

שבתי (ברת) חניה 81^{127}.

שבתי (ברת) ישיש 81^{9}.

שבתי ב׳ נבדא 2^{21}.

שבתית ברת עבריה 81^{3}.

שגא : Ha. תהשגא (2nd sing.) Aḥ. 137. השגית [Aḥ. 9]. שגי 41^{1}. שגיא [17^{2}] 27^{19} 30^{2} [38^{2}] 41^{2} 42^{1} [54^{11}] Aḥ. 29.51[58]74.106[165] Beh. 60. שגא 54^{8}. שגיאת? Aḥ. 87. שגיאן Aḥ. [11]50.116. Beh. 51.

שדך : מהשדך 37^{9}.

שדר Aḥ. 165. אשתדרו 38^{4}.

שהד verb : שהדו 82^{6}.

שהד noun 5$^{16-19}$ 6$^{17-21}$ 8$^{29-34}$ 9$^{17-22}$ 10^{21} 13$^{19.19}$ 15^{39} 18$^{4.5.5.5}$ 20$^{17.18}$ 28$^{16.16.16}$ 43$^{[12.12]12}$ 46$^{[12-14]14}$ 65, 11 Aḥ. 140. שהדיא 1^{8} 2^{19} 3^{22} 5^{15} 8^{28} 9^{16} 10^{21} 11$^{11.16}$ 13^{17} 14^{12} 15^{37} 18^{4} 25^{17} 28^{15} 43^{11} 46^{12} 49^{5}.

שהינן Aḥ. 168.

שוא pr. n. 40^{1}.

שוא ב׳ זכריה 23^{15}.

שוה to be equal to : שוה (ptcp.)

$15^{8.9.11.11.13}$. שויה 15^{12}. שוין 15^{13}. אשתוין 28^{2}.
שוי bed? 15^{15}.
שוק 82^{4}? שוקא $5^{12.14}$. שקא 13^{14}.
שור 27^{5}. שורא 27^{6}.
שורי ב׳ כדו 2^{20} [3^{22}].
שזב: שזבך Aḥ. 46. שזבוני 38^{5}. נשזבנהי 54^{9}.
שחר 37^{4}.
שחט: Niphal? ptcp. נשחט 15^{10}.
שחיק 42^{10}.
שחפימו pr. n. 73^{13}.
שחפימו ב׳ שנוט 73^{10}.
שחת: ישתתון Aḥ. 155.
שטטן 42^{8}.
שטר document $81^{5.16.17.19.20.22-26}$. שטריא 81^{14}.
שטר side 5^{5}. שטר מן except $25^{13.18}$.
שיב: שב Aḥ. 6.17. שבא Aḥ. [26]35.
שיבה pr. n. 45^{2}.
שים: שמת (2nd sing.) Aḥ. 94 (1st sing.) Beh. 35. ישימנך 30^{2} [31^{2}]. תשים (2nd sing.) Aḥ. 130. ישימון Aḥ. 115. ישימו? 69 B. שים ptcp. 38^{10}. שים טעם $26^{22.23.25}$. שימה Aḥ. 95. יתשים 27^{21} Aḥ. 80. שימא amount 38^{10}.
שים noun $26^{10.19}$.
שירית [27^{18}] 30^{11} [31^{10}].
שכח: Ha. השכח 30^{14} 31^{13}. השכחת (2nd sing.) $42^{7.8}$. השכחת (1st sing.) 13^{6} Aḥ. 76. השכחו 38^{4}. השכחן 4^{5}. יהשכח [Aḥ. 85]. תהשכח (2nd sing.) Aḥ. 34. תשכח (2nd sing.) $10^{9.10.17}$. תשכחון 38^{7}. יהשכחון 37^{10} [Aḥ. 66]. אשתכח $27^{2.13}$. אשתכחו $34^{[1]4}$.
שכר [21^{7}].
שלה [Aḥ. 22].
שלוה pr. n. $39^{1[5]}$.
שלום pr. n. 23^{8} 25^{18} [35^{2}] 63^{10}.
שלום ב׳ הודויה 44^{1}.
שלום ב׳ זכריה 22^{66}.
שלום ב׳ מנחם 22^{20}.
שלומם pr. n. 1^{2} $20^{2.17.19}$ 46^{11}.
שלומם ב׳ הו[דויה] 46^{16}.
שלומם ב׳ עזריה 1^{10} $20^{6.12.13}$.
שלומם ב׳ שנ̄ת̄ $46^{2[8]}$.
שלח [26^{1}] 30^{7} 31^{6} 40^{3} 64,20 Beh. 38. שלחת (2nd sing.) 41^{5}. שלחת (1st sing.) 16^{8} [26^{3}] 54^{2} Beh. [7.15.18] 25.26. שלחו 26^{6} 30^{19} 54^{15}. שלחן $30^{18.20.29}$ $31^{17.28}$. ישלח [49^{4}] Aḥ. 62. ישלחנך Aḥ. 201. אשלח 41^{3}. שלח (imperat.) 38^{10} $42^{10.10}$. שלח (ptcp.) 38^{9}. שלחן 17^{3}. שליח 21^{3} 26^{6}. ישתלח $26^{4.21}$ [27^{22}] 30^{24}. משלחה Aḥ. 98. Pa. inf. לשלחה? 49^{3}. Ha. השלחת? 67, 2. תהשלח? 40^{4}.
שלט: שלט (ptcp.) $2^{16.17}$ [3^{19}]. שליט $5^{11.14}$ 8^{11} $9^{6.11}$ 10^{16} 28^{6} 46^{7}. שליטה 8^{9} 9^{9} 15^{18}. שליטן $9^{7.10.13}$ 10^{8}.

שלין Aḥ. 130.

שלם: Pa. pay שלמת (1st sing.) 11^{7} 17^{2} 29^{6} [35^{7}] 82^{5}. שלמתך $10^{7.11.14}$. שלמו 10^{16}. שלמן 42^{2}. תשלם (2nd sing.) [Aḥ. 131]. אשלמנהי $11^{3.6.10}$. אשלמן 35^{5} 64, 27? אשלם [29^{4}]. ישלמון 10^{15}. לשלמה 13^{5}: greet? [Aḥ. 110]. משלם 11^{7}. משלמותה Aḥ. 131.

שלם welfare 17^{1} 21^{2} 30^{1} 34^{7} $37^{[1]2}$ 38^{2} 39^{1-3} $40^{[1]1.1}$ $41^{[1]8}$ 42^{1} 54^{10} $57^{1.1.8}$ 65, 4. 66, 9. 67, 11. 68, 1, 8. 69 C [70^{1}] 77^{1} Aḥ. 110.120. שלמך $41^{2.3.5.7}$ 56^{1} $58^{1.2}$? שלמכי 39^{1}. שלמכם 57^{4}.

שלם pr. n. 13^{20} $19^{4.9}$ $22^{41.85.88.97.116}$.

שלם ב׳ הושעיה 5^{18}.

שלם ב׳ הודו 22^{39}.

שלם ב׳ נתן 28^{16}.

שלמיה pr. n. 30^{29} 31^{28}.

שלמיה ב׳ ישוב 22^{24}.

שלמם ב׳ גלגל 49^{1}.

שלמצין pr. n.? 81^{2}.

שם Aḥ. 85.85.138.138. בשם 8^{12} 13^{9} $14^{8.9}$ [20^{12}] $25^{12.13}$ $43^{4[6.9]10}$ 47^{4}. שמי Aḥ. 170. בשמי 6^{14} 8^{16} $25^{12.13}$. שמך Aḥ. 141. בשמך 30^{26} 31^{25}. שמה $28^{4.5.9.13}$ 33^{1-5} 66, 1. Aḥ. 1.5[8]18. Beh. 2[4]7. 12.17[18.18]22.25.27*.[31.35. 38.61]. בשמן 30^{29} 31^{28}. שמהת 22^{1} $34^{2.4}$ 66, 1. שמהתהם [66, 1] Aḥ. 116.

שמו ב׳ בנופי $26^{8.21}$.

שמוח pr. n. $22^{21.28}$ [24^{7}].

שמוע ב׳ חגי 12^{5}.

שמוע ב׳ שלם 22^{41}.

שמין Aḥ. 95. שמיא [27^{15}] $30^{2.15.26}$ $31^{[2]27}$ 32^{4} $38^{[2]3.5}$ 40^{1} [Aḥ. 116].

שמע 71^{10}. שמעת (2nd sing.) [Aḥ. 98]. שמעת (1st sing.) 40^{2} $41^{2.2}$ [Aḥ. 21.76]. שמעו [Beh. 8.39]. ישמע Aḥ. 93. תשמע (2nd sing.) [Aḥ. 132]. נשמענך Aḥ. 59. שמע (ptcp.) Aḥ. 29. שמע (imperat.) Beh. 53. שמעו (imperat.) Aḥ. 59. אשתמיע Aḥ. 70. ישתמע 18^{3}. ישתמיע [Aḥ. 62].

שמעון pr. n. $81^{8.17.19[20]}$.

שמעון ב׳ חגי 81^{15}.

שמעיה pr. n. 13^{19} 19^{5} $22^{26.119}$ 24^{3} 52^{12}.

שמעיה ב׳ הושע 5^{17}.

שמעיה ב׳ חגי 33^{3}.

שמעיה ב׳ ידניה 8^{31} 9^{19}.

שמעיה ב׳ שלם 19^{5}.

שמר: אשתמר (imperat.) Aḥ. 97. 101. ישתמר? Aḥ. 125.

שמרין pl. n. 30^{29}.

שמש $6^{8.9}$ 8^{6} 13^{15} $25^{6.7}$ 67, 13? Aḥ. 92.93.108.138.171. שמשא 21^{8}.

שמשגרי ב׳ בלבן 24^{14}.

שמישלך pr. n. $26^{[4]8}$.

שמשנורי pr. n. 11^{12}.

שמתי pr. n. 81^{16}.

שנא: שנאת (1st sing.) $15^{23.27}$. תשנאנך (3rd fem.) 9^{8}. שנאי (ptcp.) [Aḥ. 176]. שנאה divorce 15^{23} 18^{1}. שנאתה his hatefulness Aḥ. 132.

שנדן pr. n. 22^{19}.

שנה change: תשתנה Aḥ. 201.

שנה year: 10^{7}. שנת 1^{1} 2^{1} 5^{1} 6^{1} 7^{1} 8^{1} 9^{1} 10^{1} 11^{3} 13^{1} 14^{1} [15^{1}] $16^{2.2.6.6}$ 17^{7} 20^{1} 21^{3} 22^{1} $24^{34[35]44}$ $25^{1.1}$ 26^{28} 27^{2} $28^{1.1}$ $29^{1.5}$ $30^{4.19.21.30}$ $31^{4.19.29}$ 32^{7} $35^{1.6}$ [42^{14} 43^{1}] 45^{1} $50^{3.5}$ 61^{12} $63^{1.8.15}$ 64, 20, 24. 66, 16. 67, [1]10. שנתא 21^{3} 71^{14} $81^{33.112}$. שנן 45^{8} 71^{9}.

שנוט pr. n. 73^{10}.

שנחאריב pr.. n. Aḥ. 3.4.4.[5.7]15. 27[47]. See also סנח׳.

שנית? pr. n. 46^{2}.

שנן? 15^{16}.

שנת to tattoo: שנית (ptcp. pass.) $28^{4.6}$. שניתת tattooing $28^{4.6}$.

שערן $2^{[3.4]5.7.8}$ $3^{4[6]}$ 4^{5} 10^{10} [24^{38}] 33^{14} 35 c 45^{8} 49^{2} 64, 18. 66, 4.

שף $26^{11.19}$.

שפה: שפותה Aḥ. 132. שפות [Aḥ. 151].

שפט 52^{7}. ישפט [Aḥ. 145]. תשפט (2nd sing.) [Aḥ. 143]. ישפטון Aḥ. 104. נשפט 52^{5}.

שפטיה pr. n. 52^{14}.

שפי: שפין Aḥ. 113.

שפל: שפל (ptcp.) [Aḥ. 150]. יהשפל Aḥ. 150. השפל (imperat.) [Aḥ. 149].

שפע: שפיען [Aḥ. 74].

שפר: שפיר Aḥ. 108 [159]. שפירה 81^{33} Aḥ. 92.

שק Aḥ. 103? שקקן $30^{15.20}$ $31^{14.19}$.

שקא: Ha. להשקיא 27^{7}.

שקא see שוק.

שקל $15^{12.12}$: = שקלן 15^{14}. שקלן 10^{3} [11^{2}] $15^{5.6.8.10.11.13.24}$ 22^{122} $29^{[3]6}$ $35^{7.9}$ 35 c $36^{2.3}$ 36 b.b 43^{3} 67, 16. 78^{6}.

שרה: ישרה 71^{7}.

שרתא $72^{2.3.10[12]13.17.18.24}$.

שרח: שרחו[תא] Aḥ. 170. שרחותה Aḥ. 85.

שרי[ה בר]ת הושע 22^{4}.

שרף: שרפו 30^{12} 31^{11}.

שרק Aḥ. 100. שריק 40^{3}.

שרר: שריר 30^{3} 31^{3}. שרירא 70^{2}.

ששי pr. n. 49^{1}.

שחברין ב׳ אתרלי 5^{16} [13^{18}].

שתה six 43^{3}. שתן 26^{12}.

שתה drink: ישתה Aḥ. 93. תשתה (2nd sing.) 71^{22}. תשתו 21^{7}. שתה (ptcp.) [Aḥ. 92]. שתין (ptcp. ?) 27^{8} 30^{21} 31^{20}.

שתק: אשתק Aḥ. 121.

שתר Aḥ. 125.

תבא pr. n. $28^{4.5.12}$ 73^{8} 81^{11}.

תבלא 26^{8}.

תבן Aḥ. 112.

תבר: תברו 30^{9}. יתבר Aḥ. 106. תביר Aḥ. 109. תבירן 26^{13}.

תגר pl. n. Beh. 2.

תוב: תתב (3rd fem. jussive?) 15^{28}. יהוב [Aḥ. 65]. אתוב 45^{5}. Ha. התיב 20^{7}. יהתיבנהי Aḥ. 126. Aph.? אתבו 34^{6}. תובא reward Aḥ. 44. תוב (adv.) 1^{7} 9^{12}.

תויא pr. n. 63^{2}.

תוגא: בתוניכם 21^{9}.

תור 33^{10}.

תורה? 82^{10}.

תחום: תחומי 6^{7} 13^{13}. תחומוהי 8^{5} $25^{4.8}$ 66, 13.

תחות month-name 6^{1} 10^{1} 11^{8} 25^{1} 81^{122}. תחות god-name 69^{9}.

תחנום pr. n. 34^{2}? 39^{2} 65, 7.

תחת 26^{12}. תחתיה 6^{10} $8^{4.6}$ $25^{5.8}$. תחתיא 13^{13}.

תימנה Aḥ. 134.

תיפתיא 27^{9}.

תירי? pr. n. 37^{13}.

תכונה 15^{6}. Cf. Nah. 2^{10}.

תלי: יתלי 81^{39}. תתלנהי 71^{19}.

תליהם 30^{8}.

תלתה $26^{10.11.15.15.15.18-20}$ Aḥ. 39. תלתא Aḥ. 92.

תמה 5^{4} 25^{6} $27^{15[17]}$ $30^{6.9.11}$ 31^{6} 33^{10} 38^{5} 77^{2} Aḥ. 48.72.

תמחי 15^{12}.

תמוז month-name $30^{4.19}$.

תמים $26^{13.20}$.

תמנין $26^{10.11}$.

תמריא 81^{111}.

תנה 4^{6} 27^{4} $30^{5.24.27}$ $31^{5.23.26}$ 34^{7} 37^{2} 54^{8} 69 D.

תנין second 10^{7} 63^{13}.

תנין dragon Aḥ. 106.

תעובי month-name [21^{4}] 42^{14} 67, 1. 68, 11. תעבי 83^{1}.

תפלה? 81^{20}.

תפכה 55^{1}.

תקותיא pr. n. 68, 1.

תקל: יתקלנהי 71^{6}. תתקל (3rd fem.) 15^{24}. תקל = שקל 10^{5}. מתקלת מלכא 28^{11}. מתקלת פרס 26^{21}.

תרוח pr. n. $16^{3.5.9}$.

תרין $26^{8.11.12.14.18.19}$ 82^{11} Aḥ. 56.58. 62[67.69.77]. תרתין Aḥ. 92. בתרתי רגליא Beh. 1 [10]. תריהם [38^{8}].

תרך: יתרכנה? 65, 13. לתרכותה 15^{30} [46^{8}].

תרע 5^{8} Aḥ. 44. תרעא $5^{12.14}$. תרען 30^{9} 31^{9}. תרעיה Aḥ. 168.

תשטרם pl. n. $24^{39[43]}$ 27^{9}.

תשרי month-name 15^{1} [Beh. 32].

APPENDIX

The following three fragments of papyrus found at Saḳḳara, were published by Mr. Noël Giron in the *Journal Asiatique*, vol. *18* (*1921*), p. 56. His text and translation are reproduced here by his kind permission, but for further information the reader is referred to his article.

Fragment A is part of a list of names, all Egyptian. In l. 4 פסמ̇שך, cf. 74^{1}.

A

1 חרחבי בר נחמסאח אמה . . .

2 . . צ̄ . ור בר נפו אמה תטחרפע . . .

3 . . . . בר וחפרע אמה ניתרטיס . . .

4 . . . . . בר פסמשך̄ אמה . . .

1 Hor(-en)-Kheb b. Nakhamsakh (?), whose mother is . . .

2 . . . . or b. Nofo (?), whose mother is Ta-te-Hor-pe' . . .

3 . . . . . . b. Wahprê, whose mother is Nêthrétis . . .

4 . . . . b. PSMŠK (?), whose mother is . . .

Fragments B and C form part of one document, but apparently not the same as A, though the writing is similar. Mr. Giron has ingeniously fitted them together and suggests that they represent government accounts. He points out that in l. 6 מנדת חילא (cf. Ezra 4^{13}) is 'tribut de la colonie', not a contribution for religious purposes as in No. 22. There was therefore a colony (חילא), military or otherwise, at Memphis (cf. 37^{11} 42^{7}, &c., 83^{2}) as at Elephantine. There is nothing to show that it was Jewish or even Semitic.

	B	C
1		 III
2		[ש]קלן III
3	. . . . רגסת . . .	. . נת מסטי . . . .
4	. . . . כסף כרשן	
5	. . . . כסף כרשן [. . . ש]ק[לן . . . .] חלרן ד II	
6	. . . . [כס]ף כרשן III II ש[קלן . . חלר]ן ר III II ▲ מנדת חילא . . .	
7	. . . . III I חלרן	
8	. . . . [כסף כרש]ן דדד שקלן III II חלרן ר III II	
9	. . . . ן III I . . . ר II שקלן	
10	. . [כסף כרשן] . . . . . . III [שק]ל I חלרן ד III III I	
11	. . . . כמרן בבתי אלהיא כסף	

1 3

2 shekels 3+

3 . . . RGST . . . NT MSṬI ??? . . .

4 . . sum of kerašin . . . .

5 . sum of kerašin . . . . . . shekels . . . . hallurin 22.

6 . sum of kerašin 5, shekels . . . . . . hallurin 15. Tax of the colony.

7 . . 4, hallurin . . . . .

8 sum of kerašin 60, shekels 5, hallurin 15.

9 . . . . . . 4, . . 12, shekels . . .

10 sum of kerašin . . . +3, shekel 1, hallurin 27.

11 . . . . the priests (who are) in the houses of the gods the sum of . .

PRINTED IN ENGLAND
AT THE OXFORD UNIVERSITY PRESS

CPSIA information can be obtained
at www.ICGtesting.com
Printed in the USA
LVHW050039140323
741536LV00033B/2153

9 780342 848720